110
On4o

103621

DATE DUE			

PHILOSOPHY
OF
PLATO AND ARISTOTLE

PHILOSOPHY
OF
PLATO AND ARISTOTLE

Advisory Editor
GREGORY VLASTOS
Princeton University

THE ORIGINS OF
EUROPEAN THOUGHT

BY

RICHARD BROXTON ONIANS

ARNO PRESS

A New York Times Company

New York / 1973

Reprint Edition 1973 by Arno Press Inc.

Reprinted from a copy in
The Princeton University Library

PHILOSOPHY OF PLATO AND ARISTOTLE
ISBN for complete set: 0-405-04830-0
See last pages of this volume for titles.

Manufactured in the United States of America

回回回

Library of Congress Cataloging in Publication Data

Onians, Richard Broxton.
    The origins of European thought about the body, the
mind, the soul, the world, time, and fate.

    (Philosophy of Plato and Aristotle)
    Reprint of the 1951 ed.
    1. Philosophy. 2. Civilization, Occidental.
I. Title. II. Series.
B72.05 1973   110   72-9298
ISBN 0-405-04853-X

THE ORIGINS OF
EUROPEAN THOUGHT

ABOUT THE BODY, THE MIND
THE SOUL, THE WORLD
TIME, AND FATE

THE ORIGINS OF EUROPEAN THOUGHT

ABOUT THE BODY, THE MIND
THE SOUL, THE WORLD
TIME, AND FATE

New Interpretations of
Greek, Roman and kindred evidence
also of some basic Jewish and Christian beliefs

BY

RICHARD BROXTON ONIANS

Hildred Carlile Professor of Latin
in the University of London

'Look unto the rock whence ye
were hewn and to the hole of
the pit whence ye were digged'

CAMBRIDGE
AT THE UNIVERSITY PRESS
1951

PUBLISHED BY
THE SYNDICS OF THE CAMBRIDGE UNIVERSITY PRESS

London Office: Bentley House, N.W. 1
American Branch: New York

Agents for Canada, India, and Pakistan: Macmillan

Printed in Great Britain at the University Press, Cambridge
(Brooke Crutchley, University Printer)

TO THE MEMORY OF
MY FATHER

CONTENTS

Preface   *page* xi

Introduction   The Earliest Greeks   1

PART I

THE MIND AND THE BODY

Chapter I   Some Processes of Consciousness   13

      II   The Organs of Consciousness   23

     III   The Stuff of Consciousness   44

      IV   Cognition—The Five Senses   66

       V   The Liver and the Belly   84

PART II

THE IMMORTAL SOUL AND THE BODY

Chapter I   The ψυχή   93

      II   The *Genius, Numen,* etc.   123

     III   *Anima* and *Animus*   168

      IV   The Knees   174

       V   The Strength   187

      VI   The Stuff of Life   200

     VII   River-Worship and some Forms of the   229
           Life-substance

    VIII   The World: Beginnings of Greek   247
           'Philosophy'

      IX   Death and Cremation   254

       X   The Offerings to the Dead and to the   271
           Gods

      XI   Nectar and Ambrosia   292

PART III

FATE AND TIME

Chapter I 'On the Knees of the Gods'   *page* 303

    II Πείρατα   310

   III Καιρός   343

   IV The Weaving of Fate   349

    V Other Peoples—Fate and Magic   352

   VI Μοῖραν ἐπιτιθέναι, πεπρωμένος, etc.   378

  VII 'Υπὲρ μόρον and the Relation of the Gods to Fate   390

 VIII The Jars of Zeus, the Scales of Zeus, and the Κῆρες   395

   IX Time—'Ημαρ   411

    X Lachesis, Klotho, and Atropos   416

   XI Phases of Body and Mind, Sorrow, Sleep, Death, etc.   420

  XII Τέλος   426

ADDENDA

    I 'Winged Words'   469

   II Mars, Woodpecker, Wolf   470

  III *Liber, liber*, 'free', *Freyr*, etc.   472

  IV Ancient Jewish Conceptions of the Mind or 'Soul', the 'Spirit', the 'Holy Spirit', the Body, and the Divinity of Christ   480

    V *Praecordia* and the Liver   505

   VI Βρότος, 'Gore', and the 'Ichor' of the Gods   506

  VII *Apocolocyntosis*   507

CONTENTS

VIII   *Mortarium,* 'Mortar'   *page* 508

IX   The 'Billie Blind' or 'Belly Blind',   509
       'The Auld Belly-Blind Man'

X   *Delubrum* and *Lustrum*   510

XI   *Finis, Fimus*   510

XII   Ancient Hindoo Conceptions of the Soul   511

Indexes   515

ILLUSTRATIONS

Fig. 1   Ariadne being deserted by Theseus   402
         From *Wiener Vorlegeblätter*, Serie D, Taf. VIII

Fig. 2   Europa on the Bull   431
         From Millingen, *Vases grecs*, Plate XXV

PREFACE

What is the nature of the mind? What are its processes?
What is the soul? What is the nature of life? What happens
at death and after? What is the significance of the body and
of its various parts in men, in animals, in plants? What is
the form of the world and how did it originate? By what
forces and what means are human destinies determined?
What are universals? What is time? This book began in an
attempt to discover the earliest answers of the Greeks and
of the Romans to these fundamental questions, the beliefs
which for centuries satisfied their minds and governed their
actions. These beliefs appear to have been embodied in and
to explain also a multitude of words and passages in literature,
of theories in later philosophy and science, and of legends,
myths, and customs. To the faithful eye and the sympathetic
imagination there emerges a strange vision, a remarkable
system of beliefs, coherent in itself and, when we grasp the
appearances of things strangely conspiring, not unreasonable.
τέχνη τύχην ἔστερξε καὶ τύχη τέχνην. This vision seems to
have been largely shared by other peoples, including Semites
and, among 'Indo-Europeans', our own Anglo-Saxon, Norse
and Celtic ancestors. For, while I have looked first and
hardest at the relevant phenomena of experience and at the
Greek and Roman evidence, I have adduced evidence also
from other languages and literatures and have occasionally
made bold with suggestions concerning its meaning, though
I am not unaware of the perils of interpreting evidence with
imperfect knowledge of its background. The work may be of
some interest to scholars in these fields and to philosophers,
anthropologists, historians of science, and students of religion,
as well as to the plain man who would penetrate into prehistoric times and the beginnings of our civilisation. There
are a good many things of general interest by the way (e.g.
the explanations of magic, of the attitude to sex, of Hell-fire,

of the Holy Spirit, of the belief that Christ is the son of God). To the student of the 'humanities' the basic Greek and Roman conceptions of human nature and human destiny and of the world, though they are relatively neglected in most of our schools and universities, should not be indifferent. Without them much of the *meaning* of ancient life and literature is lost. With them the organic unity of ancient thought, the natural growth through individual minds, is revealed; and many customs and symbols, which we still use without understanding them, can be understood. That is not to say that all these things have been achieved here.

For introduction I have been content with a brief account of the Homeric Greeks, the earliest Europeans we really know. There are no materials for a comparable picture of the early Latins. Lack of evidence for the original belief is indeed a main reason why on some points (e.g. on the form of the world or on fate) I have said much less on the Roman side. Sometimes I have been silent from a desire to avoid stating what is obvious or already established. Often the evidence is fragmentary and obscure. Where it does not seem to suffice to determine the truth I have expressed conjecturally what is only conjecture. To give scholars the actual evidence I have quoted the original language at all crucial points. I usually translate in full, but in some few passages translation would badly blur the finer shades. The main point will, I believe, always be clear to the layman. Some words that I have explained occur in countless passages. I have cited the most revealing and have omitted, so far as I am aware, none that might tell against my interpretation. For a number of words I have ventured upon new explanations of the form, and, conscious of my own fallibility, I ask to be forgiven the general observation that many current etymologies have been put forward and accepted with some regard for the form but with little for the background of life and thought on which the word came into being.

The work is knit together with cross-references, which save a great deal of space at the cost of some trouble to the reader.

Often the reference is to a point later in the book, which cannot be fairly appreciated without knowledge of what has led up to it. Indeed, such cross-references and other points to which the reader may be led by the Indexes will be much more intelligible and convincing when once the book has been read. I have tried to help by making these references reasonably comprehensive, naming perhaps a whole page or more where only a detail may be severely relevant. The reader will, I believe, easily discern what is in point. The chapter headings give only imperfect indication of the argument, but the General Index provides a summary of what has been done with each subject. In the case of proper names in the text or elsewhere consistency is scarcely attainable and I have not attempted it. I am inclined to give their own names transliterated (Aias, Odysseus, etc.) to historic or mythical personages, but the current English, often Latinised, names of authors and historic places (e.g. Plato, Athens) are almost inevitable. Having changed my practice in the course of writing, I may inadvertently have given the same name different forms in different places.

The history of the book is roughly this: I had, as an undergraduate at Liverpool, guessed the physical reference of φρένες and θυμός without realising the importance of that discovery. In 1922, I began to research into the development of ethics amongst the Greeks, but felt that I could not do justice to it till I had dealt with their basic psychological, metaphysical and religious concepts, which did not seem to have been satisfactorily explained. Fascinated in my own thinking by the problem of moral responsibility, I first worked out the main lines of what I have called 'Fate', then returned to the mind and its processes and to the soul and to their relations to the body. The Hare Prize was awarded by the University of Cambridge in 1926 for a portion of this work consisting mainly of the study of 'Fate'. I had already worked out the main ideas (φρένες, θυμός, πείρατα, etc.) of Parts I and III but had not yet put Part I into satisfactory shape and I wished to add some smaller points and further evidence, and to work out Part II. The main argument of the book was complete when I first submitted it to the Cambridge University Press in 1929, the date by which the Hare Prize regulations required publication. It was then estimated to be 272 pages. It was, however, not till 1934 that I allowed it to be set up in type, when it amounted to 424 pages. The Council of the Senate had year by year graciously extended the time for the Hare Prize, so that I felt bound to let the book go as soon as it seemed reasonably complete. I did not know how such leisure as teaching and administration left me would be curtailed by supervening family circumstances or how, in the period over which proof-correction had to be spread, subsidiary ideas and evidence would emerge as I taught, and demand admission. The second proof of the text (451 pp.) was not printed till 1937, and the third, including Addenda I and II (454 pp.), and with it the original Indexes, till 1939. The additions have, I hope, made the book a little more useful but have somewhat damaged its form. To make room for them the expression has in places been cramped and references have been intruded into the text or very much contracted. One disadvantage of not publishing till I had worked out the implications of what I had found has been that in the interval other researchers, more particularly P. T. Justesen and F. Rüsche, have discovered and published one or two of the points I had discovered. I have added a note where this occurs (see General Index). References to other workers in the field with divergent views will be found throughout.

It remains to thank the Master and Fellows of my old College, Trinity, Cambridge, for the hospitality which year by year made pleasanter my researches; the University of Cambridge for allowing me to defer publication of the Hare Prize Essay; and the Syndics of the Cambridge University Press for their patience with my delays and additions, the printer for his accuracy and the reader for his helpful care. Among scholars I gratefully acknowledge my debt particularly to Professor A. C. Pearson, one of my teachers and a most kind friend, who, being officially appointed to supervise

my research, in generous trust allowed me to follow my bent
and welcomed my ventures with the criticism of his fine
scholarship, and to Professor F. M. Cornford, who, also for
a period my 'supervisor', then and on many occasions since
helped me by his sympathetic judgement and inspiring
encouragement and has endured more than once to read my
work in whole or part. My old friend, Mr F. H. Sandbach
of Trinity College, has also read it and made helpful criticisms
at various stages, above all in proof, and my friend and former
colleague, Professor J. F. Mountford of the University of
Liverpool, has also read it in proof and helped me by
scholarly criticism. Professor H. J. Rose of the University of
St Andrews also most generously found time to read it in
proof and gave me the benefit of his wide learning. None has,
unfortunately, seen it later than the first proof; and responsibility for the defects of its present state is wholly mine.
Positive contributions of ideas or evidence I have acknowledged where they occur. My old tutor, Mr E. Harrison,
after a glimpse of the second proof kindly brought to my
notice some points in orthography. Other teachers and
friends have helped me on my way with generous encouragement. My wife has nobly assisted in proof-reading and
copying the original Indexes. Greatest is my debt to my
father, who first inspired me to love the ancient languages
and literatures and to seek the causes of things, and who,
until his death in January 1931, remained my comrade, ever
interested and critical.

R. B. O.

CHALFONT ST GILES
December 1940

POSTSCRIPT

After the above was through the press, Addendum III was
set up early in 1941. Addendum IV had seemed sufficiently
relevant and important to hold up publication for a little
while in a world which had too many other things to think

about. The pre-occupations of war in fact made research difficult and the task itself proved larger than I had thought. When with peace publication became possible, I had made enough progress to want to finish it. Then, however, unexpected family responsibilities, which I could not escape, claimed much of my time. I had also become involved in other exacting work. At last I have had to let Addendum IV go, though I have scarcely done justice to the subject. A number of small points which had accumulated by the way have been squeezed into the text and Addenda. I thought I had made these changes without upsetting the paging, but in the revision that proved impossible. To avoid further delay the Press has kindly made itself responsible for making new and much shorter Indexes, changing all the cross-references and also for the correction of the fourth proof throughout.

In addition to circulation in 1935 of the first proof, which already contained all the main ideas, the second proof was in 1941 and 1944 privately circulated to a number of scholars from whom comments were neither expected nor received. Some of the contents have, with my permission, been explicitly quoted in books already published (in Professor F. M. Cornford's *Plato's Cosmology* and Professor E. R. Dodds' edition of the *Bacchae*). Because of this and the long delay, copies of the first, second and third proofs have, by the kind permission of the authorities of the British Museum and of the Librarian of Cambridge University, been deposited in those Libraries, and can be consulted there, should any question of priority arise.

From *Origins of Greek and Roman Thought*...as at first planned, I have ventured to change the title to *The Origins of European Thought about the Body, the Mind, the Soul....* The vast bulk and the intrinsic worth of the Greek and Roman evidence, its key position as a link with more ancient civilisations, and its dominating influence in later European thought —these perhaps justify the great weight here attached to it. It happens also to be the evidence with which I am best acquainted. The 'basic Christian beliefs' referred to in the full title are those in the Holy Spirit, in the divinity of Christ

and in hell-fire. They are mentioned because they might not
be expected in a work dealing mainly with pre-Christian
origins in Europe. They are, moreover, still part of the living
faith of millions, and their difficulties are a stumbling block
to other millions. The explanation of their origins is, therefore, if achieved, the part of the book which is of most obvious
general interest. They are related to Jewish beliefs about the
body and the spirit, about the spirit of God in man and about
the nature of life itself. I have been emboldened to suggest
new interpretations of this and other evidence only because
the ideas I found among the Greeks and Romans seemed to
provide a key. It is remarkable that, with slight variations in
detail, the same basic conceptions of the body, the mind and
the soul which can be traced in our earliest evidence for the
Greeks and Romans and the Celtic, Slavonic, Germanic and
other 'Indo-european' peoples are to be seen also in early
Egypt and Babylonia and among the Jews. Influence cannot
be excluded; but the same phenomena probably led the early
Semites, the 'Indo-europeans' and other peoples to the same
conclusions.

I need perhaps scarcely add that the book is a publication
of research and not a comprehensive survey of existing knowledge. There are many details of belief about the subjects
named which are not noticed here. They are, I trust, either
not basic to the subject or not relevant to the argument. In
the footnotes will often be found matter of as much intrinsic
interest as the text. It is found there sometimes because it
is not in the main line of argument at that point, and sometimes because it occurred to me when the book was already
in page proof, and it could then most easily be squeezed in
by way of a footnote. There remain many defects in the
book, some at least of which I should have removed, had I
had time.

R. B. O.

CHALFONT ST GILES
May 1950

INTRODUCTION

The Earliest Greeks

Basic to modern European thought are Greek philosophy and science. It is usual to begin their study with Thales, Anaximander, and their successors in the sixth century B.C., not the roots but the lowest surviving branches of a far mightier tree. Through the centuries behind stretches the parent stem, the thought of the race, the system of beliefs whereby the race rendered intelligible to itself for many generations the life of man and the world in which man lives; a working faith, slightly different, doubtless, in one quarter than in another, and growing gradually with the thoughts of individuals whose contributions cannot now be distinguished and whose names are for ever lost. Its roots are buried deep as the converging races from whose happy union sprang the stock we know. Later 'philosophies', the theories of individuals and of schools, are criticisms and improvements, ever more far-reaching, upon this racial scheme, and are not likely to be understood aright except in relation to it. In itself, if it could be recovered, it must be supremely interesting, the fundamental beliefs concerning life and mind and human destiny, beliefs determining the words and the actions of every man. And not only for the Greeks. In a sense we shall be exploring the roots of civilisation in Europe and beyond. It will, I think, appear that the fundamental beliefs traceable in the language and the earliest literature of Greece and Rome were shared by the Germanic, Celtic, and other peoples; were, in some cases at least, already current in the Old Stone Age, explaining curious practices then; and live on unrecognised in customs and idioms of to-day.

Five or six centuries before Thales of Miletus was born, the inhabitants of mainland Greece and of the islands, including Crete, had shown their unity by the ten years' siege of Troy and, still several centuries before Thales, in some place not yet conclusively ascertained, had produced two lasting monuments to their ways of living and thinking, the *Iliad* and the *Odyssey*, much the earliest accounts we possess of life and thought in Europe. Behind these lies the 'Minoan-Mycenaean' world, some few of whose outward trappings the spade has revealed and some tiny fragments of whose history the memories of later Greece and the records of Hittites and Egyptians appear to have preserved, but which else is dark and silent. Of its inner life and meaning, distinctive hopes and fears, no word remains save in a script (and possibly a language) to which as yet we have no key. The treasures of graves and the debris of palaces, relics of a god (or gods), a goddess (or goddesses), caves, trees, birds, snakes, double axes, 'horns of consecration' and other symbols and cult and funeral furniture must be eked out with our knowledge of later cults, myths, and legends, of uncertain relevance, and with analogies no less uncertain. After Homer, again, for centuries there is little or nothing comparable to him —Hesiod, meagre epic fragments, hymns and lyric and elegiac poems, no continuous or nearly complete illumination of changing life and thought. When in the fifth century the clear day shines, it is through a different atmosphere and upon a different world. It is to Homer, above all, that we must look for hints of the earlier beliefs. To men of his own time and race, sharing his environment and his beliefs, his picture was clear. They understood not only with ourselves the plain story which he tells, the explicit descriptions, but also the allusive references to things and thoughts not ours. In the light of what is clear in him and of what we know from later Greek writers and from excavated remains we may approach outstanding problems, freed from the alien ways and preconceptions of modern thought. The perfection of his art and the rationalism of his race must not blind us to the strangeness of his world. Of its points of likeness to our own we need not be reminded. Many, indeed, are older than the species, than our common humanity. Many of the virtues we unite with him to honour, such as affection for wife and offspring, and courage in their defence, are also shared by the wild beasts, to which, indeed, he repeatedly likens his heroes. The points wherein we differ are more instructive. A few may serve to suggest or recall the living background of the beliefs about to be considered.

The manliest warriors weep copiously and publicly. Because the Achaeans are driven back, imperial Agamemnon stands unashamed before the assembled host, 'weeping like a fountain of black water that from a beetling crag pours its dark stream'.[1] When he is bidden visit Hades, Odysseus cries aloud and rolls about.[2] Waiting in the Wooden Horse, all the Achaean champions,[3] save Neoptolemos, weep and tremble.[4] Priam, pleading with Hector to retire, first beats his head with his hands and then plucks out his hair.[5] When Hector dies, he rolls in dung, and, gathering it up, befouls his head and neck with it and stays in the midst of it for twelve days, inconsolable.[6]

The noblest behave like savages in battle. Agamemnon, after slaying the suppliant son of treacherous Antimachos, cuts off his arms and head, then sends the trunk rolling.[7] Patroklos bids the Aiantes 'work shame' on Sarpedon's body[8] and, when Patroklos himself falls, Hector strips his corpse and drags it along in order to cut off the head and give the body to the dogs of Troy.[9] When he too falls, and Achilles has stripped his dead body, all the Achaeans near plunge their weapons into it[10] and Achilles, slitting the ankles and passing thongs through them, drags it helter-skelter in the dust behind his racing chariot.[11] He intends to give it to the dogs[12] and Priam expects him first

[1] *Il.* ix, 14 f. Cf. i, 349 ff., ix, 432 f., xiii, 88, xvi, 2 ff., xviii, 316 ff., xix, 5.
[2] *Od.* x, 497 ff. Cf. xiv, 279 f.; *Il.* xi, 130 ff.
[3] According to *Od.* iv, 280 ff. Diomedes, Menelaos, etc.
[4] *Od.* xi, 527. Cf. xx, 204 ff.
[5] *Il.* xxii, 33 ff. Cf. x, 15 f., xviii, 23 ff.; *Od.* xxiv, 316 f.
[6] *Il.* xxii, 414, xxiv, 31, 163 ff., 640.
[7] *Il.* xi, 146 f. Cf. vi, 57 ff., xiii, 202 ff., xiv, 494 ff.
[8] *Il.* xvi, 559 f. Cf. 545.
[9] *Il.* xvii, 125 ff. Cf. xiii, 830 ff., xviii, 176 f.
[10] *Il.* xxii, 368 ff., xxiv, 420 f. Cf. xxii, 335 ff.
[11] *Il.* xxii, 395 ff.   [12] *Il.* xxiii, 21.

to cut it up limb from limb.[1] To honour Patroklos Achilles 'threw four strong-necked horses swiftly on the pyre',[2] and butchered and burned there twelve captive Trojan youths, kept for the purpose, and two of his friend's dogs.[3] Telemachos, the wise and good, obeys Odysseus' command to twist the hands and feet of the unfaithful Melantheus behind his back and, by a cord fastened to them, hang him up so 'that he may long remain alive and suffer torments'.[4] Later they took him down still alive, led him through the court, 'cut off his nostrils and ears with the pitiless bronze, plucked out his genitals for the dogs to devour raw, and hacked his hands and feet with vengeful spirit', then left him.[5]

Women are an avowed aim and approved prize of war. It is to save their wives that men fight.[6] When a city is taken, the men are slain, the children are dashed to death or enslaved,[7] and the women violently dragged away to serve as slaves and concubines of their married or unmarried conquerors.[8] The *Iliad* is built upon a quarrel over such victims. There is no shame or condemnation about it. To the folk in solemn assembly Agamemnon declares that he prefers his captive Chryseis to his wife Clytemnestra,[9] and the venerable Nestor says: 'Let no man hasten to return till each have lain by some Trojan's wife and repaid his strivings and groanings for Helen'.[10] The attitude to sex is one of frank naturalism.[11]

Piracy, raiding at large for human and other booty,[12] is an honourable trade. Without offence one asks highly respectable

---

[1] *Il.* xxiv, 408 ff.   [2] *Il.* xxiii, 171 f.
[3] *Il.* xxiii, 174 ff. Cf. xxi, 27 ff.   [4] *Od.* xxii, 172 ff. Cf. 465 ff.
[5] *Od.* xxii, 474 ff. With a like fate Antinoos threatened Iros (*Od.* xviii, 85 ff.). Cf. the experience of Eurytion (*Od.* xxi, 298 ff.) and Laomedon's threats (*Il.* xxi, 452 ff.).
[6] E.g. *Il.* ix, 591 ff.
[7] *Il.* xxii, 63 ff., xxiv, 732 ff. Men too, of course, might be enslaved.
[8] *Od.* viii, 523 ff. Cf. *Il.* viii, 165 ff., 287 ff.; *Od.* ix, 40 ff. Aeschylus describes them 'young and old with their clothes all torn, dragged by the hair like horses', *Septem*, 326 ff.
[9] *Il.* i, 113. Cf. 31 f., ix, 664, 667 f., xix, 60, 291 ff., xxiv, 675.
[10] *Il.* ii, 354 ff.   [11] E.g. *Il.* iii, 441 ff., xiv, 294 ff., xxiv, 128 ff.
[12] E.g. *Od.* i, 398, xiv, 246 ff.

strangers, whom one has entertained, whether they are mer-
chants or pirates.[1] Successful theft and perjury are admired.
Odysseus visits Autolykos, 'his mother's noble father, who
excelled all men in thieving and perjury. This skill the god
himself gave him, even Hermes; for to him he burned accept-
able sacrifice, the thighs of lambs and kids'.[2] Amongst other
feats he acquired a helmet by piercing the wall of a house.[3]
The attitude to property is naïvely, often brutally, unsenti-
mental. The child with no father and the old man with no son
at hand may expect to be dishonoured and ousted from their
possessions.[4] If a son dies in early manhood, it is noted that
'he did not repay his parents the cost of his rearing'.[5]
A daughter is a commercial asset, 'earner of oxen' (ἀλφεσί-
βοια),[6] since she is usually disposed of to the highest bidder.[7]
Iphidamas is slain by Agamemnon far from his just-wed bride,
'of whom he had known no joy and much had he given for her'.[8]
Athene hastens Telemachos' return by working upon his fear
that his mother Penelope may marry, while he is away, and
carry off one of his treasures.[9] The man who successfully
exploits hospitality in visiting friends and collecting presents
is admired.[10] Even the mightiest and the noblest spoil the
slain. The arch-king, lord of 'golden Mycenae', systemati-
cally strips each victim of his spear before proceeding to
the next.[11]

[1] *Od.* III, 71. Cf. *Il.* IX, 406; *Od.* XXIII, 356 f.
[2] *Od.* XIX, 395 ff. ὅρκῳ may well mean by keeping the letter and
evading the spirit of the oath. Cf. *Il.* IV, 64 ff., 95 ff., 197 ff., etc. The
divine witnesses, if scorned, might take vengeance.
[3] *Il.* X, 266 f. There are weights, τάλαντα, but money is otherwise
unknown. For precautions taken see *Od.* II, 337 ff.
[4] See e.g. *Il.* XXII, 484 ff., XXIV, 488 ff., 540 f.; *Od.* IV, 164 ff., XI,
494 ff.
[5] *Il.* IV, 478, XVII, 302. Cf. VIII, 185 ff.
[6] *Il.* XVIII, 593.
[7] See e.g. *Od.* XV, 16 f., 367, XVI, 76 f., XX, 335, etc. There are traces
of exceptions to this rule. See e.g. *Il.* IX, 146 ff., and for discussion,
e.g. Cauer, *Grundfragen der Homerkritik*[3], pp. 333 ff., and E. Samter,
Volkskunde im altsprachlichen Unterricht. I. Homer, pp. 20 ff.
[8] *Il.* XI, 243.
[9] *Od.* XV, 15 ff. Cf. 91.
[10] E.g. *Od.* XV, 80 ff., XIX, 270–95.
[11] *Il.* XI, 100, 110, etc.

The prince is honoured like a god by his people,[1] yet lives close to nature.[2] He superintends in the harvest field[3] and herds cattle.[4] The aged Laertes digs and tends his vineyard.[5] When guests come, though there are humbler Myrmidons in plenty around, Patroklos makes up a fire and cooks the backs of a sheep and a goat, and the chine of a pig, after Achilles has cut them up.[6] The noble suitors flay goats and singe pigs for themselves.[7] Odysseus, reigning in peace, builds his bedroom and makes his bedstead with his own hands.[8] The queens, Arete, Penelope, Helen, etc., busily spin and weave,[9] and the princess Nausikaa as a matter of course helps to wash the family clothes.[10] Writing appears to be neither used nor understood.[11]

[1] E.g. *Il.* x, 33, xi, 58.

[2] Remembrance of these facts destroys the argument (e.g. of Platt, *Journ. of Phil.* xxiv, 1896, pp. 28 ff., and Cauer, *op. cit.* pp. 477 ff.) that with his frequent illustrations from nature and from farm and domestic life Homer belongs to a later age, not Achaean but Ionian; and his audience consisted not of 'heroes' and knights but of peasants, fishermen, artisans. In any case it would not be impossible for the former to live alongside of the latter and know their ways.

[3] *Il.* xviii, 556 f.   [4] E.g. *Il.* v, 313, vi, 25, xi, 106.
[5] *Od.* xxiv, 226 f.   [6] *Il.* ix, 206 ff.
[7] *Od.* ii, 299 f.   [8] *Od.* xxiii, 189 ff.
[9] E.g. *Od.* i, 357, iv, 122 ff., vi, 306.   [10] *Od.* vi, 25 ff.

[11] The only possible allusions to it in all the forty-eight books appear to be *Il.* vi, 168–78 and *Il.* vii, 175–89. The latter is no more than the scratching of a distinguishing mark, σῆμα, on a 'lot', recognised only by the man who made it; and the σήματα λυγρά and σῆμα κακόν of the former are most naturally taken either as meaning a pictorial message or as the description of writing by one who has seen it or heard of it (e.g. 'Minoan' script) but does not understand it. Some tablets have been found in a Mycenaean palace at Old Pylos. Otherwise 'thousands of inscribed clay tablets have been found in Crete but not a single one on the mainland, and this cannot be accidental. The art of writing was indeed used, but only to put marks on vessels. Several amphoras and amphora handles have been found with signs scratched in or painted on the clay' (Nilsson, *The Minoan-Mycenaean Religion and its survival in Greek Religion*, p. 20). Such unfamiliarity as the Homeric evidence suggests cannot be feigned. If the poet had belonged to an age easily familiar with writing, he could not have made one of his characters, the courtly Glaukos, refer to writing as a practice of that character's period or earlier which that character did not understand. The possibility that he wished to suggest that Glaukos was more ignorant than his fellows or forbears need not be considered. I sometimes speak of the poet himself 'writing' in the sense of composing. The bulk of the poems is not beyond the

Men unite to defend their city and homes, and the responsibilities of power are felt by some,[1] but it is an age of stark individualism, of princes dominated by personal pride and ready to sacrifice multitudes. Menelaos would have brought his friend Odysseus with all his folk to settle in Argos, and, to make room for them, he would have sacked one of his own peaceful subject-cities.[2] Achaean Achilles, whose pride is wounded by the king's removal of Briseis, asks his mother to persuade Zeus to 'hem in the Achaeans by the sea to be slain the while, that all may have the benefit of their king and that Agamemnon may perceive his blindness in that he honoured not the best of the Achaeans'.[3] She persuades Zeus and thus Zeus obliges. And Achilles prays for himself and his friend Patroklos: 'O father Zeus and Athene and Apollo, would that no single one of all the Trojans might escape death nor one of the Argives (i.e. Achaeans), but that we twain might evade destruction that alone we might unloose the sacred diadem of Troy!'[4]

Despite Homer's essential nobility of spirit and epic dignity, these are some of the features of his world, characteristics of his heroes. The difference lies not so much in their nature as in the ideas and ideals by which they lived. It is not difficult to produce a parallel to many of these features, to one here and another there,[5] in the subsequent history of Europe; but such barbarism of action, whether survival or recrudescence, is

powers of memory and oral tradition. The rhapsodes knew them both by heart and an Athenian gentleman could recite them through, having learned them in childhood (see Xenophon, *Symposium*, 3, 5). Contrast the story of the Trojan War in Schol. Ven. to *Il.* VI, 35, told apparently by Hesiod. For the gulf between Homer and Hesiod see below, p. 8, note 2.

[1] E.g. Sarpedon (*Il.* XII, 310 ff.).
[2] *Od.* IV, 179 ff. Cf. the action of Paris, e.g. *Il.* VII, 362.
[3] *Il.* I, 409 ff.   [4] *Il.* XVI, 97 ff.
[5] E.g. piracy in the Norse 'heroic age' and such barbarous treatment of enemies as of Brodir in the Njal Saga, the mutilations inflicted by mediaeval justice, the license and brutality of seventeenth-century Europe in the Thirty Years' War as reflected in *Der abenteuerliche Simplicissimus*, the scale of values which required our great-grandfathers in cold blood to hang a man for stealing e.g. a pair of shoes worth five shillings from a shop, or the pride in theft which Tolstoi found still existing in the Caucasus in 1852 (Uncle Yéroshka in *The Cossacks*). Reversions to barbarism in the 'Great War' and later need not be quoted.

almost invariably accompanied by barbarism of thought, by crude superstitions and fallacies. The circumstances cited are almost without exception not important events, essential parts of the original true story or the saga, but details such as the poet would provide. In them he betrays no disapproval or consciousness of contrast, no hint of a different world for comparison.[1] The material splendours unearthed at Knossos, Mycenae, and elsewhere, older than the saga, than Ilion's fall, are as irrelevant to this point as the advanced stage of poetic art and the manifest genius of the poet. It may be that the poet or poets to whom our greatest debt is due was or were not so far removed in time, in spirit or in cultural conditions from the age professedly described, perhaps not more than one or two aristocratic and still 'heroic'[2] centuries in a land

[1] For κακά and ἀεικέα μήδετο ἔργα see Leaf on *Il.* xxiii, 24, 176; but the transition to a moral sense has probably begun. Here and always we shall do well to remember (1) that history is a *continuum* in which men, thoughts, customs and tools of different kinds and qualities develop and overlap, (2) that even in a savage community elements from different ages and mutually inconsistent beliefs coexist, (3) that the poet *is* portraying a past age to his own, using older and in some degree strange material, (4) that, though unobtrusive, his personality may not be negligible but he may think and feel, as he writes, somewhat differently from his fellows, (5) that he is human and may like Shakespeare or Scott be inconsistent without knowing it, and (6) that short of flagrant disharmony, he may consciously vary his means with his end, the details with the effect at which he aims. In any given passage these points deserve consideration before the dividing or excising knife is applied. Between the two poems there are divergencies indicating some change or difference of spirit. Compare e.g. *Od.* xxii, 411 ff. with the practice in the *Iliad* (xiii, 373 ff., etc.).

[2] The gulf between Homer and Hesiod may be clearly seen in their use of the word ἥρως. For Homer it describes a social class, the generality of the folk, the ordinary free man as opposed to the θής or δμώς (see e.g. *Od.* i, 100 f., 272, ii, 7 ff., 41, vii, 44, xviii, 423 f., etc.), but for Hesiod it signifies demigods, an earlier and quite distinct race, who fought at Thebes and Troy and vanished from the world of men to the Islands of the Blest (*Works and Days*, 156–80). That when Homer says that the men of to-day (οἷοι νῦν βροτοί εἰσι, *Il.* v, 304, xii, 383, etc.) are not so strong as the warriors at Troy it need not imply a long interval may be seen by the fact that he represents Nestor as saying among the warriors at Troy that they, Achilles, Agamemnon, etc., are no match for the contemporaries of his youth and 'none of the men of to-day (οἳ νῦν βροτοί εἰσιν ἐπιχθόνιοι) could fight with those' (*Il.* i, 260–72).

where Dorian invaders had not come;[1] but it would be impertinent and profitless, without publicly sifting all the evidence, to beg the 'Homeric Question'. For the subsequent argument it is irrelevant. We are concerned, in each of several spheres, to discover the original thought behind a great number of passages whose fundamental unity of conception can be vindicated. The problems would remain, whatever diversity of authorship or dating were imagined. There will appear evidence that the beliefs in question arose long ages before the Homeric poems and survived into later ages. In Roman literature, beginning some two centuries before our era largely under the influences of Greek civilisation, it is inevitably more difficult to trace the original native thought; yet, as we shall find, the fundamental beliefs may still be discerned. And this is true also of the earliest surviving Celtic, Anglo-Saxon, Norse and Russian literatures, which, though later, are relatively independent.

[1] This would be possible after mainland Greece was overrun, but in view of the diffusion and importance of the Dorians in the historic period it is remarkable that in the forty-eight books there is no hint of their existence except for the loosely attached mention of Δωριέες τριχάϊκες in the catalogue of inhabitants of Crete (*Od.* xix, 177). Tlepolemos, son of Herakles (slain in *Il.* v, 628 ff.), is in the Catalogue of Ships (*Il.* ii, 653 ff.) associated with Rhodians who are much praised but do nothing and receive no mention anywhere else in either poem. Also, if the Ionians preceded the Achaeans, as is maintained for instance by Kretschmer ('Zur Geschichte der griechischen Dialekte', *Glotta*, i, 1909, pp. 9 ff.) and Nilsson (*op. cit.* pp. 28 ff.), it is—when we remember their importance and numbers in the historic period and as early as the Hymn to the Delian Apollo—also remarkable that there should be no mention of Ionians at all, except the justly suspect *Il.* xiii, 685 (see Leaf, *ad loc.*) referring to Athenians. Distinct Ionian nationality, if it existed, is either submerged or ignored. The poet seems to write not only of, but for, 'Achaeans'.

PART I

THE MIND AND THE BODY

CHAPTER I

Some Processes of Consciousness

How do Homeric notions of the main processes of consciousness differ from our own? A good deal is explicit.[1] Thinking is described as 'speaking' and is located sometimes in the heart but usually in the φρήν or φρένες, traditionally interpreted as the 'midriff' or 'diaphragm'. To deem, be of opinion, is φάναι or φάσθαι. Thus the false dream leaves Agamemnon alone, 'thinking (φρονέοντα) in his mind (θυμός) things that were not to be fulfilled. For he deemed (φῆ, lit. "said") he would take Priam's city that very day'.[2] Deep reflection is conversation of one's self with one's θυμός or of one's θυμός with one's self. Thus Menelaos, deserted in battle, 'spake (εἶπε) to his great-hearted θυμός: "Woe is me if I leave behind these noble arms....But why did my θυμός thus hold converse (διελέξατο)?...That were choicest of evils". While thus he pondered (ὥρμαινε) in his θυμός and φρήν, the Trojan ranks came on'.[3] This view of thought as speech contributed to the later use of λόγος[4] as equivalent to *ratio* as well as *oratio*. Expression may be more or less articulate. As he lay awake, the heart of Odysseus within him barked against the serving maids as a bitch with pups barks savagely at a stranger, but Odysseus 'smote his breast and rebuked his heart with words: "Endure, O heart; yet a more shameful thing didst thou endure". And his heart enduring abode fast. But Odysseus himself rolled this way and that pondering...'.[5]

Father. *What is thinking really?*
Hilda (aged four years, nine months). *Don't know.*
Father. *Well, what do we think with?*
Hilda. *Animals think with their mouths.*

[1] Terms like βουλή and μῆτις need not be discussed here. Others will more conveniently be discussed in a later context. Greekless readers will find the important Greek words transliterated in the Word Index.
[2] *Il.* ii, 36 f. Cf. iii, 366, v, 190, viii, 498, xii, 106, 165, etc.
[3] *Il.* xvii, 90–106. Cf. *Od.* v, 284 ff., 298 ff., etc.
[4] See e.g. Plato, *Theaetetus*, 206 D; *Sophist*, 263 E. More light is cast on λόγος on pp. 33, 56, 66 ff., 76, n. 9 below. [5] *Od.* xx, 6 ff.

Father. *And people?*
Hilda.   *With their tongues.*
Father. *What does a man do then when he thinks?*
Hilda.   *He speaks.*

With this record[1] of a child's view might be compared not only Homer's but also the Society Islanders' conception of thinking as 'speaking in the stomach'[2] and that of the natives of New Guinea: 'The mind, *nanola*, by which term intelligence, power of discrimination, capacity for learning magical formulae and all forms of non-manual skill are described as well as moral qualities, resides somewhere in the larynx. The natives will always point to the organs of speech where the *nanola* resides.... The man who cannot speak through any defect of his organs is identified in name (*tonagowa*) and in treatment with all those mentally deficient'.[3] It is a naïve recognition of the importance of words in thinking and a no less naïve inference that thinking is where words appear to come from (cf. p. 67). We today may regard them as sounds or auditory images, symbols, but it was natural to identify them with the breath with which they are uttered.

In later Greek φρονεῖν has primarily an intellectual sense, 'to think, have understanding', but in Homer it is more comprehensive, covering undifferentiated psychic activity, the action of the φρένες, involving 'emotion' and 'conation' also, e.g. οἱ δ' ἰθὺς φρόνεον μέμασαν δὲ μάχεσθαι,[4] to which translation can only approximate: 'their spirits pressed forward and lusted for battle'; λύκοι τε καὶ ἄρνες...κακὰ φρονέουσι διαμπερὲς ἀλλήλοισιν, 'wolves and sheep feel evil sentiments (more adequately and clumsily: "have evil psychic activities") ever towards each other';[5] εἴ κέν τοι κείνη γε φίλα φρονέῃσ' ἐνὶ θυμῷ, 'if she feel kindly (sentiments) towards thee'.[6] But

---

[1] See W. Stern, *Psychology of Early Childhood*, translated by A. Barwell from the 3rd edition, 1924, p. 384. When my little nephew, F. R. S. (three years, five months), after making a statement, was asked 'How do you know?' he used to reply 'With my tongue'.
[2] See pp. 172–3 below.
[3] Malinowski, *Argonauts of the Western Pacific*, p. 408.
[4] *Il.* xiii, 135. Cf. xii, 124.   [5] *Il.* xxii, 263 f.   [6] *Od.* vii, 75.

we must not press the contrast too far. Traces of this fuller sense, e.g. μέγα φρονεῖν, are not uncommon in later Greek; and sometimes in Homer the intellectual side predominates or is all that need be represented in ordinary translation, as in the description of Agamemnon quoted above. More may be implied. Thus when Kalypso asks Hermes why he has come, αὔδα ὅ τι φρονέεις,[1] Butcher and Lang translate, 'Tell me all thy thought', though what follows, τελέσαι δέ με θυμὸς ἄνωγεν, shows that desire is involved.

Again, οἶδα in Homer can often be rendered by 'know', its usual meaning in later Greek, as if it were purely intellectual and involved no more than cognition, e.g. οἶδ' ἀρετὴν οἶός ἐσσι, 'I know what thy valour is';[2] but it sometimes clearly involves a great deal more, e.g. λέων δ' ὡς ἄγρια οἶδεν...ὡς Ἀχιλεὺς ἔλεον μὲν ἀπώλεσεν;[3] δαΐδας φέρε κεδνὰ ἰδυῖα Εὐρύκλεια;[4] Ἀτρεΐδης καὶ ἐγώ, φίλα εἰδότες ἀλλήλοισιν;[5] τοι ἤπια οἶδε παῖδά τε σὸν φιλέει.[6] It will not do just to say with Leaf[7] that εἰδέναι in Homer 'is regularly used to express disposition of character', or to explain with Ebeling:[8] 'Homer thinks that men act rightly or otherwise according as they understand rightly or otherwise whether anything is becoming or not, although we know that in many cases they do not so act'. This does not fit the construction, the various adjectives which follow; and that men in general of Homer's time and race should imagine mere knowledge to be adequate to virtue, if it was not, is unlikely. Literal translation is impossible. Myers, Butcher and Lang render: 'he is cruelly minded as a lion...even thus Achilles hath cast out pity', 'trusty Eurykleia bare for him torches', 'the son of Atreus and I as loving friends', 'he is loyal to thee and loves thy son'. Preconceptions born of later Greek usage, and our own thought, must be abandoned. To a verb which later was reserved for the expression of cognition, intellectual awareness,[9] we are compelled to give a richer

---

[1]. *Od.* v, 89. [2] *Il.* XIII, 275. [3] *Il.* XXIV, 41 ff.
[4] *Od.* I, 428 f. [5] *Od.* III, 277. [6] *Od.* XIII, 405.
[7] On *Il.* v, 326. [8] *Lexicon Homericum*, p. 354 (B. Giseke).
[9] In χάριν οἶδα, however, feeling probably continued to be implied.

meaning, a relation to feeling, emotion, and even to conation. A condition or rather attitude of the whole mind[1] is implied. οἶδα is a perfect tense, seeming here with its accusatives to mean something like 'I have felt (and now possess) a certain attitude or feelings', savage, trusty, friendly, or kindly, in general, or towards somebody in particular, as the case may be. What is the explanation? There is a clue in the aorist of the same verb εἶδον, ἰδών κ.τ.λ., which may be used of perceiving, seeing, e.g.

> ἄσβεστος δ' ἄρ' ἐνῶρτο γέλως μακάρεσσι θεοῖσιν,
> ὡς ἴδον "Ηφαιστον διὰ δώματα ποιπνύοντα.[2]

But often[3] this clearly carries in itself emotional and active force, which once at least is defined by an accusative neuter plural adjective just as was οἶδα:

> δεινὰ δ' ὑπόδρα ἰδών "Ηρην πρὸς μῦθον ἔειπεν,

where we must be content with something like 'looking terrible things beneath his brow'.[4] Seeing merges into 'looking'. And thus the attainment not of mere perception, knowledge, but also of stable feeling, sentiment, of such an attitude active and emotional, is implied by the use of οἶδα, the perfect, in the passages quoted and in greater or lesser degree elsewhere according to the nature of the accusative which follows: λυγρά, αἴσιμα, ἀθεμίστια, οὔ τινα θεμιστά, νέμεσιν, φίλα μήδεα κ.τ.λ. We can explain this by the primal unity of mind in which perception or cognition is associated with or immediately followed by an emotion and a tendency to action varying in degree and kind according to the nature of the object, a unity

[1] Superficially it might seem possible that the verb should convey no more than cognition and its objects be emotions or sentiments; but the objects are not so defined.
[2] Il. I, 599 f.
[3] E.g. ἰδών ἐς παῖδα σιωπῇ (Il. VI, 404), τὸν δ' ἄρ' ὑπόδρα ἰδών (Il. I, 148) etc. Cf. invidere.
[4] Il. XV, 13. With δέρκομαι and βλέπω the neut. plur. acc. is common later, e.g. 'Shield of Herakles', 236 (cf. Latin torva tuens, etc.). The use with the neuter singular is fundamentally the same. In terms of grammar, the accusative is, of course, internal. Continuing the usage, Pindar has not only φθονερὰ βλέπων, 'casting glances of envy' (Nem. IV, 39), but also ὁρῶντ' ἀλκάν, 'with valour in his eyes' (Ol. IX, 111). Vivid imagination is often expressed in Homer by ὄσσομαι, e.g. κακὰ δ' ὄσσετο θυμός, Od. X, 374.

whose survival in our own processes is stressed by the 'ideo-motor' theory of modern psychology which asserts that 'every "idea" is not only a state or act of knowing but also a tendency to movement'.[1] Ordinary speech, e.g. 'to see her is to love her',[2] 'I shuddered at the thought', etc., bears witness to the same. We discriminate between the sight or thought and the feeling, and we note the latter as subsequent, but must not forget that the former may persist and also that the emotion may precede the idea, may be vaguely felt before taking definite shape in consciousness and being 'intellectualised'. A man meets another or is brought into less direct relations with him, e.g. by being told about him. According to what he learns, so he feels towards him, and his emotion takes on intellectual definition and is realised in idea. This process, at least as much the rest as the first perceiving, lies behind τοι ἤπια οἶδε, etc. Where there is no dative defining the scope (e.g. ἄγρια οἶδε) we may explain by a similar reaction to things or people at large and by the formulation of general emotional and conative tendencies. The perfect tense (οἶδα, εἰδώς) means that the process has already been achieved and is thenceforward effective. Working out the 'ideo-motor' theory, Stout writes:[3] 'All the various systems of ideas which grow up in the process of ideal construction of the world and of the Self have their conative aspect. Each system of ideas is a general tendency to feel and act in certain ways under certain circumstances. It is convenient to have a general name for ideal systems considered from this point of view'. He names them 'sentiments'. It is such that φίλα εἰδότες ἀλλήλοισιν, κεδνὰ ἰδυῖα, etc., imply.

Complementary to the subject with its activity, the object, the 'idea', has quality and may be characterised according to its emotion and the action to which it tends: ἄγρια, φίλα, κεδνά κ.τ.λ. In the passive we may compare τῷ δ' ἀσπαστὸν ἐείσατο κοιμηθῆναι.[4] The bearing upon conation appears in

---

[1] MacDougall, An Outline of Psychology, p. 290.

[2] Burns, Bonny Lesley. Cf. ὡς δ' ἴδεν, ὡς μιν ἔρως πυκινὰς φρένας ἀμφεκάλυψεν (Il. xiv, 294), ἐλεαίρεσκον...εἰσορόωντες (Il. xxiv, 23), ἴδιον, ὡς ἐνόησα (Od. xx, 204), Theoc. ii, 82, etc.

[3] Manual of Psychology[3], pp. 700 f.   [4] Od. vii, 343. Cf. v, 398, etc.

Priam's question[1] to Hecuba, when he has told her that Zeus
has sent bidding him go to Achilles:

> τί τοι φρεσὶν εἴδεται εἶναι;
> αἰνῶς γάρ μ' αὐτόν γε μένος καὶ θυμὸς ἄνωγε
> κεῖσ' ἰέναι.

Where cognition and thought are so bound up with feeling
and tendency to act, the relation of moral character, of virtue
to knowledge, is closer than where cognition is more 'pure'.
How emotional and prone to physical expression of their
emotions Homer's heroes were we have seen.[2] Greeks like
Aristotle and we to-day have apparently attained to greater
'detachment', power of thinking in cold blood without bodily
movement, as we have to a sharper discrimination and definition of the aspects and phases of the mind's activity. It is with
the consciousness, the knowing self, the spectator aware of
what happens within and without (emotions, sensations, etc.),
that a man would tend more particularly to identify himself.
As this spectator became more 'detached', the purely intellectual, the cognitive bearing of such words as οἶδα would
naturally prevail.

Whether or not Socrates, in his doctrine that virtue is
knowledge, was at all consciously influenced by the superficial
meaning of these phrases in the Bible of his race, it is interesting
to note, despite the differentiations of thought and language
which intervene, the reappearance of what is essentially the
same truth. The doctrine of 'vision' presented by Plato[3]
implies more than mere cognition, and for him what the soul
has 'seen' is all important for its condition, so that he might
have accepted κεδνὰ ἰδυῖα, λυγρὰ ἰδυῖα, ἄγρια οἶδεν, ἀπατήλια
εἰδώς κ.τ.λ. as just explanations, if not descriptions, of moral
character.

The same peculiarity emerges also in the verbs of 'learning',
'forgetting', and 'remembering', which otherwise might
appear to be concerned only with cognition, the acquiring,
losing, or recovering of knowledge. δαῆναι, 'to learn', means
'to take into the mind', but, as we might now expect, 'into

---

[1] *Il.* xxiv, 197 ff.   [2] P. 3.
[3] See e.g. *Rep.* 401 f., 411, 500; *Phaedr.* 246, 255.

the mind as a whole', including in its action feeling and conation, λανθάνεσθαι, 'to let escape' thence, μιμνήσκεσθαι and μνᾶσθαι, 'to recall' thither or 'to turn one's mind to' (something). Thus by the side of δαῆναι ἐμὸν νόον,[1] μνήσασθε ἕκαστος παίδων ἠδ᾽ ἀλόχων[2] and οὐδὲ σέθεν λελάθοντο,[3] we find δεδαηκότες ἀλκήν[4] (for ἀλκή cf. πλῆσθεν δ᾽ ἄρα οἱ μέλε᾽ ἐντὸς ἀλκῆς καὶ σθένεος),[5] εὖ εἰδότα θούριδος ἀλκῆς,[6] μνήσασθε δὲ θούριδος ἀλκῆς,[7] λάθοντο δὲ θούριδος ἀλκῆς[8] and μνήσαντο δὲ χάρμης,[9] μνώοντ᾽ ὀλοοῖο φόβοιο,[10] λήσεσθαι χόλου,[11] ἀπεκλελάθεσθε δὲ θάμβευς,[12] etc., in which the meaning is not merely that the emotion or activity is perceived or lost as an object of thought, but that it is recovered in itself, felt and perhaps visibly expressed, or (λάθοντο etc.) that the consciousness thereof, the emotion and the tendency to action, cease together.

With these findings about Homer, it is interesting to compare Lévy-Bruhl's[13] analysis of 'primitive' thought:

On entend par 'représentation' un fait de connaissance en tant que l'esprit a simplement l'image ou l'idée d'un objet....La représentation est, par excellence, un phénomène intellectuel ou cognitif. Ce n'est pas ainsi qu'il faut entendre les représentations collectives des primitifs. Leur activité mentale est trop peu différenciée pour qu'il soit possible d'y considérer à part les idées ou les images des objets, indépendamment des sentiments, des émotions, des passions, qui évoquent ces idées et ces images, ou qui sont évoqués par elles. Précisément parce que notre activité mentale est plus différenciée et aussi parce que l'analyse de ses fonctions nous est familière, il nous est très difficile de réaliser, par un effort d'imagination, des états plus complexes, où les éléments émotionels et moteurs sont des *parties intégrantes* des représentations. Il nous semble que ces états ne sont pas vraiment des représentations. Et en effet, pour conserver ce terme, il faut en modifier le sens. Il faut entendre par cette forme de l'activité mentale chez les primitifs, non pas un phénomène intellectuel ou cognitif pur, ou presque pur, mais un phénomène plus complexe, où ce qui pour nous est proprement «représentation» se trouve

[1] *Od.* IV, 493.
[2] *Il.* XV, 662 f.
[3] *Il.* IV, 127.
[4] *Od.* II, 61.
[5] *Il.* XVII, 212. Cf. 499.
[6] *Il.* XV, 527 f., XI, 710.
[7] *Il.* VI, 112, etc.
[8] *Il.* XV, 322, etc.
[9] *Il.* IV, 222, etc.
[10] *Il.* XI, 71, XVI, 771.
[11] *Od.* XI, 554.
[12] *Od.* XXIV, 394.
[13] *Les Fonctions Mentales dans les Sociétés Inférieures*, pp. 28 f.

encore confondu avec d'autres éléments de charactère émotionel ou moteur, coloré, pénétré par eux et impliquant par conséquent une autre attitude à l'égard des objets représentés.

There is, perhaps, no such thing as 'un phénomène intellectuel ou cognitif pur' for us either. It is rather a difference of degree in the 'impurity'. Most of us are, perhaps, inwardly calmer and outwardly more restrained than 'les primitifs', and we have learned to differentiate conceptually, to analyse a complex state of mind into abstract elements with separate names which create the illusion of separate existence. We lack terms like φρονεῖν for the complex unity which is the reality.

On the emotionalism of Homer's race and the difference in its categories of thought there is another curious sidelight in his language. τέρπεσθαι, which in later Greek means 'to be pleased, delighted', he applies also to experiences which later Greeks[1] and we should not deem delightful, viz. weeping and lamentation. Thus Penelope complains

αὐτὰρ ἐμοὶ καὶ πένθος ἀμέτρητον πόρε δαίμων,
ἤματα μὲν γὰρ τέρπομ' ὀδυρομένη, γοόωσα...[2]

and Odysseus rushes to embrace his mother

ὄφρα καὶ εἰν Ἀΐδαο φίλας περὶ χεῖρε βαλόντε
ἀμφοτέρω κρυεροῖο τεταρπώμεσθα γόοιο.[3]

Apparently τέρπεσθαι is used when any inclination, even if it be only an inclination to give bodily expression to grief, is realised. The stages appear to be ἵμερος or ἔρος, desire, to which the stimulus may be sorrow (e.g. Menelaos, by reminding Telemachos of his father lost, τῷ... ὑφ' ἵμερον ὦρσε γόοιο);[4] its satisfaction,[5] τέρπεσθαι or ἐξ ἔρον εἶναι, literally 'to put the desire from one', to work it off; and κόρος, 'satiety', after it

---

[1] See however Plato, *Philebus*, 47 E ff., of which Professor Cornford reminds me. [2] *Od.* XIX, 512 f. [3] *Od.* XI, 211 f.

[4] The desire might be repressed, unsatisfied, or deferred till a more fitting occasion. There was 'a time to weep and a time to laugh'. When Menelaos and Helen and their guests Telemachos and Peisistratos are settling down for 'a good cry' together, Nestor's son, worthy of his father, interrupts: 'I personally do not enjoy wailing during dinner (τέρπομ' ὀδυρόμενος μεταδόρπιος). There will be the morning...' (*Od.* IV, 193 f.). The host agrees to continue the subject then and bids them take to eating once more instead. Contrast *Il.* XXIV, 507, 514.

[5] This appears to be the root meaning of the word.

has been worked off (e.g. Odysseus confesses to have reacted violently when bidden visit Hades and continues αὐτὰρ ἐπεὶ κλαίων τε κυλινδόμενός τ' ἐκορέσθην).[1] This lack of differentiation appears to mean that men then lived more for the moment or at least shaped their language from the standpoint of the moment and its satisfaction. Later ages have not only deprived themselves of the pleasure of unrestrained weeping and the free bodily expression of other feelings, but also, taking a longer view, have restricted such terms virtually to those instincts and satisfactions which, when viewed from the outside or in cold blood, seem desirable.

In that earlier stage seems also to lie the explanation of the much disputed word χάρμη, the spirit of battle, which is most naturally connected with χαίρω, χάρμα, χαρμονή and interpreted to mean in origin something like 'joy'. Absence of these considerations has led scholars to look elsewhere, e.g. Leaf[2] prefers a root *ghar* meaning 'prick, tear' (which does not fit *Il.* xiii, 82, 104, etc.), objecting that Homer does not like war and calls it hard names; but neither does he like sorrow, and weeping itself he calls στυγερός. Within themselves war and sorrow have both their desires and their satisfactions. Boisacq (s.v.) connects both χαίρω and χάρμη with a conjectural Indoeuropean *gher(e)* expressing desire of various kinds including anger. χάρμη will be the 'battle-lust' or 'joy'[3] that comes with free play of the warrior's energies, when like the war-horse he 'smelleth the battle afar off'. Then 'warring becomes sweeter than returning home'[4] and battle —to sweep over the field with instincts and energies free—is 'joy' indeed, the supreme realisation of the pride of power. In the world of warriors which the *Iliad* shows, it would deserve to be so named, even as μέμαα, which continues to mean 'desire' in general, is used[5] alone without definition to express

---

[1] *Od.* x, 499. 　　　　　　[2] On *Il.* iv, 222.

[3] Professor Cornford reminds me that in the German word *Lust* desire and delight are still combined. They were so combined in Anglo-Sax. *lust*.

[4] *Il.* ii, 453 f., xi, 13 f.

[5] *Il.* vii, 261, viii, 327, etc. μέμαα itself may be significant as suggesting an original equivalence or unity of desire and quick movement; for it may mean either. By the side of μεμάασι κτήματα δάσσασθαι (*Od.* xx,

the warrior's 'desire' *par excellence*, the lust for battle or its expression in activity. For those warriors battle also meant shouting, ἀϋτή, and ἀϋτή like χάρμη becomes a name for battle with its original sense receding into the background, so that the poet can say that the wounded chieftains come out ὀψείοντες ἀϋτῆς καὶ πολέμοιο[1] or ῥεῖα δέ κ' ἀκμῆτες κεκμηότας ἄνδρας ἀϋτῇ/ὤσαιμεν προτὶ ἄστυ.[2] Of many[3] descriptions of the battle-lust one must suffice. Telamonian Aias echoes his namesake thus: '"Even so too my hands invincible quiver with eagerness about the spearshaft, and energy is roused within me, and both my feet beneath me urge me forward, and I burn even in single fight to meet Hector, Priam's son, who lusts (sc. for battle) ceaselessly (ἄμοτον μεμαῶτι)". So they spake, one to another, rejoicing in the joy (or "lust") of battle (χάρμη γηθόσυνοι) which the god set in their hearts'.[4] The poet here, as in οὐδ' ἔπι χάρμη,[5] 'and there is no joy of battle in them', shows what is his own interpretation; and it is not only more pointed and Homeric but even necessary to give a sense of such subjective feeling in passages like the description of the Achaeans fleeing before Hector and Aineias οὖλον κεκλήγοντες ἴσαν, λήθοντο δὲ χάρμης.... πολέμου δ' οὐ γίγνετ' ἐρωή.[6] Here too desire and enjoyment pass away and there is κόρος, satiety. 'Soon comes satiety of battle to men, when Zeus inclines his scale.'[7] But if he will, they may enjoy it long and 'know not satiety of battle' (μάχης ἀκόρητοι ἔασιν).[8] There is, we may note, a striking parallel in Sanscrit: *raṇa* has a basic meaning 'joy, delight' but in many contexts means 'battle'.

215 f.), μεμάασιν ἀκουέμεν (*Od.* XVII, 520) and even μεμάασιν αὖθι μένειν (*Il.* x, 208 f.) we find πῇ μέματον; (*Il.* VIII, 413), ἵπποι γάρ με παρήϊξαν πρόσσω μεμαυῖαι (*Il.* XI, 615) and ἰθὺς μεμαῶτε μαχώμεθα (*Il.* XXII, 243). Cf. ἰθὺς φρόνεον (p. 14 above).
1 *Il.* XIV, 37.   2 *Il.* XVI, 44 f.
3 *Il.* III, 133, XIII, 286, etc.
4 *Il.* XIII, 77 ff. Cf. Aeschylus, *Septem*, 377 f., 392 f. (Murray).
5 *Il.* XIII, 104.   6 *Il.* XVII, 759 ff.
7 *Il.* XIX, 221 ff.   8 *Il.* XIII, 621-39. Cf. XII, 335, etc.

CHAPTER II

The Organs of Consciousness

The general internal anatomy of men and beasts must have
been familiar to all through battle and sacrifice or the
domestic killing and dressing of animals; but the true functions of the several organs, with the exception of the alimentary
canal and its obvious accessories, were not known. Let us
look for the seat of consciousness. Where is it in the body?
A man is said to think his thoughts and feel emotions and
impulses in his heart (κῆρ or κραδίη) but more usually in the
φρένες, sometimes called πραπίδες, and in the θυμός. What
are these? In the latter half of the fifth century the Hippocratic
school[1] gave the name φρένες to the midriff or diaphragm and
Plato in the *Timaeus*[2] did so too. Later writers, ancient and
modern,[3] have therefore assumed that this must have been
the meaning for Homer also, while the θυμός, apparently
something 'vaporous' (cf. θυμιάω, etc.) which the φρένες are
said to contain,[4] is interpreted as the 'blood-soul'. But no
part of the body has less obvious claims to be the seat of the
'blood-soul', if such is in point, or indeed of the intelligence,
than the midriff or diaphragm, the pink muscular sheet
dividing the organs of the thorax from those of the abdomen.
Nor has that sheet any claim to be considered as a plurality,[5]
φρένες, or, as the latter are, to be described as μέλαιναι (or
ἀμφιμέλαιναι),[6] 'black', 'blackish', or whatever that means.
In defence reference can only be made to the 'midmost darkness of the body' or to the colour of other parts or entrails

[1] E.g. περὶ ἀρχ. ἰητρ. 1, 54 (Kühn).   [2] 70 A.
[3] See e.g. Buchholz, *Homerische Realien*, III, pp. 73–101; Rohde, *Psyche*,
English translation, pp. 30 f.; Bickel, *Homerische Seelenglaube*, 1926, and the
various commentaries on Homer.
[4] See e.g. *Il.* VIII, 202, IX, 458.
[5] It is recognised (e.g. by Buchholz, *loc. cit.*) that the rarer singular
φρήν is used for metrical purposes.
[6] *Il.* I, 103, XVII, 83, 499, 573; *Od.* IV, 661.

near.[1] 'His midriff black (with anger) was full of fury on both sides (above and below)' is Leaf's interpretation of one passage,[2] following Autenrieth. How a dome-shaped muscular sheet can be 'filled (πίμπλαντο) on both sides' thus is not explained. Nor is the similar difficulty met that Homer repeatedly speaks of θυμός, etc. as moving *in*, being *in* or being placed *in*, not beneath, the φρένες. These points need not be pressed. Let us remember what Aristarchus observed, what appears to have been forgotten, that a large proportion of the commonest words had changed their meaning in the interval between Homer and the Attic age.[3] We may then with an open mind examine the Homeric instances and, for further guidance, turn not to science, relatively late and original in its terminology, but to the earliest literature where, if anywhere, the tradition of language and thought might be expected to survive.

To the reader thus emancipated from respect for the traditional meaning 'diaphragm', it may at once occur, as it did to the writer and, independently, to Justesen,[4] that the 'blackish' organs (plural) containing something vaporous (θυμός) might be nothing else than the lungs[5] containing the breath. Let us examine all the evidence.

[1] Köppens pointed to the gall, Helbig to the 'adjacent muscles', Buchholz also to the 'entrails'.   [2] *Il.* I, 103 f.
[3] See e.g. Lehrs, *De Aristarchi Studiis Homericis*, Diss. II, De Aristarchea vocabulorum Homericorum interpretatione, pp. 35 ff., and Monro, *Odyssey XIII–XXIV*, Appendix, p. 450.
[4] Since this work was done, P. T. Justesen has in *Les principes psychologiques d'Homère*, Copenhagen, 1928, published the suggestion that the φρένες were the lungs and θυμός breath, but he misses the relation of breath and blood (see pp. 46 ff. *inf.*) and, instead of many of the arguments below, has others which have not been accepted. Writing since, J. Böhme (in *Die Seele u. das Ich im homerischen Epos*, Leipzig, 1929, pp. 3 ff.), F. Rüsche (in *Blut Leben u. Seele*, Paderborn, 1930, pp. 27, 33, etc.), and V. Larock (in 'Les premières conceptions psychologiques des Grecs', *Revue Belge de Philol. et Hist.* IX, 1930, pp. 385 f.) all maintain the old view that φρένες meant diaphragm, while O. Körner (in *Die Sinnesempfindungen in Ilias u. Odyssee*, 1932, p. 42; cf. *Die ärztlichen Kenntnisse in Ilias u. Odyssee*, pp. 26 f.) maintains that it means the pericardium.
[5] The pleurae also are probably included incidentally, perhaps even the diaphragm. This last and the pericardium would scarcely be differentiated by name from the organs they bound. It occurred to me that the diaphragm and pericardium together might constitute the φρένες above the liver and around the heart, but a mere envelope and partition could

Aeschylus[1] speaks more specifically of the μελαγχίτων φρήν, 'black- (or dark-)tunicked', so apt to the lung with its dark exterior.[2] 'The adult lung is bluish grey, more or less mottled with black.'[3] The 'black' need not be stressed. Homer applies μέλας not only to the dark blue κύανος and to grapes but to blood and also apparently to swart ruddiness of complexion.[4] For Pindar[5] and Theognis[6] it is the colour of the heart. It does not suit the diaphragm. Similarly, if the φρένες were the lungs, naturally thus coloured, we can understand why evil φρένες are described as λευκαί by Pindar:[7] πεύθομαι γάρ νιν Πελίαν ἄθεμιν λευκαῖς πιθήσαντα φρασίν... ἀποσυλᾶσαι βιαίως, to which existing explanations are merely: 'white, i.e. envious. Others compare λευγαλέος λυγρός' (Gildersleeve); and: '"in obedience to mad thoughts"— clearly connected with λύσσα, Att. λύττα for λυκγα. This Pindaric use is all that is wanted to confirm this explanation of λύσσα. Hesychius gives λευκῶν πραπίδων· κακῶν φρενῶν' (Fennell). The contrast, as we may now see it to be, to the colour of the healthy lung, organ of mind, will be simply analogous to that of our own ancient phrase 'white-livered', describing an unhealthy condition of the seat of passion. The quality and condition of a man's φρένες determine or are the quality and condition of his mind.[8] These phrases are further discussed below.[9]

scarcely have impressed men sufficiently to receive all the significance which they attached to the φρένες and that meaning does not so well fit the various instances and the evidence for θυμός, etc., below. The filling of the φρένες with μένος (Leaf's 'fury') perhaps suggests recognition of the flow of blood to the lungs in crises (see MacDougall, *An Outline of Psychology*, p. 322).   [1] *Persae*, 115.

[2] Possibly even alluding to the pleura in which each lung is clothed and which medical writers appear actually to have called χιτών (e.g. Galen, *de Plac.* VIII, 715).   [3] Piersol, *Human Anatomy*, 1907, p. 1846.

[4] See e.g. *Il.* XI, 24, XVIII, 562, IV, 149; *Od.* XVI, 175.

[5] Fr. 123.   [6] Line 1199.   [7] *Pyth.* IV, 109 f.

[8] Thus unlike Pelias τὸ πρὶν μὲν ἀναίνετο ἔργον ἀεικές/δῖα Κλυται-μνήστρη· φρεσὶ γὰρ κέχρητ' ἀγαθῆσι, *Od.* III, 265; cf. ἀλλὰ πατὴρ οὑμὸς φρεσὶ μαίνεται οὐκ ἀγαθῆσι, *Il.* VIII, 360. For what appears to be a misunderstanding of μέλαινα φρήν (possibly on the basis of the later meaning 'diaphragm' but cf. our 'black-hearted'), see Scol. Anon. No. 32, *Anth. Lyr. Gr.* Vol. II, ed. Diehl; cf. κελαινόφρων, Aesch. *Eum.* 459.

[9] Pp. 46–8.

Where are the φρένες? There is one passage[1] which at first sight seems to support the accepted view based on the Hippocratic attribution and may have suggested the latter. Odysseus is tempted to slay the Cyclops outright with his sword, οὐτάμεναι πρὸς στῆθος ὅθι φρένες ἧπαρ ἔχουσι, to stab him in the chest 'where the φρένες hold (or "enclose") the liver'. The diaphragm rises, as it were a thin dome, within what may roughly be called the cylinder of the thorax. Immediately beneath the dome and almost filling it is the liver; fitting neatly around the dome between it and the walls of the thorax, especially at the back and sides, are the lungs. With the membrane of the diaphragm intervening, they too 'hold the liver'. In their favour is the plural number and their size. They are conspicuous organs, and the relationship is so close that an abscess on the liver sometimes breaks through into the right lung and is discharged by coughing. In the *Iliad*, in a couplet three times used,[2] the apparently synonymous πραπίδες, also plural, appear: βάλε...ἧπαρ ὑπὸ πραπίδων, 'smote him in the liver beneath the πραπίδες', for which the same considerations hold. There is less possibility of doubt elsewhere. Patroklos hurls his spear at Sarpedon and ἔβαλ' ἔνθ' ἄρα τε φρένες ἔρχαται ἀμφ' ἀδινὸν κῆρ, 'smote him where the φρένες shut in the dense heart'.[3] ἀμφί means 'around' or 'at the sides of'. The heart rests on the top of the dome so that the diaphragm is out of the question, whereas the lungs are shaped to fit neatly around the heart and do shut it in.

A few lines later Patroklos plants his foot on Sarpedon's chest and 'pulled the spear out of his flesh and the φρένες came out after it',[4] which might indeed happen if φρένες

---

[1] *Od.* IX, 301.   [2] *Il.* XI, 578, XIII, 412, XVII, 349.

[3] *Il.* XVI, 481. Of the adjective ἀδινόν Leaf, in his commentary on *Il.* II, 87, writes: 'According to the explanation of the ancients adopted by Buttman, the primary sense is *dense*, but this gives a much less satisfactory chain of significations. It is then particularly hard to explain the application of the word to the heart'. But with φρένες meaning the light porous lungs there would be admirable point here in the contrast. Leaf wishes to trace all to an original meaning of 'quick, restless motion', but density, frequency in space or time (cf. πυκνός or *creber*), is adequate.

[4] *Il.* XVI, 503.

means 'lungs', but scarcely[1] if it means the diaphragm, taut muscle firmly attached all round. When Achilles from above plunges his sword into the chest of Tros so that the liver and blood come out,[2] there is no mention of the so important φρένες, which, if pierced, would surely have been mentioned; yet the diaphragm must have been pierced. When, on the other hand, Aias with a stone strikes Hector on the chest (στῆθος) 'above the rim of his shield near his neck'[3] and Hector vomits blood and is seized with 'sore gasping',[4] it is his φρένες which are distressed with pains (ὀδύναι),[5] as the hand is when pierced by an arrow[6] or the flesh of the foot when an arrow is plucked thence.[7] Most decisive of all, perhaps, is the word μετάφρενον, which it is recognised should mean 'the part behind the φρένες', a strange name to use at all for a large area if the φρένες meant merely the membrane dividing the thorax from the abdomen. In fact, for Homer μετάφρενον means the upper part of the back, so that scholars have been puzzled: *qua ratione eam induerit significationem, adhuc non satis explicatum est.*[8] Blows fall upon the μετάφρενον and shoulders together,[9] and four times[10] its position is actually defined as 'between the shoulders', μεταφρένῳ ἐν δόρυ πῆξεν ὤμων μεσσηγύς, 'thrust his spear into the part behind the φρένες between the shoulders'. Recognition of the φρένες as the lungs removes the difficulty. Later, just as for Homer 'the φρένες shut in the heart', Aeschylus, whose μελαγχίτων φρήν so well fits the lung, speaks of the heart (καρδία) as 'within the φρένες'[11] and as 'kicking the φρήν in fear',[12] and as 'whirling in eddies against the φρένες':[13] πρὸς φρεσὶν... δίναις κυκλούμενον

---

[1] This has been recognised and the passage said to refer to 'all the intestines near the midriff', Buchholz, *op. cit.* p. 75.

[2] *Il.* xx, 470.   [3] *Il.* xiv, 412.

[4] *Il.* xiv, 437, xv, 10.   [5] *Il.* xv, 60 f.

[6] *Il.* xvi, 510–24, xv, 394, etc.

[7] *Il.* xi, 398. Cf. v, 354, xv, 394. For φρένες= lungs as seat of 'mental' pain, grief, see below, pp. 37 f.

[8] Ebeling, *Lexicon Homericum*, s.v. μετάφρενον (Mutzbauer).

[9] *Il.* ii, 265, xvi, 791; *Od.* viii, 528. Cf. *Il.* xxiii, 380.

[10] *Il.* v, 40 f., viii, 258 f., xi, 447 f., xvi, 806 f.

[11] *Choeph.* 832 f.   [12] *P.V.* 881.   [13] *Ag.* 996 f.

28   THE ORGANS OF CONSCIOUSNESS

κέαρ, an assimilation perhaps of the heart to a spinning top. The current rendering of φρένες in these passages as 'midriff' is palpably absurd, as the latter is below the heart. We cannot fail to be reminded of Plato's view that the lungs (πλεύμων) were 'set around the heart like a cushion' (μάλαγμα v.l. ἅλμα) to receive its 'leaping' (πήδησις) in fear.[1]

Homer also describes[2] the φρένες as πυκιναί (a word used of things close together or of close texture, e.g. a thicket,[3] the twigs and branches of a tree[4] or the stones of a wall[5]), which fits admirably the multitude of branching passages and veins within each lung and the intricate tracery,[6] the polygonal lobules of the outside. It appears to be a word of praise, suggesting perhaps that the fineness and complexity of structure of the lungs, as for us of the brain with its convolutions,[7] were related to fineness and complexity of mind (cf. πυκιμηδής, πυκινὰ φρεσὶ μήδε' ἔχουσα, etc.[8]); for moving about in the passages of the lungs and conditioned by them was the θυμός, the vital principle that thinks and feels and prompts to action. Here also perhaps is the explanation of the epithet λάσιος, 'bushy, shaggy', which could be applied to a sheep, a tree or a thicket and which Homer applies to the heart, between which and the φρένες the consciousness seems to be shared, e.g. 'Αχαιοὺς ὦρσε Μενοιτιάδεω Πατροκλῆος λάσιον κῆρ, 'the

[1] Timaeus, 70 B ff. Cf. Aristotle, de Part. Anim. 669 a, 18 ff. The ancient Egyptian word 'heart' 'ib meant 'dancer'. In ḫ'ti they seem to have referred to the lungs also as a seat of thought and feeling.
[2] Il. xiv, 294.   [3] Il. xviii, 320; Od. vi, 128.
[4] Od. v, 471.   [5] Il. xvi, 212.
[6] This perhaps contributes to the recurring image of Aeschylus (P.V. 789, Choeph. 450, Eum. 275, Suppl. 179; cf. Pind. Ol. x, 2 f., Soph. Fr. 597 (Pearson) and Plato, Theaet. 191 c ff.), in an age familiar with writing: δέλτοι φρενῶν or δελτογράφος φρήν. This choice of name, if it carried with it any suggestion of Δ form (cf. the κύρβεις), suits the roughly triangular lungs as does the number, but does not suit the dome-shaped midriff. 'In man each lung is pyramidal in form' (Century Dictionary, s.v.). The epithet ἔλλοψ applied by Empedocles (B 3, Diels) to the φρήν has, when applied to fish, been interpreted 'scaly' (cf. λεπίς), and might thus refer to the lobules on the surface of the lung but possibly to the complete envelope or pleura (cf. p. 25 with note 2).
[7] In lower animals and idiots the convolutions are in fact much less marked.   [8] Od. i, 438, xix, 353; Il. xxiv, 282, xv, 461, etc.

bushy heart of Patroklos, son of Menoitios, roused the Achaeans'.[1] Elsewhere Homer appears to confine the word κῆρ to the internal organ, which makes against the current interpretation of 'hairy chest'. Plato[2] interpreted λάσιον κῆρ as a description of the internal organ indicating a quality of mind; and the scholiast's interpretation is συνετὴ ψυχή, that of Eustathius πυκινὴ ψυχή. If we look at the heart itself with the tracery of branching veins and arteries running over its surface and with the multitudinous branching veins and arteries growing immediately out of it, like bushes, many of them through the lungs, we understand the name at once. Through the lungs there stretch also the *rami* of what by an inevitable metaphor is still known to medicine as 'the bronchial tree'. Hence the old Latin name *ramites*. On either hand from the trachea or wind-pipe stretch the bronchi and from them grow the smaller tubes branching and bifurcating in a hundred directions. The origin of λάσιαι φρένες, expressive of intrigue and cunning as late as the Alexandrian period,[3] will thus be explained, as it could not hitherto. For Aeschylus, as we have seen and shall see, φρένες appears still to mean 'lungs'. It is now perhaps possible to explain a passage in which he uses the synonym πραπίδες: 'whatsoever is brought to pass by a nod of Zeus' head, it falls without tripping and not upon its back, for thick and bushy stretch the passages of his πραπίδες, not to be perceived by the eye' (δαυλοὶ γὰρ πραπίδων δάσκιοί τε τείνουσι πόροι, κατιδεῖν ἄφραστοι).[4] The word πόροι is regularly used of the passages in the body, veins, ducts, etc.; but the commentators, familiar only with the equation of φρένες or πραπίδες to the 'diaphragm', are hard put to. Thus Tucker: 'πραπίδες—not merely thoughts but

[1] *Il.* xvi, 553 f. Cf. ii, 851.

[2] *Theaet.* 194 E f. The tradition that Lysander's heart and that of Alexander's dog, when their bodies were opened, were found to be hairy (see Eustathius *ad Il.* i, 189, pp. 78 f.) shows how the Homeric phrase was interpreted. Compare also Pliny, *N.H.* xi, 37, 184 f.

[3] Alex. Aetol. *ap.* Ath. 699 c. The lungs would fit even if we thought λάσιαι φρένες referred to a 'hairy chest', which has more to be said for it in ἐν δέ οἱ ἦτορ στήθεσσιν λασίοισι διάνδιχα μερμήριξεν, *Il.* i, 188 f.; cf. *Od.* ix, 433.   [4] *Suppl.* 91 ff.

shrewd devices (of wrestling) which like chased animals run through the intricate paths of the dark mysterious mind of Zeus'. But πραπίδες does not elsewhere or here mean 'thoughts' or 'devices' but a physical organ, and perhaps by extension the mind of which it is the organ. The passages of the lungs give admirable point. The image of vegetation in the breast constantly recurs. Alcaeus¹ speaks of βρόμος, frenzy, 'growing' or 'springing up in the breast' (ἐν στήθεσσι φυίει), as Simonides² of Ceos of hope 'springing up in the breast (στήθεσσιν ἐμφύεται) of the young' and Theognis³ of 'straight thought springing up in the breast' (ἰθεῖα γνώμη στήθεσσιν ἐμπεφύῃ), while Pindar⁴ says 'By the grace of God a man blossoms (ἀνθεῖ) with wise πραπίδες', and time and again⁵ speaks of the 'fruit' (καρπός) of the πραπίδες, φρήν or φρένες, and Aeschylus himself speaks of 'reaping the fruit (καρποῦσ-θαι) of the φρένες'⁶ or more fully 'reaping a deep furrow through the φρήν out of which sprout trusty counsels' (βαθεῖαν ἄλοκα διὰ φρενὸς καρπούμενος, ἐξ ἧς τὰ κεδνὰ βλαστάνει βουλεύματα).⁷ Such a conception of the φρένες and their growth of tubes, or of θυμός within them, enables us better to understand Homer's curious and hitherto suspected⁸ simile: 'His θυμός was "melted" (or "warmed" ἰάνθη) as when (lit. "as if", ὡς εἰ) dew about the ears of a growing crop when the fields are bristling (φρίσσουσιν); even so was the θυμός in your φρένες melted, Menelaos'.⁹ Other instances of the image can more conveniently be discussed below.¹⁰

Certain people's φρένες are described as πευκάλιμαι.¹¹ As Liddell and Scott observed, 'the ancients were at a loss as to the true sense' of the word. They tried to relate it either to πυκνός in the sense of 'intelligent' or to πικρός or πεύκη in the

---

¹ Fr. 97 (Bgk.).   ² Fr. 85 (Bgk.).
³ Line 396.   ⁴ Ol. xi, 10. Cf. Soph. Antig. 683.
⁵ Ol. vii, 7 f.; Pyth. ii, 73 f.; Nem. x, 12.   ⁶ Ag. 502.
⁷ Septem, 593 f. Cf. the quotation from Lysis in Iambl. de vit. Pythag. xvii.
⁸ See e.g. Ameis-Hentze, commentary and 'Anhang' ad loc. Other points in the image are dealt with below, pp. 46 f.
⁹ Il. xxiii, 597 ff.   ¹⁰ P. 54. See also p. 46, n. 6.
¹¹ Il. viii, 366, xiv, 165, xv, 81, xx, 35.

sense of 'piercing', and modern scholars also have been uncertain and divided between these interpretations. The contexts suggest that it describes a desirable condition of the φρένες. Now Hesychius, who glosses πευκαλίμη· θερμή, θρασεῖα καὶ φλεγμαίνουσα, of which the latter part (but possibly not the basic θέρμη, 'warm') is clearly wrong for Homer, has preserved for us two words that are more clearly akin than those that have been suggested but, perhaps because no connection with the diaphragm or the mind was obvious, have been ignored: πευκαλεῖται· ξηραίνεται, ἢ ἀντὶ τοῦ ζητεῖται, 'Αριστέας and πευκαλέον· ξηρὸν ἀγγεῖον. For πευκαλέω and our word πευκάλιμος we might compare ὠφελέω and ὠφέλιμος, etc. Aristeas, the sixth-century epic poet, may have used some part of the verb or it may be quoted from the Alexandrian grammarian. What is reasonably clear and more important is the meaning, *dryness*, more particularly the dryness of a vessel. ἀγγεῖον can mean a vessel in the body and is actually[1] used of the bronchial tubes in the lungs, i.e. φρένες. Is their dryness to the point? It is, and not only for physical but also for spiritual well-being; for the breath which dwells there is the θυμός, thinking, feeling, impelling to action. It is not disease, relatively rare and less immediate in its effects upon the mind, which provides the contrast. When do consciousness and intelligence normally recede? In sleep and in intoxication. Several passages suggest that sleep was conceived as a liquid[2] or moist vapour, mist, coming to the φρένες. ὑγρὸς...ὁ ὕπνος says a scholiast.[3] It is μελίφρων, 'honey to the φρένες', a regular epithet of wine, only twice used of anything else (food), and it is 'poured'[4] upon the eyelids and the φρένες. One of the four instances of πευκάλιμος is just this. Hera hopes to deceive Zeus, τῷ ὕπνον ἀπήμονά τε λιαρόν τε/ χεύῃ ἐπὶ βλεφάροισιν ἰδὲ φρεσὶ πευκαλίμῃσι, 'and to pour sleep gentle and warm upon his eyelids and upon his dry (i.e. efficient) φρένες'.[5] This thought will also explain the *sese*

---

[1] Aristotle, *de Gener. Anim.* 787 b 3.
[2] There is, of course, also the agent, the god who brings it.
[3] On *Il.* XIV, 253.　　[4] E.g. *Il.* II, 19, XIV, 253.　　[5] *Il.* XIV, 164 f.

exsiccat somno Romana iuventus of Ennius,[1] the *mitemque rigat per pectora somnum* of Furius Antias[2] and later the *somnus per membra quietem inriget* of Lucretius,[3] the *inriguo somno* of Persius,[4] Virgil's account of the god Somnus dripping sleep from his *ramum Lethaeo rore madentem*[5] and the *illos...fessos...cornu perfuderat omni Somnus* of Statius.[6] What of wine? Not only does a man 'damage his φρένες with wine'[7] and have 'his φρένες subdued with wine'[8] but also he 'becomes heavy in his φρένες with wine',[9] and one accuses a man of being drunk by saying that 'wine possesses (ἔχει) his φρένες'[10] and quite explicitly 'the wine came about the φρένες of the Cyclops'.[11] Thus the φρένες become at once moist (with sleep or wine) and inefficient. The natural opposite to this moist condition will be the 'dry' state of alertness and sobriety, which exactly fits our interpretation of πευκάλιμος. Let us look ahead for a moment to Diogenes of Apollonia in the fifth century. His view that the soul, the conscious and intelligent element in man, consisted of 'air', is usually explained as a revival of Anaximenes' doctrine, but both, as we shall see,[12] are merely refinements upon the traditional belief. For Diogenes this air had apparently its chief seat in the chest, or region of the heart, 'whether in the lungs or, as the compiler of the *Placita* tells us, in the "arterial cavity" of the heart'.[13] What is strikingly clear is that intelligence depends upon the *dryness* of this air, and is diminished—how? 'Understanding (φρονεῖν) is the work of pure and dry air. For *moisture* hinders intelligence (νοῦν); wherefore in *sleep* and in *drunkenness* and in *surfeit* understanding is diminished. And that moisture takes away intelligence is indicated by the fact that other animals have inferior intelli-

---

[1] *Ann.* 469 (Vahlen). [2] See Macrob. *Sat.* VI, 1, 44.
[3] IV, 907 f. Cf. Virgil, *Aen.* I, 691 f., III, 511. [4] V, 56.
[5] *Aen.* V, 854 f. So too Ovid, *Met.* XI, 605–7; Val. Flac. IV, 15 ff.
[6] *Theb.* II, 143 ff. Cf. Apul. *Met.* VI, 21. [7] *Od.* XXI, 297.
[8] *Od.* IX, 454. [9] *Od.* XIX, 122. [10] *Od.* XVIII, 331, 391.
[11] *Od.* IX, 362. [12] P. 115, n. 7; pp. 251–2.
[13] See Beare, *Greek Theories of Elementary Cognition*, p. 260; also below, p. 117. The evidence is rather doubtful. The writer of the Hippocratic περὶ ἑπταμήνου (Kühn, I, 490) also places the intelligence in the left ventricle. Cf. below p. 49, n. 1.

gence (διάνοιαν). For they breathe in (ἀναπνεῖν) the air from the earth and take moister nourishment.'¹ Before Diogenes of Apollonia, Heraclitus of Ephesus, with whose school Diogenes has no apparent connection, is reported² to have taught that men received the λόγος by breathing in (δι' ἀναπνοῆς). We can now perhaps, while remembering his emphasis upon 'fire', better understand his cryptic sayings about the damage to the soul (ψυχή, apparently including intelligence and consciousness) by moisture, e.g. 'the dry soul is wisest and best', αὔη ψυχὴ σοφωτάτη καὶ ἀρίστη.³

We have seen that for Ennius awakening from sleep to normal consciousness was a 'drying' process and can now better understand the reproach of Caecilius: 'Is he so forgetful? Is his memory so wet?'⁴ Here should also be considered some other curious expressions. Sappho⁵ says 'according to my σταλαγμός' (i.e. 'my drop') and apparently wishes that her μελεδῶναι, 'cares',⁶ might carry it away. The *Etymologicum Magnum*⁷ tells us that 'the Aeolians call pain (ὀδύνη) σταλαγμός'. Aeschylus says: 'Before the heart in sleep there drips (στάζει) pain woe-recalling (μνησιπήμων πόνος) and wisdom (σωφρονεῖν) comes to the unwilling'.⁸ The explanation of these passages appears to lie in a strange thought which explains a great many other expressions, the thought that in grief or yearning the relevant parts of the body 'melt' (τήκεσθαι) and as they 'diminish' (φθίνειν, φθινύθειν) there issues liquid. This thought must have been inspired in part by the tears and wasting of grief.⁹ The heart and lungs, as the parts chiefly concerned in emotion, were supposed to

¹ A 19; Diels, *Fragm. d. Vors.*⁴
² A 16 (60, 10) Diels, but see also below, p. 76, n. 9. For thought as words, breath, see also pp. 13 f., 56, 67 ff., 169 ff.
³ B 118, Diels' textual note, taking ξηρή as gloss on αὔη which, the present argument apart, seems the simplest solution. Cf. also B 36, 77 and 117.
⁴ Fr. 30 (Ribbeck): *Itane Antipho invenitur profluia fide?... Itane est madida memoria? Profluia fide* is rather against the reference of *madida* merely to drunkenness.   ⁵ Fr. 14 (Diehl). The reading is not certain.
⁶ See pp. 67, n. 4; 85 f.; 405, n. 3.
⁷ S.v. μελεδῶναι.   ⁸ *Ag.* 179 ff. Cf. *Septem*, 918 ff.
⁹ Cf. ἀνασταλύζω in Anacr. Fr. 43 (Bgk.).

'melt'. We can thus understand why Archilochus speaks of the lungs as 'watery' with pain (ὀδύναι)[1] and Ovid of his woes in exile: *sic mea perpetuis liquefiunt pectora curis*.[2]

In this way, too, the φρένες are the reverse of πευκάλιμαι, are at once in an undesirable state and wet. In Aias' famous lines about Time that changes all, Sophocles[3] says: 'There is nothing (i.e. no change) beyond hope; the awful oath and the φρένες that are exceeding dry (περισκελεῖς, cf. σκέλλω) become his prey (ἁλίσκεται)'. They are very 'dry', unemotional, very far removed from melting or yielding, yet even they yield in time.

The current explanation of *lymphatus* and *lymphaticus* is that persons who *saw* a nymph or water-sprite went mad. Hydrophobia is quoted and *lymphatus* is supposed to refer primarily to mad fear, panic. But if we examine the earliest evidence we find that hydrophobic symptoms or fear are not implied, but the reference is to people in a state of wild excitement like that of the followers of the wine-god (cf. Horace about to drink: *non ego sanius/bacchabor Edonis: recepto/dulce mihi furere est amico*).[4] Thus Pacuvius, apparently of someone distraught with grief (or anxiety), says 'moved in *animus* (*flexanima*) as if *lymphata* or stirred by the rites of Bacchus (*Bacchi sacris commota*) she calls to mind her Teucer among the tombs',[5] while Catullus describes the Bacchantes themselves as 'raving with mind *lymphata*': *quae tum alacres passim lymphata mente furebant/ euhoe bacchantes, euhoe capita inflectentes*.[6] Both Pacuvius and Catullus elsewhere have *lympha* in its original sense of water, and the natural interpretation is that *lymphatus* meant 'watered' or 'possessed by liquid', whether involving a living agency, a spirit of the liquid, or not, and described a state of the *animus* the reverse of calm or sober. It is apparently the *chest* which is thought to be so affected. Ovid describes the

---

[1] See p. 38.   [2] *ex Pont.* I, 2, 57.
[3] *Aj.* 648 f.   [4] *Odes*, II, 7, 26 ff.
[5] 422 f. (Ribb.) quoted by Cic. *de Div.* I, 36, 80; Varro, *de Ling. Lat.* VII, 87. Plautus, *Poen.* 345 f., speaks of coins as *lymphatici*, apparently as if they were excited and would not keep still.
[6] LXIV, 254 f.

frantic women who attack Orpheus as *tectae lymphata ferinis pectora velleribus.*[1] We shall presently[2] see reason to believe that the Romans had very much the same beliefs as the Greeks about the nature and the seat of the mind. Here the mind at the same time has lost its calm and rational state and is possessed by liquid. The evidence scarcely justifies us in saying decisively whether in the original thought the liquid had been introduced from without or had been generated within. Horace's *mentemque lymphatam Mareotico,*[3] while it refers to the alarmed, suggests liquid as the direct agent, as does later Pliny's *hac pota lymphari homines,*[4] but on the other hand *lymphatus* is used repeatedly of people who are not said to have imbibed anything but are merely in a frantic state of mind, *commota mente.*[5] We shall see[6] that both Greeks and Romans believed that the mind in the lungs was in direct relation to the native liquid there, the blood, and that water or wine, alien liquid, when drunk, went to the lungs, and the power in it possessed or displaced the mind there. The Muses, *Camienae* and *Carmentis,* inspiring poetic frenzy were water-nymphs (p. 66). *Lymphari* could thus mean 'to be frenzied', possessed by such a power.

To return to Homer, his usage elsewhere and the passages discussed (pp. 31 f.) demand that φρένες should mean not merely 'wits' as usually translated, but the physical organ which is also the seat of intelligence. The lungs appear to be affected by sleep, since the breathing becomes audibly gentler. Aeschylus speaks of one 'breathing warm sleep through his πνεύματα'[7] ('through his lungs', Weir Smyth). But neither the midriff nor the lungs receive wine that is drunk. This *fact* is, however, irrelevant; for it is traditional *belief* that we are

---

[1] *Met.* xi, 3 f.   [2] Pp. 40 ff., 168 ff.
[3] *Odes,* i, 37, 14.   [4] *N.H.* xxiv, 17, 164.
[5] νυμφόληπτος to which some refer (if νύμφη meant a spirit of water or plant-juice (pp. 219 f.)) would describe the inspiring effects of drinking. See pp. 66 f.
[6] Pp. 36 f., 42 f., 61–7. Compare also *perfundere,* e.g. *quae tibi flexo animo mentis perfundat amorem,* Catullus, LXIV, 330, *ad perfundendum animum tanquam illiquefactae voluptates,* Cic. *Tusc.* IV, 9, 20.
[7] Fr. 93 (Weir Smyth). Cf. *Choeph.* 621: πνέονθ'...ὕπνῳ and Virg. *Aen.* IX, 326: *toto proflabat pectore somnum* (see p. 41), also Pliny, *Ep.* VI, 16, 13.

tracing. After Homer the φρένες continue to be spoken of as receiving wine that is drunk. Thus Archilochus speaks of himself as 'stricken (συγκεραυνωθείς) in his φρένες with wine',[1] while Epicharmus speaks of 'unmixed wine going about the φρένες',[2] and Alcaeus also speaks of 'wine about the φρένες'.[3] Not only, however, do he and Archilochus in other fragments[4] confirm that for them φρένες meant 'lungs' but, advising one to drink in the hot season, he actually says unequivocally 'wet your lungs with wine' (τέγγε πνεύμονας οἴνῳ),[5] while Euripides speaks not only of 'troubling and lulling the φρένες with strong drink'[6] but also of 'wine passing through the passages of the lungs' (πλευμόνων διαρροάς).[7] A passage in the Hesiodean 'Shield of Herakles' seems to imply that, as might be expected, not only wine, the normal drink, but other liquids upon being drunk went into the φρένες. The Keres are described as 'eager to drink the black blood' of fallen warriors, seizing the bodies and 'when they had satisfied their φρένες with human blood' casting them away.[8] This belief, thus widespread and apparently traditional, that the lungs were the receptacle for drink is not only recorded also for Eupolis, Hippocrates, etc.,[9] but appears explicitly in the Timaeus[10] of Plato and, though Aristotle[11] sought to refute it, found support in the time of Galen.[12] The immediate effects of wine upon the mind,[13] coupled with the belief that the lungs were the organ of mind, would contribute to the mistake, which will not seem so unnatural if we recollect not only the porous

[1] Fr. 77 (Bgk.).   [2] Fr. 35 (Kaibel).
[3] πε[ρὶ] φρένας οἶνος, Fr. 50 (Bgk.[4]), πε[δάσει] (Lobel).
[4] See p. 38.   [5] Fr. 39 (Bgk.).
[6] Fr. 1079, 4 (Nauck).   [7] Fr. 983 (Nauck).
[8] Lines 245 ff., but cf. p. 88 for φρένες as seats of appetite.
[9] See e.g. Plut. Qu. Conv. VII, 1=698 f. and de Stoic. Rep. XXIX, 7 ff.
θωρήσσεσθαι normally means to put on a breastplate or corselet. This belief perhaps explains its use (with or without οἴνῳ) in the sense of 'to get drunk'. See Theognis, 413, 470, 842; Pind. Fr. 72. Cf. ποτῷ φρένα θωρηχθέντες, Nic. Al. 32, ἀκροθώραξ, calda potio vestiarius est (Petron. 41).
[10] 70 C, 91 A.   [11] See de Part. Anim. B, 664 b, 7.
[12] See de Plac. VIII, 9, p. 715, referring to the fluid in the enveloping pleurae which may have contributed to the belief (cf. θωρήσσεσθαι). That appears in English, e.g. 'How often have I rinsed your lungs in aqua vitae?' Dekker, The Honest Whore, Pt II, v, 2.
[13] E.g. Horace, Odes, III, 21, 2-4, 11-20.

nature of the lungs but also the apparent connection between breathing and drinking which is implied by ἄμυστις, ἀμυσ-τίζειν, etc., and the Latin proverb *simul flare sorbereque hau factu facilest.*[1] Recalling the reproach of Caecilius: 'Is he so forgetful? Is his memory so wet?'[2] we may now also understand why *Lethe*, 'Forgetfulness', was liquid and was drunk.[3]

The substitution of πλεύμων or πνεύμων, the later words for 'lung', for φρήν may also be seen elsewhere and some hitherto puzzling passages find explanation. In Homer[4] it is the φρένες (or πραπίδες) containing the θυμός which not only think but also are affected by love or desire. But in a long fragment of Sophocles,[5] Love is praised as omnipotent, 'for it melts its way into the lungs of all who have life in them (ἐντήκεται γὰρ πλευμόνων ὅσοις ἔνι ψυχή)…it tyrannises over the lungs (πλευμόνων) of Zeus without spear, without steel; Love cuts short the designs of gods and men'. And in the lexicons of Photius and Hesychius 'lung-disease', πλευμονίαν, used apparently by some comic poet, is explained as 'the disease of love', νόσον τὴν ἐρωτικήν. Similarly grief: of one who hears bad news Homer[6] says 'sharp pain smote (τύψε) him in his deep φρήν', while Euripides[7] makes Kreousa, on similarly hearing bad news, say 'a piercing pang smote me within my lungs' (ἔτυπεν ὀδύνα με πνευμόνων τῶνδ' ἔσω) and, nearer to Homer in time, Archilochus after a national disaster says 'we have our lungs watery with pangs' (ὑδαλέους δ' ἀμφ'

[1] See Plaut. *Most.* 791. Cf. *Mil. Glor.* 818 ff.
[2] See p. 33. Thus also we can understand why one who wishes not to be thought *immemor* says *quanquam ego vinum bibo, at mandata non consuevi simul bibere una* (Plaut. *Pers.* 170). For Roman beliefs about drinking (and about hearing as drinking) see pp. 42 f. and 64, n. 3 below.
[3] See pp. 33 above and 66 f. below and cf. Eurip. *Bacch.* 282; Plut. *Quaest. Conv.* Praef. 612; Hor. *Odes*, ii, 7, 21.
[4] E.g. *Il.* iii, 139, 442, xi, 89, xxiv, 514; cf. Hymn to Aphrodite, 57.
[5] 941 (Pearson). The interpretation of Ellendt (cf. Campbell) appears sound. Jebb prefers 'It sinks deep into all who have in them the breath of the lungs'; but this not only ignores the Διὸς τυραννεῖ πλευμόνων eight lines later and the other evidence here presented, but also unjustifiably makes ψυχή the breath of the lungs (see below, pp. 93 ff.). For love and the lungs cf. below, pp. 54 f., and for the melting, p. 46, n. 6 and pp. 202 f.
[6] *Il.* xix, 125; cf. i, 362, viii, 124, xxii, 43, etc.; and for φρένα βαθεῖαν cf. the καὶ βαθὺν ἀκρήτῳ πνεύμονα τεγγόμενος of Eratosthenes (Fr. 25 Powell) quoted by Plutarch, *Quaest. Conv.* vii, 1=698. [7] *Ion*, 766.

ὀδύνης ἔχομεν πνεύμονας),[1] i.e. melting with the pangs of grief. And the lungs continue to be spoken of as the seat[2] of life, which weapons threaten.

Finally, if φρήν and πραπίς mean 'lung', we can understand how they can be described as 'porous, spongy' (χαῦνος). Of one who asserts what cannot be believed Pindar says 'with porous (or "puffed out") πραπίς he maketh empty struggles'[3] (παλαιμονεῖ κενεά), with which we may compare his κενεά πνεύσας, 'having breathed empty breaths',[4] of one who has struggled fruitlessly. To a shell sounded by blowing, Alcaeus says 'you make porous (or "puff out", χαυνοῖς) the φρένες'.[5] Now too we can see the point of the old song 'To a flute-player the gods gave not intelligence (νοῦς); while he blows, his intelligence also flies out'.[6]

Our own Anglo-Saxon ancestors, as we shall see,[7] had very similar views about the mind and the chest, and, though it appears to attract little notice, the lungs of a bird are still called its 'soul' in several counties.[8] This we may now reasonably guess to be a survival from a belief that that organ was the seat of the 'soul'. In *Beowulf* the *sawol* (2819 f.) 'departs out of (the hero's) *hreðer*'. *Hreðer* is usually rendered vaguely

[1] Fr. 9, 4 f. (Bgk. who with other editors reads οἰδαλέους). For the fitness of ὑδαλέους, the vulgate reading, see pp. 33 f. above.
[2] E.g. Aesch. *Choeph.* 639; Eurip. *Ion*, 524.
[3] *Pyth.* II, 61.   [4] *Ol.* x, 91.
[5] Fr. 51 (Bgk.). Cf. *pulmo...spongeosus ac fistulis inanibus cavus* (Plin. *N.H.* XI, 188).
[6] *Carm. Pop.* 4 in *Anth. Lyr. Gr.* Vol. II, ed. Diehl. The point of this passage is made clearer on p. 56 below. If πραπίδες was a name for lungs it is perhaps related to πρήθω, 'blow out', 'blow'.   [7] Pp. 68 f.
[8] See *English Dialect Dictionary* (ed. J. Wright), s.v. Soul (8), giving references for Durham, Westmorland, Yorkshire, Lincolnshire, Somerset, etc., but defining it merely as 'Part of the viscera of a fowl when cooked'; 'a substance which lines the inside of the back-bone of fowls; being connected with the entrails it is left in and cooked'. This is in fact the lungs. The *O.E.D.* quotes Goldsmith, *Nat. Hist.* II, 1, 1, 5: 'Their lungs, which are commonly called the soul stick fast to the sides of the ribs and the back'. I first met the use in living speech in Shropshire as a little child. Somewhere I have also heard the oath 'Upon my liver and upon my soul', which appears to rest upon a similar conception of the 'soul' in a man. In German *Seele* = 'soul' means also the air-bladder or 'swim' of a fish. I shall in the course of this book use 'soul' not with any reference to this history of the word but to express what survives death.

'heart, breast, mind', but it probably designated or included the lungs; for in another passage[1] 'his *hreðer* swelled with breath' (*aeðme weoll*). Cf. later, e.g., 'create a soul under the ribs of death'.[2]

There remains the fact that the Hippocratic treatises, Plato, and later writers give the name φρένες to the diaphragm. Why? With such fragmentary records we cannot hope to trace the change any more than with other common words.[3] ἠλακάτη, which in Homer's day appears to have meant 'spindle',[4] later bore instead the meaning 'distaff', which meaning people have been content to assume for Homer also. To the transference of φρένες several circumstances may have contributed. The diaphragm wanted a name and apparently had not yet received one, being a mere partition. The lungs had another name, πλεύμων, which, for its descriptive quality,[5] could not be transferred. That name occurs in the text of Homer, which might suggest that φρένες and πραπίδες should be referred to something else; and the diaphragm, wanting a name,[6] might succeed to the title by juxtaposition (the lungs rest upon it) and also because it co-operates in the act of breathing, and beneath it, as beneath the φρένες or πραπίδες in Homer, is the liver. That 'diaphragm' is not the meaning of those words in Homer, or indeed in the poetic tradition a good deal later, we have seen; and in fact πλεύμων occurs only once in the forty-eight books, πάγη δ᾽ ἐν πλεύμονι (or πνεύμονι) χαλκός,[7] which, were it the common or only word for 'lungs', would be

---

[1] Line 2593; cf. 2113.
[2] Milton, *Comus*, 561 f. Cf. pp. 67, n. 8; 68, n. 7.
[3] See e.g. Monro, *Odyssey XIII–XXIV*, Appendix, p. 450.
[4] See *Classical Review*, xxxviii, Feb. 1924, pp. 4, 6, to which we may add τῆς ἠλακάτης τῆς στρεφομένης δίκην μύλης (Schol. Ambros. to *Od.* vii, 104, based apparently upon Hesiod) and the fact that its secondary meanings were 'revolving topmast' (Ath. xi, 475 a) and 'windlass' (Schol. Thuc. vii, 25). See also p. 307 below. The Schol. to Proclus *in Remp.* p. 381 (Kroll), to which Mr F. H. Sandbach has drawn my attention, interpreted ἠλακάτη as 'spindle' in Homer though on false evidence.
[5] It implies 'floating' (√πλέϝ, πλέω, etc.); cf. English 'lights', now confined to the lungs of beasts. The 'swim' of a fish is not quite parallel. πνεύμων is a popular variant. For the etymology of φρένες see p. 47.
[6] διάφραγμα in *Timaeus* (70 A) has the generic meaning 'partition, barrier'.
[7] *Il.* iv, 528. For the reading in xx, 486 see Leaf, *ad loc.*

40   THE ORGANS OF CONSCIOUSNESS

remarkable, in view more particularly of the vast number of wounds described. If φρένες or πραπίδες meant 'diaphragm', that much inferior target was much oftener hit. But there is no reason why Homer should have had only one word for 'lungs' any more than for the heart which he calls both κῆρ and κραδίη, or the head which he calls κάρη, κάρηνον and κεφαλή. Nor is the transference in fact complete, as Plato himself shows. Homer indicates time and again that the φρένες should contain the θυμός, and later poets[1] are no less explicit; but for Plato still the θυμός, or as he more often calls it, τὸ θυμοειδές, is to be found not in the diaphragm but in the chest above it;[2] and medicine applied the name θυμός not to anything near the diaphragm but to the thymus gland which is between or 'within' the lungs near the neck and is separated from the diaphragm by the heart.

What did the Romans believe to be the organs of consciousness, of mind? It is obvious that for them, even more than for the Greeks, the heart (cor)[3] was important (cf. excors, vecors, etc.). But it was not only the heart; it was the whole chest: non tu corpus eras sine pectore (Horace[4]), rudis et sine pectore miles (Ovid[5]), pectus est quod disertos facit (Quintilian[6]), etc. What of the praecordia, also seat of consciousness? Lewis and Short render: 'I. Literally, the muscle which separates the heart and lungs from the abdomen, the midriff, diaphragm. II. Transferred: A. the entrails, the stomach; B. the breast, the heart; C. the body, bodies', which last rests upon a passage (Ovid, Met. VII, 559) that is satisfied by reference to the trunk or part of the trunk. Pliny tells us that people gave the name praecordia to the diaphragm 'which the Greeks have called φρένες'.[7] But it should mean organs 'in front of the heart'. The lungs overlap the heart in front and nothing else does. The diaphragm is beneath the heart. Further, it is clear that praecordia was before Pliny's time used more generally of organs in the upper part of the trunk. Pliny himself in this

[1] See e.g. Bacchylides, XVI, 21 ff.
[2] See Timaeus, 69 C; Phaedrus, 235 C, 236 C, and Republic, 441.
[3] See e.g. Cic. Tusc. I, 9, 18.   [4] Epist. I, 4, 6; cf. Sat. II, 4, 90, etc.
[5] Met. XIII, 290; cf. 326, 369; Her. XVI, 201–2; Propertius, III (IV), 5, 8, etc.   [6] Inst. X, 7, 15.   [7] N.H. XI, 37 (77), 197.

same passage limits the name *exta* to the organs above the diaphragm, which, in fact, are the heart and the lungs, and in another[1] says: 'We give the one name *praecordia* to the *exta* in a human being'. For his contemporary Celsus[2] *praecordia* unmistakably meant the organs above the diaphragm. But originally *praecordia* could not mean the heart itself (*cor*), so that again we are left with the lungs.[3] *exta* could, of course, include the liver; but that, the stomach, or any other organ below the diaphragm, has still less claim than the latter to the natural meaning of *praecordia*. The vagueness and confusion might well arise when, under the influence of Greek thought, *praecordia* was identified with φρένες and *pulmo* remained, as πλεύμων for the Greeks, to express 'lung' without reference to the mind. Traces of the original specific meaning seem to be preserved in a few phrases. Thus Lucilius says 'when I bring forth any verse out of my *praecordia* (*ex praecordiis ecfero*)'.[4] M. Caelius referred to Antony in his drunken sleep as 'snoring with the whole of his *praecordia* (*totis praecordiis stertentem*)',[5] which we may compare with Virgil's *toto proflabat pectore somnum*.[6] The only reference in Plautus appears to be that of an exhausted runner, 'I'm done for; my spleen is rebelling and invading (*occupat*) my *praecordia*. I'm done for; I can't draw my breath (*animam vertere*); I should be no good as a piper'.[7] Horace says that under Canidia's enchantments he is struggling (*labor*) night and day 'and cannot relax his *praecordia* distended with breathing' (*levare tenta spiritu praecordia*).[8] Virgil tells how a spear strikes a man's back and passes through (*transit*) his *praecordia* and he vomits the warm blood from his chest (*pectore*),[9] and how in sudden dread 'the chill blood gathers into the *praecordia*',[10] and how a man brags,

---

[1] *N.H.* xxx, 5, 42.   [2] *de Medicina*, iv, i.
[3] The pericardium, the heart's envelope, scarcely deserves to be differentiated or to be considered a plurality.
[4] 590 f. (Marx). For the thought see pp. 67 f., 71, 170, 172 below.
[5] Quoted by Quintilian, *Inst.* iv, 2, 123.   [6] See p. 35.
[7] *Merc.* 124 ff. The spleen appears to have been held responsible for the 'stitch'. It lies beneath the left lung with the diaphragm membrane between.
[8] *Epod.* xvii, 25 f.   [9] *Aen.* ix, 412 ff.
[10] *Aen.* x, 452. Cf. p. 24, n. 5 *fin.* For *Georg.* ii, 484, cf. p. 47.

puffed up with marrying a princess, *vociferans tumidusque novo praecordia regno.*[1] Cf. his *tumido in pulmone*[2] of anger, or Persius' *pulmonem rumpere ventis*[3] of pride. He has *avias tibi de pulmone revello* (v, 92 : *de tuis praecordiis*, Schol.) and *sinuoso in pectore...fibra* (v, 27–9 : cf. 1, 47), both of the mind. Livy says 'they perceived that he was alive from his warmth and the breath still in his *praecordia*' (*spiritu remanente in praecordiis*).[4] See also pp. 505 f.

Passages in Horace suggest that the *praecordia* like the φρένες were not only, with the heart, the seat of the conscious mind, but also received drink; evidence already cited[5] tends in this direction. *quid hoc veneni saevit in praecordiis?*[6] (apparently of a liquid element, garlic-juice, in a dish) and *condita cum verax aperit praecordia Liber,*[7] with which we may compare the wine, *quod cum spe divite manet/in venas animumque meum, quod verba ministret.*[8] The wine goes where the *animus* is, and we shall see[9] reason to believe that the latter was naturally associated with the lungs. The idea that wine enters *venae* direct[10] (whether *venae* includes air passages[11] or merely veins) is more natural if it was thought to go to the lungs than if to the stomach. Thus explicitly of a drink: *vacuis committere venis/nil nisi lene decet; leni praecordia mulso/prolueris melius.*[12] The belief that drink went to the lungs would also help us to explain why, for instance, Cicero says to Antony *istis lateribus...tantum vini...exhauseras*[13]

---

[1] *Aen.* ix, 596. Cf. xi, 346 *flatusque remittat.*   [2] *Aen.* x, 387.
[3] iii, 27. See also p. 55.   [4] xlii, 16.   [5] Pp. 32–5.
[6] *Epod.* iii, 5. If liquid is not intended, this example must exemplify the vaguer use of *praecordia*. For the possibility that *meis inaestuet praecordiis libera bilis* (*Epod.* xi, 15) refers to the lungs, see p. 84.   [7] *Sat.* i, 4, 89.
[8] *Epist.* i, 15, 19 f. Cf. *Od.* ii, 2, 14 f., *Georg.* iii, 482 f., Phaedr. iv, 15 (16), 9.   [9] Pp. 168 ff.
[10] Cf. Sen. *Epist. Mor.* 122, 6 *vinum recipiunt inanibus venis*; Arnob. (*adv. Nat.* v, 6) *potionem hiantibus venis rapit.*
[11] Cf. φλέβες and ἀρτηρίαι on pp. 80 f.
[12] *Sat.* ii, 4, 25 ff. Cf. Lucr. iii, 476 ff., with Juv. iv, 138 f. below. The *venas hominis tetigit et praecordia* of Lucilius (642 Marx) quoted by Nonius for *tangere=inspicere* seems also to imply the connection of *venae* with the mind. Elsewhere Lucilius has *iam disrumpetur medius iam ut Marsu' colubras/disrumpit cantu, venas cum extenderit omnis* (575 f. Marx). We may refer also to the relations of *animus* and *cor* (with p. 171, n. 1) and to what is said below (pp. 79 ff.) of θυμός in the arteries. For the effects of wine we may compare Virgil's picture of the sleeping Silenus *inflatum hesterno venas, ut semper, Iaccho* (*Ecl.* vi, 15).   [13] *Philippic,* ii, 25.

and speaks of his getting rid of drunkenness as *vinum* or *crapulam exhalare*,[1] why, on the other hand, for Lucilius 'to breathe' was *caelum bibere*[2] and 'if you want to hear this' *haec tu si voles per auris pectus inrigarier*,[3] and commonly later 'to hear' is *aure* or *auribus bibere*:[4] *adbibe puro pectore verba puer*.[5] Hence our 'instill', originally 'drip into'.[6] In *haustus e fontibu' magnis/lingua meo suavis diti de pectore fundet*[7] there is liquid in the chest of the speaker and it is imbibed by the chest of the hearer. The conception of wisdom as moisture will become clearer presently.[8] *Non ille quamquam Socraticis madet/sermonibus te negleget* says Horace[9] addressing Wine concerning his friend. *Si semel amoris poculum accepit meri/eaque intra pectus se penetravit potio* says Plautus[10] implying that the receptacle alike of drink and of love is the chest. Later passages, e.g. Ovid's *et relevant multo pectora sicca mero*[11] or Virgil's description of the man who has been knocked into the sea, *salsos revomentem pectore fluctus*,[12] are surely to be explained by reference to the lungs. Explicitly in Juvenal we read *cum pulmo Falerno arderet*[13] and in Apuleius, of a doctor's wife and a little girl who had both drunk poison unawares, *parvulae quidem tenuem spiritum et delicata ac tenera praecordia conficit protinus virus infestum, at uxor medici dum noxiis ambagibus pulmones eius pererrat tempestas detestabilis potionis, primum suspicata quod res erat, mox urgente spiritu iam certo certior, contendit*,[14] etc. Here we seem to have the same belief that was found among the Greeks.[15] Some other passages[16] suggest that drink went to the stomach.

---

[1] *Ibid.* 12 and 17 etc.   [2] 601 (Marx).   [3] 610 (Marx).

[4] Horace, *Odes*, II, 13, 32; Prop. III, 6, 8; Ovid, *Trist.* III, 5, 141, etc.; also Plaut. *Pers.* 170 on p. 37 above and *Mil. Glor.* 883. For hearing as drinking see also pp. 67, 70 below.   [5] Horace, *Epist.* I, 2, 67 f.
[6] *Ibid.* 8, 16.

[7] Lucr. I, 412 f. Cf. Pind. *Ol.* VII, 7 f. with pp. 65 f.   [8] Pp. 47 ff., 61 ff.

[9] *Odes*, III, 21, 9 f. Cf. Martial I, 39, 3 f. and VII, 69, 2 on p. 64 below, and *ut studiosi iuvenes lectione severa irrigarentur* (Petronius 4).

[10] *Truc.* 43 f.   [11] *Fasti*, III, 304.   [12] *Aen.* v, 182.   [13] IV, 138 f.   [14] *Met.* X, 28.

[15] The problem occurred to me at a late stage. This is not a complete survey of the evidence and does not demonstrate what was the original Roman belief; but, since I have not seen thus much elsewhere, I set it down for what it is worth.

[16] E.g. Juv. v, 49: *si stomachus domini fervet vinoque ciboque* (? heartburn in throat).

CHAPTER III

The Stuff of Consciousness

What was the θυμός (*thymos*)? Evidently something vaporous (cf. e.g. θυμιάω). It has been interpreted by Gomperz[1] and others after him as the 'blood-soul', receiving its name from the steam which rises from newly shed blood. Nägelsbach and Autenrieth[2] have been followed by Bickel[3] in referring it rather to the raging and boiling of the circulating blood, following the etymology of the *Cratylus*,[4] ἀπὸ τῆς θύσεως καὶ ζέσεως—not, however, for Plato of the blood but τῆς ψυχῆς—and thus losing the name's more natural and direct suggestion of something vaporous. Nor does Homer connect the θυμός directly with blood or make it behave as a mere 'blood-soul' should. It quits the body when no blood is spilt.[5] Rohde speaks of the 'untranslatable word θυμός',[6] and says that it is not taken from any bodily organ and it shows already that it is thought of as an immaterial function,[7] which, however, does not explain its origin and, unfortunately, is not true; for Homer's language makes it clear that it is not a function but a thing.

If the φρένες, in which the θυμός is said to be, are not the diaphragm but the lungs, it is no great leap of the imagination to guess that the θυμός itself is the breath,[8] which may always be felt as vaporous and sometimes is visible. With it may be compared[9] *fumus*, Sanscrit *dhūmaḥ*, 'vapour, smoke', Old Slav. *dymŭ*, 'smoke', *duchŭ*, 'breath, spirit', etc. Does this

[1] *Griechische Denker*[4], p. 206; Buchholz, *Homerische Realien*, III, p. 5.
[2] *Homerische Theologie*[3], p. 461.
[3] *Homerische Seelenglaube*, p. 261. [4] 419 E.
[5] E.g. when Andromache faints at sight of Hector's corpse (*Il.* XXII, 475) or Ares is bowled over by a stone (*Il.* XXI, 417).
[6] *Psyche*[8] (English translation), p. 365. [7] *Ibid.* p. 30.
[8] 'Breath' is among the meanings given by the unrevised Liddell and Scott. As noted above (p. 24) Justesen contends that θυμός means 'breath' but has missed the relation to blood (see pp. 46 ff.).
[9] See Boisacq, *Dictionnaire étymologique de la langue grecque*, s.v.

meaning 'breath, breath-soul or spirit' fit or otherwise throw light upon the passages in which Homer uses the word? Diores, when his leg was crushed by a stone, 'fell on his back in the dust and stretched out both his hands to his dear comrades, breathing forth (ἀποπνείων) his θυμός'.[1] An arrow pierced Harpalion and 'breathing forth (ἀποπνείων) his θυμός, he lay stretched upon the ground like a worm'.[2] Achilles wounded Hippodamas with his spear 'and he gasped (ἄϊσθε) for his θυμός and roared as when a bull etc.'[3] Sarpedon wounded the horse Pedasos 'and he bellowed gasping (ἀΐσθων) for his θυμός and fell in the dust moaning and his θυμός floated away (ἀπὸ δ' ἔπτατο)'.[4] Agamemnon sacrificing 'cut the lambs' throats with the pitiless bronze and laid them upon the ground gasping, in want of θυμός (ἀσπαίροντας, θυμοῦ δευομένους)'.[5] Apollo comes to Hector as he is recovering from the blow of Aias' stone and he was 'sitting, no longer lying; he had but late recovered (ἐσαγείρετο) his θυμός, recognising his comrades round him, and his gasping (ἄσθμα) and sweating had ceased when the will of Zeus revived him'.[6] Menelaos shuddered when the arrow struck him, but when he saw that the barbs had not entered, 'his θυμός was gathered again in his chest' (ἐνὶ στήθεσσιν ἀγέρθη).[7] Odysseus struggles to land, breathless (ἄπνευστος), but presently 'he breathed again (ἄμπνυτο, or ἔμπνυτο Aristarchus) and the θυμός was gathered into his φρήν'.[8] Andromache fainted at sight of Hector's corpse 'and she fell backwards and breathed forth her soul (ἀπὸ δὲ ψυχὴν ἐκάπυσσε), but when she breathed again and the θυμός was gathered into her φρήν, she, etc.'[9] When the spear was plucked from Sarpedon's thigh, 'his soul (ψυχή) left him and mist o'erspread his eyes. Then he breathed again and the breath of Boreas revived him, breathing upon him around, who had grievously breathed forth his θυμός'[10] (αὖτις δ' ἀμπνύθη, περὶ δὲ πνοιὴ Βορέαο/ζώγρει ἐπιπνείουσα κακῶς

[1] *Il.* IV, 522 ff.
[2] *Il.* XIII, 653.
[3] *Il.* XX, 403 f.
[4] *Il.* XVI, 468 f.
[5] *Il.* III, 292 ff.
[6] *Il.* XV, 240 ff. Cf. XXI, 417.
[7] *Il.* IV, 152.
[8] *Od.* V, 456 ff.
[9] *Il.* XXII, 467 ff.
[10] *Il.* V, 696 ff. Cf. *Od.* V, 468.

κεκαφηότα θυμόν; cf. κάπυς· πνεῦμα, Hesych.). We can now appreciate the fitness of the simile: 'Even as two winds stir up the main, the home of the fishes, Boreas and Zephyrus, that blow from Thrace...even so was the θυμός divided in the breasts (στήθεσσι) of the Achaeans',[1] and the explicit expression: 'Among the other gods fell painful grievous strife and the θυμός was blown (or "breathed") in two directions in their φρένες'[2] (δίχα δέ σφιν ἐνὶ φρεσὶ θυμὸς ἄητο, which Lang, Leaf, and Myers for instance render 'and their hearts were carried diverse in their breasts'). We saw[3] reason to believe that for Aeschylus φρένες still meant lungs, and shall later[4] see that for him θυμός was a matter of breath. Clytemnestra, after describing her murder of Agamemnon by stabbing him thrice, says 'thus fallen he drives forth his θυμός and blowing out sharp blood strikes me with dark drops of gory dew...' (οὕτω τὸν αὑτοῦ θυμὸν ὁρμαίνει πεσὼν/κἀκφυσιῶν ὀξεῖαν αἵματος σφαγὴν/βάλλει μ' ἐρεμνῇ ψακάδι φοινίας δρόσου...).[5]

But it is clear that θυμός expressed a much richer concept for the Homeric Greeks than our 'breath' or mere outer air received and expelled. They did not know that breathing helped to regulate temperature and they could not guess that it brought oxygen to the body and took carbonic acid gas away. What they must have observed is that breath is warm and moist. It contains, of course, a good deal of water-vapour from the body, which becomes visible by condensation when it meets a bright surface or air that is cooler. The suspected[6] simile: 'His θυμός was warmed (or "melted", ἰάνθη) as when dew about the ears of a growing crop is warmed when the fields are bristling (φρίσσουσιν); even so was the θυμός in your

---

[1] *Il.* ix, 4 ff.   [2] *Il.* xxi, 385 f.   [3] Pp. 25, 27 f., 29 f.   [4] Pp. 53 f.
[5] *Ag.* 1388 ff. With the interpretation of θυμόν as loosely equivalent to 'life' it has been customary to punctuate with a colon after πεσών.
[6] The meaning and the fitness of this passage and of another may be revealed if we set them side by side. Of a lion balked of his prey Homer says τοῦ δ' ἐν φρεσὶν ἄλκιμον ἦτορ παχνοῦται (*Il.* xvii, 111 f.; cf. Hesiod, *Works and Days*, 360), usually rendered by something like 'his strong heart within him groweth chill' (Lang, Leaf, and Myers). It will appear below (pp. 80 ff.) that ἦτορ cannot mean 'heart' and must mean something very close to θυμός. παχνοῦσθαι is usually translated 'to be chilled, congealed';

φρένες warmed, Menelaos', had, we saw,[1] great aptitude for the 'crop' of tubes in the lungs, but it also likens θυμός to dew, atmospheric moisture. The cognates of θυμός (θυμιάω, etc.) suggest that it should mean vapour. Whence? From what liquid but blood,[2] the hot liquid which is in fact concentrated in the heart and around it in the lungs (φρένες)? The latter are filled with blood[3] and breath that interact, giving and taking from each other. A tradition of this relation probably survives in the doctrine attributed to Empedocles[4] that slowness of wit is due to coldness of the blood around the heart and in the scholion 'θυμός is the boiling of the blood around the heart through a desire to retaliate'[5] and lies behind the Platonic explanation, 'θυμός from the seething (θύσεως) and boiling of the ψυχή'.[6] This θυμός is not the blood-soul as

but it is formed from πάχνη (cf. λάχνη, λαχνοῦσθαι), which meant not any kind of cold or frost but specifically 'hoar-frost'; so that παχνοῦσθαι should originally have meant 'to be hoar-frosted' or 'to be turned to hoar-frost'. But what is hoar-frost? Frozen dew (cf. τὸ δ' ἐπὶ γῆς συμπαγὲν ἐκ δρόσου γενόμενον πάχνη λέγεται, Plat. Timaeus, 59 E, Ov. Fasti, III, 345, 880 etc.). The lion and Menelaos had been balked each of his prize. Bitter feeling, detestation, and fear were by the early Greeks conceived as freezing, chilling (see the uses of ῥιγέω, ῥιγεδανός, κρυερός, etc. So the θυμὸς ἐρρίγει, Od. XXIII, 215 f.; ψυχρὸς ἔγεντο, Sappho, Fr. 16 Bgk., etc.); and comforting, cheering or joyful feelings on the other hand were 'warming', 'melting' (see ἰαίνω, θερμαίνω, etc.). Dew, atmospheric moisture condensed by cold, was associated with cold by Homer (see Od. V, 467). Thus in Menelaos the moisture of the θυμός in the tubes of the φρένες had condensed like dew, in the lion it had frozen, as it were, from dew to hoar-frost, and in Menelaos, when his prize is restored, it was warmed, dissolved again.   [1] See p. 30.

[2] We may compare the Eskimo belief that from flowing human blood a vapour arises which surrounds the bleeding person (see Frazer, Taboo etc., pp. 210 ff.). Such evaporation would be most obvious in a cold atmosphere.

[3] πᾶς ὁ πνεύμων φαίνεται μεστὸς αἵματος ὤν, Aristot. Hist. An. 513 b, 22; αἷμα δὲ πλεῖστον μὲν ὁ πνεύμων ἔχει τῶν ἐν τοῖς ζώοις μορίων κ.τ.λ. ibid. 496 a, 30 ff. See also p. 54 below. If φρένες described the lungs full of passages (pp. 28 ff.) for air, blood and drink, it was perhaps related to φρέω (δια-, εἰσφρέω etc.) 'give passage to' or φρέαρ, 'well', 'reservoir'.

[4] Schol. to Horace, Ars Poet. 465. See also pp. 54, 71, 141.

[5] ad Il. XVIII, 110. This is, as Professor Cornford reminds me, a blending of two views quoted by Aristotle, de An. 403 a, 30 f.

[6] Crat. 419 D; cf. Rep. 440 C; Tim. 70 B. For the Stoics too the soul was warm breath fed by exhalation from the blood (Gal. Hipp. et Plat. II, 8).

opposed to the breath-soul nor indeed mere breath but breath
related to blood,[1] not mere air but something vaporous within,
blending and interacting with the air without, something
which diminishes if the body is ill nourished, but is increased
when the body is well nourished. Circe bids Odysseus and
his comrades 'Come, eat food and drink wine till once more
you get θυμός in your chests as it was when first you left your
fatherland of rugged Ithaca; but now you are dry (ἀσκελέες)
and lacking θυμός (ἄθυμοι), mindful ever of your grievous
wandering'.[2] When a man is in trouble or pines or is wasting
physically as well as in spirit, he may be said to 'melt',
'dissolve' (τήκειν)[3] his θυμός, or to 'waste it away'[4] (ἀπο-
φθινύθειν), or to 'eat' it, i.e. consume the vapour that is the final
product of food and is the stuff of consciousness, spirit. 'Why
sit you thus like one that is dumb, Odysseus, eating (ἔδων)
θυμός and not touching food or drink?'[5] says Circe. Elsewhere,
in similar circumstances the organs of consciousness, the heart[6]
or the lungs[7] (φρένες) that contain the θυμός, are said to be
'eaten' or 'wasted' ('diminished'). This brings us to the other
side of the concept. If the stuff of consciousness was breath
thus related to blood, the relevance of blood to intelligence
and moral character appears: 'You are of good blood, dear
child, to judge from what you say[8] (αἵματός εἰς ἀγαθοῖο, φίλον
τέκος, οἷ' ἀγορεύεις)' is Menelaos' appreciation of Telemachos.
So 'white φρένες'[9] used with reference to moral or intellectual
defect perhaps meant 'anaemic, bloodless φρένες'.

---

[1] Rüsche in the work mentioned on p. 24 refers both θυμός and ψυχή
to the blood and the breath, but thinks that φρένες means 'diaphragm'
and that θυμός is the *allgemeine Lebenskraft* (*op. cit.* p. 27). The ψυχή, as
we shall see (pp. 93 ff.), is quite distinct and it, not θυμός, is the *Lebenskraft*.

[2] *Od.* x, 460 ff. Cf. Hesiod, *Theog.* 639 ff. The relation of consciousness
to moisture appears in Socrates' reason for raising himself above the
earth: ἡ γῆ βίᾳ/ἕλκει πρὸς αὑτὴν τὴν ἰκμάδα τῆς φροντίδος (Aristoph.
Clouds, 232 f.). Cf. Hippo on p. 214.

[3] *Od.* xix, 263 f. This may mean 'liquefy, condense into liquid' here,
but it carries with it the sense of 'dissolve, disintegrate, diminish' usual
with the melting of solids, and so is unlike ἰαίνειν, which carries with it
pleasant associations of warmth.

[4] *Il.* xvi, 540.   [5] *Od.* x, 378 f. Cf. 143, ix, 75; *Il.* vi, 202.
[6] *Il.* xxiv, 129.   [7] *Il.* xviii, 446.
[8] *Od.* iv, 611. See below, p. 121.   [9] See p. 25 above.

In *Il.* ix, 4 ff., xxi, 385 f. (see p. 46), the poet may possibly have imagined the breath going different ways in the main *wind*-pipe and the air passages that divide thence, but it is clear that more than a merely physical event is in point, division of the mind or minds thus conceived. This is doubtless true also of the passages quoted on p. 45; not only breath but also consciousness departs in the departure of θυμός. It is the θυμός which is most often mentioned when the poet is describing emotion. The consciousness is naturally identified with the breath not only because to be conscious is to have breath, but also because the breathing is affected when there is violent emotion, and not only the breathing but the flow of blood. There is pulsation with flushing or pallor. 'Every sudden emotion quickens the action of the heart and with it the respiration',[1] observed Darwin. 'When a fearful object is before us we pant and cannot deeply inspire.'[2] Hence it is, we perhaps may now guess, that Homer can say of those stricken with fear not only κραδίη...πατάσσει[3] but also θυμὸς ἐνὶ στήθεσσι πάτασσεν.[4] The θυμός is active and throbs, beats, i.e. pants. Similar experience may be expressed in terms of the lungs, the φρένες. Agamemnon not only weeps profusely in public; he cries alone in the night: 'In close succession came the cries in his breast from the bottom, from his heart, and his φρένες quivered within him'[5] (ὡς πυκίν' ἐν στήθεσσιν ἀναστενάχι3' Ἀγαμέμνων/νειόθεν ἐκ κραδίης, τρομέοντο δέ οἱ φρένες ἐντός). We may recall a child's sobs, 'a series of short convulsive

---

[1] *The Expression of the Emotion in Man and Animals* (Popular edition, ed. Francis Darwin, 1904), p. 283. The early Greeks appear, like the Hindoos, Hebrews, and other peoples, to have believed that there was breath in the heart as well as in the lungs. See pp. 56, 170, and for ἦτορ ἐν κραδίῃ pp. 81 f. Such belief was not unnatural in view of the compactness of lungs and bronchial tubes with the heart and its vessels, and of the fact that the 'arterial' (i.e. left) ventricle of the heart is found virtually empty after death, and of the supposed relation of breath to blood.

[2] W. James, *Principles of Psychology*, II, p. 376; cf. p. 460.

[3] *Il.* xiii, 282.   [4] *Il.* vii, 216.

[5] *Il.* x, 9 f. Cf. xv, 627, x, 492 and the 'tremulous sob' of Wordsworth's 'complaining owl'.

inspirations', and the rapid quivering of the lungs as he tries to check them. So too of the charioteers panting with eagerness as they race, πάτασσε δὲ θυμὸς ἑκάστου/νίκης ἱεμένων,[1] where, as in the last instance, 'heart' has been the usual translation of θυμός. To *pant* with eagerness, to *gasp* or *whistle* with astonishment, to *snort* with indignation, to *sob* with grief, to *yawn* with weariness, to *laugh* with mirth, to *sigh* with sadness or relief are some of the more marked variations of breathing with feeling that have found distinct expression in everyday speech. The '*breast heaving with emotion*' is a commonplace. We '*catch our breath*' at a sudden sound, '*hold our breath*' in suspense, '*breathe more freely*', and so the list might be continued. For the Homeric Greeks the θυμός is the 'spirit', the breath that is consciousness, variable, dynamic, coming and going, changing as feeling changes and, we may add, as thought changes. Thought and feeling were, we saw, scarcely separable then, and it is still recognised that thought, even the abstract thought of the philosopher, affects the breathing.[2]

Upon a man's 'spirit' or 'breath-soul' depend his fierceness or energy (μένος) and courage (θάρσος). He breathes them. Repeatedly[3] warriors are described as μένος or μένεα πνείοντες, e.g. 'the Achaeans advanced in silence breathing fierceness'.[4] The man who is furious does *breathe* visibly and audibly. 'The respiration is affected, the chest heaves and the dilated nostrils quiver. As Tennyson writes "sharp breaths of anger puffed her fairy nostrils out". Hence we have such expressions as "breathing out vengeance" and "fuming with anger".'[5] The author of the 'Shield of Herakles' says simply that the Boeotians go eagerly to battle '*breathing above their shields*'[6] (ὑπὲρ σακέων πνείοντες). Virgil describes Tyrrhus roused from a peaceful occupation to fight *rapta spirans immane securi.*[7]

We can now better understand '*inspiration*'. What conception could be more natural, when feeling and thought are the work of the lungs? Time and again, more particularly

---

[1] *Il.* xxiii, 370 f. [2] See James, *op. cit.* ii, p. 472 and below, pp. 56 ff. [3] *Il.* ii, 536, xxiv, 364, etc. [4] *Il.* iii, 8. [5] Darwin, *op. cit.* p. 249. [6] 23 f. [7] *Aen.* vii, 510. This also explains Catull. lxiv, 194.

before a great effort, we read how a god or goddess (Athene, Apollo, or Hermes, etc.) 'breathed μένος' into a hero or heroes or into horses or mules. Thus Odysseus pointed out their prey, the sleeping Thracians, to Diomedes, 'but into him Athene breathed (ἔμπνευσε) μένος and he began slaying right and left'.[1] The same goddess in the final battle of the *Odyssey* encouraged old Laertes and 'breathed into him (ἔμπνευσε) great μένος, then he praying...straightway swung and hurled his spear'.[2] A sudden access of courage or impulse or resolve with its accompanying sense of energy and power was conceived as the work of a god. He who feels it probably does in fact draw a deep breath, and it has been observed that a man commencing any violent muscular effort invariably first distends his lungs with air;[3] but while recognition of some such unpremeditated physical accompaniment may lie behind the phrase, it would be wrong to press that side as uppermost in Homer's thoughts. We shall see more fully presently[4] that at the stage of thought when these beliefs emerged there was

[1] *Il.* x, 482 f. For strength as a matter of 'breath' (πνεῦμα) later see Aristot. *Pol.* 1336 a, 37, *Probl.* 868 a, 17 ff., *De Motu An.* 703 a, 9 ff. but see also pp. 195 f.

[2] *Od.* xxiv, 520 f. Conrad describes a sailor struggling with a storm: 'For some reason Jukes experienced an access of confidence, a sensation that came from outside like a warm breath and made him feel equal to every demand' (*Typhoon*, ch. v). For the literal meaning of 'inspiration' cf. a legend of the *Cid*. He helped a leper out of a quagmire, ate with him, and 'ordered a bed to be made ready for himself and for the leper and they twain slept together. When it was midnight and Rodrigo was fast asleep the leper breathed against him between his shoulders and that breath was so strong that it passed through him, even through his breast; and he awoke being astounded and felt for the leper by him and found him not.' The leper reappeared and said 'I am Saint Lazarus...whensoever that breath which thou hast felt shall come upon thee, whatsoever thing thou desirest to do and shalt then begin, that shalt thou accomplish to thy heart's desire, whether it be in battle or aught else'—translated by Southey in *The Chronicle of the Cid*, i, 9. For the Jews the spirit was breath or wind, so, 'when he had said this, he breathed on them (or "into them", ἐνεφύσησεν), and saith unto them "Receive ye the Holy Ghost" (λάβετε πνεῦμα ἅγιον)', John xx, 22. The conception of the Holy Ghost=Spirit, however, is more complex.   [3] Darwin, *op. cit.* p. 244.

[4] Part III, below. That μένος should be conceived of as material is, however, not so far removed from later doctrines of the 'humours' or indeed our own theories about the secretions of the endocrine glands.

difficulty in conceiving anything except material entities. μένος is apparently not an abstraction or a mere state of something else, but conceived as itself something, fluid or gaseous, which for convenience we may translate 'energy', and which was felt inwardly much as we feel what we so name. It was thought to be more particularly with the θυμός in the φρένες. Hence he, who has it, 'breathes' it, and the god, who gives it, 'inspires' or 'breathes it into' him, and alternatively is said to 'place it in his θυμός',[1] or 'in his φρένες'.[2]

Similarly the gods 'place boldness (or "high spirit", θάρσος) in the θυμός'[3] of a man or 'fill his φρένες'[4] with it, and again we have the explicit alternative expression. His comrades took their stand with Odysseus about the sleeping Cyclops and 'some god breathed great θάρσος into them'[5] (θάρσος ἐνέπνευσεν μέγα δαίμων). It is something in the breath or breath-soul which gives courage and it is itself described as ἄητον, 'snorting, strongly breathing or breathed'. When strife fell among the gods and 'the θυμός was breathed (ἄητο) in two directions in their φρένες', Ares railed at Athene: 'Why with (lit. "having") θάρσος ἄητον dost thou drive the gods together in strife? Why did thy great θυμός move thee?'[6]

Again χόλος, which is 'anger' or what is felt as such, is spoken of as entering into or being in the breast[7] (στῆθος or στήθεα), or more specifically in the φρένες[8] or in the θυμός.[9] We can now understand why Achilles described it as 'waxing like smoke in the breasts of men (ἀνδρῶν ἐν στήθεσσι ἀέξεται ἠΰτε καπνός) even as Agamemnon angered me, but we will let bygones be bygones, quelling the θυμός in our breasts'.[10]

This association of the emotion with the breathing may seem strange to us, since we are in the habit of abstracting the emo-

---

[1] *Od.* II, 320, XVI, 529.   [2] *Il.* XXI, 145; *Od.* I, 89.   [3] *Od.* I, 320 f.
[4] *Il.* XVII, 570 f. Cf. *Od.* VI, 140.   [5] *Od.* IX, 380 f.   [6] *Il.* XXI, 394 f.
[7] *Il.* IV, 24, VIII, 461. For further discussion of χόλος see pp. 84 f., 87 f.
[8] *Il.* II, 241; *Od.* VI, 147; in the heart, *Il.* IX, 646.   [9] *Il.* VI, 526, etc.
[10] *Il.* XVIII, 110 f. Such thought is perhaps the ultimate root of *irai fax...fumida suffundens caecae caliginis umbram* (Lucr. III, 303 f.) and of Dante's sullen ones carrying smoke (*fummo*) within (*Inf.* VII, 123), 'fuming'. Cf. *Purg.* XVI.

tion itself from its bodily expressions and thinking that the latter are *epiphenomena* or after-effects; 'that the mental perception of some fact excites the mental affection called the emotion and that this latter state of mind gives rise to the bodily expression'. We may be less scornful of the Homeric view when we remember that Lange, James, and other psychologists have held 'that the bodily changes follow directly the perception of the exciting fact and that our feeling of the same changes as they occur *is* the emotion'.[1]

After Homer emotion is continually expressed not so much in these same phrases as in others bearing independent witness to the conceptions we have found in him. Many obscure images of the poets thus become intelligible. Aeschylus, for whom, as for Homer, φρένες and πραπίδες were seen above to mean 'lungs', will serve to illustrate. Feeling, emotion, is 'breathed' or 'blows'. Thus a maid speaks of her wooer as 'strongly breathing goodwill to me'[2] (κάρτ' ἐμοὶ πνέων χάριν). Clytemnestra 'breathes truceless war upon her friends'.[3] The goddess Justice 'breathes deadly wrath (κότος) against her foes'.[4] In warriors before battle 'no pity was there through their lips (οἶκτος οὔτις ἦν διὰ στόμα) but the iron-lunged (σιδηρόφρων) θυμός breathed flaming with valour'[5] (ἀνδρείᾳ φλέγων ἔπνει). The suppliant Danaids entreat the strange land

---

[1] James, *op. cit.* II, p. 449. Among other evidence he points (p. 459) to 'morbid fear' that has no object or external provocation: 'if inability to draw breath, fluttering of the heart and that peculiar epigastric change felt as "precordial anxiety" with an irresistible tendency to take a somewhat crouching attitude and to sit still...all spontaneously occur together in a certain person, his feeling of their combination is the feeling of dread. A friend...tells me that in his case the whole drama seems to centre about the region of the heart and respiratory apparatus, that his main effort during the attacks is to get control of his inspirations and to slow his heart and that the moment he attains to breathing deeply and to holding himself erect the dread *ipso facto* seems to depart'. Jung (*Psychological Types*, English translation, p. 522), defining emotion, maintains that the psychic feeling and the bodily change are two sides of a unity 'each of which has a cumulative reciprocal effect upon the other'.

[2] *Ag.* 1206.

[3] *Ibid.* 1235 f., reading Ἄρη after Porson for MSS. ἀράν.

[4] *Choeph.* 951. Cf. 34, and *Eum.* 840.   [5] *Septem*, 51 ff.

and its gods to welcome them 'with breath (or "breeze") of reverence'[1] (αἰδοίῳ πνεύματι). The Homeric likening of the θυμός or breath to the wind is carried further. Agamemnon at Aulis is described as 'breathing in harmony (or "blowing in the same direction") with the chances that smote him'[2] (ἐμπαίοις τύχαισιν συμπνέων) and, before the sacrifice, as 'breathing from his φρήν an impious veering wind'.[3] Hoping for the punishment of Clytemnestra and Aigisthos, the Choephoroi say 'why should I hide what nevertheless floats (or "flits", ποτᾶται used of a vapour or cloud[4]) from my φρήν? Before the prow of my heart is blown keen θυμός, wrathful hate'[5] (πάροιθεν δὲ πρῴρας δριμὺς ἄηται κραδίας θυμός, ἔγκοτον στύγος). This, with Homer's likening of divided θυμός to two winds blowing upon the sea,[6] may be seen in its full appositeness if we recall that the blood is massed in the lungs around the heart as nowhere else in the body[7] and that Empedocles speaks of the heart as 'dwelling in the sea (πελάγεσσι) of blood that leaps against it where especially is what men call thought'.[8]

If we recall more exclusively the structure of the lungs, the 'bronchial tree' and rami or ramites and the epithets λάσιος, δαυλοί τε δάσκιοί τε, etc., applied to φρένες or πραπίδες,[9] we can better appreciate other passages. For Sappho, we are told, 'Love shook her φρένες like a wind falling upon oaks down a mountain';[10] and, in a rather doubtful text, Ibycus declares that 'like Boreas from Thrace, aflame beneath the lightning, Love rushing from the Cyprian with parching

---

[1] Suppl. 27 ff.   [2] Ag. 187.
[3] Ag. 219.   [4] Eum. 378; Pers. 669 f. Cf. Il. xvi, 469.
[5] Choeph. 389 ff., reading οἶον after Hermann for MSS. θεῖον. The θυμός determines the action of the whole man. 'I am carried out of my course by the raging breath of frenzy' (λύσσης πνεύματι μάργῳ), says Io (P.V. 883 f.). The nautical metaphor may with less relation to the original thought be applied to the θυμός itself, 'His φρένες steered (ᾠακοστρόφουν) his θυμός' (Pers. 767; cf. Ag. 802), with which we may compare from Bacchylides 'you pilot (κυβερνᾷς) the θυμός within your φρένες righteous no longer', xvi, 21 f.
[6] Il. ix, 4 ff., discussed on p. 46 above.   [7] See p. 47, n. 3.
[8] B 105 (Diels). For his doctrine see below, pp. 71-2.
[9] See pp. 28 ff.   [10] Fr. 42 (Bgk.).

frenzy, dark and dauntless, by force doth shake from their base my φρένες',[1] with which we might compare from the Anthology 'Desire, blowing heavily, maketh storm'[2] (χειμαίνει δ' ὁ βαρὺς πνεύσας πόθος). 'Thou breathest two breaths, O Love'[3] (δισσὰ πνεύματα πνεῖς), says a tragic poet, referring (according to Ps.-Lucian) to spiritual and carnal love. Euripides, whose Bacchai are 'frenzied with breaths from the god'[4] (θεοῦ πνοαῖσιν ἐμμανεῖς) and for whom love is 'the breaths (or "blasts", πνοαί) of Aphrodite',[5] makes Iokaste say to Eteokles 'Check thy dread eye and the blasts (πνοαί) of thy θυμός',[6] and describes Pentheus as 'breathing forth (ἐκπνέων) θυμός' when trying to fetter Dionysos. In the *Rhesus* the horses are 'snorting, breathing θυμός from their windpipes (ἐξ ἀρτηριῶν)'.[7] With the same thought and meaning as appears in the Homeric μεγάθυμος Euripides has μεγάλα πνεῖν, 'to be high-spirited, have high thoughts', literally 'to breathe big breaths',[8] preserving something of the basis of the belief. Even in prose this equation survives. Antipho the Sophist speaks of people well matched as 'having equal thoughts, equal breaths'[9] (ἴσα φρονοῦντας, ἴσα πνέοντας). Pindar has χαμηλὰ πνέων, 'breathing lowly breaths',[10] i.e. thinking lowly thoughts, etc. He who has laboured fruitlessly 'has breathed empty breaths'[11] (κενεὰ πνεύσας), and, unlike the man who possesses greatness by birth, he who has that which is taught, 'in darkness breathing some breaths now and others at another time (i.e. having some thoughts, feelings, purposes—some motions of the breath that is consciousness—now, etc., ἄλλοτ' ἄλλα πνέων) steppeth never with sure foot but, fulfilling not a purpose completely, tastes countless excellences'.[12] To the

---

[1] Fr. 1 (Bgk.) reading πεδόθεν τινάσσει (Naeke) generally accepted for MSS. παιδόθεν φυλάσσει. Of one who is dauntless Pindar says, 'her φρένες have not been storm-tossed by fear' (φόβῳ δ' οὐ κεχείμανται φρένες, *Pyth.* IX, 32). [2] *Anth. Pal.* XII, 157.
[3] *Trag. Adesp.* Fr. 187 (Nauck). Cf. the poem of Cercidas beginning δοιά τις ἅμιν ἔφα γνάθοισι φυσῆν τὸν κυανοπτέρυγον παῖδ' 'Αφροδίτας, 2 (Diehl). [4] *Bacch.* 1094. [5] *Iph. in Aul.* 69. [6] *Phoen.* 454. [7] Line 785.
[8] *Androm.* 189 f., 327, etc. Cf. *Aen.* IX, 596, X, 387 quoted on p. 42.
[9] B 49 (§ 598, 18), Diels (*Fragm. d. Vors.*⁴).
[10] *Pyth.* XI, 30.   [11] *Ol.* X, 93.   [12] *Nem.* III, 41 f.

Hyperboreans Perseus 'went breathing with bold heart'[1] (θρασείᾳ δὲ πνέων καρδίᾳ μόλεν).

Thus we might continue;[2] but, returning to Homer, let us note that it is not only emotion that the gods 'breathe' into men but also thoughts, devices, relatively intellectual. This too we might expect, since it is with his θυμός and φρένες or, if our interpretation be right, his breath-soul and lungs, that a man thinks and knows no less than feels. Thus 'take thought in your φρήν and θυμός how you may slay the suitors',[3] or the recurring line 'and I will say something else and do you put it in your φρένες',[4] by the side of which we may set 'I will tell you an easy rede (ἔπος) and will put it in your φρένες'.[5] So to Penelope the idea of her stratagem occurred thus—'Some god breathed into (ἐνέπνευσε) my φρένες that I should set up a great loom and weave a robe'.[6] Mind, thoughts, knowledge are breath which can also be breathed out. We have already seen[7] in this the explanation of the song 'To a flute-player the gods gave not intelligence (νοῦς); while he blows, his intelligence also flies out'.

We are now better able to understand the verb πεπνῦσθαι, which has been interpreted by some as quite unrelated to πνεῖν or any notion of breathing but as formed from a verb πνύειν, whose otherwise unknown existence is argued from ποιπνύειν and ἄμπνυτο, ἀμπνύθη. This argument was elaborated at length by Schulze[8] and is followed by Leaf,[9] Boisacq,[10] and the revisers of Liddell and Scott's lexicon.[11] ποιπνύειν, it is urged, means 'to bestir oneself, to hurry', and is a reduplicated form of an original πνύειν with the same meaning of rapid physical motion. Later transferred to the mind, this by a

[1] *Pyth.* x, 44. For Pindar apparently as for Homer the heart shares the θυμός and consciousness with the φρένες. See p. 49, n. 1.

[2] The thought survived in philosophy (cf. pp. 71 f., 76 ff., 80, etc.). Thus the Epicurean Lucretius shows that minds vary according to the proportions in which they consist of hot *vapor* (felt in anger), cold *aura* (felt in fear), *aer* (characteristic of calm) and a subtler nameless element (III, 231–313).

[3] *Od.* I, 294. Cf. *Il.* IX, 423, etc.   [4] *Il.* I, 297, IV, 39, etc.

[5] *Od.* XI, 146. Cf. *Il.* XIX, 121.   [6] *Od.* XIX, 138 f. Cf. Hes. *Th.* 31, etc.

[7] P. 38.   [8] *Quaestiones Epicae*, pp. 322 ff.

[9] Commentary to *Il.* v, 697.   [10] *Op. cit.* s.v.   [11] S.v.

curious leap is made to mean 'to be conscious, to be in full possession of one's spiritual forces'. Thence ἄμπνυτο and ἀμπνύθη are derived with the meaning 'recovered consciousness', while πεπνῦσθαι is interpreted as meaning 'to be physically active' in the case of Telemachos but elsewhere 'to be fully conscious', and so 'wise'.

Now for such a root πνυ- no evidence is offered from any cognate tongue. ποιπνύω itself, on which the whole argument rests, is probably better explained¹ as meaning originally 'I pant, puff about', 'I exert myself, bustle', a man's breathing being, for the reasons we have seen, his most significant feature. For ἄμπνυτο and ἀμπνύθη we need only look back to the passages already quoted.² The θυμός is 'breathed forth' (ἀποπνεῖν) and the reverse process is described by the words 'ἄμπνυτο (or ἀμπνύθη) and the θυμός was gathered into the φρήν'. Further, to support his case Schulze is compelled to deny the natural meaning of ἄπνευστος, 'breathless', and say that it means 'faint, powerless', because the recovery of the man who is ἄπνευστος is expressed by ἄμπνυτο (Od. v, 456–8). Again, in the Homeric Hymn to Hermes,³ when the god makes a fire ἄμπνυτο δὲ θερμὸς ἀϋτμή, 'recovered consciousness' makes nonsense. Nevertheless the natural

---

¹ 'Bustling' suggests a person moving about energetically and noisily, possibly panting with his efforts, 'puffing about' as we say. Thus Phaedrus (II, 5) describes the tribe of 'busybodies' as trepide concursans...gratis anhelans. For such a sense we might compare the Middle High German phnuht, 'noisy breathing', and note that in fact initial πν- is not used elsewhere in Greek except in some connection with breath, πνέω, πνοή, πνίγω, etc. (The apparent exception, the place of assembly, Πνύξ, forms its oblique cases in πυκν-, whence its origin is usually traced.) Moreover, such expressive reduplication is common in other languages in that connection, from our own childish 'puff-puff' to the Sanscrit pupphusa-ḥ, 'lung', etc. The obvious parallel in Greek itself is ποιφύσσω, based on φυσάω, 'I blow'. The most expressive context in which ποιπνύω occurs is 'and laughter unquenchable arose among the blessed gods when they saw Hephaistos ποιπνύοντα through the halls' (Il. I, 599 f.). For what it is worth, we may note that his 'breathing' or 'blast', ἀϋτμή, is characteristic of fire for Homer (Od. IX, 389, XVI, 29, etc.) as of the fire god Hephaistos himself (Il. XXI, 366 f.). The latter is found at his bellows by Thetis and is termed πέλωρ αἴητον, apparently meaning 'puffing monster' (Il. XVIII, 410 ff.).   ² P. 45.   ³ Line 110.

reference to ἀναπνεῖν which ἀϋτμή demands and which is seen
e.g. in ἀμπνεῦσαι καπνόν,[1] etc., is ignored in favour of this
hypothetical ἀναπνύειν. 'Alternatively', Schulze suggests,
'the poet may have made a mistake.'[2] The active ἄμπνυε in
the sense of 'recover breath' (Il. xxii, 222) they cannot and do
not deny. For the formation of the middle and passive aorists
ἄμπνυτο and ἀμπνύθη from ἀνα- or ἀμ-πνέω, and indeed of
the perfect πέπνυμαι from πνέω, we may compare ἔχυτο,
ἐχύθη and κέχυμαι from χέω.

If we would pursue the case further, πέπνυμαι on the current
interpretation varies its meaning with very little justification.
The supposed original πνύειν, 'to move vigorously, bestir
oneself physically', is supported by the argument that Telemachos, repeatedly described as πεπνυμένος, is too young to
be called 'wise'. In his case, therefore, we are told it means
'nimble, active, brisk' (Schulze), 'vigorous rather than sage'
(Leaf). But by the side of τὸν δ' αὖ Τηλέμαχος πεπνυμένος
ἀντίον ηὔδα (Od. xxiv, 510) we find τὸν δ' αὖ Λαέρτης
πεπνυμένος ἀντίον ηὔδα (ibid. 375). Telemachos must thus
have had a 'nimble' and not a 'wise' grandfather or Homer
must be behaving very strangely. In fact there is no reason
why Telemachos should not be 'wise' and his grandfather
too. He is constantly represented and recognised as such,[3]
and πεπνυμένος without qualification is applied to the young
Antilochos unequivocally in that sense.[4] The arguments in
favour of a verb πνύω thus failing,[5] we are left with πέπνυμαι,
perfect middle or passive of πνέω, 'I breathe', which was
proposed long ago.[6] It means not merely 'I have received

---

[1] Pind. Ol. viii, 36.
[2] 'nisi forte error auctoris subest', op. cit. p. 324, n. 2.
[3] E.g. Od. iv, 158, 593–611, etc.   [4] Il. xxiii, 440, 570.
[5] The attempt to connect πινυτή, πινυτός, etc., is rejected even by
Boisacq.
[6] This, the obvious derivation, given by Ameis-Hentze, Merry, etc.,
failed for want of background of explanation. Since this was written it
has been revived by Justesen (op. cit. p. 43, see p. 24 above), who explained it as 'inspired' in connection with the interpretation of νόος as
'nose', and by Rüsche (op. cit. p. 40), who explains that Anhauch intensifies
the spiritual faculties, renders intelligent. Neither has discussed the current

breath' and so 'I have breath' but also something like 'I have intelligence, wisdom'. This fits exactly what we found, that consciousness and intelligence depend upon the breath and the lungs, and that wisdom is 'breathed into' a man. It explains why Homer can express the same meaning by saying that a man is πεπνυμένος as by saying that he has 'good φρένες'.[1] Similarly Achilles shows his scorn for Agamemnon by saying 'Away with him, for Zeus hath taken away his φρένες',[2] and Menelaos for Antilochos: 'Away with thee, since falsely we Achaeans said that thou πεπνῦσθαι....Antilochos, who wert aforetime πεπνυμένος, what hast thou done?'[3]

The famous description of Teiresias, whose ψυχή Odysseus is to consult in Hades, is also thus intelligible: 'the blind prophet whose φρένες are firm (ἔμπεδοι). To him, though dead, Persephone granted understanding (νόον) that he alone should πεπνῦσθαι, but the others dart about, mere shadows'.[4] Teiresias is privileged in having, though dead, a body or at least that part of it which is the organ of consciousness and intelligence, namely the φρένες or lungs, so he alone πέπνυται, has breath and the consciousness and intelligence that means. The rest are fleshless shadows without these things, ἀφραδέες, 'senseless', as they are described elsewhere.[5] Achilles ineffectually tries to clasp the ghost of Patroklos, 'and clasped it not, but the ψυχή was gone, like unto smoke, beneath the earth, squeaking'. And Achilles leapt up in wonder: 'Ah me, then there is even in the halls of Hades a ψυχή and phantasm (εἴδωλον), but φρένες there are not therein at all'.[6] Here, as in the contrast of Teiresias to 'shadows', the bodily organ appears to be implied. Thrice does Odysseus try to clasp the ψυχή of his mother but thrice she flew out of his hands 'like

alternative or prevented the revisers of Liddell and Scott from explaining: 'From root πενϝ which becomes πινυ in πινυτός...not cognate with πνέω, with which however it soon began to be confused'; so I leave what I had written above.

[1] See e.g. *Od.* III, 266; *Il.* XVII, 470.

[2] *Il.* IX, 377. The hyperbole 'Zeus has taken away his φρένες' reminds us of our own 'He has no brains', 'He lost his head', etc.

[3] *Il.* XXIII, 440, 570. Cf. *Od.* XVIII, 215 ff., 226 ff.

[4] *Od.* X, 492 ff.   [5] *Od.* XI, 476.   [6] *Il.* XXIII, 100 ff.

a shadow or even as a dream' and she explained: 'This is the way with mortals, when one dies, for the sinews no longer hold the flesh and the bones, but the mighty energy (μένος) of burning fire overcomes these (as soon as the θυμός has left the white bones) and the ψυχή like a dream flies away and flutters'.[1] The prophet Teiresias, though dead, has apparently not been burned and he retains his organs and intelligence.[2] The prophet Amphiaraos, to whom he has been compared,[3] passed beneath the ground in his body by divine intervention according to post-Homeric evidence;[4] so too other prophets and heroes who retain their powers. The ψυχαί, we may note, of Elpenor[5] and Patroklos,[6] whose bodies

---

[1] *Od.* XI, 218 ff.

[2] Its peculiar pallor might explain why Pelops was reputed to have received from the gods an unusual, an 'ivory' shoulder (see e.g. Pind. *Ol.* I, 26 f. (with Schol. *ad loc.*); Virgil, *Georg.* III, 7, etc.), but scarcely why his 'shoulder-blade' (see Paus. V, 13, 4, etc.) or his 'rib of ivory' (Pliny, *N.H.* XXVIII, 4, 34) was uniquely treasured after his death. The original reason for the emphasis upon these bones is perhaps an association with the living consciousness (cf. p. 68, n. 7), that they contained the lungs, φρένες, the organs of mind, good or bad, 'taken away' (pp. 59, 81, *Il.* XVIII, 311, XIX, 137, etc.) on occasion or bestowed (see *Od.* II, 117 f., VII, 111 f., VIII, 167 f., etc.) by a god. The same thought will explain the later practice of divination by the appearance of a victim's shoulder-blade (see Grimm, *Deutsche Myth.*[4] p. 932, Nachtr. pp. 322, 422, 433), as among the Romans of the lung itself (e.g. Cicero, *de Div.* I, 39, 85, II, 12, 29). Thus Dido sacrifices *pecudumque reclusis/pectoribus inhians spirantia consulit exta* (*Aen.* IV, 63 f.). Cf. pp. 41 (*exta*), 505 f.; Juv. VI, 549 ff. The Babylonians, from whom this divination perhaps derived through the Etruscans, believed that the state of the organ showed the state of mind of the god, who at the moment of sacrifice was believed to have identified himself with the victim (see Jastrow, *Religion of Babylonia and Assyria*, pp. 148, 155). Cf. below pp. 88–9, 228, n. 1, 236; *mentesque deum scrutantur in illis* (Ov. *Met.* XV, 137); *conscia fibra deorum* (Tib. I, 8, 3); *lubrica signavit cum deus exta notis* (II, 5, 14). Prophetic virtue was attributed to the *merry-thought*, i.e. breast-bone of a goose or other bird, among our ancestors (see e.g. Brand's *Popular Antiquities, etc.* (rev. Ellis), III, p. 220 (Bohn)), for whom, as we have seen (pp. 38 f.), the lungs were the 'soul' and the breast was the seat of thought. It is still for us the 'wish-bone'.

[3] See Rohde, *op. cit.* p. 89 and notes p. 103.

[4] See Pindar, *Ol.* VI, 14.

[5] *Od.* XI, 60. The thinness or lack of voice may have been related to the lack of φρένες=lungs. With all this cf. Lucan VI, 621–3, 628–31.

[6] *Il.* XXIII, 65 ff.

lie unburned, have consciousness and speak to Odysseus and Achilles, as does that of Teiresias to Odysseus, though the other ψυχαί, whose bodies have presumably been burned, do not speak or show sign of recognising Odysseus till they have tasted blood[1] and so got breath, θυμός, for the occasion. For, as we have seen, breath, θυμός, was conceived as vapour in connection with blood.[2] Patroklos asks for funeral, saying that till he has received it the ψυχαί of the dead will not admit him to their number, but, once he has been burned, he will not come back from the house of Hades.[3]

Light can perhaps also be thrown on *sapere* (*sapiens, desipere* etc.). Its original meaning (e.g. *occisam saepe sapere plus multo suem*[4] or *oleum male sapiet*[5]) was 'to be flavoured, have flavour'. It described an object as having something in it which could be received in tasting. It was, it is commonly[6] supposed, then transferred to the taster so as to mean 'to have the faculty of taste' and thence 'to have discrimination', 'to be wise'. But the transition is not natural[7] and there is no adequate evidence[8] for *sapere* 'to have the faculty of taste'.

---

[1] *Od.* XI, 96, 147 ff., 152 ff. Here, as in other eschatologies, there is not perfect consistency; for when, at the end of the *Odyssey*, the ψυχαί of the suitors reach Hades they find the ψυχαί of Achilles and Agamemnon (though they have not, so far as we are told, had anything to drink) holding an intelligent conversation. It might be argued that, if the same author is at work, he had subordinated consistency to dramatic opportunity or that the ψυχαί have not on this occasion to deal with a live man of flesh and blood. In *Od.* XI, 38 ff. the ψυχαί come to the pit of blood, the old men who have suffered much, the wounded, etc., and 'tender maids νεοπενθέα θυμὸν ἔχουσαι'. Here, unless the variant of the Oxyrh. Pap. νεοπενθε αωτον preserves the original version, the attempt to describe these ψυχαί as active, vocal, responsive to the offering, to suggest their different appearances fixed at death, has, perhaps unconsciously, involved the use of expressions devised to describe the living (e.g. ταλαπενθέα θυμὸν ἔχουσαν, XXIII, 15, ἀπηνέα θυμὸν ἔχουσα, 97, etc.). These lines were rejected by Zenodotus and Aristophanes for other reasons without reference to this point. For the separation of θυμός and ψυχή at death see also pp. 94 ff. below.

[2] See pp. 46 ff.　[3] *Il.* XXIII, 71 ff. Cf. VII, 410.　[4] Plaut. *Mil. Gl.* 587.
[5] Cato, *de agri cult.* 66, 1.　　[6] See e.g. Ernout and Meillet s.v.
[7] Our 'taste', *goût* etc. begin with the act of the taster.
[8] The only instance quoted by Lewis and Short is relatively late, Cicero, *de Fin.* II, 8, 24: *nec...Laelius eo dictus est sapiens quod non intelligere*

Also *sapere* often signifies 'to have consciousness' or 'intelligence' in the most general sense (e.g. referring to Parthia's return of the standards taken from Crassus at Carrhae, Propertius addresses the dead man: *gaude, Crasse, nigras si quid sapis inter harenas*),[1] and *resipiscere* 'to recover consciousness'.[2] It was the chest which *sapiebat*, e.g. *sapit hic pleno pectore* (Plautus, *Epidicus* 286), *frugi convenit esse hominem pectus quoi sapit* (*Bacchides* 660. Cf. *Miles Gl.* 786, 336 etc.). 'To have flavour',[3] more directly, will scarcely explain this. Also, *sapere* refers to something inherent rather than to the impression a man makes on others. We have, perhaps, not yet reached the full original sense of *sapere*. It looks akin to *sapa* which was used of the juice of the grape boiled but, as appears in its derivatives in the Romance languages (Italian *sapa*, French *sève* etc.) and the Germanic cognates (Anglo-Saxon *sæp*, old Icelandic *safi*, German *Saft*, etc.), it must have meant more generally 'sap, juice'. It is natural to think that the flavour of food (e.g. a piece of meat or fruit) is in its blood or juice, and not in the fibres that remain when that has been extracted. Greek χυμός and χυλός (χέω), Sansc. *rasa*, Arm. *ham* all mean both 'sap' or 'juice' and 'flavour'. Using the noun, Lucretius[4] says *in os salsi venit umor saepe saporis/cum mare versamur propter*; and quite explicitly for him[5] and other Latin writers 'flavour' was *sucus*. Thus Horace praises long eggs as *suci melioris* (*Satires* II, 4, 13). *Quae oblonga sint ova gratioris saporis putat Horatius Flaccus* (Pliny, *N.H.* x, 52, 145). In fact 'the sense of taste can be stimulated only by fluids. Solid substances must be dissolved in the mouth before they can affect it.'[6] If *sapere* meant originally 'to have sap, native juice', and was applied thus to the chest, that

quid suavissimum esset; nec enim sequitur ut cui cor sapiat ei non sapiat palatus; which in fact is satisfied by the vague contemporary sense 'is wise' in both cases (cf. *intelligeret quid suavissimum esset*).

[1] IV (v), 6, 83.
[2] See p. 169, n. 3.
[3] But *insulsus*, etc., derive from this line of thought.
[4] IV, 222, cf. II, 398 ff.   [5] IV, 615 ff.
[6] G. F. Stout, *A Manual of Psychology*[3], p. 260.

accords perfectly with what we found and shall find,[1] that the Greeks and Romans related consciousness and intelligence to the native juice in the chest, blood (foreign liquids affected consciousness for the most part adversely),[2] and to the vapour exhaled from it, breath. In fact, when used of external things, *sapere* could refer not only to juice absorbed in tasting but also to its exhalation or breath,[3] i.e. fragrance, received by the nostrils in breathing.

As we saw,[4] Germanic peoples, in particular our own ancestors, held beliefs about consciousness in the chest like those of the Greeks and Romans. Thus they intimately related *sawol* ('soul') to blood.[5] The terms for consciousness in the Germanic languages that appear to be cognate with *sapere* are perhaps to be explained similarly. Compare e.g. old Icelandic *safi* 'sap', *sefi*[6] 'mind' with *froða, froðr* (p. 68, n. 7), *vatr* 'wet' for 'wise', *þurr* 'dry' = ignorant (*Laxd.* 67, *Sturlunga* II, 227). If *animus*[7] was, like θυμός, related to blood, we may have the ground of the notion that the blood was the *sedes* of the soul.[8] The phenomena at its base continue. Tacitus describes Seneca's wife stopped from bleeding to death when

---

[1] See p. 42, n. 12, also Horace, *Odes* III, 21, 9f. etc. on p. 43, and pp. 46–8, 61 ff. *Sapiens*, originally 'juicy', *sapientia*, 'juiciness', give point to Plaut. *Trin.* 367 f.; *sapiens* 'the juicy' is the meat to which age is the seasoning.

[2] See pp. 31–8. Other 'sap' means other mind (see p. 66). *Quo me, Bacche, rapis tui plenum...mente nova?* (Hor. *Od.* III, 25, 1); *carmina vino/ ingenium faciente canunt* (Ov. *Met.* VII, 432 f.). The mind of a man is changed into that of a sea-god:

> *pabula decerpsi, decerptaque dente momordi,*
> *vix bene combiberant ignotos guttura sucos*
> *cum subito trepidare intus praecordia sensi*
> *alteriusque rapi naturae pectus amore...*   *Met.* XIII, 943 ff.

[3] E.g. *ambrosiaeque comae divinum vertice odorem/spiravere*, etc. (Virgil, *Aen.* I, 403 f.; cf. *Georg.* IV, 415 ff.) See also pp. 74–5.

[4] Pp. 38f. See also p. 68.

[5] See p. 69, n. 1.

[6] σοφός also, which the Romans translated *sapiens*, may be related.

[7] Cf., perhaps, Plaut. *Pers.* 177. *animus* is discussed below, pp. 168 ff.

[8] See Servius *ad Aen.* V, 79. Cf. *Aen.* IX, 349, Homeric Hymn to Apollo 361, also *Georgic* II, 483f. with Empedocles B 105 and pp. 42, 54.

already faint, *ore ac membris... albentibus ut ostentui esset multum vitalis spiritus egestum* (*Ann.* xv, 64).

With this background of consciousness or wisdom, native or acquired, as moisture in the chest we can better understand passages above[1] and such expressions as Martial's

> *si quis Cecropiae madidus Latiaeque Minervae artibus,*[2]

or   *cuius Cecropia pectora dote* [v.l. *voce*] *madent.*[3]

Lucilius and Horace, as we saw,[4] connected the mind with *venae* in the chest. In this original and usual sense of *vena* as a pipe or vessel containing liquid, native liquid, must lie the true interpretation of Horace's claim to *ingeni/benigna vena*[5] and his

> *ego nec studium sine divite vena*
> *nec rude quid prosit video ingenium,*[6]

not, as Wickham for instance interprets, a 'vein of metal', a metaphor from mining. The latter is not very natural for a Roman speaking of his mind or its organs and *dives* implies no more than 'abounding'.[7] Ovid,[8] also, has

> *ingenioque meo vena quod paupere manat*
> *plaudis et e rivo flumina magna facis,*

and

> *ingenium fregere meum mala cuius et ante*
> *fons infecundus parvaque vena fuit;*
> *sed quaecumque fuit nullo exercente refugit*
> *et longo periit arida facta situ,*

---

[1] Lucilius 610, Petronius 4, Horace, *Odes*, iii, 21, 9 f., etc. on p. 43. Petronius links this with the idea of the generation of poetry, creation of the mind (cf. p. 219, n. 3): *neque concipere aut edere partum mens potest nisi ingenti flumine litterarum inundata* (118, 3).

[2] i, 39, 3 f. So Hor. *Epist.* i, 2, 54, 67–70, Pers. ii, 74, etc.

[3] vii, 69, 2. See also pp. 66 f. below. Wisdom imbibed is moisture in the chest, 'dew' (if *rore* is correct here), i.e. vapour (apparently breath, words —so Pers. i, 126; cf. 123) condensed (see p. 46, n. 6). So apparently Plautus: *postquam adbibere aures meae tuae rorem orationis* (*Miles Gl.* 883 Heins. for *tuam moram*); and *inflata rore* (Ald.; *rhorso* B) *non Achaico verba* (Virg. *Cat.* v, 2. Cf. 4 with pp. 80 f. below).

[4] P. 42.   [5] *Odes* ii, 18, 9 f.   [6] *Ars Poet.* 409 f.

[7] See Lucr. i, 412 f. below.

[8] *Ex Ponto* ii, 5, 21 f., *Tristia*, iii, 14, 33 ff. See also 7, 15 f. (with p. 66) and Prop. iv, 1, 59 f.

and earlier Lucretius

> *usque adeo largos haustus e fontibu' magnis*
> *lingua meo suavis diti de pectore fundet.*[1]

Of Demosthenes and Cicero Juvenal declares

> *utrumque*
> *largus et exundans leto dedit ingenii fons*[2]

and Quintilian speaks of *sucus ingenii*[3] and *tenuis et angusta ingenii vena.*[4]   The meaning of *sapere* traced above adds point to Horace's *scribendi recte sapere est et principium et fons.*[5]

---

[1] I, 412 f. Cf. p. 43 and Hor. *Epist.* I, 3, 10 f. See also Plato, *Phaedr.* 235 c on p. 71. We can thus better understand Galaton's picture: τὸν μὲν Ὅμηρον αὐτὸν ἐμοῦντα, τοὺς δὲ ἄλλους ποιητὰς τὰ ἐμημεσμένα ἀρυτομένους (Aelian, *V.H.* XIII, 22), *adice Maeonidem a quo, ceu fonte perenni,/vatum Pieriis ora rigantur aquis* (Ov. *Amor.* III, 9, 25 f. For *Pieriis aquis* cf. pp. 66 f.), *Maeoniumque bibat felici pectore fontem/...sic flumine largo/plenus Pierio defundes pectore verba* (Petron. 5), Homer *cuius ex ore profusos/omnis posteritas latices in carmina duxit/amnemque in tenues ausa est deducere rivos* (Manil. II, 8 ff.).

[2] x, 118 f. Cf. Cicero, *de Suo Cons.* 74, Horace, *Epist.* II, 2, 120 f. etc.

[3] *Inst. Or. Proem.* 24, passing from the mind to its utterance.

[4] *Ibid.* VI, 2, 3.

[5] *Ars Poet.* 309.

CHAPTER IV

Cognition—The Five Senses

The dead prophet has φρένες, lungs, and πέπνυται, has breath, intelligence. It is by the θυμός in his φρένες or by what is breathed into them by some god that a live prophet divines. Athene and Apollo agree to stop the battle by setting Hector on to single combat, 'and Helenos, Priam's dear son (a prophet), understood (lit. "put together for himself", σύνθετο) in his θυμός their counsel'.[1] The perception is taken into the θυμός and is there correlated with the rest by the φρένες. An eagle drops a snake among the attacking Trojans—a portent from Zeus—and Polydamas interpreting to Hector says: 'Thus would a prophet expound who had clear knowledge of portents in his θυμός'[2] (σάφα θυμῷ εἰδείη τεράων). Aeschylus has the word θυμόμαντις[3] and describes[4] how Apollo is inspired as a prophet τέχνης δέ νιν Ζεύς ἔνθεον κτίσας φρένα. Cf. Enn. Ann. 18, fari donavit divinum pectus habere. θυμός is vapour from liquid, and liquid drunk goes to the φρένες or lungs. Hence it is, we may guess, that prophetic inspiration was sought by inhaling vapour,[5] or by drinking[6] blood or water, or wine or honey, or by chewing (i.e. extracting the essence in liquid),[7] not eating, the divine plant;[8] hence that the Muses

---

[1] Il. VII, 44 f.
[2] Il. XII, 228. Cf. VI, 438 f., XVIII, 224, etc. and pp. 73 f.
[3] Persae, 224. Cf. στερνόμαντις, Soph. Fr. 59.
[4] Eum. 17. Cf. Eurip. Ion, 1347.
[5] θυμός or intelligence from a deity was sought thus. Cf. e.g. anhelitus ...terrarum quibus inflatae mentes oracula funderent (Cic. de Div. I, 50, 115) and Delphi ibid. 57, 117, with Aeneid, VI, 48, 50 f., 78 f., Lucan V, 163–9 and the poets' alternative to drinking water of the Muses: nebulas Helicone legunto (Pers. V, 7).
[6] See pp. 34 f. and Eurip. Bacch. 279–84, 298–301, the drinking of the well of λήθη and later that of μνημοσύνη at the oracle of Trophonios at Lebadeia, Tac. Ann. II, 54, 4 and (with pp. 36, 42 f.) Hor. Od. II, 19, 6, Sil. Ital. IV, 777, Gruppe, Griech. Myth. u. Rel., pp. 829 f., 925. Cf. pp. 70–1 below. [7] Cf. p. 63, n. 2.
[8] See p. 456, n. 2 and e.g. laurumque momordit (Juv. VII, 19).

were water-nymphs, and poets drank of their springs[1] on Helicon or Parnassus, Castalia, etc. and τῷ μὲν ἐπὶ γλώσσῃ γλυκερὴν χείουσιν ἐέρσην,/τοῦ δ' ἔπε' ἐκ στόματος ῥεῖ μείλιχα (Hes. *Theog.* 83 f.) and a poem was water, honey or nectar of the Muses.[2] So too the *Camenae* and *Carmenta* were water-nymphs (cf. *lymphatus* (pp. 34 f.)).

Thus, too, it was natural to say that the speeches of a man who πέπνυται are themselves πεπνυμένα.[3] They come forth with the breath that is intelligence in them, they are parts of it,[4] and the listener puts them, takes them, into his θυμός, thus adding to his store, his knowledge. They pass from lung to lung, mind to mind. Penelope 'put the μῦθος πεπνυμένος of her son in her θυμός'[5] and words are continually said to be 'put in the φρένες'. Not only the evident connection between breathing and emotion already urged, but also the belief[6] that thoughts are words and words are breath—ἔπεα ἀέρια as Sappho[7] seems to have called them—would lead[8] to the be-

---

[1] Cf. pp. 34 f., 220. We can now better understand e.g. Pind. *Ol.* VI, 85 ff., *Isthm.* VI, 74 f., Lucr. IV, 2, Hor. *Epist.* I, 3, 10 f., Prop. III (IV), 1, 5; 3, 5 f.; 3, 51 f.; IV (V), 6, 75. So Arethusa (Mosch. III, 78; Virg. *Ecl.* X, 1 ff.). And so perhaps Truth was ἐν βυθῷ (Democ. B 117), in the depths of water, 'in a well'. Pythagoras, after drawing up and drinking water from a certain well, foretold that there would be an earthquake in two days' time (Andron cited by Euseb. *Praep. Ev.* X, 3, 6).

[2] E.g. Pind. *Ol.* VII, 1 ff., VI, 91; Pers. *Prol.* 1, 14; Lucr. 1, 412 f., 947 f.; Horace, *Ep.* I, 19, 44. Egeria, who inspired Numa, was a water-nymph.

[3] *Od.* IV, 204–6, XIX, 350–2; *Il.* IX, 58.

[4] Just as the whole θυμός is said to 'fly' (*Il.* XVI, 469, XXIII, 880), the words, thoughts that issue forth, portions of it, are feathered, 'winged' like birds, ἔπεα πτερόεντα, to the hearer. Unspoken, kept in the φρένες (see *Od.* XV, 445), they are 'not winged' (*Od.* XVII, 57). That troublesome thoughts were conceived as little winged creatures in the chest will be shown below (pp. 85 f., 404 f.). It was perhaps these early conceptions which suggested to Plato his image of the mind as a cage full of birds (*Theaet.* 197 C ff.). Apollonius Rhodius, using the Homeric conception, describes Medea thus: μῦθος δ' ἄλλοτε μέν οἱ ἐπ' ἀκροτάτης ἀνέτελλε/ γλώσσης, ἄλλοτ' ἔνερθε κατὰ στῆθος πεπότητο (III, 683 f.). Cf. Proverbs xxvi, 2. See also p. 469.   [5] *Od.* I, 361, XXI, 355.   [6] See pp. 13 f.

[7] Fr. 1 a (Edmonds). Cf. *Od.* VIII, 408 f. etc.

[8] Much later, when some claimed that the governing consciousness was in the head (see below, pp. 115 f.), this argument was used e.g. by the Stoic Zeno: φωνὴ διὰ φάρυγγος χωρεῖ. εἰ δὲ ἦν ἀπὸ τοῦ ἐγκεφάλου

lief that the organs of breath, the lungs, are the organs of mind. This conception of words would be natural, inevitable among men unfamiliar with writing (see p. 6). These words or thoughts are kept in the lungs. Thersites ἔπεα φρεσὶν ᾗσιν ἄκοσμά τε πολλά τε ᾔδη.[1] The poet uses both μῦθος and ἔπος for unspoken thoughts.[2]

On the other side of the world the natives of New Guinea, who, as we have seen,[3] locate the intelligence in the organs of speech and regard people who are defective in the latter as mentally defective, think that 'the memory, the store of formulae and traditions learned by heart, resides deeper, in the belly'.[4] Magic, power is in the words: 'The force of magic does not reside in the things; it resides within man and can escape only through his voice'. The survival already noted[5] of the name 'soul' for the lungs suggests that our own ancestors had similar beliefs to those of the Homeric Greeks. If we look to the earliest Anglo-Saxon poems we find that it is in that region of the body that knowledge, store of words, and the mind are supposed to be. Thus in *Beowulf*, 'began to speak' is *wordhord onleac*,[6] 'unlocked his word-hoard'. The mind is the *breosthord*,[7]

χωροῦσα, οὐκ ἂν διὰ φάρυγγος ἐχώρει. ὅθεν δὲ λόγος, καὶ φωνὴ ἐκεῖθεν χωρεῖ· λόγος δὲ ἀπὸ διανοίας χωρεῖ, ὥστ' οὐκ ἐν τῷ ἐγκεφάλῳ ἐστὶν ἡ διάνοια (cited by Galen, *de Hipp. et Plat.* II, 5, p. 241 K). See also Chrysippus, *Stoic. Vet. Fr.* (von Arnim), II, 242 f., Diog. L. VII, 55 and 159. Milton's *Comus* (244 ff.) marvels at the Lady's song, at that in her which can

'Breathe such divine enchanting ravishment?
Sure something holy lodges in that breast
And with these raptures moves the vocal air
To testify his hidden residence'.

[1] *Il.* II, 213.   [2] See e.g. *Il.* I, 541–50; *Od.* XV, 445.   [3] P. 14.
[4] Malinowski, *Argonauts of the Western Pacific*, p. 408.
[5] Pp. 38 f.   [6] Line 259, cf. *Widsith*, init.
[7] E.g. *Beowulf*, 1719, 2792; cf. Icelandic *hafa rað undir hverju rifi* = have counsel under every rib, etc. The conception of wisdom as something drunk, a liquid, Mimir's well (e.g. *Gylfaginning*, 15), or the mead *Oðrœrir* (made from honey and the blood of *Kvâsir*, the incarnation of wisdom, who was formed by the gods out of their collected *sputum*) seems to have grown out of the thoughts we have traced (pp. 34 f., 42 f., 63–7). So perhaps *froðr* 'wise' was related to *froða* 'froth, slaver' and dialect forms of Norwegian *frodig* (see Falk-Torp) = 'sappy'. Cf. also the Celtic cauldron of Ceridwen.

e.g. *wordes ord breosthord þurhbræc,*[1] 'an opening word broke from his breast-hoard'. 'Hir thoughte it swal so sore aboute hire herte/That nedely som word hir moste asterte' says Chaucer.[2] 'So shall my lungs coin words'[3] says Shakespeare. 'To get it off one's chest' is to-day a crude colloquialism for delivering oneself of a statement, and 'Do not breathe it' advises the keeping of a secret. If we recall that θυμός was particularly associated with courage, 'spirit', there may be seen another parallel in our use of 'pluck' for courage; for originally the 'pluck' meant just the heart and lungs.

Returning to Homer, we may wonder whether, though words and thoughts might naturally be believed to come *from* the lungs, they could be thought to go *to* them, be perceived, received by them, when the ears and eyes in the head must inevitably be recognised as sense organs. That they were so thought there can be no doubt. There are the many statements that the words of a speaker are 'put into the φρένες' of the hearer and the less conclusive descriptions[4] of people whose 'φρήν is delighted as they hear' singing or themselves play the lyre. Clearest of all, though it has not excited notice, is the account of how Odysseus hears Nestor calling to wake him. 'Quickly the sound (or "blast, breath", ἰωή, used of wind[5]) came about (inside[6]) his φρένες and he went forth from the hut.'[7] The sound, the breath, of which the words consist passes through the ears not to the brain but to the lungs. This, though it may seem foolish to us, is in fact a natural interpretation of the anatomy of the head, which shows an air passage direct from the outer air through the ear to the pharynx and so to the lungs. Aristotle remarks that the ear

---

[1] Ll. 2791 f. Just as the θυμός was related to blood, the Anglo-Saxon poet speaks of 'soul-blood' (*sawuldrior*, 2693) and even says 'in his *hreðer* (see p. 39) fast in mind-bonds a secret longing burned in (*wið*) his blood' (1878 ff.; cf. 1993, 2065 f., etc.). Cf. pp. 47 f., 62 ff.   [2] *Cant. T.* 6549 f.
[3] *Coriolanus*, III, 1, 76 f. Cf. *The Merry Wives of Windsor*, IV, 5, init.
[4] E.g. *Il.* I, 474; ὁ δὲ φρένα τέρπετ' ἀκούων. Cf. *Od.* VIII, 368; *Il.* IX, 186.
[5] *Il.* IV, 276, XI, 308. Cf. perhaps *anima=sonus* (Nonius, p. 347 Linds.).
[6] For the sense of περί see *Il.* I, 317 and XVI, 157 with the note of Ameis-Hentze-Cauer.
[7] *Il.* X, 139 f.

'has not a passage (πόρος) to the brain, but has to the roof of the mouth'.[1] The passage is divided by the tympanum, its lower portion being known as the Eustachian tube. The sense of smell working by the in-drawing of the breath would form an obvious basis for comparison and analogy.

If confirmation be needed, it is provided by the earliest writers after Homer. The φρένες continue to be the destination of speech. The epic phrase in which words are 'put into the φρένες' of the hearer recurs.[2] Hesiod, who uses it, also tells (in the *Eoiae*[3]) of Melampous and snakes that 'lick his ears and breathe into him prophetic knowledge' (λείχειν τὰ ὦτα καὶ ἐμπνεῦσαι αὐτῷ τὴν μαντικήν), and in the *Theogony*[4] the Muses are said to 'breathe into [the poet] a divine αὐδή that [he] might sing things past and to come'. In the Homeric Hymn to Hermes, that god sounded his lyre for Apollo 'and the lovely blast (or "breath", ἰωή) of the sound went through his φρένες and sweet desire took hold on him as he *listened with his* θυμός'[5] (ἐρατὴ δὲ διὰ φρένας ἤλυθ' ἰωή/θεσπεσίης ἐνοπῆς καί μιν γλυκὺς ἵμερος ἧρει/θυμῷ ἀκουάζοντα); while in the *Battle of the Frogs and Mice*, compact of older epic expressions, 'the speech entered their ears and disturbed their φρένες'[6] (λόγος δ' εἰς οὔατα πάντων/εἰσελθὼν ἐτάραξε φρένας). Anacreon confesses that his 'φρένες have become deaf'[7] (or perhaps 'dumb', αἱ δέ μευ φρένες ἐκκεκωφέαται; cf. Sappho's[8] ἀβάκην τὰν φρέν' ἔχω). In Theognis we read that 'In men of understanding the eyes and tongue and ears and mind (νόος) grow (φύεται, "are rooted") in the midst of their breasts'.[9] Simonides of Ceos, who in one place speaks of the wind 'preventing the spreading honeysweet voice from fitting the ear of mortals',[10] after praising a passage of Homer says 'few mortals, receiving it with their ears, stored it in their breasts'[11]

[1] *Hist. Anim.* 492 a, 19.

[2] E.g. Hesiod, *Works and Days*, 274. Cf. Homeric Hymn to Apollo, 237, 261.

[3] Fr. 149 (Rzach[3]).

[4] 31 f.

[5] 421 ff.

[6] 144 f.

[7] Fr. 81 (Bgk.).

[8] Fr. 72 (Bgk.).

[9] 1163 f.

[10] Fr. 41 (Bgk.).

[11] Fr. 85, 4 f.

(οὔασι δεξάμενοι/στέρνοις ἐγκατέθεντο). Thus in Plato's *Phaedrus*[1] Socrates can say that he 'has his chest full' of thoughts, which he has heard from others, and that he 'has been filled like a vessel (ἀγγεῖον) from some alien streams (ἀλλοτρίων ναμάτων) through the ears (διὰ τῆς ἀκοῆς)'. We saw that liquid drunk was supposed to be taken into the lungs (φρένες) and were able better to understand why words taken in were said[2] to be 'drunk down'. For Aeschylus 'speech comes through the chest[3] (ἱκνεῖται λόγος διὰ στηθέων)' and 'respect for a ruler penetrates through the ears and φρήν of the people'.[4] The belief that words were breathed forth from the φρένες also continues, as we might expect. Thus Terpander[5] says: 'Let my φρήν sing of' Apollo, and Aeschylus speaks of a 'well-tongued φρήν'[6] and of 'the φρήν raving with cries'[7] and of 'crying shrilly out of the φρήν',[8] while Pindar speaks of 'breathing forth (speech) from her immortal mouth'[9] and 'the tongue takes it from the deep φρήν'.[10]

If we turn to the private theories of the philosophers or 'scientists', we find that the first whose views on this subject are recorded, Alcmaeon of Croton, held that hearing was the result of the echoing of the air inside the ear[11] and said that 'goats breathe in through their ears'.[12] His discovery of the function of the brain is discussed below.[13] Empedocles, who located the mind in the blood around the heart, which is indeed where the lungs full of blood[14] are, taught that hearing is produced by the impact of the moving air against a piece of

[1] 235 C. Cf. *Rep.* III, 411 A.
[2] See Aristoph. *Ach.* 484 of the θυμός; Chrysippus in *Stoic. Vet. Fr.* (von Arnim), II, 257, etc.; also p. 43 and p. 64, n. 3 above.
[3] *Septem*, 563.
[4] *Choeph.* 55 ff. Cf. 450 ff.; *Septem*, 24 f. and *Ag.* 1052.
[5] Fr. 2 (Bgk.).   [6] *Suppl.* 775.
[7] *Septem*, 967.   [8] *Ibid.* 874. Cf. 864 f.; *Ag.* 546, 1491, etc.
[9] *Pyth.* IV, 11.
[10] *Nem.* IV, 8. Cf. Scol. Anon. 32 in *Anth. Lyr. Gr.* (Diehl).
[11] See Beare, *Greek Theories of Elementary Cognition*, pp. 93 f.
[12] A 7, Diels, *Fragm. d. Vors.*⁴=Aristot. 492 a, 13. Similarly Aelian, *de Nat. An.* I, 53: ἀναπνεῖ γὰρ καὶ διὰ τῶν ὤτων καὶ διὰ τῶν μυκτήρων.
[13] P. 115.   [14] See pp. 47, 54.

cartilage suspended in the ear, which rings and oscillates, when struck, like a gong.[1] Diogenes of Apollonia, who, as we have seen,[2] identified the conscious and intelligent element in man with air centred, apparently, in the chest, held that hearing resulted from the impact of sound upon the air within the ear, which, being moved, in turn moved the air within[3] (? the head). Aristotle, for whom the centre of consciousness was in the region of the heart, held the somewhat similar view that, when sound is produced, the air between the source and the organ of hearing is set in motion and the organ of hearing itself is of the nature of air, somehow perhaps connected with the air in the back of the head, but not with the brain.[4] 'The passage of the sense of hearing, since the organ of this sense is formed of air, terminates at the point where the native breath (σύμφυτον πνεῦμα) produces in some animals the throbbing of the heart and in some the respiratory process. Wherefore, also, it is that we understand what is said so as to utter again what has been heard; for as was the movement which entered through the sense organ, such back again (πάλιν), as it were from one and the same stamp, is the movement through the voice, so that a man utters what he has heard. And we hear less well when yawning or breathing out than when breathing in, because the starting point of the sense organ of hearing is at the part concerned with breath (ἐπὶ τῷ πνευματικῷ μορίῳ).'[5] 'Why do sponge-divers slit their ears and nostrils?' ask the *Problemata*. 'Is it in order that the breath may pass more freely? For it is by this way that the breath seems to pass out';[6] and again, 'Why do the deaf talk through their noses? Is it because they suffer lung trouble (ἢ ὅτι ὁ πνεύμων ἐστὶ τούτοις πεπονηκώς), since deafness is simply congestion (πλήρωσις) in the region of the lungs?'[7] It is impossible to do justice here to the supplementary details of each theory and the considerations which contributed to it. There were

[1] See Beare, *op. cit.* pp. 95 f.   [2] P. 32. See also pp. 76, 115, n. 7, 117.
[3] See Beare, *op. cit.* pp. 105 f.
[4] See *de Anim.* 420 a, 3 and *de Part. An.* 656 a, 27–b, 26.
[5] *de Anim. Gen.* 781 a, 23 ff.   [6] 960 b, 21 ff.
[7] 962 b, 35 ff.

some views[1] rather further removed from the traditional scheme traced above and others akin to it, which are more conveniently mentioned below.[2]

For Homer, though it may seem incredible that the lungs or breath should have anything to do with seeing, one also 'sees in one's φρένες' or 'lungs'.[3] Seeing 'delights the φρήν'[4] and is the work of θυμός or breath, ἴδε θυμῷ,[5] θηήσατο θυμῷ,[6] etc., like θυμῷ ἀκουάζοντα above. The mystery of vision has at a much later date produced strange theories. If the Homeric Greeks attempted to trace the passage through, the naso-lachrymal passage leading from the eye to the air of the nose and so to the throat and lungs might be supposed to be the channel by which the necessary connection was made, but evidence is wanting. Later, as we have seen,[7] Theognis speaks of the eyes and tongue and ears and mind as alike centred (lit. 'growing') in the chest. For Homer visual imagination was the work of θυμός (ὄσσοντο θυμῷ[8]) and Alcman appears to have spoken of 'memory seeing with the φρένες'[9] (μνήμη φρασίδορκος). In actual seeing, something—what is received through the eyes—is 'breathed' from the objects seen. What is received is 'breath'. This will explain the fragment from the Hesiodic Catalogue of Women:[10] 'Beauty (εἶδος—of form, *visible*) was breathed from [? her eyes]' ([βλεφάρων] δ' ἄπο εἶδος ἄητο); and a description of Alkmene in the 'Shield': 'From her head and her blue eyes was breathed (ἄητο) even as from golden Aphrodite'.[11] Similarly in the Homeric Hymn to Demeter 'the goddess changed her stature and form (εἶδος) and beauty was breathed around her (περί τ' ἀμφί τε κάλλος ἄητο) and lovely perfume was spread from her fragrant robes

---

[1] See Beare, *op. cit.* for Democritus (p. 99), Anaxagoras (p. 103) and Plato (p. 106).

[2] Pp. 76 f.

[3] *Il.* xxi, 61.

[4] *Il.* xix, 19, xx, 23.

[5] *Od.* viii, 450.

[6] *Od.* xv, 132, xxiv, 90, etc.

[7] P. 70.

[8] *Il.* xviii, 224. Cf. *Od.* x, 374, etc. and θυμόμαντις on p. 66.

[9] Fr. 145 (Bgk. after O. Müller).

[10] Fr. 245, 7 (Rz.); 7 (Evelyn-White), from Berlin Pap. 7497 and Oxyrh. Pap. 421. For the restoration see *Classical Quarterly*, vii, 217–18.

[11] Line 7.

and light shone afar from the immortal flesh of the goddess'.[1]
These passages suggest that what was 'breathed' in through
the eyes from objects was recognised in light (differentiated
by colour and form), thought of as gaseous or confused
perhaps with the air through which it passed as we saw that
sound was and as odour must have been. The same thought
will explain the Latin use of *aura*[2] of a ray or gleam,
radiance.

Sound was obviously breathed out in the voice and odour
must have been observed in the breath. According to Hesiod
Zeus wooed Europa 'breathing saffron from his mouth'.[3] As
odour is thus manifestly 'breathed' out in the air, so objects
giving off odour are said to 'breathe' it from them. Homer
describes seals as 'breathing from them the sharp smell of the
deep salt-sea'[4] (πικρὸν ἀποπνείουσαι ἁλὸς πολυβενθέος
ὀδμήν), and, in contrast, ambrosia as 'breathing most sweet'[5]
(ἡδὺ μάλα πνείουσαν). The percipient not less obviously
'breathes' in the odour through the nostrils and so to the lungs.
Thus it is with the three senses which operate through the
outer air and feed the central consciousness, the breath or
breath-soul (θυμός) in the lungs (φρένες).

This correlation of the earliest Greek evidence perhaps
enables us to realise that the Homeric and later Greek word
ἀΐω, 'I perceive', usually of hearing but also of seeing and
more generally of 'taking in' something, is really identical
with the Homeric ἀΐω, 'I breathe in',[6] as it appears to be, but

[1] 275 ff.
[2] See Virg. *Aen.* I, 590 f. and VI, 204. This goes beyond the conception
of αἰθήρ as flame, to which Conington refers. See also *Aen.* XII, 115,
Ennius, *Ann.* 588, Pind. *Ol.* VII, 70 f.
[3] Catalogue, Fr. 30 (Rzach³).   [4] *Od.* IV, 406.   [5] *Od.* IV, 446.
[6] This (or 'I gasp, struggle for breath', i.e. draw it inwards) and not,
as they are often translated, 'I breathe out', appears to be the meaning
of both ἀΐω and ἀΐσθω. The process is ἄσθμα (cf. *Il.* XV, 252 and 240 f.).
The ideas traced assist to the fuller understanding, for instance, of the
repeated cry of the Erinyes πνέω τοι μένος ἅπαντά τε κότον. οἰοῖ δᾶ,
φεῦ. τίς μ' ὑποδύεται πλευρὰς ὀδύνα; θυμὸν ἄϊε, μᾶτερ Νύξ (Aesch. *Eum.*
840 ff.), the last phrase of which is translated (e.g. by Verrall) 'Hark to
my indignation'. For Aeschylus, as we saw, θυμός is still 'breathed',
here 'breathed out', and the old sense of ἀΐω would suggest 'breathed

as it is currently¹ assumed not to be in the absence of these considerations. Similarly, we may now see that αἴσθομαι, 'I perceive' (with the resultant substantive αἴσθησις and the lengthened form αἰσθάνομαι, our 'aesthetics', etc.), is the middle of the Homeric ἀΐσθω, 'I gasp, breathe in', and we can also relate to these and explain the curious fact preserved for us by Alcaeus² and Hesychius³ that in Aeolic ἐπιπνεῖν, 'to breathe at', means 'to look at' (ἐπιβλέπειν), the eyes being in fact not only passive and recipient like the ears, but also active outwardly. Thus for the race at an early stage the primary relation of breath to consciousness appears to have been worked out to a logical conclusion in a harmonious system, surviving, though unrecognised, in these terms.

Our incredulity, if not our wonder, may be diminished when we realise that the ancient Hindoos had similar beliefs. According to the Upanishads, speech, sight, hearing, and mind were known as breaths (*prāṇa*). 'Verily, they do not call them "Speeches" nor "Eyes" nor "Minds". They call them "Breaths", for the vital breath is all these';⁴ and again: 'The vital breaths verily go into a unity, for [otherwise] no one would be able at once to cause to know a name with speech, a form with the eye, a sound with the ear, a thought with the mind. As a unity, verily, the vital breaths, every single one, cause to know all things here. All the vital breaths speak along with speech when it speaks, all the vital breaths see along with the eye when it sees',⁵ and so on. That within receives all that enters by the separate 'breaths'. It is 'the all-obtaining in the breathing spirit'. 'Speech pours all names in it, with speech it obtains all names; breath pours all odours in it;

in' by Night. The thought that what issues as speech has bodily form, is breath, vapour (see pp. 44ff., 67, 69 ff.) will help to explain δνοφεράν τιν' ἀχλὺν κατὰ δώματος/αὐδᾶται πολύστονος φάτις (*Eumen.* 380 f.), νέφος οἰμωγῆς ὡς τάχ' ἀνάψει/μείζονι θυμῷ (Eurip. *Med.* 107 f.), στεναγμῶν γάρ με περιβάλλει νέφος (*Herc. Fur.* 1140).

¹ See e.g. Boisacq, and the revised Liddell and Scott, s.v.
² Fr. 66 (Bgk.). ³ S.v. ἐπιπνεύων.
⁴ *Chāndogya Upanishad*, 5, 1, translated by R. E. Hume, *The Thirteen Principal Upanishads*, pp. 226 f.
⁵ *Kaushitaki Upanishad*, 3, 2, trans. Hume, *op. cit.* p. 322.

with breath it obtains all odours; the eye pours all forms in it; with the eye it obtains all forms',[1] and so on. There were many variations and complications of the doctrine.[2]

Let us glance at later private theories of vision among the Greeks, which, without this background, have seemed to be quite original. Alcmaeon of Croton, an associate of Pythagoras at the end of the sixth century, is the first whose views are recorded and, as we shall see,[3] the most original; he thought, apparently, that the passages from the eyes, by which perceptions are received, were full of 'natural breath'.[4] Diogenes of Apollonia, who apparently identified the governing consciousness with air in the chest and treated the air in the head as intermediate, taught that sight was effected by a fusion, through the image in the pupil, with the air inside the head.[5] Other Pythagorean teaching is discussed below.[6] An account[7] of uncertain origin tells us that the soul consists of vapour (ἀτμός) and λόγοι are 'winds of the soul' (cf. Il. IX, 4 ff., XXI, 385 f., etc. on pp. 46, 49, 54), also that 'sight is an excessively hot vapour', and a similar explanation is implied for the other senses (cf. the Stoics). Elsewhere[8] Pythagoreans are said to have taught that a ray goes forth from the eye and returns again. In the pre-philosophic evidence quoted the eyes not only receive light or what is 'breathed' from objects but are themselves stressed as sources of the same, perhaps by reason of their brightness. In Homer[9] there are

[1] *Kaush. Up.* 3, 4, trans. Hume, *op. cit.* p. 324.
[2] See e.g. A. H. Ewing, *The Hindu Conception of the Functions of Breath, A Study in early Hindu Psycho-Physics.* The doctrine helps us to understand the importance which the Yogi attaches to *Pranayama*, the regulation of the breath, control of the acts of inspiration and expiration.
[3] P. 115.
[4] See the account of Chalcid. *in Tim.* p. 279 (= A 10, Diels, *Fragm. d. Vors.*[4]).
[5] See A 19 and B 5 (Diels).   [6] Pp. 112, 118.
[7] From Alexander Polyhistor preserved by Diogenes Laertius, VIII, 28 f. = Diels, *op. cit.* I, XLIII f. (Nachträge).
[8] See Stob. *Ecl.* I, 43 f.; Plut. *de Plac. Epit.* IV, 14; Diels, *Doxog. Gr.*[2] 404 f. and *Fragm. d. Vors.*[4] Archytas, A 25.
[9] E.g. *Il.* XII, 466, XIII, 474. Alcmaeon taught that there was fire in the eye and Heraclitus implies a similar belief (B 26). We can now better

survivals of the belief that fire flamed in the eyes more particularly in anger. There is action outwardly from them; to
'look at' was in early Aeolic 'to breathe at'. To return to the
philosophers, Empedocles taught that from objects there come
emanations or effluences (ἀπορροαί) which enter the eye by
tiny passages, and that from the fire in the eye there goes forth
a ray towards the object.[1] To Timaeus, who also apparently
was connected with the Pythagoreans, Plato[2] assigns a belief
that from the object 'flows flame' and that 'the fire in the eyes
flows forth'. According to the *Placita*, Plato taught that sight
was the result of a 'fusion of rays (συναύγεια), the light of the
eyes flowing out to some distance into the kindred air and the
light from the objects meeting it',[3] with which we may compare
another account: 'raylike breath (πνεῦμα...αὐγοειδές) of the
eyes coming forth mingles with the light around objects and
blends with it'.[4] Finally, if we turn to the Stoics we find that
not only is the soul fiery 'breath' (πνεῦμα) centred in or
around the heart or, according to another view, in the head,
but also the senses are 'breaths' extending thence, that of

understand (1) the cosmic λόγος (*Logos*, B 2 etc.) so important later,
i.e. λόγος = speech, thought conceived materially as breath, spirit, πνεῦμα
(see pp. 13 f., 67 ff. and λόγοι = 'winds of the soul' above), and (2) his
reported teaching (A 16, Diels) that we become intelligent by drawing in
the divine λόγος through *in-breathing* and that in sleep when the passages
of the senses are closed the mind loses contact with the λόγος except that
one contact through the breath is preserved as a kind of root, but 'on
awakening, it (the mind) leans out again through the passages of the
senses as if through windows, and making contact with that which surrounds
us, it assumes the power of the λόγος'. Pliny (*N.H.* xi, 39, 226) records the
belief that intelligence depends on the density of the skin, the degree to
which it admits the *immeans spiritus*. There is an interesting parallel in the
Far East: 'The knowledge of all creatures depends upon their breathing,
but if their breath be not abundant, it is not the fault of Heaven which
tries to penetrate them with it day and night without ceasing, but men,
notwithstanding, shut their pores against it' (*The Writings of Kwangtse*,
Bk. xxvi, Pt. iii, Sect. iv, § 9, translated by J. Legge, *The Texts of Taoism*,
Sacred Books of the East, Vol. xl, p. 139). Heraclitus also complains that
men refuse to receive the λόγος though it is ever present (see B 1, 72, 73,
Diels).

[1] A 86, 91, 92, B 84 (Diels). Cf. Leucippus A 29; Democritus A 135, 50.
[2] *Timaeus*, 45 b ff. and 67 c ff.   [3] See Diels, *Doxog. Gr.* p. 404.
[4] See Plut. *Qu. Conv.* i, 8, 4 = 626.

sight to the eyes, that of hearing to the ears, etc.[1] Thus, despite
the widest divergency of teaching about other points affecting
the details of the views cited above, the original thought tends
to persist and recur. It perhaps contributes to such turns of
thought as Plato's:[2] Lest reared among images of evil the
young should receive evil into their souls 'we must seek out
those artists who by natural gifts are able to trace out the
nature of the beautiful and graceful, so that our young men,
dwelling as it were in a healthy spot, may receive good from
every quarter from which any emanation from noble works
may come to their eyes or ears, like a breeze bringing health
from salubrious regions' (αὖρα φέρουσα ἀπὸ χρηστῶν τόπων
ὑγίειαν). The original thought (e.g. Aeolic ἐπιπνεῖν = ἐπιβλέπειν) may be recognised in such beliefs as that expressed by
Calasiris[3] about the 'evil eye': 'This air which surrounds us
penetrates through eyes and nostrils and mouth[4] and the
other passages into the depths of the body and takes with it its
qualities from outside, and it sows in those who receive it πάθος
of the quality with which it flows in. Accordingly when anyone looks with envy at what is noble, he fills the surrounding
atmosphere with a quality of hate (δυσμενοῦς) and blows the

[1] See St. Vet. Fr. II, pp. 217 ff., 226–8.
[2] Rep. 401 C. Cf. Phaedrus, 255 C, etc. The reference of consciousness to
breath will also explain why the Athenians were thought to be intelligent
as a result of the clear air of Athens, and the Boeotians to be dull as
a result of the thick atmosphere in Boeotia (Eurip. Medea, 828 ff.; Cic.
de Fato, 4, 7; Horace, Epist. II, 1, 244; Juv. x, 50). Cf. Diog. on pp. 32 f.,
Plat. Tim. 92 B, Hor. Od. II, 16, 38. Georgic, I, 417–22 seems to be explained
by a relation of the animus to the atmosphere. Cf. p. 56, n. 2, p. 170, n. 5.
Conversely the atmosphere of Thomson's City of Dreadful Night (xv) is
'dark and dense' because 'wherever man are gathered, all the air/Is
charged with human feeling, human thought;/ Each shout and cry and
laugh, each curse and prayer/Are into its vibrations surely wrought;/
Unspoken passion, wordless meditation/Are breathed into it with our
respiration'.
[3] Heliodorus, III, 7. Cf. pp. 15 f. and Aristot. de Insomn. 459 b, etc.
[4] The MSS. have δι' ὀφθαλμῶν τε καὶ ῥινῶν καὶ ἄσθματος καὶ τῶν
ἄλλων πόρων εἰς τὰ βάθη διϊκνούμενος. I suggest that καὶ ἄσθματος is a
corruption of καὶ στόματος. The nostrils would be included in ἄσθματος
and the latter is not a πόρος. Plut. Quaest. Conv. v, 7 (Mor. 680 c ff.) would
not, I think, suggest ἄσθματος.

breath from himself (τὸ παρ' αὐτοῦ πνεῦμα...διερρίπισε) full
of bitterness into him that is near'. So perhaps the Gorgons
ἃς θνητὸς οὐδεὶς εἰσιδὼν ἕξει πνοάς (Aesch. *P.V.* 800). *Invidere* [1]
may thus be related to *animus per oculos* [2] (p. 171), and Persius'
urentes oculos (II, 34).

There remains the sense of touch. [3] How did the θυμός in
the chest receive perceptions from the skin? It is the kind of
question to which we should not expect an explicit answer or
indeed an allusion except in a scientific treatise addressed to
the problems of cognition. This is not to say that the question
would not be raised or answered in the earlier period.
Consistency would require that the transmission should be
by way of breath, θυμός. Was there θυμός elsewhere than in
the chest and the passages to eyes, ears, nose, and mouth? Yes.
Where θυμός is concerned in thought or emotion, it is the chest
or the heart or lungs that are usually referred to. These are
the organs of the mind, the central consciousness. In Priam's
company, Achilles weeps aloud for his father and for Patroklos,
but when he had had his fill of weeping '*and the desire departed
from his* πραπίδες *and from his limbs* (γυίων), he sprang from his
chair...'. [4] The line italicised has for its 'un-Homeric thought'
been rejected by some editors following Aristarchus; yet violent
grief affects the limbs as it were directly and not through the
conscious will, producing contractions and movements, as
Homer illustrates and Eustathius here realises. In a line beyond
dispute Athene '*put courage in the* φρένες *of Nausikaa and took fear*
(δέος) *from her limbs* (γυίων)'. [5] At death Homer speaks of the

---

[1] E.g. Catullus, v, 12; Cic. *Tusc.* III, 9, 20.

[2] So too we can explain the belief (Schol. Theocr. XIV, 22; Virg.
Ecl. IX, 53 f. Cf. Plat. *Rep.* 336) that if a wolf looks at one first one is
smitten with silence. A wolf is characteristically silent: *tacitorum more
luporum/ore premunt voces* (Ov. *Met.* XIV, 778 f.). In the Polish epic *Pan
Tadeusz* (Mickiewicz) 'the *Wojski*, noticing that all were thus silent,
called the meal "a supper not of Poles but of wolves"' (v, 424). Cf. Vigny,
La Mort du Loup.

[3] Taste might be explained in conjunction with Touch (through tongue
or palate) or possibly Smell. See pp. 61 ff.

[4] *Il.* XXIV, 514 f. Cf. XIII, 77 ff. on p. 22.

[5] *Od.* VI, 140.

θυμός as leaving—not the chest but—the 'limbs, members'[1] (μέλεα), which suggests strongly that θυμός was not confined to the chest, but was to be found in the body elsewhere. Thus, death might be caused by a 'disease which by a hateful wasting took the θυμός from my limbs'[2] (μελέων ἐξείλετο θυμόν), or again: 'Quickly out of her limbs (ἐκ μελέων) fled the θυμός'.[3] To the earlier, as to later, Greeks it might well seem that the arteries, which after death are found empty and dilated, contained 'breath' and perhaps also that the pores were πόροι, 'passages' inwards.[4] θυμός was not merely breath; it was vapour of blood; and ἦτορ, which means something very close to θυμός, is spoken of by Homer as in the heart as well as in the lungs, and so might naturally be thought to be in the aorta, etc., also. This lies behind later views[5] that the breath passes into the heart and thence over the body through the arteries. Before the formal division[6] of the φλέβες, the vessels throughout the body, into ἀρτηρίαι, 'air-tubes', and φλέβες, then restricted to the 'veins', there is evidence that such vessels were supposed to contain air. Thus Diogenes of Apollonia held that the stuff of consciousness and medium of sense perception was ἀήρ in the φλέβες elsewhere as well as in the chest (τοῦ ἀέρος σὺν τῷ αἵματι τὸ ὅλον σῶμα κατα-

[1] It is also said to 'leave the bones' (*Il.* XII, 386, XVI, 743, etc.), which does not mean 'come out of the bones' but 'leave the bones behind'. The bones were apparently what mattered after death. They alone are mentioned elsewhere though the whole body is present (see *Il.* IV, 174, XXIII, 222, 224; *Od.* I, 161). The reasons for this will appear in Part II.

[2] *Od.* XI, 201. Cf. *Il.* XIII, 672, XVI, 607, etc.   [3] *Il.* XXIII, 880.

[4] See e.g. the κλεψύδρα analogy of Empedocles (B 100, Diels), *de Spiritu* 483, b 15 ff., and the evidence of Pliny and Kwangtse on p. 76, n. 9.

[5] See e.g. Arist. *Hist. An.* 496 a 30 ff., Cic. *De Nat. Deor.* II, 55, 138.

[6] Anaxagoras distinguished between ἀρτηρίαι and φλέβες (B 10; cf. A 46, Diels), but one cannot be sure that ἀρτηρίαι did not mean just the bronchial tubes. The distinction appears in the Hippocratic corpus and Erasistratus and Praxagoras taught that the arteries contained πνεῦμα. The first explicit writer on these subjects, Alcmaeon, says that 'sleep occurs by the withdrawal of the blood into the blood-flowing (τὰς αἱμόρρους) φλέβες, awakening is its diffusion (διάχυσις), and its absolute withdrawal is death' (A 18, Diels=Aetius, v, 24, 1). 'The blood-flowing φλέβες' appears to be his own phrase. There must be point in the epithet. It implies that there were other φλέβες not 'blood-flowing'.

λαμβάνοντος διὰ τῶν φλεβῶν),[1] teaching for instance that
'if in general the blood, diffusing, fills the φλέβες and drives
the ἀήρ they contain into the chest and the γαστήρ beneath,
sleep occurs and the thorax is warmer; but if all that is of the
nature of ἀήρ departs from the φλέβες, death occurs'.[2]
Persistence of the idea that sensation, the sense of touch, was
the business of the blood vessels, may be seen in Pliny's
statement that fat is without feeling: *adeps cunctis sine sensu
quia nec arterias habet nec venas. plerisque animalium et pinguitudo
sine sensu, quam ob causam sues spirantes a muribus tradunt arrosas.*[3]
Thus perhaps we can better understand παχύς, applied to the
dull of perception, *pinguis*,[4] Hor. *Sat.* II, 6, 14f., Persius, III, 32 f.

Of the meaning of ἦτορ it is difficult to speak for want of
decisive evidence. It appears to mean something the same as
or in very close relation to θυμός. It may originally have
expressed the agent responsible for breathing or for the beating
of the heart and pulse. It is stirred in emotion. It is in the
φρένες[5] and in the heart[6] (κραδίη). It laughs.[7] It is concerned in speech.[8] It occurred to me that it might mean the
vessel[9] or system of vessels containing θυμός—the bronchial
tubes, aorta, etc., since often μεγαλήτωρ appears as an epithet
of θυμός and there recurs the phrase 'his knees and dear ἦτορ
were loosed'. But this evidence is not decisive. It does not
appear to have been observed that in the 'Shield of Herakles'[10]
ἦτορ is described as κελαινόν, 'swart, dark, black'. This might
conceivably fit dark vapour (cf. κελαινὴ νύξ) or one might
think of blood;[11] but ἦτορ is nowhere spoken of in terms dis-

[1] Simplic. *phys.* 153, 13=Diog. B 6, Diels.
[2] A 29, Diels. Cf. περὶ ἱερῆς νόσου, 7. [3] *N.H.* XI, 37, 213, cf. 220.
[4] Cf. *corpore tenuato pectoreque undique obeso ac mente exsensa* (Laevius,
100 B.C.), Cic. *de Am.* V, 19, Ov. *Met.* XI, 148f., Isaiah vi, 10. It survives:
'fat-head'. [5] *Il.* XVI, 242.
[6] *Il.* XX, 169. [7] *Il.* XXI, 389. [8] *Il.* II, 490 ff.
[9] Its form has been compared to Old High German *ādara*, Old English
ædre, 'vein' (see revised Liddell and Scott, s.v.). [10] 429.
[11] Justesen, *Les principes psychologiques d'Homère*, pp. 48ff., suggested blood
on the basis of *Il.* XVII, 111 f. (for which see p. 46 n. 6) and of *Il.* XV, 252,
ἐπεὶ φίλον ἄϊον ἦτορ, which he refers to *Il.* XIV, 437, κελαινεφὲς αἷμ'
ἀπέμεσσεν, but it is more reasonably to be referred to the actual gasping
and recovery of θυμός spoken of in the context, XV, 240 f. Cf. XIV, 436.

tinctively appropriate to a fluid substance as one would expect if it meant just 'blood', and such an expression as ἐμοί γε κατεκλάσθη φίλον ἦτορ, 'my ἦτορ was broken off',[1] seems to rule out that interpretation. The only other Homeric uses of κατακλάω refer to the physical snapping of a stalk or a spear-shaft. The chief objection to the view that ἦτορ meant the containing vessel is that he who slays a man is sometimes said to 'take away the ἦτορ', as elsewhere he is said to 'take away the θυμός' of his victim. To explain the expression as hyperbole is possible (cf. φρένας ἐξέλετο, *Il.* VI, 234, etc.) but not very satisfactory. In any case numerous passages show that the ἦτορ is concerned in consciousness in much the same way as the θυμός is said to be. Finally, a man is said to be hurt, struck or divided, βεβλαμμένον, vv.ll. βεβολημένον, δεδαϊγμένον, in the ἦτορ when wounded where the φρένες enclose the heart,[2] and another is said to be 'divided (δεδαιγμένον) in the ἦτορ' when wounded in the γαστήρ.[3] It is scarcely possible to avoid the conclusion that the stuff of consciousness was there also, which fits our argument that θυμός was not confined to the chest. Aeschylus[4] says: 'My ἦτορ cries out within my members' (βοᾷ, βοᾷ μοι μελέων ἔντοσθεν ἦτορ).

More important in subsequent Greek thought is νόος, e.g. εἰπέ μοι εἰρομένῃ· τί νύ τοι νόος ἔνδοθι κεύθει; (*Od.* XXIV, 474). It is located in the chest. Two passages[5] suggest an identification with the heart. But Poseidon tells Apollo that he has ἄνοον κραδίην;[6] moreover, that νόος can express a purpose, an act or the result of an act of consciousness (e.g. οὐ γὰρ δὴ τοῦτον μὲν ἐβούλευσας νόον αὐτή[7]), seems to prove that in origin it did not express a permanent organ of the body. It is, I suggest, a formation (? from νέομαι 'I go', νέω 'I move in liquid, swim') like πνόος a 'blowing' or a 'wind' from πνέω, ῥόος a 'flowing' or a 'river' from ῥέω. It expresses either the particular movement, purpose, or, relatively permanent,

---

[1] *Od.* IV, 481, etc.
[2] *Il.* XVI, 481, 660.
[3] *Il.* XVII, 519, 535.
[4] *Persae*, 991.
[5] *Il.* III, 60–4, IX, 553 f. with 646.
[6] *Il.* XXI, 441.
[7] *Od.* V, 23, etc.

that which moves, the purposing consciousness. It darts
(ἀίξῃ[1]), rushes (ὄρνυται[2]), is restrained (ἴσχανε[3]), turned
(τρέπεται,[4] cf. ἐπιγνάμπτει[5]). It is not identical in meaning
with θυμός but is rather something in, a defining of, this[6] as
e.g. a current in a sense consists of but defines, controls air
or water. It makes the difference between uncontrolled and
intelligent, purposive, consciousness (e.g. μὴ χαλέπαινε παρὲκ
νόον[7]) as in a different way the defining frame of the φρένες
did.[8] Thus, like φρένες, it gets something of the value of
'intelligence' or 'intellect' but, unlike φρένες, it is not obviously
material, tangible, pierced by weapons, etc. It is not mere
intellect; it is dynamic, as we have seen, and emotional:
θεουδής, ἀπηνής, ἀτάρβητος as the case may be: νόος δέ οἱ
ἄλλα μενοινᾷ,[9] χαῖρε νόῳ,[10] etc. We can thus better understand its function in Greek philosophy, e.g. for Anaxagoras
as the dynamic ordering factor in the universe. In man,
as the current of consciousness, of θυμός, it perceives through
the senses, e.g. τὸν δὲ μάλ᾽ αἶψ᾽ ἐνόησε[11] whence later, e.g.
νοῦς ὁρῇ καὶ νοῦς ἀκούει· τἄλλα κωφὰ καὶ τυφλά.[12]

[1] *Il.* xv, 80. [2] *Od.* i, 347. [3] *Od.* xix, 42.
[4] *Od.* iii, 147. [5] *Il.* ix, 514.
[6] See *Od.* x, 492 ff. on p. 59, *Od.* i, 322, xiv, 490, xviii, 228, etc.
[7] *Il.* xx, 133; cf. x, 391, xxiv, 358, Hymn to Aphr. 254, etc.
[8] See pp. 28 f. [9] *Od.* ii, 92, etc. [10] *Od.* viii, 78.
[11] *Il.* xvii, 682, etc. [12] Epicharmus, Fr. 249 (Kaibel).

CHAPTER V

The Liver and the Belly

χόλος, usually translated 'wrath', appears to be another form of the un-Homeric χολή, 'bile'. With angry emotion there is often obvious biliary disturbance, and Homer's 'On χόλος your mother reared you, pitiless one!'[1] shows that χόλος was conceived as substantial. For Homer the heart and lungs (φρένες) were the emotional centre of the body and so χόλος was believed to enter those organs. It is spoken of as in the θυμός, in the heart, in the φρένες or in the chest. Bile was indeed believed to enter the organs above the diaphragm as liquid. Thus it is that in the *Agamemnon* Aeschylus has ἐπὶ δὲ καρδίαν ἔδραμε κροκοβαφὴς σταγών, 'to my heart has run a saffron-dyed drop',[2] and in the *Choephori* explicitly κἀμοὶ προσέστη καρδίας (καρδίᾳ Scal.) κλυδώνιον/χολῆς, ἐπαίσθην δ' ὡς διανταίῳ βέλει.[3] Anaxagoras taught that χολή 'was the cause of acute disorders (νοσημάτων), because overflowing it spurted to the lung and the veins and the ribs'.[4] With this also should be related the belief manifest in Aeschylus and the other tragedians that painful emotion strikes the liver. Thus in the *Agamemnon* πολλὰ γοῦν θιγγάνει πρὸς ἧπαρ,[5] δῆγμα δὲ λύπης οὐδὲν ἐφ' ἧπαρ προσικνεῖται,[6] and in the *Eumenides*—the task of the Furies—ἄλγησον ἧπαρ ἐνδίκοις ὀνείδεσιν.[7] The κροκοβαφὴς σταγών is caused by an awful feeling, stirred by the words of Kassandra, that tragedy is on its way, and the κλυδώνιον χολῆς was raised in Elektra by the emotional shock of seeing a lock of hair of the long-missing Orestes. The deep-seated organ thus believed to secrete with violent emotion

[1] *Il.* XVI, 203.　　　　　　　　　　[2] 1121 f.
[3] 183 f. Cf. Hippocr. περὶ καρδίης 11 (IX, 88 and 90 Littré).
[4] A 105, Diels. Cf. Hippocr. περὶ νούσων, I, 30 (VI, 200 Littré) and *Epist. Pseudhipp.* 17, 15; 23, 7.　　[5] 432.　　　[6] 791 f.
[7] 135. Cf. Soph. *Aj.* 938: χωρεῖ πρὸς ἧπαρ, οἶδα, γενναία δύη; Eur. *Hipp.* 1070: αἰαῖ· πρὸς ἧπαρ δακρύων τ' ἐγγὺς τόδε, etc.

must almost inevitably be believed to be moved by the emotion. It would seem that the liver thus came to be regarded as the inmost spring[1] of the deeper emotions, stirred only by powerful stimuli. It is central, enclosed immediately beneath the dome formed by the diaphragm and by the heart and lungs above that. Its appearance strongly suggests blood. In fact, not only does it secrete bile, but it is a huge blood-gland.[2] From it, moreover, the blood passes on up to the heart (and lungs) by way of the 'largest vein' (φλέψ μεγίστη), the *vena cava*. Thus before Homer's day it might well be believed to send up to heart and lungs not only χόλος but also blood and so θυμός. In Homer the only evidence for a more than physical significance (apart from the implications of his uses of χόλος) appears to be that it is Achilles' liver, which Hecuba in her feeling for Hector slain would like to devour,[3] and it is the liver of guilty Tityos that the vultures do devour in the *Nekuia*.[4] This last has been interpreted by ancients and moderns as punishment of the organ of desire, but, as we have seen, for Homer desire is the work of the θυμός in the φρένες. Moreover, in the parallel punishment of Prometheus, the sin was not such desire but the deceiving of Zeus on behalf of men. Instead of trying to make the punishment exactly fit the crime it may perhaps be explained for Tityos in the light of the above that the vultures eating into the liver were a magnification of the concrete image under which were originally conceived[5] the painful thoughts (calling up bile, assailing and using up the liver)

[1] It is commonly the organ aimed at in suicide (Eurip. *Orestes*, 1063; *Phoen.* 1421; *Med.* 40, 379; *Hel.* 982 f., etc.). It is easily accessible under the ribs.
[2] It receives from the adjacent stomach and alimentary canal products of digestion for chemical treatment before their distribution in blood. Empedocles called it πολυαίματον (B 150) and believed that it converted the food into blood (B 61, Diels). Cf. Cicero, *Nat. Deor.* II, 55, 137 for the view that the *sucus* from food was converted by the liver partly into bile and *umores* of the kidneys, the rest into blood flowing by the *vena cava* to the heart. Burton calls the liver 'the shop of blood' (*Anat. Melan.* I, 1, 2, 4).
[3] *Il.* XXIV, 212.   [4] *Od.* XI, 578 ff.
[5] Cf. the backgrounds of Ixion's wheel (p. 452), and of the *Cestus* of Aphrodite and of the Helmet of Hades (pp. 424 f.).

which his defeat in love brought; in Prometheus, it is an eagle[1] which exacts these pains. In Homer's picture of Tityos, he lay flat upon the plain 'and did not ward them off with his hands', while in Hesiod's picture of Prometheus, the latter also cannot ward it off; his liver recovers during the night (? sleep, rest from grief), and as for the eagle that gnaws during the day, Herakles killed it—the language is noteworthy—'he warded off the evil νοῦσος from the son of Iapetus and freed him from his bitter thoughts'[2] (ἐλύσατο δυσφροσυνάων). This explanation is not an alien rationalisation but is in harmony with the Homeric beliefs, e.g. that pain and disease were arrows shot by a god,[3] in harmony with the concrete imagery noted below.[4] The idea that emotional thoughts, 'cares', were living creatures troubling the organs in one's chest has not, I think, been adequately recognised. It seems to explain, e.g. Homer's

πυκιναὶ δέ μοι ἀμφ' ἀδινὸν κῆρ
ὀξεῖαι μελεδῶναι ὀδυρομένην ἐρέθουσιν.[5]

They are winged as if birds:

φροντίδες ἀνθρώπων ἔλαχον πτερὰ ποικίλ' ἔχουσαι
μυρόμεναι ψυχῆς εἵνεκα καὶ βιότου,[6]

from which aspect, as we have suggested above,[7] may have developed Plato's image of the mind as a cage full of birds. As the bird is said to tear or devour the liver of Tityos and Prometheus, Pindar seems to have spoken of κῆρες ὀλβο-θρέμμονες μεριμνάτων ἀλεγεινῶν as 'tearing' (σπαράττειν) a man.[8] According to Theocritus, Herakles was distraught,

[1] A type of winged creature appropriate through its relation to Zeus.
[2] *Theog.* 523 ff.
[3] See e.g. *Il.* I, 10, 47 ff. Cf. Pind. *Pyth.* III, 9 f. etc.
[4] In Part III (Fate).   [5] *Od.* XIX, 516 f.
[6] Theognis, 729 (Bgk.). They are little winged creatures as the κῆρες were often represented on vase-paintings, κῆρες within (see pp. 404 f.) as it were. Cf. οἶστρος. For the thought of winged creatures within we may compare the old German student-song: *Mein Herz das ist ein Bienenhaus* ('My heart is a hive of bees'). Cf. also our 'maggot'='fancy', 'A maggot in the brain', and the playful 'a bee in your bonnet', etc.
[7] P. 67.
[8] Fr. 277 (Schr.). Cf. Hom. Hymn to Hermes, 44 f., Hor. *Od.* II, 16, 11 f., etc.

seeking in vain for his love Hylas, χαλεπὸς γὰρ ἔσω θεὸς ἧπαρ
ἄμυσσεν.[1] Moschus thus describes Eros:

καὶ πτερόεις ὡς ὄρνις ἐφίπταται ἄλλον ἐπ’ ἄλλῳ,
ἀνέρας ἠδὲ γυναῖκας, ἐπὶ σπλάγχνοις δὲ κάθηται.[2]

Hecuba may well have singled out the liver to cling to and
devour as the source of Achilles’ χόλος and perhaps also as the
source of his θυμός. For Homer χόλος ‘waxes as smoke in the
breasts of men’,[3] and later there is some curious evidence of
a reverse movement. Breathing, so vitally necessary, must
have been conceived as replenishing θυμός;[4] and if we look we
find that later, at any rate, breath was believed to reach and
be absorbed by the liver, perhaps by way of the aorta, in
accordance with what was suggested above for the distribution
of θυμός. In a passage of Aeschylus, preserved in translation
by Cicero, we read that the eagle returned ‘when the liver
has been restored by breathing’ (inflatu renovatum est[5]); and, in
Bion’s dirge for Adonis, Kypris asks for a kiss lasting ‘until from
your soul your breath flow into my mouth and into my liver’.[6]
For Plato’s Timaeus it is by a ‘breath’, ἐπίπνοια, that the liver
receives images from the διάνοια,[7] and the ‘movement produced (by the stroke that is sound), beginning from the head
and ending in the region of the liver, is hearing’.[8] This belief
about the liver does not appear to have been satisfactorily
explained.[9] It may well be a relic of the beliefs traced above:

---

[1] XIII, 71.   [2] II, 16 f.   [3] See p. 52.
[4] Compare vesci vitalibus auris Lucr. v, 857, also Aen. I, 546 f.
[5] Fr. 193 (Nauck).   [6] 45 ff.   [7] 71 C.   [8] 67 B.
[9] Archer-Hind says: ‘The liver appears to be selected because that
region is the seat of the nutritive faculty of the soul, 70 D, and since the
sensation of sound does not appeal to the intellectual organ it is transmitted to that faculty which is specially concerned with sensation’. There
is not, I think, any evidence that sensation, or the sensation of sound in
particular, was not supposed to appeal to the intellectual organ or to
θυμός but was supposed to appeal to τὸ ἐπιθυμητικόν. A. E. Taylor
says: ‘It (sc. the liver) is supposed to be specially the seat of τὸ ἐπιθυμητικόν and presumably the continuance of the reaction in hearing to that
region is meant to account for the shock unfamiliar noises or those which
indicate the presence of something hostile to the organism and some
others (e.g. the squeak of a pencil on a slate) give to the whole bodily
system’. The present question apart, the liver is not, I think, ‘specially

that sound was breathed in through the ears to the θυμός in the chest,[1] and that breath reached the liver; and this would be helped by the consideration, e.g. in the passages from Aeschylus discussed on p. 84, that painful news reaches the liver.

For the Platonic doctrine that θυμός, τὸ θυμοειδές, is in the region above the diaphragm and ἐπιθυμία, τὸ ἐπιθυμητικόν, below in the region of the γαστήρ, we may note that Homer speaks occasionally of the γαστήρ as if it were an independent being in man 'commanding'[2] him (in hunger) as θυμός is said to 'command'. This does not appear to affect the identification of consciousness with the θυμός. The θυμός is said to 'have need of food and drink'[3] and to be filled by them[4] and in the Homeric Hymn to Demeter we read of 'the φρήν sated by food'.[5] Already in Democritus[6] appeared the belief that not only desire for food and drink but also sexual appetite is the concern of the γαστήρ. To this the association of the liver with the yearning pain of love may have contributed (cf. Theocritus above). This association appears in the Latin poets[7] and was perhaps helped by change of colour: *nimius luto corpora tingit amor*.[8] It may have been derived from the Greeks, but the association of bile with anger appears to be

the seat of τὸ ἐπιθυμητικόν'. This was already (see 70 D ff.) chained there in the space between the diaphragm and the navel, which contained the stomach naturally associated with such appetite for nourishment. The liver was then (71 f.) introduced into that region by God to be an instrument or intermediary of the highest part of the soul whereby the latter could show visions to and terrify or appease τὸ ἐπιθυμητικόν. The liver is the means whereby τὸ ἐπιθυμητικόν receives intimations from the higher part of the soul or from the outer world.

[1] Pp. 69 ff.

[2] *Od.* VI, 133, XVIII, 53 f. Cf. XVII, 473 f.   [3] *Od.* I, 460.

[4] *Od.* XVII, 603, XIX, 198.   [5] 174 f.

[6] See B 235 (Diels). If Epicurus followed him in this it helps to explain why for him the pleasure of γαστήρ ('belly', not 'stomach') was 'the beginning and root of all good' (Athen. XII, 546 f.). For Plato here and Democritus there may have survived something of the belief traced below (pp. 484–90, esp. p. 489, n. 1) that with the γαστήρ was associated the procreative life-soul.

[7] See e.g. Horace, *Odes*, I, 25, 15; *Epist.* I, 18, 72.

[8] Tibull. I, 8, 52. Cf. *tinctus viola pallor amantium* (Hor. *Odes* III, 10, 14, the *viola* apparently being yellow; see Virg. *Ecl.* II, 47) and Sappho Fr. 2, 14.

native to the Romans. Biliary disturbances perhaps explain
the use of *stomachus*, *stomachor*, etc., in connection with anger.
In the Babylonian culture, to which Etruscan divination by
the liver (followed by the Romans) seems to have affinities,
the liver had great importance as organ of the mind (see
p. 60, n. 2). In Rome also it appears to have been the seat of
consciousness not limited to love and anger. Thus Pacuvius
scorned *haruspices*: *plusque ex alieno iecore sapiunt quam ex suo*.[1]
The meaning of *animus* and other phases of body and mind
are discussed below.[2]

[1] Fr. 83 Ribb. (The original sense of *sapiunt*—pp. 61 ff.—might add
point since the liver is a huge blood gland, p. 85.) Cf. Persius I, 24 f.,
v, 129 f. and pp. 505 f. below.
[2] See esp. pp. 168 ff. and 420 ff.

PART II

THE IMMORTAL SOUL AND THE BODY

CHAPTER I

The ψυχή

The ψυχή is currently explained[1] as the 'breath-soul'. It is
thought to be the breath-soul because ψύχω means 'I blow'.
The fact that in one passage the ψυχή is governed by ἀπό...
ἐκάπυσσε and that when disembodied it is described as dis-
appearing beneath the earth 'like smoke', ἠΰτε καπνός,[2] is
not conclusive; because the mouth[3] is the natural passage to
and from the interior of the body and any kind of 'soul' might
well be conceived as thus gaseously insubstantial though visible.
If our view of θυμός as the 'breath-soul' is correct, in favour
of the same meaning for ψυχή and its equivalence to θυμός,
though not decisive, are the descriptions of Andromache's
swoon already quoted: 'she breathed forth (ἀπό... ἐκάπυσσε)
her ψυχή... (seven lines) ...but when she breathed again
(ἄμπνυτο) and the θυμός was gathered into her φρήν';[4] of
Sarpedon's: 'his ψυχή left him and mist o'erspread his eyes,
then he breathed again and the breath of Boreas around him
revived him, breathing upon him who had grievously breathed
forth (κεκαφηότα) his θυμός';[5] and Nestor's plea that if
Peleus heard that the Achaeans were cowering before Hector,
he would pray 'that his θυμός might pass from his limbs into
the house of Hades',[6] which the ψυχή is commonly said to do.
But this is a rhetorical wish and not a description of what
anywhere happens; θυμός may on this occasion be substituted
for ψυχή as suggesting the life-factor which perceives and feels

---

[1] See e.g. Rohde, *Psyche*⁸, 1, § 2; Nilsson in Ch. de la Saussaye, *Lehrb. d.
Religionsgesch*⁴. v, ii, p. 298; Bickel, *op. cit.* p. 49; Rüsche, *op. cit.* p. 48 ff.;
Larock, *op. cit.* p. 390. There has already been some discussion of the
ψυχή above (pp. 59 ff.).

[2] *Il.* xxiii, 100.

[3] It could equally well leave through a wound, e.g. in the flank (see
p. 94, n. 5 and p. 197).

[4] *Il.* xxii, 417–75. The last line also follows ἀποψύχοντα in *Od.* xxiv,
348 f.   [5] *Il.* v, 696 ff.   [6] *Il.* vii, 131.

the shame. That the θυμός and the ψυχή are separate entities is implied by their juxtaposition elsewhere: 'The mighty force of burning fire overcomes these (as soon as the θυμός has left the white bones) and the ψυχή like a dream-phantom flies away';[1] 'This bow shall deprive many champions of θυμός and ψυχή';[2] 'The son of Tydeus deprived them of θυμός and ψυχή and took away their glorious arms'.[3] There is also the clear implication that none of the ψυχαί except that of Teiresias has breath or intelligence (πέπνυται), and, above all, a fundamental difference of usage in the multitude of passages throughout the poems. The θυμός is constantly spoken of as feeling and thinking, as active in the lungs (φρένες) or chest (στῆθος) of the living person, and as departing at death, but is not spoken of in connection with the succeeding state. The ψυχή, on the other hand, is 'in'[4] the person but is not spoken of as being in the lungs or chest[5] nor as thinking or feeling while a person lives. Rather it seems to be a 'life-principle' or soul not concerned in ordinary consciousness and to be what persists, still without ordinary consciousness, in the house of Hades, there identified with the εἴδωλον, the visible but impalpable semblance of the once living.

It might be suggested that while in the body actively alive within the confining and controlling organs of intelligence (the lungs), the soul, being a warm vapour, was called θυμός, but when it passed out with the last breath and became 'cold', it was called ψυχή. But we have seen the evidence against such identity or unity. θυμός and ψυχή are both said to leave the body as if separately and simultaneously. And we may add, what does not appear to have been noticed, that while

[1] *Od.* xi, 220 ff.

[2] *Od:* xxi, 154, 171. For the persistence of the difference see e.g. Tyrtaeus, xii, 18 (*P.L.G.*[4] Bgk.).

[3] *Il.* xi, 333 f.   [4] *Il.* xxi, 569.

[5] In *Il.* xvi, 504 ff., when the spear is pulled out of Sarpedon's chest the φρένες follow. With the spear-point itself the ψυχή was drawn out. This does not involve any special relation of the ψυχή to the chest as has been suggested by Rüsche (*op. cit.* p. 48), but as on another occasion from the flank the ψυχή is said to issue by way of the wound, ψυχὴ δὲ κατ' οὐταμένην ὠτειλὴν/ἔσσυτ' ἐπειγομένη (*Il.* xiv, 518 f.), see below, p. 197.

the ψυχή leaves the body ἠΰτ' ὄνειρος (as a phantom of the person such as is encountered in a dream) and persists in the house of Hades as an εἴδωλον, i.e. preserves its form and does not disintegrate, the θυμός is 'destroyed', and 'shattered' by death. Deadly drugs are φάρμακα θυμοφθόρα,[1] death-dealing foes are δήϊοι θυμοραϊσταί[2] and more generally death itself (θάνατος) is characterised as θυμοραϊστής, i.e. 'θυμός-shattering'[3] (ῥαίω). If then the ψυχή is not the θυμός or 'breath-soul' proper but represents something else in the living man, we are left with something gaseous and so liable to be 'breathed forth', possibly identified with the shadow, as which after death it is in fact described by Homer,[4] σκιά (cf. umbra, etc.), and which is relatively 'cold'.[5] Darkness was thought to be vapour and not recognised as mere absence of light till a much later date.[6] The old ideas of θυμός and ψυχή perhaps lie behind the moralising words of Sophocles, 'Man is but a breath and a shadow'[7] (πνεῦμα καὶ σκιά).

In any case, the ψυχή was, I suggest, associated more particularly with the head,[8] whence it would naturally be

[1] Od. II, 329. Cf. Il. VI, 169. [2] Il. XVI, 591, XVIII, 220.

[3] Il. XIII, 544, XVI, 414, 580. See also pp. 59 ff. 119, where it does not appear to be finally destroyed till the destruction of the body.

[4] Od. X, 495. Cf. XI, 207. In later Greece he who entered the precinct of Lykaian Zeus was believed to lose his shadow and die within a year (see Paus. VIII, 38, 6; Polyb. XVI, 12, 7; Plut. Q.G. 39). For instances of belief in modern Greece that a man's shadow is his soul, see Frazer, Golden Bough, Taboo and the Perils of the Soul, p. 89. How the shadow-soul has been conceived by other races may be instanced from China by the custom of coffin-bearers and grave-diggers who, being endangered by proximity to the dead, attach their shadows firmly to their persons by tying a cord tightly round their waists, and by the belief that a man's shadow ought to be deep so that he will attain to greatness (ibid. pp. 79 f.).

[5] As are also the dead; see e.g. Il. XI, 477; Soph. Oed. Col. 621 f., and Alex. Ἀσωτ. I, 10: ψύξει σε δαίμων τῷ πεπρωμένῳ χρόνῳ. The cold stiffness of death is perhaps the reason why the death-river (e.g. Il. VIII, 369) was Styx (Στύξ) affecting as with death (Hes. Th. 786, 793–8). See p. 202, n. 5. The significance of the name ψυχή will appear below (pp. 119 f.).

[6] Cf. Hesych. αὐερός· σκιά from αὔηρ (Aeolic for ἀήρ).

[7] Fr. 13 (Pearson).

[8] The ψυχή is twice said to fly forth from the ῥέθη, which meant 'face', as we know, in Aeolic (see Schol. ad Il. XVI, 856, XXII, 68), but the θυμός also is once taken thence (Il. XXII, 68); so the reference probably is merely to the mouth (and nostrils?) as a way out (cf. Il. IX, 409 f.).

'breathed forth'. It has apparently attracted little notice
hitherto[1] that while the chest (στῆθος) and its organs, the φρένες
(or πραπίδες), the κῆρ, κραδίη, ἦτορ, and the θυμός are continually mentioned in the poems as the seat of consciousness
and intelligence, feeling and thought, the head is also important
in a different way, is in fact regarded as in a unique degree
precious or holy, identified with the person and equated with
that soul or principle of *life* which the ψυχή appears to be.

The head is the life or the seat of life: 'I will save you,' says
Hermes to Odysseus, confronted by the perils of Kirkē's drugs
and magic; 'go with this goodly herb to Kirkē's halls that it
may ward off from your head the evil day'.[2] 'I am afraid not
so much for the corpse of Patroklos as for my head, lest any
thing should happen to it (μή τι πάθῃσιν), and for yours',[3]
says Aias to Menelaos, though the danger that threatens is
the general danger of battle. For helping Odysseus 'you shall
pay with your head',[4] says one of the suitors to the pretended
Mentor. Perjury goes not unpunished, says Agamemnon, 'for
even if the Olympian make not fulfilment immediately, yet at
last doth he fulfil and the transgressors pay with heavy price,
with their heads and their wives and children'.[5] The man who
is making oath and imprecating death upon himself, should he
not fulfil, as in the modern 'Strike me dead if...', does not pray
that he may be thus struck or his heart pierced, but 'Let my head
be no longer on my shoulders if...',[6] or 'May a stranger cut off
my head if...'.[7] By the belief that it contained the 'life' or ψυχή
we should also perhaps explain the practice of cutting off the
head of the fallen foe[8] and the use of δειροτομεῖν for 'to kill'.[9]

---

[1] See p. 99, n. 7.   [2] *Od.* x, 286 ff.

[3] *Il.* xvii, 240 ff. For the persistence of the idea, see e.g. Bacchylides,
v, 89 f.: ἦ τάχα καλλίζωνος Ἥρα κεῖνον ἐφ' ἁμετέρᾳ πέμψει κεφαλᾷ,
'will send to take my life' (Jebb); Soph. *Oed. Col.* 564 ἤθλησα κινδυνεύ-
ματ' ἐν τώμῷ κάρᾳ.

[4] *Od.* xxii, 218.   [5] *Il.* iv, 160 ff.
[6] *Il.* ii, 259 f.   [7] *Il.* v, 214 f.; *Od.* xvi, 102 f.
[8] E.g. *Il.* xiii, 202 ff., xvii, 126 f. Cf. the Celtic practice mentioned
in note 4 on p. 101 below.
[9] See *Il.* xxi, 89, 555, and compare *Od.* xxii, 328-9, 349, x, 438 ff. etc.;
also Hesiod, *Theog.* 280.

The head is supremely honoured or holy. 'Patroklos, whom
I honoured above all my comrades equally with my head',[1]
says Achilles. It is the head that suffers when a man is dishonoured. They 'poured shame upon my head'[2] (ἐμῇ κεφαλῇ
κατ' ὀνείδεα χεῦαν), says Telemachos of the guilty serving-
women. 'I am not blind to your great sin which you shall
wipe off upon your head',[3] says Penelope to one of them.
'I beseech you by the sacrifice and the god and also by your
own head and (those of) your comrades',[4] says Theoklymenos
to Telemachos, as Hector says to Achilles 'I beseech you by
your ψυχή', etc.[5] So too among the anthropomorphised gods:
'By Earth and Heaven and Styx and by your sacred head
(σή θ' ἱερὴ κεφαλή) and by our bridal couch I swear',[6] says
Hera to convince Zeus. Thus we may explain the sanctity of
the nod.[7] When an action in the future has been spoken of,
a man to guarantee fulfilment nods his head,[8] thus, I suggest,
involving in the undertaking his ψυχή, the soul that is his life
and is also, as we shall see,[9] the executive power, his physical
strength.[10] Similarly, after saying that he will do as Thetis
asks, Zeus adds: 'Come now, I will nod with my head, that
you may believe. For that is the greatest sign from me among
the immortals. For no decision of mine may be taken back or

[1] *Il.* xviii, 82.
[2] *Od.* xxii, 463. For the persistence of the idea that it is the *head* which
receives honour or dishonour see e.g. 'Shield of Herakles', 104; Pind.
Ol. vi, 60, vii, 67; and Eurip. *Androm.* 110 quoted on p. 145.
[3] *Od.* xix, 91 f. See below, p. 108.   [4] *Od.* xv, 261 f.
[5] *Il.* xxii, 338. See below, p. 174.
[6] *Il.* xv, 36; lit. 'be witness' (ἴστω) Earth, etc., but cf. Hymn to
Hermes, 274 and Hymn to Aphrodite, 26 f.
[7] It will be discussed further on pp. 104 f.
[8] κατανεύειν. See e.g. *Il.* iv, 267, xiii, 368. Similarly ἀνανεύειν, to throw
the head back in refusal (e.g. *Il.* vi, 311, xvi, 250, 252), would mean a
withdrawal of the ψυχή.   [9] Pp. 140, 187 ff. etc.
[10] Thus I would explain also the sanctity of the right hand given with
a promise (see e.g. *Il.* ii, 341, iv, 159, x, 542, Cic. *Deiot.* iii, 8, etc. with
pp. 133, n. 1 *fin.*; 139, n. 4 below, also our 'Your hand upon it' and the
use of a glove as gage of honour), that it was the executive member
representing and pledging the life soul. Cf. Juv. iii, 48. See also p. 198,
n. 1, 226, n. 1. The mediaeval vassal pledged *hominium*, his 'manhood'
service as his lord's 'man', by putting his hands within those of his lord.

false or unfulfilled that I nod with my head'. He nods and Olympos shakes.[1] The importance of the god's nod has already been illustrated.[2]

The head is in some sense the person. A man is referred to as a 'head': 'Teukros, dear head'[3] (φίλη κεφαλή) is Agamemnon's greeting. But with the exception of this one instance it is the *dead* that are thus referred to in Homer. 'Why, trusty head (ἠθείη κεφαλή), hast thou come hither?'[4] says Achilles to the ψυχή of Patroklos. 'Such a head (τοίην κεφαλήν) do I regret',[5] says Penelope of her husband presumed to be dead.[6] 'Such a head did the earth take possession of',[7] says Odysseus of the defeated Aias, and to him, 'We mourn continually for thee dead as much as for the head of Achilles'.[8] 'But now I go to reach the slayer of that dear head',[9] says Achilles himself, and having reached him and wounded him unto death, 'There is none that shall keep the dogs away from thy head'.[10] 'Make a huge blaze and I will raise a whirlwind which shall burn up the heads of the Trojans and their arms',[11] says Hera to the fire-god, though the complete bodies are there. So too it is a 'ransom for Hector's head' that Priam takes[12] and Achilles accepts,[13] though quite clearly[14] the whole body is in question. It is as if the head were all that mattered after death. Striking is the action of Hecuba and Andromache when Priam approaches with Hector's body. They 'first plucked out their hair for him, darting upon the fair-wheeled wagon and laid hold of his head'[15] (ἁπτόμεναι κεφαλῆς). They took him home still on the wagon, laid him upon a bed and set singers of dirges beside him and 'white-armed Andromache led their lament, holding in her hands the head of man-slaying

---

[1] *Il.* I, 524 ff. Cf. 514, XV, 75, VIII, 246, XVII, 206–10, etc.
[2] P. 29. See also *Hom. Hymn to Hermes* 518 f.
[3] *Il.* VIII, 281.
[4] *Il.* XXIII, 94.
[5] *Od.* I, 343.
[6] See e.g. *ibid.* 161, 396.
[7] *Od.* XI, 549.
[8] *Ibid.* 556 ff.
[9] *Il.* XVIII, 114.
[10] *Il.* XXII, 348.
[11] *Il.* XXI, 333 ff.
[12] *Il.* XXIV, 276.
[13] *Ibid.* 579.
[14] E.g. *ibid.* 581.
[15] *Ibid.* 710 f.

Hector'.[1] So too in the midst of a procession of chariots and footmen 'his comrades bore Patroklos. And they heaped all the corpse with the hair which they cut off and cast upon it, and, behind, noble Achilles carried the head, grieving, for he was escorting a blameless comrade unto the house of Hades'.[2] There is the complete parallelism of the lines 'sent many mighty ψυχαί to Hades'[3] and 'send many mighty heads to Hades'[4] (πολλὰς ἰφθίμους κεφαλὰς "Αϊδι προϊάψειν, cf. 'Αΐδῃ κεφαλὰς ἀπὸ χαλκὸν ἰάψ[ει]ν, Hes. Fr. 96, 80 Rz.), and the parallelism of the descriptions of people who follow dangerous courses 'staking their ψυχαί'[5] or 'staking their heads'[6] (παρθέμενοι κεφαλάς). Finally, the ψυχαί themselves in Hades are four times spoken of as 'passionless heads of the dead'[7]

---

[1] *Il.* xxiv, 723 f. There is perhaps a remote survival of such a practice recorded in the 'Last Request' of a Greek robber (Klepht) to his beloved:

'And hold my head up in thy hands
Till flies away my soul...
Then as the hen her feathers plucks,
So pluck thy hair for me'.

trans. E. Martinengo-Cesaresco in 'The Inspiration of Death in Folk-Poetry' (*Essays in the Study of Folk-Songs*). Hair is discussed below, pp. 107 f., 229 ff.

[2] *Il.* xxiii, 134 ff. This practice explains Hesych. τριχῶσαι· θάψαι.

[3] *Il.* i, 3.   [4] *Il.* xi, 55.   [5] *Od.* iii, 74.   [6] *Od.* ii, 237.

[7] *Od.* x, 521, 536, xi, 29, 49. I find that Bethe (*Rhein. Mus.* LXII, 1907, p. 465) noticed these two Homeric phrases, νεκύων ἀμενηνὰ κάρηνα and κεφαλὰς "Αϊδι προϊάψειν, and a vase with the head of Troilus (Baumeister, III, p. 1902) as evidence that 'the head from which the soul goes out in the breath was understood as a representation of the soul by the Greeks'. To this 'soul' he ascribes the moral characteristics of the conscious self which, as we have seen, belong to θυμός and he enumerates heart, liver, blood, hair, and phallus as similar seats of the soul. His evidence did not suffice. Radermacher (*Archiv. f. Relig.-wiss.* XI, 1908, p. 414) points out as a possible alternative interpretation that 'people have been counted by *capita* and so the head has taken the place of the whole man'. Waser (*ibid.* XVI, 1913, pp. 378 ff.) referring to more vases thought 'the bodiless head, the seat of intelligence (*Sinne*), could be conceived as seat of the soul and be employed in word and picture as a kind of abbreviation for the *eidolon* or for the human-headed soul-bird as a symbol of the soul'. Otto (*Die Manen oder Von den Urformen des Totenglaubens*, 1923, p. 25) interprets κεφαλάς as 'persons' as in Radermacher's suggestion and dismisses Bethe's interpretation as 'baseless conjecture' (p. 22). Kern (*Religion d. Gr.* p. 71) notices the use of the head for the soul as *Abkürzung* for the whole body. Justesen, Böhme and other recent writers upon the subject have ignored it.

(νεκύων ἀμενηνὰ κάρηνα). That the ψυχή was the head or in the head will help us to understand why the distinctive appurtenance[1] of Hades was a κυνέη, a helmet enclosing the head, i.e. enclosing the ψυχή, and rendering invisible.

Many other peoples have considered the head peculiarly sacred as the seat of the soul.[2] Thus among kindred 'Indo-Europeans' the Persians dedicated the top of the head to Haoma that at death he might receive the immortal part. Resultant from such a belief, as might be expected, is the head's preservation.[3] Thus the Germanic tribes, who appear to have shared this belief,[4] fastened up human heads on trees[5] and, if the ghost of a person who had been buried was thought to be responsible for misfortune, the head of the corpse was cut off and burnt.[6] By this belief we can perhaps also explain a number of expressions in *Beowulf*. It is the head that matters in battle. Wiglaf 'bears his war-head (*wigheafolan*) to help his lord'.[7] Men who fight 'guard their heads'[8] (*hafelan weredon*) and it is the head of the dead warrior that matters and is mentioned. When Beowulf and the Worm have slain each other and are lying dead, Wiglaf 'keepeth guard over the heads (*heafodwearde*) of friend and foe'.[9] It is the head that goes to the Norse realm of Death (*Hel*, i.e. hell).[10] The Celts, likewise, cut off the heads of the slain and 'had a cult of human heads and fixed them up on their houses in order to obtain the

[1] See *Il*. v, 845; 'Shield of Herakles', 227. See also below, pp. 135 f., 421 ff.

[2] Many instances from other peoples have been collected by J. A. MacCulloch, s.v. 'Head', in Hastings, *Encyclopaedia of Religion and Ethics*, and by Frazer, *Taboo, etc.* pp. 252 ff.; also 44, 47 f., 53 ff., 58, 67, etc.

[3] E.g., for the hope of Dyak head-hunters that the soul of the victim will be at home in his captured head, see Frazer, *Taboo, etc.* pp. 71 f. and cf. below p. 127, n. 2.

[4] See E. Mogk in Paul's *Grundriss der germ. Philol.* III, p. 254, also in Hoops, *Reallexikon der germ. Altertumskunde*, s.v. 'Seelenglaube'.

[5] See Tacitus, *Ann*. I, 61 with Nipperdey's note.

[6] See Mogk in Paul's *Grundriss, loc. cit.* He adduces, however, very little evidence as ground for the generalisation.

[7] Line 2661 f. 'War-head' would be a strange expression for 'helmet', the usual interpretation, and not less strange would be the resultant statement: 'Wiglaf bears his helmet to help his lord'. See also pp. 195 f. below.

[8] Line 1327. This survived for centuries. Thus in *Robin Hood and the Monk*, 'He gaf hym a gode swerd in his hond/his hed therwith for to kepe' (*Oxford Book of Ballads*, p. 597). [9] Line 2909 f.

[10] E.g. *Sigurðarkv*. II, 1, 6; *Helr. Brynh*. 2. See also pp. 106, 154 ff. below.

protection of their ghosts',[1] just as Herodotus[2] tells us the
Tauri did. Apparently related to the Homeric evidence for
early Greece are such traditions as that Oinomaos wanted to
build a shrine of the heads of his daughter's suitors;[3] that when
Eurystheus fell in battle against the sons of Herakles, his head
was cut off by Iolaos and buried separately at Trikorynthos
—the place was known as 'Eurystheus' Head' (Εὐρυσθέως
κεφαλή) till Strabo's day—and the body at Gargettos;[4] that
the heads of the sons of Aigyptos were buried in the tomb
named after them at Argos, though their bodies were at
Lerna;[5] that two of the Korybantes (or Kabeiroi) after killing
their brother wrapped his head in a crimson cloth and buried
it separately, carrying it on a bronze shield to the foot of Mount
Olympos;[6] that Kleomenes of Sparta kept the head of his
friend Archonides in a vessel of honey and professed to consult
it before every undertaking;[7] and that the body of Orpheus
was torn to pieces but his head buried in a tomb or shrine
(e.g. in Lesbos) and thence continued long to utter prophecies.[8]

[1] J. A. MacCulloch, *The Religion of the Ancient Celts*, p. 34; cf. pp. 240 ff.,
337. In the Mabinogi of *Branwen* Bran commands his followers to cut off
his head and it keeps company with them afterwards without corrupting.
This and further Celtic evidence is discussed on pp. 156 ff. below.

[2] IV, 103. Cf. the Slav evidence on p. 155, n. 2 below.

[3] Tzetzes *ad Lyc.* 160. Cf. Schol. *ad Il.* IX, 557.

[4] Strabo, VII, 6, 9, p. 377. Cf. Pind. *Pyth.* IX, 80 f. The occasional
burial of the head apart from the body perhaps derives from practices
and ideas resembling those of the Irish Celts who like some Homeric
warriors (see pp. 3, 96) cut off the heads of those they slew as
trophies but 'when the retreating friends of a fallen warrior succeeded
in cutting off his head before his enemies could secure it and in piling
a Carn of stones over it, it was saved from being a trophy; for independently of the difficulty of removing the stones in the face of the enemy,
the Carn was regarded as a sanctuary for the remains of the fallen warriors
which should not be violated without dishonour' (E. O'Curry, *Manners
and Customs of the Ancient Irish*, I, p. cccxxxvii).

[5] Paus. II, 24, 2.

[6] See Clem. Alex. *Protrept.* II, p. 16, ed. Potter (I, p. 80, Migne).

[7] Aelian, *Var. Hist.* XII, 8.

[8] For the evidence of literature and art see J. E. Harrison, *Prolegomena
to the study of Greek Religion*, pp. 465 ff., and Gruppe, *Griechische Mythologie
u. Religionsgeschichte*, p. 297. The legends that the heads of Orpheus (*ibid.*),
Osiris (Lucian, *de Dea Syria*, 7), and Battos (Heraclides Ponticus, IV, 4)
were thrown into river or sea perhaps rest upon the same view of the
stream as appears in the offering of hair from the head discussed below,

The body of Pentheus also, we may remember, was torn to pieces and left behind by the Maenads but the head carried off (in the *Bacchae*, on the end of the thyrsus[1]). We should perhaps add the detached human head on the sealstone from the necropolis at Phaistos[2] and the heaps of skulls found in Minoan tombs elsewhere,[3] back to which culture there appears to be continuity of thought in other respects.[4]

For Pindar the αἰῶνος εἴδωλον (=ψυχή), which 'alone comes from the gods' and survives death, 'sleeps while the limbs are active, but, to those that sleep, in many a dream it shows decision of things delightful and grievous creeping on'.[5] So too in Homer the ψυχή apparently has no part in ordinary waking life and might well be thought to be resident in the head, the contents of which, unlike those of the breast, also seem not to move in ordinary waking life. It may be significant that alike the dream-spirit[6] (ὄνειρος), the ψυχή of the dead,[7] and the god[8] appearing to a man in sleep are

pp. 229 ff., and represent the path of the ψυχή to a new life, but the others may be derivative from the story of Osiris who was intimately associated with the fertilising Nile. An olive-wood head of Dionysos also was reputed to have been fished out of the sea (see Paus. x, 19, 3 and Gruppe, *op. cit.* p. 297, 12).

[1] 1137 ff. For the thyrsus as the god, the life-power, see p. 456, n. 2 and for identification of god with victim 105 f., 228, 236.

[2] See Nilsson, *The Minoan-Myc. Rel., etc.*, Fig. 66, p. 199. Cf. pp. 143 f., below.

[3] See Xanthoudides, *The Vaulted Tombs of Mesara* (trans. Droop), p. 7; also p. 92.　　　　[4] See e.g. pp. 236 f., 239, 260 f., 273.

[5] Fr. 131 (96). For the relationship of Orphism, which Pindar sometimes reflects, see below, pp. 111 f. In Aesch. *Eum.* 104 f. it is the φρήν which is spoken of as seeing in sleep, though prevision is denied during the day. As opposed to what Homer would call the ψυχή and what for Pindar gives the warning, it represents perhaps the recipient consciousness that has knowledge on waking, but cf. *Ag.* 179 ff. and pp. 116 f. below. The fusion of conceptions had already begun.

[6] *Il.* II, 20, x, 496; *Od.* IV, 803.

[7] *Il.* XXIII, 68. The ψυχή is εἴδωλον and described as ἠΰτ' ὄνειρος (*Od.* XI, 222) and the ὄνειρος as εἴδωλον (*Od.* IV, 796). In dreams of distant places or friends the ψυχή might be thought to see the vision by going thither, leaving the body visible at home. Compare the Swedish belief on p. 196.

[8] *Il.* XXIV, 682; *Od.* VI, 21, XX, 32. Eurykleia takes the same position to wake Penelope (*Od.* XXIII, 4). Cf. also *Od.* XX, 94. Awakening may have been thought of as a recalling of the ψυχή to its home.

described as standing not at the side nor at the feet, but, in all the seven passages in point, at or above the head[1] of the recumbent sleeper. The Jews attributed consciousness to the heart (Dan. ii, 30; vii, 28, etc.) and seem also originally to have regarded the head[2] much as we have found the Greeks doing. This would explain why, when a dream foreshadowing what is to come is vouchsafed to Nebuchadnezzar and, on waking, the latter does not know what it was, Daniel declares to him 'Thy dream and the visions of thy head upon thy bed are these:' (ii, 28). The phrase 'visions of the head' recurs (iv, 5, 13; vii, 1, 15). Later Jews and other Semites took and kept human heads in the belief they could prophesy.[3] If the ψυχή was resident in the head and had faculties dissociated from waking consciousness,[4] we can explain the importance attached to a sneeze, a strange happening the real cause of which was unknown. Heads, we saw, were preserved in Greece and supposed to have prophetic knowledge. A sneeze would naturally be traced to something inside the head, be regarded as a spontaneous expression of that something, independent of the body and the conscious will. It was regarded as prophetic, a sign from a power with other know-

[1] Our ghosts used to come to the bed's *foot*. See Brand, *op. cit.* III, p. 70.

[2] This is apparently not recognised, but seems to be implicit in many expressions and practices of the Old Testament (Gen. xlix, 26; Ex. xxix, 10; Numb. vi, 5–19; I Sam. xxviii, 2; II Sam. i, 2; Is. i, 5, etc. Cf. Matt. v, 36; etc.) and in the Talmudic belief that on HOSHA'NA RABBAH eve, when destinies for the year are distributed, one's head casts no shadow if one is to die within the year (cf. p. 95, n. 4), and the custom of greasing just the head and face of the dead with egg-yolk (*The Home and Synagogue of the Modern Jew*, pp. 37, 120), life-renewing stuff (cf. pp. 153, n. 1, 167, 271 ff.). Arabs referred to the souls of the dead as 'skulls' (Wellhausen, *R. Arab. Heid.*[2], p. 185). See also pp. 144, 185, n. 1, 188 ff., 234 f., 239, n. 6, 287 f., 483 ff. below. The original beliefs would be confused by tendencies like those traced on pp. 115 ff. and 168 ff.

[3] See D. Chwolsohn, *Die Ssabier*, etc. II, pp. 15, 19 ff., 130 f., 150 ff. Arab prophets veiled their heads for inspiration. It was conceived as activity of the *ginn* (=soul) within (Wellhausen, *op. cit.* pp. 135, 156). Cf. I Kings xix, 13 and Moses on p. 153, n. 1 *infra*. That the departed soul was a god (cf. pp. 131 f., 405, n. 8) with prophetic powers explains I Sam. xxviii, 13 ff.

[4] ψυχή seems to have served for the early Greeks many of the purposes which the concept of the Unconscious serves for us (see also pp. 161 ff.).

ledge.[1] Penelope says to Eumaios: 'Oh, if Odysseus might come and reach his fatherland, soon would he with his son avenge the violence of these men'. So she spake and Telemachos sneezed loudly (μέγ' ἔπταρεν) and around the roof rang terribly. And Penelope laughed and forthwith spake to Eumaios winged words: 'Go, I pray; call the stranger even so before me. Dost thou not see that my son has sneezed at (ἐπέπταρε) all my words. Wherefore not unfulfilled should be death for the suitors nor shall any of them escape death and the doom-sprites'.[2] Later, at least, a sneeze from one's own head was regarded as an indication that what one was thinking of just then would be fulfilled.[3] This incidentally fits our explanation[4] of the sanctity attached to a nod; a nod pledged in the name of the ψυχή fulfilment of words previously spoken. A sneeze is also a nod, a nod not expected or controlled by the conscious self but an apparently spontaneous expression of the life in the head.[5] When a person sneezed it was customary to do reverence (προσκυνεῖν) to his head.[6] The *Problemata*[7] of the Aristotelian corpus explain the sanctity of the sneeze by the fact that, unlike eructation and other πνεύματα, it comes from the head, the holiest part of man. If the sneeze that had no obvious prophetic relevance was interpreted as a disturbance of the life-soul, the gaseous ψυχή—the relation of the name to 'blowing', ψύχειν, appears below[8]—we can also understand why it was customary for a man who sneezed to say 'Zeus, save me'[9] (Ζεῦ, σῶσον). Jewish bystanders uttered a prayer

---

[1] The Celts, who similarly thought the head contained the soul (see pp. 100f., 156 ff.), also regarded a sneeze as a prophetic sign (see P. W. Joyce, *A Social History of Ireland*, I, p. 231). The interpretation of similar signs in the body independent of the conscious will is dealt with on pp. 197f.

[2] *Od.* XVII, 539–47. For the Romans cf. Catull. XLV, and p. 226, n. 1.

[3] *Anth. Pal.* XI, 375. That originally the ψυχή was concerned in the prophetic act will explain why the head of Pythia or Sibyl was veiled. Cf. pp. 133, n. 1, 152 f.   [4] Pp. 97f.

[5] 'Nodding' in sleep also may have been interpreted as activity of the ψυχή, which was thought to be especially active during sleep. For Pliny (*N.H.* XI, 37, 135) such nodding is the work of the brain. To the above conception of the head would perhaps be related its tossing in madness or ritual frenzy. See Catull. LXIV, 255; Aristoph. *Wasps* 8, with Pliny *l.c.* and pp. 138 ff., 146 ff.   [6] See Eustath. 757 *ad Il.* IX, 378.

[7] 962 a.   [8] Pp. 120 f.   [9] See *Anth. Pal.* XI, 268.

for the sneezer's life, and Hindoos said 'Live'.[1] Rabbinic tradition[2] explains that originally God decreed that each man should sneeze but once and his soul should depart in that instant.

For the Kabbalah[3] with its anthropomorphic conceptions of deity the Spirit 'proceedeth from the concealed brain into the gallery of the nostrils'. In the seventeenth century sneezing was regarded as a 'motion of the brain'.[4] 'Physitians generallye define itt to be the trumpet of nature upon the ejection of a vapour from the braine.'[5] Now animals as well as men have ψυχαί for Homer[6] and are referred to as 'heads'.[7] In later Greece, as we know, there was a superstition, attested more particularly for Attica, against eating the brain or contents of a creature's head (ἐγκέφαλος). Ancient crones, the usual guardians of belief, threw them away. There was μύσος involved.[8] Such taboo would be natural in connection with what was identified peculiarly with the life or soul.[9] Thus, perhaps, also we may explain the practice of preserving and fastening up the heads of the animals burned and eaten in sacrifice,[10] a practice that seems to go back to the Minoan

[1] See Tylor, *Primitive Culture*[4], I, p. 161, also below, p. 132.

[2] See *Pirkê de Rabbi Eliezer*, Chap. LII.

[3] See *Ha Idra Rabba Qadisha*, x, 175, 179, 199; *Ha Idra Zuta Qadisha*, v, 136–8, translated by S. L. M. Mathers, *The Kabbalah Unveiled*, pp. 131, 133, 273.

[4] Sir Thomas Browne, *Pseudodoxia Epidemica*, IV, 9.

[5] Christopher Wren (father of the architect) commenting upon Browne, *ad loc.* Cf. Cowper's praise of tobacco snuffed to provoke a sneeze:

> 'Whether pulverized it gain
> A speedy passage to the brain
> Or whether, touched with fire, it rise
> In circling eddies to the skies'

in lines 'To the Rev. William Bull'.

[6] See *Od.* XIV, 426. [7] *Il.* IX, 407, XXIII, 260.

[8] See Schol. B. and Eustath. *ad Il.* IX, 378; also Athenaeus, *Deipn.* 65 f., and Plut. *Quaest. Conv.* II, 3, 1=635.

[9] See pp. 111f.

[10] See e.g. Theophr. *Characters*, 21, 7 and Schol. *ad* Aristoph. *Plut.* 948. Cf. Herodotus, II, 39 and 41; Aelian, *de Nat. Anim.* x, 21; and, for the significance of the head in Egypt, Budge, *Osiris and the Egyptian Resurrection*, I, pp. 169 ff. and *infra* p. 236, n. 2. They wrapped up their heads to sleep and protected them from cold more than any other part (see Erman, *Lit. of the Anc. Egyptians* (trans. Blackman), p. 289).

period,[1] and that we find also among the Germans,[2] who likewise believed that the head contained the soul[3] and objected to eating it.[4] We can perhaps catch a glimpse of it in Homer, where the completion of the picture is left to the hearer's knowledge of usage, and at the same time we may perhaps explain the otherwise extravagant putting of gold about the victim's horns. Homer tells us that this was done 'in order that the goddess might rejoice seeing the ἄγαλμα',[5] a hundred and sixty lines after saying that Aigisthos 'burned many thighs on the holy altars of the gods and fastened up (ἀνῆψεν) many ἀγάλματα, robes and gold'.[6] Agathias[7] asks Τρόψ:

ὦ πτόλι, πῇ σέο κεῖνα τὰ τείχεα; πῇ πολύολβοι
νηοί; πῇ δὲ βοῶν κράατα τεμνομένων;

Originally, perhaps, the deity was in the ἄγαλμα.[8] According to Herodotus the Issedones, when a man's father died, scoured his skull, covered it with gold and treated it as an ἄγαλμα (ἅτε ἀγάλματι χρέωνται), sacrificing to it.[9] Nicolaus of Damascus[10] tells us that the Panebi of Libya, when their king dies, bury the body, but, upon the head, which is cut off, they put gold and set it up in a temple. The gold may originally have had more than an ornamental significance, being as elsewhere[11] thought to be stuff of life or immortality. Gold was found upon the face and head of the dead at Mycenae.[12]

[1] See Nilsson, *The Minoan-Mycenaean Religion, etc.* pp. 196–200, and for the preservation of human heads separately, p. 102 above.

[2] Tac. *Ann.* 1, 61, *Saxo Gr.* p. 75, 'Die Gänsemagd' (Grimm, *Kinderm.*).

[3] See p. 97.

[4] See e.g. the evidence for Bavaria as late as the fifteenth century in Usener, *Religionsgesch. Untersuch.* II, p. 84.

[5] *Od.* III, 437 f. Cf. 384; *Il.* x, 294.

[6] *Od.* III, 273 f. Cf. VIII, 509, XVI, 184 f., XII, 347.

[7] *Anth. Pal.* IX, 153.

[8] See pp. 60, n. 2, 102, 228. Cf. pp. 126 f., 134 f. The Sabaians chose human victims resembling different deities and kept the head, believing that the deity's soul entered it and prophesied (Chwolsohn, *op. cit.* II, pp. 19 ff., 388 f., etc.).

[9] IV, 26.   [10] Fr. 44 (Dind.).

[11] See e.g. *Satapatha Brahmana*, V, 2, 1, 20; 3, 5, 15; 4, 1, 14; VI, 7, 1; XII, 5, 2, 6; XIII, 1, 1, 4. The thought will become clearer on pp. 146 ff. (esp. pp. 156, n. 2, 165 ff.); see also pp. 183, n. 1, 330, 456, n. 2.

[12] See Schliemann, *Mycenae* (Engl. trans.), pp. 155, 289, 291, etc. and

With this preservation of the head, in the belief, as I suggest, that it contained the soul, we should probably connect the ἀπαρχαί, the important 'first act' of the sacrifice, the offering in the fire of 'hair from the head',[1] κεφαλῆς τρίχας, of the victim before the slaughter. The head itself is then spared, the axe falls upon the neck and the throat is cut.[2] To this 'first act' I would relate the last. After the thighbones and fat have been burned for the gods and after flesh and organs (σπλάγχνα) have been eaten by men, then at nightfall the tongue is cut out[3] and burned with wine poured over it. This also implies that the head remained. The offering of the hair was perhaps in origin a substitution for or dedication of the head and soul,[4] the whole being sympathetically involved by the fate of the part (cf. p. 246 fin.). In Euripides (Alcestis, 73 ff.) the human victim is dedicated the property of the gods below when the Death-god cuts hair from his head.[5] In Homer's day one clasped the head of a dead comrade or kinsman and gave him hair from one's own head[6] as he set out for the house of

---

note 1, p. 183 below. At Troy (see Schliemann's Excavations by Schuchhardt, trans. Sellers, p. 78), with the exception of two skeletons embedded in the layer of the second city, he found no bodies but only urns containing nothing but fine ashes, all but one, which contained a skull minus its lower jaw (cf. below, p. 236, n. 2).

[1] Il. III, 273; Od. III, 446, XIV, 422.

[2] See Od. III, 449 ff.

[3] This is the most natural interpretation of τάμνετε μὲν γλώσσας (Od. III, 332); cf. γλώσσας δ' ἐν πυρὶ βάλλον (341). Cf. also Aristoph. Birds, 1711; Peace, 1060; Ap. Rhod. I, 517 f., and for the jaw, pp. 233 ff. below.

[4] Similar, perhaps originally in relation to the life or soul, was Jewish circumcision (Gen. xvii, 10 ff., Exod. iv, 24 ff.). Cf. pp. 103, 108 ff., 234 f., 483 ff., 495.

[5] Cf. Phryn. Fr. 3 (Nauck), Aen. IV, 698 ff. The life of Nisos was believed to be bound up with the preservation of a hair of his head (Aesch. Choeph. 619; Paus. I, 19, 5), which suggests a relation to the ψυχή. Other offerings of hair from the heads of men are discussed below, pp. 229 ff. For loss of hair as a sign of approaching death see also p. 130 below.

[6] See pp. 98 f. above and p. 278, n. 1. Not only the plucking out or cutting off of hair from the head but also the covering of the dead with it, the heaping of dust, grain, etc., upon the head and other attentions to it at other times, e.g. the pouring of water over the head after meeting pollution (see Theophr. Characters 16, Δεισιδ. fin.), become more intelligible if the head is the honoured seat of the ψυχή.

Hades. The significance attached to hair will appear more clearly below.[1]

Similarly, a belief that it contained the soul, the surviving being, would explain the custom of wiping off upon the victim's head the blood (and with it the pollution or guilt of the 'murder'[2]) from the knife. Clytemnestra, as we hear in later literature,[3] after murdering Agamemnon 'wiped off upon his head the stains' (κάρᾳ κηλῖδας ἐξέμαξεν). It is to such usages Penelope appears to refer in the *Odyssey*, chiding the serving-maid: 'sin (μέγα ἔργον), which thou shalt wipe off upon thy head'.[4]

There is this various evidence that the head was holy with potency by which to swear and make appeal and was thought to contain the life or ψυχή apparently in its actual contents, the ἐγκέφαλος, the somewhat uncanny brain and cerebro-spinal fluid, 'the most peculiar of the parts' of the body as it appeared even to scientific Greeks.[5] The formula bý which death was invoked, namely a prayer that one's head might be removed, is varied at the treaty in *Iliad* III: Achaean and Trojan call down a curse upon the party that transgresses the oath: 'May the ἐγκέφαλος of themselves and of their children flow (ῥέοι) to the ground even as this wine does and may their wives be mingled with other men'.[6] Homer and his audience knew that during life and for some time after death the brain is a fluid mass. It was holy, not to be eaten. It had nothing to do with ordinary consciousness (perception, thought and feeling being the business of the chest and its organs), but instead was the vehicle of life itself, of that which continues and does not die. But life does not merely persist in the individual; it issues forth[7] and a new life begins. This is

[1] See pp. 130 f. and 231 ff.

[2] That to slay an animal is 'murder' is witnessed by the legends of the βουφονία.

[3] See Soph. *Electra*, 445 f.   [4] *Od.* XIX, 91 f. See above, p. 97.

[5] See Aristotle, *de Part. Anim.* 656 a, 26.

[6] *Il.* III, 299 ff. Other good MSS. have δαμεῖεν for μιγεῖεν.

[7] Cf. Democr. B 32 (Diels): ξυνουσίη ἀποπληξίη σμικρή· ἐξέσσυται γὰρ ἄνθρωπος ἐξ ἀνθρώπου καὶ ἀποσπᾶται πληγῇ τινι μεριζόμενος. If procreation was the work of the ψυχή, we can understand why those who

the greatest miracle, the holiest mystery. Elsewhere[1] and, as we shall see, in earliest Greece[2] it was those parts of the body, that were the seats and sources of life in this sense, that were revered, counted holy, so that men made appeal or oath by them. It was natural[3] and logical to think that the 'life' or ψυχή issuing from a man must come from the 'life' or ψυχή in him, from his head therefore, and, helping that location, to see in the seed, which carries the new life and which must have seemed the very stuff of life, a portion of the cerebro-spinal substance[4] in which was the life of the

lost their shadow (= ψυχή, see p. 95) also lost the power of procreation (Schol. ad Callim. Hymn. 1, 13; cf. Petron. 140 with p. 170, n. 2), also perhaps why for a boy to sit upon a tomb (i.e. receptacle for ψυχή, place of ψυχαί liable to steal or damage one's ψυχή. Cf. pp. 95, n. 4, 186) was believed to endanger his virility (Hesiod, W. and D. 750 ff.). After speaking of the maddened φρένες of the daughters of Proitos, Bacchylides describes them as 'still with virgin ψυχή' (παρθενίᾳ γὰρ ἔτι ψυχᾷ, x, 47 ff.). For him elsewhere the ψυχή is the life-soul surviving death. Cf. also Anacr. 4.

[1] E.g. in ancient Israel the oath imposed by Abraham (Gen. xxiv, 2 f. and 9): 'Put thy hand under my thigh and...swear'. Cf. also Jacob's request, Gen. xlvii, 29 and Gen. xlvi, 26; Exod. i, 5, where the procreative significance of yarekh (there translated 'loins') appears. This explains also its part in the curse of Num. v, 21 ff. See also W. Robertson Smith, Kinship and Marriage in Early Arabia², p. 38 and pp. 182 f., 188 below.

[2] See pp. 174 ff., 207 ff., 232 f., 236 f. It was particularly by the heads of Demeter and Praxidike (see p. 114, n. 5) that the local inhabitants swore (Paus. VIII, 15, IX, 33). The genital organs themselves were αἰδοῖα, 'inspiring awe, reverence', no less than 'shame'. Cf. verenda. We must not be misled by the limitations of pudenda. The sentiment attached to them may not only in Greece but elsewhere (cf. pp. 153 ff., 448, n. 5) derive largely from the thought that they were the organs of the ψυχή or life-soul and of the life-process. Cf. ἱερὸν ὀστέον, etc. (p. 208) and, in vulgar Latin, curses upon linguam ni (= ne) dicere possit...viscum sacrum ni possit urinam facere (Amer. J. Philol. Suppl. xxxiii, 1).

[3] See e.g. Aristotle on p. 111, n. 6; Ait. Aran. II, 5, 1, 2, on p. 196; and Swedenborg: 'man's life being in his seed' (Divine Providence, § 144); and 'Everyone's soul is derived from his father and it is only clothed with a body by the mother...the soul is in the seed which causes conception, and the seed is clothed with a body by the mother' (ibid. § 277). Thought of seed as ψυχή would help πᾶσι δ' ἀνθρώποις ἄρ' ἦν ψυχὴ τέκνα (Euripides, Androm. 418).

[4] That the testes were necessary to procreation must have been well known from the effects of gelding (see ἔνορχα, p. 232 below), but they do not seem to have been regarded as the source of the seed, perhaps

parent. It will indeed appear that this interpretation of the cerebro-spinal substance as the seed is vital to the whole thought. To this interpretation, we shall see,[1] there contributed the head's demonstration of fertility in producing hair.

We should not expect this aspect of the head to appear explicitly in Homer, but there is evidence to be discussed presently. In Hesiod it is visible, though it has escaped notice. He describes midsummer: 'then women are most wanton (μαχλόταται) but men are most impotent[2] ("feeblest", ἀφαυρό-

because secretion was not understood and they were seen to have no relation to the 'life' of the parent that was thought to be transmitted. They were a cache by the way, part of the channel, removal of which prevented issue. As late as Aristotle, de Gen. Anim. A, 717 a, 20 ff., they were believed merely to retard the seed. See also the Problemata, 879 b and 897 b, 23 ff. This suggests that the chief purpose originally behind the religious practice of self-castration was not, as has been thought, the bestowal of the seed-vessels wholesale upon some deity (see e.g. Frazer, Golden Bough, Attis, I, pp. 268 ff.) or the loss of virility or the avoiding of defilement but the positive conservation of the seed, the life-stuff, the soul-stuff, with which the ψυχή was particularly identified. This will explain why it was believed (see Arnobius, adv. Nat. v, 7, Paus. VII, 17) that Attis, being castrated, did not suffer death in the ordinary way: his body did not corrupt (σήπεσθαι, cf. Il. XIX, 24 ff. discussed on pp. 200 ff.), his hair continued to grow (cf. pp. 130 f., 231 ff.) and his little finger to move (cf. pp. 195 f., 198, n. 1), why also the 'Gospel to the Egyptians' (quoted by Clement, Strom. III, 13, 92) made the cessation of death dependent on the cessation of procreation. Cf. τὸν αἴτιον τοῦ θανάτου ἔρωτα ὄντα (Poimandres, in Hermetica, I, 18 ed. Scott) and in the Fall the linking of death with sexual shame (Genesis ii, 17–iii, 19). The Gnostics did not castrate or abstain from intercourse but religiously avoided begetting offspring and practised 'self-collection', collection of ψυχή, whenever seed was emitted: τὴν δὲ δύναμιν τὴν ἐν τοῖς καταμηνίοις καὶ ἐν ταῖς γοναῖς ψυχὴν εἶναί φασιν, ἣν συλλέγοντες ἐσθίομεν (Epiphan. Panar. I, 2, 26, 9; cf. 11, 13, etc). They believed that they thus remained 'virgin' (ibid. 13). A better understanding also of the religious value of chastity in antiquity (for examples, see E. Fehrle, Die kultische Keuschheit im Altertum) is now possible. Cf. Galahad, etc. in the mediaeval legend of the Grail on pp. 187, n. 7; 156, n. 2. The value attached to the ψυχή thus conserved will appear more fully below. The gallus might at the same time think that he was bestowing upon the goddess a portion of the seed (cf. Hesiod, Theog. 180 ff.) and abandoning mortal propagation. Cf. χλούνης on p. 177, n. 9. The analogy with plants was felt (111 ff.). For many plants to seed is to die. Sexual intercourse brought to Alexander a sense of mortality (Plut. Vit. Alex. 22). Cf. p. 187.   [1] Pp. 130 f., 231 ff.
  [2] Pliny interprets for both Hesiod and Alcaeus in N.H. XXII, 22, 86. The usual sense of ἀφαυρός is 'physically weak, powerless'. Cf. p. 187.

τατοι) because Sirius dries up the head and knees (κεφαλὴν
καὶ γούνατα...ἄϳει) and the flesh is dried up with the heat'.[1]
Similarly Alcaeus: 'Now women are lewdest (μιαρώτατοι)
and men lean (λέπτοι) because Sirius dries up the head and
knees'.[2] The 'knees', as we shall see,[3] strengthen the argument. Thus, too, can now be understood the hitherto mysterious belief, also recorded by Hesiod,[4] that when Zeus wished
to have a child and dispense with a mother he 'gave birth' to
it (Athene) 'from his head' (ἔτικτε...ἐκ κεφαλῆς). The author
of the Homeric Hymn to the Pythian Apollo[5] says that he
'engendered' it 'in his head' (γείνατ'...ἐν κορυφῇ). Later
in Greece, as we shall see,[6] it was generally believed that the
seed was ψυχή and was stored in the head. This belief may
also explain why at a Cretan festival Molos was represented
as headless with the explanation that he had been found
to be thus after he had ravished a nymph,[7] and why at
Tanagra Triton likewise was represented headless as a result
(? punishment) of a similar act.[8]

If the head was the beginning, the source of generation,
we can explain the Orphic line Ζεὺς κεφαλή, Ζεὺς μέσσα, Διὸς
δ' ἐκ πάντα τελεῖται with the variant Ζεὺς ἀρχή κ.τ.λ. (Fr. 21 a,

---

[1] *Works and Days*, 586 ff.   [2] Fr. 39, 6 f. (Bgk.).   [3] Pp. 174 ff.

[4] *Theog.* 924. The story of Μῆτις put into his νηδύς (886–900) seems
to be an inessential accretion to the myth and will be dealt with more
suitably below (p. 489). Hera's retaliation which follows (927 ff.) and
the version in the Hymn imply that Zeus was sole parent. Here too we
may explain the birth of Pegasos when the head was cut off Medousa
(e.g. *caesae gravida cervice Medusae prosiluisse*, Ovid, *F.* 451; cf. p. 124,
n. 4) as of Aphrodite when the μήδεα were cut off Ouranos (see p. 121).

[5] 130 ff. (307–10). Cf. the Homeric Hymn to Athena (xxviii), 4 f.:
ἐγείνατο...σεμνῆς ἐκ κεφαλῆς. The conception of the brain as an embryo
is implicit in *dura mater* and *pia mater* (derived from the Arabic).

[6] Pp. 115, 118 ff. For the view that the new life came from the father
see Aesch. *Eum.* 658–66, and in Diels, *Fragm. d. Vors.*[4] Alcmaeon, A 13,
for Diogenes, Hippo and the Stoics. Contrast e.g. Hippo, A 13; Anaxag.
A 107. Aristotle taught that the ψυχή is contributed by the seed of the
male and that a woman cannot provide it (*De Gen. An.* 737 a, 30 ff.). Cf.
pp. 109, n. 3, 230, n. 8. Such thought has perhaps facilitated the widely
held belief that a woman has no soul.

[7] See Plut. *de Defect. Orac.* xiv=p. 417 e. He may have been a vegetation
spirit (? cf. μολεύω, μολούω). Cf. p. 113, n. 2.   [8] Paus. ix, 20, 4 f.

2; 21, 1; cf. 168, 2 Kern) and the fuller Orphic hymn (xv) to Zeus as παντογένεθλος: ὦ βασιλεῦ διὰ σὴν κεφαλὴν ἐφάνη τάδε ῥεῖα,/γαῖα θεά...καὶ πόντος καὶ πάνθ' ὁπόσ' οὐρανὸς ἐντὸς ἐέργει. These beliefs will also explain[1] the Orphic and Pythagorean saying ἴσον τοι κυάμους τε φαγεῖν κεφαλάς τε τοκήων, 'to eat beans (κύαμοι) is equal to eating the heads of one's parents'. κύαμοι were interpreted by the ancients as eggs, vessels of seed, of generation, and connected with κυεῖν,[2] so that there is point in the equation and special emphasis in making them as taboo as the heads of one's parents. The aim of these food prohibitions of the Orphics and Pythagoreans seems to have been to prevent the eating of the ψυχή in its various abodes.[3] We have seen that Orpheus' head was honoured without the body and believed to contain what was immortal. On these points at least Orphics and Pythagoreans appear to be at one with Homer and the Olympianism with which they are usually contrasted. Exactly as in Homer we have ψυχή and κεφαλή interchanged in line and phrase, so we have two versions of the Pythagorean oath, identical except that one[4] begins 'By him who gave to our ψυχή the tetraktys' ([οὐ]μὰ τὸν ἁμετέρᾳ ψυχᾷ παραδόντα τετρακτύν) and the other[5] 'By him who gave to our head (κεφαλᾷ) the tetraktys'.

[1] They would make easier also the myth that the father of the crested lark was buried in its head (see Aristoph. Birds, 471 ff., with Schol. ad loc. and ad Theocr. vii, 23). Cf. the myth of the Phoenix (p. 207 below).

[2] See Plut. Quaest. Conviv. ii, 3, 1, p. 635; Hippolytus, Ref. Omn. Haer. i, ii, 14 f. (= Diels, Doxog. Gr. p. 557); Gellius, iv, 11, 9; Diog. Laert. viii, 34. For Empedocles (B 79 Diels) olives were 'eggs': οὕτω δ' ᾠοτοκεῖ μακρὰ δένδρεα πρῶτον ἐλαίας. The bean may have been singled out as containing ψυχή because it was believed that διεγείρει τὰ σώματα πρὸς συνουσίαν ἐσθιόμενος (Joan. Lyd. de Mens. iv, 42) and on account of its flatulence (see Porph. in Hor. Serm. ii, 6, 63). Cf. Hom. Hymn to Hermes, 295–303 (so perhaps Hesiod, W. and D. 759) with pp. 119 f. below.

[3] See p. 280 below and Rohde, Psyche[8], ch. x, note 54, ch. xi, notes 42 and 47; also see p. 105 above.

[4] See Plut. de Plac. Phil. Epit. i, 3, 18 (= Diels, Doxog. Gr. p. 282).

[5] See Stob. Ecl. i, 10, 12. Association of the head with generation would help to explain why in the Orphic Theogony bulls' heads were attached to the loins (λαγόνες) of Phanes = Eros, who contained the seeds of all life (Fr. 54 Kern).

The idea that the soul and seed of new life were in the head was, we may now suggest, helped by that assimilation of man to other[1] children of Mother Earth, more particularly to the corn,[2] which seems to lie behind the Eleusinian and other mysteries.[3] That assimilation appears in the stories that aforetime men grew out of the earth as 'sown ones' (σπαρτοί), etc.[4] In the Phrygian mysteries we know that the god was a 'sappy ear of corn reaped' (χλοερὸν στάχυν τεθερισμένον), and that was also the supreme revelation at Eleusis.[5] That in Phrygia the head of man was assimilated to the 'head' (ear) of corn appears in the story of Lityerses, who feasted strangers and made them reap with him, then reaping with his sickle 'the man-high corn' (τὸν ἀνδρομήκη πυρόν) rolled the stranger together with the sheaf and cut off his head (τὸν ξένον δὲ δράγματι/αὐτῷ κυλίσας κρατὸς ὀρφανὸν φέρει[6]). In

[1] Pausanias tells us that on the way to Eleusis was the shrine of 'Him of the Bean' (κυαμίτης) and, after doubtful talk about the sowing or discovering of beans, says: 'Whoever has already seen the rite at Eleusis or has conned the so-called Orphica knows what I mean' (I, 37, 4. Cf. VIII, 15, 4).

[2] Equation of brain to the contents of a corn-ear (cf. pp. 221 f.) will explain the German idiom, *er hat Grütze im Kopfe*, 'he has oats [peeled grain] in his head' = 'he is intelligent'. The grain is the seed. The lament of a Paiute Indian, after losing his son, runs:

'The corn-stalk comes to the ear again!
But I here,
I am the stalk that the seed-gatherers,
descrying empty afar, left standing.
Son, my son,
what is my life to me now you are departed?'

Trans. Mary Austin in *Anthology of World Poetry*, selected by M. Van Doren, p. 1156.

[3] See, e.g., p. 274, n. 2 *fin.*

[4] Cf. γηγενεῖς, αὐτόχθονες, e.g. αὐτόχθονες δ' ἔφυμεν.../εἰ δ' ἦν ἐν οἴκοις ἀντὶ θηλειῶν στάχυς ἄρσην (Eurip. Fr. 360, 8, 22, Nauck) or Θῆβαι...ἔνθ' ὁ γηγενὴς σπαρτῶν στάχυς ἔβλαστεν (Eurip. *Her. Fur.* 4 f.). In the *Politicus* (272 E, cf. 269 B) of Plato the ψυχαί are spoken of as seeds falling into the earth and in the *Timaeus* (42 D, cf. below, pp. 118 f.) as 'sown' into the earth and other worlds. Cf. pp. 230, n. 8, 269 ff., 285 ff. The same thought explains the winnowing-basket cradle, *liknon*.

[5] See Hippolytus, *Refut. omn. haer.* v, 9 (ed. Duncker and Schneidewin).

[6] Sosith. 2, 19 f. (*Trag. Gr. Fragm.* Nauck², p. 822); cf. *Mythogr. Westerm.* p. 346, 16, etc. The equation appears in the various versions of the

many districts in antiquity reapers cut off just the 'head' (the ear) and left the stalk. Two of the three methods described by Varro[1] involve this. So also we find it in ancient Egypt,[2] Israel,[3] and Gaul.[4] It was a custom once widely spread in England and elsewhere in Europe to treat the last sheaf as the corn spirit and cutting it to say that one is 'beheading' or 'cutting the neck' of the Boba, etc.[5] Homer speaks of men as 'corn-stalks' (καλάμη) and their slaying in battle as the mowing and falling of such,[6] or just says their 'heads fell'[7] (πῖπτε κάρηνα). The flower or fruit of a plant, i.e. what contained the seed, was called its 'head'. Thus Homer describes a warrior wounded: 'Even as in a garden a poppy droops aside its head (κάρη) being heavy with fruit and the moisture of spring, so bowed he aside his head (κάρη) laden with the helmet'[8] and, in the Homeric Hymn to Demeter, for her daughter 'the flower-faced maid' (καλυκώπιδι κούρῃ)

symbolic advice given by Thrasyboulos of Miletus (Herod. v, 92, 6; cf. Eurip. *Suppl.* 448 f.; Livy, I, 54) and Shakespeare's 'Go thou and like an executioner/Cut off the heads of too fast growing sprays' (*Richard II*, Act III, Sc. 4). It will help us also to understand δρέπων μὲν κορυφὰς ἀρετᾶν ἀπὸ πασᾶν, Pind. *Ol.* I, 13.

[1] See *de Re Rustica*, I, 50. Cf. Columella, *de Re Rustica*, II, 20 (21); Virgil, *Georg.* I, 317, etc. So Catullus' *praecerpens aristas* (LXIV, 353).

[2] See Wilkinson's *Ancient Egyptians*[3], IV, pp. 85 f., 95.

[3] See Job xxiv, 24.   [4] Palladius, VII, 2, 2 ff.

[5] See Frazer, *Spirits of the Corn, etc.* I, pp. 217–68. The goddess whose head and neck or head and shoulders are seen emerging from the ground on several vase paintings (see e.g. J. E. Harrison, *Prolegomena, etc.* pp. 277 ff.) perhaps belongs to this circle of thought. The smiting of her *head* there is now more intelligible as a stimulus to fertility (cf. the smiting of the head of Zeus to bring Athene to birth). The thoughts traced help to explain also why the corn mother, Demeter, was represented by a head at Pheneos in Arcadia (see Paus. VIII, 15) and why Praxidike, whom *Hymn. Orph.* xxix identifies with Persephone (the corn maiden, mistress of the buried ψυχαί or 'heads' of men) and who is an avenging spirit like an Ἐρινύς or angry ψυχή, was represented as just a head and the offerings to her were heads (see Hesych. Phot. Suid. *s.v.*). So perhaps the Γοργείη κεφαλή from Perseph. (*Od.* xi, 634 f.). In one legend Perseus cuts it off with a sickle. A chthonic Gorgon appears in art. Perseus (? 'Destroyer') who wore the helmet of Hades and covered his victim's head (p. 446, n. 4) was for the Etruscans *Pherse*. Did they connect *Phersu* (p. 429, n. 1)? Cf. Φερσεφόνη.

[6] See *Il.* xix, 221 ff., xi, 67 ff.   [7] See *Il.* xi, 158, 500.

[8] *Il.* viii, 306 ff. Cf. xiv, 499.

Earth produced a wondrous narcissus and from its root 'grew a hundred heads (ἑκατὸν κάρα ἐξεπεφύκει[1])', i.e. buds or flowers. The contribution of Alcmaeon of Croton can now be better appreciated. He is the earliest writer whose explicit teaching on these subjects is recorded. In the absence of facts here collected it has been assumed that he was the first to attach importance to the brain (ἐγκέφαλος). He held that it was the seat of the 'leading factor' in man. But thus far there may be little that is new.[2] He was, however, empiric in method and was reputed to have practised dissection. He held that the seed came from the brain; but against an existing view that it came exclusively thus from the 'marrow' he tried to show that the flesh, more particularly the fat, was also drawn upon.[3] But even this was not new.[4] He discovered 'passages' leading from the eyes to the ἐγκέφαλος and urged that the latter received the perceptions of sight, sound, and smell, and was the seat of thought.[5] This is a very real advance. Whether Orphic and Pythagorean belief, by assigning a richer existence (more particularly after death) to the ψυχή that resides in the head and by a doctrine of retribution naturally tending[6] to the identification of the party punished after death (what survives, the ψυχή) with the party responsible for good or bad deeds in life (the conscious agent), gave him an even better lead[7] in this direction, we cannot tell; but a very important

---

[1] Lines 8 ff. Cf. our own folk-song: 'I will give my love an apple without e'er a core....My head is the apple without e'er a core'.

[2] ἐν τῷ ἐγκεφάλῳ εἶναι τὸ ἡγεμονικόν (Aet. iv, 17, 1 = A 8, Diels). What original expression the Stoic term τὸ ἡγεμονικόν covers we cannot tell.

[3] A 13.   [4] See below, pp. 177f., 187 ff., etc.   [5] A 5, 8, 10, 11.

[6] See e.g. Pind. Ol. II, 68 ff. cited again below and, for the general principle δράσαντι παθεῖν, Aesch. Choeph. 313 and Ag. 1562 ff., etc.

[7] Cf. also Heraclitus' ἦθος ἀνθρώπῳ δαίμων (B 119) with p.118 and p.405, n. 8. Professor A. E. Taylor in his learned commentary upon the Timaeus (pp. 519 f.) argues that the central importance of the brain was suggested to Alcmaeon by Anaximenes' doctrine that ἀήρ is τὸ θεῖον (which he had met, it is urged, through Pythagoreanism) and by the belief that the brain contained ἀήρ; but no evidence is adduced for the latter belief earlier than the Hippocratic writers and Diogenes of Apollonia, who are later than Alcmaeon himself. In fact, the ψυχή conceived of as gaseous and located in the head by popular belief as early as Homer suffices to have suggested these views to Anaximenes (see p. 252, cf. 32), Alcmaeon, Diogenes (see p. 117), etc.

change can now be traced. The ψυχή gradually ceases to be merely the life or life-soul which it was in Homer and Hesiod, etc., and begins to be conceived of and spoken of as concerned in perception, thought, and feeling, which had formerly passed as the work of θυμός, φρένες, and κῆρ in the chest. In it as a single entity, 'life' and consciousness, which had formerly been divided, centred in head and chest respectively in ψυχή and θυμός, are now united.

The transition can be traced in literature. We have seen that, with Homer and the intervening writers, Pindar often refers to the θυμός and the organs of the chest as concerned in feeling and thought, and we have cited[1] his statement that 'the body of all men is subject to most mighty Death but there is left still alive αἰῶνος εἴδωλον. For it alone is divine 'lit. "from the gods"). And it sleeps when the limbs are active', which is the conception of ψυχή = εἴδωλον seen in Homer. Pindar himself elsewhere uses ψυχή of that which survives death and passes to the realm of Hades,[2] that which is the 'life' of the living.[3] Like Homer, too, he speaks of the 'head' as the seat of honour[4] and of life.[5] But, unlike Homer, he also speaks of the ψυχή as concerned in the feelings of ordinary waking life, which is perhaps why he does not use that name in referring as above to the older conception of a soul explicitly not so concerned. If he still thought of the head as pre-eminently the seat of the ψυχή but thought of the ψυχή as feeling and active in waking life,[6] e.g. 'Bring to mind in what (οἵαις) battles he stood fast with daring ψυχή (τλάμονι ψυχᾷ παρέμεινε)',[7] we can better understand why he thus speaks of the nymph Cyrene wrestling with a lion, 'admire what a contest she is waging with unfearing head (οἷον ἀταρβεῖ νεῖκος ἄγει κεφαλᾷ), girl with a spirit (ἦτορ) that does not yield to toil'.[8] This in the past has been emended with

[1] P. 102.   [2] See e.g. Pyth. iv, 159; Isth. i, 68; Fr. 133 (98) 3 (Schr.).
[3] E.g. Pyth. iii, 101; Ol. viii, 39.
[4] Ol. vi, 60, vii, 67.   [5] Pyth. ix, 80 f.
[6] See Ol. ii, 70; Pyth. i, 48, iii, 41; Nem. ix, 32; Isth. iv, 53. Both uses occur in Aeschylus. Cf. e.g. Pers. 630; Ag. 965 with ἀπὸ ψυχῆς κακῆς, Ag. 1643.
[7] Pyth. i, 48.   [8] Pyth. ix, 31 f.

κραδίᾳ ('heart', Schneidewin) for κεφαλᾷ or explained[1] unconsciously in terms of our own psychology or as referring merely to outward appearance. Pindar's only other instance of ἀταρβής is ἀταρβεῖ φρενί,[2] in harmony with the old psychology, and the passage discussed is followed immediately by 'and her φρένες are not storm-tossed with dread (φόβῳ)'.[3] Transition in the opposite direction may be seen in the second Olympian: 'Of the dead here forthwith the feckless φρένες pay the penalty',[4] the φρένες being the responsible organs of consciousness in life; but for Homer[5] they were lacking in the surviving soul, the ψυχή or 'head'. The confusion of the new and the old conceptions may also be illustrated by the relatively late Homeric Hymn to Ares (VIII):

> ὥς κε δυναίμην
> σεύασθαι κακότητα πικρὴν ἀπ' ἐμοῖο καρήνου
> καὶ ψυχῆς ἀπατηλὸν ὑπογνάμψαι φρεσὶν ὁρμὴν
> θυμοῦ τ' αὖ μένος ὀξὺ κατισχέμεν ὅς μ' ἐρέθῃσι.... [6]

The transition and the blending may be illustrated among philosophers by Diogenes of Apollonia, who appears to have identified the ψυχή with the conscious element, air, and to have placed its controlling part in the chest[7] but to have explained seeing, hearing, and smelling as affecting more immediately the air in or around the brain.[8] The great dispute between subsequent thinkers[9] as to whether the head or the chest is the seat of the ruling part follows this breakdown of the original duality ψυχή and θυμός, and their fusion in a more complex ψυχή.[10]

---

[1] Gildersleeve says 'A steady head is a compliment as well as ἀταρβεῖ κραδίᾳ, which Schneidewin reads. Note the serenity of the heads of combatants in Greek plastic art'. But 'a steady head' (cf. 'Der Mensch verliert aus Angst...den Kopf oder lässt ihn hängen...ein klarer Kopf', Schroeder) is an expression resting upon our present views of the brain and ignores the fact that before Pindar's time, and indeed after it, Greeks did not speak of the head as the seat of emotions.

[2] Pyth. v, 51. [3] See p. 55. [4] Lines 57f. [5] See pp. 59 ff. [6] Lines 12 ff.
[7] See above, p. 32. [8] A 19, 21, B 5 (Diels).

[9] E.g. Plato favoured the head, Aristotle the heart, and Epicurus the chest, while the Stoics were divided.

[10] How little the course of this development has been recognised appears in the statement of Dr W. D. Ross in his presidential address to the

Nevertheless, the old ideas about the ψυχή can be seen to persist. Probably attached to Pythagorean tradition, Hippo of Samos or Magna Graecia in the fifth century found the ἀρχή in moisture[1] (τὸ ὑγρόν) and said that the ψυχή was the ἐγκέφαλος[2] (or brain and fluid in the head), in substance 'water',[3] according to one account 'generative water'[4] (ὕδωρ γονοποιόν), and referred it explicitly to the 'seed' which flowed, as he thought, from the marrow.[5] It is important to note that the same name, 'marrow', μυελός, was applied to the brain and its fluid,[6] which are merely a continuation of the spinal 'marrow' and inevitably considered one with it. For Leucippus also, the 'seed' was ψυχῆς ἀπόσπασμα,[7] and for Democritus the ψυχή was bound and rooted in the marrow.[8] That such a view was not mere philosophic doctrine is suggested by the Nurse's remark in the *Hippolytus*[9] of Euripides, that mortals should mingle their affections in moderation and 'not to the limits of the marrow of the ψυχή' (πρὸς ἄκρον μυελὸν ψυχῆς). But the best testimony to the survival in essentials of the racial scheme discovered in Homer is to be found in the *Timaeus* of Plato, which should probably be grouped under the Pythagorean tradition. The head is what really matters, the body is added merely to carry it.[10] The head is the divinest and dominant[11] part and is

Classical Association: 'It seems to me highly probable that as Professors Burnet and Taylor have mentioned, Socrates was the first person who brought into Greek thought the notion of the soul not as a pale ghost-like entity associated especially with dreams and with death, but as the whole spiritual part of our being' ('The Problem of Socrates', *Proceedings of the Classical Association*, 1933, p. 23).

[1] See A 4 and 6 (Diels).   [2] A 3.
[3] A 3 and 10.   [4] A 10.   [5] A 3 and 12.
[6] See Soph. *Trach.* 781 with *Il.* xx, 482, etc.
[7] Leucippus, A 35 (Diels).
[8] B 1 (Diels). This perhaps refers to the nerves that are joined to the spinal cord. These may have been observed long before and have contributed to the idea of the ψυχή.
[9] 255. So also perhaps τὴν ψυχὴν ἐκπίνουσιν (Aristoph. *Cl.* 712). For love in the marrow cf. Archil. *Fr.* 84 Bgk. πεπαρμένος δι' ὀστέων, Theocritus xxx, 21 τῷ δ' ὁ πόθος καὶ τὸν ἔσω μυελὸν ἐσθίει.
[10] 44 D.   [11] *Ibid.*

inhabited (οἰκεῖν) by ψυχή, that is a δαίμων,[1] and survives death.[2] For the mortal part of the soul (ψυχή), we are told that that which partakes of courage and θυμός resides in the chest above the diaphragm (i.e. where the lungs and heart are) and the baser or appetitive part between the diaphragm and the navel,[3] which region, as we have seen,[4] also had its own significance earlier. But this extension of the term ψυχή, to correspond with the θυμός, etc., of Homer, is presently ignored and its original limitations suggested; for it is planted and fastened, we are told—not in the organs of thorax and abdomen but—in the marrow, the divine part in the marrow of the head called the ἐγκέφαλος.[5] In this fastening life (βίος) is involved.[6] The ψυχή is itself 'seed'[7] (σπέρμα), or rather is in the 'seed',[8] and this 'seed' is enclosed in the skull and spine,[9] and explicitly identified with the marrow[10] or, as it is once called, 'generative marrow'[11] (γόνιμος μυελός) and flows thence in the propagation of a new life.[12] It breathes through the genital organ.[13] This appears to be original popular belief. Aeschylus speaks three times of Io as rendered pregnant by the ἐπίπνοια of Zeus.[14] That the seed was itself breath or had

---

[1] 90 A. Cf. Ξενοκράτης φησὶν εὐδαίμονα εἶναι τὸν τὴν ψυχὴν ἔχοντα σπουδαίαν· ταύτην γὰρ ἑκάστῳ εἶναι δαίμονα (Aristot. *Top.* II, 6, 112 a 32) and the ψυχὴ οἰκητήριον δαίμονος of Democritus (B 171, Diels), who also (B 1), exactly as does Timaeus (73 B), speaks of the ψυχή as 'bound' and 'rooted' in the marrow. Timaeus later varies the image with 'anchors' (73 D) and 'cables' (85 E) to suit the 'stream' (cf. 43 A ff.).   [2] 69 C.

[3] 69 C ff. θυμός has been narrowed down to a sense of 'spirit' appearing in anger and courage. Cf. 'pluck' (p. 69). It is interesting to note that the head, in which normally no physical change is felt accompanying changes of consciousness (contrast the chest, pp. 49 ff.), was in the original belief the seat of an entity not concerned in consciousness, consciousness then being emotional (see pp. 3, 14 ff.). Its calmness now becomes the seat of the dispassionate intelligence, which has been distinguished and separated from the emotional and appetitive elements.

[4] See pp. 84 ff.   [5] 73 B ff.; cf. 85 E.
[6] *Ibid.*   [7] 73 C.
[8] Cf. 91 A f. [9] 73 f. [10] 91 A f. [11] 77 D. [12] 86 B ff. and 91. [13] 91 B.
[14] *Suppl.* 17, 44, 577. Aeschylus does not use the word elsewhere except in a somewhat doubtful text (1043), where it appears to refer to mortal husbands. To this conception may also belong εἰσπνεῖν, εἰσπνήλας, and ἀΐτας (cf. ἀΐω), which Bethe (*Rhein. Mus.* LXII, 1907, pp. 460 ff.), without the evidence here cited, has referred to physical inter-

breath (πνεῦμα) and that procreation itself was such a breathing or blowing is very explicit in Aristotle.[1] For the Stoics also the seed was πνεῦμα.[2] Procreation and sneezing[3] appear to be the distinctive manifestations of the ψυχή. Here then, strange as it may seem, must be sought the origin of the name, if its nearest kin be ψύχειν, 'to blow'.[4] This may also explain why the τριτοπάτορες, recognised as ancestral ψυχαί and still active agents of generation, were conceived to be winds (ἄνεμοι),[5] and how the 'Orphic' world-egg could be thought to be begotten by a wind (ὑπηνέμιον ὠιόν).[6] That the ψυχή was not the breath-soul proper, the breath in the lungs, to which all manifestations of the conscious self belonged, we have shown.

course. Cf. also ζάει, which Hesych. explains by πνεῖ (? δι-άει) but records the sense βινεῖ. Boisacq and Liddell and Scott (ed. 9) resort to βία!

[1] See e.g. *Hist. Anim.* 586 a, 15 f.; *de Gen. Anim.* 728 a, 9 f., 736 b, 33 ff. with *Problemata*, 879 b, 1 ff., 880 a, 30. This thought was, indeed, English; see 'blow', 'blow-through', 'blower', in, e.g., Partridge, *Dict. of Slang*. Cf. 'blow' of flies, etc.

[2] See Plut. *de Plac. Epit.* IV, 21, 2 (*Dox. Gr.* p. 410).

[3] See pp. 103 ff. and the emphasis in the names *genius*, *anima* (pp. 127–173).

[4] This appears to be the original meaning whence 'cool' could easily be derived (cf. 'Save your breath to cool your porridge') but not the converse. If ψυχή did originally connote something 'cold' (cf. p. 95), beliefs about the pale cerebro-spinal marrow to which it appears to have been related, as θυμός was to blood, might help. In later times while blood was associated with heat or fire, the brain was regarded as the 'coldest (ψυχρότατον) of the parts of the body', the very 'metropolis of the cold and the viscous' (see Aristotle, *de Part. Anim.* 652 a, 28; cf. 444 a, 9, 457 b, 30, 495 a, 6, etc., and the Hippocratic περὶ ἀρχῶν or σαρκῶν, I, 427). For Pliny, *N.H.* XI, 37, 133, the brain was *omnium viscerum frigidissimum*. For the belief that it burned on critical occasions see pp. 147 ff.

[5] See Demon and Phanodemos quoted by Photius and Suidas, s.v. τριτοπάτορες. Cf. the souls (pp. 154 ff.) of the dead = winds in the northern 'Wild Hunt'.

[6] Aristoph. *Birds*, 695. Cf. Varro, *de Re Rust.* II, 1, 19 (hens and horses), Cat. LXIV, 282, Lucr. I, 11, etc. For the world-egg in relation to ψυχή = πνεῦμα, see pp. 249 ff. See also p. 112, n. 2. The belief about horses might derive from an imagining of the winds as horses (*Il.* XVI, 149 f., XX, 223 ff.), but Virgil in *Georg.* III, 273 ff. and Varro cited by Servius *ad loc.* imply conception from the wind through the mouth (cf. p. 233, n. 5).

Thus the ancient view persisted. Against this harmony we have fragments of knowledge that in the latter half of the fifth century Hippocrates and Democritus held that the seed was drawn from the whole body;[1] but the writer of the more complete Hippocratic περὶ γονῆς, while maintaining this,[2] also makes it plain that it gathers to the spinal marrow[3] and that most of it flows from the head;[4] and Democritus, we saw, regarded the marrow as the stronghold of the ψυχή. For him, too, the δύναμις of the seed was πνευματική.[5] Diogenes of Apollonia, explaining the word ἀφροδίσια, urged that seed was foam (ἀφρός) of the blood[6] 'of the nature of breath' (πνευματῶδες[7]). This is evidently derived from Hesiod's story[8] of the birth of Aphrodite from the foam not of blood but of the severed μήδεα of Ouranos. Blood itself was not ignored in the original belief. The new-born child obviously owes its blood to its parents and, from the relation[9] of blood to θυμός and the conscious self, noble or ignoble, the continuity was important. Thus, after telling of the greatness of his ancestors, Glaukos says: 'Of this generation and blood do I claim to be'.[10] And Odysseus spurs Telemachos to act wisely and faithfully, saying: 'If you are really mine and of our blood, let no one hear that Odysseus is in the house'.[11] The later Pythagorean already quoted[12] taught that 'the seed is a drop of the brain containing in itself warm vapour (ἀτμός)', which vapour becomes the ψυχή and αἴσθησις (i.e. virtually what had been θυμός) in the new creature.[13] The persistence

[1] Democr. A 141, B 124 (Diels). [2] I, 371 and 374 (Kühn).
[3] 372. [4] 373. [5] A 140 (Diels).
[6] A 24 (Diels). [7] B 6. [8] *Theog.* 188 ff.
[9] See p. 48 (αἵματος εἰς ἀγαθοῖο, etc.). Cf. Eurip. *Heraclid.* 539 ff.
[10] *Il.* VI, 211; cf. XX, 241.
[11] *Od.* XVI, 300 f. Thus Zeus promises lordship to one of the race of men 'who are from me in blood' (οἵ θ' αἵματος ἐξ ἐμεῦ εἰσί), *Il.* XIX, 105; cf. III and *Od.* VIII, 533. [12] P. 76.
[13] See Diels, *Fragm. d. Vors.*[4] I, p. xliii (Nachträge). The ἀρχή of the ψυχή extends from the heart to the brain. There are some strange features: the φρένες, presumably as identified with intelligence or reason, are transferred to the head and denied to lower animals, while the θυμός is placed in the heart. Cf. the variations of 'Philolaos' (Fr. 13, Diels).

of the association of the ψυχή with the head may be illustrated by the story of Timarchos, who, according to Plutarch,[1] after Socrates' death descended into the cave of Trophonios and lying there it seemed to him 'that his head was struck and at the same time there came a great noise and the sutures of his head parted and allowed the ψυχή to issue forth'.

We can now, perhaps, explain the strange form of Hermes from prehistoric times (e.g. Herodot. II, 51), a squared pillar, having just a head at the top and genital organs, phallus erect, in the middle; also why a similar pillar or stele was often set up over a grave ,to represent the dead,[2] i.e. what survived death, the ψυχή (cf. pp. 135 f., 496 f.). We have seen that the generative power was thought to be in the head and to be the ψυχή. Head and genital organs are its outward essentials. Hermes was the generative power in the world at large, as it were the universal fertilising ψυχή (cf. the individual *iuno* and *Iuno*, pp. 143, 501), so giver of increase, wealth. At his home, Kyllene (e.g. *Od.* XXIV, 1), he was in historic times worshipped in the form of an erect phallus (e.g. Paus. VI, 26, 5). He is thus naturally ψυχοπομπός (cf. p. 252, n. 11), responsible for the bringing of ψυχαί into this world and the taking of them hence to the underworld with his 'golden branch' or 'rod', the life-power,[3] διάκτορος, 'he who brings through'—like διάκτωρ or ἄκτωρ best related to ἄγω—and so the divine messenger or herald, and the god of travellers. Other aspects of the ψυχή are discussed below.

---

[1] *De Genio Socr.* XXII=590 B.

[2] See Cic. *de Leg.* II, 26, 65; Babr. 30; *Epigr. Gr.*, ed. Kaibel, 108; and Pfuhl in *Jahrb. d. kais. deutsch. Arch. Inst.* XX (1905), pp. 76 ff.

[3] See p. 456, n. 2. The union of the two serpents round the wand might for the Greeks represent the life-power complete by the union of male ψυχή and female ψυχή. They were believed to appear as serpents (pp. 206 f.). Cf. the union in Hermaphroditos.

CHAPTER II

The *Genius, Numen,* etc.

We have seen the parallelism between the Roman conception of *cor, praecordia,* etc., and the Greek conception of κῆρ, φρένες, etc. For both peoples the seat of consciousness was in the chest. What was the Roman view of the head, *caput,* whose importance appears so strikingly in legal and other phrases? It has been generally recognised—indeed is obvious—that it was used as loosely equivalent to 'life'. Why has not been explained. The figure *pars pro toto* and the fatal results of decapitation have perhaps sufficed. I suggest, what does not appear to have been suspected, that it was thought to contain the seed, the very stuff of life, and the life-soul associated with it. This seems to be the explanation of the early phrase, *caput limare cum aliqua* (or *aliquo*), 'to diminish (lit. "file away", cf. *molere, terere*) one's head with someone', which has been taken to mean 'to kiss'. One might speak of 'snatching kisses from' someone but it would be strange to speak of kissing as 'filing away one's head' with the help of somebody. It is not a jest but an indirect way of referring to some quite important act. Thus a character in a tragedy of Livius Andronicus says: 'Believe it that she never with my will diminished her head with him'.[1] In comedy it seems to be used of courtesans or the like: 'This I demand of you that you never hereafter diminish your head with my son';[2] 'For your father has never up to the present diminished his head with her';[3] 'I was afraid lest in love (*amoris causa*) you had diminished your head with her'.[4] Finally, beyond these fragments we have a clear context. A girl, who has been bought by a young man after being lent to him without ceremony or previous acquaintance, says after two years in his possession: 'It is two years now since he began

---

[1] 28 (Ribbeck).
[2] Caecil. Stat. 140.
[3] Plaut. Fr. 112 (Lindsay).
[4] Sex. Turp. 112.

his liaison with me (*rem habere mecum*) and we swore between ourselves, I to him and he to me, that neither of us would diminish his or her head in debauch (*stupri causa*), I with a man except with him or he with a woman except with me', to which her new owner replies: 'Good heavens! Is he not to lie even with his wife?' (*di inmortales! etiam cum uxore non cubet?*[1]). Thus also we can better understand another[2] passage in Plautus and hitherto mysterious expressions, e.g. Catullus' 'plot against my head', *nostrum insidiis caput lacessas,*[3] i.e. 'attempt to win the favours of my love'; Juvenal's *capitis matrona pudici,*[4] Festus' *progenies quae ab uno capite procedit* (s.v. *procapis*) or Propertius (to Pecunia): 'the seeds of trouble come from your head', *semina curarum de capite orta tuo.*[5] The use of *caput,* τὸ κεφάλαιον (our 'capital'), for money which produces interest can now be seen to arise from this thought; 'interest', what the 'head' produces, was τόκος, 'offspring', *fenus* which the Romans rightly (*fe-nus* as *pig-nus* (p. 375, n. 7), *facinus,* etc., see p. 182) thought to have the same origin: *dictum a fetu et quasi a fetura quadam pecuniae parientis et increscentis.*[6] That the

[1] See Plaut. *Merc.* 100 ff., 533 ff. Cf. *Bacch.* 14 f. So we can explain the emphasis on union of heads (Tib. I, 5, 8; Prop. II, 14, 22; Ov. *Her.* III, 107; Petron. 22). [2] *Bacch.* 1191 ff. on pp. 198 f.

[3] XV, 16 (where *nostrum caput* has been not very appropriately explained e.g. by Robinson Ellis: "'me' with the further notion of something virtually affecting my life and fortunes').

[4] VI, 49. The idea that the head was directly affected by sexual intercourse will explain the ridiculed belief of Catullus (LXIV, 377 f.) and the recently surviving Italian belief (quoted by Robinson Ellis, *ad loc.*) that the virginity of youth or maid, when it had been in danger, could be tested by measuring the neck and head for growth of the latter. Cf. *gravida cervice* on p. 111, n. 4; also Petron. 131 (binding the neck to restore the impotent).

[5] III (IV), 7, 4. For birth direct from the head, not just as ultimate source, Terence uses not *de* but *ex capite: si ex capite sis meo natus item ut aiunt Minervam esse ex Iove* (*Heaut.* 1035 f. Cf. pp. 111 f.).

[6] Varro (Fr. 57) quoted by Gellius, XVI, 12. We may perhaps relate *semina quae magno faenore reddat ager* (Tib. II, 6, 22), also *fenum* (*quotannis novum parit,* Fest.). The custom of making money-boxes in the form of the female breast and other shapes of fruitfulness (see e.g. the collection in the Basel Museum) seems to derive from the same thought. So, I suggest, the Babylonian *birku,* 'knee', for money-box (cf. p. 176). For them the head (*rêšu, qaqqadu*) had similar value (cf. p. 234, n. 6) and was 'capital'.

head was believed by the early Romans to contain, to be the source of, the seed will also explain, as nothing else can, why in the vegetable kingdom not only the blossom or fruit containing the seed but also, in old Latin, that from which a plant sprung, its root, was called *caput*,[1] and why in nature at large, from Plautus onwards, the source[2] of a stream was called its 'head', e.g.

> *Nile pater, quanam possim te dicere causa*
> *aut quibus in terris occuluisse caput?*[3]

Aristaeus, son of Apollo, *ad extremi sacrum caput adstitit amnis...* *Penei genitoris ad undam* (*Georg.* IV, 319, 355). Cf. the definition of the Digest: *caput est unde aqua nascitur.*[4]

Now also the Roman name for the contents of the head, the brain, *cerebrum*, can be better understood. It has been vaguely connected with κάρα, etc., with a suggested basic meaning, 'the topmost part of the body';[5] but, as may now[6] be seen, the obvious Latin cognate is the old verb *cereo*, more familiar as *creo*, 'I beget, engender'. This helps to explain Ennius, *cere comminuit brum*. Cf. *deluo, delubrum*; *lavo, lavabrum*; *voluto, volutabrum*, and for *cerebellum*: *flo, flabrum, flabellum*, etc. We may compare also *Ceres*, the name of the goddess of fertility identified particularly with the seed in the 'head' of the corn-stalk,[7] and the masculine *Cerus* (with various Italic by-forms[8]) meaning 'engenderer'. *In carmine Saliari cerus manus intellegitur creator*

---

[1] E.g. Cato, *de agri cult.* 33, Virgil, *Georg.* II, 355. Cf. Macrob. I, 7, 34 f.

[2] Only later (in Caesar, etc.) is *caput* used of the *os*, 'mouth', i.e. 'entrance', quite a different thought.

[3] Tibullus, I, 7, 23 ff.

[4] XLIII, 20. See also below, pp. 231 f.

[5] See Walde-Hoffmann, also Ernout and Meillet, s.v., and against, p. 238 below.

[6] Further evidence appears on pp. 148 ff. and 238 ff.

[7] Cf. pp. 112 ff., 471, n. 3 and *prima Ceres docuit turgescere semen in agris,/ falce coloratas subsecuitque comas...deciderant longae spicea serta comae*, Ovid, *Am.* III, 10, 11–36, etc.

[8] See Wordsworth, *Fragments and Specimens of Early Latin*, pp. 405 and 163; and for the connection of *cerebrum* with *cerus* see also pp. 148 ff. below.

bonus.[1] A garland for the head, formed of corn-ears or 'heads', was the distinctive offering to Ceres.[2]

If, moreover, the head contained the seed, the principle of fertility, several other ancient Roman customs can be better understood. In the ceremony of the 'October Horse', which is recognised as a 'therio-morphic corn deity',[3] the sacrifice was said to be on account of corn fertility, and so bread (i.e. seed from heads of corn) was attached to the head[4] and the latter was fought for[5] with the utmost fierceness by the men from two districts of the city in order that it might be set up in the victors' territory. Thus, too, we can explain Virgil's account of the founding of Carthage when the wanderers dug up an omen which Juno had shown:

> *caput acris equi; sic nam fore bello*
> *egregiam et facilem victu per saecula gentem,*[6]

'the head of a spirited horse, for by this sign it was shown that the race would be distinguished in war and abound with the means of life'. Virgil shows in III, 537 ff. that the finding of a horse signified war. It is therefore the *head* which is the sign

---

[1] Festus, s.v. *Matrem Matutam* (p. 109 Lindsay, Teubner).

[2] See Tibullus, I, I, 15 f., II, I, 4; Ovid, *Met.* X, 433; Horace, *Carm. Saec.* 30, etc. The heads of the Arval brothers were wreathed with corn-ears (see Pliny, *N.H.* XVIII, 2, 6; Gellius, VII, 7, 8; *C.I.L.* I, 28, 8). The thoughts here traced will also explain the *modius* or corn-measure head-dress. See also p. 133, n. 1.

[3] See Sir James Frazer's *G.B.*[3] VIII, p. 43, and Professor H. J. Rose on Plut. *Rom. Quest.* XCVII. It appears in fact to be an embodiment of Mars (pp. 142, n. 3, 470 f. *inf.*), on whose field and in whose honour the ceremony took place. In 46 B.C. human heads seem to have been treated thus (Dio Cassius, XLIII, 24, 4). The tail at the other end of the spinal marrow and associated with fertility by its hair (see pp. 130 f., 231 ff.) was also important. It consists largely of fat, the significance attached to which appears below (pp. 177, n. 9, 188 ff.). The tail-end of the spine was the 'holy bone' for the Greeks (see pp. 208 ff.) and, as it were, the seed that grew into a new body according to Jews and Mohammedans (see pp. 287 f.). Such thoughts will explain why special value was attached to the tail of the October Horse, and to the liquid from it. See also p. 472.

[4] See Festus, s.v. *panibus redimibant caput equi idibus Octobribus in campo Martis quia id sacrificium fiebat ob frugum eventum* (p. 246). Cf. pp. 226, n. 5; 240, n. 7 *infra.*

[5] So the head of the boar fertility god in the north (pp. 154 f. below).

[6] *Aen.* I, 444 f. For *facilem victu,* cf. *Georg.* II, 460.

of abundance. In the past it has been suggested that 'the horse may be a symbol of plenty either as an appendage of wealth or because a war-horse is high-fed' (Conington). Palladius tells the farmer to set up the skull of a horse or ass *sed non virginis* on his land; *creduntur enim sua praesentia fecundare quae spectant.*[1] The same idea about the head seems to prompt the custom of hanging *oscilla* on trees, imaged heads of the god of fertility particularly associated with the vine, Liber equated to Dionysus-Bacchus. Of hanging such Virgil says: 'Therefrom all the vineyard becomes fertile (*pubescit*) with plenteous progeny (*fetu*) and the valleys teem (*complentur*) and the deep glades and wheresoever the god has turned his noble head[2] (*caput honestum*)'. 'Probus', commenting on Virgil,[3] tells us that *oscilla* were also hung up when seed was being sown.

Now, too, perhaps we can understand the *genius* (feminine *iuno*), obviously some kind of spirit in relation to man, but hitherto very differently interpreted. Thus for Birt the *genius* was originally the generative principle in a man, but 'the content of the personal *genius* had early been enriched and all the governing, determining instincts in the man, his instinct for happiness generally, were included and comprehended in the *genius*: it was the personality, the character projected out of the man and made into a god...above all the *genius* is the instinct for enjoyment and natural optimism in the man generally. He who yields to this instinct *indulget genio*'[4] For Wissowa it is 'the divine embodiment of the generative power active in the man and looking to the continuation of the family. This significance is then enlarged, inasmuch as the *genius* remotely mirrors and represents the total strength, energy,

[1] 1, 35, 16. See also Colum. x, 344 f., with pp. 144 f., 226, n. 5, and 245. The thought traced may explain the relation of horse's or ass's seed to head in Plin. *N. H.* xxviii, 11, 181.

[2] *Georg.* ii, 388 ff. The Dyaks appear to have hunted heads in the belief that they were supremely sources of fertility (see Spencer St John, *Life in the Forests of the Far East*, i, p. 204). Cf. also p. 100, n. 3 above.

[3] On *Georg.* ii, 385.

[4] S.v. *genius* in Roscher, *Lexicon d. gr. u. röm. Myth.*

capacity for enjoyment, in a word, the whole personality of the
man, his higher and inner nature....It dies with him.'[1] But
in opposition to this and to Birt's view we shall see later[2] that
the personality of a man, his capacity for enjoyment, etc., are
matters of the conscious self which the *genius* does not mirror
or represent. For Otto, it does not dwell in a man but is thought
of as 'his companion'; it has nothing to do with death and is
the counterpart of the Homeric θυμός.[3] But the θυμός is not
external, a companion, and such could scarcely be active in
procreation, which was undoubtedly the function of the *genius*.
Professor Rose has surveyed and criticised the existing interpretations and himself urges that 'the *genius* is the life, or
reproductive power, almost the luck, of the family, appearing
as is usual with Roman manifestations of *mana* in a masculine
and a feminine form, naturally appropriated to the male and
female heads of the house....The *genius* then is one, and one
only, for each family, and probably originally only one for each
gens.'[4] The *genius* and *iuno* 'were spirits belonging to no
individual alive or dead but to the clan'.[5] The *genius* was, he
thinks, transmitted by the *pater familias* at death to the succeeding male and the *iuno* by the *mater familias* to the succeeding
female in the known custom of receiving the last breath.[6] To
this view also there are objections. If procreation was explained by the idea of the *genius*, yet sons and slaves beget
children while the *pater familias* lives, the 'embodying' of the
genius in the latter must have been very loosely conceived.
For the theory that the receiving of the last breath was the
receiving of the *genius* from the dying *pater familias* by his
son it is unfortunate that the clearest and earliest evidence[7]
represents mothers receiving the last breath of their sons.

[1] *Religion u. Kultus der Römer*², pp. 175 f.   [2] Pp. 224 f.
[3] W. F. Otto, *Die Manen u.s.w.* 1923, pp. 59 ff.
[4] 'On the original Significance of the *Genius*', *Class. Quart.* XVII, 1923,
pp. 59 f. Cf. *Primitive Culture in Italy*, pp. 149 ff.
[5] 'Ancient Italian Beliefs concerning the Soul', *Class. Quart.* XXIV, 1930,
p. 135.
[6] *Class. Quart.* XVII, pp. 59 f.; *Primitive Culture in Italy*, p. 152.
[7] Cic. *In Verrem, Act.* II, v, 45, 118. Cf. Virgil, *Aen.* IV, 684; Ovid, *Met.*
VII, 861; *Consol. ad Liv. Aug.* 97; Seneca, *Cons. ad Marc.* 3; Statius, *Silv.* V,
1, 195 f. etc.

Further, that the *genius* of the *pater familias* was worshipped in family cult is not evidence that no other member of the household possessed a *genius*. We should expect the *genius* of the *pater familias* to be honoured in this way. Finally, in fact our earliest evidence shows that even a slave had his personal *genius*.[1]

We have seen[2] and shall see[3] that the Roman conception of the conscious self was virtually identical with that of the Greeks. It has a slightly different emphasis in surviving literature, but the *genius* was, I suggest, in origin the Roman analogue to the ψυχή as here explained, the life-spirit active in procreation, dissociated from and external to the conscious self that is centred in the chest. This will explain many facts not hitherto accounted for. The *genius* was believed to assume the form of a snake,[4] as was the ψυχή.[5] The ψυχή was believed to be in the head. We have seen that for the Romans the head was the source of the seed and concerned in procreation. The name (cf. *gigno, genus*, etc.) and the association with the *lectus genialis* show that procreation was the concern of the *genius*, which therefore should be particularly associated with the head. But there happens to be preserved for us the information that the forehead was considered sacred to the *genius* and it was usual for a Roman when honouring his *genius* to put his hand to his forehead.[6] It was a habit of the race, a habit most evident in ritual acts, to touch whatever was in question[7] (see e.g. legal and other uses of *manus*). There is perhaps also

---

[1] E.g. Plaut. *Pers.* 263.   [2] Pp. 40 ff., 61 ff. etc.   [3] Pp. 168 ff.

[4] See p. 159, n. 2 and Otto in Pauly-Wiss.-Kr. s.v. *genius* (1162).

[5] See pp. 206 f. For the ψυχή as holy or divine see pp. 97, 102 ff., 108 f., 405, n. 8.

[6] See Servius *ad Aen.* III, 607; *Ecl.* VI, 3. Cf. below, p. 146, the rubbing and p. 184, the striking of the forehead. So too it was, I suggest, that a woman's brows belonged to *Iuno* (? her *iuno*) (Varro, *L.L.* V, 69, Fest. p. 396). Cf. pp. 127, 143.

[7] This explains *Aen.* VIII, 69 f. and the touching of the ear of him one asks to witness a summons (Plaut. *Pers.* 747 ff.; Horace, *Sat.* 1, 9, 75 ff.; Pliny, *N.H.* XI, 45, 103). Cf. Sen. *Apoc.* 9. The importance of touching is constantly apparent, e.g. Juv. XIV, 219 or Plautus' *Rudens* (333 ff.): Gripus administers an oath to Labrax thus: *Tange aram hanc Veneris.* La. *Tango.* Gr. *Per Venerem hanc iurandum est tibi.* He dictates the formula *tum ego huic Gripo, inquito et me tangito.* Cf. pp. 132 f., 183 f.

reference to the association of the *genius* with the head when
Horace says that there is a *genius*, a god 'for every head, a god
changeful of countenance (*in unum quodque caput, voltu muta-
bilis*[1])'. Belief that the *genius* is in the head will also explain
why the hair, which as we shall see[2] was naturally related
to the generative life-soul and the life-substance, is for
Apuleius *genialis*. He not only speaks of the *capitis aurei
genialem caesariem*[3] of the sleeping Cupid, but also describes
an old man mourning thus: *maestus in lacrimis, genialem canitiem
revellens senex.*[4] For Ovid the rose is *flos genialis,*[5] apparently
because it was used for garlands about the head, which were
thus an attention to the *genius*: *data sunt capiti genialia serta.*[6]

> *florea serta, meum mel, et haec tibi carmina dono:*
> *carmina dono tibi, serta tuo genio....*[7]

So too we may better understand a passage of Propertius:

> *me iuvat et multo mentem vincire Lyaeo*
> *et caput in verna semper habere rosa;*
> *atque ubi iam Venerem gravis interceperit aetas*
> *sparserit et nigras alba senecta comas,*
> *tum mihi naturae libeat perdiscere mores....*[8]

The poem of Apuleius quoted just before continues:

> *serta autem ut laeto tibi tempore tempora vernent,*
> *aetatis florem floribus ut decores.*

Association of the life and the procreative life-soul with the
head would be helped by the fading and loss of hair in age.
Of one who has lost his hair Petronius writes:

> *ut mortem citius venire credas/*
> *scito iam capitis perisse partem,*[9]

---

[1] *Epist.* II, 2, 188 ff.   [2] Pp. 231 ff.   [3] *Met.* V, 22.
[4] II, 27. Laevius (100 B.C.) says to his love, *capiti meo...plexti munera.*
[5] *Met.* IV, 2. For the equation and association of head and flower see
pp. 112 ff. and 124 f. above, also pp. 141 f., 217 ff., 227 and 272, n. 4 below.
[6] Ovid, *Met.* XIII, 929. The relation of the *genius* and the head to con-
viviality is discussed below (pp. 224 ff.).
[7] Apul. *carm. fr.* 4. 2 (Baehrens).
[8] III (IV), 5 (4), 21 ff. Cf. *arida/pellente lasciuos amores/canitie* (Horace,
Odes, II, 11, 6 ff. etc.).
[9] 109. Cf. the Greek belief on p. 107 above.

i.e. part of his life or life-soul. Cf. his

> ...*transfudimus hinc et hinc labellis*
> *errantes animas. valete, curae*
> *mortales. ego sic perire coepi* (79).

Further evidence that the *genius* was the spirit in the head and identical with the *anima* appears below.[1]

Despite Wissowa's view that it perished with the body,[2] the *genius* appears, like the ψυχή, to have been the part of man which survived death. It was the one part of a man that during his life was honoured as a god, a status naturally associated with immortality; and we know that the part which survived death was a 'god',[3] *deus parens*, 'engendering god',[4] honoured

---

[1] See pp. 168 ff., 197 f., 226, etc.

[2] The *naturae deus humanae mortalis* in Hor. *Epist.* II, 2, 188 ff. just alluded to is adduced as evidence to this effect, but the description appears to deviate elsewhere from the original Roman conception (in *natale...qui temperat astrum* for which see pp. 163 f. below); and in any case *mortalis*, if it is taken with *deus* rather than *naturae*, may be satisfied by the fact that the *genius* or 'head' (see Petronius above and pp. 132 ff. below) suffered from death when the body perished, unlike the great gods who were not touched by death. See below (pp. 137 f.) Cicero's argument about the worship of the 'dead' (*mortuus*) as opposed to that of the *immortales*, also the title of the departed souls of the γένος ἀργύρεον : μάκαρες θνητοί (Hesiod, *W. and D.* 141), μάκαρες normally signifying gods (136 etc.).

[3] See the evidence of Varro in Plutarch quoted below (p. 263). Aeneas buried *divini...ossa parentis* (*Aen.* V, 47).

[4] There is no valid reason why the beliefs of the Gracchi and their mother as implied in the letter attributed to her: *ubi mortua ero, parentabis mihi et invocabis deum parentem*, should be impugned as non-Roman. Catullus (LXIV, 404) speaks of *divos parentes*, and for references to *di parentes* in inscriptions see Jordan, *Hermes*, XV, pp. 530 ff. The passage of Catullus can now be interpreted more convincingly: *ignaro mater substernens se impia nato/impia non verita est divos scelerare parentes*. This has been explained (see Robinson Ellis, Kroll, Lenchantin de Gubernatis, etc.) of giving offence to the deified spirits of her parents, 'cast a slur on the memory of her sainted parents' (Simpson); but the natural meaning of *scelerare* is to 'pollute, involve in sin', which she could not be said to do to the spirits of her parents but did to the 'engendering deities' involved in her act, his *genius* and her *iuno*. Cf. Epict. *Disc.* II, 8, 11–16, Marc. Aur. III, 16, I Corinth. iii, 16f., vi, 15–19. For the lust of the conscious self in which the *genius* or *iuno* might thus be implicated see pp. 224 f. Recognition of this sense in *parens* (cf. its regular use of the male, and Caecilius, 18; Nonius, 464, 22) may also save the MSS. reading in LXVI, 15 ff., where *parentum*, interpreted as 'of their parents', has been felt by many scholars to be unsatisfactory and emended: *amantum* (Owen), *aventum* (Munro), *maritum* = *maritorum* (Schmidt, Postgate, Palmer), *patrantum*, etc.

by the surviving family in the *Parentalia*, the 'rites of the
engendering ones'. The departed spirit is in fact sometimes
referred to as the *genius*[1] of the dead person; but since, when
thus disembodied, its procreative activity is no longer to the
fore, we find, as we should expect, that it is commonly referred
to by terms expressive of its present state, *umbra* and *anima*, or
by the vaguely flattering *manes*. If *anima* was used by the
early Latins of the surviving soul, the *genius*, it may, like ψυχή
(cf. ψύχω), originally have described the life-spirit that
'blows'[2] in procreation and sneezing and is also the vaporous
ghost or shade, *umbra* (cf. σκιή). Innumerable passages imply
that for a Roman the 'head' (*caput*) meant the 'life'. We have
seen[3] that among the Greeks a sneeze with no prophetic
relevance was treated as a disturbance—perhaps a sign of
departure—of the life-spirit in the head. The similar significance attached to a sneeze by Romans—when a man sneezed,
bystanders said *Salve*[4] (in Italy in 1823 *Viva*[5]), prayed for his
safety (*salutem ei imprecari*[6])—can most naturally be explained
by a similar reference to the life-soul in the head, the *genius*.
Of this there appears to be confirmation below.[7]

If the spirit in the head was the *genius*, there is further reason
for believing that what survives death, what goes to the nether
gods, is the *genius*. For it is, we find, the 'head' (*caput*) that does
so. The Greeks, for whom also it was the 'head' and who referred to the ψυχαί in Hades as 'heads',[8] touched the chin,
γένειον,[9] apparently with reference to the generative ψυχή.
In the rite of *devotio*, in which a Roman commander dedicated
himself and the enemy host to the *di manes* and Earth, to the
world of departed souls, it was his 'head' which he offered
to them, *sua capita voverunt*;[10] he covered his head and 'thrust

---

[1] E.g. Ovid, *Fasti*, II, 421, Aeneas makes offering *patris genio*: it is the
first *Parentalia*. This identity explains Stat. *Silv.* II, 7, 132, 135.

[2] See pp. 120 f.   [3] P. 104.

[4] E.g. Pliny, *N.H.* xxviii, 2, 23; Petronius, 98.

[5] See J. T. Blunt, *Vestiges of Ancient Manners and Customs discoverable in
Modern Italy and Sicily*, 1823, p. 174.

[6] Apul. *Met.* IX, 25.   [7] Pp. 225 f.

[8] See pp. 99 f.   [9] Discussed below (pp. 233 f.).

[10] Cicero, *de Fin.* V, 22, 64.

up his hand beneath the *toga* to his chin'[1] as he made the
dedication, then rushed into battle to die. Again the relevant
object is touched. In a similar rite in which a Roman general
promises three black sheep to the *manes*, Dis, and Vediovis, if
they will take the enemy, he calls Earth and Jupiter to witness.
'When he says Earth, he touches the earth with his hands;
when he says Jupiter, he raises his hand to heaven; when he
says that he takes upon himself the promise, he touches his

---

[1] See Livy, VIII, 9 f. The covering of the head also appears to be an
attention to the seat of the life-soul. In the *ver sacrum* an Italian community promised, if it were saved, to sacrifice all creatures born in the
following spring. But, as a substitute for putting to death the children
born then, they allowed them to grow to maturity and covered their
heads (*velabant*) and drove them out beyond their borders. (See Festus,
s.v. *ver sacrum*.) Thus, too, when a man was condemned for treason his
head was veiled and he was hanged on a barren tree (Cic. *pro Rab. perd.* 13;
Livy, I, 26; cf. x, 38, 3). Those who committed suicide, or knew that they
were about to die, first veiled their heads. Thus numbers of plebeians,
desperate for want of food, 'wrapped up their heads (*capitibus obvolutis*) and
threw themselves into the Tiber' (Livy, IV, 12; cf. Horace, *Sat.* II, 3, 37 f.).
'Let us bind (*praeligemus*) our heads with our garments and plunge into
the deep' says one of Petronius' characters, desperate (102). And Julius
Caesar, when he knew his fate, wrapped his head in his *toga* (Suet. *Jul.*
82). See also pp. 428 f. below. The Greeks, with their beliefs about the ψυχή
and the head, covered the heads of themselves or others destined to die and
of the dead (see e.g. Eurip. *Hippol.* 1458, *I.T.* 1207; Plato, *Phaedo*, 118;
compare *Aen.* XI, 77 and the Germanic practice, p. 154 below). The
Roman practice of covering the head when sacrificing would also seem to
be an attention to the life-soul (cf. pp. 144, 152 f. and the binding of the head
when sacrificing, pp. 457 f. below, with *vittas...sacrati capitis, Aen.* III, 510 f.).
So too in marriage (pp. 152 f., 233, 446 ff.) for Greece as Italy and in
initiation in the 'mysteries' not only the veiling of the head but also the
putting of loaves in the fertility vessel, the liknon (p. 113, n. 4), upon it.
(For instances see Miss J. E. Harrison's *Prol. to the study of Gr. Religion*,
pp. 519–33, and cf. the loaves attached to the head of the October Horse,
p. 126 above with p. 274, n. 2.) So too the sprinkling of the victim's head
(p. 228, n. 1) and in various rites the putting of leaves etc. upon the head
(see e.g. in the making of a 'father' Livy, I, 24; also *Aen.* III, 370 f., XII, 120;
Prop. IV, 8, 86; Ovid, *Fasti*, I, 358 ff., IV, 655; Plut. *Rom.* XXI, 10, etc. See
also pp. 107, n. 6, 228). Wrapping, as binding e.g. with fillet or crown,
might consecrate or change the state of what was wrapped or bound and
might also be thought to separate off the soul (see below, pp. 152 f., 353 ff.,
420 ff.). The wrapping of the head of the sacrificer is like the wrapping of
the hand (cf. p. 97, n. 10) in the rites of *Fides* (Livy, I, 21, Horace, *Odes*,
I, 35, 21 f.).

breast with his hands.'[1] He touches the breast (*praecordia*, etc.), the seat of the conscious self that makes the promise,[2] as in the other cases he touches the head, the seat of the life-soul he is offering to the *manes*, or, explicitly, of the *genius* he is honouring (p. 124). The touching was an important part of the ceremony. Ovid warns against having a tirewoman (*ornatrix*) who hates her mistress, for

devovet et dominae tangit caput illa.[3]

Persistence of the belief that the soul was in the head will also explain other passages: e.g., why *mors ad caput adstitit* (Lucr. III, 959); why when Dido's soul cannot pass and Iris is sent *quae luctantem animam nexosque resolveret artus,* Virgil explains

nondum illi flavum Proserpina vertice crinem
abstulerat Stygioque caput damnaverat Orco,[4]

i.e. the head to the realm of the dead; why Euryalus' mother, seeking to die, says

invisum hoc detrude caput sub Tartara telo;[5]

why for Horace   *nullum*
saeva caput Proserpina fugit;[6]

why Propertius says

cum capite hoc Stygiae iam poterentur aquae;[7]

and in his poem on Marcellus' death

Stygias vultum demisit in undas....
ille licet ferro cautus se condat et aere,
mors tamen inclusum protrahet inde caput;[8]

and Seneca   *cur caput tenebris grave*
non mitto ad umbras Ditis aeternas? quid hic
manes meos detineo?[9]

---

[1] Preserved in Macrob. *Sat.* III, 9.

[2] For touching the chest, an appeal to the conscious self, see pp. 183 f. below.

[3] *Ars Am.* III, 241. We can now better understand why, to send a message *Stygias ad umbras,* a witch cuts off a head and breathes the message into it (Lucan VI, 566 ff.).

[4] *Aen.* IV, 698 f. For the hair see p. 349 below and pp. 106 f., 130 f. above. Compare *Aen.* IV, 640 with *Il.* XXI, 333 ff. etc. on p. 98.

[5] *Aen.* IX, 496.   [6] *Odes,* I, 28, 19 f.   [7] II, 9, 26.

[8] III (IV), 18, 9, 25 f. Cf. IV (V), 11, 10.   [9] *Phoen.* 233 ff.

We can now understand some curious Italian practices. An *oscillum*, a mask or likeness of a head, was, we saw,[1] hung up to secure fertility, which is the natural work of the *genius* or procreative spirit. Such an *oscillum* was also hung up for the departed spirit when a man died by hanging.[2] On the same principle, apparently, a copy of the head might be put in the grave when a man received normal funeral.[3] Here, too, perhaps is the reason why *larva* meant 'ghost' and 'mask';[4] here the explanation of the *imagines*: namely, that each head or mask in its 'shrine[5]', honoured on festal days with a garland, served for the *genius* of the departed ancestor the same purpose as his image served for one of the ordinary gods.[6] Cicero speaks of the *imago* of a man's *parens* as laurelled (cf. *genialia serta*[7]) in the hour of rejoicing and as disfigured with dishonour and 'mourning' (*lugentem*) when the son is put to shame.[8] This belief that the surviving soul is in or is a head appears to go back into prehistoric times; for it surely is the explanation of the 'Villanovan' practice of covering the inurned ashes of the dead with a bronze or pottery helmet[9] (cf. the Greek 'helmet

[1] See pp. 126 f.
[2] See Varro quoted by Servius *ad Aen.* XII, 603. To hang the *oscillum* thus was *parentare*. Cf. the hanging of *pilae* at the *Compitalia*, etc.: *tot pilae quot capita* (Fest., s.v. p. 272 f. Lindsay), Macrob. I, 7, 28 ff.; 11, 48 f.
[3] See e.g. Dennis, *Cities and Cemeteries of Etruria*, I, p. 427; II, pp. 84, 459.
[4] Thus also we may explain med. Lat. *masca*, 'goblin', 'mask'. Cf. pp. 143, 154, n. 4. *Maniae turpes deformesque personae*, Festus, s.v. (p. 129, cf. 128, 114, 115 Lindsay) and μορμολυκεῖον, Schol. Aristoph. *Peace*, 474; also Γοργείη κεφαλή, *Od.* XI, 634 (see p. 114, n. 5). Lucretius, making a 'bogey' of 'Religion' (I, 64), mentions only her *caput*. Cf. IV, 173.
[5] ναίδιον, Polyb. VI, 53. [6] Cf. p. 106.
[7] See pp. 130, 141 f., 227.
[8] *Pro Murena*, XLI, 88; cf. *pro Sulla*, XXXI, 88, etc.
[9] See D. Randall-MacIver, *Villanovans and Early Etruscans*, pp. 47 f., etc. The Villanovans inhabited Etruria before the Etruscans and had settlements at Rome and in the Alban hills. The vessel itself beneath the helmet has an outline rather like that of a head (back and sides), with a neck at the base swelling to the level of the ears then contracting slightly towards the top. The helmet fits it just as it would a head and is made for a head of that scale. Such a vessel was *testa*. 'Then when the fire set beneath has turned me to ashes', says Propertius, 'let a little *testa* receive my *manes*' (II, 13 [III, 5], 31 f.). For later Romans the head or skull was *testa*, whence It. *testa*, Fr. *tête*. There appears to be confirmation of this interpretation at Chiusi, where in Etruscan times the predominance of

of Hades', pp. 99 f.) and, long before, of the palaeolithic and neolithic Ligurian practice,[1] found also in Corsica,[2] of protecting, roofing over with stone, the *head*, but not the body, in its grave. In the Ligurian graves it is clear that this attention to the head was confined to adults, which is exactly what we should expect if the soul was believed to be in the head[3] and potent in procreation, manifest thus only after the attainment of puberty. Discrimination of adult from child funerals in classical Rome is discussed below.[4]

> *Tarda sit illa dies et nostro serior aevo*
> *qua caput Augustum, quem temperat orbe relicto,*
> *accedat caelo faveatque precantibus absens*[5]

says Ovid. Of the mushroom that killed Claudius Juvenal says that it 'stopped (*pressit*) the *praecordia* of one old man and bade the trembling head and lips dribbling with saliva descend to heaven'.[6] We appear incidentally to have traced the native roots[7] of Caesar-worship, the worship of the emperor's *genius*

cremation suggests the persistence of an unusually strong Villanovan element. There bronze or pottery faces to scale were actually attached to the *testa* (see Randall-MacIver, *op. cit.* p. 223; also F. von Duhn, *Italische Gräberkunde*, I, pp. 350 ff.). The bowl-like covering which is alternative to the helmet perhaps represented a more pacific form of hat like the *petasus*. In some cases a hybrid between this and the helmet appears (see Randall-MacIver, *op. cit.* p. 47). *Caput* itself can perhaps be explained as the 'container', what mattered being the life or soul. Cf. Daniel vii, 15 and our 'soul-case'. For the diminutive *capillus* (hair) see pp. 231 ff. with 99, 107, 129 f. The practice of putting an image of the head in or on the tomb (as on Etruscan ossuaries; e.g. Nogara, *Les Etrusques*, etc., p. 132) may explain 'bust' (*bustum*). Cf. *Aen.* IV, 640, Prop. IV, 11, 9 f.

[1] See von Duhn, *op. cit.* pp. 6, 11, 197.   [2] *Ibid.* p. 112.
[3] The contemporary practice of trepanning should perhaps be related to this (? an attempt to make a way out to rid the head of a spirit possessing it. See pp. 147 ff., but also p. 157).
[4] P. 264.   [5] *Met.* xv, 868 ff.
[6] vi, 621 ff. Cf. e.g. *emerito sacrum caput insere caelo* (Sil. It. vii, 19), of Fabius. Representations of the emperor's head upon a *cornu copiae* (e.g. *Camb. Anc. Hist. Plates*, IV, p. 159 b, c) can now be seen to mean his *genius*. Cf. pp. 239 f. His *imago* seems to have meant essentially a head or bust (cf. Plin. *Paneg.* 52). Offerings made to it (e.g. Plin. *Ep.* x, 96, 5) were made to his *genius* (e.g. *Paneg.* 52).
[7] Traditions of worship of the ruler himself were at work in the provinces and slowly affected Roman thought (see e.g. Professor Lily R. Taylor, *The Divinity of the Roman Emperor*, pp. 1 ff.), but in Italy it was

during his life and also, as we may now see, after his death. The worship of the dead emperor, *divus Augustus*, etc., as *divus Iulius*, was the worship of his *genius*. For, as we have seen, the dead man is identified with the *genius*, since it is what represents him, what survives of him. The plain Roman at death could be said to become a god,[1] i.e. *deus*, *divus*. But we do not hear much of this as deification, for the very good reason that the god was there even during life, the *genius*, a god important only for the man himself and his family. When his daughter dies, Cicero uses a Greek word, speaking of her ἀποθέωσις, and would build a private shrine for her.[2] His objection to the honours Antony would pay to the dead Julius (*supplicatio*) was not that they implied divinity[3] but that they were such as were traditionally reserved for the great gods that knew not death, the *immortales*, the gods of the state—*ut cuius sepulchrum usquam exstet ubi parentetur, ei publice supplicetur*[4]—i.e. that instead of family worship as a *deus parens*, it was to be a matter of the worship of the whole state. In essence what was new, what was distinctive in the position of the Caesars alike during life and after death, was just this, that while the *genius* of the ordinary citizen was a private god and privately worshipped, the *genius*

---

to his *genius* that the cult was directed. We learn from Dio Cassius (LI, 20) that neither Augustus nor any other emperor allowed himself to be worshipped in Rome or elsewhere in Italy during his lifetime. The *genius* is not just 'his shadowy attendant spirit' (Taylor, *op. cit.* p. 203) but, as we have seen and shall see, his life-soul, which was worshipped also after death.

[1] See pp. 131 f., 263.   [2] See *ad Att.* XII, 18, 19, 20, 36.

[3] It is noteworthy that he opposes not *homo* to *deus* nor *humanus* to *divinus* but *mortuus* to *immortalis* and *parentalia* to *supplicationes*.

[4] *Phil.* I, 6. This aspect of the imperial cult was helped by the supposed precedents of Aeneas and Romulus. Association of the head in particular with such divinity might contribute to Virgil's reference to the *divinum caput* of Aeneas (*Aen.* x, 639; cf. Silius' reference to Fabius in p. 136, n. 6 above and pp. 159 ff. below). The offering of the *supplicatio* was incense and wine, for which see p. 282 below. Already to Marius there had been such a *supplicatio* by the people (see Seneca, *de Ira*, III, 18 and p. 276). Factors which helped the belief that Caesar's soul passed to the heavens and did not, as had been believed usual, abide with the *manes* in the earth are discussed on pp. 147 ff. Special reverence prescribed that his *imago* might not be carried with the *imagines* of other kin at funerals.

of the Caesar was a state god and publicly worshipped,[1] a useful recognition that he was uniquely 'public', a *parens* or *pater patriae,* as important for the state as the *pater familias* was for the family. Julius Caesar was already, before his death, officially *parens patriae,*[2] and when citizens made libation to the emperor's *genius* they addressed him explicitly as *pater patriae,*[3] *Laribus tuum miscet numen* (Hor. *Od.* IV, 5, 33; cf. p. 158, n. 5). Further evidence for the identity of the deified surviving soul of Julius (and later Caesars) with the *genius* in the head will appear.[4]

We found[5] that among the Greeks the reason why a nod was the peculiarly binding and sacred form of promise, expression of will, was that thus the ψυχή in the head, the ψυχή that was the holy life-soul and the executive power, was involved in the promise. We saw that the same significance was attached to the spontaneous nod of a sneeze, i.e. that that same power in the head ensured fulfilment of some event. This interpretation of the spontaneous nod was, perhaps, the origin of

---

[1] Cf. Lucan, VII, 457 ff.:

> *bella pares superis facient civilia divos;*
> *fulminibus manes radiisque ornabit et astris*
> *inque deum templis iurabit Roma per umbras.*

For the worship during life we may compare the fact (see Dio Cassius, LVIII, 2, 7 f.; 4, 4; 6, 2; 8, 4; 11, 2; Suet. *Tib.* 65) that to his minister Seianus, as to Tiberius himself, statues were set up and worshipped and his birthday (i.e. festival of his *genius=Natalis*) made a public holiday (cf. Julius Caesar in Dio C. XLIV, 4, 4). We can now better understand Juvenal's reference to his *adoratum populo caput* (X, 62). Cf. p. 163, n. 3.

[2] See Dio Cassius, XLIV, 4, 4. Cf. the inscription on the statue erected on the Rostra by Antony after Caesar's death: *Parenti Optimo Maximo,* and Suetonius, *Jul.* 85. The relationship was pressed. The Ides of March was *Parricidium* (*ibid* 88), the assassins *parricidae.* It is, I suggest, Cicero's pride in being acclaimed as *parens patriae* (*in Pis.* 3; *pro Sest.* 57, 122; Pliny *N.H.* VII, 30, 117; Juv. VIII, 244, etc.) that explains *O fortunatam natam me consule Romam!* (See Juv. X, 122.) When Romulus was *pater patriae,* he gave that people birth. (So Ennius known to Cic. *de Rep.* I, 64.) It was his *progenies* (Liv. I, 16). Cf. Augustus: *duas habere se filias...rempublicam et Iuliam* (Macrob. II, 5, 4). The title derived, I suggest, from a view of the community as a family. It was the *pater patratus populi Romani* who negotiated with, e.g., the *pater patratus populi Albani* (Liv. I, 24).

[3] E.g. Ovid, *Fasti,* II, 637 f. (cf. 127 ff.); Petronius, 60.

[4] Pp. 163 ff.   [5] See pp. 97 f. and 104.

the deliberate nod. Movement, such movement, is the characteristic manifestation of the ψυχή during life,[1] speech being the
expression of the breath-soul, the conscious self.[2] The Romans,
who appear likewise to have interpreted the sneeze as a manifestation of the *genius*,[3] moved the head in the same fashion
in expressing decisions[4] (*adnuo*; cf. Plaut. *Ps.* 629). It was

[1] See pp. 195 f.
[2] See pp. 41, 67 ff., 170, 172. This may explain *muto*, i.e. as meaning 'the
dumb one' (cf. *nasus, naso*, etc.), the generative soul and so the generative
organ (of man or woman apparently; Hesychius' *Lex.* interprets μυττός
as 'dumb' and also as τὸ γυναικεῖον) as opposed to the spirit of ordinary
consciousness in the chest, the *animus*, to which speech belongs. We can
thus understand why Horace, to make the former articulate, lets the
animus act as its mouthpiece in the case of an adulterer who has been
thrashed: 'If to him, as he witnessed such calamities, his *animus* were to
speak as follows on behalf of his "dumb one"' *huic si mutonis verbis mala
tanta videnti/diceret haec animus* (*Sat.* I, 2, 68 f.). *Huic* represents vaguely
the person, as when in Homer a man's θυμός talks to him and he—not
the ψυχή—replies (see p. 13). *Mutunus* appears to be formed like
tribunus (*tribus*), *Portunus* (*porta, portus*), *Fortuna* (*fors*). *Mutinus* would
resemble *marinus* (*mare*), *Matutinus* (*matuta*), *Lucina* (*lux*). Souls after death
also were known as the *silentes*, cf. *Tacita, Muta* and pp. 59 ff. above, esp.
p. 60, n. 5. Lust is the wrath (*ira*) of the *muto* (Horace, *ibid.* l. 70).
[3] See pp. 131 f., 225 f. For the brow twitching (Plaut. *Ps.* 107) cf. p. 129,
n. 6.
[4] Analogous movement was similarly expressed: νεῦον τὸ αἰδοῖον,
Herodotus, II, 48; *innuebatque digito*, Pliny, *Ep.* VII, 27, 9, etc. We may
here explain 'Thumbs up!', the practice of lowering the thumb to show
favour (e.g. *pollices cum faveamus premere etiam proverbio iubemur*, Pliny, *N.H.*
XXVIII, 2, 25; cf. Horace, *Epist.* I, 18, 66), and turning it back, up and
away from the suppliant to show hostility (*pollicem vertere, convertere*, Juv.
III, 36, etc.). In the latter position it is *infestus* (see Quintil. XI, 3, 119;
Apul. *Met.* II, 21; Wilkins on Horace, *Epist.* I, 18, 66). The movement of
the thumb is, I suggest, like that of the head explained above, down and
towards one in consenting, showing favour (*adnuere*, κατανεύειν, cf.
propitius = προπετής), and up, back, away in refusing, showing hostility
(*abnuere*, ἀνανεύειν, cf. *aversari*, ἀποτρέπεσθαι, etc.). The fallen gladiator
asked for mercy and the victor waited for the decision of the spectators
thus expressed. It was obviously more convenient to keep the head still,
watching the arena, and use the thumb thus. For the use of the hand to
represent the executive power see pp. 97, 198 f. In the past it has been explained that 'those who wished the death of a conquered gladiator turned
their thumbs towards their breasts as a signal to his opponent to stab him;
those who wished him to be spared, turned their thumbs downwards as
a signal for dropping the sword' (Mayor on Juv. III, 36; cf. Duff, *ad loc.*;
Wilkins on Hor. *Ep.* I, 18, 66, etc.). But there appears to be no evidence

probably to the *genius,*[1] as it was to the ψυχή,[2] that physical
strength and executive power belonged. We can perhaps now
better understand why 'deity' was commonly expressed by
numen, i.e. 'nodding' or something that nods or is nodded
(cf. *fluo, flumen*; *sugo, su(g)men*; etc.). According to Catullus,
after Ariadne's prayer

> *adnuit invicto caelestum numine rector,*
> *quo motu tellus atque horrida contremuerunt*
> *aequora....*[3]

Livy refers to Campanian envoys as saying to the Roman
senators *annuite, patres conscripti, nutum numenque vestrum invictum
Campanis*[4]—the nod is all powerful, irresistible, an unfailing
promise, sign of action; and Lucretius describes the Curetes as

> *terrificas capitum quatientes numine cristas.*[5]

---

that the thumb was pointed at the breast except Prudent. *contra Symm.*
II, 1096 ff.: *et quoties victor ferrum iugulo inserit illa/delicias ait esse suas
pectusque iacentis/virgo modesta iubet converso pollice rumpi,* which not only is
extremely late (*circa* A.D. 400) and may be merely a conceit of the poet's
own, but also *proves* no more for the poet's own thought than that the
turning-back of the thumb was the signal for the death of the fallen,
supposed on this occasion (and perhaps usually) to be achieved by piercing
his breast. And there appears to be no evidence or inherent probability
that the lowering of the thumb symbolised the dropping of the sword.
The movement of the thumb was a reply to a similar movement on the
part of the suppliant gladiator, the showing of his finger asking for life and
certainly not representing his sword any more than in *digitum ostendere* (see
p. 198). The scholiast on Persius, V, 119, *digitum exere,* says *tractum a gladiatori-
bus qui victi ostensione digiti veniam a populo postulabant*; cf. Sidon. Apoll. *Carm.*
XXIII, 129 f., and *ad digitum pugnavi,* Quintil. VIII, 5, 20; *ad digitum posita con-
currere palma,* Mart. *Lib. Spect.* XXIX, 5. It should be added that on the
strength of a relief in which the thumbs of four spectators are turned up
and there is a defective inscription, NANTES MISSI, Friedländer (*Darst.
aus der Sittengesch. Roms etc.*[5] II, p. 346) argued that the thumb was turned
down as a sentence of death, and up as a signal to spare—the modern
'Thumbs up!'—but *sperat et in saeva victus gladiator harena,/sit licet infesto
pollice turba minax* (*Anthol. Lat.* ed. Riese, 415, 24 f.) and the literary
evidence cited above is decisively against this view.

[1] See pp. 193 ff., 224 ff. A friendly *genius* meant good bodily health
and fortune. Contrast *genio sinistro,* Persius, IV, 27.
[2] See pp. 194 ff.   [3] LXIV, 204 ff.
[4] VII, 30. Cf. VIII, 34, 2. *Aen.* VIII, 78 (cf. II, 691).
[5] II, 632.

Speaking to Caesar of his *genius*, Horace says 'your *numen*'.[1] If a Roman believed that the god whose relation to a body he knew, his own *genius*, was in a head, was indeed after death, when unaccompanied by the conscious self of life, a head without a body, and manifested his will by nodding, he would naturally think of other gods as beings of like nature, each a head or having his deity and life and power, including generative power, in the head and *characteristically* nodding when manifesting his will. For Empedocles, who placed the human soul, the mind, in the φρένες,[2] God had no other limb or part but φρὴν ἱερὴ καὶ ἀθέσφατος ἔπλετο μοῦνον.[3] We have seen that among the Romans an image of a god's head was hung up to ensure fertility.[4] More striking still, we find that at the solemn banquets offered to the gods (*lectisternia*) the guests were 'gods' heads', *capita deorum*, as if they *were* the gods (cf. p. 106). This is not a Greek custom. On one occasion Livy tells of a miraculous moving: 'in the *fora* where there was a *lectisternium* the gods' heads, which were on the couches, turned away and a dish which had been set near Jupiter fell down'.[5] We learn elsewhere[6] that for the 'heads of the gods' on the couches in Rome (and also for Castor similarly at Tusculum) there stood *struppi* defined as 'bunches (*fasciculi*) of *verbena*'. *Verbena* appears to have meant twigs with leaves, etc., of olive, laurel, or other plant, perhaps as most obviously containing sap[7] and life. Virgil[8] characterises *verbena* as *pinguis*,

---

[1] *Odes*, IV, 5, 34 f.; *Epist.* II, 1, 16. Cf. Ovid, *Fasti*, v, 145, etc., and Preller-Jordan, *Römische Myth.*[3] II, p. 440, and for other texts in which *numen* is virtually equivalent to *genius, ibid.* I, p. 86.

[2] See pp. 47, 54, 71.

[3] B 134, Diels. Cf. Xenophanes, B 23, 24, 25.   [4] See pp. 126 f.

[5] XL, 59. Perhaps to the thought here suggested belongs the holiness of the 'place of the head' (or 'heads'), the *Capitolium*, and the legend that, when the foundations were being cleared for the famous early temple, there appeared a human head intact (Livy, I, 55; Varro, *Ling. Lat.* v, 41, etc.). Cf. the horse's head at Carthage, p. 126 above.

[6] See Festus, s.vv. *capita deorum, stroppus, struppi* (pp. 56, 12; 410, 6 ff.; 472, 15 Lindsay). Eating was the affair of the *genius* or head (pp. 222 ff.).

[7] It should perhaps be related to *ver* (p. 177, n. 9). So too *verber*. Cf. *virgae* (use in Plaut.). In French 'whip' *fouet* originally meant 'beech-twig'. Cf. 'to birch'.

[8] See *Ecl.* VIII, 66. With such apparently the early Roman replenished

i.e. full of oily sap. It was with *verbena* that the *fetialis* touched
a man's head and so made him *pater patratus*;[1] and what the
fetialis took with him, going to make a treaty, was the stone
(? 'thunder-stone'; cf. p. 218, n. 1, *Aen.* XII, 200) identified
with Jupiter and such *verbena* from the Capitol.[2] It may be
that with *verbena*, as in the *lectisternia*, the early Latins commonly represented their gods.[3] Varro[4] tells us that for over
a hundred and seventy years the Romans worshipped their
gods without portrait-images (*sine simulacro*). To our explanation of *numen* and *capita deorum* it may be relevant that there
are references[5] to the *genius Iovis, genius Martis, cerfus Martius*[6]
etc., e.g. *Priapi genio pervigilium deberi* (Petron. 21), and that

his gods (see Ov. *Fasti*, I, 341 ff. and pp. 282 f.). Homeric Greeks (*Od.* XII,
357 f.) used oakleaves instead of barley-groats (=marrow, see pp. 222,
228, n. 1, 279).

[1] P. 133, n. 1. Slavs made a chief by putting a clod of earth on his
head. See Gogol, *Taras B.* III with p. 155, n. 2 *inf*. Did *patratus* mean
'begotten', 'created a new person'? See Pers I, 18, Quintil. VIII, 3, 44, etc.
with pp. 188 f., 228 *inf*. Did *creare regem*, etc. begin thus? Cf. e.g. Liv. I,
8, 3, 7; 17, 2 with 3, 7 and pp. 125, 188 ff. Were the *fetiales* concerned
with what was 'engendered' (p. 182)?

[2] See Livy, XXX, 43. The *verbena* was described as *sagmen*, cf. *ius
sacratum Iovis iurandum sagmine*, Naevius, *trag. inc.* 219 (Festus, p. 426, 4).
O. Mueller transposes *ius* and *Iovis*. *verbena* was put upon altars; carrying
it the *fetialis* or *legatus* was inviolable. See also p. 456, n. 2. C. Saturninus
showed how *nullam gratiam floris, nullam laetitiam frondis, nullum caespitem aut
palmitem non alicuius* (sc. *dei*) *capiti invenias consecratum* (Tert., *de Cor.* 7).

[3] A similar thought (cf. p. 456, n. 2) may explain how a bundle of
grass, *manipulus*, came to be the standard which the ancient Romans
carried into battle and whence the unit got its name. It was holy:

*illa quidem faeno; sed erat reverentia faeno
quantum nunc aquilas cernis habere tuas.*

(Ovid, *Fasti*, III, 115 f.)

The standards were gods (Cic. *in Cat.* I, 9, 24 f., Tacitus, *Ann.* II, 17, *Hist.*
VI, 10, etc.). The eagle represented Jupiter. The bundle of grass was, I
suggest, the presence of the war god himself: *Marti...gramen est consecratum*
(Servius, *ad Aen.* XII, 119; cf. Horace, *Odes*, III, 7, 26), *Gradivus Mars ap-
pellatus est...quia gramine sit ortus* (Festus, 86, 17 s.v. *Grad.*). The truth of
the association of *gramen* with Mars is not affected by the falsity of this
etymology of *Gradivus*. Cf. Ovid, *Fasti*, V, 251 ff. See also pp. 126, 470 f.
Corn is a grass. Its relation to the war-god will help us to understand
adorea (ᾰδορ νίκη, Gloss. II, 8, 21) and why the supreme honour for a soldier
was *corona graminea*, given only to him who had saved the whole army.
The significance of a crown appears below (pp. 376 ff., 445 ff., esp. p. 456,
n. 2).   [4] See Aug. *de Civ. Dei*, IV, 31.

[5] See Wissowa, *op. cit.* pp. 180 f.   [6] P. 125.

Juno, the name of the great goddess, was also the name of the female counterpart of the *genius*, the deity, the private generative spirit, of a woman[1] as the *genius* was of a man. It has been denied that early Roman religion was anthropomorphic. Well-defined and complex personalities with histories such as the Homeric gods possess the Roman gods doubtless had not, but the description of the latter as 'fathers', e.g. *Iuppiter*, and the word *numen* itself imply that degree of transference from conceptions of man which is here suggested. Vague explanations of *numen* as a 'being with a will' do not fit the precise early meaning of the root or the character of the Roman imagination elsewhere, its love for what is concrete and can be visualised.[2] The traditional importance of the divine head may be a reason why it alone is mentioned in Lucretius' picture of *Religio*:

> *quae caput a caeli regionibus ostendebat*
> *horribili super aspectu mortalibus instans.*[3]

We saw the ox-heads of Cretan and Greek cult.[4] Cf. *boum capita et capita vervecum et immolatis et colitis*, Min. Fel. (*Oct.* 28) to the Romans. In mediaeval art, when the association of the soul with the head still persisted,[5] cherubim were conceived

---

[1] Pp. 129, n. 6, 264.

[2] The functional activity of *Sondergötter* is no exception to this. Gods were of course worshipped in their actual manifestations, Vesta in the burning hearth, etc. It is now easier to refer *Aen.* iv, 357 to 'both gods'.

[3] i, 64 f. But cf. p. 135, n. 4. For traditional identification by him of the life with the head, see iii, 1041. For iv, 173, cf. 137 and 'thunder-head' ('One of the round compact swelling cumulus clouds which frequently develop into thunder clouds', *Cent. Dict.* s.v.) perhaps contributing to the conception of the Gorgon's head with lightning glance. Belief that the gods are primarily 'heads' might be helped by the form of this, of globular lightning, of the moon and the sun, 'at whose sight all the stars hide their diminish'd heads'. See e.g. *caput obscura nitidum ferrugine texit*—of the sun's eclipse, Virg. *Georg.* i, 467. For the explanation of the Gorgon's glance as lightning (see Aesch. *P.V.* 356; cf. *Ag.* 469 f., Aristoph. *Ach.* 566 f., *Trag. Adesp.* 278) cf. the Celtic conception of lightning as the deadly glance from the eye of the lightning god (for which see H. D'Arbois de Jubainville, *Le Cycle mythologique irlandais et la Mythologie celtique*, pp. 185 ff.), also Mickiewicz, *Pan Tadeusz* viii, *init*.

[4] See pp. 102, 105 f., 236 ff.

[5] See e.g. the representation of the weighing of souls in the form of heads in *Revue Archéologique*, i, 1844, p. 238. Cf. p. 135, n. 4 above.

and represented just as heads with wings, with which we may compare the Cretan sealings representing animal or human heads with wings[1] and the Platonic conception of the δαίμων as complete in the head, the body being attached merely as a means of locomotion.[2] Representation of the corn-mother, Δημήτηρ, as a head has been mentioned.[3] It was a charge against the Templars that they worshipped heads. Thus in the Articles of Accusation despatched by Pope Clement V:[4] *Item quod ipsi per singulas provincias habeant Idola, videlicet capita quorum alia habebant tres facies et alia unam et aliqua cranium humanum habebant'.* This cult can now be better understood. For this divine head was worshipped as the source of wealth, as making trees to bloom and earth to germinate (*Item quod facit arbores florere. Item quod terram germinare*) much as did the head of *Liber.*[5] There is reason[6] to believe that among the Jews originally the head was believed to contain the life or life-soul. In the Kabbalah the supreme deity is conceived just thus, as a 'head', a head containing the liquid of life.[7] His name is *Arik Anpin*, the Vast Countenance. Further evidence of the importance of the divine head will be found below.[8]

The belief that the head contained the seed and the *genius* will explain why it was adorned with a cap (*pilleus*) during the festival of the fertility god *Saturnus* associated with seed, with nuts,[9] why *oscilla* (pp. 127 f.) were associated with his festival.[10] To this festival, it is suggested,[11] Horace refers in

---

[1] See Figs. 76 ff. of the Zacro sealings published by Hogarth (*J.H.S.* 1902, pp. 76 ff.) and compare the Minoan evidence on p. 102 above.

[2] *Timaeus,* 44 D, 90 A. He sees the head as a sphere, the proper form of deity.

[3] P. 114, n. 5. For Greece see also pp. 228, n. 1, 236.

[4] See M. Michelet, *Procès des Templ.* I, pp. 92 ff. Cf. p. 157, n. 1 below.

[5] See pp. 126 f., 264.   [6] See pp. 103 ff., 234 ff., 239, n. 6, 287 f.

[7] See pp. 234 f., 287 f.

[8] Pp. 164 ff. *Panim* 'face' is used like 'person' (Lev. xix, 15, etc.). Men beseech 'the face of Yahweh' (Ex. xxxii, 11, etc.). The 'shew bread' was 'bread of the face' (I Sam. xxi, 6).

[9] See e.g. Martial, V, 30, VII, 91, XIV, 1 and cf. Catull. LXI, 128 ff., Virg. *Ecl.* VIII, 30, Festus 179, 8 f. etc.

[10] Macrob. I, 11, 1 and 48 f.; cf. 7, 22, 28 ff.

[11] See Warde Fowler, *Roman Festivals,* p. 272, with Martial, XIV, 70.

cras genium mero | curabis et porco.[1] Ovid calls that month *acceptus geniis.*[2] It will also explain why, though the head was normally covered in sacrificing, it was uncovered when a man sacrificed to Saturn.[3] The legal concept of *caput* in relation to a man's existence in the community can also now be better understood. In Greece, as we saw,[4] it was the head, seat of the life-soul, the ψυχή, that was affected by honour or shame. Euripides' Andromache says that she was taken from her home to the Greek ships 'putting hateful slavery about my head' (δουλοσύναν στυγερὰν ἀμφιβαλοῦσα κάρᾳ[5]). This will explain why in Rome from early times a band[6] was put about the head of one sold into slavery (*sub corona*); why loss of status, e.g. banishment or slavery, was *deminutio capitis*; why when a slave was manumitted it was his *head* which was concerned. Thus a master promises: *liberum caput tibi faciam paucos cis menses,*[7] and whoever buys his freedom for a slave pays the money 'for his head' (*pro capite*[8]). A freeman's *genius* controlled him.[9] A slave was subject to another. As restoring the head, thus interpreted, to honour, inaugurating a new state for the *caput*, I would explain the ceremonies of emancipation: the slave was touched on the head with the *vindicta* (cf. pp. 456, n. 2, 471, n. 4), shaved his head and bound it with white wool or put on a *pilleus*, thus the 'cap of freedom' (e.g. *raso capite calvos capiam pilleum*[10]), and received a name[11]

---

[1] *Odes*, III, 17, 14 f. For the wine, see pp. 215 ff., 227 f.; for the pig pp. 154 f. and 177, n. 9.

[2] *Fasti*, III, 58. For *cerei* at the *Sat.* cf. p. 282, n. 9; 156, n. 2.

[3] See Festus, 432, 1 ff.; 462, 28 f. (Lindsay); Plut. *Q.R.* 11; Serv. *ad Aen.* III, 407, etc. This was the usual way of sacrificing for Greeks, and the cult of Saturn was subjected to Greek influences, but other native Roman cults so influenced still had the head covered in sacrifice. Cf. pp. 133, n. 1, 152 f.

[4] Pp. 97 f. Such thought explains *huic capiti insultans* (*Aen.* VIII, 570).

[5] *Andr.* 110. Cf. p. 377.   [6] Explained in Part III, esp. pp. 376 ff., 445 ff.

[7] Plaut. *Merc.* 152 f. Cf. Juv. III, 33, Seneca, *de Ira*, I, 2, 1, etc.

[8] E.g. Plaut. *Most.* 211, 242; *Pseud.* 175.   [9] See pp. 160 ff.

[10] Plaut. *Amph.* 462. Cf. Martial, XIV, 132. Cf. the *pilleus* or *apex* of kingship on Tarquin (Liv. I, 34; Cic. *Leg.* I, 1, cf. Hor. *Od.* I, 34, 14 and pp. 376 ff.). Various 'capping' ceremonies, e.g. in universities, appear to derive from the same thought.

[11] See Horace, *Sat.* II, 5, 32; Pers. v, 75 ff.

(*praenomen*), elsewhere[1] associated with the *genius* and given with the *toga virilis* or *libera* when a boy's *genius* became effective and he a citizen. Cf. *per genium eius Gaium appellando rogare coepit* (Petron. 75). Since the rites with *oscillum* and *imago* are explained[2] by this conception of *caput*, we may thus also explain the legal *persona*, lit. 'mask' (cf. p. 429, n. 1), 'that attribute in a man which renders him capable of the enjoyment of rights'.[3]

In the belief that the *genius* was in the head and in the touching of the forehead in referring to him (see p. 129), we have probably the origin of the curious Roman custom of rubbing the forehead when blushing.[4] That a blush is confined more or less to the head would foster the belief that it is the head which is primarily affected by honour or dishonour, shame. It is a strange phenomenon for which the conscious self feels no responsibility and which it cannot control. It would therefore seem to be a sign from the *genius*[5] and the rubbing would be an attempt to propitiate him, as other evidence[6] appears to confirm. It was not a matter of improving or restoring one's appearance (for it would not), and when quite alone a man, who felt that he was blushing, rubbed.[7] The face also belonged to the *genius* and sometimes it was rubbed. The reddening of the blush is accompanied by a burning sensation and an actual rise in the temperature of the skin.[8] We speak of 'burning' with shame; the Romans spoke of 'fire' in this and

---

[1] E.g. see p. 264. [2] Pp. 126 f., 135.

[3] *The Commentaries of Gaius*, annot. F. Tomkins and W. G. Lemon, p. 57.

[4] Quintil. IX, 2, 25; Martial, XI, 27, 7; Juv. XIII, 242, and reff. given by Mayor and Duff. Hence, too, uses of *frons*, 'effrontery', etc.

[5] Cf. pp. 103, 138 f., 197 f., *pudor* (e.g. Ov. *Met.* II, 450), *pudicitia*, αἰδοῖα, p. 109, n. 2. The belief that besides the conscious self there was in the body another spirit was perhaps based mainly upon such unwilled phenomena as a sneeze, not least upon sexual excitement and the autonomy of the genital organ independent of the will. Cf. Plat. *Tim.* 91 B–C., Petron. 140 (p. 170, n. 2). [6] Pp. 180, 184 f.

[7] E.g. Petronius, 132, 12 f. For the significance of a blush for the Romans, see also below, pp. 153, 403 and for the smiting of the forehead p. 184. The forehead obviously covers the *cerebrum* (cf. p. 129).

[8] E.g. (of the blushing of the Aymara Indians in Bolivia) 'even in the dark a rise of temperature of the skin of the face can be felt exactly as occurs in the European', Forbes, *Transact. of Ethn. Soc.* II, 1870, p. 16.

other connections. Thus Virgil describes Lavinia, when in her presence her parents try to dissuade Turnus from his desire to marry her and its attendant dangers:

> *flagrantes perfusa genas cui plurimus ignem*
> *subiecit rubor et calefacta per ora cucurrit.*[1]

This 'burning' happens to the head thus not only when the occasion is shame but also in rage or other disturbance. The conscious self, the *animus* and its organs, *cor* and *praecordia*, in the chest are concerned in ordinary anger (cf. *stomachari*[2]); but when a man becomes frantic, the head is obviously affected. It becomes 'inflamed', red; the eyes glare and flash (e.g. *ardent oculi*[3] as if mad) and in some cases the hair bristles.[4] Later such frenzy was treated by bleeding the head (e.g. *quotiescumque coeperis a te exire, sanguinem tibi a capite mittam*[5]). This conception of fury as fire burning in the head, the brain, will explain why in Plautus when a pander, meeting the slave and confederates who have tricked him, says 'my heart is burning *(uritur cor mi)*', the other takes it up with 'Give him a tankard if his heart is burning lest his head catch fire *(caput ne ardescat)*',[6] the life-soul thus becoming dangerously involved and the man going 'out of his mind'; why a young man, almost frantic with love and anxiety, says: 'Love is making such a fire in my breast and my heart. If tears in my eyes did not prevent it, my head would already be on fire, I believe *(iam ardeat, credo, caput)*';[7] and why of what is maddening people one says 'their brain is now on fire at this *(id nunc his cerebrum uritur)*'.[8] This is the Roman background behind a strange passage in the *Aeneid*. Turnus raging for battle 'is stirred by these furies and from all his face, as he burns, leap sparks; from his fierce eyes darts fire':

> *his agitur furiis, totoque ardentis ab ore*
> *scintillae absiliunt, oculis micat acribus ignis.*[9]

---

[1] *Aen.* XII, 65 f. So Theocr. XIV, 23, etc.   [2] See p. 88.
[3] Plaut. *Capt.* 594.   [4] Cf. pp. 129 f., 231 ff. and Cuchulain on p. 157.
[5] Petron. 90.   [6] *Pers.* 801 f.   [7] *Merc.* 590 f.
[8] *Poen.* 770. So *caldicerebrius* (Petron. 45; 58).
[9] XII, 101 f. In VII, 787 f. the Chimaera on his head flames more fiercely in proportion to the fierceness of his warfare.

In madness and what seems to be a brief spasm of madness, violent rage (cf. Horace's *ira furor brevis est*,[1] and the use of *furo, furor*, etc.), when the head was thus 'on fire', the normal rational consciousness, whose seat is the chest, is no longer in control (cf. e.g. *a te exire* above). The man appears to be 'possessed', dominated by some other spirit, and might well seem to be dominated by that potent other spirit in him, dissociated from normal consciousness, the spirit in the head, more particularly in the brain (*cerebrum*), the *genius*.[2] Thus we may understand not only references to the head as what was concerned in madness[3] but also the use of *cerebrum*, *cerebrosus* and *cerritus* in reference to one who is furious or mad. He who was frantic, 'possessed', was *cerritus* or *cerebrosus*. These two words can scarcely be dissociated from each other; or *cerebrosus*[4] from *cerebrum*; or *cerritus*[5] from *cerus, kerus* (equivalent in meaning to *genius*[6]) and the adjective *kerriios* applied to generative powers on the tablet of Agnone.[7] It fits our interpretation of the rubbing of the forehead, when blushing, as a propitiation of the *genius* that the conscious self was afraid of the anger of the *genius*.[8] In oath a man says *ita genium meum*

---

[1] *Epist.* 1, 2, 62.

[2] I mean, of course, here and below that this was probably the original belief, not that it was always present to those who later used the expressions quoted. With the blurring (see pp. 168 ff.) of the original dualism of *animus*, the normal conscious mind associated particularly with the chest, and *genius*, the procreative life-soul associated particularly with the head (and marrow), vagueness and confusion would inevitably arise.

[3] See e.g. Horace, *Sat.* II, 3, 128 ff.: *tun sanus?...insanum te clament... incolumi capite es? Ars Poet.* 300: *tribus Anticyris caput insanabile.*

[4] See e.g. *insanum hominem et cerebrosum*, Lucil. 509 (Marx). Cf. Horace, *Sat.* I, 5, 21 and for *cerebrum* I, 9, 11 f., II, 3, 75, also Plaut. *Men.* 505 f.: *non tibi sanum est...sinciput.* On the materialistic interpretation the brain had gone wrong. Cf. below, p. 160, n. 4. Juv. XIV, 57 f., XV, 23, seem to imply that in madness the brain has gone from the head, a development perhaps of this last or of the view traced on pp. 115 f., 118 f. (cf. Pliny, *N.H.* XI, 37, 134). But cf. Juv. VII, 159, etc.

[5] *cerritus* seems to mean 'possessed by a *cerus*' as *larvatus* 'possessed by a *larva*' (see e.g. Plaut. *Men.* 890; *Amph.* 776). *larva* was a term for the departed soul, or, as we have seen reason for believing, *genius* or *cerus*, conceived as inhabiting a head (cf. *larva*='mask', pp. 135, 429, n. 1). An alien spirit of the kind might be supposed to take possession of one's head. Cf. p. 136, n. 3.   [6] See pp. 125 f.   [7] Zvetaieff, *Osc. Syll. Inscr.* p. 116.

[8] Cf. *genio sinistro* (Pers. IV, 27); pp. 162 f., 224 f.

propitium habeam, curabo,[1] etc., a woman of the *iuno*, the feminine counterpart of the *genius: iunonem meam iratam habeam si unquam....*[2] Belief that the deity to whom one belonged, the *genius* or *iuno*, was in the brain and took cognisance of what the conscious self said or did may explain the custom or customs described by Pliny in two passages, in one of which he says that to escape retribution for one's words one asked divine pardon by touching the mouth with a finger and then applying the finger to the head behind the right ear[3] and in the other that to 'propitiate disquietude of mind' people applied saliva with a finger to the head behind the ear.[4] It fits an original attribution of fury to the *genius* that while one character in Petronius, announcing his impending fury, says *experieris cerebrum meum,*[5] another vouches for his truth to the assembled company by saying *ego si mentior genios vestros iratos habeam*[6] (cf. *genius tuus ignoscet mihi,*[7] etc.).

It is as natural to refer to the *caput* or *cerebrum* instead of their indwelling spirit, the *genius*, as to refer to the *pectus, cor,* or *praecordia* instead of their indwelling spirit, the *animus. Caput* was regularly referred to thus after death.[8] But, as we have seen and shall see, there is evidence that the life-soul was particularly associated not only with the brain but with the whole of the cerebro-spinal 'marrow'. Through the vertebrae 'the marrow descends from the brain (*a cerebro medulla descendente*). That it is of the same nature as the brain is inferred from the fact that if only the thin surrounding membrane is pierced one immediately expires'.[9] Thus Pliny; and there is evidence[10] a good deal earlier that for the Romans the marrow was the stuff of vitality and strength. By recogni-

---

[1] Petron. 74. [2] *Id.* 25.
[3] *N.H.* XI, 45, 251. His idea that this part of the head was the seat of Nemesis is like the explanation of the sanctity of the knees as the seat of Misericordia (see Serv. *ad Ecl.* VI, 3; *Aen.* III, 607) and as certainly is not the true explanation (see pp. 174 ff. below). [4] XXVIII, 2, 5.
[5] 75, 6. The charms of a low forehead (*minima,* Petron. 126, cf. Hor. *Od.* I, 33, 5; Mart. IV, 42, 9) were perhaps originally acclaimed in a belief that it betokened less *cerebrum.*
[6] 62, 14. [7] 37, 3 discussed below, p. 226.
[8] See pp. 132 ff. [9] *N.H.* XI, 37, 178. Cf. Macrob. VII, 9, 22.
[10] See p. 210 with 206 f., Lucan, VI, 750 ff. (*subrepens vita medullis*), etc.

tion of this unity and of the thought just traced other strange passages may be explained, where in frenzied grief or rage there is said to be fire in the marrow, in the bones. Thus, according to Virgil, when by his steersman's fault Gyas is passed in the race, *exarsit iuveni dolor ossibus ingens*, and he knocks the steersman into the water (*Aen.* v, 173 ff.); and when his attack upon the Trojans is baffled,

> *Rutulo ... tuenti*
> *ignescunt irae et duris dolor ossibus ardet.*[1]

Catullus thus describes Berenice distraught by the loss of her brother:

> *quam penitus maestas exedit cura medullas!*
> *ut tibi tum toto pectore sollicitae*
> *sensibus ereptis mens excidit!*[2]

There is frenzy, the marrow is consumed and the normal consciousness, the mind whose seat is the organs of the chest, is dethroned.

Other passages also may now be better understood. They confirm our interpretation[3] of *caput* as containing the stuff of life, the seed; of *cerebrum*, the brain or cerebral marrow itself as the source of procreation (*cereo, creo*), seat of the procreative power (*cerus = genius*); and of frenzy as a becoming active, a burning and, as it were, eruption of the same. Plautus speaks

---

[1] Lucan IX, 65 f. So too in great terror or anxiety there is 'chill trembling' in the bones. Not only the chest, seat of the conscious mind, *animus*, but also the seat of the life-soul is affected, e.g. *obstipuere animi gelidusque per ima cucurrit/ossa tremor* (*ibid.* II, 120 f.; cf. III, 57, VII, 458 f., etc.). The involuntary quivering would naturally be attributed to the *genius* (see pp. 138 f., 146, 197 f., 207 f.). It feels the peril. To Cassius of Parma at Actium there is recorded to have appeared a huge figure, black and with hair unkempt, i.e. *sordidatus*, in distress or mourning (cf. Plut. *Vit. Cic.* 30 f.), apparently his *genius* (cf. Plut. *Vit. Brut.* 36, 48 and Preller-Jordan, *op. cit.* II, p. 198 f.). Cassius soon afterwards suffered *supplicium capitis* (Val. Max. I, 7, 7). Thus the *genius*, whether within a man or without (see pp. 159, n. 2, 184, 197 f.) at the time, foresees danger and may give an indication. For the ψυχή thus outside the waking man see e.g. the implications of Aeschylus' ψυχοστασία (pp. 397 f., 405, n. 8 *fin.*).

[2] LXVI, 23 ff. Cf. Ovid, *Am.* II, 19, 43.

[3] Pp. 123 ff. Similar thought will explain our own name for the surviving life-soul in the head (pp. 100, 154 f., 238 ff.): Anglo-Saxon *gǽst*, 'ghost', German *Geist*, etc. if it originally referred to fury, frenzy. Cf. Old Norse

of 'loving with one's marrow' (*medullitus amare*[1]), and of love, figured as a storm, not only as flowing into one's chest[2] but also as flowing into one's marrow.[3] Explicitly of sexual excitement, the *furor*[4] of love, Catullus says *cum vesana meas torreret flamma medullas*;[5] so on other occasions *ignes interiorem edunt medullam*;[6] *ignis mollibus ardet in medullis*,[7] etc.; while Virgil in the third *Georgic* says that all men and birds and beasts

> *in furias ignemque ruunt: amor omnibus idem.*[8]

For him explicitly this sexual fire of the marrow expresses itself in fury.[9] Unwarlike deer become fierce. Man himself when thus possessed, with his marrow burning, is mad:

> *quid iuvenis magnum cui versat in ossibus ignem*
> *durus amor?*[10]

And

> *scilicet ante omnis furor est insignis equarum....*
> *continuoque avidis ubi subdita flamma medullis*
> *vere magis, quia vere calor redit ossibus, illae....*[11]

So time and again in the *Aeneid*. Venus fondles and embraces her husband,

> *ille repente*
> *accepit solitam flammam notusque medullas*
> *intravit calor et labefacta per ossa cucurrit....*[12]

---

geisa 'to rage' and pp. 155 ('hag'), 245, n. 2. For reference to terror in Anglo-Saxon *gœstan* 'gast', 'aghast', etc. cf. perhaps p. 150, n. 1.

[1] *Most.* 243, i.e. affecting not only the chest, organs of ordinary consciousness, but the inmost seat of life itself.

[2] *Ibid.* 142 f.   [3] *Fragm. dub.* 1 (Lindsay).

[4] Prop. 1, 13, 20; Horace, *Epod.* xi, 6; *Sat.* ii, 3, 325 f., etc., and below. For Democritus it was a kind of 'possession': τὴν συνουσίαν εἶναι μικρὰν ἐπιληψίαν (quoted by Macrob. ii, 8, 16; cf. B 32 Diels on p. 108, n. 7).

[5] c, 7. The cerebro-spinal marrow must be primarily intended in these passages. For other bones and marrow, however, see below, pp. 178, 182 f. That marrow burns, is readily transmuted into flame, may have helped the thought (cf. pp. 262 f. below); but the cerebro-spinal 'marrow' has much less fat than the rest.

[6] xxxv, 15.   [7] xliii (xlv), 16.   [8] 242.

[9] The belief here traced that the burning of the marrow signified alike the wrath and the sexual excitement of the *genius* makes it easier to understand how Horace can speak of sexual indulgence as called for by the 'glowing wrath' of the sexual agent in man, *Sat.* i, 2, 68 ff.; cf. pp. 21, 139, n. 2. Ovid speaks of the unhappy Sabine women as *genialis praeda* (*Ars Am.* i, 125).   [10] *Georg.* iii, 258 f.   [11] *Ibid.* 266 ff.

[12] viii, 388 ff.

She sends Cupid to Dido so that he may

> *furentem*
> *incendat reginam atque ossibus implicet ignem.*[1]

Later

> *est mollis flamma medullas*
> *interea et tacitum vivit sub pectore volnus.*
> *uritur infelix Dido totaque vagatur*
> *urbe furens....*[2]
>
> *ardet amans Dido traxitque per ossa furorem.*[3]

Ovid thus describes 'love at first sight':

> *vidit et ut tenerae flammam rapuere medullae,*
> *hinc pudor, ex illa parte trahebat amor.*[4]

Propertius refers to love as 'fire in the bones' (*in ossibus ignes*[5]) which when unsatisfied might be assuaged by wine entering through the temples, i.e. to the cerebro-spinal marrow:

Bacche, tuis per fervida tempora donis/accersitus erit somnus in ossa mea.[6]

With the same breath he speaks of the god Love as haunting his breast and asks 'what pleasure he can find living in dry marrows'[7] (sc. such as the poet's had now become). Popular belief that in the body of the lover two systems are involved: (*a*) the organs of the chest, seat of the *animus*,[8] the mind of normal consciousness disturbed by the emotions, and (*b*) the marrow associated with the procreative life-soul, will also explain why Horace's Canidia, to make the old man she wants 'burn' for her, is at pains to prepare the liver and marrow of a boy as a 'cup of love' (*amoris poculum*) for him.[9] Among the organs Horace elsewhere singles out the liver as concerned in love.[10] This is perhaps also the ultimate explanation why the person loved is said to be 'fixed in the marrow and organs' (*in medullis ac visceribus haerere*) of the person who loves.[11]

We have already[12] seen that the veiling of the head was

---

[1] I, 659 f.   [2] IV, 66 ff.   [3] *Ibid.* 101.
[4] *Am.* III, X, 27 f. Cf. *Her.* IV, 15, *Met.* IX, 485, XIV, 351, *Ars Am.* III, 793.
[5] III (IV), 17, 9.   [6] *Ibid.* 13 f. Cf. pp. 227 f.
[7] II, 12 (III, 3), 17. See p. 213, n. 4 below.
[8] See e.g. Plautus' *fixus animus clavo cupidinis*, p. 373.   [9] *Epod.* V, 37 f.
[10] See pp. 87 ff.   [11] See Cic. *Phil.* I, 15, 36; also p. 161, n. 6.   [12] Pp. 132 f.

probably for the benefit of the *genius* or *iuno* in the head. It is this that is primarily concerned in marriage. We can now better understand why the veil had so important a part in the ceremony (*nubere, conubium*, etc.), why it was flame-coloured[1] and called *flammeum,* not just to hide a blush,[2] as has been suggested, but to suit or perhaps rather to induce the appropriate state[3] of the generative soul. Thus too the bridal torch.[4]

---

[1] Cf. p. 403 and *tollite, o pueri, faces./flammeum video venire*, Catull. LXI, 114 f., and his association of the *ignis* of the Evening star with marriage: *nec iunxere prius quam se tuus extulit ardor*, LXII, 29. Women also wore the *flammeum* to sacrifice (Non. 541, 28), the soul apparently being then present in power. Cf. pp. 133, n. 1; 145. Moses' veil was associated with the condition of his head as he spoke with the Lord: 'the skin of his face shone and they were afraid to come nigh him' (*Ex.* xxxiv, 29–35), which should perhaps be related to the belief that the soul is in the head (pp. 103, 234) and to the statement in the *Talmud* that on the head of a child (in the womb apparently) a light burns (*Niddah*, 30 b). Cf. pp. 155 ff.

[2] Blushing itself had quite other importance for the Romans than for us (see pp. 146 ff. Cf. pp. 159 ff., 403, n. 1). The veil might indeed be thought to screen off the generative spirit expected to be present in power at this rite. In Scandinavia maidens went bareheaded but the head of a woman who was married or who, though unmarried, had once had sexual intercourse, was believed to have dangerous potency and had to be covered indoors or out. For evidence, see P. Lugn, *Mitteil. d. Anthrop. Gesellsch. in Wien*, 1920, pp. 81 ff. He explains merely by a widespread belief that the *Macht* is in the hair. Cf. the similar Slav custom (Hastings, *E.R.E.* VIII, 471).

[3] See also pp. 156, 403, esp. n. 1. There is the 'love-light' still:

> 'And love is fire; and when I say at need
> *I love thee*...mark!...*I love thee!*...in thy sight
> I stand transfigured, glorified aright,
> With conscience of the new rays that proceed
> Out of my face towards thine'.
>
> (From 'Yet love, mere love...' in Mrs Browning's
> *Sonnets from the Portuguese.*)

Sanscr. *rakta* 'red' meant also 'in love', i.e. sexually excited. Savara bridesmaids warm their fingers at a lamp and rub the bridegroom's cheeks (Risley, *Tribes...of Bengal* II, 243). Cf. Ap. Rhod. III, 962, 1016 f., Theoc. II, 140 f., Claud. *Nupt. Hon.* 1 ff. (*hauserat insolitos promissae virginis ignes...incanduit ore confessus secreta rubor*), etc. For Sappho λέπτον/δ' αὔτικα χρῶ πῦρ ὑπαδεδρόμακεν (II, 9 f.). We can now explain why statues of Priapus were painted red, *ruber* (Tibull. I, 1, 17; Ovid, *Fasti*, I, 400, 415, etc.). Cf. p. 403, n. 1 and pp. 156 ff.

[4] Associated with Ceres (see pp. 125 f., 471, n. 3), Fest. 77, 21. Cf. Serv. *ad Ecl.* VIII, 29, etc., Love's torch, ἀμφίκαυστις, etc. and p. 156, n. 2.

In old Germanic belief likewise the mind, the conscious self, was believed to be in the chest[1] and the surviving soul to be in the head.[2] Thus we can understand in the same way[3] as for the Greeks and Romans the custom referred to in *Beowulf* and the Norse sagas of wrapping up the head of the dead.[4] And we may perhaps suggest that among the Germanic peoples also the head and the life-soul were thought to be specially concerned in procreation.[5] This will explain the custom constantly alluded to in *Beowulf* and common to both the nations described (Geats and Danes), the custom of carrying the image of a boar upon one's helmet. The head contained the life and life-soul so that men who defended themselves were said to 'guard their heads'.[6] The helmet or 'head-protector' (*heafod-beorg*) is referred to simply as 'the boar'.[7] It is 'the boar, the head-sign' (*eafor heafod-segn*).[8] 'The boar kept ward' (*ferh wearde heold*[9]). This seems to mean that the head was committed uniquely to the protection of the god of procreation and fertility, Freyr, whose emblem the boar was.[10] Its head

---

[1] See pp. 38f., 68f.   [2] See p. 100.   [3] See pp. 101, 132f.

[4] Hoops (*Englische Studien*, LIV, 1920, pp. 19 ff.) reviews the evidence but makes no suggestion as to the origin of the custom. Belief that a ghost appeared as a head will explain Anglo-Saxon *gríma* (1) 'mask', 'helm', (2) 'spectre'. Cf. pp. 135, 148, n. 5. For the wrapping of the heads of northern prophetesses then as in the later witch-cult cf. pp. 102 ff., esp. p. 104, n. 3.

[5] See also pp. 153, n. 2, 239 ff., 267 ff. Anglo-Saxon *heafod-gemæca* (= 'head-consort or companion, mate'), *heafod-maga* (= 'head-son'), etc., are usually explained by the metaphorical interpretation of *heafod* as 'chief', but perhaps originated rather in the belief that marriage, kinship and comradeship were affairs of the head. *Heafod*, like *caput*, was used for the source of a stream, cf. pp. 125, 231.   [6] See p. 100.

[7] 1111 f.   [8] 2152.

[9] 305. Cf. *Elene*, 76, etc.

[10] See e.g. *Skaldskaparmal*, 35; *Gylfaginning*, 49. Tacitus (*Germ.* 45) tells us of the Aestii on the northern sea that 'they worship the mother of the gods and as emblem of the superstition they wear images of wild boars. This serves instead of armour or any other protection and renders the worshipper of the goddess free from anxiety even amidst the foe'. 'The mother of the gods' was presumably a fertility goddess like that familiar to the Romans, like Freyja, female counterpart of Freyr. That the boar on the helmet in *Beowulf* was probably an emblem of Freyr has long been recognised. But why the head should be under his care has, I think,

appears to have been the chief feature of his festival, Yule, surviving when the latter became Christmas.[1] We shall find below[2] other evidence that for the Germanic peoples the head and brain were associated with fertility and see (p. 213) that the marrow, of which the brain was conceived to be part, was for the later English as for Greeks and Romans the seed and the seat of animal vitality and strength. We referred fire in the head to the *genius*; in old Germanic belief the soul appeared as a flame.[3] So perhaps it was in England a flame was believed to appear at night on a man's head or a horse's mane and called a 'hag', a term for a ghost, sprite, or fury. In the sagas fire was to be seen at the graves of the dead.[4] *Bruni* meant

---

lacked explanation. It was, perhaps, because it procreates so many off-spring at once that the pig seemed the embodiment of fertility in northern Europe and in parts of the Mediterranean, e.g. at the Thesmophoria. See Schol. to Lucian, *Dial. Mer.* II, 1, and note 9 on p. 177 below.

[1] It was garlanded and treated with great ceremony. We hear that in 1170 it was preceded by trumpets (Holinshed. *Chron.* III, 76). 'A Carol bryngyng in the Bore's Hede' was recorded, printed by Wynkin de Worde in 1521, declaring that 'The bores hede, I understande, Is the chefe servyce in this lande, Loke wherever it be fande'. 'Loke' usually means 'look' but the original text must surely have meant 'luck wherever it is found'. It is the still familiar *Caput apri defero Reddens laudes Domino....* The boar's head thus important was reinterpreted by Christians as a symbol of Christ. See *The Early English Carols*, ed. R. L. Greene, p. 92 with note *ad loc*. In many places the head was wrestled for and carried off by the victor. Cf. the head of the October Horse, p. 126 above. A belief in its potency thus may explain why the head (and skin) of the Calydonian boar were fought for with such eagerness (*Il.* IX, 548 ff.). For the skin, see p. 235, n. 4.

[2] Pp. 239 ff. Now also we may guess why heads were the offering to the god of procreation among their neighbours in Slavonia (Dulaure, *Histoire abrégée de différents cultes*[2], II, p. 245). Cf. p. 153, n. 2. If the ancient Slavs associated the surviving soul with the head it will explain the offering of animals' heads to the death-god and incidents in e.g. W. R. Ralston, *Songs of the R. People*[2], pp. 129 f., 135, 175 and above p. 142, n. 1. They believed that it appeared as fire (see Ralston, *op. cit.* p. 116. Cf. p. 158, n. 5 below) and seem to have identified consciousness with the breath (cf. p. 44 above) in the air passages of the lungs (e.g. Ralston, *op. cit.* p. 117). A myth made man's thought out of the wind (Ralston, *Russian Folktales*, p. 328).

[3] See R. M. Meyer, *Altgerm. Rel.* pp. 75 f.; E. H. Meyer, *Myth. d. G.* p. 75.

[4] *Hauga Eldr*, 'Cairn-Fire'. The dragon or serpent, 'fire-drake', with which it was sometimes associated, as in *Beowulf*, was perhaps originally

'burning, heat; burning passion, lust, etc.' and *brundr* meant 'seed' (animal).[1] Cf. German *Brunst,* etc. This will also explain English 'spunk' (= 'spark, flame') for 'seed'.[2]

In many parts of Wales there existed comparatively recently the belief[3] that, when he is about to die, a flame like that of a candle quits a man and precedes the corpse on its way to the grave. Such was believed to appear upon the womb of a mother before a child was born. This was surely, in origin, the soul thus conceived. For the Celts the seat of the soul was the head.[4] The belief in such a flame passing to the grave is instanced also from the Isle of Man, and among the Gadhelic Celts we find further striking evidence of a conception like that traced among the Romans. The Gaelic word for 'brain', *eanchainn,* was used to express 'boldness, audacity, impudence', and the derivative adjective *eanchainneach,* 'brainy', meant

the northern counterpart to the snake-form of ψυχή and *genius* (see pp. 129, 206 f., 233 f., Paul. Diac. *H. Langob.* III, 34). Its treasure seems to be that buried with the dead (e.g. *Beowulf,* 2211 ff.). Thus perhaps in *Voluspa* (42) a room in the Land of the Dead covered with the backs of serpents. 'So have I seen a fire-drake glide at midnight/Before a dying man', etc. (Chapman, *C. and P.* III, 1).

[1] Saxo Grammaticus (VII, p. 222, ed. Holder) tells us that Sewald said of Halfdan: 'it was not strange that a bachelor empty of offspring (*prole vacuum*) should refuse the combat offered, since his nature was without heat and had struck a shameful frost into his body and mind'.

[2] See s.v. in Wright, *English Dialect Dictionary.* In *Morte d'Arthur* (XVII, 18), the chaste Galahad comes to a hot well. He touched it 'so that it burnt no more and the heat departed. For that it brent it was a sign of lechery, the which was that time much used'. This conception of the procreative principle as active in fire (cf. p. 158) will explain the widespread kindling of fires to produce fertility as the merely solar and purificatory theories hitherto current will not. For examples of such fires see Frazer, *The Golden Bough, Balder,* etc., I, pp. 106–346. Often it was an embodiment of the life or fertility spirit (e.g. the Yule log; cf. pp. 153, n. 4, 219 ff., 268, n. 1, 456, n. 2) which was thus kindled. For some the sun was its supreme embodiment, kindling to renewal of life. For gold=fire, see p. 166. To the Hindoos gold was seed, the seed of Agni = Fire (see *Satapatha Brahmana,* II, 1, 1, 5, etc.), of the immolated horse (*ibid.* XIII, 1, 1, 3 f.) or of Indra (*ibid.* XII, 7, 1, 7), the god who fertilises in the thunderstorm, lightning. We can now better understand the virtue of Thor's hammer (=lightning) in the lap of the bride (e.g. *Þrymskviða* 30), Semele conceiving Dionysos πυρόσπορος (cf. Hes. *Theogony,* 699 ff.), Danae (Pind. *Pyth.* XII, 17; Soph. *Ant.* 950, etc.), and Aphrodite linked with Hephaistos.

[3] See Brand's *Pop Antiq.* (publ. Bohn), III, pp. 237 f.   [4] See pp. 100 f.

'bold, impudent, *audax, impudicus*'.[1] A belief in its potency[2] will explain why the ancient Irish used to take just the brain from the head of a fallen warrior and mix it with earth, moulding it into a ball to be used as a missile weapon, a *tathlun*. In the *Táin Bó Cúalnge* there are striking descriptions of the hero Cuchulain in a fit of fury which remind us of Virgil's picture of Turnus.[3] On such an occasion when he was a boy his hair stood on end and 'thou wouldst have weened it was a spark of fire that was on every single hair there'.[4] On another such occasion Ailill utters a warning that there is no hope of forcing a way past him: 'Ye will

[1] See Celt. Dict. of the Highl. Soc. of Scotl., s.v. If the head was the source of procreation, fertility, we can perhaps also explain the Welsh version of the Grail (*Peredur ap Efrawg* in the *Mabinogion*) in which the Grail vessel, which has long been recognised as a fertility symbol and which like the *cornucopia* (see pp. 239 f.) was a miraculous source of supply, is replaced by a head on a dish. Miss J. L. Weston (*Romania*, XLIX, pp. 273 ff.) has related this version to the curious statement in the York Breviary: *Caput Iohannis in disco: signat Corpus Christi: quo pascimur in sancto altari*. But that too has lacked explanation; with the significance traced his severed head was perhaps a reason why John was chosen by the Church to replace the fertility god worshipped at Midsummer (for his 'Fires', cf. p. 156, n. 2). Cf. the account of the head worshipped by the Templars on p. 144. John the Baptist was their patron. The loss of the head in the Peredur story, like the loss of hair noted below (p. 231, n. 1), is associated with the maiming (see p. 183, n. 3) of the Grail king. R. S. Loomis (*Revue Celtique*, 1930, pp. 39 ff.), correlating various versions, urges that the head in the dish is the head of Bran=Bron, i.e. the Grail king. If this is so, since the point of the maiming of the king in the Grail legends is his loss of procreative power (see pp. 182 f., 220 below and Miss Weston, *From Ritual to Romance*), attended by loss of fruitfulness in nature, this alternative form of maiming, the loss of his head—the other was a wound in his thigh—would be a loss of that power and would imply for the head the value I have suggested. To the Celtic belief that the head contains the soul we related above (p. 101) the story of the 'Entertaining of the noble Head'. Bran commanded that his head should be cut off, and his comrades feasted with the head. It was as pleasant company as it had been when possessed of a body, and it continued thus during their feasting and journeying till after eighty-seven years they buried it in London, and its potency was such that the island could not be invaded so long as it was buried there.

[2] See also pp. 191, n. 1, 193 f. The ideas traced (cf. p. 136, n. 3) may explain the brain-extraction at Maiden Castle (neolithic). See *The Times*, Feb. 25, 1938, p. 18.

[3] See p. 147.

[4] *Op. cit.* trans. Dunn, pp. 48 f. Cf. p. 17.

not go past him by force, now that his flame of valour has risen'. For it was usual in him when his hero's flame arose in him that 'his feet would turn back on him and his buttocks before him and the knobs of his calves would come on his shins, etc.' His body becomes unrecognisable as if animated by a different spirit. His normal consciousness is no longer in control. 'He would recognise neither comrade nor friend.'[1] Later the 'flame of valour' is more fully described. 'There were seen... the sparks of glowing red fire, blazing and flashing in hazes and mists over his head with the seething of the truly wild wrath that rose up above him. His hair bristled all over his head like branches of a red-thorn thrust into a gap in a great hedge....The champion's light stood out of his forehead so that it was as long and as thick as a whetstone, so that it was as long as his nose, till he got furious handling the shields, thrusting out the charioteers, destroying the hosts.'[2]

Among the evidence[3] of the ancient Italian association of procreation with fire are the legends that Servius Tullius was begotten by a phallus of fire which appeared on the hearth[4] and that Caecilius, the reputed founder of Praeneste, was begotten by a spark from the hearth.[5] Our interpretation of the fire in the head and in the cerebro-spinal marrow as a manifestation of the *genius* active within will help to explain the beliefs that 'men's heads at nightfall shine with light around

---

[1] *Op. cit.* p. 144.

[2] *Ibid.* p. 191. Homer's story of the flame about the head of Achilles may be a vestige of such a belief (*Il.* xviii, 207 ff.). Cf. *Od.* xviii, 353 ff.

[3] See e.g. Gruppe, *op. cit.* p. 726, n. 2.

[4] Pliny, *N.H.* xxxvi, 27, 204 says that the *Lar familiaris* (worshipped on the hearth) was believed to have begotten him thus; Ovid, *Fasti,* vi, 631 *Volcanus.*

[5] See Serv. *ad Aen.* vii, 678. The association of the procreative impulse with fire and these stories of the hearth as source of procreation (see also Plut. *Rom.* ii, 7) support the assimilation of *Lar* and *genius.* So far from it being against the interpretation of the *Lares* as ancestral *genii* that they made the fields fertile, such fertility is elsewhere expected from the dead, e.g. ἀπὸ γὰρ τῶν ἀποθανόντων αἱ τροφαὶ καὶ αὐξήσεις καὶ σπέρματα, Hippoc. περὶ ἐνυπν. ιι, p. 14. Cf. τριτοπάτορες on pp. 120; 127, n. 2; 234, n. 1; 424, n. 7. Among the Slavs (cf. p. 155, n. 2) the soul of an ancestor was believed to be in the fire in the stove (see Ralston, *op. cit.* pp. 119 ff.).

them, a great sign for the future' (Plin. *N.H.* II, 37, 101) and before Salvidiemus Rufus' greatness his head flamed (Dio Cass. XLVIII, 33) and Servius Tullius, though born of a slave mother, was as a boy marked out for great fortune by the prodigy that while he slept—a time when, as we saw (pp. 102 f.), for the Greeks not the conscious self in the chest but the life-soul in the head was active—'his head blazed in the sight of many people' and in alarm water was brought to quench it, but on the advice of the queen was not used, and presently 'with the departure of sleep the flame also departed'. Later, in his hour of crisis the queen appeals to the flame: *nunc te illa caelestis excitet flamma.*[1] To the ideas traced we may now relate the Persian belief (cf. p. 100) that about the head, more particularly of a king or great man, was 'light' or 'glory', *hvarenō.* Cicero relates Servius' flame to his remarkable sagacity in speech and action, saying that when he attended upon the king *non latuit scintilla ingenii quae iam tum elucebat in puero.*[2] It is perhaps to outbursts of the genius, to the *furor*[3] of the poet, that Ennius alludes:

> *Enni poeta, salve, qui mortalibus*
> *versus propinas flammeos medullitus,*[4]

---

[1] See Livy, I, 39 and 41 and the references on p. 158, n. 4. Whether these stories arose together or one grew out of the other is hard to say. His begetting by fire fits the manifestation of his *genius* in fire. This manifestation showed not only the presence but the active power of the *genius*. For the veiling of his head (Ov. *Fasti* VI, 570 ff.) cf. pp. 133, n. 1, 153, nn. 1, 2.

[2] *De Republica*, II, 21, 37. Very similar is the story of the child Roscius around whom sleeping it was noticed with alarm that a serpent was coiled. Consulted by his father about it, the *haruspices* replied that the child would be most distinguished and famous (Cic. *de Div.* I, 36, 79). That this was the child's *genius* showing its favour is the most natural interpretation in view of the regular representation of the *genius* as a serpent and its generally acknowledged appearance in that form on similar occasions (see e.g. Cic. *de Div.* I, 18, 36; Livy, XXVI, 19, etc., and pp. 129 above and 206 f. below). Association of the *genius* with the head and with serpent form perhaps lies behind the story in Dio Cassius, LVIII, 7, 1 f., the smoke there being a sign of consuming by fire. Cf. Juv. x, 62.   [3] See e.g. Cic. *de Div.* I, 37, 80.

[4] *Sat.* III, 1. See Nonius, pp. 33, 139. *capitalis* applied to the gifted (see Ovid, *Fast.* III, 839, Cic. *ad Q. fratr.* II, 11, 4) perhaps derives from the association of the prompting *genius* or of originality (cf. pp. 124 f.) with the head.

with which we may compare Catullus' picture of Ariadne, who at first sight of Theseus

> *cuncto concepit corpore flammam*
> *funditus atque imis exarsit tota medullis,*[1]

and, when her love is frustrated by his desertion, prays:

> *meas audite querellas*
> *quas ego, vae, misera extremis proferre medullis*
> *cogor inops ardens amenti caeca furore.*

She is frenzied, 'possessed', on fire; her utterance is compelled and comes from her marrow. In the third century B.C., the story went that, as Marcius was addressing the troops, 'without his feeling it, flame streamed out of his head to the great alarm of the soldiers standing round'.[2] Cf. perhaps Moses' face shining (p. 153, n. 1). The Syrian Eunus, simulating the prophetic state, contrived flames from his mouth.[3] Further evidence appears below.[4]

Not only was his *genius* thus apparently liable to intervene or take possession of a man but we shall[5] also see reason to believe that it was, in the time of Plautus, thought to enjoy knowledge beyond what was enjoyed by the conscious self and to give the latter warning of impending events. Other uses[6] in Plautus imply that a man's *genius* was his protector

---

[1] LXIV, 93 f., 196 ff. In both cases Catullus refers immediately afterwards to the organs of the chest as concerned. Cf. p. 152.

[2] See Livy, xxv, 39, 16; Pliny, *N.H.* II, 107, 241; Val. Max. I, 6, 2.

[3] Diod. Sic. XXXIV, 2 Fr.

[4] Pp. 163 ff. A belief that the element in the head flamed perhaps lies behind the use of φλέγμα for the liquid of the head. Its form suggests and we know in fact that originally it meant 'flame' (*Il.* XXI, 337). Herodotus (IV, 187) describes how Libyan nomads apply fire to the heads of their children so that κατάρρεον φλέγμα ἐκ τῆς κεφαλῆς may never afterwards hurt them. φλέγμα was regarded as responsible for epilepsy (cf. p. 151, n. 4 with p. 148 and n. 4) or frenzy (cf. above), also for κατάρροι, *pitnita*. Sweat was supposed to come especially from the cerebro-spinal fluid mass (p. 193). It comes out in πυρετός and might seem to be the stuff of its 'flame'. Cf. e.g. ἀπύρετος, φλέγμ' οὐκ ἔχων (Antiph. Fr. 226), *caput incensum fervore gerebant* (Lucr. VI, 1145). For this 'humour' (phlegm) as cold, cf. p. 120, n. 4.

[5] Pp. 197 f., 207, 226, n. 1; cf. 150, n. 1.

[6] See *Capt.* 879; *Curc.* 301; *Men.* 138.

or 'good angel'. Thus in essence it will be the native Italian conception of the *genius* and not, as has been suggested, the Greek conception of the δαίμων which lies behind Horace's dictum[1] that the reason why one man chooses one course of action and his brother another 'is known to his *genius*, the companion[2] who tempers his natal star,[3] mortal god of human nature, one for every head,[4] changeful of countenance, fair and gloomy'. If a man's *genius* was believed to affect his behaviour for good or ill and was associated more particularly with the brain, we can understand another mysterious expression. As we saw,[5] Petronius' Trimalchio announced an impending fit of fury to its victim by *experieris cerebrum meum*. Telling how by serving his master's pleasure in his youth he began his fortune, he says not 'I won my master's *animus* or heart' (i.e. 'conscious self') but 'I won my master's brain (*cepi ipsimi cerebellum*). What need to say more? He made me coheir with Caesar.'[6] Another grateful freedman says *genio illius gratias, enatavi* (57). The idea of the *genius* seems to have served in great part as does the twentieth-century concept of an 'unconscious mind',[7] influencing a man's life and actions

---

[1] *Epist.* II, 2, 187 ff. See also p. 165.

[2] Cf. Hadrian's *animula vagula blandula/hospes comesque corporis* (Ael. Spart. *Hadr.* 25). For the identity of *anima* and *genius* see pp. 168 ff.

[3] This can scarcely belong to native Roman thought. See pp. 131, n. 2, 164 f. *Hvarenō* (p. 159) was sometimes derived from the heavenly light. For Slavonians (p. 155, n. 2) the soul was a spark of heavenly fire originally kindled by the lightning god (Ralston, *Songs of the Russian People*[2], p. 116. Cf. pp. 156, n. 2; 230, n. 8 *inf.*).

[4] See p. 129 above.   [5] P. 149.

[6] 76, 1. Some have read *ipsi mi* which, if it could stand without being unnaturally emphatic, would mean 'I got a brain for myself' and might be related to the restoration of *caput* to the emancipated slave (see pp. 144 f.). To *cepi ipsimi cerebellum* should perhaps be related in origin the expressions by which a person loved is said to be 'fixed in the marrow' (*haerere in medullis*, Cic. *ad Fam.* xv, 16, 2), as elsewhere 'fixed in the marrow and in the organs' (see p. 152), of him who loves him; and even a thing or idea is said to be 'shut up in one's marrow' (Cic. *ad Att.* xv, 4, 3). Cf. *Append. Verg. Dirae* 101, Ovid, *Trist.* I, 5, 5–10, etc. At times the writer may mean little more than that the person or thing is where one's very life is.

[7] The emphasis in the name *genius* reminds us of that in the Freudian *libido*. Cf. p. 103, n. 4.

apart from or even despite his conscious mind. It is now possible to trace the origin of our idiom that a man 'has' or 'has not genius', meaning that he possesses or does not possess a native source of inspiration beyond ordinary intelligence. At the end of the first century A.D. a man who ignored, or was ignored by, his *genius* might hyperbolically be said not to have one.[1] Juvenal says that an astrologer to be believed to have insight into the future must have been banished or imprisoned: 'No astrologer who has not been condemned will have (i.e. will be deemed to have) a *genius*'[2] (*genium...habebit*). How little the native Roman conception has been understood may be illustrated by the fact that Zilsel, who has examined the question most recently and exhaustively, says that this is 'nothing but a jesting reminiscence of Socrates with his Greek Daimonion'.[3] The Roman conception here traced of the *genius* as life-soul as well as divine helper, prompter of the conscious self, is happily employed in a poem of Martial in the same period. He says of a contemporary book reputed to be 'talented' (*ingeniosa*) that that is not enough to ensure that it shall live: *victurus genium debet habere liber*.[4]

Plutarch[5] tells us that, according to his soothsayer, the fortune of Antony was dimmed by the fortune of Octavian, his δαίμων (apparently = *genius*) afraid and humbled in the presence of Octavius' δαίμων and in fact, when they drew lots or competed in any way together, Antony always came off second best. We should not expect the *genius* of one man to be uniform with or of equal power with the *genius* of another.[6] There is, moreover, clear evidence of the belief that, while one man was favoured by his *genius*, to another his *genius* was unpropitious.[7] Thus between the man who had a powerful *genius* active on

---

[1] See Martial, VII, 78, 4, discussed below (p. 225).

[2] VI, 562.   [3] *Die Entstehung des Geniebegriffes*, 1926, p. 11.

[4] VI, 61, 10.

[5] See *Ant.* 33. δαίμων can represent nothing but *genius* in Roman belief. It seems to be the departed soul or *genius* in *Consol. ad Apoll.* 14 (109 D).

[6] Cf. in the conception of the soul as *umbra* 'the belief that a man's shadow ought to be deep so that he will attain to greatness' (note 4 on p. 95 above).   [7] See pp. 140, n. 1, 224 ff.

his behalf and the man who had a *genius* which was feeble or which ignored or hindered him there was a vast difference. The flame about the head of Servius Tullius, when a child asleep, marked him out for greatness. Virgil[1] uses the same idea in his account of the fall of Troy, telling how when Anchises and Aeneas were in despair, flame poured from the top of the head of the child Iulus and around his temples and his hair flamed, and while the rest wished to quench the 'holy fires' with water, Anchises prayed to Jupiter and asked for confirmation of the omen, and in answer there was thunder and a star with trailing light shot down to Mount Ida. Belief that the *genius*, the divine soul that survives, thus manifested itself in fire in the head would make easier the belief of the common people at Rome that the 'star with hair' (*stella crinita, cometes*), which appeared during the games celebrated soon after the death of Julius, was the soul of the latter thus shown to be *inter deorum immortalium numina receptam*.[2] Augustus himself after these words continues: 'explicitly for this reason (*quo nomine*) a star was added to the image of his head which we dedicated in the forum soon after'.[3] The greater the

---

[1] *Aen.* II, 680 ff. Similar was the portent when her marriage was in question and the maid Lavinia was standing at the altar before Aeneas' men reached the court of her father Latinus. Her hair and crown caught fire, so that wrapped in smoky yellow flame she scattered fire throughout the palace, which was interpreted that she herself would be *inlustrem fama fatisque* but to the nation boded a mighty war (VII, 71 ff.): this last being perhaps the interpretation of the fire scattered through the palace.

[2] See Pliny, *N.H.* II, 25, 93f.; Suet. *Jul.* 88; Virg. *Ecl.* IX, 47 with Servius *ad loc.* and *ad Aen.* VI, 790; Ovid, *Met.* xv, 749 ff.; Dio Cassius, XLV, 7. The ideas here traced explain the belief that the appearance of a comet means a change of rule (Lucan I, 529, Tac. *Ann.* XIV, 22 *regis*; Sueton. *Ner.* 36, etc.).

[3] Cited by Pliny, *loc. cit.* Cf. the representation of Augustus placing (or touching) a star upon the head of a figure of Agrippa in a coin of the year of the latter's death (Mattingly, *Coins of the Roman Empire in the British Museum*, Pl. IV, 14) and Dio Cassius, LIV, 29, 8. In the Augustan age the souls of other great Romans seem to have been thought to pass to the stars as did that of Caesar (cf. p. 138, n. 1). Thus Propertius (III (IV), 18, 33 f.) speaks of the dead Marcellus passing

> *qua Siculae victor telluris Claudius et qua*
> *Caesar ab humana cessit in astra via.*

energy, the potency of the soul, the brighter the flame, the star:

micat inter omnes
Iulium sidus velut inter ignes
luna minores. [1]

Augustus, we are told, [2] liked to believe that the appearance of this star portended good fortune for himself, and had a star shown on his own helmet. Virgil represents him at Actium:

geminas cui tempora flammas
laeta vomunt patriumque aperitur vertice sidus.[3]

A planet or star was itself conceived as a 'head' or 'face', *os sacrum.*[4] Pliny speaks of *sidera...ut existimat vulgus singulis attributa nobis, et clara divitibus, minora pauperibus, obscura defectis* (*N.H.* II, 8, 28).

At the end of the *Metamorphoses* just before the poet's prayer that not yet *caput Augustum...accedat caelo faveatque precantibus absens*[5] Venus complains of the plot to kill Julius: *quanta... caput cum fraude petatur* (xv, 766) and presently took his *anima* from the body and carried it away,

dumque tulit, lumen capere atque ignescere sensit
emisitque sinu. luna volat altius illa
flammiferumque trahens spatioso limite crinem
stella micat.[6]

That the departed soul or 'head' of the emperor was believed thus to ascend to the heavens fitted the belief that the *genius* manifested itself in flame and the Stoic belief that souls passed at death as fire to the heavens.[7] Virgil says of men and animals

igneus est ollis vigor et caelestis origo
seminibus,[8]

---

[1] Horace, *Odes,* I, 12, 46 ff.

[2] Pliny, *loc. cit.*   [3] *Aen.* VIII, 680 f. and Servius *ad loc.*

[4] *Aen.* VIII, 591, *Georg.* IV, 232. Cf. p. 143, n. 3.

[5] See p. 136 above. See also *Apocolocyntosis*, Addendum VII, p. 507.

[6] xv, 847–50. It is *stella iubata.* Jupiter had said: *hanc animam interea caeso de corpore raptam/fac iubar* (840 f.). *iuba* and *iubar* are perhaps thus related. *iubar* was a star or other light emitting rays, *iuba* the mane or hair, sometimes golden, radiating from the head. Hair was naturally regarded as stuff of the *genius* (see pp. 130 and 231 ff.).

[7] See references in Arnold's *Roman Stoicism,* pp. 263 f., and Lucan's account of Pompey (IX, 1 ff.). This belief is much older in Greece (e.g. Aristoph. *Peace,* 832 f.). It appears to have been held by the Orphics. Cf. p. 230, n. 8.   [8] *Aen.* VI, 730 f.

and for Horace the *genius* (elsewhere itself *natalis*) 'rules the *natale astrum, naturae deus humanae mortalis*, one for every head'.[1] Stoicism and astrology thus blended harmoniously with native Roman belief.

It is now possible better to understand the *nimbus* and representations of rays of light radiating from the head, also the rayed crown. It has long been believed[2] that they originally represented light as the attribute of deity (as belonging, it is suggested,[3] to the bright *aether* above), but it has not been adequately recognised that they express not mere light but fire, energy, power, nor has the question why the head should be shown thus radiant but not the rest of the body[4] been satisfactorily explained. Reference to artistic convenience or the principle of 'the part for the whole', etc., will not suffice. The chief reason[5] surely is that, as we have found, the head was believed to contain the life-soul, the divinity in each man, his *genius*, and the radiance belonged to the latter. It is impossible to say how early the story of the flame about the head of Servius Tullius was current. In the Greek world there is evidence of the use of the radiate crown at least three centuries[6] before our era. The Romans were not necessarily the first to use this means of representing radiance but had, as we have seen, their own reasons for believing that the power in the head manifested itself as fire and had, apparently, from remote antiquity covered the head with the *flammeum*[7] at

---

[1] See pp. 130f., 160f.

[2] See L. Stephani, 'Nimbus u. Strahlenkranz, etc.', *Mém. de l'Acad. des Sciences de St Pétersbourg*, VI Série, Sc. pol. hist. philol. IX, 1859. For the 'cloud' (*nimbus*) thus illumined cf. *inf.* pp. 421, 424, n. 7, *Aen.* II, 616, etc.

[3] So Stephani, *op. cit.* Sometimes the rays have a solar or stellar significance (e.g. Virg. *Aen.* XII, 162 ff.).

[4] In early Greece the gleaming beauty of a god might belong to all his body (see Homeric Hymn to Demeter, 188 ff. with Hymn to Aphrodite, 173 ff. and p. 197 below).

[5] So too we found that the head was bound, covered, etc., because it contained the soul (see pp. 132f., 144f., 152f.).

[6] Rather different but still with the sense of glorifying, making splendid, is Pindar's τηλαυγέσιν ἀνέδησεν Ὀρτυγίαν στεφάνοις (*Pyth.* II, 6; cf. III, 73; *Ol.* VIII, 1). Gold would be used for crowns to represent fire, flame and so divine energy, life. See p. 106 and note 2 on p. 156, also p. 183, n. 1 and p. 330.

[7] See pp. 152 f.

marriage. To Julius Caesar, whose departed soul it recognised in the 'star with hair', the Roman people had during his lifetime awarded 'a crown with rays' *(corona radiata)*[1] as a sign not of kingship but of deity.[2] *Vultus ubi tuus affulsit populo* says Horace of Augustus *(Od.* IV, 5, 6) and Seneca *flagrat nitidus fulgore remisso/vultus et adfuso cervix formosa capillo (Apoc.* 4) of Nero. He allowed himself to be represented with 'radiate head', as did his successors.[3] To Trajan Pliny says of his services: *Horum unum si praestitisset alius, illi iamdudum radiatum caput et media inter deos sedes auro staret aut ebore....Tu delubra non nisi adoraturus intras....*[4] The emperor Gallienus to make his head shine not only wore rays in public but sprinkled gold filings upon his hair.[5] To the emperor a little later a panegyrist speaks of 'that light surrounding your divine head in a bright circle' *(illa lux divinum verticem claro orbe complectens).*[6] It is in harmony with the belief that radiance about the head was an expression of the divine power, the *genius* there, and with the argument about *numen* and *capita deorum* above,[7] that we find, e.g. on the wall-paintings at Pompeii and Herculaneum,[8] the immortal gods, including those who had no obvious connection with the heavenly fires or with other fire, represented with a *nimbus* or with rays about their heads, and in literary records the faces of divine images gilded.[9] So perhaps *flagrantis dei vultus*[10] *(Aen.* I, 710), *divini signa decoris/ardentisque notate oculos* (V, 647 f.; cf. Suet. *Aug.* 79) and Venus reveals her divinity: *avertens rosea cervice refulsit* (I, 402). So the Parcae *roseo vertice* (Catull. LXIV, 309; cf. Lucr. V, 610, 976).

---

[1] See Florus, *Epit.* IV, 2, 91. Cf. Dio Cassius, *R.R.* XLIV, 6.

[2] See Dio Cassius, *loc. cit.*; Lucan, VII, 457 ff. cited on p. 138, n. 1 above and the evidence here given for the significance of the radiate crown. Florus goes on to tell us that the emblems of royalty were offered to him later.

[3] See Stephani, *op. cit.* p. 116. [4] *Panegyr.* 52.

[5] Trebell. *Vit. Gall.* 16. [6] Mamert. *Pan. Maximin.* 3.

[7] Pp. 141 ff. [8] See Stephani, *op. cit.* pp. 13 ff.

[9] See *auro sacras...perducis facies,* Pers. II, 55 f., 58, Juv. XIII, 151 f. (cf. p. 183). For Greece cf. p. 158, n. 2 and perhaps the fire on the heads of the Bacchae (Eur. *Bacch.* 757 f.) in relation to pp. 102, 111 f., 156, n. 2, 456, n. 2 and that on the fertility god on p. 240, n. 7.

[10] For Love, cf. pp. 152 f.

Servius tells of the *nimbus* that *deorum vel imperantium capita quasi clara nebula ambire fingitur*[1] and again *est enim fulgidum lumen quo deorum capita cinguntur, sic etiam pingi solet.*[2] This, harmonising with Jewish belief (p. 153, n. 1), explains the Christian use of the *nimbus* on deity, angel and saint (cf. II Corinthians iii, 7, 18; iv, 6).

Here too perhaps is the explanation of the custom[3] of painting the face of Jupiter's statue and also the triumphing general with red lead. Martial describes Domitian triumphing *purpureum fundens Caesar ab ore iubar* and adds that the people *salutavit voce manuque deum.*[4] Among the gods in the *igneae arces* Horace pictured Augustus with gleaming face: *purpureo ore.*[5] Red was used on the ancient images of the gods.[6] See also p. 470.

---

[1] *Ad Aen.* iii, 587. Cf. pp. 159 f. So, perhaps, representations of the head in gold, e.g. of the emperor (*The Times*, 22 Apr. 1939, p. 11) or Lucan (Stat. *Silv.* ii, 7, 129 ff.; cf. 132, 135 on p. 132, n. 1, and iv, 2, 40–4).

[2] *Ad Aen.* ii, 616. Cf. *ibid.* ix, 111, etc.

[3] See Pliny, *N.H.* xxxiii, 7, 111 f., Servius *ad Verg. Ecl.* x, 27. Greetings of the triumphing general as the god whose garb he wore will explain not only Juv. xi, 194 f. but also Hor. *Od.* iv, 2, 49 ff., *te* being Caesar.

[4] viii, 65. Seneca (*Tro.* 448) pictures Hector *vultus flammeum intendens iubar.* Cf. pp. 147 f.

[5] *Odes*, iii, 3, 10 f. Scarcely 'lips'. Cf. iv, 5, 5–7, 32–5.

[6] Plut. *Q.R.* 98. Cf. Virg. *Ecl.* x, 27.

CHAPTER III

Anima and *Animus*

Let us now look at *animus* and *anima*. The problem of their original meanings is one of great difficulty, owing to the nature of the terms themselves, two words obviously cognate, differing in fact only in declension and gender and both connoting entities or substances of the nature of wind or breath (cf. ἄνεμος), intangible, invisible, and easily confused. We have very little evidence before about the beginning of the second century B.C. By the fifth century B.C. the Greeks had completely changed and confused their conceptions of ψυχή and θυμός, so that ψυχή, from meaning originally the vaporous life-soul associated particularly with the head, had come to include the θυμός in the chest, and the original identity of θυμός with the physical breath was obscured. This evolution was, as far as can be seen, not hastened by foreign influences. The Romans, though more conservative by nature, were increasingly influenced by Greek thought, educated Romans by the various schools of philosophy. These later and more personal developments are fairly obvious, but even without them there remains confusion and overlapping of terms. The present state of the question may be illustrated from the recent survey of 'Ancient Italian Beliefs concerning the Soul' by Professor Rose:[1] '*anima* is the breath of the living as much as the soul (breath-soul, as I take it to be) of the dead; *animus*, to judge by the Plautine *animo malest*, is the vital principle of a living person'. But for the Romans the vital principle, the life, was unquestionably in the head and was not the *animus* but, as we have seen, the *genius*, and might also be described as *anima*. *Animus*, on the other hand, was overwhelmingly, throughout Latin literature, not the vital principle but the principle of consciousness. As the early tragedian Accius tersely says,

[1] *Class. Qu.* xxiv, 1930, pp. 133 f. Cf. his *Primitive Culture in Italy*, p. 148.

sapimus animo, fruimur anima;[1] introducing which several centuries later the grammarian Nonius[2] says, *animus est quo sapimus, anima qua vivimus*. Consciousness with all the variations of emotion and thought is a matter of *animus*. To contemplate some action is 'to have it in one's *animus*'; to turn one's attention to something, an idea within or an object in space, is 'to turn the *animus* towards it'; courage, despair, etc., are matters of *animus*; to feel faint, to be on the way to losing consciousness,[3] was in the Plautine phrase quoted 'it goes ill with one's *animus*'; when a man loses consciousness his '*animus* leaves him'; to collect one's faculties and spirits is 'to collect one's *animus*'—and so we might continue. *Animus* is concerned with consciousness and *anima* has nothing to do with consciousness. So much is clear. In *anima* there is apparent confusion. In surviving literature it means 'breath' and it means life-soul; but the life-soul originally was not in the chest, where the breath as ordinarily conceived was, but was in the head, the *genius*. Whether it was also called *anima* by the early Latins we cannot tell. If it was, the explanation appears to be that the word *anima* was generic. It was in fact applied to anything of the nature of vapour, air, or wind, to breezes, exhalations, etc., and so could be applied both to the physical breath coming from the chest and to the life-soul conceived as vaporous and manifesting itself in sneezing and perhaps in the 'breath' of procreation like the ψυχή,[4] the name of which also means something like wind. Thus confusion would arise and the life-soul, being described as *anima* and breathed out at death as was the ψυχή, might seem to be the breath-soul proper which originally it was not. Happily, while these terms lent themselves to confusion and were obscure at the relatively late period illustrated by surviving literature, the original significance of the relative parts of the body is clear and should be our guide to the original significance of these terms. Horace appears to refer to the two elements in man

---

[1] 296 (Ribb.), cf. pp. 61 ff. [2] P. 426, 27. Cf. *vita=anima* (*Aen.* x, 819 etc.).
[3] See e.g. *Mil. Glor.* 1331–4 (cf. 1345), where the converse of *animo male factumst* is *resipiscit*. [4] Pp. 119 f.

in his *animi capitisque labore.*[1] The significance of the head helps
with *anima.*[2] What of *animus*? It is not generic. It cannot like
anima be applied to any and every thing of the nature of air
or breath but means something specific of that nature. What?
We must proceed from the known to the unknown. *Animus*
was originally some 'breath' in the chest;[3] also *animus* was the
stuff of consciousness, and the consciousness was in the chest;[4]
therefore *animus* was breath that was consciousness[5] in the
chest. What breath was there in the chest? The ordinary
breath of respiration, the breath in the form of which pride,
spirit, etc., i.e. *animus*, appears,[6] and in the form of which—
words—consciousness issues forth,[7] thoughts are uttered. We
have shown[8] that the *praecordia*, organs of the consciousness, of
animus, were the lungs. So perhaps: Labrax: *animo male
fit....* Charmides: *pulmoneum...nimi' velim vomitum vomas*
(Plaut. *Rud.* 510f.). And Horace, challenged to produce verses:

> *di bene fecerunt inopis me quodque pusilli*
> *finxerunt animi, raro et perpauca loquentis;*
> *at tu conclusas hircinis follibus auras*
> *usque laborantes dum ferrum molliat ignis*
> *ut mavis imitare,*[9]

which Juvenal echoes:

> *tunc immensa cavi spirant mendacia folles.*[10]

---

[1] *Epist.* I, 1, 44 (see p. 195). *Anima recens* (e.g. Tib. III, 2, 15), like *umbra recens*, suggests that *anima* was not the usual name for the life-soul till after death.

[2] The conception of the *anima* as a serpent (under which form the *genius* was conceived, see p. 129; p. 159, n. 2) will help Martial's reference to a bronze bear in which lurked *vipera scelerata: vivebatque animā deteriore fera* (III, 19, 6). Cf. p. 291, n. 1 and Stat. *Silv.* I, 1, 58 (*genius*), cf. 86 (*ora*). Petronius speaks of the return of sexual potency as the return of *anima* (140). Cf. pp. 108, n. 7, 130 f., 146, n. 5.

[3] See Plaut. *Ps.* 34; Virg. *G.* IV, 83; *Aen.* V, 363, VII, 356, X, 485-7.

[4] See pp. 40 ff.

[5] How natural was the association of consciousness and breath may be seen in Plaut. *Epid.* 204 f.: Epid. *Mane, ⟨mane⟩, sine respirem, quaeso.* Periph. *Immo adquiesce.* Epid. *Animo male est.* Ap. *Recipe anhelitum.* Virgil suggests a connection in *tenuisque subibit/halitus atque animos tollent sata* (*Georg.* II, 349 f.). Cf. pp. 76, n. 9, 78, n. 2 and *Aen.* X, 899, Hor. *Sat.* II, 2, 78 f. (*animum quoque praegravat una/atque afficit humo divinae particulam aurae*).

[6] See e.g. *Aen.* IX, 596, XI, 346 (cf. 366), X, 387 on p. 42 and *Aen.* VII, 510 on p. 50.

[7] Pp. 41, 63, 67 f.   [8] Pp. 40 ff.   [9] *Sat.* I, 4, 17 ff.   [10] VII, 111.

Animus thus appears to have been the same in origin as θυμός, the breath that was consciousness in the chest. That this was in the heart no less than in the lungs seems to have been believed by Greeks and Romans.[1] *Animus*, like θυμός, appears in relation to sense perception.[2] With *animum advertere* we may compare such phrases as *animus per oculos male defit*.[3] *Animus*, like θυμός, must have been used constantly and predominantly to describe the various states and changes of consciousness. Occasions to refer to the physical aspect of breathing are relatively rare. Accordingly, when men better understood what physical breath was and that it was *not* the stuff of consciousness, *animus*, like θυμός, would naturally continue its connection with consciousness and cease to be identified with the physical breath. But the original conception still appeared in the uses of *spiritus* and of *spiro, conspiro, anhelo, inflo*, etc., to describe activities of the *animus*. They confirm that consciousness was a matter of the breath, as do πνεῖν, πνεύματα, etc., above.[4] For the mere physical breath dissociated from any reference to consciousness the generic *anima* was used. Being necessary to life, it might be confused with the life-soul when the conception of the latter had become indistinct. Like the Greeks, and doubtless influenced by them, educated Romans tended to unify, to identify the surviving soul with that which consciously controls a man in life. But such developments[5] need not be pursued here.

This investigation may, perhaps, also throw light on the origin of the custom whereby a relative caught with his mouth

[1] See p. 49, n. 1 and e.g. Cic. *Nat. D.* II, 54, 136, *pulmones et cor extrinsecus spiritum ducunt*, etc., also pp. 62 ff. above.   [2] See pp. 67 ff.
[3] Plaut. *Mil. Glor.* 1261. See also p. 79 above.   [4] See pp. 53 ff.
[5] E.g. Sall. *Jug.* 2; *Aen.* IX, 580, X, 601 (but there 'the breath' is possible) and *Aen.* XI, 408 f. if we ought not there to read *animum*. *Talem* refers to the characteristics of the conscious self and elsewhere in Virgil (see note 3 on p. 170) the *animus* is thus referred to the chest. If *anima* was used by the poet, there and in Propertius, II, 10, 11 it might be evidence merely that the physical breath was still recognised as the conscious spirit, but *Aen.* VI, 817 f. (cf. 827 ff.) gives to the surviving *anima* in the world of the dead the characteristics of the conscious self, i.e. *animus*. Propertius' description of Cynthia angry as she appeared to him in a dream after her death: *spirantisque animos et vocem misit* (IV, 7, 11) suggests a reference of *animus* to breath.

the last breath of the dying—*postremum spiritum ore excipere.*[1]
This has been vaguely described as transmission of the soul,
and it has recently been suggested that it was the *genius*; but the
evidence quoted above[2] precludes that, and the *genius* (= *anima*)
continued, as we have seen,[3] with independent existence in
the world of the dead. It was therefore not the *genius*. What
remains but the *animus*?[4] There is no indication that it
originally was thought to maintain an independent existence
after death. It was precious, the stuff and agent[5] of mind,
which might otherwise perish. Who could better inherit and
preserve it than the next of kin? The 'last kiss' is virtually
inspiration, as discussed above,[6] with the recipient more, and the
transmitter less, active. Thoughts, words, were 'breath',[7]
animus, from the *cor* and *praecordia*. We saw that the natives of
New Guinea and the Society Isles had somewhat similar
conceptions.[8] Of the Society Islanders we are told[9] that they
called thoughts by a word which signifies 'words in the belly'
and 'when one of their sacred recorders (*harepo*), who had been
famous in his life for his knowledge of the ancient traditions,
was at the point of death, it was customary for his son and
successor to place his mouth over the mouth of the dying man
as if to inhale the parting soul at the moment of quitting the
body; for in this way he was believed to inherit the lore of his
father. The natives, it is said, were convinced that their sages

[1] Cic. *Verr. Act.* II, v, 45, 118. See also p. 128.

[2] P. 128.   [3] See pp. 131 ff.

[4] It is in the chest (p. 171). When Procris dies *incauto paulatim pectore
lapsus/excipitur miseri spiritus ore viri* (Ov. *Ars Am.* III, 745 f.). *Mens* is
secondary and belongs to *animus*. So *mens animi, amens animi.*

[5] With the last breath there was probably thought to depart the agent
of breathing.

[6] Pp. 50–6.

[7] See pp. 67 ff., 171 and cf. Lucil. 590 f. on p. 41; *clamantis revocaverit
aura puellae* (Propertius, II, 27, 15); *tenuis famae perlabitur aura* (Virg. *Aen.*
VII, 646), etc.

[8] Pp. 14, 68.

[9] See Frazer, *Belief in Immortality*, II, pp. 297 f. He seems to imply that
this is the immortal soul but it lives in the *viscera* of the body, while other
evidence which he quotes (pp. 288, 311, 324) suggests that it is the skull
with which the surviving soul is associated. As with ψυχή in later Greece
there may have been conflation of two souls into one.

owed their learning to this expedient'.[1] The conception of his words as portions of his spirit perhaps lies behind the poet's claim: Let no man mourn me. *cur? volito vivos per ora virum.*[2] As of Dido dying her sister says *extremus si quis super halitus errat/ore legam,*[3] Ovid, referring to his poems, claims in dying *ore legar populi perque omnia saecula fama/...vivam.*[4] It is, perhaps, after a kiss conceived as a passing of *spiritus* that Lucretius pictures Venus with Mars in her lap: *eque tuo pendet resupini spiritus ore.*[5]

[1] *Ibid.* p. 98. This is adduced by Professor Rose as supporting his reference to the *genius*.
[2] Ennius, *Epigr.* II, quoted by Cic. *Tusc.* I, 15, 34.
[3] *Aen.* IV, 684 f.
[4] *Met.* XV, 878 f. 875 f. seem to refer to the *genius* (pp. 163–7).
[5] I, 37.

CHAPTER IV

The Knees

The head, we have seen, was holy, as being seat and source of the 'life' and the life fluid. The knees too have sanctity, though it has attracted little notice and has not been explained. The suppliant regularly clasps and appeals to them.[1] To ask a favour in return for her rescue of him Thetis sat down before enthroned Zeus and 'clasped his knees with her left hand and with her right took hold of him by the chin beneath'.[2] 'This act', it is suggested, 'perhaps symbolises the last resource of the disarmed and fallen warrior who can only clasp his enemy's legs to hamper him and turn aside his face so that he cannot see to aim the final blow until he has at least heard the prayer for mercy.'[3] Were this really a symbolism based upon the action of a 'disarmed and fallen warrior' threatened by a standing or onrushing foe, imagination would show us a nimble long-armed victim clasping at once the knees and chin of an obligingly passive conqueror whose legs are more dangerous than his arms. There is in fact no hint here or elsewhere of turning aside the face, and the legs of sitting Zeus on this occasion[4] scarcely called even for 'symbolic' hampering. Hera tells us just that Thetis 'kissed his knees and took his chin in her hand'.[5] Faint and dying on the ground with Achilles' spear through his neck, Hector says: 'I beseech you by your ψυχή and your knees and your parents let not the dogs devour my body'.[6] This indicates the value set upon the knees, the order of ideas to which they belong and shows that the clasping was secondary, as in the similar appeal by the head[7] or the chin.[8]

[1] *Il.* IX, 451, XI, 608, XVIII, 457, etc., and the verb γουνάζομαι.
[2] *Il.* I, 500 f.   [3] Leaf, *ad loc.*
[4] Cf. *Od.* X, 481 f., etc.   [5] *Il.* VIII, 371. Cf. *Od.* XIV, 279.
[6] *Il.* XXII, 338 f.; cf. 345.   [7] See p. 97 and Hom. Hymn to Aphr. 27, etc.
[8] This is explained below (pp. 231 ff.).

With no reference to this evidence for Greece, it has been observed[1] that in the Indo-European group of languages the name for 'knee' (Irish *glun*, Latin *genu*, Greek γόνυ, etc.) appears to be cognate and sometimes interchangeable with the term for 'generation', and many unsatisfying and conflicting attempts have been made to explain this: by the metaphor of the family as a human body and the knee as a branch;[2] by urging that knots or joints on grasses and plants were known as γόνατα (surely a secondary use of the word) and thus the idea of branches or members[3] (*Glieder*) arose; by the fact that one of the postures assumed by mothers in giving birth was kneeling;[4] and by two other widespread customs, that a wife gave birth upon the knees of her husband and that a child was placed upon the knees of his father or foster-father as a sign that he was acknowledged as his or adopted.[5] These customs are, however, not fundamental but themselves need explanation. Rather, I suggest, with the name they bear witness that the knee was thought in some way to be the seat of paternity, of life and generative power, unthinkable though that may seem to us. Professor Meillet[6] explains *genuinus* as meaning one who has been acknowledged by his father as 'authentic', his own offspring, by being

[1] By J. Loth, 'Le mot désignant le genou au sens de génération chez les Celtes, les Germains, les Slaves, les Assyriens', *Revue Celtique*, XL, 1923, pp. 143–52. See also *ibid.* p. 495 and XXXVII, p. 66, and E. Benveniste, 'Un emploi du nom du «genou» en vieil-irlandais et en sogdien', *Bull. de la Soc. de Ling.* XXVII, 1926, pp. 51 ff.

[2] M. Cahen, '«Genou», «Adoption» et «Parenté» en germanique', *ibid.* pp. 56 ff.

[3] H. Güntert, 'Weiteres zum Begriff «Winkel» im ursprünglichen Denken', *Wörter u. Sachen*, XI, 1928, pp. 124 ff.

[4] R. Back, 'Medizinisch-Sprachliches', *Indogerm. Forsch.* XL, 1922, pp. 162 ff. and S. Simonyi, 'Knie und Geburt', *Kuhn's Zeitschr. f. vergl. Sprachforsch.* L, 1923, pp. 152 ff. R. Meringer ('Spitze, Winkel, Knie im ursprünglichen Denken', *Wörter u. Sachen*, XI, 1928, pp. 114 ff.) also argues that points and corners were symbolic of power and explains the clasping of the knee by Homeric suppliants as a stroking of the seat of the person's feeling and thoughts!

[5] Loth, *loc. cit.*

[6] See *Bull. de la Soc. de Ling.* XXVII, 1926, p. 54 f. Cf. *Comptes Rendus de l'Acad. des Inscr. et Belles Lettres*, 1926, pp. 45 f.

received on his *genua*, which may be correct so far as it goes. But he also explains *genua* by suggesting that the root of *genus*, γίγνομαι, γένος, etc., meant 'to recognise, know' and so 'to recognise as belonging to a family'. His suggestion of a 'purely juristic' meaning in this idea of recognition (curiously surviving within so limited a sphere and with so little trace of that meaning in the terms in question), and his denial of connection with the physical process of generation, are more than bold. Consider e.g. the traceable uses of *gigno*, *genius*, *genialis*, *genitalis*, etc., and of the Greek cognates of γόνυ: γείνομαι, γίγνομαι, γονεύς, γόνος, γονή, γονάρ (='womb', Lacon.), etc. Moreover, he offers no hint why the jaw should have been referred to with this same adjective *genuinus* and γένυς, etc. (see p. 233), or why the knees should be so decisively the part of the body wherewith to suggest or recognise paternity and that in particular; and he does not reckon with the other facts here presented and hitherto unexplained.

Euripides refers to the knees as 'generative members' (γόνιμα μέλεα).[1] Lucilius has the form *genus* for 'knee'[2] and *genu(s)*[3] apparently for the male organ. He associates it with the *testes*. Cf. *penu* or *penus* with genitives *penus*, *penoris* or *peneris*. For the Assyrians and Babylonians of race and language quite unrelated to Greek and Latin the word *birku*[4] signified either the knee or the male organ of generation. Russian *koleno* (Pol. *kolano*)[5] means either 'knee' or 'generation, race'; the same association appears in Lap, Finnish and other Finno-

---

[1] See *Electra*, 1208–15, comparing *Troades*, 1305–7.

[2] 162 (Marx).

[3] 534 (Marx). Hittite *genu* apparently had two meanings, 'knee' and 'sexual organ'. See J. Friederich, 'Einige hethitische Etymologien', *Indogerm. Forsch.* XLI, 1923, p. 375.

[4] See Holma, *Die Namen der Körperteile im Assyrisch-Babylonischen*, pp. 95 f., 132 ff. The only explanation he can suggest is euphemism. See also p. 124 and *inf.* p. 491. The knees so named were, like the γόνατα, believed to contain the strength (pp. 180 f., 187, 491 *inf.*).

[5] A departing son embraces his parents' knees (e.g. Jendrek in Bol. Prus, *The Outpost*, cap. x). A man thanking another for help embraces his knees (Slimak, *ibid.*).

Ugrian tongues. Thus Finnish *polvi* means both 'knee' and 'generation', and with this we should, I suggest, connect the old Finnish belief that the nest for the cosmic egg was made on the knee of the water-mother, Ilmatar, which she thrust up from the waves[1] or, in other versions,[2] upon the knees of her son Väinämöinen. We may guess that the ancient Finns believed that the *knee* was the source of generation; for elsewhere in the *Kalevala* we find that Ukko, the sky-god, generates the Luonnotars, cloud-maidens, thus:

> Ukko maker of the heavens
> Firmly rubbed his hands together,
> Firmly pressed them on his knee-cap;
> Then arose three lovely maidens,[3]

and a maiden by similar action produced a squirrel,[4] a marten[5] and a bee.[6]

The clue to all may now perhaps be found in the remark of Hesiod quoted above[7] that at midsummer 'women are most wanton (μαχλόταται) but men are most impotent ("feeblest", ἀφαυρότατοι) because Sirius dries up the head and knees (γούνατα) and the flesh is dried up with the heat'. Alcaeus in his similar explanation[8] mentions only the head and knees. This suggests that the fluid or liquefiable content of the joint, its true function not being known, was classed with the cerebro-spinal fluid or liquefiable substance, the fluid of life,[9]

---

[1] See *Kalevala*, Runo I.
[2] E.g. in the First Recension of the *Kalevala*.
[3] Runo IX, English translation by J. M. Crawford, p. 107.
[4] *Ibid.* p. 305. (The hands are discussed below on pp. 198, n. 1, 494 ff.)
[5] *Ibid.* p. 307.   [6] *Ibid.* p. 309. She rubs a pod on her knee.
[7] Pp. 110 f. and *inf.* p. 187.   [8] See p. 111 *supra*.
[9] As will appear (see pp. 215 ff.), this fluid was correlated with the 'sap', the vital fluid, of plants and χλοερός, χλωρός was used to mean 'sappy, having sap' (χλωρόν· ὑγρόν, Hesych.), where greenness is not in question (see p. 255 and cf. χλωραὶ ἐέρσαι, Pind. *Nem.* VIII, 40; χλωρὸν δάκρυ, Eurip. *Med.* 906, 922, *Hel.* 1189; also 'if they do these things in the green (ὑγρῷ) tree, what shall be done in the dry?' Luke xxiii, 31). Sap or sappiness seems to be the meaning of χλοῦνις in Aeschylus' σπέρματός τ' ἀποφθορᾷ παίδων κακοῦται χλοῦνις (*Eum.* 187 f., the text is doubtful) and thus it is Theocritus not only speaks of bride and bridegroom χλοεροῖσιν ἰαινόμενοι μελέεσσιν (XXVII, 66) but also (XIV, 70) says

and thought to contribute to the seed. Of this fluid Hesiod implies both sexes feel the want in the dry season. The general structure of the joint suggesting a containing chamber might help the thought.[1] In fact the joint-cavity of the knee is the largest in the body. It is lined with the synovial membrane which secretes the fluid and it may also contain fat or 'marrow', thought perhaps with the cerebro-spinal 'marrow' to melt into the fluid.

We saw[2] that the story of Zeus engendering a child in his head without the help of a mother was explained by the belief that the head contained the seed. There appears to have been preserved a striking variant in a folk-tale of Zakynthos recorded some seventy years ago. It tells how the greatest king in

---

'a man must do something while his knee is χλωρός', i.e. 'has sap in it'. This appears to be the origin of Horace's *dum virent genua* (*Epod.* XIII, 4). Cf. Laberius, 116 (Ribb.). Recognition of the boar (see pp. 154 f.) as supremely full of sap, of the procreative fluid, will explain χλούνης. Its later application to the castrated might arise out of their greater plumpness (so *maialis*?), the apparent conservation of the fluid (see n. 4, p. 109. Cf. p. 246). In several Indo-european tongues the term for 'male' refers to liquid emitted, i.e. the seed (e.g. ἔρσην, cf. ἔρση, Sanscr. *vár* 'water', *vṛṣan*- 'male', O. Norse *ver* 'water, sea'). For the Latins this belonged *par excellence* to the boar: *verres*. I suggest that *ver* meant originally the liquid or sap, seed, new growth, 'offspring' (so *ver sacrum* and *verna*, p. 225, n. 2), then spring (cf. p. 220—the Grail—*it ver et Venus*, Lucr. v, 737 with Juv. IX, 51, *Pervigil. Veneris*, etc.), and that ἔαρ 'spring', which is cognate, was the same word as ἔαρ 'sap, juice'. *Vir* and cognates O. Norse *verr*, *ver*, Anglo-Saxon *wer* = 'male', 'husband' referred, I suggest, originally to this liquid, sap that was the seed and strength (pp. 187 ff.), the most important characteristics of the male. So *virus* and *vires*, *vis* (p. 187; cf. p. 234, n. 6). The relation of greenness to sap just traced will thus also explain *vireo* and its kin. 'Green', Ger. *grün*, etc., meant originally 'growing'. *Virga* 'twig' perhaps originally referred to sap as opposed to dry wood. Cf. p. 213, n. 6, our 'sapling', etc. So too *virgo*. Cf. p. 219, n. 7, θάλος (*Od.* VI, 157, etc., cf. p. 202), *Epigr. Gr.* (Kaib.) 368, 7, etc. The same thought as for *vir*, *ver* but a different root *ma-* as in *madeo*, *mano*, etc. may explain (with *mare* 'sea') *mas*, *maris* (whence *masculus*, our 'male'), *maritus* (perhaps from a rite like those on p. 230 *init.* below) and *Mars* (pp. 470 f.). Neptunus was linked with *Salacia* and in N. Italy with *Vires*, sometimes *Lymfae* (*Lymphae*) *Vires* (p. 219, n. 7).

[1] The idea that knees were sources of generation may have been helped by the growth of shoots from the 'knees', γόνατα, of plants. Cf. Pliny, *N.H.* XVII, 21, 152 f. on p. 220 below.

[2] Pp. 111 f.

the world in his virtue had resolved never to take a wife, yet would have liked to have children and one day he sat and wept and 'there appeared to him an angel and said he must not weep; he would get a child out of his ἄτσα. (This is a rare dialect word for part of the leg. Schmidt renders it *Wade*, i.e. "calf".) Soon after, one of the king's legs swelled and one day as he was hunting he stuck a thorn into it. Then all at once a wonderfully beautiful maiden with all her body armed and carrying lance and helm sprang out of his ἄτσα'.[1] This story can only be explained by the belief that the seed of new life was to be found in the leg, where in fact, as we have seen,[2] the ancient Greeks believed it to be even as in the head. In the evidence above, not only for the Greeks and other Indo-European peoples but also for Semites and others, the knee was associated with generation. I have happened upon a story of the Masai, a Nilotic people, beginning thus: 'There was once an old man who had no wife and lived alone in his hut. One night he went to sleep and when he awoke in the morning he found his knee (*guñgu*) was swollen. There was nobody there to look at it, so he kept quiet thinking that he had a boil. After waiting for six months he asks himself in his heart why the boil does not ripen so that he can break it. He waits two months more and, finding that it will not ripen, he fetches a knife and says "Even if I die, I will break it", and he stabs it with the knife and out come two children. He picks them up, takes them to the hut, and feeds them until they grow up. And he tells them to sit by the door of the cave while he goes to look for food, and not to open to people they do not know. On his return he sings "It has become soft and it does not break, my children of the knee. Go, my darlings, open to me." The children open the door to him and he enters and gives them their food....'[3] Popular association of the knees with generation will explain not only the name (γόνυ, etc.) and the customs at childbirth and adoption mentioned above but also the wide-

---

[1] Trans. B. Schmidt, *Griech. Märchen u. Volksl.*, pp. 76 ff. Cf. p. 246 *inf.*
[2] Pp. 175 f.
[3] Recorded by Hollis, *The Masai, their Language and Folklore*, pp. 147 f.

spread superstition[1] that an enemy, by interlocking his fingers,[2] can hinder childbirth, more especially if he interlock them *around one or both knees*.

As in the case of the head, the source should also be the seat of life. In fact the knees are strangely prominent in Homer as the seat of vitality and strength.[3] 'As long as I live' is expressed by 'As long as I am amongst the living and my knees are active (ὀρώρῃ)',[4] and to slay is repeatedly expressed by to 'loose the knees[5] of' the victim. The Romans appear, with the similar name *genu*, to have had similar ideas about the knees. To appeal to a man they 'rubbed'[6] (*fricare*) or 'clasped'[7] his knees or from a distance stretched out their hands towards them.[8] *Protendo igitur ad genua vestra supinas manus*, says one.[9] It was the characteristic gesture in prayer to extend towards the power entreated, towards the heavens or, if present, towards the

[1] See Pliny, *N.H.* XXVIII, 6, 59f., and cf. Ovid, *Met.* IX, 298–311 (Ilithyia and Alcmene). For evidence of the belief in Sicily, etc., see Samter, *Geburt, Hochzeit, Tod*, pp. 16 f., and for the same superstition in Norway, Ploss-Bartels, *Das Weib in der Natur und Völkerkunde*, II, p. 247. In Italy the superstition seems to have been extended to other spheres, which indeed fits the belief also noted here that the knees contain the strength, executive power. In Armenia 'as many times as the bride strikes her knee against the dais on which the altar stands, so many years will she bear no child' (see C. F. Lehmann-Haupt, *Armenien Einst u. Jetzt*, II, p. 174).

[2] Why the *hands* of birth-goddesses, etc. were opened to loose the generative power and why representations of a *hand* were offered after safe delivery is explained by pp. 198, n. 1, 494 f.

[3] E.g. *Il.* IV, 313 ff.; XIX, 354.

[4] *Il.* XXII, 388—perhaps the original of 'alive and kicking'. Cf. IX, 610; X, 90; XI, 477; *Od.* XVIII, 133.

[5] *Il.* V, 176; XV, 291; XXI, 498, etc.

[6] See Plaut. *Asin.* 670 f. and 678. We explained (pp. 146 ff.) the rubbing of the forehead as propitiation of the *genius* thought to be responsible for fury and saw that fury was associated not only with the brain but also with the marrow of other bones (pp. 149 ff.).

[7] See e.g. Petron. 101 (cf. 80, 3); *prensare circumstantium genua* (Tac. *Ann.* I, 21); *ambulantis Tiberii genua advolveretur* (ibid. 13), etc.; *aegros vide, si mortis periculum...*, *medicorum genua tangentes* (Sen. *Brev. V.*, 8). Anyone who clasped a flamen's knees (or feet, cf. p. 246) could not be whipped (Serv. *ad Aen.* III, 607).

[8] E.g. Tacitus, *Ann.* I, 11, where the senators, appealing to Tiberius to accept empire, *ad deos, ad effigiem Augusti, ad genua ipsius manus tendere*.

[9] Petronius, 17.

image of the god, the palms thus upturned.[1] Attention to the
knees[2] was, I suggest, an appeal to the *genius* in act as so often
in word. With *per tuum te genium opsecro*,[3] etc., we may compare
per tua genua te opsecro, 'I beseech you by your knees to tell
us',[4] etc. The life-soul, being responsible for begetting, would
in Italy, as in Greece, be associated with the knees (*genua*).
Appealing for help one clasped the knees or explicitly 'im-
plored (*adorare*) the *genius*'[5] of another. Apuleius says that
'those prayers by which men entreat the *genius* and the knees
(*genium et genua*) seem to me to bear witness to the union and
bond in our nature, since they comprehend under two names
body and spirit of which we are a communion and linking'.[6]
The elder Pliny remarks that in a man's knees 'there is a certain
sanctity observed by the nations. It is these that suppliants
touch, towards these that they extend their hands, these that
like altars they worship, perhaps because in them is the life
(*vitalitas*). For in the joint of each knee, left and right, there
is in front a certain bulging cavity (lit. "an empty space of
cheeks", *buccarum inanitas*) on the piercing of which, as of the
throat, the spirit flows away'.[7] Finally, reverting to Homer,
we may point out that when Theoklymenos with second sight
tells the doomed as a sign of death: 'Your heads and faces and
beneath your *knees* are wrapped in darkness'[8] (i.e. mist, cloud;[9]
νυκτὶ μὲν ὑμέων/εἰλύαται κεφαλαί τε πρόσωπά τε νέρθε τε

[1] Cf. ὑπτιάσμασιν χερῶν, Aesch. *P.V.* 1005. This I believe to be in
origin merely a begging gesture, one with the act of the beggar who holds
out his hand to the passer-by. The suppliant holds out his hands for the
favour desired as if for a material gift. Similarly perhaps προσκυνεῖν and
adoratio will be the giving to the god of the blessing first breathed by the
worshipper into his own hand. Cf. Lucian, *de Salt.* 278, Apul. *Met.* iv, 28,
etc. and the meaning of *salutatio* and 'blessing' (p. 186 with pp. 491 ff.).
[2] Including perhaps *genua incerare deorum* (Juv. x, 55). See p. 282, n. 9.
[3] Plaut. *Capt.* 977. Cf. Hor. *Epi.* i, 7, 94; Tib. iii, 11, 8; Sen. *Epi.* 12, 2.
[4] Plaut. *Curc.* 630. The speaker clasped the knees (*Poen.* 1387-97).
[5] E.g. Propertius, iv (v), 8, 69.
[6] *De deo Socratis*, cap. xv, § 152. The association of the knees with the
genius and the life may explain the old taboo attributed to Numa Pom-
pilius: SI HOMINEM FULMEN IOVIS OCCISIT NE SUPRA GENUA
TOLLITO, quoted by Festus, s.v. *occisum* (p. 190 Lindsay).
[7] *N.H.* xi, 45, 250, reading *qua perfossa ceu iugulo spiritus fluit.*
[8] *Od.* xx, 351 f.   [9] See p. 95.

γοῦνα), he means what he says, just heads and knees, and not, as is currently explained,[1] 'from head to foot', which Homer expresses quite clearly and differently when he wishes to.[2] The 'darkness' perhaps originated[3] in the mist that darkens the eyes in faintness, λιποψυχία, departure of ψυχή (e.g. τὸν δ' ἔλιπε ψυχή, κατὰ δ' ὀφθαλμῶν κέχυτ' ἀχλύς, *Il.* v, 696), when also the knees are loosed.[4]

The seed from the head was believed to issue by way of the 'marrow' in the spine. That from the knee would naturally be thus associated with the marrow of the thigh-bone, to which the knee-cap particularly belongs.[5] The thigh-bone is the largest bone in the body and the Latin name for thigh, *femur*, *femoris*, or *femen*, *feminis*, should according to its form mean 'that which engenders', from √*fe-*, whence *fetus*, *fecundus*, *femina*. Cf. √*flu-*, *flumen*, etc. As we explained the legend of

---

[1] See e.g. Ameis-Hentze-Cauer and Monro, *ad loc.*

[2] See e.g. ἐκ κεφαλῆς εἴλυτο διαμπερὲς ἐς πόδας ἄκρους (*Il.* xvi, 640), or just κάλυψαν/ἐς πόδας ἐκ κεφαλῆς (*Il.* xviii, 352 f.), whereas the description of the suitors is paralleled rather by that of Aias, μειδιόων βλοσυροῖσι προσώπασι νέρθε δὲ ποσσὶν/ἤϊε μακρὰ βιβάς, 'smiling with grim face but beneath with his feet hugely striding he went' (*Il.* vii, 212 f.; cf. xiii, 77 ff.), or of Andromache, πάλλεται ἦτορ ἀνὰ στόμα νέρθε δὲ γοῦνα/πήγνυται, 'in my breast my ἦτορ leaps up to my mouth and beneath my knees are frozen' (*Il.* xxii, 452 f.; cf. xvii, 386 f., etc.). [3] See pp. 421 ff.

[4] See e.g. *Il.* v, 68, 309 f., xvi, 344, xx, 417, xxii, 466 f., etc. Cf. Plaut. *Curc.* 309, *tenebrae oboriuntur, genua inedia succidunt*, with *Il.* xix, 354, also Ovid, *Her.* xiii, 23 f., *Met.* ii, 180 f. This and the association of the soul with the head help to explain Ἄϊδος κυνέη.

[5] According to the *Oxf. English Dictionary* and others 'marrow-bones' used to mean 'knees' in such expressions as 'Down upon your marrow-bones', but the word may rather have designated originally the thigh-bones which are the 'marrow-bones' *par excellence*, and to which he who kneels descends. It is usual to explain the Greek word for 'thigh' or 'thigh-bone', μηρός (μηρία), by the Old Irish *mir*, 'piece', Latin *membrum*, Sanscrit *māmsam*, 'meat' (see e.g. the revised Liddell and Scott lexicon), but, form apart, these words have general meanings and there is no reason why in Greek the thigh or thigh-bone should be so called or why only the thigh or thigh-bone should. Instead I would relate Anglo-Saxon *mearh*, Old High German *marag*, Welsh *mer*, etc., all meaning 'marrow'. In addition to what follows here, evidence that the *marrow* of the thigh was uniquely important for the early Greeks appears below (pp. 279 f.).

the paternal birth of Athene from the head, etc., above, so now
the legend that Dionysos was born out of the thigh (μηρός) of
Zeus¹ can be seen to have similar explanation. So too probably the Hindu legends of the birth of Aurva out of the left
thigh of his mother Vâmoru and of Nishâda out of the left
thigh of the prince Vena² and the legend in an old French
poem that St Anne, mother of the Virgin Mary, was born
direct from the thigh of her father Phanuel which he touched
with a knife.³ The ancient Hebrews spoke of the thighs as
sources of procreation.⁴ In Egypt his pyramid tells us that
king Wn'is 'issued from both the thighs of the Nine Gods and
was carried in the womb of the goddess Sḥmt'.⁵ Further
evidence that for the early Greeks and Egyptians the thigh
contained the life will be more conveniently discussed below.⁶

The smiting of the thigh⁷ in Homer has been passed over
as a mere emotional gesture, but quite clearly it is no mere

¹ See e.g. Eurip. *Bacch.* 94 ff., 243, 286 ff., 523 ff. On a Vth-century *krater*
(*J.H.S.* LIV (1934), Pl. IX) the birth is from the knee end. The alternative
name of the town Nysa near the Maeander, where there were Cretan
connections (see e.g. Methodius quoted by *Et. Magn.* 45, 16 ff.), was
Akara and there happens to be preserved for us the information that this
was Cretan for 'legs' (σκέλη, see *ibid.*). The significance of the thigh seen
here (pp. 182 ff.) will explain the gold found upon the thigh as upon the
face in Mycenaean graves (cf. pp. 106 and 427) and with it the story that
Pythagoras tried to inspire reverence at Olympia by showing his thigh as
of gold (τόν τε μηρὸν ὑποφῆναι χρυσοῦν, Plut. *Numa*, 8), and the custom
of gilding not only the faces of the statues of the gods but also their thighs
(see Juv. XIII, 151 f. referred to on p. 166, and for the significance of the
gold, pp. 106; 156, n. 2; 165 ff.; 330); also the emphasis upon the thighs
and hips in early 'steatopygous' images. In dreams οἱ δὲ μηροὶ τὰ μὲν
ἄλλα πάντα ἐπίσης τοῖς αἰδοίοις σημαίνουσι (Artemidorus, *Onir.* I, 46).
² See F. F. A. Kuhn, *Die Herabkunft des Feuers*, etc., pp. 167 ff.
³ See S. Hartland, *Legend of Perseus*, I, p. 130. See also the Grail king
(p. 157, n. 1), the maiming of the thigh of Adonis (e.g. Bion, I, 7 f.) and
Morte d'Arthur, XIV, 9 f.
⁴ See p. 109, n. 1. In the Apocalypse the name is written not only upon
the forehead (xiv, 1, xxii, 4, etc.) but also upon the thigh, μηρός (xix, 16;
cf. 12). Amongst the Jews, as amongst the early Greeks (see pp. 279 f.), the
thigh was important in sacrifice (see Exod. xxix, 22, 27, etc.). For the
fat see also pp. 188 ff., 286 f.
⁵ See Ebers, *Abh. der k. bayer. Akad. der Wiss.* I, Cl. XXI, Bd. I, p. 154.
⁶ P. 280.
⁷ The ancient Jews did it (Jerem. xxxi, 19; Ezek. xxi, 12).

instinctive movement; the practice must have rested on some
basis of thought. The man (or woman) strikes both thighs[1]
with both hands[2] and does so when standing up and armed
in the midst of the battle,[3] which is not 'impossible', as the
scholiast says (ad loc.), but might involve difficulties. In none
of the instances recorded[4] is it a matter of surprise or any light-
hearted occasion, but in all cases the person is in distress, in
grief or anxiety. Also in the other instances of smiting one's
own body, the part in question is chosen as containing that
to which one's attention is directed,[5] even as when Althaie in
her anguish beats the ground she does so calling to the powers
beneath.[6] The beating of the breast was addressed to the
conscious self, the θυμός or its organs. Thus Odysseus when in
indignation 'his θυμός was disturbed in his chest, smote his
chest and chid his heart with speech: "Endure, O heart, etc."
(στῆθος δὲ πλήξας κραδίην ἠνίπαπε μύθῳ κ.τ.λ.)'.[7] So too
the touching of the head.[8] Our explanation of the significance
attached to a sneeze suggests that the ψυχή was originally
believed not only to be that on which the life of the body
depends, but also to be interested in and affect one's destiny[9]
(cf. the genius[10]). A suppliant may clasp one's head or make
appeal in speech by it as seat of one's ψυχή[11] and one honoured
it oneself and showed it honour;[12] but in distress one might
treat it less gently—still, I suggest, as seat of one's ψυχή.
Priam in extreme anxiety, trying to save his son who is endangered, smites his head, and when nevertheless his son is
killed he puts dung upon it,[13] as Achilles puts dust upon his

[1] The dual is invariably used, cf. ἄμφω κ.τ.λ., Hymn to Demeter, 245.
[2] See Il. xv, 113 f., 397 f.; Od. xiii, 198 f.
[3] See Il. xii, 162. Cf. Od. xiii, 197 f.
[4] Il. xii, 162, xv, 113, 397, xvi, 125; Od. xiii, 198. Cf. Hymn to
Demeter, 245.   [5] See also pp. 129, 132 f.
[6] Il. ix, 568 ff. Cf. Stat. Theb. i, 54 f.; Val. Flacc. vii, 312 ff., etc.
[7] Od. xx, 9 f. Cf. Il. xviii, 31, 51 and Plaut. Mil. Glor. 202: pectus digitis
pultat; cor credo evocaturust foras, Nahum ii, 7: 'mourn...tabering upon
their hearts'.
[8] See pp. 129, 132 ff., 145 f., and 233.   [9] Cf. pp. 197, 405, n. 8.
[10] See pp. 160 ff.
[11] See p. 97 and Homeric Hymn to Aphrodite (v), 27.
[12] See pp. 97 f., 129 f., 144 ff.   [13] Il. xxii, 32, xxiv, 163 ff.

in similar circumstances.¹ I suggest that the knees with the thigh-bones were treated as the other seat of the ψυχή. A suppliant may clasp them or make appeal by them in speech; one may oneself in distress stir them less gently, striking the thigh rather than the knee because it is more convenient to do so. This (in relation to the *genius*) appears to be also the origin of similar practices among the Romans.² Not only so. If the knees had this significance as containing the life and the life-soul, kneeling itself was in origin primarily an affair of the knees and not, as has been assumed, merely incidental to putting one's body on a lower level than his whose favour one is seeking. He who clasped or caressed the knees of another might also humble his own, even as more extremely he might humble his head by laying his forehead in the dust. His mother knelt to Orestes ἰώ μοι, πρὸς πέδῳ τιθεῖσα γόνιμα μέλεα.³ By the side of such expressions as πρόσπιπτε δ' οἰκτρῶς τοῦδ' 'Οδυσσέως γόνυ⁴ we have προσπίτνω σε γόνασι,⁵ Plautus' *nunc tibi amplectimur genua egentes opum...te obsecramus/aram amplexantes hanc tuam lacrimantes genibus nixae,*⁶ Virgil's *genua amplexus genibusque volutans,*⁷ etc. Tibullus declares that, if he has sinned against Venus, he will *tellurem genibus perrepere supplex/et miserum sancto tundere poste caput.*⁸

Among the ancient Irish⁹ its name implies the same valuation of the knee. We can now perhaps also explain—as

¹ *Il.* xviii, 23 ff. With the belief that the head contains the ψυχή we may relate the Attic idiom of one in distress, 'loudly to bewail one's head', not with the revised Liddell and Scott (s.v. κλαίω), 'suffer terribly in the head' (κλάειν μακρὰ τὴν κεφαλήν, cf. ὀτοτύξεσθαι μακρὰ τὴν κεφαλήν, Aristoph. *Lys.* 520), and compare perhaps the frequent cry οἴμοι κακοδαίμων, etc. For the ψυχή as originally δαίμων see pp. 118, 405, n. 8, etc. For the Jewish practice (II Sam. xiii, 19, Jer. ii, 37), cf. pp. 103, 234 f., etc.

² For the striking of the forehead see Cic. *ad Att.* 1, 1; Apul. *Met.* 1, 7, 32 and pp. 129, 145 f. above; for the striking of the thigh (*femur*) as of the forehead, Cic. *Brut.* LXXX, 278; *ad Herenn.* III, 15 (it continued; cf. Dante, *Inf.* xxiv, 9, etc.); and for touching or beating the breast, p. 132 and *plango.*

³ See p. 176.   ⁴ Eurip. *Hec.* 339.
⁵ Soph. *Phil.* 485.   ⁶ *Rudens,* 274, 694 f.   ⁷ *Aen.* III, 607.
⁸ 1, 2, 85 f. Cf. Juvenal vi, 525 f. etc.   ⁹ See p. 175.

blessing or honouring by raising what had this significance—
the curious gesture of salutation (cf. the baring[1] or bowing[2] of
the head) by which one who was seated showed honour to
another. He raised his knee or thigh.[3] And, perhaps to
humble it beneath one's life-soul, one placed beneath one's
thigh[4] the severed head of an enemy, which also was associated with the life-soul.[5] Among the Germanic peoples,
too, not only does the head[6] appear to have had such
significance as it had for the Greeks and Romans but also the
words for 'knee' (Anglo-Saxon *cneów*,[7] Icel. *kné*, etc.) have
clearly the same origin as γόνυ, *genu*, etc. Among the Norsemen the way to lay a ghost was to cut off the head of the
dead and place it between his thighs. Thus Grettir deals
with Kar after a struggle in the latter's grave[8] and with
Glam outside Thorkall's house.[9]

In this singling out of head and thigh (with knee) as containing the life-substance and the life-soul, we have perhaps
found the origin of a symbol that is still with us, just these,
the skull and thigh-bones (crossed), singled out to represent
the person after death. These associations will also explain
use of the skull or the thigh-bone in magic. Thus in India[10] to
curse another one places a human thigh-bone under his bed.[11]
Possibly it was originally believed to draw away or receive
the life-soul or the departed soul was, as often, regarded as
an agent of death.[12]

---

[1] See Plut. *Q.R.* 10, 13; *Pomp.* 8; *Crass.* 6; Pliny, *N.H.* xxviii, 6, 60
(before men) and pp. 144 f. *supra* (before a god). Cf. pp. 132 f., 152 f. See
also the baring of the *head* and the *knees* in drinking referred to on p. 228.

[2] See pp. 97 f., 104 f., 138 ff.

[3] See P. W. Joyce, *A Social History of Ireland*, ii, p. 489.

[4] *Ibid.* i, p. 150. [5] See pp. 100 and 156 ff. [6] See pp. 100, 105, 154 ff.

[7] The same original significance will explain, e.g., the term for
'kinsman', *cneó-maégas*, lit. 'knee-relation'. Cf. p. 154, n. 5.

[8] *Grettir's Saga*, cap. xviii. [9] *Ibid.* xxxv.

[10] Cf. p. 183.

[11] See C. Sorabji, *India Calling*, pp. 204 f. and *The Times*, 29 June 1939,
p. 15.

[12] Cf. p. 108, n. 7 and p. 361, n. 2.

CHAPTER V

The Strength

If the knees get their name and their sanctity thus, there still remains to be explained the belief that in them in a special degree is the strength.[1] In weariness or exhaustion the limbs (? 'joints', γυῖα) 'are loosed',[2] the knees are 'impaired'[3] (βλάβεται) or 'heavy'.[4] Feelings in the knees are not adequate to account for the belief; and in the passage quoted[5] Hesiod seems to imply that the strength is in the liquid there which is also the seed. He and other early poets characterise sexual love as 'loosing the limbs'[6] (λυσιμελής) and, as biologist, Aristotle observed that 'the enfeebling ("loosing, relaxing", ἔκλυσις) consequent upon the issuing of even very little of the seed is conspicuous'.[7] That the strength is in the seed and has its source in the source of the latter seems to be implied by the Latin use of vires[8] and virus (cf. vir). The same notion appears

---

[1] See pp. 180f.   [2] E.g. Il. vii, 6, xiii, 85.

[3] Il. xix, 166; Od. xiii, 34.

[4] See Theocr. Idylls, xviii, 9 f.   [5] See pp. 110f., 177f.

[6] See e.g. Hesiod, Theog. 910 f.; Archilochus, Fr. 85; Sappho, Fr. 40.

[7] De Gener. Anim. 725 b, 6 f. The result is 'lack of strength' (ἀδυναμία) and conversely where there is lack of strength there is lack of seed (ibid. ll. 17–21). Venus enervat vires (Anth. Lat. ed. Riese, 633, 3). In dreams τὸ αἰδοῖον images ἰσχὺς καὶ ἡ τοῦ σώματος ἀνδρεία ὅτι καὶ αὐτὸ τούτων αἴτιον (Artem. Onir. 1, 45). In the legend of the Holy Grail the perfect strength of Galahad depends upon his perfect chastity (cf. n. 4, p. 109).

[8] Cf. p. 177, n. 9. By the disabling effects of gelding we can perhaps explain Il. xv, 466 and xvi, 119. When Zeus breaks Teucer's bowstring as he is aiming at Hector, Teucer shudders and says to Aias: 'A god is cutting the μήδεα of our battle (μάχης ἐπὶ μήδεα κείρει/δαίμων ἡμετέρης). He has knocked the bow out of my hand and snapped therefrom the newly twisted sinew which I bound thereon this morning that it might bear the arrows oft leaping thence'. And in the next book when Hector with his sword cuts through Aias' spear the latter 'shuddered at the deeds of the gods that Zeus cut the μήδεα of battle'. In these two, the only instances of the idiom, μήδεα has been interpreted 'purposes, plans'; but reference to these is not natural (see xvi, 102 ff.), reference to physical cutting destroying physical effectiveness is, and the regular meaning of

(p. 196) in ancient Hindoo thought, among the Zulus[1] and elsewhere. In the *Zohar* of the Hebrew Kabbalah it is said that in the *testes* 'are gathered all the oil, the dignity and the strength of the male from the whole body'.[2] This conception of the seed as oil[3] will explain the practice of

κείρειν is 'to cut' something material, hair, wood, etc. Neither it nor its compounds appear to be used otherwise in Homer except perhaps διακέρσαι ἐμὸν ἔπος (*Il.* VIII, 8). The use of ἐπικείρειν is 'to cut' corn, troops, etc. Also, μήδεα in the sense of 'plans' does not seem to be used elsewhere with a genitive except that of the person planning. The Homeric Greeks imaged the battle as a living creature but scarcely as a planning creature. They imaged it as a creature with bodily parts acting physically (πολέμου στόμα δύμεναι αἱματόεντος, *Il.* XIX, 313; τοσσῆσδ' ὑσμίνης ἐφέποι στόμα, XX, 359, cf. X, 8). μήδεα has such a bodily sense in Homer (*Od.* XVIII, 87, etc.). Hesiod says of Kronos φίλου δ' ἀπὸ μήδεα πατρὸς/ ἐσσυμένως ἤμησε (*Theog.* 180 f.). Cf. Archilochus' ἵνας δὲ μεδέων ἀπέθρισεν 'cut (like corn) the sinews of the μέδεα' (= μήδεα), Fr. 138, Bgk. In the most explicit of the two instances what is cut is the sinew (νευρή) of the bow. If Homer spoke thus of the maiming, rendering ineffective, of the fighting of one side, here may be the earliest form of our 'sinews of war', Cicero's *nervi belli* (*Phil.* V, 2, 5). Cf. *legionum nostrarum nervos nonne his consiliis incidemus?* (*Phil.* XII, 3, 8), *morte Africani castratam esse rempublicam* (*De Or.* III, 164). Pindar speaks of Achilles cutting down Trojan warriors as Τρωΐας ἵνας ἐκταμών (*Isth.* VIII, 52 f.), Aeschines says ὑποτέτμηται τὰ νεῦρα τῶν πραγμάτων (*In Ctes.* 166). κείρειν was naturally so used, e.g. by Alcaeus of a Gallus κειράμενος γονίμην φλέβα (*Anth. Pal.* VI, 218).

[1] See J. Macdonald, in *Journ. Anthr. Inst. of G. B. and I.* XX, 1891, p. 116.

[2] *Ha Idra Zuta Qadisha*, XXII, 741, translated by Knorr von Rosenroth (*Kabbala Denudata*) and S. L. M. Mathers (*The Kabbalah Unveiled*) after him. The prime source was the head (see *op. cit.* XXII, 759 and *infr.* pp. 234 f., 287 f.). The interpretation of the seed, the stuff of life and strength, as 'oil' fits and perhaps explains the belief among the Semites and elsewhere that the fat contains the life, and more particularly why the fat about the kidneys has been singled out as the seat of life and strength by Arabs, Australian natives, etc. (see e.g. Robertson Smith, *Religion of the Semites*, re-ed. S. A. Cook, pp. 380 ff.). That region was thought to be the source of the seed as it is in fact of the urine. See *Problemata*, 876 b, 20 f. and the significance of the loins, *ḥᵃlaçayim*, (Gen. XXXV, 11, etc.), and in imperial Latin *lumbi* (Juv. VI, 314 f., IX, 59, etc.), the 'reins' (e.g. Drayton, *Polyolbion*, I, 127 f., etc.). These thoughts may have contributed to the Hebrew belief that the 'reins'—kidneys—were seats of soul; similar thoughts about the *omentum* will explain its importance for the early Greeks, Hindoos, etc. (see pp. 280, 208, n. 2).

[3] Cf. pp. 239, n. 6, 280 f., 286. This may explain the Greek belief in the dependence of the supply of olives upon chastity and the rule that they must be planted or gathered only by the chaste (e.g. Pallad. *Res Rust.* I, 6, 14). So too among the Cilicians nearer the Jews (*Geoponica* IX, 2, 6). Identification of oil with the fat or marrow of the thigh, i.e. the seed (pp. 109, n. 1,

'anointing',[1] infusing oil into, kings, i.e. as a begetting, a
bestowing of new life, divine life, and is of vital importance for
an understanding of the belief that Jesus was not only the king
of the Jews but also divine, the son of God.[2]

177 ff., esp. 182), may explain the term for the base of a lamp: *yarekh*
'thigh' (Exod. xxv, 31, etc.). The base usually contains, is source of, the
oil.   [1] Cf. p. 228, n. 1.

[2] In the Old Testament the king was 'the Yahweh-anointed' and, as
we may now see, by the anointing became the son of Yahweh. 'I have
found David, my servant; with my holy oil have I anointed him....He
shall cry unto me "Thou art my father, my God and the Rock of my
salvation". I also will make him my first-born, the highest of the kings
of the earth' (Psalm lxxxix, 20, 26 f. Cf. II Sam. vii, 12–14). Thus, too,
the contemporary king in the second psalm: 'The rulers take counsel together, against the Lord (Yahweh), and against his anointed....The Lord
shall have them in derision. Then shall he speak unto them in his wrath...
"Yet I have set my king upon my holy hill of Zion". I will tell of the
decree. The Lord said unto me, "Thou art my son. This day have I
begotten thee. Ask of me and I will give thee the nations for thine
inheritance"....Be instructed, ye judges of the earth. Serve the Lord
with fear, and rejoice with trembling. Kiss the Son, lest he be angry and
ye perish in the way...'. And thus it is that centuries later Paul tells the
Jews in the synagogue at Antioch how God gave unto them as kings Saul
and David. 'Of this man's seed hath God according to promise brought
unto Israel a saviour, Jesus....We bring unto you good tidings of the
promise made unto the fathers, how that God hath fulfilled the same
unto our children, in that he raised up Jesus, as also it is written in the
second psalm, "Thou art my son. This day have I begotten thee"'
(Acts xiii, 23–33). Saul, the son of Kish, and David, the son of Jesse,
who were Israel's saviours in times of Philistine oppression, were the first
kings, the prototypes of the king who was looked for. The anointing was
a begetting, a giving of new life, a making of a new person, a person with
a different spirit, the spirit of Yahweh. Thus 'The spirit of the Lord God is
upon me because he hath anointed me...' (Isa. lxi, 1; cf. xliv, 3) claimed
by Jesus (Luke iv, 18, 21). Cf. Joel ii, 28, etc. The prophet Samuel at the
prompting of God chose Saul and anointed him, telling him that he would
meet a company of prophets 'and the spirit of the Lord shall come mightily
upon thee and thou shalt prophesy with them and shalt be turned into a
different man...and it was so that when he turned his back to go from
Samuel God gave him another heart and those signs came to pass that
day' (I Sam. x, 1 ff.). So too when the prophet Samuel saw David, 'the
Lord said, "Arise, anoint him, for this is he". Then Samuel took the
horn of oil and anointed him in the midst of his brethren: and the Spirit
of the Lord came mightily upon David from that day forward' (I Sam.
xvi, 12 f.). Thus too Jesus was foreknown by the prophet John and appears
to have become the Christ (i.e. the 'anointed', χριστός = Aramaic *Messiah*)
and so the son of God at his baptism by John: 'Straightway coming up
out of the water he saw the heavens rent asunder and the Spirit as a dove
descending upon him and a voice came out of the heavens, "Thou art

From a different angle, for the belief that the strength is in the fluid of the knee-joint, we may recall our own old-fashioned wish, 'More power to your elbow!', implying that strength is

my beloved son, in thee I am well pleased". And straightway the Spirit driveth him forth...' (Mark i, 10 ff.). So 'Prophesy unto us, thou Christ' (xiv, 61–5, Matt. xxvi, 68). Now we may understand 'Except a man be born anew....Except a man be born of water and the Spirit he cannot enter into the kingdom of God' (John iii, 3, 5), διὰ λουτροῦ παλινγενεσίας καὶ ἀνακαινώσεως πνεύματος ἁγίου, οὗ ἐξέχεεν ἐφ' ἡμᾶς (Titus iii, 5 f.; cf. p. 272, n. 8). We may relate the custom seen in David's command that Solomon be taken to the water of Gihon (see II Chron. xxxii, 30) to be anointed king (I Kings i, 30–9). For Acts Jesus was 'thy holy servant Jesus whom thou didst anoint' (iv, 27; cf. Isai. xlii, 1), 'Jesus of Nazareth, how God anointed him with the holy Spirit and with power' (x, 38). He was thus the son of God who was the 'Son of Man'. It was of a son of David (Matt. xxii, 42, xii, 23, xxi, 9, 15), son of God by anointing, that contemporaries thought. 'Art thou the Christ (i.e. "anointed"), the son of the Blessed?' 'Yes.' (Mark xiv, 61 f.) According to Luke (ix, 20, cf. ii, 26) Peter said, 'Thou art the Christ (i.e. anointed) of God'. It was through Joseph and not Mary that Jesus was of David's seed (Matt. xvi, 16; Luke i, 27, iii, 23–31). Paul is quite explicit. He preached 'the Gospel of God ...concerning his son who was born of the seed of David according to the flesh, who was ordained ("separated off", ὁρισθέντος) son of God in power according to the spirit of holiness...' (Rom. i, 1–4. Cf. Matt. xii, 18, iii, 16 f., Luke ix, 35, xxiii, 35). Mark, the earliest Gospel, begins with the baptism and says nothing of the begetting by the Holy Spirit upon the virgin Mary, which if he had heard and believed he could not have omitted. Christians, those who received the Spirit, became 'sons of God... joint-heirs with Christ...the firstborn among many brethren' (Rom. viii, 14–19, 29; cf. John i, 12). 'Ye have an anointing (χρῖσμα, chrism, oil, etc. infused) from the Holy One and ye know all things...the χρῖσμα which ye received of him abideth in you and ye need not that anyone teach you....Beloved, now are we the children of God....Whosoever is begotten of God doeth no sin because his seed abideth in him' (I John ii, 20, 27, iii, 2, 9. Cf. II Corinthians i, 21 f.). At baptism still the baptised becomes 'the child of God, and an inheritor of the kingdom of heaven' (Catechism in the Book of Common Prayer). In early forms of the rite he was anointed. In the form cited below (p. 299) God is described as the 'Father of all unction'. In the Armenian church the chrism was described as 'life-creating' (ζωοποιὸν χρῖσμα, see *Rituale Armenorum*, ed. Conybeare and Maclean, p. 404) and the ministrants prayed 'that when we cast it into this water, it may regenerate those about now to be baptised...' (*ibid.* p. 104). Recognition of the original thought will also explain why in the baptism among witches actual human seed was used in the chrism (see pp. 247 f. of *The Witch-cult in Western Europe*, by M. A. Murray). Oil was in fact the liquid of seed, the seed of the olive tree (cf. pp. 217 f.). We may better understand how the holy oil could

in the joint, and the more explicit noun 'elbow-grease' which connotes strength, vigour, and should naturally express the 'grease', the lubricating synovial fluid (Anglo-Saxon *lith-ule*, 'joint-oil') of that joint. It is, I am told, still applied by butchers to that in the knees of beasts. There was, however, another side to this belief. Sweat was referred to as 'elbow-grease'.[1] Sweat would naturally seem to be the stuff of strength, vigour, since it is expended when strength, vigour, is expended,[2] and conversely he who sweats through external heat feels loss of strength, of vigour. The Nubians suppose it will give them strength to apply the sweat of their horses to their own bodies.[3] In the Torres Straits men drink the sweat of famous warriors in the belief that in it they are getting their valour.[4] The thought traced among our own forefathers, that sweat, the pale liquid coming out of the flesh, and synovial fluid, the liquid in the joints, are one and are the stuff of strength, vigour, appears (with emphasis instead upon the knee-joints) to have been part of the earliest Greek physiology, which also assimilated with these the cerebro-spinal fluid and the seed. The various elements may be seen in the quotation from Hesiod that at midsummer 'women are most wanton but men are most impotent ("feeblest", ἀφαυρότατοι) because Sirius dries up (ἄзει) the head and knees and the flesh is dried up (αὐαλέος) with the heat (ὑπὸ καύματος)'.[5] An expression in the 'Shield of Herakles'[6] suggests that the drying is by sweating:

be regarded as the seed of God if we compare the belief that the bread and wine after consecration are the body and blood of God. Zechariah refers to anointed king and anointed high priest as 'the two oil-sons that stand by the Lord' (iv, 14). For the horn see pp. 236 ff. See also pp. 482 ff.

[1] See e.g. the *Oxford English Dictionary* and Brewer's *Dictionary of Phrase and Fable*, s.v. The original concrete meaning appears to have been lost sight of in the jesting use to-day. Cf. perhaps 'beauty, wit,/high birth, vigour of bone...are subjects all/to...time', Shak., *Troil. and Cress.* iii, 3 and pp. 213 f. below. Irish *smior*, 'marrow', is used also to express 'strength' (cf. *smioramhlachd*, 'activity, manliness, briskness') and *smuis* means both 'marrow' and 'sweat', while *allur mo cnám*, lit. 'the sweat of my bones', is used of sweating through exertion. Cf. p. 289, n. 5.

[2] Sweating was not unimportant for Homer, e.g. *Il.* iv, 25 f.

[3] See p. 210 below.   [4] See Haddon, *Journ. Anthr. Inst.* xix, p. 312.

[5] See pp. 110 f., 177 above.   [6] 397. Cf. also *Works and Days*, 575.

ἴδει ἐν αἰνοτάτῳ ὅτε τε χρόα Σείριος ἄӡει (cf. ἔλπομαι πολλοὺς μὲν αὐτῶν Σείριος καταυανεῖ ὀξὺς ἐλλάμπων, Archilochus[1]).

It is liquid or something liquefiable which gives the flesh its fullness, fatness. Other Greek evidence is more conveniently discussed below.[2] The Romans with the same belief[3] spoke of this liquid as *umor*, more usually *sucus*, 'sap'. Thus in an age when, as to-day, 'slimming' was the general fashion, Chaerea rejoiced that the object of his affections was *corpus solidum et suci plenum*[4] (cf. *sucidus*, 'plump', *aridus*, 'lean'), and in the figure of a young man Apuleius speaks of *cervix suci plena, malae uberes*.[5] This *sucus* appears to have been identified with sweat[6] and recognised as the stuff of vigour. Apuleius argues that a little image of Mercury (patron of the wrestling school) is not as alleged a spirit of the dead, a *larva* or *sceletus* (σκελετός, i.e. one 'dried up'): *En, vide quam facies eius decora et suci palaestrici plena sit*,[7] 'how full of the sap of the wrestling-school' (cf. e.g. *cum ⟨in⟩ stadio, in gymnasio, in duplici corpus siccassem pila*, Lucilius).[8] It is the stuff of life, e.g.

> *quasi quom caletur cochleae in occulto latent,*
> *suo sibi suco vivont, ros si non cadit:*
> *item parasiti rebus prolatis latent*
> *in occultis, miseri victitant suco suo,*
> *dum ruri rurant homines quos ligurriant.*[9]

---

[1] Fr. 61. The use of αὖος of one afraid (αὖός εἰμ' ἤδη τρέμων, Aristoph. *Lys.* 383, αὖός εἰμι τῷ δέει, Menand. *Epit.* 480, etc.), which the revised Liddell and Scott explains as '*trembling, shivering* (like a dry leaf)', originates rather, I would suggest, in the cold sweat of fear leaving the body 'dry'. So too ξηρός (Theoc. xxiv, 61). 'That the skin is much affected under the sense of great fear we see in the marvellous and inexplicable manner in which perspiration immediately exudes from it...the mouth becomes dry', Darwin, *Expression of the Emotions*, pp. 290 f. Cf. *Probl.* 947 b 35; Lucr. iii, 154 f.; also *siccus*, in n. 8 and p. 223, n. 3.   [2] Pp. 201 ff., 212 ff.

[3] Other evidence will be discussed on pp. 209–212, 215 f., 222 ff., etc.

[4] Terence, *Eun.* 317. Cf. Horace, *Odes*, iii, 27, 53 ff., etc.

[5] *Florida*, ii, 15, p. 52.

[6] Varro tells us that sheep are sheared *cum sudare inceperint oves; a quo sudore recens lana tonsa sucida appellata est* (*R.R.* ii, 11, 6).

[7] *De Magia*, 63.

[8] 641 (Marx). Cf. Hor. *Sat.* ii, 2, 14 on p. 223, n. 3. This sense of *siccus*, surely, gives the true interpretation of Lucan iv, 638 f. Juno sees Hercules taxed by Antaeus: *videt exhaustos sudoribus artus/cervicemque viri siccam cum* ['though';? better *quae* or *qua*] *ferret Olympum*. Cf. vi, 542 f., etc.

[9] Plaut. *Capt.* 80 ff. Cf. *siccus* (pp. 212, 223 f.).

The sexual aspect is illustrated by an old man's claim:

> *et ego amoris aliquantum habeo umorisque etiam in corpore;*
> *nequedum exarui ex amoenis rebus et voluptariis.*[1]

To return to Greece, Alcaeus' version of Hesiod's point implies that the liquid in the flesh is dependent upon that in the head and knees: 'Now women are lewdest and men are lean ("thin", λέπτοι) because Sirius dries up the head and knees'.[2] We have explicit record later that the sweat was believed to come from the cerebro-spinal fluid and marrow,[3] and we can perhaps now better understand why, twenty lines after the quotation discussed, Hesiod's advice to the farmer after the corn-harvest is just to 'cool again (ἀναψῦξαι) the dear knees of the serfs and to loose the oxen',[4] and why Homer says that the comrades of Aias 'received his shield when distress and sweating assailed his knees (κάματός τε καὶ ἱδρὼς γούναθ' ἵκοιτο)'.[5]

That the knees should be imagined to be seats of a man's strength is strange, but it would be stranger still if the head was thought to be such also;[6] yet that is what the beliefs traced should involve and what in fact we find. Of the epic adjectives expressive of strength, ἄλκιμος means 'brave, strong in battle' and κραταιός and κρατερός more generally 'powerful, effective' (e.g. βασιλεύς τ' ἀγαθὸς κρατερός τ' αἰχμητής), κρατερός sometimes 'masterful, violent' (cf. κράτος); but the epithet

---

[1] Plaut. *Mil. Glor.* 639 f.   [2] See pp. 111, 177 above.

[3] See e.g. *Problemata*, 867 a, 23 ff., 867 b, 23 f. and 34 ff., 868 a, 1 ff., 965 b, 3 ff. and Theophr. Fr. IX, *de Sudore*, § 33. It is, Pliny tells us, a sign that individuals have no marrow that they 'do not thirst or sweat' (*N.H.* VII, 18, 78). In the 'sweat of the brow' (πρῶτον καὶ μάλισθ' ἱδρῶσι τὸ μέτωπον, Theophr. *l.c.*; cf. *Probl.* 868 a, 1 ff., Theoc. II, 106 f.) and the liquid inside (see pp. 108, etc.) lies, I suggest, the explanation of the name for the front part of the head, βρεχμός, βρέγμα, etc. (cf. βρέχεσθαι, e.g. Herodotus, III, 104), to which it is usually suggested our 'brain', Anglo-Saxon *brægen*, is akin. 'From his brain...flows a cold sweat', Jonson, *Volp.* I, 1. The Zoroastrian first man was born from the sweat of Ormazd.

[4] *Works and Days*, 608.

[5] *Il.* XIII, 710 f. Cf. XVII, 385 f., XIX, 166 f., 354.

[6] We have seen that the ancient Irish had similar ideas about the soul and the head (pp. 100 f., 156 ff.) and believed that the marrow was the strength (pp. 191, 289, n. 5). Belief in its 'strength' perhaps explains why they mixed a man's brain with earth to form a weapon.

more narrowly expressive of bodily strength is ἴφθιμος, which is frequently applied to persons (e.g. Sarpedon at the wall of the Achaeans says to his comrades: 'it is hard for me, though I am ἴφθιμος, alone to break through and make a path to the ships'),[1] occasionally to women[2] (ἄλοχος, etc.), but, apart from this use and one reference to rivers[3] perhaps personified,[4] it is used more specifically by Homer[5] eight times in all: once of 'shoulders'[6] and six times with the different words for 'head' (κρατὶ δ' ἐπ' ἰφθίμῳ κυνέην εὔτυκτον ἔθηκε,[7] βοῶν τ' ἴφθιμα κάρηνα,[8] πολλὰς δ' ἰφθίμους κεφαλὰς Ἄϊδι προϊάψειν[9]), and once of ψυχαί equated by the context to the 'heads' in the last instance: πολλὰς δ' ἰφθίμους ψυχὰς Ἄϊδι προΐαψεν.[10] The ψυχαί of the dead are described as ἀμενηνὰ κάρηνα,[11] not, as often translated, 'strengthless heads', but rather 'passionless, devoid of μένος', i.e. of active eager energy or fury, which even during life is characteristic not of the head but of the chest and limbs.[12] Leaving the warm body and the light of day, the ψυχή was, indeed, not envied; but practices long

[1] Il. xii, 410 f.
[2] E.g. Il. v, 415, xix, 116; Od. x, 106.
[3] Il. xvii, 749.
[4] They are prominent as fathers, see below, pp. 229 ff.
[5] Similarly in the Homeric hymns ἴφθιμος is used five times in all, once of shoulders and four times in the phrase βοῶν ἴφθιμα κάρηνα. In Hesiod's Works and Days and Theogony and the 'Shield of Herakles', apart from its application to persons (Works and Days, 704, etc.), ἴφθιμος is used only of the 'head': κρατὶ δ' ἐπ' ἰφθίμῳ, etc. This evidence suggests that the words for the 'head' itself, κράς κρατός, κρανίον, etc., may be closely related to κράτος, κραίνω, etc. (cf. φάος, φαίνω, etc.), the head being from remote prehistoric times the supposed seat of the strength, of the power which creates and brings to pass (cf. pp. 97; 125; 138 f.; 198, n. 1; 238; 241 f.).
[6] Il. xviii, 204. Cf. Il. xvii, 569: ἐν δὲ βίην ὤμοισι καὶ ἐν γούνεσσιν ἔθηκεν.
[7] Il. iii, 336, xv, 480, xvi, 137; Od. xxii, 123. [8] Il. xxiii, 260.
[9] Il. xi, 55. For strength in the head see also pp. 210f. below.
[10] Il. i, 3.
[11] Od. x, 521, 536, xi, 29, 49.
[12] For a description of the μένος χειρῶν (Il. v, 506) see p. 22 above. In Il. xvii, 451 ff. Zeus puts μένος into the knees and into the θυμός of horses lingering disconsolate and threatened with capture. For μένος see also pp. 24 f., 51 above and cf. μενεαίνω, μενοινάω.

after Homer's time[1] show that it was reckoned with as a power, not a *mere* 'shadow'. If among the Romans there lingered on some sense of the head as the source of the bodily strength, the executive power, we can better understand Horace's

> *exiguum censum turpemque repulsam*
> *quanto devites animi capitisque labore;*
> *impiger,*[2] etc.

Further evidence in this direction will be discussed below.[3]

This various evidence suggests that the ψυχή was not simply the 'life' but was the living strength which sustains the body, giving it vital tone[4] and movement. When the advancing warrior is stricken, there 'are loosed his ψυχή and his μένος'.[5] In a swoon, consciousness fails with the θυμός; the departure of ψυχή will correspond to the departure of the vital strength, the loosing of the knees, the collapse of the body into so much 'dead' weight. Perhaps the reason why to announce the ceasing of a swoon[6] Homer tells us that the θυμός is recovered, but does not specify the return of the ψυχή, is the fact that deep breathing and consciousness return before strength and the power of movement, which come gradually later. We can thus understand why at death the primary characteristic of the ψυχή, that has left the inert body and is separated from the θυμός, is rapid motion; why to Teiresias alone was it granted to have φρένες and the breath of living consciousness, οἴῳ πεπνῦσθαι, τοὶ δὲ σκιαὶ ἀΐσσουσιν;[7] why early philoso-

---

[1] E.g. in connection with ἥρωες (see pp. 8, 206). Cf. Hesiod, *Works and Days*, 121 ff., 140 ff., etc.

[2] *Epist.* I, 1, 43 ff. Wickham interprets 'risk of life', which was doubtless included in the sense but can scarcely be the full force of the expression. Wilkins says '*animi capitisque*, "of mind and body"'; *caput* seems to be used somewhat generally for the body but it is difficult to find an exact parallel'. See pp. 169 f. above and *animum...caput* in *Odes* III, 24, 5 ff. cited on p. 374, also p. 226.

[3] Pp. 223 ff., etc.

[4] This will explain the words of Anaximenes quoted below (p. 252). To this aspect of the gaseous ψυχή should perhaps be related the Aristotelian theory on p. 51, n. 1.

[5] See *Il.* v, 296, viii, 123, 315.

[6] See pp. 45, 93.   [7] *Od.* x, 493 ff.

phers[1] seem to have considered that the primary function of the ψυχή is *moving*. In the Babylonian Gilgamish epic the earth is opened and the ghost of Eabani is 'caused to rise up like a wind'[2] (cf. ψυχή, *anima*[3]). It is called his *utukku*, a general word for 'spirit', with associations suggesting strength. Nearer home, in the translated report of a Swedish witch-trial concerning children, each of whom said that in the night, when supposed to be in bed, he or she had been taken by the Devil to see and take part in the rites at the Blockula, we find that, on 'being asked whether they were sure of a real personal transportation and whether they were awake when it was done, they all answered in the affirmative and that the Devil sometimes laid something down in the place that was very like them. But one of them confessed that he did only take away her *strength* and her body lay still upon the ground, yet sometimes he took even her body with him'.[4] The radical unity of βία 'strength' and βίος 'life' (cf. *vis* and *vita*) may now be seen. For the identification with the seed also we may compare the statement from ancient India: 'Verily, from the beginning he (the self) is in a man as a germ, which is called seed. This (seed) which is strength gathered from all the limbs of the body he (the man) bears as self in his self (body)'.[5] In the early Greek scheme the ψυχή seems to be the informing spirit in the fluid, leaving it in vaporous form. The 'steaming' of perspiration (cf. διαπνεῖν, ἀτμίζειν, etc.) in strenuous effort may

[1] Aristotle introduces his own discussion of the subject (*de Anima*, 403 b, 25 ff.) with the views of earlier Greeks, Democritus, the Pythagoreans and others: 'all these seem to hold the view that movement is what is closest to the nature of the soul (οἰκειότατον...τῇ ψυχῇ)'. It is 'mover' as well as itself moving. Cf. in Diels, *Fragm. d. Vors.*[4]: Thales, A 22 f.; Alcmaeon, A 1 and 12; Anaxagoras, A 19; also Plato, *Phaedr.* 245, etc.

[2] See *The Epic of Gilgamish*, translated by R. Campbell-Thompson, p. 59.

[3] See pp. 120 f. and 169.

[4] See 'An Account of what happened in the Kingdom of Sweden in the years 1669 and 1670', translated by A. Horneck, p. 7 (an appendix to Glanville's *Sadducismus Triumphatus*). Cf. note 7 on p. 102 above. It would give point to *Beowulf*, 2661 f., quoted on p. 100 above, if the head contained with the soul the strength.

[5] *Aitareya Aranyaka*, II, 5, 1, 2; about the *ātman* or 'self', cf. p. 512.

have helped the thought. An Orphic verse of doubtful date ran ἔστιν ὕδωρ ψυχή (ψυχῇ, Sylb.), θάνατος δ' ὑδάτεσσιν ἀμοιβή.[1] Heraclitus taught that ψυχαί are exhaled from liquids.[2] In the original scheme, the fluid, while concentrated particularly in the head[3] and in a lesser degree in the knees, is found also in the flesh elsewhere, and the ψυχή, while associated or equated particularly with the head, is seen of similar size and form to the living body,[4] which it quickens, and it can depart not only from the face but through wounds in the flank,[5] etc. The same thought will explain why the *genius* was interpreted as the executive power.[6]

We saw[7] that a sneeze was believed to be a sign from a power with prophetic knowledge not possessed by the conscious self and that that power was almost certainly the ψυχή, and that similarly a sneeze and a blush were treated as if signs from the *genius*. The belief that a movement, quivering, throbbing, etc. (παλμός), of a part of the body without any apparent influence from the conscious self was a warning of some happening beyond the ken of the latter can now be explained. The nature of the happening was indicated by the choice of part moved. Thus a lover talking of his love suddenly says: 'My right eye is quivering. Shall I see her then?'[8] When the ear tingles or rings, someone is speaking or will speak concerning you.[9] The itching palm signifies that it presently will receive (money). And so on. The ψυχή or *genius*[10] was the power with just such superior knowledge, such relations to the body and such independence of the conscious self. It fits this and there is confirmation of the argument above[11] (that the

---

[1] Fr. 226, 1 (Kern).
[2] See p. 252 below. If the ψυχή was the vital strength and substance as indicated, and not merely 'life' or 'soul', we can better understand the crux of Heraclitus: 'It is difficult to fight with one's θυμός; for whatever it wishes for, it purchases at the cost of ψυχή' (B 85, Diels).
[3] See pp. 108 ff., 217 ff., etc.   [4] E.g. *Il.* XXIII, 66.
[5] *Il.* XIV, 517 f. Cf. XVI, 505.
[6] See Festus, s.v. and *genialis* (p. 84, Linds.); Mart. Cap. II, 152; *inf.* pp. 223 f.   [7] Pp. 103 ff., 132, 138 f., 225 f.   [8] Theocr. III, 37 f., etc.
[9] See Lucian, *Dial. Meret.* 9, 2; Pliny, *N.H.* XXVIII, 2, 24.
[10] See pp. 102 ff., 146 f., 149 f., 207 f., etc.   [11] Pp. 123 ff.

genius, the generative soul, was associated particularly with the head) in a hitherto unexplained passage of Plautus. A courtesan offers her embraces to an old man and, about to yield against his original purpose, he says: 'My head itches! I am done for! (*caput prurit. perii.*) I am scarcely saying No',[1] just as a man

---

[1] *Bacch.* 1193. *Prurire* could express not only itching but also wanton desire. Similarly for Plato's Socrates lust, above all that of the κίναιδος, was an itching (ψωρᾶν) to be relieved by scratching, scraping (κνῆσθαι), *Gorg.* 494 c ff., cf. Xen. *Mem.* I, 2, 30, also Hesych. ψωρός· παιδεραστής and *caput limare* (pp. 123 f.). This thought about the head will also explain why to say that a man 'scratched his head with one finger' was to insinuate that he was a sexual pervert or *pathicus*, why Juvenal (IX, 132 f.) refers to such as *omnes/qui digito scalpunt uno caput* and why, according to Plutarch, trying to defame Pompey Clodius with a gang of licentious fellows shouted τίς ἐστιν αὐτοκράτωρ ἀκόλαστος; τίς ἀνὴρ ἄνδρα ζητεῖ; τίς ἐνὶ δακτύλῳ κνᾶται τὴν κεφαλήν; (*Pomp.* 48. Cf. Calvus in Seneca, *Contr.* VII, 4, 8, *Digito caput uno scalpit. Quid credas hunc sibi velle? Virum,* and Ammianus Marc. XVII, 11). If Pompey did scratch his head with one finger, mere reference to that act without further associations of thought or *double entente* will not suffice for Calvus or for Clodius' climax. The explanation in the past has been merely that foppish avoidance of disarranging the hair was described. From the use of the expression to describe sexual inverts and a belief, based upon the ideas just traced, that the act betrayed a desire for such sexual experience, probably derives Seneca's *impudicum...ostendit...relatus ad caput digitus* (*Epist.* LII, 12), which can scarcely be true to-day or the result of simple observation at any time (unless indeed among men who touched the head when thinking of something sexual, cf. above pp. 129 and 144 f.). For the equation of finger and phallus see *digitus infamis, impudicus*, also Mart. I, 92, II, 28, 2 and the evidence cited by Mayor on Juv. x, 53 for *ostendere digitum*, etc. with pp. 226, n. 1, 233, n. 5. For *scalpere* cf. Pers. I, 20 f.

Above (p. 97, n. 10) we suggested that the hand, more particularly the right hand, was regarded as an embodiment of the executive power, the life-soul. If the hand was felt to be peculiarly related to and expressive of that, the procreative agent, the use of the hand as an embodiment not only of power but, apparently, of procreative power, e.g. as the symbol of the fertility god Sabazios, can be understood, also how Zeus begot Epaphos by touching Io with his hand (Aesch. *P.V.* 849 f., *Supp.* 313) and why women, to be made fertile, were struck on the palm (cf. p. 226, n. 1) by the hide (see p. 235, n. 4) wielded by the *Luperci* (Ovid, *Fasti*, II, 425 ff.). Not only was Nishâda born out of the left thigh of Vena (p. 183) but also Pṛithâ out of his right hand. See also the passages from the *Kalevala* on p. 177; and for other instances of birth from a hand and of the setting up of a hand to make fields fertile (cf. pp. 126 f., 144) see s.v. 'Hand' in Hastings' *Encyl. of Rel. and Ethics* (MacCulloch), p. 493. These can now be better understood. See also pp. 180 above, 208, n. 3, 221, 226, n. 1, 246, 494 ff. below. That the hand was peculiarly related to the life-soul will explain

in danger from another's fists thinks he is warned by such an indication in his teeth that presently his teeth will be involved: *perii; dentes pruriunt*[1] (cf. a few lines later the other's threat: *pugnos edet*), and a slave that he is warned of impending punishment, a flogging: *timeo quid rerum gesserim, ita dorsus totus prurit.*[2]

cheiromancy or palmistry, the belief that one's life is defined in the lines of one's hand (e.g. Aristot. *Hist. Anim.* 493 b 32 ff., Juv. VI, 583 f.), even as the relation of the life and life-soul to the head, the forehead (pp. 129, 145 f.) will explain metoposcopy (Juv. *loc. cit.*, Artemid. *On.* II, 69, etc.).

[1] Plaut. *Amph.* 295. Cf. *Poen.* 1315 and Novius, *Maccus*, 1.
[2] *Mil. Glor.* 397. Cf. *Pers.* 36, *Asin.* 315 f. etc.

CHAPTER VI

The Stuff of Life

Let us now look at the word αἰών (*aiōn*, whence 'æon'), which is associated with ψυχή. On the assumption that its nearest cognates are ἀεί and *aevum* it is generally agreed that the fundamental meaning for Homer and later is 'period of existence' and so, from the meaning 'lifetime', that of 'life' is derived. But the passages, from which this is inferred for Homer, can be put thus: 'If I go home, my αἰών will exist for a long time'[1] (ἐπὶ δηρὸν...ἔσσεται. Homer elsewhere uses εἶναι for 'to live, survive') and 'Briefly-lasting was (μινυνθάδιος ἔπλετο) his αἰών for him vanquished beneath the spear of Aias'.[2] Here the time is expressed by the other words. Usually the person himself is described as μινυνθάδιος. And elsewhere in Homer αἰών clearly is not a period of time but a 'thing' of some kind like ψυχή persisting through time, life itself or a vital substance necessary to living. At death 'ψυχή and αἰών leave'[3] a man, or we are told merely that 'αἰών leaves'[4] him or that he 'is deprived' of it[5] or of it and ψυχή.[6] 'I fear', says Achilles, 'lest meanwhile flies enter into the stalwart son of Menoitios by the bronze-dealt wounds and breed worms therein and defile his body—for the αἰών is slain therefrom—and so it should rot in all its flesh.'[7] 'Husband, you perished young from your αἰών (ἀπ' αἰῶνος νέος ὤλεο) and are leaving me widowed',[8] says Andromache. Of the husband or wife who yearns for his or her mate 'the αἰών is

---

[1] *Il.* IX, 415 f. Ebeling interpreted *vis vitalis* and Professor A. C. Pearson in *Verbal Scholarship and the Growth of some Abstract Terms* (pp. 26 ff.) urged that αἰών meant 'vitality', 'living stuff', 'the principle of continuity, that which marks the persistency of the living force, the lasting thing'.

[2] *Il.* IV, 478 f. and XVII, 302 f.   [3] *Il.* XVI, 453.

[4] *Il.* V, 685; *Od.* VII, 224.   [5] *Il.* XXII, 58.   [6] *Od.* IX, 523 f.

[7] *Il.* XIX, 24 ff.   [8] *Il.* XXIV, 725 f.

wasted'[1] (φθίνεσθαι, φθινύθειν) as he or she weeps. Explicitly[2] related to this and most significant of all is the only remaining instance—about the husband: 'nor were his eyes ever dry of tears, but there flowed down the sweet αἰών as he lamented for his return' (οὐδέ ποτ' ὄσσε/δακρυόφιν τέρσοντο, κατείβετο δὲ γλυκὺς αἰών/νόστον ὀδυρομένῳ). This has hitherto been ignored and paraphrased away: 'his life ebbed', etc., but its natural interpretation in fact is that the liquid flowing down was αἰών and that it is the same liquid which is said to be 'wasted' when husband or wife weeps. κατείβω, whose middle we have translated 'flow down', is used fifteen times elsewhere in Homer but never except literally of tears[3] or water.[4] Thus also we can understand a line which happens to be preserved for us by the *Etymologicum Magnum*:[5] τῆς δ' ὀλοφυρομένης ἀμφ' ἀχνύι εἴβεται αἰών.

Let us examine Homer's belief as to the origin of tears. When Demodokos sang of Troy, 'Odysseus was melted (τήκετο) and a tear wet his cheeks beneath his eyelids'; as a woman falls weeping about the body of her wounded and dying husband 'and with most piteous grief her cheeks are wasted ("diminish", φθινύθουσι), even so piteous a tear Odysseus poured forth (εἶβεν) beneath his brows'.[6] When Odysseus in disguise spoke of himself to Penelope, 'her tears flowed as she listened and her flesh was melted (τήκετο δὲ χρώς). Even as the snow is melted (κατατήκετ') on the mountain tops... and with its melting (τηκομένης) the rivers flowing become full, even so were her fair cheeks melted as she shed tears'.[7] These passages make it clear that there was believed to be in the flesh, filling or forming it, liquid or a liquefiable element which

---

[1] *Od.* v, 160, also XVIII, 204.

[2] It is part of the context, eight lines earlier, *Od.* v, 151 ff.

[3] *Il.* XVI, 11, XIX, 323, XXIV, 794; *Od.* IV, 153, VIII, 531, XI, 391, XVI, 219, 332, XXI, 86, etc.

[4] *Il.* XV, 39, XXI, 261; *Od.* v, 185. Cf. καταλείβομαι, *Il.* XVIII, 109.

[5] 182, 1, s.v. ἀχνύς.

[6] *Od.* VIII, 522 ff.

[7] *Od.* XIX, 204 ff. The point is unfortunately missed by Monro, whose commentary bids us 'note the difference in the sense of τήκω, first (in 204) "to moisten" but in the simile "to melt"'.

could come out of it and be lost. This belief we have met already,[1] the liquid being recognised in sweat. Later also, as we know, tears and sweat were thought to be the same liquid.[2] It is this liquid which Homer calls αἰών.

But αἰών in Homer and later in some way represents the 'life'. The earlier evidence[3] implied that this liquid in the flesh was one with the cerebro-spinal fluid and the seed, the stuff of life and strength. There is other evidence for it as issuing at the eyes. Sexual love is repeatedly described as a process of 'liquefying, melting' (τήκεσθαι) and is characterised as ὑγρός, 'liquid, wet'.[4] Thus, according to the Homeric Hymn to Pan (XIX), Hermes went as herdsman to a mortal, 'for coming upon him there burgeoned liquid desire'[5] (θάλε γὰρ πόθος ὑγρός... ἐπελθὼν νύμφῃ...φιλότητι μιγῆναι, cf. Homer's τεθαλυῖά τ᾽ ἔερση, θαλερὸν δάκρυ, etc.). It flows at the eyes. Ἔρως ὃ κατ᾽ ὀμμάτων στάζεις πόθον, cry the Chorus of the Hippolytus.[6] This adjective 'wet' (ὑγρός) was com-

---

[1] Pp. 191 ff.

[2] See e.g. the Problemata, 884 b 22 ff. Empedocles speaks of tears and sweat together as produced by a 'melting' (τήκεσθαι) of the blood (which his system singled out for notice), more explicitly a separation of the watery liquid thence (see A 78, Diels, cf. Plut. de Plac. Phil. v, 22). Compare also the Greek use of ἱδρώς and δάκρυ alike for anything exuded and our own 'Thou hast not swette out of thyn eye a tear' (Pilgr. Sawle (Caxton) I, XXII (1859); cf. Shak. Cor. v, 3, 196) with 'He wept not with his eyes only but with all his limbs' (Ancren Riwle, p. 110).

[3] Pp. 191 ff.

[4] E.g. Alcman, Fr. 36; Anacreon, Fr. 169 (Bgk.); Plato, Phaedr. 251; Xen. Symp. 8, 3; Plut. de Tu. Sanit. Praec. XXV; Amat. IV, etc.

[5] Ll. 33 f. No satisfactory etymology has been found for ἐράω (ἔρως Eros, etc.) applied to one moved sexually. It was, I suggest, in origin just ἐράω 'I pour out (liquid)', related to ἔρση. Cf. p. 177, n. 9. This use of ἐράω occurs in compounds (ἐπ-, ἐξ-, κατ-, μετ-, etc.). The simple form seems to have developed early the specialised application and so the sense of 'love'. ἔραμαι would thus originally mean 'I pour out myself, emit liquid' (Middle) or 'I am poured out', ἔρος εἵπετο (Hes. Theog. 910). Cf. ῥεῖν καὶ λείβεσθαι τὸν ἐρωτικόν, ὅταν ἐμβλέπῃ τοῖς καλοῖς, οἷον ἐκχεόμενον εἰς αὐτούς (Plut. Q. Conv. v, 7, 2). στυγέω 'I hate' originated in the physical 'I freeze, stiffen at' (see p. 46, n. 6 and Boisacq, s.v.). Cf. the development of μέμαα, χάρμη, and 'breath' = 'emotion' on pp. 21 f., 49 f., 53.

[6] Ll. 525 f. Cf. Aesch. P.V. 902 f. etc. There is sometimes the suggestion that thus love comes; 'It is engender'd in the eyes, with gazing fed': amor ut lacrima ab oculo oritur, in pectus cadit (Publ. Syri Sent. 40, Ribbeck).

monly applied to the swimming eyes of sexual passion: ὑγρὸν βλέμμα;[1] ὑγρὰ δερκομένοισιν ἐν ὄμμασιν;[2] ἐπ' ὄμμασιν ὑγρὰ δεδορκώς;[3] ὀφθαλμοὶ κλυჳόμενοι, κυμαίνοντες ἑαυτούς, ἐπαφρόδιτον καὶ ἐμπαθῆ ἄνδρα δηλοῦσιν,[4] etc. Thus perhaps it is that in a (? Orphic) poem, part of which Proclus has preserved, men are engendered by the tears of the Creator,[5] and thus perhaps that for Empedocles tears seem to have been identified with the seed in a line[6] about the elemental water, Nestis: Νῆστίς θ' ἣ δακρύοις τέγγει κρούνωμα βρότειον, 'Nestis, that wets the human well-spring with tears', which has been preserved for us with the explanation 'Nestis and human well-spring the seed and water (τὸ σπέρμα καὶ τὸ ὕδωρ)'.[7] Aristotle tells us that the region round the eyes was the region of the head most fruitful of seed ('most seedy', σπερματικώτατος), pointing[8] to generally recognised effects upon the eyes of sexual indulgence and to practices which imply that seed comes from liquid in the region of the eyes.

It is this liquid from the eyes which Homer calls αἰών and three times says 'wastes' or 'flows down' as husband or wife weeps, yearning for the other. That he does not refer to it thus in any of the many other cases[9] of weeping or separation

---

[1] *Anacreont.* xxviii, 21.   [2] *Anth. Pal.* vii, 27.   [3] *Anth. Plan.* 306.

[4] Polemon, *Physiogn.* 1. Cf. Rose's *Physiognomon*, p. 123; Lucian, *Amor.* 3, 14 *fin.*; Catullus, xlv, 11, etc.

[5] Fr. 354 in *Orphicorum Fragm.* (ed. O. Kern), quoted from Procl. *in Plat. Rep.* 1, p. 128 (Kr.). It runs: δάκρυα μὲν σέθεν ἐστὶ πολυτλήτων γένος ἀνδρῶν,/μειδήσας δὲ θεῶν ἱερὸν γένος ἐβλάστησας. Cf. the account of creation in *pap. Lugd.* iv, 1395 (Dieterich, *Abraxas*, 17, 29 ff. Kern *ibid.*), ἐκάκχασε τὸ ἕβδομον ἀσθμησάμενος/καὶ κακχάჳων ἐδάκρυσε καὶ ἐγένετο ψυχή. The Egyptians spoke of men as coming from the eye of the god, as his tears (see Ebers, *Abh. d. k. bay. Ak. d. Wiss.* 1, Cl. xxi, Bd. 1, p. 153).

[6] B 6 (*Fragm. d. Vors.*), where Diels translates 'Nestis, die ihren Tränen sterblichen Lebensquell entfliessen lässt'. Burnet (*Early Gk. Phil.*³ p. 205) renders 'Nestis, whose tear drops are a well-spring to mortals'. In *Doxog. Gr.* (p. 287) Diels punctuated ... τέγγει, κρούνωμα.

[7] A 33 (*Fragm. d. Vors.* Diels), *Alleg. hom. script.* in Stob. *Ecl.* 1, 10, 11 b, p. 121 W. Cf. *ibid.* Aetius, 1, 3, 20: Νῆστιν δὲ καὶ κρούνωμα βρότειον οἰονεὶ ('as if' i.e. 'meaning') τὸ σπέρμα καὶ τὸ ὕδωρ.

[8] *De Gen. An.* 747 a, 13 ff.; Fr. vii, 285 (Rose). Cf. *Probl.* 876 a 30 ff., 880 b 8 ff.

[9] E.g. Laertes weeping for Odysseus or Penelope for Telemachos.

suggests that it is the conjugal relationship[1] which occasions its mention with frankness that is characteristic.[2] We can perhaps now understand a passage of Hesiod, whose beliefs have already been illustrated:[3] Woman is a great evil; the man who does not marry has no one to care for him in old age and when he dies his possessions are divided; on the other hand if a man marries and has obtained a good wife, 'for him from his αἰών evil contends with good for existence (ἀντιφερίζει ἔμμεναι). He who gets (τέτμῃ) a mischievous progeny lives with ceaseless pain for his θυμός and heart in his breast, and the evil is irremediable'.[4] It is difficult to see how for Hesiod ἀπ' αἰῶνος could mean 'always' (Paley), 'continually' (Evelyn-White), 'all his life' (Mazon) or 'of old' (Liddell and Scott), which it has hitherto been made to do. To Hector dead Andromache says as she holds his head, 'Husband (ἄνερ), you perished young from your αἰών (ἀπ' αἰῶνος) and are leaving me widowed in the halls and the child that we begot, you and I unhappy, is still but an infant nor methinks will he grow to puberty'.[5] What we were told at Hector's death was that his ψυχή, 'flying forth from his face, was gone to the house of Hades, bewailing his fate, leaving his virility (or "manhood", ἀνδρότητα, v.l. ἀδροτῆτα, "fulness, strength of body") and puberty (ἥβην)'.[6] His father, trying to save him, urged as an inducement that he should 'not give great glory to Peleus' son and himself be reft of his dear αἰών (αὐτὸς δὲ φίλης αἰῶνος

[1] See the context of the crucial passage (*Od.* v, 151–61). Cf. Penelope's summing-up (XXIII, 210–12).   [2] See p. 4.

[3] See pp. 110f.

[4] *Theog.* 607 ff. It may mean something like 'from his fate' (or '*genius*', see below, pp. 405 f.), but that scarcely fits the ἀντιφερίζει ἔμμεναι and I know of no evidence for this development of meaning till about three centuries later. The reference to αἰών in the 'Shield' is Homeric: γλυκερῆς αἰῶνος ἀμέρσῃς, 331; cf. *Il.* XXII, 58. The *Melampodia* quoted by Tzetzes *ad* Lyc. 682 makes Teiresias address Zeus ὅς γέ με μακρὸν ἔθηκας ἔχειν αἰῶνα βίοιο, which is quite un-Homeric.

[5] *Il.* XXIV, 725 ff.

[6] *Il.* XXII, 362 f. Cf. XVI, 856 f. and Simonides, 117 (Bgk.): 'Ah, fell disease, why dost thou grudge to the ψυχαί of men to remain with lovely youth (ἐρατῇ πὰρ νεότητι)? Thou didst rob Timarchos, unmarried, of his sweet αἰών before he saw a wedded wife.'

ἀμερθῇς)᾽.¹ It is precious, the stuff of life and strength, the 'sweet (γλυκὺς) αἰών flowing down'.²

This liquid was, we saw, thought to be concentrated particularly in the head, to be dependent upon the cerebro-spinal fluid and 'marrow'. Homer³ expects the flesh to corrupt when 'the αἰών is slain therefrom', unless in its stead a god drips immortal fluid through the nostrils, apparently into the cerebro-spinal cavity.⁴ In any case we know that later writers used αἰών to mean 'spinal marrow' (νωτιαῖος μυελός). The 'marrow' includes the fluid; the same name (μυελός) was applied to the brain and its fluid, which are merely a continuation of the spinal 'marrow'.⁵ In the Homeric Hymn to Hermes, the god, before cutting up two cows to cook, 'threw both on their backs snorting on the ground and bending them inwards rolled them over when he had pierced (or "penetrated") their αἰῶνες'⁶ (ἐγκλίνων δ᾽ ἐκύλινδε δι᾽ αἰῶνας

---

¹ *Il.* xxii, 57 f.   ² See *Od.* v, 160, quoted on p. 200.
³ See *Il.* xix, 24 ff., quoted on p. 200.
⁴ Sneezing apparently was thought to come from the life-principle there (see pp. 103 ff.). Plautus says *cerebrum e capite emungere* (*Most.* 1110) and the Egyptian embalmers used to extract the brain through the nostrils by means of a curved instrument and fluid thus introduced. An inkling of this last will not, as is usually suggested, serve as the explanation of Homer's story. For it was only a small part of the Egyptian process. It preserved and professed to preserve only the skull. To prevent the corruption of the flesh—the aim of Thetis—there was other and not less striking procedure: the bowels were removed, the cavity cleansed and filled with spices, the whole body pickled in natron for seventy days, then swathed in mummy wrappings and gum and fitted into its coffin (Herodotus, ii, 86). Cf. *Il.* xix, 352 f., where, however, αἰών is not mentioned nor the nostrils, and it is nourishment to the erect and living that is given.   ⁵ See pp. 118 ff., 149 ff.
⁶ Ll. 118 ff.; cf. δειροτομῆσαι, 405. This is an alternative to the use of an axe on the back of the neck of the standing beast (see above, p. 107, also Deut. xxi, 4–6). In one passage (*Aj.* 298 ff.) Sophocles, describing Aias' slaughter of cattle, says 'some he necked (ηὔχένιϡε, meaning perhaps by smiting with sword or axe. See ll. 55 f. and 236 f. quoted on p. 206 with *Od.* iii, 449 ff., etc.) and others he turned up and cut their throats and their spines' (τοὺς δ᾽ ἄνω τρέπων ἔσφαϡε κἀρράχιϡε). The meaning of ἄνω τρέπων is perhaps 'turning over' (on to their backs as Hermes does; cf. ἀνατρέπειν and ἄνω κάτω τρέπειν, Aesch. Fr. 311, etc.) rather than 'bending back the throat' (Jebb), a religious act (see Leaf on *Il.* i, 459) scarcely likely in this episode. More doubtful is Hermes'

τετορήσας, v.l. αἰῶνος). To divide the 'spinal marrow' at the neck is the most expeditious way of rendering unconscious and killing. Hippocrates too spoke of the spinal marrow as the αἰών,[1] and Erotian, who gives us that information, also preserves, as an example of the same use, a fragment of Pindar.[2] It describes the fatal blow dealt with a club, apparently by Herakles, after smaller wounds: 'Finally lifting it up, πρὸς στιβαρὰς σπάραξε πλευράς, αἰὼν δὲ δι' ὀστέων ἐρραίσθη'. The spine is, apparently, broken through. Thus some of his victims among the herds Aias πλευροκοπῶν δίχ' ἀνερρήγνυ.[3] Cf. Athene's version, ἔκειρε πολύκερων φόνον κύκλῳ ῥαχίζων[4] ('severing the spine'). It is doubtless with knowledge of this use that the scholia on Homer's 'the αἰών is slain therefrom' actually give 'spinal marrow' (νωτιαῖος μυελός) as the meaning of αἰών there.

It was, we found, more particularly with the cerebro-spinal marrow that the ψυχή, the life-soul that lives on after death, was associated. This is confirmed by and throws light upon two other beliefs which we may now put together: (1) that —an alternative to the εἴδωλον—a dead man's ψυχή assumes snake form[5]—it was represented thus at tombs—a belief which lingered on chiefly in association with the mighty dead, i.e. 'heroes'; and (2) that the spinal marrow of a dead man turns into a snake (e.g. ῥάχις ἀνθρώπου νεκροῦ φασιν ὑποσηπόμενον τὸν μυελὸν ἤδη τρέπει ἐς ὄφιν· καὶ ἐκπίπτει τὸ θηρίον).[6]

procedure when, as a preliminary to making a lyre, he had carried a tortoise home (40 ff.): 'ἀναπηλήσας with knife of grey iron he gouged out (ἐξετόρησεν) the αἰών of the mountain tortoise'. ἀναπηλήσας is otherwise unknown and its meaning obscure. It is possible that αἰών here means more generally the moist substance, the life-fluid throughout, as opposed to the dry shell.

[1] See *Epidem.* 7, 122, Erotian (*Gloss. Hippocr.*), p. 49, Klein, also Hesych. and *Et. Magn.* s.v.

[2] Fr. 111.   [3] Soph. *Aj.* 236.   [4] 55 f.

[5] See e.g. Harrison, *Prolegomena to the Study of Greek Religion*[2], pp. 235–7, 325–31; Nilsson, *The Minoan-Mycenaean Religion*, pp. 273 f. There are references to 'heroes' in this form, e.g. Sosipolis (Paus. 6, 20, 4 f.); cf. Erichthonios (*ibid.* 1, 24, 7), Trophonios (Schol. Arist. *Clouds*, 508).

[6] Aelian, *de Nat. Anim.* 1, 51. Cf. *sunt qui, cum clauso putrefacta est spina sepulchro,/mutari credunt humanas angue medullas*, Ovid, *Met.* xv, 389 f.;

Both may be illustrated by what befell after the death of the Spartan king, Kleomenes. 'A few days later those who were guarding the impaled body of Kleomenes saw a good-sized snake coiled about his head and covering his face so that no carrion birds approached. Wherefore a superstitious fear fell upon the king and dread which moved the women to other purifications, on the ground that a man of higher nature and beloved of the gods had been slain. The Alexandrians also showed reverence, visiting the spot and calling Kleomenes a hero and child of the gods, until those who were wiser stopped them explaining that...from the bodies of men, when the fluids (ἰχῶρες) around the marrow have flowed together and thickened ("solidified", σύστασιν ἐν ἑαυτοῖς λαβόντων), there issue snakes and, being well aware of this, the men of old associated the snake rather than any other animal with heroes'[1] (i.e. the mighty dead). The identification of the marrow and the serpent with the seed of new life appears in the myth of the Phoenix, a creature of smaller scale, which itself thus becomes more intelligible. Before death, it builds a nest 'and dies upon it, then from its bones and marrow there is born first of all as it were a worm (cf. the old English and German use of "*worm*" for "serpent"), thence it becomes a chicken and renders funeral due to its predecessor'.[2]

The common interpretation of a shudder down the spine as a premonition of death[3] may well be explained by an original belief that there was the life and the life-soul. In other

---

anguem ex medulla hominis spinae gigni accipimus a multis, Pliny, *N.H.* x, 66, 188. Here perhaps we have the main reason (cf. p. 291) why the soul was believed to appear as a snake (pp. 129, 155, n. 4, 159, n. 2, etc.): it was identified particularly with the spinal cord and the latter resembles a snake.

[1] Plut. *Vit. Cleom.* 39. Cf. p. 159, n. 2 above.

[2] Pliny, *N.H.* x, 2, 4. According to Tacitus, *Ann.* vi, 28, it builds the nest *eique vim genitalem adfundere ex qua fetum oriri; et primam adulto curam sepeliendi patris*. The belief traced about the marrow will help to explain the belief in the generation of bees from an ox: *teneris tepefactus in ossibus umor/aestuat et visenda modis animalia miris/trunca pedum*, etc. (Virgil, *Georg.* IV, 300 f.). Its nostrils, etc. were first blocked, perhaps, to seal in the life.

[3] For references see Halliday, *Greek Divination*, p. 177. For the spinal marrow as the life see Pliny, *N.H.* xi, 37, 178 and English evidence below, p. 213, n. 4.

such signs the part of the body affected indicates thus the nature of the event portended.[1] In the belief that it contained the stuff of life and the ψυχή we have perhaps also the reason[2] why the lower end of the spine was called the 'holy bone', ἱερὸν ὀστέον (whence *os sacrum*), and the canal within the spine the 'holy tube' (ἱερὰ σῦριγξ. Cf. σπέρματα ἔχουσα θύεται τοῖς θεοῖς, Schol. *Aesch. P.V.* 497 concerning ὀσφύν). That Jews and Mohammedans believed it to be the source of renewed life will appear below.[3]

'The αἰών is slain therefrom' and those Homeric passages which speak of 'αἰών leaving' a man suggest the transition from the meaning 'life-fluid' to that of the 'life' which the fluid contains and represents. Similarly, even in Homer,[4] ψυχή from its concrete meaning 'soul' comes to mean *not* that entity but the life which it confers, and later θυμός, which to begin with meant the physical breath, vehicle of feeling, came to mean 'emotion' and more restricted still 'anger'. It fits the original sense of fluid for αἰών that unlike ψυχή and θυμός it is not said to leave the body in a swoon or go to Hades. It flows away in tears. The unmistakable use of αἰών for 'spinal marrow' has been regarded as later and derivative. That the meaning 'marrow' or 'fluid' could arise out of a supposed primitive meaning 'period of existence' is difficult to believe, and in fact, as we see, the earliest evidence lends no support to the latter meaning. On the other hand it is not

[1] See pp. 197 ff.
[2] See also pp. 109, n. 2; 126, n. 3, and p. 280, n. 2. A notorious rite of the witch-cult was the kissing of the deity's posterior. He was a fertility god. It was perhaps this part thus interpreted that was honoured. For the variant (e.g. Brand, *op. cit.* I, p. 313), the goat's tail, cf. pp. 126, n. 3, 471 with 240, n. 7. So too the kiss at initiation in the Templars' fertility cult (cf. p. 144): *in ore, in ventre nudo* (cf. the *omentum* on pp. 188, n. 2, 280) *et in ano seu spina dorsi. Item aliquando in virga virili* (Clement, in Michelet, *op. cit.* I, p. 91, cf. p. 183, etc.).
[3] P. 288. Cf. p. 280, n. 2. Similar thought will explain the Egyptian *ded* pillar representing the spine, which was sometimes used as an amulet of life (e.g. *Book of the Dead*, ch. CLV). The spine and phallus of Osiris were found at Mendes. The vital fluid (*sā*) is repeatedly shown as transmitted by laying the hand on the top of the spine or passing it down the spine.
[4] See *Od.* IX, 523 f.

difficult to see how a word designating the life 'fluid' might come to mean the life which the fluid represents and so the life temporally considered, the lifetime[1] dependent upon it. The first two instances cited[2] from Homer also show how the interpretation of the word might change thus. The temporal suggestion appears gradually to have increased by popular association of the word with ἀεί, αἰεί, till at last it meant 'eternity'. For light upon the original force of αἰών and its variant αἰώς (extant accusative αἰῶ) we should look not so much to ἀεί or αἰεί and *aevum*, the precise original force of which is obscure, as to αἰό-λλω, 'I move rapidly', αἰό-λος, 'quick-moving', to which have been related our 'soul', Anglo-Saxon *sawol*, Gothic *saiwala*.[3] Nearer to αἰών, αἰώς are Gothic *saiws*, 'a body of water', Sanscrit *ayúḥ*, 'mobile, living', *áyuḥ*, 'vital element, life, lifetime'.

In any case, for our discovery, that αἰών connoted *liquid* in relation to the body, there is confirmation in a series of words hitherto unexplained in themselves and, since they seemed to have no connection with αἰών as currently interpreted, ignored in dealing with it: αἰονάω, 'I moisten, foment, apply liquid to the flesh' used by Aeschylus, Hippocrates, etc.; ἐπαιονάω, 'I bathe' (transitive); καταιονάω, 'I pour upon'; αἰόνημα, αἰόνησις, etc. We may compare δαίμων, δαιμονάω, etc. The original idea behind fomentation, the application of salutary liquid, would appear to have been that thus the liquid, i.e. αἰών, was conferred upon, introduced into the body. Further

---

[1] For later uses see pp. 405 f. below.   [2] On p. 200 above.

[3] R. M. Meyer (*Altgermanische Religionsgeschichte*, p. 74) quotes from Goethe: 'Man's soul (*Seele*) resembles water'. For the connection of *sawol* with blood in *Beowulf*, see p. 69, n. 1. In view of the development from an original duality to a single in-dwelling spirit of life and consciousness, illustrated by the early fusion of ψυχή and θυμός (see pp. 115 ff.) among the Greeks and by the Roman confusion of *anima* and *animus* (see pp. 168 ff.), it is difficult without a similar study of all the Germanic evidence to establish the original connotation of *sawol*. It perhaps began as the conscious self, breath in relation to blood centred in the chest, and was later, with a growing belief in the continuance of the conscious self, identified with the surviving ghost. As among the Greeks and Romans, there are clear traces of an original association of the head with life (see pp. 100 and 154 ff.) and of the chest with consciousness (see pp. 38 f., 68).

evidence in this direction appears below.[1] After strenuous effort and sweating a bath seemed to restore vitality: (*de balneis*) *hic lavet: hic corpus reparans...membra fovebit aqua;*[2] *hospes dulciflua dum recreatur aqua.*[3] Plautus says *mihi...prae lassitudine opus est ⟨ut⟩ lavem* (*Truc.* 328) and again: Charinus. *at tu edepol sume laciniam atque absterge sudorem tibi.* Acanthes. *nunquam edepol omnes balineae mihi hanc lassitudinem eximent* (*Merc.* 126 f.). Cf. *medullam lassitudo perbibit* (*Stich.* 340); *defessus omnibus medullis* (Catull. LV, 30), etc. We can also now better understand anointing, the application to the body of oily liquids or unguents, practised from the Homeric age onwards usually after the bath. It is generally dismissed as part of the toilet, cleansing and perhaps perfuming the skin or 'so that the skin might not be left harsh and rough',[4] but was, I suggest, thought to feed, to introduce into the body through the pores, the stuff of life and strength,[5] which appears to come out through the pores in the form of sweat. The head, seat of strength,[6] seems to sweat most,[7] and was apparently in Homeric times, as later, specially anointed.[8] Sweat itself might be used. The Nubians suppose it will give them strength to apply the sweat of their horses to their own bodies. After a ride they scrape off the sweat from their horses' backs with the hand and rub it about their persons as if it were one of their ordinary greasy ointments.[9] Anointing was thought so essential to a Greek athlete[10] that ἀλείφεσθαι came to mean 'to be in training for athletics'. Sweating, as we saw,[11] was naturally regarded as the issuing of the watery cerebro-spinal liquid or lymph and of marrow or fat, the liquefiable element, the stuff of life and strength, from the body. 'Why is it that the fat is consumed in those who exert themselves?' ask the *Problemata*. 'Is it because fat melts

---

[1] See pp. 228, 230, 271 ff.   [2] *Anth. Lat.* (Riese), 119, 7.   [3] *Id.* 120, 4.

[4] Rich, s.v. *balneae* in Smith's *Dictionary of Greek and Roman Antiquities*², p. 184. Cf. I. v. Müller, *Die gr. Priv. u. Kriegsalt.*² pp. 135, etc.

[5] See pp. 191 f., 201 ff.   [6] See pp. 193 ff.   [7] See p. 193, n. 3.

[8] See *Od.* xv, 332. Cf. *Il.* xxiii, 281 f., Petron. 47, 1; 65, 7 and below, pp. 227 f.

[9] See E. Crawley, *Mystic Rose*², rev. Bestermann, I, p. 144.

[10] E.g. λίπα μετὰ τοῦ γυμνάζεσθαι ἠλείψαντο, Thuc. I, 6 (of the Spartans).   [11] Pp. 191 ff.

when heated?'[1] ἀλοιφή, 'unguent', is for Homer animal fat,[2] but the analogous[3] plant substance, the oil of the olive, was also used. It is possible in England to experience the penetrative virtue of goose-grease or camphorated oil or, if one is an athlete, olive-oil itself, and our twentieth-century life-essence, vitamin-vehicle, cod-liver oil is now absorbed by *inunction*. If we realise that the Greeks thought of unguents essentially as penetrating, we can also understand how χρίω commonly used of 'anointing' can be used by Aeschylus[4] in the sense of 'penetrate, pierce'. 'Why is it that fatigue ceases more readily if one mixes water with the oil with which one rubs oneself?' continue the *Problemata*.[5] 'Is it because the oil sinks in more (μᾶλλον εἰσδύεται) when mixed with water but by itself does not penetrate so well because of a tendency to remain on the surface?' So too among the Romans. Thus Plautus[6] speaks of 'filling a man up' (*repplere*) with unguents; and of those who are exhausted Petronius writes: *intraverunt palaestritae complures et nos legitimo perfusos oleo refecerunt. utcumque ergo lassitudine abiecta cenatoria repetimus.*[7] When Democritus, who was fond of eating honey, was asked 'how one might live in health', he replied 'by moistening one's inside with honey, one's outside with olive-oil (εἰ τὰ μὲν ἐντὸς μέλιτι βρέχοι, τὰ δὲ ἐκτὸς ἐλαίῳ)'.[8] External application does not trouble the stomach and may have seemed a more direct and economic way to recruit the layer of fat (just beneath the skin)[9] that

---

[1] 880 b, 36 f.

[2] *Il.* IX, 208, XVII, 390; *Od.* VI, 220, XVIII, 179. Cf. ἄλειφα, Hesiod, *Theog.* 553 and below, pp. 279 ff.

[3] See pp. 188 ff., 239 f., 286, 296, n. 7.

[4] *P.V.* 566, 597, 675, 879 f. Cf. Plato, *Phaedr.* 251 D. We may compare the German *einschlagen, Einschlag.*

[5] 881 a, 4 ff. [6] *Poen.* 701.

[7] 21. Cf. Seneca, *Ep. Mor.* 53, 5 *corpus unctione recreavi* (after seasickness).

[8] A 29 (Diels); cf. *Anab.* IV, 4, 12 f., etc.

[9] Various attempts have been made to explain the word δῆμος (*dēmos*), 'deme, people, democracy, etc.': by δάμνημι, 'subdue', δῆ, 'earth', δόμος, 'house', δαίομαι, δατέομαι, 'divide', Sanscrit *dāti*, 'reap', etc.; but it is, I suggest, merely the word for fat, a fat part of an animal, applied specifically to land. Homer seems to have thought so. He uses it of the

appears to exude in sweat. For Horace[1] he who was sleek with ample food was *unctus* and opposed to him who was 'dry', *siccus*, with poor living. We saw[2] that the *sucus*, the liquid of life and strength in the body, was recognised in sweat. How natural it was to think thus of the fat may be seen e.g. in Pliny's *pingue inter carnem cutemque suco liquidum*.[3] A few lines later he assimilates marrow to fat: *et medulla ex eodem videtur esse*.

There was perhaps further reason for the use of αἰών to land occupied by a community—which would be the fertile land well covered with soil as opposed to the bare and barren rocks—speaking repeatedly of the Boeotians, etc., 'having exceedingly plump δημος (πίονα δημον)', 'in the plump δημος (πίονι δημῷ) of Lycia', 'in the plump δημος of the Thesprotians', etc. Exactly thus he speaks of 'the plump δημος (πίονα δημον) of sheep' or of thigh-bones 'covered with plump δημος (πίονι δημῳ)'. This use of δημος will thus rest upon the same thought as the immemorial Greek cult of Earth, the Mother, and the derivative legend of Deucalion and Pyrrha, for whom rocks were 'the bones of their mother', and Homer's use of ὀφρύς, etc., of land. Instead of saying 'he came to deep-soiled (ἐριβώλακα) Phthia', etc. (*Il.* IX, 475), Homer may equally well say 'he went to Ephyra, a plump ploughland' (πίειραν ἄρουραν, *Od.* II, 328; cf. XXIII, 311, etc.) or 'he came to Achaian Argos, an udder [or "breast"] of ploughland' (οὖθαρ ἀρούρης, *Il.* IX, 141, 283; cf. Varro, *R.R.* I, 7, 10; Virgil's *uber agri* with *pinguis ager*, etc.), or 'he came to the plump δημος of Ithaca' (*Od.* XIV, 329, XIX, 399). It is striking that 'in Greece the land falls not into valleys but into plains.... If they rise at all, they rise not at the base of the mountains, but towards their own centre, like upturned saucers' (Zimmern, *The Greek Commonwealth*[2], p. 47). On each such δημος a community would develop and be referred to as a δημος just as we use 'parish', 'country', etc., for the inhabitants of the same (e.g. 'all the parish will be there', 'tell the country', etc.). The thought appears also in Hebrew: 'He shall enter peaceably even upon the fattest places of the province' (Dan. xi, 24). Cf. Gen. xxvii, 39, 28, also Is. v, 1 in note 6 on p. 239 and the use of 'ḥelebh in·Gen. xlv, 18. For the Egyptian conception of the earth as a body see Ebers, *op. cit.* p. 121. Old Norse myth conceived of earth as the flesh, mountains as the bones, and stones as the teeth and bits of bone of Ymir (see *Gylfaginning*, 8). That each fertile area should form a separate community was particularly natural in Greece, divided up, as it is, by mountain ridges. 'Greece is not fat and well-fed like England but a naked land with all her bones showing' (Zimmern, *op. cit.* p. 42). For parallel development of a word and divergence of accent cf. pp. 346, 506, 511.

[1] *Epist.* I, 17, 12. Richer food was *unctius* (*ibid.* 15, 44), *unctior cena* (Mart. v, 44, 7).

[2] Pp. 192, etc.   [3] *N.H.* XI, 37, 212, speaking of animals.

represent the 'lifetime'. This liquid (or liquefiable element) in the body appeared in fact to be the stock of life, vitality, strength. Not only did it deserve to be identified with them as expended in tears and sweat and seed,[1] but also in the normal course as it increases in amount they increase and as it diminishes they diminish. Thus in serious illness, when the patient 'is melted',[2] wasting with sweating and loss of vitality go together. 'Loss of flesh' is loss of the liquid. So we can understand many expressions in the poets, e.g., in Aeschylus, Prometheus' description how, before he came, when men were stricken with disease 'there was no defence, neither eatable nor drink nor unguent (χριστόν), but for lack of remedies they were *dried up* (κατεσκέλλοντο) '.[3] In the normal lifetime or the early Greeks as for our own ancestors[4] youth is the time of abundant marrow,[5] and with their soft and supple flesh the young were said to 'abound in liquid'[6] (πολὺ ἔχειν τὸ ὑγρόν);

---

[1] Cf. Sir T. Browne, *Vulgar Errors* III, 9, 'excess of venery which...is supposed to shorten the lives of cocks, partridges and sparrows'.

[2] See e.g. *Od.* v, 395 f., XI, 201.   [3] Aesch. *P.V.* 479 ff.

[4] See e.g. the old terms 'sappy', 'saphead', etc., for the young and foolish (but 'sapless age' *I Henry VI*, IV, 5) and the belief that the marrow was the seed of life and that with age it shrank and with death it disappeared. The early examples of it as 'the seat of animal vitality and strength' quoted by the *Oxf. English Dictionary* are: *circa* A.D. 1425, *Seven Sages* (P) 1685: 'My lordys merryghe hys welne gone' (of an old husband); A.D. 1576, Fleming, *Panopl. Epist.* 154: 'If I were in the pearl of my youth and had in my bones marrow...I wold not'; A.D. 1601, Shakespeare, *All's Well etc.*, II, 3, 298: 'Spending his manly marrow in her arms'; A.D. 1602, 2nd Part, *Return from Parnassus*, IV, 3, 1935: 'Spending the marrow of their flowering age In fruitelesse poring on some worme-eate leafe'. To these we may add Spenser (*F.Q.* I, 4, 26) on Lechery 'that rotts the marrow and consumes the braine'; *Hamlet*, III, 4, 82 f.; Tourneur, *Rev. Trag.* I, I: 'O, that marrowlesse age should stuffe the hollow bones with dambd desires' (against 'gray hayrde adultery'. Cf. *Quid tibi iucundum siccis habitare medullis*, Prop. II, 12 (III, 3),17 addressed to Amor) and Macbeth's cry to Banquo's ghost *just* after his murder: 'Let the earth hide thee! Thy bones are marrowless, thy blood is cold', comparing with this last Achilles' remark about Patroklos' νεκρός: ἐκ δ' αἰὼν πέφαται.

[5] See Aesch. *Ag.* 76 f., quoted on p. 221 below.

[6] Diog. of Ap. A 19 (45), Diels. This (but see also p. 177, n. 9) explains why the young were called ἕρσαι (*Od.* IX, 222, cf. ἐερσήεις p. 254) and δρόσοι (Aesch. *Ag.* 141, cf. Psalm cx, 3) and why 'soft', 'supple' was commonly

but with advancing years this gradually dries up and simultaneously life and strength diminish to their close. To age was to lose flesh,[1] i.e. to lose liquid, to 'dry up'. Thus, to convert Odysseus into an old man, Athene 'dried up the fair flesh (κάρψε μέν οἱ χρόα καλόν) on his pliant limbs, destroyed the yellow hair from his head, set the skin of an old man on all his limbs, and bleared his eyes that before were beautiful'.[2] 'No longer do you bloom (θάλλεις)[3] the same in your soft flesh; for it is drying up already (κάρφεται γὰρ ἤδη)' says Archilochus.[4] 'Hated old age is withering and drying me up' (μαραῖνον ταριχεύει) says Sophron,[5] and again 'shrivelled skin instead of a man'[6] (σῦφαρ ἀντ' ἀνδρός). Hippo, who identified the life-principle with the 'water' of the cerebro-spinal marrow,[7] thought that 'there is in us our own liquid (or "moisture", οἰκείαν...ὑγρότητα) according to which we are sensible and by which we live; when this liquid is in its proper condition, the living creature is healthy, but when it is dried up, the living creature lacks sense and dies; on this account indeed old men are dry (ξηροί) and lack sense because they

expressed by ὑγρός often in antithesis to σκληρός, 'hard, rigid', perhaps originally connoting 'dry' (cf. σκέλλω). Thus we find an older man σκληρὸν ἤδη ὄντα loth to wrestle with one who is νεώτερός τε καὶ ὑγρότερος, Plat. *Theaet.* 162 B; cf. *Symp.* 196 A. The idea is perhaps clearest in its application to plant life (e.g. ὑγρὸς ἄκανθος, Theoc. I, 55), where the green and sappy is soft and bends easily but the dry is hard, rigid, brittle.

[1] It is this idea that ageing means continual diminution which is carried to its logical conclusion in the story of the Sibyl of Cumae, who by divine favour was permitted to live on long after the normal span:

> de tanto me corpore parvam
> longa dies faciet, consumptaque membra senecta
> ad minimum redigentur onus.   (Ovid, *Met.* XIV, 147 ff.)

Trimalchio professed to have seen her in her later days suspended in a bottle (Petron. 48, 8). So too *longa Tithonum minuit senectus* (Hor. *Od.* II, 16, 30). Cf. *minui senio* in Pers. VI, 16.

[2] *Od.* XIII, 430 ff. Cf. ἀσκελέες in *Od.* X, 460 ff., quoted on p. 48.
[3] See p. 202.   [4] Fr. 100 (Bgk.⁴).
[5] Fr. 54 (Kaibel). For ταριχεύει see pp. 256 ff., and cf. e.g. *Anth. Pal.* XI, 392, 4.
[6] Fr. 55. Cf. much later πρόκριτός ἐστι, Φίλιννα, τεὴ ῥυτὶς ἢ ὀπὸς ἥβης, *Anth. Pal.* V, 258, 1, and Plaut. *Mil. Glor.* 639 f., quoted on p. 193. *Liquor vitalis longaevitate siccatus est* (Macrob. VII, 10, 8).
[7] See p. 118.

are without liquid (χωρὶς ὑγρότητος)'.[1] The observations which seem to have determined the traditional system reappear. For Aristotle 'the living creature is by nature moist ("liquid", ὑγρόν) and warm, and to live is to be such, but old age is cold and dry and so is what has died...it is inevitable that one who grows old should dry up (ξηραίνεσθαι)'.[2] It was thus natural to regard the liquid (αἰών) as the life, the stock of life inevitably diminishing with the passage of time, the measure of lifetime like the diminishing sand in the glass. For later Greeks with their κλεψύδρα time was water. Thus in the courts to allot different lengths of time to individuals, different amounts of water were allotted to them, and as 'his water' ran out, the allotted time of each ran out, so that we get phrases like ἐν τῷ ἐμῷ ὕδατι,[3] 'in' or rather 'during my water'.

The conception of the life as diminishing liquid inside a man will explain such language as that of Sophocles' Electra:[4] 'Dropping myself at this gate friendless I shall dry up my life (αὐανῶ βίον)', such turns of thought as that of the comic poet Antiphanes: 'The life in us (lit. "of us") approximates to wine (ἐστὶν ἡμῶν ὁ βίος οἴνῳ προσφερής); when but little remains it becomes vinegar (ὄξος)',[5] amplified by a nameless epigrammatist: 'Of sweet wine if a little be left in vessels, this that is left turns into sour (εἰς ὀξύ). So when he has drained away the whole of life (ἀπαντλήσας τὸν ὅλον βίον) and comes to old age at the bottom, the old man becomes sour-bile(d)'[6] (or

---

[1] A 11, Diels (? Hipponax).

[2] *De Long. et Brev. Vit.* 466 a, 19 ff. Cf. *De Gener. Anim.* 784 a, 34, etc. We may now guess that ὑγιής was in origin akin to and expressed something like ὑγρός. Cf. διερός on pp. 254 f. and the proverb ὑγιέστερος ὄμφακος (see pp. 216 ff.) or κολοκύντας (e.g. Epich. Fr. 154). The κολ. is notably ὑγραντική, εὔχυλος (Diph. Siph. in Athen. 59 B); *in aequario copones et cucurbitae*, Petron. 39; *veteres medici de cucurbita ita senserunt ut eam aquam dicerent coagulatam*, Garg. Mart. *med.* 6. So Diph. 98 ἢ κολοκύντην ἢ κρίνον, i.e. either living or dead; Hesych. κρί(ν)ον· τὸ ξηρόν. τάσσεται καὶ ἐπὶ πτωχοῦ (cf. pp. 222 ff.) καὶ νεκροῦ.

[3] Demosth. *de Cor.* 274, 9 and *de Falsa Leg.* 359, 6. Cf. Aesch. *in Ctes.* § 198, etc. Also Chaucer, *Cant. Tales, Reves Prol.* 3888–91.

[4] 818 f. Cf. *Philoct.* 952 ff. below (p. 222). [5] Fr. 240 a (Kock).

[6] *Anth. Pal.* IX, 127. Cf. *suam senectutem ducat usque ad senium sorbilo*, Caecil. 73 Ribb.

'quick to anger', ὀξύχολος). The beloved could be addressed thus:

ὀμφαξ οὐκ ἐπένευσας· ὅτ' ἦς σταφυλή, παρεπέμψω.
μὴ φθονέσῃς δοῦναι κἄν βραχὺ τῆς σταφίδος.[1]

Utrum est melius: virginem an viduam uxorem ducere? virginem, si musta est, says Naevius.[2] Lucilius speaks of old men as if they were raisins: *rugosi passique senes*.[3] Wine was in a peculiar degree equated to, identified with the life-fluid, and not less in Italy than in Greece. The Romans believed in a diminishing 'sap' (*sucus*) or liquid of life in the body as in a plant,[4] and Trimalchio, when century-old wine is served, says: 'Alas, alas; then wine lives longer than a man (*homuncio*, "manikin"). Wherefore let us moisten ourselves. Life is wine (*vita vinum est*)'.[5] The ancient Roman festival of the spirit of the year, Anna Perenna, on the Ides of March is now more intelligible. Its distinctive feature was that the assembled crowd drank wine 'and they pray for as many years as they take ladles full and they drink up to that number. There you will find a man who drinks up the years of Nestor, a woman who has been made a Sibyl by her cups'[6] (i.e. very long-lived). And at other times of the year to a

---

[1] *Anth. Pal.* v, 303.   [2] 53 f., Ribbeck.
[3] 557 (Marx). See also p. 264 below.
[4] See p. 192. It is the same thought when Horace refers to those who are old and past loving as *aridas frondes, Od.* I, 25, 19 f. Cf. IV, 13, 9 f.
[5] Petron. *Satir.* 34, 7. By 'let us moisten ourselves' I have given the meaning that seems to underlie the corrupt '*tangomenas faciamus*', which has been variously emended '*tengo menas*'=τέγγω μήνας Heins., τέγγω πνεύμονας Munk., τέγγε πνεύμονας οἴνῳ Chrus. Perhaps the simplest change is *tengomenous*=τεγγομένους (Reines) but not (with R.) understanding *nos*, 'Let us make ourselves wet', but just 'Let us act the drinkers (lit. "self-moisteners")'.
[6] Ovid, *Fasti*, III, 523 ff. That wine was the stuff of life and health may be seen also in the ceremony at the end of the vintage, at the first tasting of the new wine. The formula used has been preserved: 'New, old wine I drink; new, old malady I remedy' (*novum vetus vinum bibo, novo veteri morbo medeor*). This was the importance of the occasion. Thence it received its name (*Meditrinalia*). See Varro, *de Ling. Lat.* VI, 21, Festus, 110 Linds. s.v. *Med.* At Athens, the same occasion, the πιθοίγια, had similar significance. Plutarch tells us that men poured libation before drinking the new wine and prayed that 'using the remedy they might suffer no hurt but be saved' (ἀβλαβῆ καὶ σωτήριον αὐτοῖς τοῦ φαρμάκου τὴν χρῆσιν γενέσθαι, *Quaest. Conv.* III, 7, 1).

friend, as he was drinking wine, it was customary to cry 'May you live', i.e. 'Life to you'.[1] '*Vivas*', '*Bibe multis annis*', πιε, ƷΕΣΕΣ, Ƒησαις, etc. were inscribed on wine cups.[2] In this same thought doubtless lies also the origin of the ancient custom of drinking a little from a full cup of wine and then bestowing it upon one to whom one wishes well, προπίνειν, *propinare*.[3] In Greece the bride's father (or the bride) gave the cup of wine thus to the bridegroom. Thus Pindar says: 'Even as when a man gives from wealthy hand a cup bubbling within with the dew of the vine to the young man, the bridegroom, drinking therefrom first and giving it (προπίνων) from home to home, all golden, the head of his possessions, drinking with him (συμποσίου χάριν) and honouring the connection...so I am sending liquid nectar...'.[4] That this was a gift of the liquid of life is confirmed below[5] in a variation of the custom. The drinking of a little before makes of it a 'communion', a sharing of the same life. So in Homer[6] one honours another by holding out one's cup of wine for him to take and drink therefrom.

Why this treatment of wine as the liquid of life? We have seen[7] that the early Greeks recognised the kinship between men and plants. This liquid in man was correlated with, recognised as the counterpart of the liquid, the sap, of plants.[8] In man it was particularly concentrated in the head, the seed-vessel;[9] in plants also in the 'head',[10] i.e. the fruit or seed-vessel. We can now understand why in the Homeric treaty-curse wine

---

[1] E.g. Dio Cas. LXXII, 18, 2. Cf. Apul. *Met.* x, 16 ('*salus*', cf. pp. 275–7).

[2] See *Bonner Jahrb.* XIII, 107 ff., XVI, 75 f. The ancient Jews used to cry 'Wine to your life!' (L. Blau, *Altjüd. Zauberw.* p. 67). Cf. pp. 234, 287, n. 2. In Babylonia the vine was 'the tree of life' (see Dhorme in *Rev. Bibl. Intern.* 1920, p. 477).

[3] See pp. 228, 275 f.; cf. *Hoc mea manu' tuae poclum donat ut amantem amanti decet* (Plaut. *Pers.* 775); *Propino tibi salutem plenis faucibus* (*Stich.* 468).

[4] *Ol.* VII, 1 f. For other instances see Athenaeus XIII, 575 D ff.

[5] Pp. 275 ff.

[6] See e.g. *Od.* XIII, 56 ff., XVIII, 121 f. Cf. *Il.* IX, 671, XV, 86, XXIV, 101.

[7] See pp. 113 ff.   [8] P. 177, n. 9.

[9] See pp. 108 ff., 123 ff., etc.

[10] See pp. 112 ff., 125 f., 130 etc. and for the olive, an 'egg' as conceived by Empedocles, p. 112, note 2.

represented the life-fluid, the contents of the head [1] (ἐγκέφαλος) of the men concerned. Wine appeared to be the liquid of the seed of the vine and was assimilated to the seed of man.[2] The cùlt of Dionysos identified with wine was notably phallic.[3]

---

[1] See p. 108. We may compare the similar Babylonian treaty-curse with the head of an animal: 'This head is not the head of the ram. The head of Mati'-ilu (the contracting party) it is, the head of his children, etc.... If Mati'-ilu trespass against this oath, even as the head of this ram is cut off...let the head of Mati'-ilu be cut off' (see Peiser, *Mitteil. der Vorderas. Ges.* 1898, pp. 228 ff.), and indeed the Roman rite: *Si prior defexit... tu ille Diespiter populum Romanum sic ferito ut ego hunc porcum hic hodie feriam* (Livy, I, 24). The *pater patratus* then struck the victim with a stone that appears to have represented Jupiter (see p. 142). The Greeks and Trojans on this occasion cut 'hair' off the heads of two sheep and put it into the hands of the 'contracting parties' (see *Il.* III, 273 ff.; cf. pp. 107 f.) and then cut their throats and let the blood flow (cf. IV, 159); then the wine is used explicitly to represent the ἐγκέφαλος of the two parties, the life-liquid in the sense traced, and with it the curse is made. This use of wine is the origin of the lasting institution of σπονδαί, i.e. 'libations' (see *Il.* IV, 159, II, 341), the essential rite in a treaty. Cf. *spondeo*. Kircher in *Die sacrale Bedeutung des Weines im Altertum* says that for the early Greeks and Romans 'wine represents blood'. He is preoccupied with the idea of 'blood-brotherhood' and produces no early evidence for the substitution he suggests. The implication that, when digested, corn and wine were productive of blood (*Il.* V, 340 ff.) and food and wine productive of liquid and θυμός (*Od.* X, 460 ff.) could as well be quoted to show that corn or food represented blood. Homer sometimes speaks of red wine, yet we cannot assume that his other references to wine always imply such, or that wines of paler colour familiar later were then unknown. In the solemn treaty-rite the wine represented the pale fluid contents of the head. Thus considerations of function as illustrated above are more to the point. They fit other uses of wine where an equation to blood is impossible (see pp. 227 f. and 271 ff.). In the sacrificial rite there is no early evidence that the blood so readily available was offered to the gods. Wine was and there is no reason for the substitution. The head on the other hand, seat of the ψυχή, was preserved (see pp. 105 ff.) and wine may here as in the treaty libation be a substitution for its life-fluid. Cf. p. 241, n. 2.

[2] See e.g. the oracle in Plut. *Thes.* 3. Homer applies ἡβάω only to man and to the vine (*Od.* V, 69). Cf. Virgil's *pubesco* on p. 127; Cic. *Tusc.* I, 28, 69, etc. *Vitis* might seem to be the plant of *vita*. *Uva* appears to be in fact related to *uvidus*, ὑγρός, etc. That relationship would show that the ancient Latins were uniquely impressed by grapes as *liquid* (cf. αἰών).

[3] See e.g. Herodotus, II, 48 and below, p. 252, n. 11. Cf. μάχλον ἄμπελον, Aesch. Fr. 325 Nauck². The relation here (see also pp. 108 ff., 271 ff.) traced of wine to the seed, the ψυχή (so too the *genius*, see pp. 126 f., 227 f.), will explain why the Anthesteria (πιθοίγια, χόες, χύτροι) was also the festival

The Italian Liber,[1] according to St Augustine, *praeest virorum seminibus*.[2] We shall see that wine was believed to go to the brain and the *genius*.[3] It was believed to stimulate and feed sexual appetite, so that indeed the latter was said to depend upon the supply of wine.[4]

Upon its liquid depends the life of a plant. As it dries up, the plant withers and ultimately dies. The correlation with the body is exemplified by the dryads, tree-nymphs sometimes the brides of men.[5] Pindar[6] describes them 'having for their lot as limit αἰών equal to that of a tree (ἰσόδενδρον τέκμαρ αἰῶνος λαχοῖσαι)'. The Homeric Hymn to Aphrodite (264 ff.) tells how 'together with them when they were born there grew upon the earth either firs or oaks...but when the fate of death is nigh, there are dried up first of all upon the earth the beautiful trees and the bark dwindles about them and the twigs fall, and at the same time the ψυχή of the nymphs quits the light of the sun'. For the relatively scientific *Problemata*[7]

---

of ψυχαί (cf. the identification of Dionysos with Hades, p. 252, n. 11), and throw light upon the conception of the 'Αγαθὸς Δαίμων. Flowers with which the ancients connected the name 'Ανθεστήρια (see Harpocration and *Et. Magn.* s.v.) were, as we have seen, the seed-vessels, which is perhaps why Persephone was associated with them (see pp. 114 f.).

[1] See pp. 127, 264.　　　　　　　　　[2] *De Civ. Dei*, IV, 11.

[3] Pp. 226 ff. These ideas help Hor. *Epist.* I, 5, 19: *fecundi calices* (cf. *Georg.* II, 325; Ov. *Met.* IV, 698) and Prop. IV (V), 6, 76: *Bacche, soles Phoebo fertilis esse*, the generative power being there referred to the generation of ideas or poems in the mind (see pp. 35 f., 42 f., 63 ff.). Cf. ὕδωρ δὲ πίνων οὐδὲν ἂν τέκοι σοφόν, Cratin. 199, 2 (Kock), quoted by Ath. 39 c, γόνιμον ποιητήν, Aristoph. *Frogs*, 96; Socrates as 'midwife' of ideas (Plato, *Theaet.* 150 f.) and ὁ γὰρ νοῦς κύει πάντα τὰ νοήματα, ἀγαθὰ μὲν ὅταν ὑπὸ τοῦ θεοῦ τὰ σπέρματα λάβῃ, κ.τ.λ. (*Hermetica*, IX, 3, ed. W. Scott). We speak of 'creative minds'.

[4] οἴνου δὲ μηκέτ' ὄντος οὐκ ἔστιν Κύπρις, Eurip. *Bacch.* 773. Cf. *Anth. Pal.* V, 134, 3; *Problemata*, 953 b, 30 ff.; Horace, *Epist.* I, 15, 21; Ovid, *Ars Am.* I, 230 ff.; Apul. *Met.* II, 16 f., etc. Chaucer, *Cant. T.*, 6046–50, etc.

[5] See e.g. the story of Rhoikos, *Et. Magn.* s.v. ἀμαδρ. (75, 25 ff.), Schol. Theocr. III, 13, etc. Cf. Meleager and the piece of wood (p. 262), also various *metamorphoses* of human beings into plants.

[6] Fr. 165 (Schr.).

[7] 928 a, 12 ff. Not realising the fitness of ἐκφύεται to the liquid ψυχή, some read ἐκφυσᾶται. For the identification of the ψυχή with the life-fluid cf. pp. 118 ff., 247 ff. A 'nymph' appears to have been the ψυχή, the

a good deal later 'wheat has in it a certain sweet and sticky juice, which is so to speak its ψυχή (ὅς ἐστιν αὐτοῦ καθάπερ ψυχή). This is shown by the fact that when it is dried, it is quite shrivelled ("emptied", κενοῦται), but when it is moist, it is propagated (ἐκφύεται)'. Similarly in Italy *feracissima semina* were to be obtained from the *caput* of the vine. Columella[1] explains: *reliquas trunci partes humor omnis et alimentum, quod a solo ministratur, transcurrit dum ad ultimum perveniat. naturali enim spiritu omne alimentum virentis quasi quaedam anima per medullam trunci veluti per siphonem...trahitur in summum*, while Pliny[2] speaks of the budding (*gemmae*) of the vine as the bursting forth of the *medulla sive illa vitalis anima est* from the *inguen*. The vine was strikingly assimilated to a human being with *pedes, crura, lumbi, umeri*,[3] etc. Columella urges that as *semina* should be taken *ipsa membra genitalia conceptu atque foetu gravida*.[4] Cf. his *spadones*.[5] The same unity appears in the belief illuminated by Mann-hardt and Frazer, that a particular human being is the vegeta-tion spirit incarnate.[6] To it Homer most nearly approaches in his picture of the blameless king 'under whom the black earth bears wheat and barley and the trees are weighed down with fruit,[7] etc.' (compare Theoc. VIII, 41 ff. quoted below[8]). The varying legends of the Grail appear to concern such a king associated particularly with water. By the failure of the Quest he lost his virility and the land with its plants dried up and became waste, and by the achieving of the Quest he was restored to health and youth and as one version says 'the waters flowed again through their channel and all the woods were

reproductive life, in a tree, etc. In the earliest evidence, the *Iliad*, νύμφαι are clearly identified usually with water, springs, etc. Cf. pp. 34 f., 67. *Lympha* seems akin. Cf. the water-goddesses, givers of fertility among the Celts, and p. 177, n. 9. νύμφη described also a bride or marriageable girl (cf. νυμφεύω 'marry'). Such ideas may explain *rivalis*. For the Persians the tutelary spirit of the female sex was the spirit of water, Anāhita.

[1] *De Re Rustica*, III, 10, 1 f.
[2] *N.H.* XVII, 21, 152 f.
[3] See e.g. Columella, *op. cit.* III, 10, *de Arb.* III, 1.
[4] *De Re Rustica*, III, 10, 12.   [5] *Ibid.* III, 10, 15. Cf. *castrare*.
[6] Cf. pp. 113 ff., p. 157, n. 1 above.
[7] *Od.* XIX, 109 ff.   [8] P. 222, n. 11.

turned to verdure'.[1] Thus perhaps it was the distinctive power of Dionysos or the human βάκχη or βάκχος[2] to produce liquids (water, wine, milk, honey) from the stalk or branch[3] (θύρσος) directly or by striking the earth with it or by scraping the earth with the fingers.[4]

The vital sap of the human body was spoken of in terms of plant life. Homer speaks of the body of an old man whose strength is gone as καλάμη, a cornstalk that has seeded, lost the virtue that was in its head.[5] Hesiod speaks of the finger nails as dead wood on the living hand: 'At a banquet of the gods do not with bright iron cut the dry from the green (or "sappy") on the five-twigged (μηδ' ἀπὸ πεντόзοιο...αὖον ἀπὸ χλωροῦ τάμνειν)'.[6] Or we may instance from Aeschylus[7] the lament of the old men left with the youthful to guard the land when the men of military age have gone to Troy: 'The youthful marrow (νεαρὸς μυελός) shooting up within the chest is on a par with old age and Ares (i.e. warriors—the mature) is not at his post and the old man with his foliage now drying up (φυλλάδος ἤδη κατακαρφομένης) walks on three feet' (i.e. with a stick). And Aristophanes[8] refers to Cleon's 'harvest' of prisoners from Sphacteria as 'ears of corn' (στάχυς) which he is 'drying' (ἀφαύει), i.e. making lean. The equation of the vital sap of men to that of plants, the vine, corn, etc., was helped by the phenomenon of nourishment, the replenishing of the former by the latter. Thus not only animal fat but alternatively olive-oil could be infused by anointing.[9] Αἰονάω, etc., the infusion of αἰών, may also be

[1] See J. L. Weston, *From Ritual to Romance*, pp. 12 ff., also above, p. 157, n. 1 and Isaiah lvi, 3, 'Neither let the eunuch say Behold, I am a dry tree....Unto them will I give...better than sons.'
[2] See p. 456, n. 2.   [3] See *ibid*.
[4] See e.g. Eurip. *Bacchae*, 141, 704 ff. and for the fingers, p. 198, n. 1 above, also p. 226, n. 1 and pp. 494 ff.
[5] *Od.* XIV, 212. Cf. Aristotle, *Rhet.* 1410 b, 14, also pp. 113 ff. above, and for strength in the head, pp. 193 ff.   [6] *Works and Days*, 742 f.
[7] *Ag.* 76 ff. A family that has perished is a 'dried up stem' or 'stock', αὐανθεὶς πυθμήν, *Choeph.* 260; cf. 204; *Suppl.* 106.
[8] *Knights*, 392 ff.
[9] See pp. 209 ff.

exemplified by the bathing in wine of invalids at Epidaurus [1] and of babies at Sparta. [2] Similarly with what enters through the mouth. Homer equates barley-groats to marrow: 'barley-groats, the marrow of men' [3] (ἄλφιτα, μυελὸν ἀνδρῶν), or 'barley-groats and wheat-groats, the marrow of men'. [4] Circe bids Odysseus and his comrades 'eat food and drink wine till again you get θυμός in your chests such as you had when you left your fatherland of rugged Ithaca; but now you are *dried up* (ἀσκελέες) and lacking in θυμός, remembering ever your dire wandering'. [5] As we have seen, to lose flesh is to lose liquid; to become thin is to dry up. Hipponax [6] speaks of 'becoming dry with starvation' (λιμῷ γένηται ξηρός). Sophocles' Electra apparently expects to 'dry up her life', [7] lacking food; his Philoctetes, robbed of the bow with which he furnished his larder, says to his cave home: 'I shall enter thee again empty-handed, not having nutriment (τροφήν), but I shall be dried up (αὐανοῦμαι) alone in this cell'. [8] Thus also we can explain Herodas (waking a slave-girl): τὴν δὲ χοῖρον αὐόνη δρύπτει...ἐς νομὴν πέμψον. [9] The thought persists; thus Babrius [10] speaks of one 'dried up with starvation' (λιμῷ κατεσκλήκει), while for Lucian [11] 'dry' (αὗος) applied

[1] See *Inscr. Gr.* IV, 955, 13.

[2] Lycurgus, 16. Cf. Demeter and the infant Demophoon below, pp. 293 f.

[3] *Od.* II, 290. This will help us to understand ἄλφιτά τοι πρᾶτον πυρὶ τάκεται...τὰ Δέλφιδος ὀστία πάσσω (Theoc. II, 18 ff.). Cf. p. 113, n. 2 and Burns, *John Barleycorn*: 'They wasted o'er a scorching flame/The marrow of his bones.'

[4] *Od.* xx, 108.   [5] *Od.* x, 460 ff.   [6] Fr. 9 (Bgk.⁴).   [7] See p. 215.

[8] *Philoct.* 952 ff.   [9] VIII, 2 ff.   [10] 46, 8.

[11] *Tox.* 16; *Dial. Meret.* 14, 1. The externals that bring the body to its 'dry', i.e. lean, thin state (cf. Electra's ξηρὸν δέμας, Eurip. *Electra*, 239 f.) are themselves 'dry'. Thus the spendthrift at the last is 'worn by dry poverty' (καρφαλέη τειρόμενον πενίῃ, *Anth. Pal.* IX, 367, 4). For Aristophanes austere ways, diet, etc. are 'dry ways' (ξηροὶ τρόποι, *Wasps*, 1452). Realisation of this use, these associations of 'dryness', will perhaps help to a better understanding of the much disputed scene carved on the bowl in the First Idyll of Theocritus (46 ff.). A boy is sitting on a wall to guard a vineyard, but instead is busy with a locust-trap; while one fox wanders about the rows eating the grapes that are fit for the table, the other, apparently with a different taste, at greater risk has designs upon the boy's wallet, and says he will not let him go till he sets him (or 'makes him sit', καθίξῃ) to breakfast 'upon dry fare' (ἐπὶ ξηροῖσι), i.e. upon lean,

to a person means 'destitute', i.e. without livelihood, food, etc.

Thus we may explain in Latin such expressions as Aquilius' *maior pars populi ⟨iam⟩ aridi reptant fame*,[1] Petronius' description of the wealthy as *sucossi* (38) with *mulier aliquot dierum abstinentia sicca . . . avide replebat se cibo*,[2] and why for Horace the poor man is 'dry', *siccus*.[3] Romans shared the belief that there is in the

meagre or no fare. This fits the scholiast's ἄγευστον, ὁ δὲ μὴ γευόμενος καὶ ξηραίνεται and gives a clear point. Theocritus elsewhere (VIII, 41 ff.) expresses 'lean' by ξηρός. He describes herds and pastures thriving where beautiful Milon is, but if the latter departs 'then the shepherd is dry (ξηρός, i.e. "lean, withers") and the grasses too', and from a balancing scene where all things flourish in the presence of a beautiful maiden, if she departs, 'both he who herds the cows and the cows themselves are drier (αὐότεραι)'. And we should perhaps now read αὔη in his description of the Graces (poems) turned away from men's doors empty-handed: 'In anger they come home, bare-footed, often upbraiding me for a journey in vain. Shrinking (ὀκνηραί) again at the bottom of their empty coffer they stay with heads thrown upon their cold knees. There they have dry sitting (ἔνθ' αὔη σφίσιν ἕδρα) when they come home profitless' (XVI, 8 ff.), i.e. there they sit in lean conditions, in cheerless poverty; cf. 'empty' and ἐπὶ ξηροῖσι καθίξῃ above. Current texts (Ahrens, Wilamowitz-Moell., Legrand) read the easier and weaker ἔνθ' αἰεί of other MSS.: 'there always they sit'. For I, 51, the tendency of the scholium quoted has been recognised by some as a possibility but without realisation of the background of thought and without this evidence. Instead πολλάκις δέ τοι / ξηρὰ βαθεῖαν γῆν ἐνίκησε σπορά (Eurip. *Andr*. 636 f.) and τὸν βαθὺν οἶκον ἀνεξήραναν ὀδόντες (Callim. *To Dem*. 113) are quoted. Other interpretations proposed ('wreck the breakfast', 'dock the breakfast', etc.) may be seen in Cholmeley's notes. More recently, Mr A. S. F. Gow, comparing Eurip. *Bacch*. 274 ff., has suggested that 'the ξηρά... must somehow be the bread in the boy's wallet' (*Class. Rev*. XLIV, 1930, pp. 9f.) and Professor A. Y. Campbell (*Class. Quart*. XXV, 1931, pp. 93ff.), referring to καρποὶ ξηροί as opposed to καρποὶ ὑγροί, urges that we must imagine that the wallet contains grapes and the fox wants them and thus says that he will condemn the boy to cereal food left at home. The poet can, however, scarcely have made his point of this and intended us to think of the fox as desiring merely to eat grapes, which it could obviously have had, like the other, in greater abundance and with less risk from the vineyard. More recently still Mr A. D. Knox (*Class. Quart*. XXV, 1931, pp. 205 ff.) argues that the subject of καθίξῃ is the boy and ἐπὶ ξηροῖσι stands for ἐπὶ ξηροῖς (= ἀδακρύτοις) τοῖς ὀφθαλμοῖς= 'rejoicing': 'the fox will chortle'.

[1] *Boeot*. 9 (Ribbeck, *Com. Frag*. p. 38).   [2] 111 *fin*.
[3] *Epist*. I, 17, 12. How literally this was understood of absence of liquid from the body may be seen in Catullus' poem *Furei cui neque servos*, etc.

body a liquid, a 'sap' (*sucus*) on which life depends, giving the body its fullness and drying up into the leanness of old age, a liquid associated with sexual power.[1] Such a liquid would naturally be related to and be the concern of the life-soul to which sexual power belongs, the *genius*, as it was to the Greek ψυχή. This will explain many expressions from the time of Plautus, which imply that to take nourishment, i.e. *vita*,[2] was to benefit one's *genius* and to take little or none was to rob one's *genius*, expressions which do not easily fit earlier theories that the *genius* is just the procreative power in man or the luck of the family, an external guardian spirit, etc. For Plautus he who serves up food sparingly 'wages war upon' (*Truc.* 183) or 'cheats (*defrudat*)'[3] his *genius*; on the other hand a man intending to obtain a feast says: 'I shall do a lot of good to my *genius* (*genio meo multa bona faciam*)';[4] to the man who knows how to dine, one says: 'You are pretty wise as to how to treat your *genius* (*multum sapis ad genium*)'.[5] In such passages the *genius* does not, as has been suggested, represent 'the capacity for enjoyment',[6] it is not a 'hypostatisation of the warmer desires',[7] it is not a matter of a man's *genius* being 'pleased when he lives enjoyably',[8] rather when his body is well nourished. Conscious desire, whether for the pleasures of the table[9] or indeed for sexual gratification,[10] is a matter of the conscious

---

(XXIII). Horace uses *siccus* also (*Sat.* II, 2, 14) of one who has taken violent exercise, i.e. sweated. We may compare the *cum ⟨in⟩ stadio, in gymnasio, in duplici corpus siccassem pila* of Lucilius above (p. 192). Horace's use of *siccus* elsewhere (*Od.* I, 18, 3, IV, 5, 39) with special reference to wine fits the unique importance of the latter (see pp. 217 f. and 227 f.).

[1] See pp. 192, etc. Like the ψυχή (cf. p. 197), the *genius*, though associated particularly with the head (and the knees), where the life-fluid was concentrated, was concerned with it throughout the body. Like the ψυχή it was later at any rate represented by an image of a man and imagined to be, when disembodied, a 'shadow' of the whole body.

[2] *Stich.* 462, *Tri.* 477.   [3] *Aul.* 724 f. Cf. Terence, *Phorm.* 44.
[4] *Pers.* 263.   [5] *Pers.* 108.
[6] See pp. 127 f.
[7] See H. J. Rose, *Primitive Culture in Italy*, p. 149; *Class. Quart.* 1923, XVII, p. 57.
[8] See *ibid.*   [9] See e.g. Plaut. *Trin.* 334–9.
[10] See e.g. Plaut. *Amph.* 290; *Epid.* 45, 91 and p. 131, n. 4. Cf. pp. 37, 54 f.

self, the *animus*, as in Homer of the θυμός. The *genius* is a second
party distinct from and not reflecting the conscious self. It is
friendly or hostile as it is treated well or ill (cf. *curare corpus,
curare genium*) by the latter. The need and inclination of the
genius for what will replenish the life-liquid in the body is of
course known[1] to the conscious self. For Roman writers,[2] in
the man who is *satur* the sexual element is strong and active.[3]
To make concessions to that need and inclination is to 'indulge
one's *genius*'.[4] The man who does is *genialis*, while he who
does not is *aridus*, 'dry'. Both parties may be mentioned. In
Plautus the man who is thus *aridus*,[5] who has lived on niggardly
fare, confesses 'I have defrauded myself, my *animus* and my
genius';[6] while three centuries later Martial says to such a one
'You have neither heart (*cor*, seat of *animus*) nor *genius*'.[7] On
pp. 132f. we saw that the importance attached to a sneeze could
best be explained by an original belief that it was a sign from
the spirit in the head, i.e. the *genius*. We can, perhaps, now also
explain a table superstition recorded by the elder Pliny, implying that if someone sneezed when a dish was being removed
it was brought back: 'if a dish or course is recalled by a sneeze
and something is not tasted therefrom afterwards, it is counted

[1] It follows from the very concept of the *genius* and observation of
bodily thinness, weakness, and even pain, resulting from inadequacy of
nourishment. For interpretation of manifestations in the stomach as
signs from the *genius* see p. 197. The demands of the stomach could also
be referred directly to it by both Greeks and Romans (see p. 88).

[2] E.g. Catull. 21, 9; 32, 10; Pers. 6, 7; Petron. 112. Thus interpreted
Tibull. II, 1, 23, *turbaque vernarum, saturi bona signa coloni* suggests that
children were *liberi* because this meant just 'free ones' and that the name
was chosen to express social status thus and not relation to parents,
because Roman citizens commonly had other offspring by slave women,
i.e. begot slaves, *vernae* (p. 177, n. 9), in their households and so distinguished
their offspring in legal wedlock as the 'free ones'. The child of a slave
mother and a free man was a slave. See e.g. Catullus LXI, 66f.; Gaius,
I, 82.

[3] Cf. Eurip. Fr. 845 (Nauck[2]), *Trag. Gr. adesp.* 186 (N.[2]), Menand. Fr. 345
(Kock). Christians still pray for 'pride of sinful flesh subdued/Through
sparing use of daily food' (*Hymns Ancient and Modern*, 1).

[4] Pers. v, 151. For the ψυχή, cf. perhaps Simon. 85 (Bgk.); Aesch.
Pers. 841; Theocr. XVI, 24; Xen. *Cyr.* VIII, 7, 4.

[5] *Aul.* 291–7. [6] *Aul.* 724f. [7] VII, 78, 4.

among things accursed ',[1] i.e. if the *genius* indicates that another helping is wanted and the hint is ignored, it is a terrible offence. Even to speak of depriving a man of food may offend his *genius*, so that one says: 'Your *genius* will forgive me, but you would have refused to accept bread from her hand'.[2]

The life-fluid was, as we saw, concentrated particularly in the head, the seat of the *genius*. We can now understand why one who looked after his *genius*, eating a great deal, was not only termed *genialis* but in Plautus' time was nicknamed '*Capito*',[3] 'Head', as if that were all that mattered for him (cf. *gula*, *gulo*, etc.); and a curious fragment of Lucilius can thus, perhaps, be better appreciated: 'he himself destroys the head that has been nourished' (*nutricatum...caput opprimit ipse*).[4] So too the *caput...nepotis alit* of Catullus.[5] We have

---

[1] *N.H.* XXVIII, 2, 26. Reference to the *genius* may explain other superstitions there (cf. Petron. 74), why it was inauspicious, (1) if the table (with food, doubtless) was removed while one was drinking, (2) if one did not eat at all, (3) if fires were mentioned while people were eating, which omen was removed by pouring water under the table (cf. pp. 229, 254ff., 263, 274 ff.), and why (just as a sneeze, pp. 103 f.) the dropping of food and having it restored to one was a sign, apparently adverse, concerning what the conscious self was saying or thinking at the time. Reference to the *genius* will also help us to understand the belief (*ibid.* 6, 57) that sneezing could be stopped by moving the ring on to the longest finger (= *digitus impudicus*, the only finger normally kept unringed, Pliny, *N.H.* XXXIII, 1, 24) of the right hand or *palmam alterna manu scalpere* or plunging the hands into hot water (cf. pp. 177, 198, n. 1) or kissing a she-mule, cf. the ass in n. 5 below. Reference to the *genius* may also explain the custom of removing the ring from one's finger when food was brought (*N.H.* XXVIII, 2, 24) and the birthday ring (Plaut. *Curc.* 653–6, Pers. 1, 16).
[2] Petronius, 37.
[3] *Pers.* 60. Parasites appear to be 'hardy Capitones'. Ussing explained that in *Captivi* (l. 89) one may have a pot broken on his head. The fattening and the gain to the head by castration (pp. 109, n. 4, 123, 177, n. 9, 246) suggest that *capus*, *capo*, 'capon' originally referred to the head. Cf. *procapis* (p. 124) and Assyr. for 'eunuch', *ša rêši*, 'he who is head'.
[4] 1090 (Marx).
[5] LXVIII, 120 (80), followed four lines later by a reference to the *canum caput* of the grandfather as what matters in life and death. 'A free Roman citizen' (R. Ellis) will not do. There is no hint of a slave. The dining couch was *genialis* (*Aen.* VI, 603 f.). Association of the recipient of food and drink, the *genius*, with the head perhaps explains why in early days the head-rest was ornamented with a male head apparently representing the *genius* of the master (Prop. IV, 8, 68 f., Juv. VI, 21 f.) and with the head of an ass garlanded with vines (see Juv. XI, 97, Hyginus, *Fab.* 274, *Classical Review*,

seen[1] that wine was in a peculiar degree related to the life-fluid in the head. It was life-fluid itself and did not merely, like most food, contain life-fluid among other elements. Trimalchio offering his guests wine to drink says: 'Let us moisten ourselves; life is wine (*vita vinum est*)'.[2] At the ancient Roman festival of the year wine was drunk and the amount of wine was the amount of life.[3] Ovid calls it *festum geniale*.[4] This thought perhaps explains why the sacrifice to one's *genius*, one's life-spirit, consisted primarily or exclusively of wine. Horace tells of 'the *genius* appeased with wine on holidays'[5] and how 'the farmers of old...used to propitiate Earth with a pig, Silvanus with milk, and the *genius*, mindful of life's briefness, with flowers and wine'.[6] 'Pour wine for your *genius*'[7] is Persius' terse command. The traditional connection persisted. When at the close of the fourth century Theodosius I formally suppressed paganism, he forbade 'honouring the Lar with fire, the *genius* with wine, the Penates with incense' (*larem igne, mero genium, penates odore veneratus*).[8] A Roman honouring his *genius* touched his forehead: *venerantes deum tangimus frontem*.[9] The brain with its fluid was the stuff, as the *genius* was the spirit, of life, of generation.[10] Wine was apparently believed to go to the brain. One of Trimalchio's guests, who has been drinking, says: 'The wine has disappeared into my brain' (*vinus mihi in cerebrum abiit*;[11] cf. *capiti vina subisse meo*[12]). Some passages suggest that wine was applied to the

III, 322 ff.), the ass being an embodiment of the procreative principle (see s.v. *asellus* and ὄνος in the lexicons, Gruppe, *op. cit.* 797 f. and 1311 etc.). It was the animal sacred to Priapus (Ovid, *Fasti*, VI, 345 ff., etc.). The fastening of loaves about its head or neck (*ibid.*) is probably to be related to the same practice with the 'October horse' (see p. 126, also note 1 on p. 133). For the ass's head as source of fertility, see p. 127.

[1] Pp. 215 ff.   [2] See p. 215.   [3] See p. 216.
[4] *Fasti*, III, 523.   [5] *Ars Poet.* 209.
[6] *Epist.* II, 1, 144. Cf. *Odes*, III, 17, 14 ff.; IV, 5, 34 f.; Ovid, *Fasti*, V, 145 and II, 632 ff.; Tibullus, II, 2, 7 f., etc. This offering of flowers to the *genius* was appropriate since the flower was the head and contained the seed (see pp. 113 ff., 125 ff.), and it should probably be related to the use of garlands (see pp. 130, 135) and of *verbena* (pp. 141 f.).
[7] II, 3.   [8] Cod. Theod. XVI, 10, 2.   [9] See p. 129.
[10] See pp. 123 ff., 127 ff.   [11] Petr. 41.
[12] Prop. IV, 2, 30. To the belief that the life-soul was in the head, etc., perhaps goes back the custom of uncovering the head (cf. pp. 132 f.,

outside of the head perhaps as a more direct infusion. Horace tells that Teucer 'is said to have bound with a poplar wreath his temples wet with wine (*uda Lyaeo*)';[1] and Ovid says of himself waiting at the door of his mistress: 'with me are Love and a little wine around my temples (*modicum circum mea tempora vinum*) and a wreath that has fallen from my dripping hair'[2] (cf. *data sunt capiti genialia serta*,[3] etc.).

144 f., 153 f., 186) when drinking a health (see e.g. Brand's *Pop. Antiq.* rev. Ellis, publ. Bohn, ii, pp. 328 f. and 339) or eating, and of uncovering the *knees* and kneeling when drinking a health to one's mistress, etc. (see *ibid.* pp. 343, 345, 349, 353 with pp. 180 f., 185 f. above and 276 f. below).

[1] *Odes*, i, 7, 22 f. With Festus (p. 368 Lind.) *vinum in caput infun[debatur sollemni cum pre]catione* cf. *Aen.* iv, 61, vi, 244. For the victim's head cf. pp. 105 ff., 236 f. Was this 'increasing' (cf. pp. 281 f.) by wine or meal (*infra*) the original sense of *mactare*, a part of sacrifice stressed euphemistically? Cf. *immolare*. Like the anointing of the head or baptism (pp. 142, 187, 189 ff., 288, 299), this pouring of wine upon it might perhaps originally have been thought to infuse a new spirit, possibly the god himself (? thus ἱερεύειν). See pp. 60, n. 2, 236, 450 with 456, n. 2, 101, n. 8 with 105 f. At Delphi the Pythia could not prophesy unless the victim trembled all over when the wine was poured on its head (Plut. *De Defect. Oracl.* 46, 49, 51). In ordinary Greek sacrifices water was poured on its head, and unless its head shook or nodded, the victim was not sacrificed (Plut. *ibid.* 46, *Quaest. Conv.* 8, 8, 7). Not dealing with head or wine or water Frazer (*G.B., The Magic Art*, i, pp. 384 f.) compared the Yakut belief that the spirit to whom the sacrifice is being made enters the victim and manifests itself in tossing and bellowing. Similar, perhaps, to this pouring was the sprinkling of barley-groats or meal (οὐλοχύται) on the victim's head (cf. *immolare*). Barley-groats too were seed (? so Aristoph. *Peace*, 966 f.), 'marrow' (p. 222, cf. 272, 274, n. 2, 279) being identified perhaps rather with the more solid part or phase of the cerebro-spinal life-substance (cf. p. 113, n. 2) as wine or water (pp. 118, 229 ff.) with the liquid. With barley-groats the heads of the prophetesses (? Thriai) near Delphi were sprinkled (*Hymn to Herm.* 554) and the heads of the initiates at the mysteries similarly with corn, bran or flour (Demosth. *de Cor.* 259, Aristoph. *Clouds*, 260–8 with schol.). Cf. pp. 113 ff., 274, n. 2, 456, n. 2 (initiate receives divine nature. Cf. Pentheus p. 102 with n. 1). So too, apparently, the κανηφόροι (Hermippus, Fr. 26).

[2] *Am.* i, 6, 37 f. Cf. Tib. i, 2, 3; i, 7, 49 ff. and Prop. iii (iv), 17, 13 f. on p. 152. A fellow character of Trimalchio (Petron. 109, 8) wishing well to her paramour sprinkles him with wine from her cup. Cf. αἰονάω (p. 209) and the custom (pp. 217 f.) of drinking a little from a full cup of wine and then bestowing it upon one to whom one wishes well: προπίνειν, *propinare*. Another fellow character of Trimalchio (113, 8) grumbles that his beloved did not think him worthy of a *propinatio*. But *propinatio* may mean a pouring (pp. 275 f.).

[3] Ovid, *Met.* xiii, 929. Cf. p. 130 and Tib. ii, 2, 6.

CHAPTER VII

River-Worship and some Forms of the Life-substance

It is now perhaps possible to appreciate more justly Pindar's twice delivered maxim, 'water is the best thing' (ἄριστον μὲν ὕδωρ,[1] εἰ δ᾽ ἀριστεύει μὲν ὕδωρ[2]), 'best' not in comparison with wine or other liquids which in its widest sense it included [3] but best of all things. For it is the elemental liquid, the life-substance. Homer tells us that the hair which Achilles put into the hand of Patroklos was to have been offered to the river Spercheios in his fatherland.[4] It is a custom reported elsewhere [5] in early Greece that on attainment of puberty a lock at least of a youth's hair was cut off and offered to the neighbouring river.[6] We can now see why. At puberty the αἰών of the body, the liquid that is life and that issues in new life, has been brought to fullness, thanks mainly to the local god of liquid, the life-giving stream, which has in fact produced not only the water he has drunk but also in large degree that which he has absorbed in plants—'wine and barley-groats, the marrow of men', etc.—and animals nourished thereby.[7] 'The rivers are regarded as youth rearers (κουροτρόφοι) because the liquid gives growth', say the scholia [8] about Achilles and Spercheios, and go on to tell us that the ancients

---

[1] *Ol.* I, I.   [2] *Ol.* III, 42.

[3] E.g. ὕδατος εἴδη τὰ τοιάδε· οἶνος, οὖρον, ὅρρος κ.τ.λ., Aristotle, *Meteor.* 382 b, 14 f.   [4] *Il.* XXIII, 142 ff.

[5] See Aesch. *Choeph.* 5 ff.; Paus. I, 37, 3; VIII, 20, 3; 41, 3; Poll. III, 30.

[6] The offering of the hair to other gods, Apollo, Artemis, etc., does not appear to be evidenced till later (see e.g. Hesiod, *Theog.* 347 with schol.).

[7] See pp. 222 f., 285 f. (*kianag* and the grave-reliefs).

[8] *Ad loc.* Cf. *ad Il.* XIV, 246. The beliefs here traced about streams perhaps explain the legends of heads thrown into them (see above, p. 101, note 8). For the Neopythagorean reference of the Styx of Hesiod and the Orphics and the ἐκροή of Pherekydes, as also Plato's Ameles (of which ψυχαί coming to birth partake *Rep.* 621 A), to the seed, see Porphyr. =Pseudogall. *ad Gaurum*, ed. Kalbfl. (*Abh. Berl. Ak.* 1895) 34, 26 (Pherekydes, B 7, Diels), also pp. 247 ff. below.

'used to bring the bath for the bridegroom from a river as an omen of seed or procreation' (γονὴν οἰωνιζόμενοι V, cf. τέκνων τε γενέσεως καὶ παιδοτροφίας οἰωνὸν τιθέμενοι AD); while another source tells us that it was customary for the bridegroom to go to the local river to bathe and sprinkle himself with its water, 'praying by this token for the begetting of children since the water is life-begetting and generative' (περιρραίνεσθαι...συμβολικῶς παιδοποιίαν εὐχόμενοι ἐπεὶ ζῳοποιὸν τὸ ὕδωρ καὶ γόνιμον[1]), i.e. water from a river is, represents or confers seed, αἰών. Αἰονάω we saw[2] meant 'bathe, foment', as if thereby infusing αἰών. With this rite for the bridegroom we should relate that for the bride as reported from the Troad. When marrying she had to go to the local river, Scamander, and bathing herself with its water, said, as if it were something holy, 'Take, Scamander, my virginity'. The record[3] of this implies similar happening with the river Maeander in Magnesia. Spercheios and other rivers appear in the Homeric poems chiefly as fathers[4] of ordinary mortals by mortal women. Later we know it was believed, e.g. of the Charadros in Achaia, that cattle drinking thence had male offspring[5] and that 'in some places they say that the water is child-engendering (παιδογόνον) for women as also in Thespiae'[6] and by drinking the 'offspring-giving Nile' the Egyptians were enabled to produce more than three children at a birth.[7] And so the evidence might be continued.[8] It is clear that rivers were regarded as generative powers and givers of seed, as which their waters were conceived.

[1] Schol. to Eurip. Phoen. 347.   [2] See p. 209.

[3] The tenth of the letters attributed to Aeschines.

[4] Il. v, 546, xvi, 176, xxi, 141; Od. xi, 260, etc. (For evidence of the belief elsewhere that women conceive by water from springs see e.g. Hartland, Primitive Paternity, i, pp. 64 ff.) A lake, on the other hand, is a mother; thus Γυγαίη τέκε λίμνη Mesthles and Antiphos who fought at Troy (Il. ii, 864 f.).

[5] Paus. vii, 22, 11.   [6] Theophr. Hist. Plant. ix, 18, 10.

[7] See Pliny, N.H. vii, 3, 33. Cf. Aristotle, Fr. vii, 284 (Rose); Seneca, Quaest. Nat. iii, 25, 9, also Plut. De Is. et Os. xxxvi.

[8] E.g. Aeschylus characterises rivers as πολύτεκνοι (Suppl. 1028). Apart from its natural assimilation to the conception of αἰών in man, a river fertilises the land through which it flows and seems to bring vegetation

Thus also it was appropriate that offering should be made to them at puberty and appropriate that the offering should be hair[1] of the head. For Homer[2] the inmost point of a creek (λιμήν), as if it were its source, was called its κάρη. In Herodotus (translation of Darius' inscription) a river's source (πηγή) is called its κεφαλή,[3] and as we have seen[4] *caput* is the usual Latin for the same. In the human body the head was thought to be the source, the fountain-head, of the seed. 'The head seems to be the fountain-head (πηγή) of liquid, wherefore also its growth of hair on account of its abundant liquid', says the *Problemata*.[5] The victims Achilles was to have offered with the hair are explicitly and unusually specified as

to birth, e.g. *quales Eurotae progignunt flumina myrtus* (Catull. LXIV, 89); see also p. 221. The rain-water, which does likewise, was also regarded by the Greeks as seed. See e.g. Procl. *in Plat. Tim.*, vol. III, p. 176 Kr., ἐν τοῖς ᾿Ελευσινίοις εἰς μὲν τὸν οὐρανὸν ἀναβλέποντες ἐβόων 'ὗε', καταβλέψαντες δὲ εἰς τὴν γῆν 'κύε'; cf. in Plut. *Amat.* XXIV Eur. Fr. 898, 7 N., ἐρᾶν μὲν ὄμβρου γαῖαν, Aesch. Fr. 44 N., Virgil, *Georg.* II, 324 ff. and Lucr. I, 250 ff., II, 991 ff., for whom plants, animals, and men were begotten by rain in Earth's womb. If the body of a child was its mother's contribution and the ψυχή or soul was its father's seed (pp. 109, n. 3, 111, n. 6), the belief that the soul returns to Heaven or αἰθήρ (cf. p. 165) is explained: Γαῖα μεγίστη καὶ Διὸς Αἰθήρ,/ὃ μὲν ἀνθρώπων καὶ θεῶν γενέτωρ,/ἣ δ' ὑγροβόλους σταγόνας νοτίας/παραδεξαμένη τίκτει θνητούς.../τὰ μὲν ἐκ γαίας φύντ' εἰς γαῖαν,/τὰ δ' ἀπ' αἰθερίου βλαστόντα γονῆς εἰς οὐράνιον πάλιν ἦλθε πόλον (Eur. Fr. 839 Nauck²). The Orphic soul said Γῆς παῖς εἰμι καὶ Οὐρανοῦ ἀστερόεντος,/αὐτὰρ ἐμοὶ γένος οὐράνιον (Fr. 32 a Kern). Cf. the Slav belief in n. 3, p. 161.
[1] The foliage produced by the sap of plants was from Homer onwards equated with and termed hair (κόμη). See e.g. *Od.* XXIII, 195. The hair that Achilles offered ποταμῷ τρέφε τηλεθόωσαν, which epithet Homer uses almost exclusively of plants. He describes Euphorbos with his hair as 'like a blooming (ἐριθηλές) olive sapling which a man reareth in a clear spot where water springeth in plenty, a sapling fair and blooming (τηλεθάον)' (*Il.* XVII, 51 ff.). To the water a sapling owes its foliage, a man his hair. In the Grail legend (see pp. 157, n. 1, 221) one of the accompaniments of the drought was human baldness and of the 'freeing of the waters' the recovery of hair (see the *Perceval le Gallois* version, translated by Sebastian Evans, *The High History of the Holy Grail*, II, 1 and XXXV, 20). As Ben Jonson ('It is not growing like a tree...') observed, the oak 'must fall a log at last, dry, bald and sere'.
[2] See *Od.* IX, 140, XIII, 102, 346.
[3] IV, 91. See also p. 232.   [4] P. 125.
[5] See 867 a, 23 ff.–b. Cf. *cincinnos...usque ex cerebro evellam*, Plaut. *Truc.* 288; *comae quoque alimenta ex cerebro*, Tert. *Anim.* 51; cf. pp. 234f. below.

ἔνορχα[1] and the place as the river's fountain-head (πηγαί) 'because', says Eustathius,[2] 'it is that which generates (γονίμους εἶναι) the whole river'. These thoughts perhaps also explain the custom of setting up a bearded head at the source of a stream.[3] Growth of hair was, as we learn later, popularly associated with sexual vigour. 'Hairy' men were believed to have the strongest sexual bent[4]—and loss of hair, baldness, was believed to be dependent upon loss of seed.[5] This belief would naturally arise in the converse. At puberty, when hair of the head is thus sacrificed, the hair of the beard and the hair of the pubes begin to grow. Both could scarcely fail to be associated with the coming of generative power and to help the association of the head with the latter. Alcmaeon remarks[6] that the hair comes with the seed 'just as plants when about to bear seed first blossom (ἀνθεῖν)', with which we may compare the name of the chin, ἀνθερεών, the ἥβης ἄνθος of Homer,[7] Hesiod,[8] etc., and Pindar's descriptions of a young man σὸν δ' ἄνθος ἥβας ἄρτι κυμαίνει[9] and of a boy 'not yet showing on his jaws the fruit-season, tender mother of the vine bud' (οὔπω γένυσι φαίνων τέρειναν μάτερ' οἰνάνθας ὀπώραν).[10] Those who

---

[1] 'Entire' and, as Eustathius explains, γόνιμα.   [2] Ad loc.

[3] See Wieseler, Abh. der königl. Gesell. der Wissensch. zu Göttingen, xx, 1875, pp. 6 ff. with fig. at end, also Preller's Theogonie u. Götter, rev. Robert, p. 549.

[4] See e.g. Aristotle, Fr. vii, 285, 8 and Probl. 880 a, 35 ff. Cf. Pliny, N.H. xi, 39, 229 ff. and pp. 130f. above. To Roman beliefs that procreation was the concern of the head (see pp. 123 ff., 198f.) should probably be related the combing of the bride's hair with the hasta caelibaris (see p. 472, n. 1 and Ov. Fa. ii, 560; Fest. 55, 2 ff. Lind.; Plut. Qu. Rom. 87. Cf. the Vedic rite of parting a woman's hair in the middle of pregnancy to secure an easy birth, Sīmantonnayana), the flammeum (see pp. 153 f.), the garland (cf. genialia serta, p. 130) of the bride (Fest. 56, 1 f.; Catull. LXI, 6), the vitta and the crines of the married woman (Plaut. Most. 226; Mil. Glor. 791 f., etc.). See pp. 133, n. 1; 144 f.; 153 with nn. 1, 2.

[5] See Problemata, 878 b, 21 ff., 897 b, 23 ff.; Pliny, N.H. xi, 37, 131. The sexual appetite of a mare might be extinguished by cutting off her mane (ibid. viii, 42, 164; Aristotle, Hist. Anim. vi, 572 b, 9). See also pp. 129 f.; cf. p. 126, n. 3.

[6] See Aristotle, Hist. Anim. 581 a, 12 f.=Alcmaeon, A 15 (Diels).

[7] Il. xiii, 484.   [8] Theog. 988.

[9] Pyth. iv, 158. Cf. Fr. 123 (88), 3; Pyth. ix, 109 f.; Aesch. Suppl. 1001, etc.   [10] Nem. v, 6.

cannot procreate are beardless. How close was the natural association of thought may be seen in such statements as Aristotle's that 'boys maimed in their sexual organs are sterile (ἄγονοι) so that they do not get a beard (γενειᾶν) but continue as eunuchs'.[1] This evidence suggests what does not appear to be recognised, that the jaw like the knee was associated with generation and that the other names of the chin or jaw, γένυς and γένειον (cf. γενειάς, 'beard', Latin gena,[2] German Kinn, Danish kind, etc.), were related to γένος, γενεά, genus, Kind, 'kin', etc., expressive of generation. This would also explain why in one version[3] Athene was born from the chin, 'from the beard', of Zeus and with it why the chin, as if holy in the same way as the knee (γόνυ, genu, etc.), was clasped by the Greek suppliant.[4]

The legends that men were born of snake's teeth—the so-called 'dragon's teeth'—in the ground can thus be understood. They imply the equation of the teeth to seed[5] and the importance of the jaw which produces them (e.g. Menoikeus, ὅς δράκοντος γένυος ἐκπέφυκε παῖς, Eurip. Phoen. 941). The ψυχή after burial assumed the form of a snake (pp. 206 f.). These thoughts may also explain why such snakes were

---

[1] De Gener. Anim. 746 b, 21 ff.
[2] Cf. genuini = of the back teeth, with pp. 175f.
[3] See Myth. Vat. I, 176, II, 37 and pp. 111, 178 f. above.
[4] See pp. 97, 133, 174 ff., 235 and such passages as Iphigeneia's

> οἴμοι· κακῶν γὰρ τῶν τότ' οὐκ ἀμνημονῶ
> ὅσας γενείου χεῖρας ἐξηκόντισα
> γονάτων τε τοῦ τεκόντος ἐξαρτωμένη
> λέγουσα τοιάδ'· ὦ πάτερ,... (Eurip. Iph. Taur. 361 ff.)

[5] Cf. genuini (n. 2) and ? φράτερες (Frogs, 422). For the belief that loss of teeth was dependent upon loss of seed (prevented by castration) and that when the teeth have been lost fertility has been lost see Pliny, N.H. XI, 37, 168 f. Unmistakable similar interpretations of saliva (see e.g. Hartland, Primitive Paternity, I, pp. 12, 68, 73 f., Aristot. de Gener. Anim. 747 a, 9 ff., Fragm. 285, 3 ed. Rose) should perhaps be related to this view of the jaw. To restore sexual power or avert the evil eye (from one's life-soul) it was applied to the brow (p. 129) with the digitus infamis (see Persius, II, 32 f., Petronius, 131 and p. 198, note 1). The thought traced (cf. pp. 108 ff.) may have encouraged e.g. Anaxagoras to his belief that the procreative intercourse of crows and ibises was by their mouths and that weasels gave birth by the mouth (A. 114).

represented with beards,[1] though no snake in nature is so equipped. Such a snake was, we saw,[2] popularly supposed to be a form of the cerebro-spinal fluid or marrow with which the seed and ψυχή were identified. One modern Greek name for the 'returning dead' is ἀνάρραχο, used in Cythera,[3] perhaps connected with ῥάχις, 'spine'. Another more generally used is βρυκόλακας, and there is a proverb ὁ βρυκό-λακας ἀρχίζει ἀπὸ τὰ γένειά του, 'The *vrykolakas* begins with his beard', which is popularly understood as a 'half jocose, half euphemistic' equivalent for 'begins with (i.e. attacks first) his family'.[4] The sanctity of a man's beard among the Jews and the Turks and in mediaeval Europe (e.g. in Spain, where the Cid, going to face his enemies in the Cortes, bound his beard with a cord[5]) perhaps goes back to this circle of ideas. In the Jewish Kabbalah, where, as we shall see,[6] the liquid in the divine head is the vehicle of life, 'each hair is said to be the breaking of the hidden fountains issuing from the concealed brain'.[7] The Nazirite's offering of his hair to Yahweh[8] may perhaps be explained as an offering of the life-substance from within the head[9] and his abstention from the

---

[1] See Harrison, *Prolegomena to the Study of Greek Religion*, pp. 326–9. A 'dropped jaw', which Miss Harrison suggested, was clearly not intended by the artists and could scarcely have been thus misinterpreted; and to say that it was added as a human characteristic does not explain why a human characteristic should be added or the beard selected. It fits our explanation that Zeus Meilichios, a fertility spirit with chthonic cult like that of the dead and their deities, was also represented as a bearded snake (see *ibid.* pp. 15–21, esp. 17 ff.). For the association of the snake and the dead with fertility, see e.g. Nilsson, *The Minoan-Mycenaean Religion*, pp. 278 f., 503 ff.   [2] Pp. 206 f.   [3] Lawson, *op. cit.* p. 381.

[4] *Ibid.* p. 389.   [5] See Southey, *op. cit.* IX, 6, 9, 12, 18.

[6] P. 287. If for the Jews originally, as for the Greeks, Romans, etc., the head contained not only the life-soul (p. 103) but also the life-fluid, the seed, and was the source (cf. pp. 188, n. 2, 239, n. 6), we can understand their use of the term for 'head' *rosh* for the 'source' of a river (cf. pp. 125, 231; so too Bab. *rêš nâre*) and for 'beginning' (cf. pp. 111, 124 f.). For them too (Jer. iii, 3) the forehead was the seat of shame (cf. pp. 146 f.).

[7] *Ha Idra Rabba Qadisha*, VII, § 74; cf. § 70.   [8] Numb. vi, 2–21.

[9] See pp. 99, 106 f., 129 f., 163 ff. For the Arabs the *ginn* (= 'souls', p. 103) were hairy (Wellhausen, *op. cit.* p. 51). If a woman uncovered, loosed her hair, it was as if she uncovered herself naked (*ibid.* p. 199). Cf. p. 153, nn. 1, 2, and Isaiah xlvii, 2.

grape-vine by a belief, like that traced above,[1] of its relation to the life-liquid in the head. Of the 'ninth conformation of the beard' of the deity, the Vast Countenance,[2] it is said 'These are the hairs which are mingled with those which hang down and they are called "the deep places of the sea" because they depart from above in the fluid places of the brain'.[3] 'No beard is found which doth not arise from the brain of the head.'[4] 'The beard is the praise and perfection and dignity of the whole countenance.'[5] 'Worlds of desires and great pleasures ...are all concealed in the commencement of the beard, which representeth strength.'[6] Strength was in the Kabbalah associated with the seed thought to come from the brain.[7] In the legend of Samson the Nazirite it is said to be in the man's hair.[8] 'Whosoever seeth (in sleep) that his beard existeth in proper form, in him is found courage and strength.'[9] 'Whosoever seeth in his sleep that he toucheth the beard or moustache of the supernal man with his hand or extendeth his hand unto it, let him know that he is at peace with the supernals and that those who afflict him are about to be subjected unto him',[10] with which we should perhaps compare II Samuel xx, 9 and the act of the Greek suppliant. Such thoughts as we have traced may explain the legend of the might of the jawbone used by Samson and the issuing of water from it when he had

---

[1] Pp. 215 ff., esp. 217, n. 2, 227 f.

[2] See p. 144.

[3] *Ha Idra Rabba Qādisha*, xx, § 439.

[4] *Id.* xii, § 287. The conception of hair as concrete stuff of ψυχή or *genius* explains the ritual uses not only of wool but also of animal skins with their hair, e.g. the putting on of a fox-skin so that the worshipper, 'possessed', became a fox (βασσάρα, βασσαρίς), the striking with goat-skin (*verbera...saetosa*, Prop. iv (v), 1, 25) by the *Luperci* to give fertility, the Δῖον κῴδιον, etc. The hair on an animal's body might, like sweat, seem to be an outcrop from the layer of fat under the skin; for which see pp. 211 f. and Democ. on p. 237. Cf. p. 155, n. 1; p. 280, n. 2. The expression *spolia opima* was perhaps transferred as a whole from skins stripped from animals, prime ones, the original sense of *spolia*. Cf. Hor. *Od.* iii, 16, 35 f.; *Epod.* x, 21; Val. Fl. iii, 143. 'Fatness' was an attribute important in offerings (see pp. 279 ff., Sen. *de Benef.* i, 6, 3, etc.), which the *spolia* became.

[5] *Id.* xxxiv, § 756.   [6] *Id.* xii, §§ 297 f.   [7] See p. 188.   [8] Judg. xvi, 17 ff.
[9] *Ha I.R. Qad.* 34, § 776.   [10] *Id.* § 817.

cast it down,[1] the custom of cutting one's beard and hair for the dead (Is. xv, 2; Jer. xvi, 6, etc.; cf. pp. 99, 278 with n. 1, 287 f.) and why among the Baganda it is to the lower jawbone that the ghost of a person attaches itself. The lower jawbone of the dead king is cut out with the words 'Show me your grand-child' and preserved with great ceremony in a new house or shrine, and the lower jawbone and genital organ of the war-god are preserved together.[2]

The classical Greek practice of preserving and fastening up at the shrine the head of the ox sacrificed was explained above[3] by the belief that it contained the ψυχή, the life-power and the life-substance. This practice dated from Minoan times. The importance attached to the horns can now be explained. In Homer's time they were peculiarly honoured, being coated with gold[4] before the animal was slain.[5] In Minoan-Mycenaean times they had special sanctity, whence they have been called 'horns of consecration', actual horns or conventional representations of them.[6] Their usual position is upon an altar or a shrine. They are 'the place of consecration'.[7] The victim may in the sacrifice have been identified with the deity[8] as in the ὠμοφαγία and in Babylonia. The horns of the altar had special sanctity[9] amongst the Jews and have been recognised as

---

[1] Judg. xv, 15–19. Cf. Hippocrene on p. 246.

[2] See Roscoe, *The Baganda*, pp. 7, 109, 282; also Budge, *Osiris and the Egyptian Resurrection*, II, pp. 91 ff., 96 ff., 102, illustrating the preservation of the jawbone by the Egyptians. In such thoughts as have been traced above lies, perhaps, the explanation why in tumuli in Ireland the lower jawbone is often missing from the skull (see W. G. Wood Martin, *Elder Faiths of Ireland*, p. 337). Cf. p. 106, note 12 above. For the ancient Irish attitude to and treatment of the head and brain see pp. 100 f. and 156 f. above.   [3] Pp. 105 ff. See also pp. 143 f.

[4] For the significance of gold see pp. 106 f., note 2 on p. 156, pp. 165 ff., p. 183, n. 1, with 147 ff.

[5] See *Od.* III, 437 f., 384 and *Il.* x, 294.

[6] See Evans, *Journ. of Hell. Stud.* XXI, pp. 107, 135 ff.; Nilsson, *The Minoan-Mycenaean Religion*, p. 154.   [7] Nilsson, *op. cit.* p. 152.

[8] See pp. 60, n. 2, 102, 105 f., 228, n. 1. Those who eat, partake of him. Cf. 'the Lamb of God' and 'communion', John, vi, 51 ff., etc.

[9] E.g. he who sought sanctuary clasped them (I Kings i, 50, ii, 28 ff.). See also p. 239, n. 6. Satan dances between the horns of the ox returning from pasture (Blau, *Altjüd. Zauberw.* p. 79).

originating, like the Minoan 'horns of consecration', in actual horns. With the Minoan we may reasonably relate not only the Homeric practice (see pp. 105 ff.) but also the survival at Delos of an altar consisting of horns.[1] That cows, etc., on occasion use horns as weapons[2] (as other animals use teeth and claws or hoofs) will not explain these facts. Why were the horns thus holy as if in them were concentrated the divine potency? Because, it can now be seen, they were a permanent concentration, an outcrop, of the life-substance in the head, of the seed that was also the strength, of the ἐγκέφαλος in which was the ψυχή. What grows out of the head is almost inevitably believed to be an issuing of what is within the head. Thus, according to Aelian,[3] Democritus[4] explained the growth of the horns of deer: 'The bone enclosing the brain is very thin and membrane-like and porous, and thick ducts rise from it to the top of the head. The nourishment, and indeed the most generative part of it (ταύτης γε τὸ γονιμώτατον), is most speedily sent up and the fat is spread around the animals outside while the strength of the nourishment (ἡ δὲ ἰσχὺς τῆς τροφῆς) leaps up into the head through the ducts. From it therefore the horns grow forth, watered by the abundant moisture. The moisture, being continuous and flowing in, thrusts out the parts in front of it and the emerging liquid outside the body becomes hard, the air congealing it and turning it to horn'. The soft moisture below thrusts this forward and itself becomes hard and thus the growth proceeds.[5] So too Plutarch tells the story that 'from his estate there was brought to Pericles the head of a ram with one horn, and Lampon the soothsayer, seeing that the horn had grown firm and strong out of the middle of the

---

[1] See Aristotle, Fr. 489 (Rose); Callimachus, Hymn (to Apollo), 60 ff.; Plut. de Sollert. An. xxxv, 9 (983 e), etc.; and compare Oinomaos' shrine of skulls (p. 101 above).

[2] This is the usual explanation. See e.g. MacCulloch (s.v. Horn in Hastings' Encycl. of Rel. and Ethics), who adds the further suggestion that it resulted from the use of reindeer's horn and stag's horn for tools and weapons.

[3] De Nat. Anim. xii, 18–21.   [4] A 153 f. (Diels).

[5] Suggested perhaps by the solidification of sap exuding (pp. 278, 282 ff.).

forehead, declared that there being two powers in the city, that of Thucydides and that of Pericles, the might would pass into the one man with whom the portent was found. Anaxagoras however dissected the skull and showed that the brain (ἐγκέφαλος) had not filled its base but tapering like an egg had gathered out of the whole cavity to that spot whence the root of the horn had its beginning. And Anaxagoras was admired then by those who were present' (*Vit. Per.* VI). He and they evidently thought it obvious that the horn was the result of the concentration of brain in that direction.

If horns were thus believed to be outcrops of the brain, the procreative element, we can understand why the name for horn and for brain should be akin. It has long been recognised [1] that *cornu*, κέρας, *cerebrum*, κάρα, horn, *Hirn* ('brain'), etc., are related, but they have been explained as having in common the notion 'top of'. This is only [2] a guess from the fact that head and horns are usually at the top, but they are not strikingly and distinctively so in the case of the usual horned, i.e. four-footed, creatures—cows, sheep, etc. Still less would 'top' be a naturally distinctive definition of what is *inside* the head, the brain. We have seen that the distinctive importance of the head for the earliest Greeks, Romans, etc., was that it contained the stuff of life, the seed, and in it the procreative life-soul, and that *cerebrum* is related to *cereo*, *cerus*, etc., and expressive of procreation, fertility. That we may now see to be the root meaning of κέρας, *cornu*, horn, *Hirn*, etc. There was also a further reason why horns should be connected with procreation. Not only does castration produce marked change in the

[1] See e.g. Boisacq, s.v. κέρας; Ernout and Meillet, s.v. *cerebrum*; Falk and Torp, s.vv. *Hjerne, Horn*. That the head contains the seed appears to have been implied in another substance, *spermaceti*, i.e. 'seed of a whale', wax found mostly in the head of what therefore is called a 'sperm whale'. Norsemen called amber (or ambergris) *hvals auki* 'whale's seed'. *Auki*, akin to *augeo*, meant 'increase' or 'seed'; 'wax'=grow, 'wax forth'=be born, created, are akin. This surely is the origin of (bees') 'wax'. Cf. *cera* (p. 282, n. 9).

[2] The occasional use of κάρηνα, etc., with reference to mountains, etc., is most naturally explained as a transferred use. Cf. *Aeneid*, IV, 246 ff., etc.

growth of horn[1] but also, just as hair was believed to be an outcrop of the procreative power since it grows upon the face and *pubes* at puberty, so it was observed that horns tend to develop fully at a similar stage.

With this background of ideas we can better understand why Horace thus refers to the forehead and horns of a kid:

> *haedo,*
> *cui frons turgida cornibus*
> *primis et venerem et proelia destinat.*[2]

Not only are horns thus an outcrop of the procreative power but their use is largely sexual. Quoting many examples Darwin declared that 'tusks and horns appear in all cases to have been primarily developed as sexual weapons',[3] i.e. for use by the male to defeat rivals in approaching the female.

We may confirm our explanation of the horns in Cretan cult and at the same time explain what also has not hitherto been satisfactorily explained, virtually the only horn or horns separated from the head in Greek myth, the 'horn of plenty'. It was Cretan, the horn of Amaltheia, foster-mother of Zeus. Why[4] was a horn believed to be the source of new-born creatures, fruits,[5] etc.—*fertile cornu?*[6] Because it was itself an

---

[1] See e.g. Democritus, A 154 (Diels) = Aelian, *de Nat. Anim.* XII, 19, and Darwin, *The Descent of Man*, Part II, Chap. XVII, pp. 772 f. (1901 ed.).

[2] *Odes*, III, 13, 3 ff. So perhaps *proterva fronte*, II, 5, 15 f.

[3] *Op. cit.* p. 775.

[4] For the problem in the past see e.g. MacCulloch (*loc. cit.*): 'Probably a horn became a symbol of fruitfulness because it belonged to an animal associated with fertility, bull or goat [But why the horn? R. B. O.] and perhaps also because it was a drinking vessel not only among primitive but also among civilised peoples'. But that in turn does not indicate any connection with fruitfulness, and the 'horn of plenty' is *not* a drinking-vessel. For a horn and liquid see pp. 241 f.   [5] Cf. Priapus' burden of fruit.

[6] Ovid, *Fasti*, V, 127. We might expect the horns of the Jewish altar to have had the same significance (see p. 236) as those upon Minoan-Mycenaean altars. This is confirmed by 'a horn, the son of oil' (Isaiah V, 1), which implies that a horn is an outcrop of 'oil', the procreative element. It is used to signify very fruitful land. 'A very fruitful hill' is the English version. We saw (pp. 188 ff.) reason to believe that the oil with which kings were anointed was thought of as seed; and may now suspect that the use of a horn to contain it (I Sam. xvi, 1, I Kings i, 39) was not

embodiment of the seed, the procreative power.[1] The 'horn of plenty' was a symbol of the *genius* (cf. p. 136, n. 6) and sometimes represented containing *phalli*. Thus we can also explain the alternative legend that it was the horn[2] of the prime river-god (cf. pp. 247 f.) Acheloos.[3] A river was, as we saw,[4] itself the fertilising liquid of life with which the head and its other outcrop, hair, were particularly associated. The horn of Amaltheia was believed[5] to be the source of the fertilising liquid above, rain.[6] The ancient Germanic peoples here in the North had names[7] for brain and horn cognate to the Greek and Roman names and themselves mutually related,[8] and we have seen[9] reason to believe that for them also the head con-

accidental (cf. p. 241) and that the frequent use of 'horn' expressive of strength derives not merely from the observed uses of horns by animals but is related to the thought traced and to what we have seen (pp. 234 f.) of the Jewish belief that that other outcrop of the head, hair, was the strength or life-substance. Honour was a matter of the head (cf. pp. 97 f., 145 f., etc.). In honour the head is exalted (Job x, 15 f.; Gen. xl, 13, 20; Ps. iii, 3, xxvii, 6, etc.). It is affected by reproach (Neh. iv, 4). Dust is put upon it (II Sam. i, 2, cf. pp. 184 f., etc.). The sprouting of a horn (Ps. cxxxii, 17; Ezek. xxix, 21) or exalting of a horn (Ps. xcii, 10, etc.) or defiling of it with dust (Job xvi, 15) can thus be understood as a sprouting, exalting, or defiling of the strength or life-substance. The story of Pericles and Lampon above (pp. 237 f.) and of Cipus in Ovid, *Met.* xv, 565 ff., Val. Max. v, 6, 3, probably rest upon the same ideas. Unusual growth of life-substance thus meant unusual greatness (see pp. 95, n. 4, 162 ff.).

[1] The use of horns as amulets in Crete and elsewhere (and the making of horns with the fingers, the *mano cornuto*, as a sign with protective power) should probably be related to this and to the 'horns of consecration'. Cf. the use of *phalli*. [2] River-gods' horns can now be better appreciated.

[3] It was also associated with Hercules, apparently as a fertility-power.

[4] See pp. 229 ff.

[5] See Ov. *Met.* iii, 594; Stat. *Theb.* vi, 423.   [6] See p. 230, n. 8.

[7] See p. 238 f. The thought here traced may explain the emphasis upon horns in other cults, e.g. in the case of the Celtic horned god whose name Cernunnos appears to be related to κέρας, *cornu, cereo, cerebrum* and who was represented as the source of wealth. For the Celtic view of the head and brain see pp. 100 f., 157 f. The horned fertility god ('Auld Hornie', etc.) worshipped by the witches had a fire on his head (see M. A. Murray, *The God of the Witches*, p. 126), perhaps to be related to the thought on pp. 146 ff. above. At the so-called Mass bread was attached to his horns (Murray, p. 128). Cf. pp. 126 f., 226, n. 5. From some such roots perhaps grew the saying 'Luck had horns' (see Dekker, *The Shoemaker's Holiday*, ii, 5).

[8] See Falk and Torp, *loc. cit.*   [9] Pp. 154 ff.

tained the procreative element. For them too horns were the source of fertilising liquid. In *Grimnismal* the poet describes Valhalla, and 'Eikthyrnir is the name of the stag before the Hostfather's hall which feeds on the leaves of Lærath. From its horns fall drops to Hvergelmir; therefrom derive all rivers, Sith and With, etc.'[1] Thus too one can understand the association of the horn with liquid that meant fertility in Saxo Grammaticus. He tells us that at Rügen there was a horn in the hand of the god Svantovit and the priest each year filled it with wine 'to foresee from the liquid itself the abundance of the following year (*ex ipso liquoris statu sequentis anni copias prospecturus*). On the following day, while the people kept watch before the doors, he took the vessel from the image and examined it carefully. If there was any diminution from the measure of the liquid put in, he thought it was related to dearth in the year to come. If he saw that there was no diminution from the level of usual fertility, he announced that times of fertility in the land were coming (*si nihil ex consuetae fecunditatis habitu deminutum vidisset, ventura agrorum ubertatis tempora praedicabat*)'.[2]

The conception of horns as embodiments of the generative and executive, fulfilling element and the making of altars with horns thus (see p. 237 and e.g. Callim. *Hymn to Apollo*, 61 ff. δεί-

---

[1] Verses 26 f. Cf. *Gylfaginning*, 39. In ancient Iranian belief *Gaokerena*, i.e. 'ox-horn', was the 'tree of life', *haoma* (see p. 299), at the source (*Bundah.* XXVII, 4) of the water of Ardvi Sura (=fertility in plants, animals and men), from which all the rivers of the world flow.

[2] XIV, 564 ff. This suggests that the use of horns as vessels for drinking rested not merely upon their convenience but also upon the thought that a horn naturally would contain life-substance. Pagan belief in the potency of a horn must lie behind the Church's order forbidding converts to drink from a horn. Only if no other vessel were available might it be used and then only after the sign of the cross had been made over it (see Widlak, *Synode v. Liftinae*, 30). In N.E. Scotland it was believed that 'medicine or healing water was efficacious only when drunk out of a horn, especially one taken from a living animal' (see MacCulloch, *loc. cit.*). The use of skulls for drinking vessels and for pouring libation (cf. pp. 216 ff., 272 ff.), e.g. among the Celts (see Livy, XXIII, 24, etc.) who believed that the skull contained the life-soul (see pp. 100 f. and 156 f.), probably rested upon a similar thought, which may also explain the Minoan-Mycenaean use of rhytons in the shape of heads (cf. pp. 101 f., 105 f., 144, 217 f., 272 ff.) or complete animals to contain liquid to pour in libation. Cf. the offering of the life-substance of actual animals (pp. 279 ff.).

ματο μὲν κεράεσσιν...) may help us to a fuller understanding of what lies behind the Homeric myth[1] according to which dreams that are fulfilled (ἔτυμα κραίνουσι) issue διὰ ξεστῶν κεράων, through gates made of horns (κεράεσσι τετεύχαται). Recognition that horn had a procreative significance may also help the understanding of Diomedes' taunt to Paris: τοξότα, λωβητήρ, κέρᾳ [v.l. κέρα] ἀγλαέ, παρθενοπῖπα,[2] 'Bowman, reviler, glorious in horn (i.e. sexual power), ogler of girls'. Most commentators from the scholiast onwards have explained κέρᾳ (or κέρα) ἀγλαέ as a second reference to his bow, but this would be feeble and there is no particular reproach in the horn part of the bow and the transition to παρθενοπῖπα is thus more difficult. Others have suggested that Paris wore his hair in a peculiar fashion to look like horns, but for this we have' no evidence. If it were an idiosyncrasy of Paris, the poet would have explained, and if it were a common practice, reference to it elsewhere in Homer might be expected; and it would be a feeble taunt. On the other hand the reference to sex fits not only παρθενοπῖπα but also Hector's taunt to Paris: γυναιμανές, ἠπεροπευτά[3] and his actual behaviour.[4] In some counties[5] 'to

[1] *Od.* xix, 562–7. Thus apparently Homer related κέρας with κραίνω, which seems in fact to be related to κράς, κάρα, etc. (see p. 194, n. 5), κέρας (see p. 238). How far this relation contributed to the myth in origin and whether ἐλέφας and ἐλεφαίρομαι were original elements or neatly added to balance it is impossible to say. Here too Homer is perhaps near the truth. ἐλεφαίρομαι has not been explained. All other Greek words beginning ἐλεφ- appear to be related to ἐλέφας, 'tusk, ivory'. For the formation cf. γέρας, γεραίρω, etc. The current assumption that the verb meant 'deceive' may well be wrong. 'To tusk, strike from the side, obliquely (e.g. of a wild boar, Homer, *Il.* xii, 148, *Od.* xix, 450 f., Horace, *Odes*, iii, 22, 7, Ovid, *Met.* viii, 343, etc.), rend, make havoc' will better fit the extant examples: dream-phantoms inflicting injury by false messages (*loc. cit.*), Apollo striking the μάστιξ from Diomedes' hand in the race (*Il.* xxiii, 388), and the Nemean lion making havoc of men (Hesiod, *Theog.* 330). Homer's term elsewhere for a misleading dream is 'destructive', οὖλος ὄνειρος (*Il.* ii, 6, 8). Cf. *ferio*, 'strike'='cheat'. [2] *Il.* xi, 385.

[3] *Il.* iii, 39, xiii, 769. Such interpretation of horns might be helped by the thought that stags go from one female to another (Aristot. *Hist. An.* 578 b, 11 f., Pliny, *N.H.* x, 63, 174); 'the almost unparalleled excess of venery which every September may be observed' (Sir T. Browne, *Vulgar Errors*, iii, 9).

[4] Exemplified *Il.* iii, 427 ff.   [5] See Wright's *Dialect Dict.* s.vv.

have got the horn' = 'to lust, be lustful' and the epithet 'horny' meant 'amorous'. There is clear evidence that early Greeks, e.g. Archilochus,[1] referred to the male organ itself as 'horn', κέρας, and Aristotle in fact explained κέρᾳ ἀγλαέ thereby.[2]

In any case, if 'horn' had in early times such sexual significance, we can understand, as it has not been possible hitherto, how a man's wife, who receives lovers, prostituting herself (πορνεύειν), could be said 'as the saying is, to make horns for him' (τὸ λεγόμενον, κέρατα αὐτῷ ποιήσει).[3] She thus supplements him. Possibly there is a joking suggestion also of her working for his benefit. From such an idiom it would be but a step to say that the husband who 'has many a Paris in his house' (ἔνδον ἔχων πολλοὺς σῆς Ἑλένης Πάριδας)[4] has horns. The lemma to this epigram describes him as κερασφόρος. These appear to be the earliest references to this association. Mediaeval poems[5] (e.g. in the thirteenth century) show a belief that a horn grew upon the forehead of him whose wife had received a lover. Presently it was a custom in England and elsewhere in Europe for neighbours to put actual horns upon the head of the husband, apparently to show with what his wife had supplemented him. Possibly on occasion the association of horns with the pugnacious anger (see pp. 148 ff.) of the sexual element played a part. In *The Story of Rimini* Leigh Hunt describes how an enemy

> Had watched the lover to the lady's bower
> And flew to make a madman of her lord.

The putting of horns upon the head of the patient cuckold might by some be intended to endow him with that which he seemed to lack, sexual power and pugnacity,[6] what belonged

---

[1] Fr. 171. Cf. Eurip. Fr. 278, etc.   [2] See Eustath. *ad Il.* xi, 385.

[3] Artem. *Oneir.* II, 12 (not in some MSS. See Hercher, *ad loc.*).

[4] *Anth. Pal.* xi, 278. Since it produced wealth, the horn or the wife responsible might jokingly be referred to as a 'horn of plenty'. See *Anth. Pal.* xi, 5, Jonson, *Every Man in his Humour*, III, 3, Shakespeare, *Part II* of *King Henry IV*, I, 2.

[5] See Grimm, *Deutsches Wörterb.* s.v. Horn, col. 1817.

[6] The stag (or roe) loses his horns each year after breeding and receives horns for next time. Cf. p. 239. In the interval he is inactive sexually and timid. This striking loss may explain our names for boar or bull,

to the element in the head. Their use (see pp. 148f.) of *cerebrum* and *cerebrosus* (cf. *eanchainneach*[1]) implies that for the Romans to have more brain was to have more of the substance active in aggressive anger, and the conception traced of the horns as an outcrop of that substance will help us to understand Ovid's reference to his becoming angry at last because his mistress receives other lovers: *venerunt capiti cornua sera meo*,[2] and Petronius' *aerumnosi quibus prae mala sua cornua nascuntur*,[3] also

castrated after mating prime: 'boar-stag', 'bull-stag', if these do not derive from the use of 'stag' for an inadequate husband. That name or horns might be attached to a husband to show his kind.

The current explanation of 'horns' (see *Oxf. English Dict.* s.v., 7; Falk and Torp, s.v. *Horn*, etc.) appears to be that of Dunger (*Germania*, XXIX, 59 ff.) that German *Hahnreh* (lit. 'cock-roe') was applied both to a cuckold and to a capon and it was a custom to graft the spurs of a castrated cock in the root of the excised comb. That the same name should be applied to cuckold and capon is not unnatural since both are sexually inadequate and lacking in pugnacity. This German trick with capons (from the sixteenth to the nineteenth century apparently) may explain this German name for a cuckold but will not explain or fit the earlier evidence. The trick itself needs explanation. But why such strange and elaborate marking? We may suggest that it followed the name or was a humorous application of the custom of adding horns to cuckolds, inadequate males. MacCulloch (*loc. cit.*) suggests that the practice of making horns with the fingers to avert the evil eye gave rise to the phrase 'to give horns'. But we have no evidence that the making of horns with the fingers to the cuckold was not an insult concerning his condition but an attempt to avert the evil eye. In any case the evil eye was not a monopoly of cuckolds, to whom alone horns have stuck, and the origin, so far as the earliest evidence shows, is in the saying about a wife, that she makes horns for her husband. This objection applies also to Brewer's suggestion (*Phrase and Fable*, s.v. Horn) that a cuckold was horned because a stag is sometimes beaten in combat by a stronger stag and driven from his females. The analogy is lacking, as he seems to have felt; for s.v. Cornette he prefers to believe that the wearing of horns by the cuckold meant that the man wore the woman's head-dress, the cornette, 'the mob-cap anciently worn by the women of France'; but again the relevance to cuckolds is hard to see and mediaeval French costume will not explain the Greek phrase.

[1] See p. 156.

[2] *Am.* III, 11, 6. This is of course a reference to the power, as well as to the propensity, to attack. It scarcely suffices to explain the Greek evidence.

[3] 39. Also Horace's praise of wine (*Odes*, III, 21, 18):

viresque et addis cornua pauperi;

and Ovid's praise of the same (*Ars Am.* I, 239):

tunc pauper cornua sumit.

Virgil's *irasci in cornua*[1] of a bull extending its anger into its horns (cf. Ovid's *armenti modo dux vires in cornua sumo*[2]).

The view traced that the head contains the sexual element will also explain the curious belief concerning another out-growth from it, the belief[3] that from the forehead of a foal there grows something which, if eaten, introduces sexual desire into him whom it enters. It was called *hippomanes*; Virgil[4] terms it *amor*, presumably because it was the concrete stuff of sexual passion. This explanation by relation to the head thus understood is supported by the *hippomanes* from mares: *lentum destillat ab inguine virus*;[5] *hippomanes, fetae semina...equae*,[6] and by Aelian's statement that *hippomanes* grew on the foal 'some say from the forehead, others from the loins (for the sexual significance of which see p. 188, n. 2), others indeed from the αἰδοῖον' (*de Nat. Anim.* XIV, 17). See also pp. 126 f.

Thus also we can better understand the virtues attributed to the horn of the unicorn or 'Scythian ass' (i.e. rhinoceros). It was the concentrated substance of the procreative element from the animal that was the supreme embodiment of pro-creative power.[7] Aelian tells of the Arcadian Styx[8] that no vessel could hold it, not even iron ones, none except the

---

[1] *Georg.* III, 232; *Aen.* XII, 104. The phrase owes something to Eurip. *Bacch.* 743: εἰς κέρας θυμούμενοι.

[2] *Met.* VIII, 882. These expressions help to a better understanding of our own 'horn-wood' or 'horn-mad' applied to beast or man that is furious, which we should perhaps relate to the use of 'braine' (like *cerebrosus*) meaning 'furious'. Cf. p. 150, n. 3. 'Horn-mad' was some-times brought into relation with the horns of the cuckold. In the *Merry Wives of Windsor*, Ford, who believes he has the latter, says: 'If I have horns to make me mad, let the proverb go with me, I'll be horn-mad' (III, 5, *fin.*).

[3] See e.g. Aristotle, *Hist. Anim.* 577 a, 9, 605 a, 2.

[4] *Aen.* IV, 515. For Lucan it was 'swollen with sap' (*suco*), VI, 455.

[5] *Georg.* III, 281 f. Cf. Aristotle, *Hist. Anim.* 572 a, 21 ff.

[6] Propertius, IV (v), 5, 18.

[7] See note 5 on p. 226. While this is in the press, an appeal for pro-tection is issued: 'the world's rhinos are being slaughtered, because of the belief of Indians and Chinese in the aphrodisiac qualities of their horns' (*The Times*, Jan. 21, 1938, p. 14).

[8] See above, p. 229; see also p. 247.

horns of 'Scythian asses'.[1] Receiving such a horn, Alexander dedicated it

ὁ Στυγὸς ἀχράντῳ Λουσήιδος οὐκ ἐδαμάσθη
ῥεύματι, βάσταζεν δ' ὕδατος ἠνορέην.[2]

In mediaeval belief a unicorn could not be caught by force or skill but would run to a maiden's bosom.

This horn was a great rarity. Elsewhere[3] it is the hoof of an ass which is said to be the only thing which can hold the water of Styx at Taenarum. The hoof substance was naturally identified with horn and called *cornu*[4] (cf. κεροβάτης, *cornipes*). To the evidence about knees[5] we may add that the legs of eunuchs were believed to swell with the imprisoned fluid;[6] and the idea that seed comes thence will explain the belief that 'binding' of the feet (ὑπόδεσις) facilitates sexual intercourse.[7] Belief that the hoof was a concentration of the life-fluid may explain the legend that a spring (Hippocrene) appeared where the hoof of Pegasus struck the rock.[8] If hoofs and nails (*ungulae* and *ungues*) were regarded as outcrops of the life-substance[9] from the limbs as horns from the head, that would fit in with and perhaps contributed to the attribution of peculiar significance to the hand[10] and to nail-parings, as to detached hair,[11] in magic. What is done to them affects sympathetically the life of him to whom they belonged.[12]

---

[1] *de Nat. An.* x, 40.

[2] See Aelian, *N.A.* x, 40. Cf. Ἀχέροντος ἄρσενας χοάς, Soph. Fr. 523.

[3] E.g. Plutarch, *de Prim. Frig.* xx, 3. In variants it is a horse or mule.

[4] E.g. Cato, *de Agri Cultura*, 72; Virgil, *Georgic*, III, 88.

[5] Pp. 174 ff.   [6] *Problemata*, 876 b, 31 f.

[7] *Ibid.* 877 a, 4 ff. So too the belief about thick ankles in Schol. to Aristoph. *Birds*, 1620, and the flame-coloured shoes of marriage (e.g. Catull. LXI, 10, 163). Cf. pp. 153, 403.

[8] Cf. Judges, xv, 15–19 on pp. 235 f. above, also p. 221.

[9] This helps to explain the Pythagorean ἀπέχεσθαι...ποδῶν καὶ κεφαλῆς on p. 280 below.   [10] See note 1 on p. 198.   [11] Cf. p. 235, n. 4.

[12] See, e.g., Frazer, *Taboo*, etc., pp. 267 ff. Cf. p. 107 above.

CHAPTER VIII

The World: Beginnings of Greek 'Philosophy'

The thought traced that it is the 'fluid' in which life is and by which life is generated not only appears from Homer onwards in the recognition and worship of rivers as the generative powers (see pp. 229 ff.), but it also has its cosmic correlate. For Homer the 'generation' (γένεσις) 'of all' (πάντεσσι) is the river 'Ὠκεανός[1] (Okeanos) which surrounds the earth and is associated with 'mother Tethys'. τὸ γὰρ ὕδωρ πάντων ἡ ζωή says the scholiast, which reminds us of the concept of αἰών above. γένεσις suggests the process or, in this context, the *substance* rather than the *agent* of generation. That Homer uses it twice of the cosmic river and not elsewhere of gods, men, or animals, which are *agents*, 'fathers', can scarcely be accidental. In the body it is, we have seen,[2] the sources of generation for which men feel awe and by which they swear. Thus perhaps (cf. ἠνορέην on p. 246) we can better understand why the 'greatest and most awful oath for the blessed gods'[3] is by the *water of the river* of the underworld, the water of Styx proper to the dead.[4]

If such beliefs were current and traditional, we might expect them to be the starting-point of the earliest (Ionian) 'philosophers' in their views of φύσις or, as Plato[5] interprets, γένεσις, 'generation', in their discussions of the primary substance from which all developed. In fact Thales,[6] the first of them, declared that it was 'water' and that the earth rested upon (therefore was surrounded by) water. Aristotle,[7] our earliest source upon this point, suggests as the reasons for his so doing

[1] *Il.* xiv, 246; cf. 201, 302. Cf. *patrem rerum*, Virgil, *Georg.* iv, 382; *parens rerum*, *Anth. Lat.* (Riese) 718, 14.   [2] Pp. 108f., etc.
[3] E.g. *Il.* xv, 35–40; Hymn to Hermes, 519. See also note 8 on p. 229.
[4] See p. 95, n. 5 and cf. pp. 276f. (esp. Theramenes).
[5] *Laws*, 892 c.   [6] A 12, 13, 14, 15 (Diels).
[7] *Metaphys.* A 3, 983 b, 17 ff.

that he saw that the nourishment of all things is liquid and that the warm is born therefrom and lives thereby and that 'the seed of all is wet (or "liquid") by nature' (τὸ πάντων τὰ σπέρματα τὴν φύσιν ὑγρὰν ἔχειν); and he gives it as the opinion of some people that this view of Thales was the 'very ancient' view to be seen in the description of Okeanos and Tethys as 'fathers of generation' (τῆς γενέσεως πατέρας) and in the swearing by the waters of Styx.[1] But, in the absence of the above evidence, Burnet[2] and others think this suggested reason was simply one of Hippo's arguments at a later date, wrongly transferred to Thales, and they themselves suggest instead that it was meteorological observations[3] which led Thales to fix upon water. The authority of 'some people' Burnet dismisses as 'merely a fancy of Plato's taken literally'. But the passages of Plato,[4] which he claims to have been Aristotle's source, in fact refer not to Thales but to Heraclitus and make no reference to the Styx as Aristotle's authority did. Thales' contemporary, Pherekydes of Syros, unequivocally taught[5] that it was from the seed (γόνος) of Χρόνος that fire and air and water were produced.

We shall see[6] that Ὠκεανός was believed to be a bond around

[1] Cf. p. 229, note 8.   [2] *Early Greek Philosophy*[3], p. 48.

[3] There is little or no evidence for this in the case of Thales; and Burnet's statement that 'in the days of Thales the prevailing interest was not physiological but rather what we should call meteorological' is without foundation and begs the question. *After* Thales, Anaximander and Anaximenes are known to have been much interested in τὰ μετέωρα, but the interest in 'generation' is the primitive approach to the problem and, as we see, it persisted. For the question whether Thales followed tradition, we may note that when he explained earthquakes by the motion of the surrounding water (A 15, Diels) he was following the traditional view which appears in the Homeric epithets of the sea-god Poseidon, Ἐνοσίχθων, Ἐννοσίγαιος, etc.; and πάντα πλήρη θεῶν εἶναι is primitive.

[4] *Theaet.* 180 D; *Crat.* 402 B.   [5] A 8 (Diels), reading αὐτοῦ.

[6] Pp. 315 ff. It is, I suggest, the same belief which underlies the doctrine of the Orphics (Fr. 29 K.) and of Pherekydes (B 4 D.), that the first cosmic power was Ὀφίων or Ὀφιονεύς (ὄφις = serpent) with his consort described as Ὠκεανίς and that after a struggle with Κρόνος he dwelt in Ὠκεανός or Ὠγηνός. *Myth. Lat.* 1, 204 says that he was called *Ophion et secundum philosophos Oceanus*. Philo derives Pherekydes' teachings from Phoenician sources. Cf. pp. 249 f.

the earth, apparently of serpent form even as Acheloos, the primal river or water,[1] was conceived as a serpent with human head and horns.[2] The procreative element in any body was the ψυχή,[3] which appeared in the form of a serpent.[4] 'Ωκεανός was, as may now be seen, the primal ψυχή and thus would be conceived as a serpent in relation to procreative liquid. The conception of 'Ωκεανός has no basis in observation. It can now be explained as the imagined primal cosmic ψυχή or procreative power, liquid and serpent. The name appears to have been borrowed from the Semites[5] (? Phoenicians) and to mean 'circling'.[6] The surface of the earth would, as the dome above and the circle of the horizon suggest, naturally be conceived as circular, the Roman *orbis terrarum*, and was apparently so conceived by the early Greeks[7]—as a disk or cylinder.[8] Above this was the dome of Οὐρανός, conceived apparently as a hard shell[9] arching down to the surface of the earth[10] at the rim, round which 'Ωκεανός flows so that the stars are washed by the water of the latter.[11] Below, corresponding to this dome, was Τάρταρος, apparently of similar dimensions.[12] Thus, we may see, for Homer, who refers

[1] See Gruppe, *op. cit.* pp. 344, 828.   [2] *Ibid.* p. 476₆.

[3] See pp. 108 ff.   [4] See pp. 129, 159, n. 2, 206 f.

[5] The belief traced is strikingly like the Babylonian; the earth was encircled by the male element, Apsu, a serpent identified with or in water. With him was another serpent, Tiamat, 'mother of them all' (*Epic of Creation, init.*). Cf. pp. 315 f. Euphrates, thought of as a serpent, was 'the soul of the land'.

[6] See Weizsäcker s.v. in Roscher, *op. cit.* 816, also pp. 442 f. below.

[7] Homer appears to mean Achilles' shield to be circular and puts 'Ωκεανός at its outmost rim (*Il.* XVIII, 607 f.). So too in the Hesiodic 'Shield of Herakles' πᾶν μὲν γὰρ κύκλῳ... ἀμφὶ δ' ἴτυν ῥέεν 'Ωκεανός πλήθοντι ἐοικώς, πᾶν δὲ συνεῖχε σάκος πολυδαίδαλον (141, 314 f.). See also pp. 316 f. below and τὸ... ῥέον περὶ κύκλῳ ὁ καλούμενος 'Ωκεανός ἐστιν, Plato, *Phaedo*, 112 E.

[8] See Hesiod, *Theog.* 790 f., referred to on p. 316.

[9] It was χάλκεος or σιδήρεος and 'rang' (*Il.* XXI, 388). If these adjectives were meant to convey not merely extreme hardness but literally 'brazen' or 'iron', we must rid our minds of modern views of minerals and think rather of the ancient conception of stone as bone (see pp. 212, 509) and of the 'birth' of silver (*Il.* II, 857; cf. Hes. *Theog.* 161 and p. 281).

[10] See *Od.* I, 53 f.   [11] See *Il.* v, 6, VIII, 485, XVIII, 489, XIX, 1, etc.

[12] See *Il.* VIII, 13 ff., 478 ff.

allusively to the conception shared by his contemporaries, the universe had the form of an egg girt about by ''Ὠκεανός, who is the generation of all'. While identified with or believed to be in the procreative liquid, the ψυχή was πνεῦμα.[1] We can now understand as a survival of the earliest Greek conception the picture attributed by Epiphanius to Epicurus, who said almost the last word of Greek science about the structure of the universe. He is credited with saying that 'the all was from the beginning like an egg, and the πνεῦμα in serpent wise around the egg was then a tight band as a wreath or belt around the universe' (εἶναι δὲ ἐξ ὑπαρχῆς ᾠοῦ δίκην τὸ σύμπαν, τὸ δὲ πνεῦμα δρακοντοειδῶς περὶ τὸ ᾠὸν ὡς στέφανον ἢ ὡς ζώνην περισφίγγειν τότε τὴν φύσιν).[2] It is the same conception which appears in two versions of the Orphic cosmogony which we may now correlate: (1) that the world egg was begotten by a wind (ὑπηνέμιον ᾠιόν);[3] (2) that it was engendered by a serpent which arose out of water and slime;[4] the upper part of the egg became Οὐρανός and the lower part Earth, including Τάρταρος in its nether depths (cf. βαθὺς γαίης Τάρταρος,[5] νείατα Τάρταρα γαίης,[6] etc.). We can perhaps also better understand at one and the same time why in this Orphic version the serpent was called Χρόνος and why, when asked what Χρόνος was, Pythagoras answered that it was

[1] See pp. 93 ff., 102, 108 ff., 119 ff. According to the view preserved for us by Hesychius 'Ὠκεανός was ἀήρ. In *cyaneoque sinu caeli tu diceris oras/ partibus ex cunctis immenso cingere nexu* addressed to Oceanus (*Anth. Lat.* ed. Riese, 718, 7 f.) it surrounds and binds Οὐρανός as apparently in Homer.

[2] See *Dox. Gr.* (Diels), p. 589. The attribution has, not unnaturally, been suspected. Epicurus did, however, hold that some universes were egg-shaped (ᾠοειδεῖς, Diog. Laert. x, 74). The traditional thought is perhaps also the origin of the teaching of his masters, Leucippus and Democritus, that the universe was enveloped in a ὑμήν or χιτών (Leuc. A 1 and 23 Diels), these terms being used by the Orphics of the enveloping membrane of the world-egg (60, 70 Kern, B 12 Diels). In the Gnostic *Pistis Sophia* (319) the Outer Darkness (cf. ἀήρ, n. 1 above) was a serpent, surrounding the whole world, with its tail in its mouth.

[3] See pp. 119 f.

[4] See *Orphicorum Fragmenta* (Kern), 54, 57, 58, Orpheus, B 12 f., *Fragm. d. Vors.* (Diels). Cf. Emped. A 50.

[5] *Id.* 121, 3 (Kern).   [6] *Id.* 167 b, 3.

the ψυχή of the universe.[1] According to Pherekydes it was from the seed of Χρόνος that fire and air and water were produced.[2] This conception of Χρόνος, the usual meaning of which is 'Time', may be related to that of αἰών, which was not only the procreative life-fluid with which the ψυχή was identified,[3] the spinal marrow believed to take serpent form,[4] but also came to mean 'lifetime',[5] 'period of time' and so 'eternity'. For Pindar αἰών meant not only the life-fluid[6] but also a compelling destiny, a δαίμων controlling life.[7] It is the name Heraclitus gave to the power controlling the changes of the world.[8] For the Orphics Χρόνος was mated to Ἀνάγκη, 'Necessity', which also, according to the Pythagoreans, lies around the universe.[9] Below[10] it will appear how for the earliest Greeks time and fate were circles. The process of time was the movement of the circle around the earth.[11]

Let us look a little further into the first original 'philosophers'. Though Anaximander with his 'Unlimited' (ἄπειρον) as the primary substance made a bolder break than Thales from the traditional scheme of things, he found reasons for believing that originally the surface of the earth was all liquid[12] and the first living creatures were engendered in liquid[13] (ὑγρόν). Just

---

[1] See Plut. Quaest. Plat. VIII, 4 (1007 A f.). For Χρόνος as a circling stream around the universe see Eurip. Fr. 594 (Nauck) = Krit. B 18 Diels: ἀκάμας τε Χρόνος περί τ' ἀενάῳ/ῥεύματι πλήρης φοιτᾷ τίκτων/αὐτὸς ἑαυτόν.
[2] See p. 248.   [3] See pp. 108 ff.   [4] Pp. 206 ff.
[5] See pp. 200, 208, 212 ff.   [6] See p. 206.   [7] See pp. 405 f.
[8] See p. 252.   [9] See p. 332.   [10] Pp. 442 ff.
[11] The Orphics sometimes called the serpent which engendered the egg Ἡρακλῆς instead of Χρόνος, which may point to an identification with the sun or rather with the circle of the sun's path, itself perhaps conceived as a rim or ring around the earth (cf. Emped. A 50, Metrod. A 13 Diels). According to Mimnermus (Fr. 12, Bgk.) and Stesichorus (Fr. 8, Bgk.) the sun passed along Ὠκεανός in a golden vessel. Herakles was said to have travelled thus (see Athen. XI, 781 D, 469 D). The conception of Ὠκεανός as a hoop or bond circling round the earth thus might contribute to Anaximander's conception of the sun, moon and stars as bright points in hoops or circles circling round the earth (A 10, 11, 18, Diels) and to the 'bonds' (see p. 332) and 'crowns' (στεφάναι) of Parmenides (A 37, B 12, Diels). See also pp. 315 ff. below.   [12] A 27 (Diels).
[13] They developed in husks and later emerged (A 30).

as the Homeric Greeks appear to have believed that in the generative 'fluid' (αἰών) was the gaseous ψυχή, Thales[1] held that the elemental liquid and its developments were permeated by ψυχή. It was this last which Anaximenes emphasised. He derived all things from 'vapour' (ἀήρ) and expressly argued from the microcosm to the macrocosm: 'Just as our ψυχή being ἀήρ holds us together (συγκρατεῖ),[2] so do breath (or "air", πνεῦμα) and ἀήρ encompass ("surround", περιέχει) the whole world'.[3] Anaximander had taught that the Unlimited encompasses every world (πάντας περιέχειν τοὺς κόσμους)[4] and the Pythagoreans taught that there was 'unlimited πνεῦμα' outside the οὐρανός.[5] Despite his emphasis upon fire (derived perhaps mainly from religion, from the idea of an all-subduing God, Zeus, who is fire, who is lightning and αἰθήρ[6]), 'Heraclitus', says Aristotle,[7] 'declares that the first principle (ἀρχή), the exhalation (or "vapour", ἀναθυμίασις) from which everything else forms, is ψυχή'. According to the *Placita*,[8] he taught that 'the ψυχή of the universe was exhalation from the liquid (τῶν ὑγρῶν) in it'. He said that 'ψυχαί are exhaled from liquid',[9] and, we are told,[10] likened ψυχαί to rivers in the fragment: 'Upon those who step into the same rivers fresh waters are ever flowing'. An explanation of his doctrine of transformation tells us that the fire was changed 'by way of vapour (ἀήρ) to liquid, the seed as it were of the world-order, which he calls "sea" (θάλασσαν), and from this the earth and the heavens and their contents are generated (γίνεται) again'.[11] He calls the cosmic

---

[1] So at least Aristotle thought. See A 22, 23. This is not, as we can see, to assert his belief in an ordering Νοῦς.

[2] For this function of the ψυχή see p. 195 above.   [3] B 2 (Diels).

[4] 11 (Diels).

[5] Aristotle, *Phys.* IV, 6, 213 b, 22, reading πνεύματος.

[6] See e.g. B 32, 64, 66, 120 (Diels) and Pherekydes, A 9, also 8 (Diels). He was worshipped as the lightning, and his home is the αἰθήρ from Homer onwards. See also p. 230, n. 8.

[7] *De Anima*, A 2, 405 a, 24 = A 15 (Diels).

[8] Aet. IV, 3, 12 = Diels, *Fragm. d. Vors. ibid.* and *Dox. Gr.* p. 389.

[9] B 12 (Diels).

[10] Arius Didymus *ap.* Euseb. *P.E.* xv, 20 = Diels, *ibid.*; cf. B 91.

[11] B 31; cf. B 76 and A 8. Thus perhaps we can better understand why

principle αἰών and conceives it as a child playing.[1] The interest in 'generation' which the term φύσις, applicable alike to plant and animal life, suggests, explains also why Empedocles should call his elements 'roots' (ῥιζώματα), Anaxagoras his primary bodies 'seeds' (σπέρματα), and Democritus an aggregate of such πανσπερμία.[2] Thus it survived into the atomic system, the crowning development of Greek 'physics'.

in the microcosm 'for ψυχαί it is enjoyment or death to become liquid (ὑγρῆισι); the falling into generation (τὴν εἰς γένεσιν πτῶσιν) is enjoyment for them' (B 77). The second opinion may not belong to Heraclitus, but the existence of the reference of ὑγρὴν τὴν ψυχήν in B 117 below to drunkenness does not preclude it and indeed may be the reason why the reference is here defined. Condensation of the vaporous ψυχή into liquid seems to be implied (cf. B 36, etc.). It is death, for 'we live their death and they live our death' (B 77; cf. B 21, 36, 62, 76), i.e. as begotten new lives and as ghosts respectively. It may be thus he identifies Hades, keeper of the ψυχαί, with phallic Dionysos (B 15). Cf. Hermes ψυχοπομπός and Petron. 140, 12. That the meaning of ψυχή was enlarged to include θυμός (see pp. 115ff.) makes interpretation of these fragments more difficult. αὕη ψυχὴ σοφωτάτη (B 118; see p. 33 above) seems to imply the larger meaning, as probably does the description of one drunk, as οὐκ ἐπαΐων ὅκη βαίνει, ὑγρὴν τὴν ψυχὴν ἔχων (B 117; cf. pp. 35 f. above), but θυμός has its Homeric meaning in B 85, where it is set over against ψυχή (see p. 197), and the passages above fit the early associations of ψυχή. Heraclitus' remoter disciple, the Stoic Zeno, held that the seed was a portion of the ψυχή, πνεῦμα μεθ' ὑγροῦ (see Arius Didymus ad Euseb. P.E. xv, 20 = Dox. Gr. p. 470).

[1] See B 50, 52 (Diels), also C 5 with the addition ⟨συμφερόμενος⟩ διαφερόμενος and p. 405 below.

[2] See Cornford, From Religion to Philosophy, pp. 165 f.

CHAPTER IX

Death and Cremation

So much for life. We have seen that normally the liquid diminishes with the passing of life so as to seem in a sense its measure. What of death? The sweat that comes out of the dying[1] would, like other sweat, seem to be loss of αἰών, but it is unnecessary to suppose that, when the conception was formed, the αἰών was believed to depart completely with the last breath. Soon, very soon in a warm dry climate, as Homer and others[2] observed, the body dries up. Thus, by the great favour of the gods the corpse of Hector was shaded so that the 'sun should not dry up (σκήλειε) the flesh about the sinews and limbs',[3] and it is a marvel how twelve days after death he is 'dewy as if just slain'[4] (ἐερσήεις, which the scholiast interprets ὑγρότητα ἔχων, οὐ κατεσκελετευμένος). Indeed, the dead were for the Greeks pre-eminently 'dry'. It fits our finding that αἰών, the 'life', was the 'liquid', that Homer expresses 'living, alive' by 'moist, wet', διερός. Nausikaa reassures her attendants that Odysseus is not an enemy: 'That mortal is not διερός and never will be born who shall come with war to the land of the Phaeacians; for very dear are they to the immortals'.[5] Elsewhere for διερὸς βροτός Homer has ζωὸς βροτός.[6] For it here, Butcher and Lang, for instance, give a characteristic of life recognised by ourselves: 'That mortal breathes not and never, etc.' That the liquid was thought to be the stuff of vigour is also confirmed. In the raid upon the Kikones after they had got the spoil, Odysseus bade his men 'flee with διερός foot'[7] (B. and L. 'With a swift foot'), but they did not and were attacked by the other Kikones. In the absence

---

[1] See e.g. Soph. *Antig.* 1236; Eurip. *Phoen.* 1439.
[2] E.g. Herodotus, III, 125; cf. the general statement τὰ νεκρούμενα ξηραίνεται, Simpl. *Phys.* 23, 21, Lucan VI, 542f., 621–3, etc., and p. 215, n. 2.
[3] *Il.* XXIII, 190 f.   [4] *Il.* XXIV, 414 ff. and 757 ff.
[5] *Od.* VI, 201 ff.   [6] Cf. XXIII, 187.   [7] IX, 43.

of the thought we have been tracing διερός has been supposed[1]
to mean simply 'active, alive' and to be distinct from and
different in origin from διερός meaning unquestionably 'wet,
liquid' opposed to 'dry', αὖος (e.g. in Hesiod, *Works and Days*,
460). Hesychius has preserved not only χλωρόν· ὑγρόν (see
p. 177, n. 9) but also χλωρὸν καὶ βλέποντα· ἀντὶ τοῦ ʒῶντα.
We may compare ʒῶντα καὶ βλέποντα (Aesch. *Ag.* 677).

We have seen that the liquid or liquefiable stuff of life and
strength identified with the seed was the 'marrow' of head and
spine and of the thigh-bones and knees, and with this that
element in the flesh which melts and issues as sweat and tears
and appears to be above all the pale liquefying fat. These were
called αἰών and with them the immortal ψυχή was particularly
associated. How the red liquid with which the θυμός was
associated, the blood in the blood vessels concentrated above
all in the chest, was related to αἰών we have no clear evidence,
but it is part of the 'moisture' that is opposed to the dryness
of the dead. For the 'avengers of blood', the Erinyes, of
Aeschylus, it is blood that matters. To Orestes one of them
says: 'Your mother's blood is on the ground hard to recall,
alas! τὸ διερόν ("the moist" or "liquid") poured on the plain
is gone (πέδοι χύμενον οἴχεται). But you in return must give
(*sc.* to me) to drain from you alive the red fluid from your
limbs. From you would I take nurture of drink evil to drink
and having dried you up alive I will lead you below'.[2]

We can now understand why one who is dead should say:
'My mortal body became dry (αὖον ἐγένετο) and my immortal
part rose to the air',[3] and why Aeschylus should speak of 'the
dead in whom there is no moisture (ἰκμάς)'.[4] One name for
the dead, ἀλίβαντες, was explained by the ancients themselves

[1] See the revised Liddell and Scott and Boisacq, s.v. and contrast the
scholia and Eustath. *ad loc.*   [2] *Eum.* 261 ff.   [3] Alexis, *Olymp.* 1 ff.
[4] Fr. 229 (Nauck), reading οἷσιν (Boeckh). Nauck preferred ἰσίν,
'in the muscles of the dead'. *Etym. Gud.* p. 321, 58 and *Etym. in Anecd.
Paris.* (Cra.) IV, p. 35, 22, not only tell us that Apollodorus explained κῖκυς
(usually interpreted as 'strength') to mean ἰκμάς, 'moisture', which fits
the belief traced (see pp. 187 ff.), but also preserve this fragment of Aeschylus
and the next (230 N²) addressed to the dead: 'In thee is no κῖκυς nor
blood-flowing veins'. Cf. *vires, virus* etc. p. 177, n. 9.

as meaning 'without moisture'[1] (α-λιβας) and another δαναοί
(=νεκροί) as 'dry'[2] (ξηροί). Δᾱνός meant 'dry' as applied
to plants, to timber, in Homer and later. With it we may
perhaps relate also δάνος, which the Macedonians applied to
death.[3] σκελετός, our 'skeleton', applied to the dead body[4]
and also to shrivelled live bodies,[5] meant indisputably just
'dried up' (cf. σκέλλω). This thought helps us also to explain
why in the *Frogs*, when Charon is indirectly asked where he
will land his passengers, he replies 'By the Stone of Drying
(Αὑαίνου λίθος) at the resting-places'[6] (ἀπὸ τοῦ αὕους τοὺς
νεκροὺς εἶναι, schol. *ad loc.*). According to Orphic belief the
soul arrives in Hades 'dry'[7] (αὖος).

Now, perhaps, it is possible to solve the problem of cremation
and understand the purpose of burning the dead—it expedites
the 'drying', the evaporation of the liquid of life—and with it,
we can explain Homer's name for the funeral process, ταρχύειν,
and what appears to be merely a variant form,[8] ταριχεύειν,
supposed to mean 'preserve, embalm', etc. Of these the
original meaning and the etymology have hitherto been
lacking.[9] The essence of the Homeric funeral, which ταρχύειν
would naturally express, was the treatment of the body with
fire,[10] treatment incompatible with any sense of 'embalming',[11]
which it has been usual to seek. Fire was in its action 'drying'

---

[1] See schol. to *Od.* VI, 201 and Ar. *Frogs*, 186, 194; Plut. *Qu. Conv.* VIII, 10.

[2] See *Et. Magn.* 247, 49, δάνειον.

[3] See Plut. *de Aud. Poet.* VI = 22 c, δάνον...τὸν θάνατον καλοῦσι. For
the accent, cf. pp. 211, n. 9, 346. For Death conceived like the dead,
cf. p. 361, n. 2.

[4] E.g. Phrynichus, *Com. Incert.* 69, 3 (Kock); Plut. *Quaest. Conv.* 736 A.

[5] E.g. *Anth. Pal.* XI, 392.   [6] Ll. 194 f.   [7] See p. 274.

[8] As ταριχηρός = ταρχηρός. Cf. ταραχή, τάρχη; σκάριφος, σκαρφίον, etc.

[9] See e.g. Boisacq, s.vv.

[10] See e.g. *Il.* VII, 77–86, equating πυρὸς λελάχωσι with ταρχύσωσι and
showing that the entombing, heaping of a barrow, was additional. For
the dative τύμβῳ τε στήλη τε in XVI, 457, 675, cf. e.g. XVIII, 506: τοῖσιν
ἔπειτ' ἧισσον, 'they started up with these (the sceptres)'. Barrow and
stele were honorific and useful accessories.

[11] In the many descriptions of disposal of dead bodies in the poems,
there is no evidence that the Homeric heroes practised embalming, only
the temporary attentions of washing and anointing which were not
expected to prevent corruption (see *Il.* XVIII, 350 f. with XIX, 24–33).

(apparently so characterised by Homer: κήλεος, cf. κηλός, περίκηλος). The original meaning of both ταρχύειν and ταριχεύειν was, I suggest, just 'to dry'; it thus falls easily into place with a number of Indo-European cognates: ταρρός, ταρσός, 'a drying basket', τέρσομαι,[1] 'dry', 'bake', Latin torreo, 'dry by heat, bake, scorch', Danish tørke, 'dry, desiccate', etc. Desiccation, drying, is in fact the simplest and therefore probably the first mode of 'preserving'.[2] Thus ταριχεύειν = ταρχύειν, 'to dry', would naturally come to connote 'preserve' and include smoking, drying with salt and other methods.[3] If we look, we find that the ancients themselves

[1] This meaning and affinity with τερσ- was suggested long ago (see Curtius, Gr. Etym. p. 719) and was, I find, used by Dörpfeld (Mélanges Nicole, pp. 97 ff.; Neues Jahrb. f. d. klass. Alt. 1912, pp. 8 f.) in his explanation of Mycenaean burial, of which I learned just before this goes to print, from Glotz, The Aegean Civilisation, p. 277. He sums up: 'D. has maintained that the bodies underwent a partial cremation, a desiccating, a bucanning for the purpose of preserving them without reducing them to ashes and frequently with the object of making them contract. These hypotheses have scarcely any supporters now'. The background of thought, belief in a liquid of life, etc., has been lacking; and the explanation of ταριχεύειν, ταρχύειν as 'dry' in relation to τερσ- has been rejected because the original meaning was thought to be 'pickle, embalm', which I here show it was not, but in fact 'to dry'. Failing this, in Glotta, xv, 1927, pp. 78 ff., R. Blümel has tried to separate ταρχύειν from ταριχεύειν (but without justification in meaning or form; see note 8 on p. 256) and to treat it as not Greek in origin but related to Lycian-Etruscan Tarquinius, Tarchon, etc. He proposes that tarchu meant 'einen Mann der weit über die gewöhnlichen Sterblichen erhaben ist' and so ταρχύειν 'wie einen Gott oder (königlichen) Heros oder Helden, also prächtig bestatten und zwar mit einheimischen, ungriechischen Brauchen bestatten'. Why should Homer at all or specifically of the Achaeans use such a word or, if it had such a sense, speak of it as the due of the dead in general: τὸ γὰρ γέρας ἐστὶ θανόντων (see Il. vii, 85, xvi, 456 f., 674 f.)? Blümel (p. 80) attempts to ignore Il. vii, 77–85, where ταρχύειν is used of Achaeans, on the ground that it is there opposed to πυρὸς λελάχωσι, the Achaean practice, but it is not opposed and might be replaced by καίειν or some other term for the same process. He produces no evidence for the meaning of Etruscan tarqu- except that it occurs in names of distinguished men, but whether as a proper or a common noun he is not sure. If it is a proper name—which appears to be the case—he asks us to derive ταρχύειν from it as mausoleum from Mausolus.

[2] The lasting preservation of dried up tissues must have been noticed from very early times.

[3] The effect of placing a body in honey, sometimes recorded later, would be to dry it by the action of the sugar.

support this. On ταριχεύειν Suidas has σημαίνει δὲ καὶ τὸ ξηραίνειν; and what appear to be the earliest instances extant (of the verb or τάριχος) refer to the shrinking, shrivelling, the 'drying up' [1] of the body with starvation or old age, and exclude any notion of preserving or embalming. Thus Aeschylus [2] speaks of the outcast, whom none will assist, as 'perishing at last κακῶς ταριχευθέντα παμφθάρτῳ μόρῳ' (cf. ἄφιλος αὐανῶ βίον, αὐανοῦμαι, etc. above [3]), while for Sophron, as we have seen, [4] old age 'wastes and dries up' (μαραῖνον ταριχεύει) its victim. τάριχος was applied especially to dried or smoked fish, but also to the remains of men. The Greek chieftain Protesilaos, who received funeral in the Trojan war, was early in the fifth century, according to Herodotus, [5] described as 'dead and τάριχος', and, showing his vitality then by taking vengeance on the Persian who robbed his tomb, he was miraculously symbolised by 'dried fish' (τάριχος) leaping and quivering in the fire as if newly caught.

We can thus explain not only Homer's term for the funeral by cremation of his day, ταρχύειν, but also perhaps its original basis—the curious practices of earlier ages. Thus the second shaft-grave at Mycenae contained three human bodies with golden diadems, etc. 'They had evidently been burned simultaneously in the very same place where they lay. The masses of ashes of the clothes which had covered them, and of the wood which had partially or entirely consumed their flesh, as well as the colour of the lower layer of stones and the

[1] See pp. 212 ff., 221 ff.   [2] *Choeph.* 296.   [3] Pp. 215, 222.

[4] P. 214. Later Demosthenes, *Aristog.* 1, 60 (788), contrasts a man as young and fresh, νεαλὴς καὶ πρόσφατος, with one who is τεταριχευμένος with long confinement, and ταριχεύειν (προταριχεύειν) continued to be used to describe the thinning, i.e. 'drying', of a person by starvation.

[5] IX, 120. In Egyptian mummification, to which also the word ταριχεύειν was applied (e.g. by Herodotus, II, 85 ff.), the body was 'dried' by surgical and chemical means. Herodotus describes it by the verb ἰσχναίνειν, 'dry up', 'wither' (III, 24). Cf. Lucan VIII, 689 ff.

Was Τάρταρος an intensive reduplication (cf. γάργαρα, κάρχαρος, μάρμαρος, etc.) of this ταρ-='dry' (cf. *terra*) or 'scorch' (cf. its relation to volcanic Τυφωεύς, Hes. *Th.* 820–68)? Cf. Hell (pp. 287 f.) and the Slavonic death realm, Russ. *Peklo*, from *pech*'='to parch' or (subst.) 'a stove'. Οὐρανός, its counterpart (cf. p. 249), seems to have referred to moisture. Cf. οὐρεῖν, οὐράνη and Sanscr. *Varuṇa* with p. 177, n. 9.

marks of the fire and the smoke on the stone wall, which at the bottom of the sepulchre lined all the four sides, can leave no doubt whatever on this point....The funeral pyres...could not have been large and had evidently been intended to consume merely the clothes and partly or entirely the flesh of the deceased; but *no more* because the bones and even the skulls had been preserved.'[1] Similarly, in the fourth shaft-grave were found the bodies of five men. 'The bodies had evidently been burned in the very spot on which each lay; this was shown as well by the abundance of ashes on and around each corpse as by the marks of the fire on the pebbles and on the wall of schist.'[2] So too in the others, the first,[3] third,[4] and fifth[5] graves. Their discoverer, Schliemann, claimed that these exemplified cremation as practised in the Homeric poems, but quite obviously they do not, and various other attempts have been made to explain them. Thus Helbig[6] thinks that the fire was used merely to burn sacrificial victims, whose hot ashes were then strewed over the corpse—a curious and unexplained practice—while Rohde,[7] concentrating instead upon the evidence of fire underneath, argued that 'traces of smoke, remnants of ashes and charcoal point to the fact that the bodies were laid on the spot where were burnt the offerings to the dead which had previously been offered there...the offerings were burnt and then, when the fire had gone out, the bodies were laid thereon'. Why? Also, this does not square with the fact that ashes were found on as well as under the bodies, and we may ask why burn animals, garments, and other objects if not to accompany the dead by the same path?[8]

[1] See Schliemann, *Mycenae*, p. 155.
[2] *Ibid.* p. 214.   [3] *Ibid.* p. 294.
[4] *Ibid.* p. 164.   [5] *Ibid.* p. 291.
[6] *Das homerische Epos aus den Denkmälern erläutert*[2], p. 52. He is not justified in stating (p. 53) that the later Greeks recognised the remains of Pelops (Paus. v, 13, 4), Theseus (Plut. *Thes.* 36), Ariadne (Paus. II, 23, 8), Protesilaos (Herodotus, IX, 120) and Orestes (*id.* I, 68) in 'von Feuer unberührten Skeletten'.
[7] *Psyche*, Chap. I, Sect. 8.
[8] *Il.* XXII, 512 implies that if the body could not be burned by relatives they might in its honour burn garments, but these did not profit the dead unless at the time he were clothed in them; cf. *Il.* VI, 416 ff.; *Od.* XI, 74, XXIV, 59.

Instead, it has been suggested that the Mycenaean funeral rite comprised an act of ceremonial cremation.[1] But it is exceedingly unlikely that, if full cremation was the original process with such importance as Homer attaches to it, the dead would be deprived of the full rite so easily accorded. This explanation also reverses the actual time sequence as we know it. Instead of Homer's full cremation, we find from very early times partial application of fire. In 'the earliest tholos burials of which we have any evidence in Greece, the primitive ossuaries of Early Minoan Crete,...considerable traces of charring and smoke stains are visible on the skeleton remains'.[2] On the various evidence Professor Nilsson[3] sums up: 'No satisfactory explanation of these fires has been given, for the attempts to show that cremation was in use in the Mycenaean age are not to be taken seriously. Only one possible explanation seems to remain, that fire was introduced in the funeral rites and in the cult of the dead either for burning sacrifices or for a purificatory purpose, as Sir Arthur Evans thinks'. This refers to the latter's preface to Dr Xanthoudides' *The Vaulted Tombs of Mesara*, where he suggests deodorisation and 'mighty house-warmings for the dead'[4] (as elsewhere[5] 'fumigating the tomb'), in harmony with Dr Xanthoudides' own view, who yet admits that it is not satisfactory: 'There is no satisfactory explanation of the fires in these tholoi....It is certain large fires were lit inside, fierce enough to fuse stones and metal objects and to bake the clay flooring, while on the other hand it does not appear that the dead were burnt'.[6] 'In places the floor was burnt almost to terra cotta and stones were split by the heat. In the Porti tholos almost the whole of the thick burial stratum was blackened by the fire and smoke and many of the skulls and bones were made quite

---

[1] See J. C. Lawson, *Modern Greek Folklore and Ancient Greek Religion*, pp. 493 ff.
[2] Sir A. Evans, *The Shaft Graves and Beehive Tombs of Mycenae*, 1929, p. 3.
[3] *The Minoan-Mycenaean Religion and its Survival in Greek Religion*, p. 524.
[4] P. xii.   [5] *The Shaft Graves* etc., p. 3.
[6] *Op. cit.* p. 90.

black. Yet other scholars' examination of these remains has confirmed my views that there is no case of burning the body after burial. The fire came later and the bones turned black from exposure to the heat and smoke at close quarters. What was the purpose of lighting these fires inside the tholoi? Frankly, we do not know. It might have been to obtain light or to fumigate the tomb from the flavour of death or for a funeral sacrifice or feast. Yet no one of these suggested reasons would have necessitated so large a fire.'[1]

The difficulties disappear in the light of the ideas found above in the earliest literary evidence: the vaporous ψυχή or life-soul was closely bound up[2] with the life-liquid filling the flesh. Ταριχεύειν was used to describe the 'drying up' of this liquid, which meant the shrivelling of the flesh, the reduction of the body 'to a skeleton', as we say, a σκελετός, i.e. 'dried-up' body, and τάριχος to describe alike the remains of a Homeric warrior and a dried or smoked fish recognised to be in the same condition. And the essence of the Homeric funeral described by ταρχύειν was the treatment of the body with fire. We can thus believe that these fires in the early Cretan ossuaries, which smoked and dried up, but did not consume the bodies, were made for that purpose, ταριχεύειν, ταρχύειν. These were communal tombs receiving great numbers of bodies and huge fires might be needed. If in these early Cretan ossuaries a body was not at its funeral brought into contact with the embers, the Mycenaean shaft-graves—later in time —will represent an advance towards the Homeric stage in that the bodies they contained were found with ashes above and below them. But the multitude and confusion of the bones found in the Cretan ossuaries[3] seem to have precluded such observations on the part of the excavators as could be made upon the well-spaced personages in the Mycenaean tombs. In any case, the funeral practised by the Achaeans of Homer, to which this term ταρχύειν was applied and in which, after the extinction of the pyre, the clearly recognisable bones of

[1] *Ibid.* p. 135.   [2] See above, pp. 191 ff., 200 ff.
[3] See Xanthoudides, *op. cit.* p. 7.

the individual remained and were honoured with burial,[1] seems to be merely a slight development of the process, carrying rather further by a fiercer fire or its more intimate application the 'drying', the elimination of flesh or moisture and so of the vaporous ψυχή. It is not a totally different process and need not imply an originally different culture or different race, as has been maintained. Homer tells us that the burning enables the ψυχή to depart. Though it may be said to leave the body almost immediately[2] the latter is stricken, yet it does not pass to the house of Hades till the fire has done its work and then it comes not back.[3] The ψυχή of Odysseus' mother explains why she cannot be grasped: 'This is the way with mortals when one dies. For no longer do the sinews hold the flesh and the bones, but the mighty energy of burning fire overcomes these (as soon as the θυμός has left the white bones) and the ψυχή like a dream-phantom flies away hovering'.[4] The burning completes the drying up of the life-sap and the release of the ψυχή. Meleager's life was exactly correlated with that of a piece of wood and came rapidly to an end when the latter was burnt.[5] The ψυχή is ἠΰτε καπνός, 'even as (or "like") vapour (or "smoke")',[6] the visible form of what passes from the body when it is being reduced by fire, dried to a σκελετός or mere bones. It is a commonplace in European folk-lore that when a dead man is felt to be active in this world, the corpse is found to be full-fleshed still; the soul or ghost is still with it. In Greece till quite recently in such a case fire was used,[7] but the important thing was that the body should be speedily reduced to dry bones (cf. our 'dry as a bone'); we are told[8] that instead of fire on occasion knives have been used and the bones scoured.

If we turn to Italy we find similar facts from the Old Stone age onwards: 'There are signs of these palaeolithic bodies

---

[1] See Il. xxiii, 165-9, 252 f.; Od. xxiv, 72 f.

[2] Compare αἰών (p. 200).

[3] See pp. 60 f. As preventing corruption and releasing the ψυχή fire was welcomed by the dead (πυρὸς μειλισσέμεν, etc.).   [4] Od. xi, 218 ff.

[5] See Paus. x, 31, 4 (quoting Phrynichus, Fr. 6, Nauck); Aesch. Choeph. 604 ff. and more fully Apollod. i, 8, 2; Hygin. Fab. 171; Diod. iv, 34; Ovid, Met. viii, 451 ff., etc. Cf. nymphs in relation to trees on pp. 219 f.

[6] Il. xxiii, 100.   [7] See Lawson, op. cit. pp. 365 ff.   [8] Ibid. pp. 540 f.

having been not indeed burnt but subjected to the action of fire, a ceremonial whose meaning has not yet been made out. ...Neolithic man treated his dead in much the same way. Here again we find signs of the roasting or scorching process, whatever it may have meant, but the body is seldom or never really cremated'[1] Contemporaneously with this was practised the rite which has been called *scarnitura*, the stripping of the bones before burial,[2] i.e. virtually what has just been noted for modern Greece. That the early Latin name for what is under the skin covering the bones (i.e. the flesh and organs) was *viscus*[3] seems to show that its chief significance for them lay in its moistness or sticky liquid analogous to that in the pulp around the stone or seedcase of a fruit. The purpose of both these Italian rites we need not doubt is that which we have discovered in ancient Greece—the elimination of the liquid of life, with which as we have seen in Italy as in Greece the vaporous life-soul, the divine *genius* (= *anima*), was bound up. *Qui neque terraest datus nec cineris causa umquam evasit vapos* runs a line of Accius.[4] When the Roman burned his dead father, Varro tells us that 'as soon as he came upon a bone, he said that he (the dead man) had become a god',[5] i.e. a *genius* freed. We have seen[6] reason to believe that during life the *genius* was thought to be manifestly active in burning flame. That in palaeolithic graves fire was apparently applied only to those who had reached puberty[7] suggests that none but they were thought to have a soul worth liberating, and that the soul in question manifested itself in power only after puberty, i.e. was associated with procreation, as was the historic *genius*. In these same graves the head was pro-

[1] H. J. Rose, *Primitive Culture in Italy*, p. 23. In historic times the body was sometimes not subjected to the extreme action of fire. The description of Cynthia (Prop. IV (v), 7, 1 ff. referred to on p. 269 below: *eosdem habuit secum, quibus est elata, capillos,/eosdem oculos; lateri vestis adusta fuit;/ et solitum digito beryllon adederat ignis*, etc.) may not imply just the partial burning of the prehistoric graves, but suggests the essential oneness of the latter with the more complete cremation.

[2] See T. E. Peet, *The Stone and Bronze Ages in Italy*, pp. 120, 187, 194.

[3] See Plaut. *Mil. Glor.* 29, etc. For the other declension and meaning of *viscus* cf. *penus -i* or *-eris*, etc.   [4] Fragm. Trag. 112 (Ribbeck).

[5] See Plut. *Quaest. Rom.* XIV; cf. *bonos leto datos divos habento* (Cic. *Leg.* II, 9, 22).   [6] Pp. 146 ff.   [7] See Von Duhn, *Ital. Gräberk.* p. 6.

tected, but not the body, and this attention to the head was confined to adults (p. 136). Even in historic times there seems to have been a different funeral for those who had not reached puberty.[1] To such, as to fruits, grapes, etc. that have not ripened, their juice not yet mature, the word *acerbus*, 'unripe, sour', was applied[2] (cf. Horace's *tolle cupidinem inmitis uvae*,[3] to one whose love is too young to wed) and the funeral given to them seems to have been called *funus acerbum*.[4] Puberty was marked by the assumption of the *toga virilis* and this took place at the festival of *Liber*, the Italian god of seed and fertility, who *praeest virorum seminibus*,[5] was worshipped with *phalli* and identified particularly with the juice of the vine.[6] The identification or intimate relation of soul and name is a commonplace elsewhere and appears to lie behind the rite of calling the name over the dead and calling his name when praying for the safety of one who sneezed (*nomine quoque consalutare religiosius putant*[7]). It was, we saw,[8] to the soul, the *genius*, that a sneeze appeared to be referred. A Roman got his name with his *toga virilis*.[9] Cf. p. 146. His *genius* then manifested itself as effective.[10]

The use of the plural *manes*, 'good ones', for what survives

---

[1] For evidence see e.g. H. J. Rose, *Class. Quart.* xvii, 1923, pp. 191 ff.

[2] E.g. *maiores nostri virginis acerbae auris veneriis vocabulis imbui noluerunt* (Varro, *Men.* 11). [3] *Odes*, ii, 5, 9 f. Cf. *Anth. Pal.* v, 303 on p. 216.

[4] See e.g. Plaut. *As.* 595, *Aen.* vi, 429 with Servius' note. [5] See p. 219.

[6] See Varro in Augustine, *De Civ. Dei*, vii, 21, vi, 9; cf. vii, 2, iv, 11, and above, pp. 215 ff., 224 ff.

[7] Pliny, *N.H.* xxviii, 2, 23. [8] Pp. 132 f., 225 f.

[9] Though names must in fact have been used and were later at any rate assigned on the *dies lustricus* eight or nine days after birth, we have it on the authority of Q. Scaevola that it had been the custom that the individual name (*praenomen*), e.g. *Marcus*, as opposed to the name shared by the *gens*, e.g. *Tullius*, and that shared by the *familia*, e.g. *Cicero*, was not given to a boy before he assumed the *toga virilis* or to a girl before she wed (see the *De Nominibus* usually appended to Valerius Maximus). He then dedicated to the *Lares* (cf. p. 158, n. 5) the protecting 'bubble', *bulla*, that had been about his neck. Had it done duty for the *genius* = *anima*? Cf. the idiom *animam ebullire* (Petron. 42, 62; Sen. *Apoc.* 4) or just *ebullire* (Pers. ii, 10). It contained a *fascinum* (p. 448, n. 5).

[10] *iuno* designated, I suggest, the power manifest in a woman more particularly in the period of fertility, the body's prime (see pp. 187 ff.), i.e. while she was *iuvenis*. Cf. *coniuges...munere assiduo valentem/exercete iuventam* (Catull. lxi *fin.*). *iuveno* might become *iuno* as *iuvenior iunior* and *iuvenix iunix*.

when an individual has died, the soul(s) worshipped at the tomb (e.g. *si potuit manis arcessere coniugis Orpheus, Aen.* VI, 119), is strange. It is not satisfactory just to say that it originally represented the collective dead and was transferred to describe one of them. The problem would remain. How was it felt possible to apply a plural term to what survived when one man died? The doctrine of some Greeks (Censorinus[1] attributes it to Euclides of Megara) that two δαίμονες, controllers of fate, prompters one to good, the other to evil, attended each human being has been proposed,[2] but is

---

[1] III, 3. Its roots may perhaps be seen in the Homeric διχθάδιαι κῆρες (see note 3 on p. 391 and pp. 397 ff., esp. note 1, p. 404 and note 8, p. 405).

[2] See e.g. Servius, *ad Aen.* VI, 743 and, following the latter and to some extent Norden (*Aeneis*, VI², pp. 33 f.), P. Boyancé in *Revue de Philologie*, IX, 1935, pp. 189 ff., to which last my attention was drawn by Mr F. H. Sandbach. Their basis is the uncharacteristic instance in Anchises' account (*Aen.* VI, 739 ff.) of what happens to souls after death:

> *ergo exercentur poenis veterumque malorum*
> *supplicia expendunt: aliae panduntur inanes*
> *suspensae ad ventos; aliis sub gurgite vasto*
> *infectum eluitur scelus, aut exuritur igni;*
> *quisque suos patimur manis.*

Here a twofold fate, good and evil, is not suggested; and the pair of δαίμονες is nowhere else called *manes*. The alternative interpretation of Virgil's phrase, which is currently considered (see e.g. Professor H. E. Butler, *ad loc.*), is that defended by Warde Fowler: 'Each individual of us must endure his own individual ghosthood'; but such sense of an accusative of a person with *pati* is very strange. It more naturally would express the afflicting agency. The original sense of *manes*, at which Conington glances as slightly contributory, surely has strong claims. *Manes* included not only the dead but meant (e.g. 150 lines later, *Aen.* VI, 896, *Georg.* IV, 489 f. etc.) underworld powers, the agencies which the departed soul encounters after death. Thus Lucretius argues, lest

> *post hinc animas Acheruntis in oras*
> *ducere forte deos manis inferne reamur,*
> *naribus alipedes ut cervi saepe putantur*
> *ducere de latebris serpentia saecla ferarum* (VI, 762 ff.)

and the phantom of the *Culex* complains to the goatherd it has saved that he is comfortable and safe;

> *at mea manes*
> *viscera Lethaeas cogunt tranare per undas;*
> *praeda Charonis agor; vidi ut flagrantia taedis*
> *lumina conlucent infernis omnia templis;*
> *obvia Tisiphone serpentibus undique compta*
> *et flammas et saeva quatit mihi verbera; pone*
> *Cerberus* etc. (214 ff.)

scarcely likely to have occasioned this change among the
Romans. There are, we have seen, according to native
Roman belief, two spirits in the living man—the *genius*

and says of Eurydice returning to the world of life

> *illa quidem nimium manis experta severos*
> *praeceptum signabat iter....*
>
> (289 f. Cf. *C.I.L.* II, 4427; IX, 175, etc.)

In *Aen.* x, 39 ff. *manis* is used with reference to the horrid Fury, Allecto.
quisque suos patimur manis could thus naturally mean 'each suffers those
infernal agencies which are his due'. Not all the infernal powers afflict
each individual. There are particular agencies of punishment and purga-
tion for each. In her preliminary account of the underworld the Sibyl has
given instances: Tityos having his liver devoured by a vulture, Tantalus
with *Furiarum maxima iuxta* brandishing her torches at him when he would
eat, Ixion, etc. (VI, 566–627). Etruscan grave pictures represent the soul
being handled (in some cases tormented) after death by one, two, or
three underworld gods (see F. Weege, *Etruskische Malerei*, pp. 27 ff.) i.e.
manes. Statius describes the earth opening and the seer Amphiaraus with
chariot and horses violently entering the realm of Hades. The latter is
outraged and cries out, threatening to launch Tisiphone and other troubles
at the powers responsible above; then he turns to the man:

> '*at tibi quos*', *inquit*, '*manis, qui limite praeceps*
> *non licito per inane ruis?*' *subit ille minantem.*
>
> (*Theb.* VIII, 84 f.)

This sense of *manes* or reference to the spirit(s) of the dead person suffices
for the two grave inscriptions adduced by Boyancé: *te di manes tui ut
quietam patiantur atque ita tueantur opto* (8393 Dessau, slightly later than
Virgil apparently) and (beginning *dis Manibus Meniae Sophes C. Maenius
Cimber coniugi sanctissimae*),...*nunc queror aput manes eius et flagito Ditem aut
et me reddite coniugi meae, quae mecum vixit tan concorde ad fatalem diem. Mevia
Sophe, impetro si quae sunt Manes, ne tam scelestum discidium experiscar diutius*
(8190 Dessau. Cf. 8006, a similar appeal just to *Manes sanctissimae*).

Boyancé supports his reference of *quisque suos patimur manis* to the Greek
belief in two δαίμονες by the fact that in her new home

> *libabat cineri Andromache manisque vocabat*
> *Hectoreum ad tumulum, viridi quem caespite inanem*
> *et geminas, caussam lacrimis, sacraverat aras.*
>
> (*Aen.* III, 303–5.)

But here *manis* clearly refers to what survived of the dead, not to the
powers that afflict the latter. Servius suggests that the two altars were
dedicated one to Hector, one to Astyanax; but a plurality of altars were
raised at Polydorus' funeral (*stant manibus arae*, III, 63) and at that of
Anchises (*maestasque sacravimus aras*, v, 48) and, if they were not raised to
the infernal powers, might, like a plurality of candles or candlesticks set

(=*anima*) and the *animus* which, however, like the Greek θυμός, does not seem originally to have been believed to survive independently after death,[1] though it might by the end of the Republic when this use of *manes* appears. This use of the plural may, I suggest, have been helped by the plurality of bones, the visible surviving representatives of the dead. When a Roman burned his dead father, 'as soon as he came upon a bone, he said that he (the dead) had become a god'.[2] Returning to his father's tomb Aeneas says *salvete, recepti/ nequiquam cineres animaeque umbraeque paternae.*[3] The bones were perhaps likened to the hard seeds (or roots) left when the softer parts of a plant or a fruit, e.g. a grape or an ear of corn, have been dried away. That each bone was conceived to have an indwelling potency appears from the rite of the *os resectum*, the custom of cutting off a finger before burning; the presence of this one 'bone' rendered the house *funesta* till it was buried. It appears also in the long surviving cult of relics, bones together or separated (the head of Phocas, the finger of Thomas, etc.), which were believed to show their powers by healing the sick, etc. Thus, 'St Briocus of Great Britain died

up to a single deity or saint, be just a multiplication of service or honour (cf. pp. 279 ff., 286). Thus in Eclogue v, 65 f.:

> *en quattuor aras:*
> *ecce duas tibi, Daphni, duas altaria Phoebo.*

No better as evidence is Dido's (=Elissa's) appeal for vengeance to *Sol, Iuno, Hecate,*

> *et Dirae ultrices et di morientis Elissae.* (iv, 610.)

It is difficult to say whether she thought of the *manes* she became or joined by dying or of those powers whose help the injured could claim, claim with greater strength by reason of his or her death, as when Iokasta, learning what Oidipous had done, committed suicide:

> τῷ δ᾽ ἄλγεα κάλλιπ᾽ ὀπίσσω
> πολλὰ μάλ᾽ ὅσσα τε μητρὸς ἐρινύες ἐκτελέουσι.

(*Od.* xi, 279 f. Cf. ii, 134 f.; *Il.* ix, 566–72, 454–6, etc.)

We may compare *di morientis Elissae* with the cry of the beggar Odysseus when ill-treated by Antinoos:

> ἀλλ᾽ εἴ που πτωχῶν γε θεοὶ καὶ ἐρινύες εἰσίν,
> Ἀντίνοον πρὸ γάμοιο τέλος θανάτοιο κιχείη.

(*Od.* xvii, 475 f.)

[1] See p. 95.   [2] See Varro, quoted on p. 263.   [3] *Aen.* v, 80 f.

A.D. 502. In 1210, the Father Superior of Angers wished to obtain some of his bones; two ribs, an arm and a vertebra were given to him. When these bones entered the Cathedral they jumped for joy at the honour conferred upon them'.[1] The surviving power, or powers, of the dead are often clearly identified by the Romans with the burnt remains. Thus Virgil's Dido repents:

non servata fides cineri promissa Sychaeo (v.l. *Sychaei*),[2]

and his Aeneas, contemplating vengeance on Helen for being the ruin of his race, says 'it will be a joy to have sated my *animus* with vengeance *et cineres satiasse meorum*'.[3] For Propertius quite unmistakably the surviving powers of the dead that are carried to the other world, that receive judgment, are the bones:

> *aut si quis posita iudex sedet Aeacus urna*
> *in mea sortita vindicat ossa pila...*
> *moribus et caelum patuit: sim digna merendo*
> *cuius honoratis ossa vehantur aquis* (*avis* Heinsius).[4]

The bones appear to be referred to as the *manes*. Livy attributes to the Athenians this complaint against the Macedonians: *omnia sepulchra monumentaque diruta esse in finibus suis, omnium nudatos manes, nullius ossa terra tegi*,[5] with which we may compare inscriptions on the graves of ordinary men and women, e.g.

> *Ummidiae manes tumulus tegit iste simulque*
> *Primigenae vernae, quos tulit una dies,*[6]

or *dis manib./Anteiae P. f./Crispinae/cinerib. sacr.*[7] or *dis manibus*

---

[1] Dom Lobineau, *Lives of the British Saints*, cited by E. Cobham Brewer, *Dictionary of Miracles*, p. 262. Pp. 149ff. (esp. 156, n.2), 213, n.4 above and the conception of bones as seeds or containing the seed, the life, will explain 'bonfires', i.e. fires made of bones to produce fertility, luck. For instances see e.g. *Oxf. Eng. Dict.* s.v.; Frazer, *Golden Bough: Balder* I, pp. 203f. For bones with similar significance but different use see pp. 279f.

[2] *Aen.* IV, 553.   [3] *Aen.* II, 586 f.

[4] IV (V), 11, 19 f., 101 f.; cf. III, 18, 31 f.   [5] XXXI, 30.

[6] 8524 in Dessau's *Inscr. Lat. Sel.*   [7] *Ibid.* 7985.

Iulia Urbana/mater cineribus Iuliae/Secundillae filiae fecit.[1] Propertius curses a bawd thus:

> *nec sedeant cineri manes et Cerberus ultor*
> *turpia ieiuno terreat ossa sono;*[2]

and says of himself

> *deinde ubi suppositus cinerem me fecerit ardor*
> *accipiat manes parvula testa meos.*[3]

Further light on the thoughts behind the drying of the bones, usually by heat, may perhaps be shed by the belief traced that animal and plant life work on the same principles. Drying helped to separate and to preserve from corruption, from maggots, etc. the seeds, e.g. of the bean: *cum in area exaruerit, confestim, priusquam luna incrementum capiat, excussam refrigeratamque in granarium conferto: sic condita a curculionibus erit innoxia.*[4] Corn was dried by the burning sun before threshing, e.g. *opportunis solibus torrefacta proteritur.*[5] In Sweden and Kurland it was usual for the corn to be parched by fire in a building (the *Hitzrige*) before threshing.[6] So too in Russia.[7] It is and was easy to observe not only that most mature plants inevitably pass through a season of dryness, saplessness, of rest or death, but also that most seeds need to become dry, as it were dead, before they will germinate. This will explain 'That which thou sowest is not quickened

[1] *Ibid.* 7986.
[2] IV (V), 5, 3 f.
[3] II, 13, 31 f.; cf. 57 f.; Pers. I, 38 f., etc. How the ghost might be identified with the plurality may be seen in his vision of the *manes* of Cynthia, recognisable but *rattling*:

> *sunt aliquid manes: letum non omnia finit*
> *luridaque evictos effugit umbra rogos.*
> *Cynthia namque meo visa est incumbere fulcro...*
> *et solitum digito beryllon adederat ignis*
> *summaque Lethaeus triverat ora liquor*
> *spirantisque animos et vocem misit: at illi*
> *pollicibus fragiles increpuere manus.* IV (V), 7, 1 ff.

See also Seneca, *Ep. Mor.* 24, 18; Petronius, 34. For the elder Pliny the corpse itself was *manes: pleraeque alitum e manibus hominum oculos potissimum appetunt* (*N.H.* XI, 37, 148). Cf. XVI, 44, 234.
[4] Columella, *de Re Rustica*, II, 10, 11.
[5] *Id.* II, 20, 3.
[6] See Schneider's commentary on Columella, *loc. cit.*
[7] See Ralston, *The Songs of the Russian People*, p. 123.

except it die; and that which thou sowest, thou sowest not
the body which shall be but a bare grain, it may chance of
wheat...'.[1] This period of rest, of drying and apparent death,
of the seed is in reality a period of maturation, in which
certain changes, necessary preliminaries to germination, as
we now know, are taking place. In the Mediterranean world
with which we are dealing this drying takes place in the
burning heat of Midsummer, which is practically rainless.
That there is the period of death, of rest, for plants. Life
begins again with the autumn rains. The sap appears in the
dry plant and it lives again.

[1] I Corinthians xv, 36 f. Cf. S. John xii, 24.

CHAPTER X

The Offerings to the Dead and to the Gods

What of the bones from which the life-liquid and the vaporous life-soul have been liberated? The drying process of age and death has been helped to completion by the fire. The sap appears in the dry plant and it lives again. The bones have been dried even as seeds must be dry before they can spurt into new life.[1] The dry seed needs moisture anew if it is to begin life anew. So[2] the dry bones, it might be hoped, receiving life-liquid, might live. Those of which we have fullest account in Homer, the bones of Patroklos and Achilles, are treated in a way for which no satisfactory reason has hitherto been forthcoming. They are not preserved in a dry vessel, as we might expect, but in the *Iliad* those of Patroklos are taken from the ashes after quenching with wine, and are laid in 'twofold fat (δίπλακι δημῷ) ',[3] and in the second *Nekuia* in the *Odyssey* those of Achilles are 'gathered in unmixed wine and grease (ἀλείφατι, "unguent") '.[4] But we have seen that fat or grease (including marrow, and the vegetable equivalent, oil) was particularly identified with the liquid and liquefiable element of life, i.e. with αἰών.[5] In the treaty curse the Homeric heroes represented the fluid of the brain (which could not be

---

[1] See pp. 269f.

[2] An old oracle referred to the bones of Rhesus as Ῥήσου καλάμη, 'the cornstalk of Rhesus' (Polyaenus, VI, 53; cf. Lucian, *Dial. Mort.* 18). For the ancient Athenians the dead were 'Demeter's folk', Δημήτρειοι (Plut. *De Fac. in Orb. Lun.* XXVIII). For the idea that living bodies come out of the earth as the corn did, see pp. 112 ff. and 233. Cf. p. 274, n. 2.

[3] *Il.* XXIII, 243, 253. This was the *omentum*. Cf. pp. 272, n. 8, 279f., 484f., 511f.

[4] *Od.* XXIV, 73. With this practice I would relate the funeral λήκυθος, vessel for oil or unguent, put with the dead or represented on the grave, and the pouring of oil there (see e.g. Aristoph. *Eccl.* 1110f. and perhaps 1101; Plut. *Arist.* 21).

[5] For renewal of life by scorching, then steeping in liquid, compare the Eagle on pp. 290f. below.

stored as fat was) by wine.¹ The dead were above all the 'dry ones'.² Alike the bones and the ψυχή (still associated with them and the grave) were dry. Their great need, therefore, was liquid—preferably actual life-liquid of animal or plant or just the elemental liquid, water—what would help them to the state of the 'living' otherwise known as 'wet' (διερός).³

The characteristic offerings to the dead were in fact 'pourings' (χοαί).⁴ Over the great fourth shaft-grave at Mycenae was an altar with a round tube-like opening to the grave beneath. It has been recognised as a device (paralleled elsewhere) by which to pour libations, perhaps we should just say liquid, down to the dead. In the tomb itself Schliemann found a large quantity of broken pots, 'on seeing which Mr Panagiotes Eustratiades, Director-General of Antiquities, reminded me of the habit still existing in Greece of breaking vessels filled with water on the tombs of departed friends'.⁵ In classical times,⁶ also, water was poured for the dead. It was received, drunk, by the ψυχή;⁷ to the bones it was a 'bath' (λουτρόν),⁸ not to cleanse but, like the bridal-bath (pp. 229ff.), conferring life-fluid (cf. αἰών, αἰονάω, pp. 209ff. etc.), like the

---

¹ It occurred to me that it might represent blood, but see pp. 218f. Blood was on occasion poured for the dead as different from wine and had a different effect (see *Od.* xi, 26 ff., 36, 96, 147 ff., 152 ff. and below, note 4).   ² See pp. 255f.   ³ See pp. 254f.

⁴ E.g. honey-mixture, wine, water and barley-groats (*Od.* xi, 26 ff.; cf. p. 274, n. 2; p. 296, n. 7); milk, honey, water, wine, oil, and flowers (Aesch. *Pers.* 610 ff. For flowers cf. pp. 113 ff., 130 and 218, n. 3); water, milk, wine, and honey (Eurip. *Iph. Taur.* 159 ff.). Odysseus' trench of blood had, we saw (pp. 60f.), a relation rather to θυμός, to restoration of the living consciousness. Later Greece had its αἱμακουρίαι (see e.g. Plut. *Arist.* 21).   ⁵ Schliemann, *Mycenae*, p. 284.

⁶ See e.g. the law against it at Iulis (*Inscr. Gr.* Vol. xii, Fasc. v, 593, 22).

⁷ See e.g. the cup held out by the 'hero' in the Spartan grave reliefs mentioned on p. 285.

⁸ See Soph. *Electra*, 84, 434; Eurip. *Phoen.* 1667; Hesychius, s.v. χθόνια λουτρά, and the χθόνια λουτρὰ τοῖς νεκροῖς ἐπιφερόμενα (Zenob. vi, 45). Did the rites at death or its anniversary, γενέσια, originally imply 'begetting' or 'birth' to new life (cf. pp. 287 ff. and the baptismal λουτρὸν παλιγγενεσίας κ.τ.λ. p. 189, n. 2 *ad med.*)? In the womb a baby is covered with fat or grease (*vernix caseosa*) and surrounded by the clear or brown 'waters'. These must have seemed to fit into the evidence for the fat or oil and water or wine of life.

wine and fat about the bones of Patroklos in the containing vessel (ἀμφιφορεύς). Here perhaps we have the explanation of the long known Minoan practice of burying in a bath[1] (cf. πύελος, δροίτη); and it was perhaps originally with reference to the liquid of life, as vehicle or symbol, that a vessel, often pierced at the base, was set up over graves.[2] Thus perhaps also we may explain the belief that the 'unholy' or uninitiated are, in the world below, ever vainly trying to get water, trying to fill a vessel (πίθος), but it leaks away[3] and the 'holy' enjoy 'everlasting drunkenness'.[4] 'There to them alone is it

---

[1] See e.g. H. R. Hall, *The Civilisation of Greece in the Bronze Age*, p. 90. This practice will be referred to again below (p. 285).

[2] See e.g. the Dipylon vases. The ancients interpreted the bridal bath (λουτρόν) as conferring or betokening seed (see p. 230). Over the grave of the unwed it was customary to set a λουτροφόρος (usually a vessel pierced at the base) 'as a token that they had died without receiving the bridal bath and without seed' (Eustath. *ad Il.* XXIII, 141; cf. schol. *ad loc.*). The Danaids, who deprived themselves of husbands, were also believed to be in the underworld trying to get water in a vessel that leaks (*Axiochus* 371 E). In Mandaean belief, if one does not mate, his or her soul 'dries up and dies' (Brandt, *Mand. Schr.* p. 120). Danaids may have been assimilated to the uninitiated, though originally bringers of water to thirsty Argos (see Hesiod, Fr. 24). Some interpreted them as well-makers (see Eustath. *ad Il.* IV, 171; Strabo, VII, 6, 8, p. 371), which would fit human immigrants from Egypt. If the story is a myth, as is more probable, they were perhaps not well-nymphs as has been suggested, but rather rain-cloud spirits aptly conceived as bringing water in leaky vessels (cf. διὰ κοσκίνου, Aristoph. *Clouds*, 373). Traditionally they came flying across the sea from, or having done away with, the sons of Aigyptos (= Nile). The Cloud-maidens came to Athens: εἶτ' ἄρα Νείλου προχοὰς ὑδάτων χρυσέαις ἀρύτεσθε πρόχοισιν (*Clouds*, 272; cf. Aesch. *Suppl.* 1024 f.). Having drawn their water, the rain clouds almost all left Egypt (see Herodotus, III, 10; Diod. Sic. I, 10 and *Clouds*, 1130) and rain came to Greece (Argos, etc.) mainly on the South wind, Νότος. In the *Rig Veda*, *Danu* is a female spirit of cloud or rain (see e.g. Macdonell, *Vedic Mythol.* p. 158, Griswold, *Rel. of the Rigv.* p. 183), but Δάναος was perhaps the 'Dry one' (see p. 256). Δανάη received a shower (cf. pp. 156, n. 2, 230, n. 8).

[3] See Plato, *Rep.* 363 D, quoting Musaeus; Xen. *Oec.* VII, 40; Paus. X, 31, 9 ff., quoting Polygnotus; and the figures on the lekythos in *Arch. Zeit.* 1871, Taf. 31.

[4] Plato, *loc. cit.*, quoting Musaeus. The 'mud' of the underworld was a natural concomitant of the river(s). The idea might be helped by horror of a dank grave, towards which the Homeric Ἀΐδεω δόμον εὐρώεντα (*Od.* X, 512, etc.), οἰκία σμερδαλέ' εὐρώεντα τά τε στυγέουσι θεοί περ in the ground beneath men's feet (*Il.* XX, 64 f.), already point.

granted to live', says Sophocles;[1] 'for the rest all things are evil there.' Plato had heard that the vessel meant the ψυχή.[2]

According to Orphic belief the ψυχή arrives in the house of Hades 'dry' (αὖος). 'I am dry with thirst and perish' was its cry (on tablets[3] in tombs in the south of Italy and in Crete); but if it has been initiated it asks or is offered cold water from a certain spring.[4] A Greek epitaph (from Rome) consists of the wish: 'May Aidoneus, lord of those below, give thee cold water, for thou didst lose the dear flower of youth'[5] (ἥβης γάρ σοι ἀπώλετο φίλτατον ἄνθος). It is interesting to read another

[1] Fr. 837 (Pearson); cf. Homeric Hymn to Demeter, 480 ff., etc.

[2] In connection with the doctrine σῶμα σῆμα—that the body is a 'token', a tomb or grave-monument—he explains (Gorg. 493), apparently from some Pythagorean (or Orphic) source, that the pierced πίθος was used in myth to symbolise the sensual part of the ψυχή that leaked and could not be filled, and that the leaky vessel or 'sieve' (cf. Rep. 363 D) carried by the uninitiated (ἀμύητοι) in Hades was itself the ψυχή. He appears to mean ἀμύητος to be interpreted 'not closed', i.e. 'leaky', with allusion to μύειν ('to close an opening'). The conception of ψυχή had perhaps changed since the belief arose (see pp. 115 ff.) and the moral turn which he gives to the interpretation (ἀμύητος= ἀνόητος, etc.) was probably not there originally. If the objections, which have been raised to the explanation of μύστης as one who shuts his mouth, keeping the secrets he has learned, are valid, it is perhaps not necessary to turn to μύσος or some other root (see J. Harrison, Prolegomena[3], p. 154). The truth may be that at the earlier stage to which the name was applied, the initiate closed his eyes (possibly also his mouth) or they were closed by the veiling of the head (see e.g. figs. 147, 148, 155 in Harrison, op. cit.) while ceremonies were performed, and that at the later stage he saw and was therefore ἐπόπτης. Cf. Pap. Mag. Paris. (IV Preis.) 585f., 625f. It may be relevant to his advantage after death that the claim of the initiated at Eleusis was that with a preliminary fast and with certain manipulations with the aid of basket and chest he had 'drunk the κυκεών' ('Ενήστευσα, ἔπιον τὸν κυκεῶνα, ἔλαβον ἐκ κίστης, ἐργασάμενος ἀπεθέμην εἰς κάλαθον καὶ ἐκ καλάθου εἰς κίστην, preserved by Clem. Al. Protr. II, 18). It appears from the Homeric Hymn to Demeter, 208f., that the κυκεών was made of barley-groats (ἄλφιτα) and water flavoured with pennyroyal. Homer (see p. 222) termed barley-groats 'the marrow of men', μυελὸς ἀνδρῶν. By ritually partaking of this—the corn-life—with the accompanying ceremony (e.g. corn or flour on the head, p. 228, n. 1; liknon and loaves on the head, p. 133, n. 1) one secured life, or a fuller life, in the world below. Cf. Δημήτρειοι in n. 2, p. 271 and ἀμβροσία in n. 7, on p. 296.

[3] See O. Kern, Orphicorum Fragmenta, 32, a, b.

[4] For the possibly late reference to Μνημοσύνη and Λήθη, i.e. not to vitality but to consciousness, see pp. 66f., etc. [5] Epigr. Gr. (Kaibel), 658.

record of the modern Greek custom: 'As the bier passes along
the road, the friends and neighbours of the dead man empty
at their doorway or from their windows a vessel of water and
usually throw down the vessel itself to be broken on the stones
of the road.... Some interpret the custom as a symbol of what
has befallen the dead man; the vessel is his body, the water is
his soul; the pouring out of the water symbolises the vanishing
of the soul and the dead body will fall to pieces like the broken
crock. Others say that they pour out the water "in order to
allay the burning thirst of the dead man", a notion ominously
suggestive of the boon which Dives sought of Lazarus.[1] But
the real purpose of the rite is still known in some of the Cyclades
where exactly the same custom is followed also on the occasion
of a man's departure from his native village to live, as they say,
in exile. And the purpose is to promote the well-being of the
dead or the exile in the new land to which he is going.'[2] It is,
we might explain, a gift or an earnest, by sympathetic magic,
of the liquid that is life and strength; which conception also
lies behind the present native interpretation of the water spilt
at a funeral as symbol of the life or soul. Trimalchio declared
'life is wine'. Perhaps to this should be related his direction
that on his grave-monument should be represented not only
himself with ships, money, and guests, and his wife and his
boy Cario, but also 'plenteous wine-jars well-covered with
gypsum so that they do not let the wine escape and one of them
you may represent as broken and over it a boy weeping'.[3] In
this same thought we found[4] the explanation of the custom
of bestowing a cup of wine upon a person to whom one wished
well, προπίνειν, *propinare*, which term appears also of libation
to the dead. Thus at the annual ceremony at the graves at

---

[1] The significance of this is suggested below (pp. 285 ff.).

[2] Lawson, *op. cit.* pp. 520 f. This much is implicit in his sources. He
betrays no suspicion of our explanation but suggests that 'the pouring
of water is a rite of sympathetic magic designed to secure that the unknown
land shall also be well-watered and pleasant and plentiful.... This custom
then in itself bears witness how widespread is, or has been, the conception
of the other world as a land of delight wherein the pleasant things of this
world shall still abound.'

[3] Petronius, 71.   [4] P. 217.

Plataea the archon took a κρατήρ and pouring it forth said:
'προπίνω to the men who died for the freedom of Hellas'.[1]
Another custom also becomes more intelligible, that of pouring
wine or other liquid for the benefit of someone living. Like
the bestowing of the cup[2] this also was found at marriage.
Thus Sappho tells how 'the κρατήρ of ambrosia had been
mixed and Hermes took the ὄλπις to pour out (οἰνοχοῆσαι)
for the gods and they all held cups and poured it (sc. on the
ground, ἔλειβον) and called down blessings on the bridegroom'.[3] Similarly, on Helen's bridal night, according to
Theocritus, the Spartan maids say they will go to the tree of
Helen and 'drip liquid unguent from a silver ὄλπις'.[4] It is
a gift of the liquid of life as in the surviving practice of the
Cyclades. In a grim parody of the custom Theramenes, after
drinking from his cup of hemlock, poured out (sc. on the
ground) what remained with the words 'προπίνω this to the
noble Critias'.[5] In this cup there was death and, as he hoped,
Critias died soon after. The liquid poured was evidently
believed to benefit in some mysterious way him in whose name
it was poured, to be received perhaps by his life-soul, his ψυχή
or *genius*. Even thus indeed wine was regularly poured for one's
own *genius* or that of another.[6] So after death all through the
night, while the body of Patroklos was burning, Achilles was
pouring out wine and calling his ψυχή.[7] To this also should
probably be related the otherwise strange custom of pouring
unmixed wine—usually reserved[8] for the dead, i.e. the ψυχή—
into one's cup and saying the name of someone present or absent
to whom one wished well, usually one's beloved. The name
was in the genitive, meaning apparently that the liquid was his[9]

---

[1] Plut. *Arist.* 21.
[2] See pp. 216f.
[3] Fr. 51 (Bgk.).
[4] xviii, 46f.
[5] See Cicero, *Tusc.* i, 40, 96.
[6] See p. 227 and cf. e.g. the libations decreed by the Roman state to
Marius as to the gods (Plut. *Mar.* 27).
[7] *Il.* xxiii, 218 ff.
[8] It stood for the life-fluid at the treaty (pp. 108, 217f.).
[9] This perhaps is the meaning of Trimalchio's *suum propinasse* (reported speech, Petronius, 28) of wine spilt by others; but the text is
doubtful.

(or hers) and he (or she) benefited by it. Thus Theocritus describes a symposium:

ἤδη δὲ προϊόντος ἔδοξ' ἐπιχεῖσθαι ἄκρατον
ὧτινος ἤθελ' ἕκαστος· ἔδει μόνον ὧτινος εἰπεῖν.
ἁμὲς μὲν φωνεῦντες ἐπίνομες, ὡς ἐδέδοκτο.[1]

That it was subsequently drunk by him who called the name did not destroy the virtue of the act but was perhaps, like the drinking by two of the same wine above,[2] felt to be a 'communion', a 'transfusion' binding life to life. Something of the same thought seems to lie behind the custom of our forefathers, whereby he who was about to drink said *wæs hal*[3] (i.e. 'be hale') to him to whom he wished well and the other replied *Drinc hal*, and our custom still of 'drinking someone else's health', of holding out the glass with the words 'Here's to you', 'Here's your health' or 'Here's long life to you', then drinking it.

With their conception of the 'sap'[4] of life and equation of life and wine the Romans put not only unguent but wine upon their bodies, above all upon their *heads*,[5] and thought that what the life-soul, the *genius*, wanted was wine.[6] How did they, after death, treat the incinerated bones? One of Trimalchio's guests, who has just left a funeral feast (*novendial*), says: 'It was pleasant, although we had to empty half our drinks upon his bones'.[7] Trimalchio himself commands: 'Bring out the *vitalia* in which I wish to be carried out (sc. to cremation). Bring out also the unguent and a taste from that jar, with wine from which I command that my bones be washed.'[8] Not only was the body anointed before burning,[9] but, as in Homer, wine

---

[1] XIV, 18 ff. Cf. II, 151 f.; Horace, *Odes*, III, 8, 13 ff., 19, 9 ff., etc.
[2] Pp. 216f.
[3] To give it health that was fertility, *wæs hal*, 'wassail', was said also to each fruit tree, with fruit juice drunk (e.g. cider for an apple tree), and some of it thrown over the tree. Cf. pp. 477 ff.   [4] See p. 192.
[5] See pp. 227 f., and for unguent upon the head e.g. Petronius, 47, 65.
[6] See p. 227.   [7] Petronius, 65.
[8] *Ibid.* 77; cf. 42, Sen. *Ep. Mor.* 99, 22. That the things put upon the corpse when it goes to be burned should be called *vitalia* suggests a relation to 'life'. Blümner's suggestion (*op. cit.* p. 495₇) that the name was 'euphemistic' is scarcely adequate.
[9] E.g. *crassisque lutatus amomis*, Pers. III, 104.

was poured over the bones. They were then wiped and unguents poured upon them in the urn.[1] For this treatment, as for the wine and fat of Homer, no satisfactory reason seems to have been advanced,[2] and we need not doubt that here too it was originally life-fluid that was thought to be given. Horace opposed him who lives well to him who lives ill as *unctus* to *siccus*.[3] Not only the oily sap of the olive but also myrrh, incense[4] (*tus*), and other exudations, 'tears' or 'sweat' as the Greeks and Romans termed them, from trees were used, sap to compensate for the 'sap'[5] (*sucus*) the dead had lost. On the ninth day after the funeral there was a sacrifice and a meal was eaten at the tomb and wine was sprinkled on it, the *vinum respersum*.[6] Many of the urns have been found with an opening in the cover through which offerings of liquid might be poured,[7] while elsewhere[8] (e.g. in the ancient cemetery discovered at

[1] See e.g. Tibullus, III, 2, 19 ff.; Stat. *Silv.* II, 6, 90; Pliny, *N.H.* XIV, 12, 88; Propertius, IV, 7, 34. Tears would be doubly welcome (e.g. Tibullus, III, 2, 23–5; Ovid, *Fasti*, III, 561 f.; *Heroides*, XIV, 127; Stat. *Silv.* III, 3, 212 f., etc.). See pp. 201 ff. above, and compare the giving of hair, pp. 99, 229 ff. (cf. Ovid, *Met.* XIII, 427 f.). The Egyptians believed that the tears of Isis and Nephthys lamenting restored the body of the dead to life (see Ebers, *op. cit.* pp. 149 f., and pp. 283 f. below, also note 5 on p. 203 above).

[2] Cumont (*After Life in Roman Paganism*, 1922, pp. 50 ff.) discusses offerings to the dead and refers to the view that wine was a substitute for blood 'but its use in connection with the dead can be explained also by its own virtue. It is the marvellous liquid which gives divine drunkenness and which in the mysteries ensures immortality to such as are, thanks to this sacred draught, possessed by Bacchus' (p. 52).

[3] See pp. 210 ff., 223 f. above.

[4] There is evidence of incense in early graves. See e.g. the censer (with cup as if for wine) with the helmeted ossuary described by Randall MacIver, *op. cit.* p. 49. [5] See p. 192.

[6] See e.g. Festus, 318 f. (*resparsum vinum*). It is to that Trimalchio's guest refers. For the pouring of wine at the grave see e.g. Dessau's *Inscr. Lat. Sel.* 8154, 8156, 8198, 8204 or Bücheler, *Carm. Epigr.* 838.

[7] See e.g. Blümner, *Die Römischen Privataltertümer*, p. 503₉: 'eine Oeffnung zum Eingiessen der flüssigen Totenopfer'.

[8] See Mau, *Röm. Mitt.* III, 1888, pp. 137 f., X, 1895, p. 156. Blümner (*op. cit.* p. 507) of the larger family graves says: 'Wenn die Urnen oder Sarkophage frei aufgestellt waren, so hatte es keine Schwierigkeit den Überresten die Totenspenden zukommen zu lassen; waren sie aber an unzugänglichen Stellen oder eingemauert, so brachte man tönerne oder metallene Röhren an, die von oben zur Urne hinabreichten und durch die man die Libationen hinabgoss'. Such will explain *Georg.* IV, 265.

a considerable depth in the Forum near the later temple to Faustina) there are tube-like passages to convey liquid to the remains of the dead.[1]

Why in the early Greek sacrifice were the essential offerings to the gods wine and bones wrapped in fat? 'Never has my altar lacked fair repast, even libation and κνίση. For that is our privilege',[2] says Homer's Zeus. It has puzzled men since Hesiod's time why the sacrificers should have the tasty flesh and organs of the victim and the gods get bones and fat. It was, suggests Hesiod, a trick of Prometheus: 'For when the gods and mortal men were having their differences decided at Mekone, then with eager spirit having divided a huge ox, he set it before them, trying to deceive the wit of Zeus. For the one portion he placed the flesh and inwards rich with fat in the hide, covering them with the stomach; for the other he placed the white bones, arranging them well and covering them with gleaming fat, intending a crafty trick'. Seeing the two heaps Zeus said: 'How unfairly you have divided the portions!' But Prometheus with a smile bade Zeus choose which portion he would, and Zeus 'knew and was not unaware of the trick, but in his spirit boded ills for mortal men, which were also about to be fulfilled. With both his hands he lifted the white grease (ἄλειφα) and was wroth in his φρένες and anger came about his spirit when he saw the white bones of the ox by the crafty trick. It is in consequence of this the tribes of men on earth burn for the immortals white bones on the fragrant altars'.[3] So in the many sacrifices in Homer the essential offering to the gods is the μηρία, the bones, more distinctively the thigh-bones (or more loosely μηροί, 'thighs'), enclosed in fat, with or without wine.[4] We can now see that the gods were not cheated; they were getting the stuff of life.[5] Just these, wine and fat, were put with the bones of the dead.[6]

---

[1] See Boni, *Not. d. Scavi*, 1903, p. 169.   [2] *Il.* iv, 48 f.; cf. xxiv, 69 f.

[3] *Theog.* 535 ff. For the bareness of the bones cf. the quotation in Clem. Alex. *Strom.* vii, 6, 34 and Menander, *Dyscolus*, 129 (Kock).

[4] See *Il.* ii, 423 ff., viii, 240, xi, 774; *Od.* iii, 455 ff., etc. and pp. 215 ff.

[5] So too when (*Od.* iv, 761) instead Penelope offers barley-groats, i.e. seed, 'marrow' (pp. 222, 228; cf. 282). Cf. the use of skulls and rhytons on p. 241, n. 2.   [6] See pp. 271 f.

The fat in both cases was the *omentum*, life-stuff.[1] The bones offered to the gods contain marrow, the thigh-bones in particular marrow that was identified with the life.[2] The thigh(s) of the sacrificial victim, apparently as the seat of life, was used in the ancient Egyptian ritual for restoring the god Osiris or the dead man to life.[3] In Homer's imagination the young prince Astyanax, the hope of Troy, 'ate exclusively marrow and the rich fat of sheep',[4] a diet not very satisfactory in practice but ideal according to the beliefs here traced. The life-substance was released from the dead body by the funeral fire, departing in vaporous form. In vaporous form the offering to the gods departs, released by the altar fire. κνίση was applied not less to the fat before it was offered than to the vapour which it became. There is a Greek record that, when Tyrian Herakles died, his friend Iolaos wished to bring him back to life, so took a quail, of which bird Herakles was fond, and 'burned it alive and from the κνίση Herakles came to life again (ἐκ δὲ τῆς κνίσης ἀναβιῶναι τὸν Ἡρακλέα)'.[5] Hesiod terms the fat thus transmitted ἄλειφα, 'unguent, stuff for anointing'. In the same sense as a direct gift of the stuff of life, infusing vitality, we can also understand the otherwise puzzling anointing of the polished stones that formed the throne or judgment seat of Nestor and of his father before him. When

[1] Cf. pp. 188, n. 3, 208, n. 2. This was for the ancient Hindoos the essential part of the sacrificial victim, the life-principle, and it was burned for the gods. The rest of the carcase was cut up and boiled and the fat, gathering on the top, was also burned for them. See e.g. *Rig Veda*, III, 21, 5.

[2] See pp. 182 ff.; also for the ὀσφύς, p. 208 and n. 3, p. 126. We can now better understand ἔλεγε δ᾽ ἀπέχεσθαι τῶν καταθυομένων ὀσφύος καὶ διδύμων καὶ αἰδοίων καὶ μυελοῦ καὶ ποδῶν καὶ κεφαλῆς, Porph. *Vita Pythagorae*, 43. See pp. 111 f. above, and for ποδῶν, pp. 174 ff., 246. In the Prose Edda (*Gylfaginning*, 44) the bones and the skin (cf. note 5, p. 235) of Thor's goats suffice and become alive and complete when consecrated by the hammer (see p. 156, n. 2). A thigh-bone had been tampered with to get at the marrow.

[3] See Budge, *Osiris and the Egyptian Resurrection*, I, p. 400. With the thigh, the heart, seat of the heart-soul (see pp. 283, 398, n. 3 below), was used. For the thighs as sources of new life among the Egyptians see p. 183 above. Evidence for similar significance of the thighs among the Jews will be found on pp. 109, 183, 188f. and for their importance in sacrifice on p. 183, note 4.   [4] *Il.* XXII, 501.

[5] Zenobius, *Cent.* v, 56, *Paroemiogr.* ed. Schneid. u. Leutsch, I, p. 143.

Nestor sat upon them they were glistening with ἄλειφαρ,[1] not as the scholiasts suggest: 'as if with ἄλειφαρ', nor as modern commentators explain, varnished to protect them, but as Homer says 'glistening with grease ("unguent")'. The Semites had similar beliefs about fat, and Jacob anointed as 'the house of God' (Beth-el), as if God were in it, the stone by resting on which he had received inspiration.[2] Such a seat of inspiration[3] was the oracular omphalos stone[4] identified with the Earth-goddess at Delphi. There men daily anointed the stone that represented Zeus when Kronos swallowed his children.[5] The unity of this practice with the burning of the fat appears among the Ainianes who worshipped a stone as holy and 'sacrifice to it and cover it with the fat of the victim' (θύουσιν αὐτῷ καὶ τοῦ ἱερείου τῷ δημῷ περικαλύπτουσι).[6]

[1] Od. iii, 408. Counsellors sit 'upon polished stones (ξεστοὶ λίθοι) in a holy circle (ἱερῷ ἐνὶ κύκλῳ)' in a scene of the 'Shield' (Il. xviii, 503 f.). For stone or metal as alive, born, see p. 249, esp. n. 9. This belief persisted and was the inspiration of alchemy. Indeed, the belief here traced, that life might be restored to a stone (including metal) in the form of a liquid, is the explanation of the name: al (Arabic) = 'the', chymeia from χυμός (cf. p. 62) 'juice', the restoring liquid which was the great object of search. See Addendum viii on p. 509.

[2] Gen. xxviii, 11 ff.

[3] See Aesch. Eum. 616 (μαντικοῖσιν ἐν θρόνοις), Eurip. Iph. Taur. 1281 f. These ideas will help us to understand the importance attached to the tripod of Pythia or Sibyl, the throne of a king, the cathedra of bishop or pope, and the Chair of teacher or bard and, ultimately, of the 'man in the chair', the 'chairman'. Taliesin speaks of his 'splendid chair, inspiration of fluent and urgent song' (see MacCulloch, The Relig. of the Anc. Celts, p. 117). So too perhaps the θρόνος of the initiate. Cf. Clouds, 254 ff. (pp. 449 f.) with schol.

[4] I suggest that the design under the gypsum throne at Knossos originated in an omphalos girt by a fillet or serpent. Incorporated in a similar position in the throne used in the coronation of our kings is the Lia Fail or 'Prophetic Stone', which was brought by Edward I from Scone. Tradition claimed that on it the head-kings of Ireland were installed and it roared like a lion when a legitimate king was upon it. Christians identified it with Jacob's stone. See W. G. Wood Martin, Elder Faiths of Ireland, ii, p. 257. A fresco from Knossos (Sir A. Evans, The Palace of Minos, ii, pp. 839 f., fig. 555) appears to depict an omphalos with a band irregularly wound about it.

[5] See Paus. x, 24, 6. Elsewhere (e.g. at Athens) it was customary thus to anoint with oil the stones at crossroads (see Theophr. Characters, xvi, Δεισ., Lucian, Alex. xxx).　　　　[6] Plut. Quaest. Gr. xiii.

At Rome it appears certain that the deity was conceived to be 'increased' or 'strengthened' (*mactus*) by the wine or other offering.[1] There was a tradition that originally the offering was not animal but grain (cf. p. 279, n. 5) with salt and wine or milk.[2] Animal sacrifices there almost certainly were on occasion, and in the later period they are familiar; the god received not only the fat (*omentum*) but also the parts concerned in consciousness—heart, lungs, liver and gall—perhaps in connection with *extispicium*.[3] Grain with salt (*mola salsa*, cf. οὐλοχύται) and wine were before the slaughter sprinkled over the victim (cf. p. 228), and there was a preliminary offering of incense (i.e. the exudations, sap of trees) and wine. Incense had apparently replaced native grain or aromatic leaves, as e.g. of the laurel with their gum and oil, *pinguis verbena*,[4] of which, as we have seen, the 'heads of the gods' consisted. 'Incense and wine' appear to have been the customary offering in a *supplicatio*, and we hear that they were supplied by the state to private citizens for that purpose at the beginning of the third century B.C.[5] They were also what the dead received,[6] not in vapour as to the gods but directly, as the grease and wine to the bones and the grease to the stones in Homer.[7] Roman deities also received unguent directly. Thus the Arval Brothers 'anointed the goddesses';[8] the Lar was anointed;[9] Terminus

---

[1] See Warde Fowler, *Religious Experience of the Roman People*, pp. 182 ff. To this idea (*alo* = 'feed, increase'; cf. *adoleo*), rather than to mere height or burning, should perhaps be related *altare* designating an 'altar' or, upon the main structure, that which receives the offering, or the offering itself. For instances of these uses see Nettleship, *Contrib. to Latin Lex.* s.v.

[2] See e.g. Ovid, *Fasti*, I, 337 ff.; Pliny, *N.H.* XVIII, 2, 7; XIV, 12, 88. For pouring milk on the burnt bones see Tib. III, 2, 20.

[3] See pp. 60, n. 2, 89.

[4] See Ov. *l.c.*; Virg. *Ecl.* VIII, 66, etc. with pp. 141 f.

[5] See Livy, X, 23, 1. Cf. Plaut. *Aul.* 24; Suet. *Aug.* 35, *Tiber.* 70; *C.I.L.* XII, 4333. [6] See pp. 277 f.

[7] See pp. 271 f. and 280 f. [8] See *C.I.L.* I, 28, 16.

[9] *saxa inlita ceris/viderat unguentoque Lares humescere nigros* (Prud. *contra Sym.* I, 203 f.). Cf. *incerat lapides fumosos idololatrix/relligio* (id. *Hamartig.* 404 f.). This waxing satisfies and is the natural explanation of his *genua incerare Dianae* (*Apoth.* 457) and Juv. X, 55 (p. 181); XII, 88. *cerei* (candles, cf. pp. 145, 287) and incense were burnt before statues of the living (Cic. *de Off.* III, 20, 80), i.e. for his *genius*. Cf. pp. 135, 138, n. 1, 144. Wax was

(the boundary stone) was anointed;[1] upon Pales milk was poured, etc.[2]

Native Greek and Roman evidence has led us to these conclusions. Let us glance at funeral practices of the older civilisations in Egypt and Babylonia. In the Egyptian ritual of embalming, the dead who had been dried up,[3] i.e. reduced virtually to skin and bone by means less drastic than fire, was, in the oils and aromatic exudations that were used, believed to receive life and renewal of his body. He was identified with Osiris, e.g. 'O Osiris N, thou hast received an aromatic that makes thy limbs (or members) perfect. Thou art receiving the source [of life].... It comes to thee, the anointing to create thy limbs...it enters into thee, the sweat of the gods, the virtues of Ra penetrate into thy limbs',[4] or again: 'Behold, thou art anointed, O Osiris N; thou hast received this oil, thou hast received this liquid, thou hast received this fluid of life'.[5] This corresponds to the wine and grease, oil or fat, put around the bones of Homer's heroes before burial and the similar attentions to the Roman dead. There were also libations made at the tomb, and the Pyramid texts tell us unequivocally what was their significance: e.g. 'These thy libations, Osiris!... I offer thee the moisture that has issued from thee that thy heart may not be still (i.e. may not be motionless, may live), possessing it' or 'The offering of libations. Thy water belongs

---

naturally used as fat, a life-substance (cf. p. 287). Its appearance of generating a multitude of bees (cf. p. 207) suggests that *cera* κηρός originally meant 'generative' substance, cf. *cereo, cerus* (p. 125), possibly κήρ (p. 405, n. 8 *fin.*), also 'wax' (p. 238, n. 1). Cf. *sine concubitu textis apis excita ceris* (Petron. Fr. 26, 7 Buech.). The young appears at first *adhaerens ita ut pars cerae videatur* (Plin. *N.H.* xi, 16, 48) and it was commonly believed that bees neither copulate nor give birth (e.g. Aristot. *H.A.* 553; Virg. *G.* iv, 198f.).

[1] See Siculus Flaccus, *de Cond. Agr.* p. 441, ed. Lachm., and, for the anointing of the *genius*, Tib. ii, 2, 5f. Belief that fat was life-substance perhaps lies behind the old Norse practice of smearing the gods with it at a sacrifice (*disablót*). See *Frithj-saga* ix, Du Chaillon, *Vik. Age*, i, pp. 375f. Cf. p. 476, n. 1 *inf.*

[2] See Tib. i, 1, 36; Ov. *F.* iv, 746.   [3] See pp. 254 ff.

[4] See 'Le Rituel de l'Embaumement', in *Mémoire sur quelques Papyrus du Louvre*, by Maspero—*Notices et Extraits, etc.*, xxiv, p. 18.

[5] *Ibid.* p. 20.

to thee, thy flood belongs to thee, the fluid that issued from the god, the exudations that issued from Osiris'.[1] Reviewing these and others, Blackman says: 'The general meaning of these passages is quite clear. The corpse of the deceased is dry and shrivelled. To revivify it, the vital fluids that have exuded from it must be restored, for not till then will life return and the heart beat again'.[2]

Incense was burned to the gods with a like meaning. It is 'the incense of the god which has issued from him and the odour of the fluid which has issued from his flesh, the sweat of the god which has fallen to the ground, which he has given to all gods.... If it lives, the Rekhyt lives, thy flesh lives, thy flesh lives, thy members are vigorous'.[3] Discussing this and other passages, Blackman says: 'Like the body of the dead, that of the god too is conceived of as shrivelled and dry and needing its moisture restored to it, which is we see accomplished by fumigating him with "living" incense, the grains of which are the crystallised exudations from a divine body'.[4] Incense was also in the Middle Kingdom burned for the dead. Thus: 'Her head is fumigated with incense. This N is vigorous by means of incense. The god's dew [approaches] towards thy flesh'.[5] In the Pyramid Texts incense is used for purification, but also the dead can thereby 'enter into communion with certain gods who are accompanied by their Kas and, apparently, he can at the same time be reunited with his own Ka'.[6] The Ka was very like the ψυχή or *genius* (see p. 495).

In Babylonia it is much the same. There a kind of embalming was practised, but also in a number of burials a use of fire,

---

[1] See 'The Significance of Incense and Libations in Funerary and Temple Ritual', by A. M. Blackman, *Zeitschrift für ägyptische Sprache und Altertumskunde*, L, 1912, pp. 69 f.

[2] *Ibid.* p. 71. This is strikingly shown in the tale of *The Two Brothers*.

[3] Ritual of Amen, XII, 7, quoted by Blackman, p. 72.   [4] *Ibid.* p. 73.

[5] *Ibid.* It needs to be said that 'purity' and 'holiness', in Egypt as elsewhere, meant more than a negative absence of defilement: the positive 'wholeness' of vital power (cf. pp. 109 with n. 4, 477, n. 2, and ἱερός, 'strong', 'holy'); and 'purification' or 'washing' was a bestowal of new life, vital power (cf. pp. 189 f., 209 ff., 221 f., 271 ff.). Pollution meant loss of it.   [6] *Ibid.* pp. 74 f.

which seems to have had the same object as that discovered for Greece and Italy, i.e. the 'drying' rather than the destruction of the body. The body was enclosed in clay and the fire applied to the latter.[1] In other cases, as later in Greece and Italy, there was complete cremation. But in all cases it is clear that the need of the dead was water. Often cisterns were provided in the grave itself. Archaeologists have recognised that the form of the baths in which bodies were placed in late Minoan burials was just that of the baths used for that purpose in Babylonia. But there the essence of the service of the dead was to 'pour water'. The festival of all souls was called *kianag*, 'place where one gives to drink', but 'the notion of "place" is often lost and the idea of drinking is made to cover sacrifices of animals, bread, cakes, etc. as well as liquors'.[2] In Greece and Rome[3] food contributed to the liquid of life and he who lacked food 'dried up'. This perhaps is why, in Spartan and Boeotian grave-reliefs,[4] the 'hero' holds out a cup, though the offerings actually brought are a cock and something which may be a cake, an egg or a fruit, and why *libare* was used of such offerings. In Babylonia this service of the dead fell to the nearest kinsman, so that he was known as a man's 'pourer of water' and we get the form of curse: 'May God deprive him of an heir and a pourer of water'. Asurbanipal tells how to his slain enemies he 'denied the Dirge of the Water-pourer' and how he ravaged the tombs of the kings of Elam: 'Their bones I carried with me to Assyria, unrest laid I on their shades and cut them off from the funerary rites of libation'.[5] On the other hand it is the reward of the man who dies in battle that he 'on a pillow reposeth drinking pure water',[6] and the prayer

[1] See e.g. R. Koldewey, *Zeitschr. f. Assyriologie*, 1887, p. 403.
[2] S. Langdon, s.v. Death and Disposal of the Dead (Babylonia) in Hastings' *Encyclopaedia of Religion and Ethics*.
[3] Pp. 221 ff.
[4] See e.g. *Ath. Mitt.* 1877, pl. XXII; Wolters, *Archäol. Zeitung*, 1882, pp. 299 ff. and Miss Harrison's *Myth. and Mon. of Ancient Athens*, p. 590.
[5] See *The Babylonian Conception of Heaven and Hell*, by A. Jeremias (trans. J. Hutchison), pp. 14 f.
[6] See *ibid.* p. 39.

that the stranger will respect the remains of the dead asks 'may his kindness be recompensed. Above may his name be blessed; below may his soul drink clear water'.[1] Why this stress upon water for the dead? Because for plants and men water is life, life is water. A lament for young Tammuz dead runs: 'Thou, O shepherd, art a seed-corn that drank no water in the furrow, whose germ bore no fruit in the field, a young sapling that has not been planted by the water course,[2] a sapling whose root has been cut, a plant that drank no water in the furrow'.[3] And how can the dead have life except by water? The question is asked and answered in the *Journey of Ištar through Hades*, through 'the land without return'. The goddess goes down through the seven doors and suffers the fate of the dead and is held fast by the Queen of the Underworld, Ereškigal, but at last the other gods send and compel the latter to restore her to the world of life. How? She says to her servant Namtar: 'Pour upon the goddess Ištar the water of life and send her away'. The water was poured upon Ištar and she returned.[4]

In the Babylonian funeral ceremonies with the sprinkling of water there was also the burning of incense[5] (cf. Egypt and Rome). The dead were believed to inhale the incense of offerings.[6] We have seen the belief that Tyrian Herakles was restored to life by the κνίση of a sacrificial quail. For the gods, also, men poured libation (e.g. 'To the gods of heaven I offer water'[7]) and burned animals and incense offerings. Reference to libations of oil and wine is most frequent; and even as the stones whereon the Neleid dynasty sat were anointed,[8] so it was customary in Babylonia to anoint inscribed stones. Referring to the pouring of oil thus and the burning of frankincense

---

[1] See A. Jeremias, *Handbuch der altorientalischen Geisteskultur*, p. 319.
[2] Cf. the Sumerian idiogram for 'life' (ZI): a reed growing by running water.
[3] See A. Jeremias, *The Babylonian Conception of Heaven etc.*, p. 10.
[4] *Ibid.* p. 45.
[5] See M. Jastrow, *The Religion of Babylonia and Assyria*, p. 603.
[6] See *ibid.* pp. 575, 579.
[7] Quoted *ibid.* p. 285; cf. p. 281.
[8] See pp. 280f.

in a temple, Jastrow notes that 'Much importance was attached to this rite and the kings take frequent occasion to adjure their successors...to anoint these stones with oil and offer sacrifices'.[1]

It was thus that Jacob anointed the stone 'Beth-el'. The essential equivalence of oil and animal fat has been seen. For the ancient Hebrews not only the blood but also the fat was holy.[2] The fat of an animal might not be eaten under any circumstances. When the animal died not by the hand of man, the fat might be used for any purpose except eating. If the animal were killed by man, the fat had to be burned to Yahweh. Though early referred merely to light or the symbolism of light, the offering of 'candles'—often by day—is in fact an offering of oil or fat and the same ideas may lie behind.[3]

Youth, the fullness of life and strength, was identified with the marrow, the moisture, in the bones.[4] It was dew (Job xx, 11; xxi, 24; Ps. cx, 3). The 'strength is dried up' (Ps. xxii, 15). 'Dry bones' express complete death, the absence of life (Ezek. xxxvii). But 'thy dead shall live; my dead bodies shall arise. Awake and sing, ye that dwell in the dust: for thy dew is as the dew of herbs, and the earth shall cast forth the dead' (Isai. xxvi, 19; cf. Ps. cxxxiii, 3, etc.).[5] In the Kabbalah the

[1] *Op. cit.* p. 664.

[2] See e.g. Lev. iii, 16f.; Num. vii, 22f. The Jewish view of wine (pp. 217, n. 2, 234f.) and oil or unguent (pp. 188ff.) as life-stuff helps to explain how the Apostles 'anointed with oil many that were sick and healed them' (Mark vi, 13; James v, 14), why the Samaritan 'poured oil and wine' on the wounds (Luke x, 34; cf. p. 235), why precious ointment was poured on the head before burial (Matt. xxvi, 7ff.), 100 pounds' weight of myrrh and aloes on the whole body (John xix, 39f.).

[3] The fat is clearly equated to life-substance in the practice of sticking pins into a candle and burning it before a saint in the belief that one's enemy's life is consumed thus; see e.g. M. A. Murray, *The God of the Witches*, p. 156 and cf. Theoc. II, 28f., etc. For wax cf. p. 282 (n. 9).

[4] Cf. pp. 213ff.

[5] For resurrection see also Deut. xxxii, 39; I Sam. ii, 6; Hosea vi, 1f., xiii, 14; Dan. xii, 2; Ezek. xxxvii, 1ff. The thought here traced explains the words attributed to Jesus in John iv, 10ff., vii, 37ff. Cf. iii, 5, etc., and, for baptism, pp. 188ff., 290. Resurrection was also rebirth (Coloss. i, 18; Rev. i, 5; cf. p. 269). Not all believed. Cf. Job xiv, 7ff.

dead are restored to life by the 'dew' (i.e. marrow or liquid) of the head of the deity:[1] 'In that skull distilleth the dew from the White Head which is ever filled therewith; and from that dew are the dead raised unto life'.[2] Rabbinic tradition[3] taught that in the grave, while the rest of the body perishes, the lower end of the spine remains (known as *Luz*), which when the dew falls upon it will become a complete body again and live. Thus is solved the mystery of the Resurrection of the Body. Hell-fire (named from Gehenna) may now be seen to mean extremity in death, in that unhappy dryness (cf. p. 258, n. 5). It is contrasted with the water of life, which is with God (Ps. xxxvi, 9), coming out from his throne (Rev. xxii, 1, 17).[4] So Dives' burning torment and need for water (Luke xvi, 24). In the judgement after death the reward of the righteous is the water of life, and the part of sinners 'shall be in the lake that burneth with fire and brimstone, which is the second death' (Rev. xxi, 6–9; cf. xx, 14f., vii, 17).

Not less illuminating is the Mohammedan view. In the Koran we read that 'God created every beast from water'.[5] Like the Rabbinic teaching is the doctrine that in the grave the earth consumes the whole of the body except the bone *al Ajb*, the bottom of the spine, which will remain till the blast of resurrection.[6] 'For this birth the earth will be prepared by the rain above mentioned which is to fall continually for forty years and will resemble the seed of a man and be supplied from the water under the throne of God which is called living water; by the efficacy and virtue of which the dead bodies

[1] See p. 144. Professor Cornford has drawn my attention to Hippol. *Ref. Haer.* v, 17 (Peratae) likening God the Father to the *cerebrum* and the Son to the *cerebellum* which μεταδίδωσι τῇ Ὕλῃ τὰς ἰδέας, τοῦτ' ἔστιν ἐπὶ τὸν νωτιαῖον μυελὸν διαρρέει τὰ σπέρματα καὶ τὰ γένη τῶν γεννωμένων.

[2] *Ha Idra Rabba Qadisha*, xxvii, § 546, trans. Mathers, *op. cit.* p. 178. Cf. *ibid.* iv, § 45, p. 116. See also *Pirke de Rabbi Eliezer* xxxiv.

[3] See e.g. the evidence collected by Pocock in his notes to *Porta Mosis* (portions of Maimonides), p. 117, and Kohler, *Jewish Theology*, p. 288. It is worth noting that this (*Luz*) was the ἱερὸν ὀστέον (pp. 207f.).

[4] Knowledge of this belief in the East explains Plaut. *Trin.* 940.

[5] Chap. xxiv, 44 (Palmer's translation).

[6] See Pocock, *op. cit.* pp. 255f.

shall spring forth from their graves as they did in their mother's womb or as corn sprouts forth by common rain, till they become perfect; after which breath will be breathed into them and they will sleep in their sepulchres till they are raised to life at the last trump.'[1] Then, when they are judged, those believers whose evil actions outweigh the good are said to be scorched for a time in hell, but, according to some, Mohammed taught that 'while they continue in hell they shall be deprived of life or (as his words are otherwise interpreted) be cast into a most profound sleep that they may be the less sensible of their torments; and that they shall afterwards be received into paradise and there revive on their being washed with the water of life'.[2]

Thus in this thought, that life is liquid, and the dead are dry we have found the reason for the widespread conception of a 'water of life'. It appears in Greece in the legend of Glaukos, who obtained immortality from the ἀθάνατος πηγή,[3] and in Euripides' account of the Garden of the Hesperides at the western edge of the world, where 'flow immortal springs (κρῆναι ἀμβρόσιαι) by the bridal-couches (κοῖται) of the halls of Zeus, where Earth divine, life-giving, increaseth felicity for the gods'.[4] The same thought will explain the legends of rejuvenation of the aged by 'boiling'. It is by an infusion of the liquid of life, of αἰών into a man, when his own is nearly exhausted (cf. αἰονάω).[5] Medea 'forthwith made Aison a dear youth at puberty (θῆκε φίλον κόρον ἡβώοντα) after

[1] Sale in 'The Preliminary Discourse' (to the Koran), Sect. IV (p. 65 in Warne's edition). Cf. πρωτότοκος ἐκ τῶν νεκρῶν, Coloss. i, 18.

[2] Sale, op. cit. p. 72.

[3] See schol. Plato, Rep. x, 421 B. 'Immortal water' (ἀθάνατο νερό) is common in modern Greek folk-tales, see e.g. Lawson, op. cit. p. 281.

[4] Hippol. 742–51. See p. 295 below and Epig. Gr. 366, 5 f. (Kaibel).

[5] See pp. 208 f. Among the ancient Irish there was similar belief in the restoration of life and strength by infusion of liquid. Thus in the Táin Bó Cúalnge (4426 ff., ed. Windisch) the wounded Cethern is placed in a 'marrow-vat' (smir-ammair) for three days and three nights absorbing the 'marrow' and then emerges in strength. For the Irish view of marrow see p. 191. In the story of Branwen in the Mabinogion the Irish warriors were restored even after death, if put into the 'caldron of renovation'.

peeling away (ἀποξύσασα) old age with knowing mind, boiling many drugs in (ἐπί) golden caldrons'.[1] Life-liquid at its full is restored to him. In some forms of the legend, possibly in this, the liquid is drunk.[2] The same thought will help us also to understand 'baptism', not mere washing but the infusion of water, new life.[3] We may also recall Herodotus' story of the 'long-lived Aethiopians' who, when visited by messengers from the Persians and told that the Persians lived on corn and wine, said that the wine must be responsible for such length of life as the Persians enjoyed and 'when the messengers showed surprise at the length of life of their hosts, led them to a fountain, and, when they washed with water therefrom, they became sleeker, as if it were olive-oil'. 'It would', says Herodotus, 'be because of this water, by using it for everything (τοῦτο τὰ πάντα χρεώμενοι), that they were long-lived (μακρόβιοι).'[4]

Much as I suggested[5] for the Homeric practice of scorching, 'drying', the dead body by fire and then putting the dry bones in wine and grease, it was believed in late classical antiquity and the middle ages that the Eagle, when he has become old

[1] The author of the Νόστοι, vi (Allen). For other reff. see e.g. the Hypoth. to Euripides' *Medea*, and Gruppe, *op. cit.* p. 546₁. The suggestion of sloughing (cf. pp. 430 f.) appears in the Gilgamish epic, where at an enchanted fountain the hero's leprous skin is removed and his whole body made once more sound and healthy. In the same place he found also a plant whereof whosoever ate regained the strength of his youth.

[2] See Gruppe, *loc. cit.* The 'water of life' in the Ištar legend could also be drunk. The messenger of the gods asks Ereškigal that he may drink it.

[3] Cf. pp. 272, n. 8, 284, n. 5, 287, 493. Baptism 'in the language of the world is called Life' (*Rituale Armenorum*, ed. F. C. Conybeare and Maclean, p. 106). Like the 'boiling', baptism might also be conceived as rebirth (see pp. 189, n. 2; 287). In the *Havamal* (158): 'This I can make sure when I suffuse a young boy with water: he shall not fall when he fights in the host' (cf. Achilles in Styx). See also p. 476, n. 1. Magic unguent or liquid infused or drunk that transforms one into a new shape (e.g. *Od.* x, 234 ff., 392 ff.) was perhaps originally thought of as liquid or seed of the new life. Cf. pp. 188 f., 228, n. 1.

[4] III, 22 f.

[5] Pp. 256 ff., 271 f.

and his strength is nearly gone, seeks out an ever-flowing well
and from it flies upwards till he comes to the sun:

> Scorched are his feathers all
> And downwards he needs must fall
> E'en to the well's deep ground,
> Where he waxeth both whole and sound
> And cometh forth all anew,

and that the Adder, when his strength fails in old age, gets rid
of his skin by fasting and creeping through a narrow hole, spits
out his venom and, having come to water,

> When he his fill hath ta'en,
> Then is he renewed again.[1]

That water is life is nowhere more strikingly illustrated
than in the actual experience of frogs in Mediterranean and
similar climes. There is a hymn in the *Rig Veda* about their
reawakening after the dry season: 'When the waters from
the sky fall upon them as they lie like a dried skin in the
(dried up) pond, the voice of the frogs rises in concert like
the lowing of cows which have calves.'[2] This helps us to
understand why the frog was a symbol of resurrection.

[1] From the *Bestiary*, ed. by Morris (Early English Text Society, Vol.
XLIX), a version of the *Physiologus*. I have taken this modernisation from
Miss J. L. Weston's *The Chief Middle English Poets*, pp. 325 f. See *Physiologus*,
ed. Sbordone, pp. 22 f., 38 ff. Its emerging new from its old skin is one
reason why the form of a snake would seem appropriate to the immortal
soul (see pp. 206 f.), but lizards, crabs and lobsters do likewise. Dwelling
in the earth also is a characteristic not peculiar to snakes. The deer,
which sheds its horns, was believed to renew its life by swallowing a
snake, then water (see *Physiologus*, ed. F. Sbordone, pp. 171 f.), i.e. by receiving, as we may now guess, a new life-soul (cf. p. 170, n. 2) and new
life-fluid. That perhaps is why it breathes the serpent in through its
nostrils (cf. pp. 103 ff., 205): *cervinus gelidum sorbet sic halitus anguem*
(Mart. XII, 28 (29), 5; cf. Ael. *Nat. An.* II, 9 and Lucr. VI, 764 f. (p. 265)).
So the virtue of *cervi pasti serpente medullā*, Lucan VI, 673. Cf. 753 on p. 149
with pp. 206 f.

[2] VII, 103, 2 (J. Muir, *Orig. Sanscr. Texts*, V, p. 431).

CHAPTER XI

Nectar and Ambrosia

What was ambrosia? Bergk[1] and Roscher[2] with Gruppe[3] and other scholars following them have explained that it was the early interpretation of wild honey. But against this there are many reasons. Wild honey, which is in point, must have been familiar from immemorial antiquity to the Indo-European peoples and it has its own names. The same holds for non-Indo-European peoples in the Mediterranean basin. Ambrosia, unlike such honey, is the stuff of immortality and is not available for men. Honey is freely eaten by mortals. It is stored in vessels[4] and used by the Homeric warriors as a normal article with cheese and wine.[5] So too beeswax. Odysseus had a 'huge wheel' of it on board.[6] So far from being thought to belong peculiarly to the gods, honey is not offered to them or associated with them in any way in either Homer or Hesiod. Wernicke,[7] arguing that ambrosia is food, asks, 'What else can it be but a kind of bread?' But against this there are the same objections; and ambrosia is used in ways unthinkable for anything bread-like. The adjective ἀμβρόσιος shows that ἀμβροσία was expressive of immortality. It is, like αἰών, concrete, the stuff of immortal life. Putting wine and nectar on one side for the moment, what in fact was the stuff of life, as the earliest Greeks conceived it, and what did they think

---

[1] *Kl. Philol. Schr.* II, pp. 669 ff.

[2] *Nektar u. Ambrosia*, 1883, Leipzig, and s.v. in his *Lexicon*.

[3] *Griech. Myth. u. Religionsgesch.* p. 8194. That honey figures in some of the later legends, e.g. as the food of the infant Zeus, does not show that it was the origin of ambrosia. It is eminently suitable for children, and Roscher recognises that the Greeks gave it to such. Milk, which in other versions was the food of Zeus, has as good a claim. Ambrosia was used as an unguent or as a cleansing application. Honey is not convenient and was never in common use as either. For honey on the pyre see p. 298, n. 8.

[4] *Il.* XXIII, 170 f.   [5] *Il.* XI, 624; *Od.* X, 234, 316, XX, 69.

[6] *Od.* XII, 173.   [7] In Pauly-Wissowa's *Realencykl.* s.v.

was the proper nourishment for the gods? These are the questions that should be asked and, as we have seen,[1] they have one answer—the liquefiable grease (marrow and fat) with the analogous vegetable sap, olive-oil, as alternative. It was this that was offered to the gods, ἄλειφα, ἄλειφαρ, 'stuff for anointing'. Ambrosia is, I suggest, just the divine counterpart to this.

What are Homer's references to ambrosia? Once[2] certainly and once[3] almost certainly ambrosia is said to be 'eaten' by a god, when nectar is drunk. This in a later age begot the idea that ambrosia was solid, as nectar liquid, nourishment; but the other clear Homeric evidence implies that ambrosia was of a fluid or melting nature, and we can achieve consistency only by thinking of it as fat or oil that might be eaten as we 'eat' oil, soup, or butter, or as Prince Astyanax, privileged with the ideal diet, 'ate exclusively marrow and fat'.[4] Ambrosia is used by Hera as a cleansing substance on her own body;[5] by the gods to anoint the body of Sarpedon[6] after washing it, as men anoint with oil or fat (ἄλειφαρ), after washing, themselves or the bodies of the dead;[7] by Thetis to 'drip' with nectar into the nostrils of Patroklos to keep his flesh uncorrupted and fresh, when 'the αἰών has perished therefrom';[8] and by Athene to 'drip' with nectar into the chest of Achilles to save him from the effects of fasting.[9] Polyphemos declares that the wine given to him by Odysseus 'is a drop ("effluent", ἀπορρώξ; cf. *Od.* x, 514; *Il.* II, 755) of nectar and ambrosia'.[10] In the Homeric Hymn to Apollo[11] it appears to be liquid yet 'eaten', and the Homeric Hymn to Aphrodite[12] suggests that it was liquid nourishment, as does also Sappho;[13] while in the Homeric Hymn to Demeter[14] the goddess nourishes the infant Demophon and makes him grow 'not with corn to eat or milk' taken

[1] See pp. 187 ff., 205 ff., 271, 279 ff.   [2] *Od.* v, 93 f.
[3] *Od.* v, 199.   [4] See p. 280.
[5] *Il.* xiv, 170.   [6] *Il.* xvi, 669 f., 679 f.
[7] See e.g. *Od.* xxiv, 44 f.   [8] *Il.* xix, 26, 38 f.
[9] *Il.* xix, 347 f.   [10] *Od.* ix, 359.
[11] Ll. 123 ff. (ἐπήρξατο yet κατέβρως ἄμβροτον εἶδαρ).
[12] Ll. 231 f.; cf. l. 206 for nectar.
[13] Fr. 51 (Bgk.). See below, pp. 296 f.   [14] Ll. 235 ff.

through the lips but by 'anointing (χρίεσκε) him with ambrosia', just as according to our earlier argument by anointing with grease or oil the liquid of life was believed to be infused through the skin.[1] Ambrosia gives off a pleasant smell[2] just as do fat[3] and oil.[4]

If we must think of ambrosia as a divine counterpart to the ἄλειφαρ possessed by men, i.e. to animal grease or its equivalent, olive-oil, we may ask 'Did the Homeric Greeks eat olives or olive-oil?' This has been denied[5] on the ground that there is no reference to such a practice. But the argument from silence is inconclusive. It is difficult to believe that olives and olive-oil were possessed but not tasted and there is perhaps unrecognised positive evidence. To torment Tantalus, over his head 'tall trees hung their fruit, pear-trees and pomegranates and apple-trees with bright fruit and sweet fig-trees and blooming olive-trees, which when the old man reached out his hands to clutch them, the wind tossed to the shadowing clouds'.[6] It is clear, surely, that olives were a fruit he wished to eat. Also after cleansing her skin with ambrosia, Hera 'anointed herself with ambrosial olive-oil, εδανός, fragrant',[7] and the line recurs of Aphrodite in the Homeric Hymn[8] in her honour. εδανός is taken by the scholiasts and grammarians, and by modern scholars following them, as belonging to ἡδύς, ἥδομαι, and so they say it ought to be aspirated and it means 'sweet'. It would, however, make at least as good sense and be at least as natural a formation if it meant 'fit to eat, edible' from ἔδω, as στεγανός from στέγω, ἱκανός from ἵκω, etc. For the meaning 'sweet', a meaning which should be common, there is no parallel or confirmation, whereas in Aeschylus, who is earlier and more 'Homeric' than the grammarians, ἐδανός occurs in just this sense of 'edible'.[9] In the historic period it was, as we might expect, the best olive-oil that was

---

[1] See pp. 209 ff. Cf. Virgil, *Georg.* IV, 415–18.   [2] *Od.* IV, 445.
[3] E.g. *Il.* VIII, 549 f.; *Od.* X, 10.
[4] *Od.* II, 339; cf. *Il.* XIV, 171 ff. discussed below.
[5] See e.g. Seymour, *Life in the Homeric Age*, pp. 216, 335.
[6] *Od.* XI, 588 ff.   [7] *Il.* XIV, 170 ff.
[8] 61 ff. The MSS. have ἐανῶ, ἑανῶ.   [9] *Ag.* 1407.

reserved for eating, the second best that was used as unguent.[1]
There would thus be natural point in saying that the oil used
by the goddess as unguent was fit to be eaten, i.e. was of the
best quality.

Whence did the gods get ambrosia? If the question were
raised, the simplest answer would be that somewhere in-
accessible to ordinary mortals it flowed forth or it grew as a
plant with oily sap like the olive or myrrh. Homer tells us no
more about it except that the river-god Simoeis 'made
ambrosia come up (ἀνέτειλε) for the horses of Hera to feed
upon[2] (νέμεσθαι, "range over") and that doves brought ambrosia to Zeus by way of the Πλαγκταί',[3] the way back for
Odysseus from Okeanos and the underworld. What picture
was in Homer's imagination it is hard to say. The divine
horses may, like the gods themselves, have partaken of liquid
ambrosia or again it might be a plant. Late writers gave
the name to various plants. Euripides thought of κρῆναι
ἀμβροσίαι, meaning perhaps 'springs of ambrosia', in the
land of evening at the edge of the world 'by the bridal couches
of the halls of Zeus where Earth divine, life-giving, increaseth
felicity for the gods'.[4] εὐδαιμονία, rendered 'felicity', was
used of abundance of good things. Homer's 'blameless
Aethiopians', to whom Zeus and the other gods went to feast,
dwelt, some where the sun rises and the others where the sun
sets[5] (i.e. in the land of evening), on the river Okeanos[6] at the
edge of the world. In Herodotus' story,[7] whatever its source
and connections, the 'long-lived Aethiopians' had not only
the 'table of the Sun' ever replenished, being a meadow full
of the boiled flesh of all manner of beasts supposed by the
inhabitants to be sent up by Earth, but also a fountain as it
were of oil to which they attributed their long lives.

[1] See e.g. Zimmern, *The Greek Commonwealth*², p. 50.
[2] *Il.* v, 777.
[3] *Od.* xii, 62. Moero, the epic poetess of the third century B.C., made
the doves bring the ambrosia to Zeus ἀπ' Ὠκεανοῖο ῥοάων (Fr. 1
Powell from Athenaeus, 491 B).
[4] See p. 289.   [5] See *Od.* i, 22 ff.
[6] *Il.* i, 423 f.   [7] See p. 290.

There remains nectar. Bergk, Roscher, Gruppe and other scholars have thought that nectar and ambrosia were originally the same thing,[1] honey. But it would be strange to find two names for one imaginary concept or one real substance, and, as we have seen, these two names are used in the same breath by Homer to represent different things. If our line of inquiry be correct, nectar should be the divine equivalent of the other form of nourishment which men thought proper to offer to the gods—wine. It is. The allusions above imply that it was liquid. Like wine it is 'mixed' in a κρατήρ and it is poured out like wine (οἰνοχόει) for the feasting gods[2] and they drink it and pledge each other in it as men do with wine.[3] Unmixed wine is sometimes described as 'red',[4] ἐρυθρός, and twice[5] we hear of νέκταρ ἐρυθρόν.

Thus all the Homeric evidence for ambrosia and nectar is satisfied. Without the clue, that evidence is confusing and appears contradictory, and centuries later, when the original conceptions had faded in popular belief, it might well lead to misunderstanding. Polyphemos' praise of the wonderful wine offered by Odysseus as a 'drop of nectar and ambrosia' does not imply that both were conceived as wines, but at most that they were liquids or might be combined in a liquid most pleasant to taste.[6] In Sappho's reference to a libation of ambrosia at a marriage[7] κρατήρ and οἰνοχοῆσαι suggest wine;

---

[1] For the references see p. 292.
[2] Il. i, 598, iv, 3; Od. v, 93 f. Cf. Hymn to Aphrodite, 206.
[3] Il. iv, 3 f. Cf. Hymn to Apollo, 10 f.
[4] E.g. Od. v, 165. Honey on the other hand was χλωρόν (Il. xi, 631; Od. x, 234; cf. Hymn to Hermes, 560).
[5] Il. xix, 38; Od. v, 93.   [6] See note 6 on p. 298.
[7] Fr. 51 (Bgk.). Hermes was peculiarly associated with the ψυχή (pp. 122, 253). Athenaeus, who preserves this fragment, elsewhere (xi, 46, 473) preserves for us not only a fragment of Strattis (22 Kock), which shows that Hermes was himself identified with a real liquid in cult: 'Hermes whom some draw from a little ewer (προχοίδιον), others mixed half and half from a καδίσκος', but also a fragment of Anticlides (13 Müll.) which tells us that the καδίσκος (which stood for Zeus Ktesios, a similar deity) should contain ambrosia and that this meant 'pure water and olive oil and παγκαρπία', which last is the same as πανσπερμία, a collection of seeds. Though this is not the original ambrosia, an imaginary substance beyond the reach of men, it is still a life-substance in harmony with the

but it is striking that nevertheless the vessel then used by Hermes is not one associated with wine (κύαθος, etc.) but ὄλπις, which appears normally to have meant an oil flask as when on the similar occasion—Helen's wedding—the Spartan maids in Theocritus say they will go to the tree of Helen and pour libation, 'drip liquid ἄλειφαρ from a silver ὄλπις'.[1] Elsewhere, Sappho says: 'Come, Cyprian, in golden κύλικες pouring (οἰνοχοεῦσα) nectar mixed for the banquet',[2] i.e. as the wine. While Homer's other references to ambrosia as liquid and the hyperbole of Polyphemos explain her reference to ambrosia, Hesiod's lines 'nectar and ambrosia which the gods themselves eat'[3] (τά περ θεοὶ αὐτοὶ ἔδουσι) and (of the perjured god) 'he goes not ever near ambrosia and nectar to eat thereof (οὐδέ ποτ' ἀμβροσίης καὶ νέκταρος ἔρχεται ἆσσον/ βρώσιος) but lies breathless and speechless…'[4] might suggest that nectar was 'eaten' rather than 'drunk'; but they do not imply it any more than that is implied for water or milk in such expressions as 'bread and water, the food of gaolbirds' or 'they shall eat milk and honey all their days'. When, however, the idea of nectar had become vague and people were dependent upon such 'fossils' in literature, the false inference might easily be made. It is also possible that, as later generations represented ambrosia as oil enriched with other ingredients,[5] so they thought nectar was wine enriched with other ingredients, what was in fact a familiar drink, κυκεών. Such a κυκεών, in which cheese, barley, and honey are mixed in with the wine, is said to be 'drunk' (ἔκπιον) and yet called 'food' (σῖτος) even by Homer.[6] There is preserved for us a fragment of Alcman,[7] νέκταρ ἔδμεναι, which the context might have shown could be explained as Hesiod's lines can, but which is set by

thought here traced. With or instead of the grease offered to the gods by men (to which we have related ambrosia) there were barley-grains, οὐλαί, οὐλοχύται. Cf. pp. 228, 279, also the κυκεών of the Mysteries, p. 274, n. 2 above and 'wheat and barley-groats, the marrow of men', p. 222.

[1] XVIII, 46 f.
[3] *Theog.* 640.
[5] See note 7 on p. 296.
[6] *Od.* X, 234 ff. Cf. *Il.* XI, 638 ff.

[2] Fr. 5 (Bgk.).
[4] *Theog.* 796 f.

[7] Fr. 100 (Bgk.).

Athenaeus¹ in the second century A.D. beside the unequivocal lines of Anaxandrides (fourth century B.C.) : τὸ νέκταρ ἐσθίω πάνυ/μάττων διαπίνω τ' ἀμβροσίαν. It was natural that the two forms of divine nourishment should be interpreted as food and drink, and here the transition of meaning in each of the two terms, the temptations towards which we have seen, is complete and Homer's scheme is reversed. This later exchange of functions has fostered the idea that nectar and ambrosia were originally the same thing, but the Homeric evidence is much the fullest and the nearest in time to any origin and it differentiates, as we have seen, quite clearly between the functions of the two substances so named. That difference between the oil or grease-like ambrosia and the wine-like nectar is maintained by the Homeric Hymns and indeed seems general. Thus for Aristophanes ambrosia is 'poured'² (κατασπένδειν) yet it is eaten (σιτεῖσθαι,³ φαγεῖν,⁴ λείχειν⁵), while wine is described as 'nectar-dropping' (νεκταρο-σταγής).⁶ Other terms⁷ for real objects completely changed their meaning after the time of Homer. With nectar and ambrosia the different interpretation is the exception (all the relative evidence has been quoted) and there are factors conducing to just such misunderstanding.

We have related ambrosia not only to the ἀλοιφή, ἄλειφαρ, offered by men to the gods but also to that put with the bones of the dead; and we have related nectar not only to the wine offered by men to the gods but also to that put with or poured out for the bones or ψυχή of the dead.⁸ The name ἀμβροσία

---

¹ II, 39 A (=Anax., Fr. 57, Kock). Cf. Eustath. 1633, 1 (ad Od. IX, 359).

² Knights, 1094 f. ³ Peace, 724.

⁴ Peace, 852. ⁵ Peace, 854.

⁶ Fr. 563. Polyphemos' hyperbole also recurs: truce-libations (σπονδαί) 'have the smell of ambrosia and nectar' (Ach. 196).

⁷ See pp. 24, 39. For the blood of the gods and an explanation of βρότος see Addendum VI, pp. 506 f.

⁸ Honey appears in relation to the dead. 'For all the dead' Odysseus 'poured a pouring (χοήν), first with honey-mixture (honey with? water or milk or wine, μελικρήτῳ), then with sweet wine, and the third time with water and sprinkled white barley-groats thereon' (Od. XI, 26 ff.). One cannot be sure of the significance of what is burned with the body on the pyre; but it is worthy of note that, with the carcases of animals

is expressive of immortal life; the name νέκταρ should be related to νέκυς, which signifies either the body or the ψυχή after death. With νέκυς all other Greek words beginning with νεκ- are unmistakably connected. Ambrosia is the oily or greasy and nectar the watery liquid of life. In old Persian belief the food of immortality consisted of sap of the heavenly *haoma* (like the juice of the vine) and the marrow of the ox killed by *Saošyant*.[1] Later, Mithraism taught that the god will come to earth and the dead arise from their graves and he will sacrifice the divine bull and mixing its fat with the holy wine, will offer to the righteous the cup of eternal life.[2] The same elements may be seen in Christian Baptism. Water and oil were used in early forms of the rite. Thus in the Gotho-Gallican rite: 'Holy Lord, Almighty Father, Initiator of the Saints, Father of all unction and author of a new sacrament through thine only Son, our Lord God; Who through the ministry of water…bestowest thine Holy Spirit'. 'While touching with the chrism thou shalt say: "I anoint thee with the unction of holiness, the clothing of immortality, which our Lord Jesus Christ first received, bestowed by the Father, that thou mayest present it entire and undiminished before the judgement seat of Christ and mayest live for ever and ever".'[3]

around it, the body of Patroklos was covered from head to foot with their fat, and vessels of honey and ἄλειφαρ were leaned against the bier before kindling (*Il.* xxiii, 167 ff.). Similarly with Achilles (*Od.* xxiv, 67 f.). Honey appears to have been a substitute for wine where wine was inconvenient. Wine was 'honey-sweet' and honey was mingled with the wine of a κυκεών. Wine would have hindered the fire in its work. It is wine and not honey that Achilles pours out all through the night, calling the ψυχή of Patroklos, while the body burns. It is with wine that the burning is quenched and, when fire has not to be considered, it is wine and not honey that with ἄλειφαρ is used, put with the bones; and the drink which men thought proper to the gods and offered to them with ἄλειφα was not honey but wine.

[1] *Bundahish*, xxx, 25. See also p. 244, n. 1.
[2] See Cumont, *Mystères de Mithra*[2], trans. T. J. McCormick, p. 146.
[3] Quoted by Smith and Cheetham (*Dict. of Christ. Antiqu.*), s.v. Baptism, p. 158. For the chrism as 'life-creating' see p. 189, n. 2. For the water see also pp. 287 ff.

PART III

FATE AND TIME

CHAPTER I

'On the Knees of the Gods'

In Homer, one is struck by the fact that his heroes with all their magnificent vitality and activity feel themselves at every turn not free agents but passive instruments or victims of other powers. It was not merely that they and their foes 'lived dangerously' and life and fortune were precarious possessions. A man felt that he could not help his own actions. An idea, an emotion, an impulse came to him; he acted and presently rejoiced or lamented. Some god had inspired or blinded him. He prospered, then was poor, perhaps enslaved; he wasted away with disease, or died in battle. It was divinely ordained (θέσφατον), his portion (αἶσα, μοῖρα) appointed long before. The prophet or diviner might discover it in advance; the plain man knew a little about omens and, merely seeing his shaft miss its mark or the enemy prevailing, concluded that Zeus had assigned defeat to himself and his comrades. He did not wait to fight further but fled.[1] What are the details of this fatalism? A good deal is clear for him who runs to read—uses of αἶσα, μοῖρα, μόρος, μόρσιμον, ὑπὲρ μόρον, θέσφατον, etc. But there are other expressions the significance of which lies deeper.

ταῦτα θεῶν ἐν γούνασι κεῖται (*Il.* XVII, 514, XX, 435; *Od.* I, 267, 400, XVI, 129)—'It lies on the knees of the gods'. This famous phrase, still current, is a picturesque way of saying that some issue rests with a higher power whose will is not yet known. While this, its general significance, is clear, its origin is lapped in obscurity. Ancient scholiasts and modern scholars[2]

---

[1] See e.g. note 8, p. 187, and note 2, p. 326. It is the rare and splendid exception when Hector, in face of an omen and its interpretation by Polydamas, cries: 'One omen is best, to defend our fatherland'—εἷς οἰωνὸς ἄριστος ἀμύνεσθαι περὶ πάτρης (*Il.* XII, 243).

[2] More recent attempts upon the problem will be found in *Socrates*, 1914 *init.* (Weniger); E. Schwyzer, 'Die Götterknie—Abrahams Schoss', in Ἀντίδωρον *Festschr. Jak. Wackernagel*, 1923, pp. 283 ff.; R. Meringer, 'Spitze, Winkel, Knie im ursprünglichen Denken', in *Wörter u. Sachen*,

alike have failed to give any satisfactory answer to the question:
'What mental image must be reconstructed to explain why
the gods' *knees* are mentioned?' The ancients were content
to offer various equally inconclusive interpretations, and the
moderns do little more than defend one or other of these.
Whatever their choice, their method, as also that of the
scholiasts, has been to seek the truth in one or other of the
various explicit uses of γούνατα in Homer: as symbols of
strength, as clasped in supplication, or as the lap of the god
whereon gifts were dedicated. There is none other which could
conceivably apply; and, apart from slight modifications of the
above, there remain only two other suggestions—one that of
a scholiast, which for its apparent nonsense has been ignored;
and the other, that hesitatingly supported by Merry and
Riddell[1] on the basis of a παροιμία, which runs: πέντε κριτῶν
ἐν γούνασι κεῖται. It is sufficient to read their applications of
the latter and to examine the paroemiographer's explanation:
παροιμιῶδες, οἷον ἐν ἀλλοτρίᾳ ἐξουσίᾳ εἰσίν. εἴρηται δὲ ἡ
παροιμία παρόσον πέντε κριταὶ τοὺς κωμικοὺς ἔκρινον, ὥς
φησιν Ἐπίχαρμος. σύγκειται οὖν παρὰ τὸ Ὁμηρικόν, θεῶν
ἐν γούνασι κεῖται, ἐπειδὴ οἱ κριταὶ ἐν τοῖς γόνασιν εἶχον ἃ νῦν
εἰς γραμματεῖα γράφεται.[2] If this phrase originated with
reference to the five judges of competitions in comedy,
possibly in the mind of Epicharmus himself (see fr. 229,
Kaibel), it would seem to be later than Homer; while in any
case the paroemiographer's explanation shows that he is
groping after a meaning, and can take refuge only in vagueness.
It appears that instead of explaining, this phrase is rather
derivative from the Homeric figure, and presupposes it, being
a natural parody to suit a particular issue.

There is another way of attack, apparently as yet untried
—namely, to examine the forms under which the Homeric

xi, 1928, pp. 114 ff. (see note 4 on p. 175 above). The significance of the
knees traced above (pp. 174 ff.) does not, I think, throw any new light
upon the phrase. There is no evidence that in the knees was the determining intelligence or that an event could naturally be said to be 'in the
knees' thus.

[1] Note to *Od.* I, 267.   [2] Zenob. III, 64. For writing see p. 6 above.

Greek conceived the gods as controlling the fortunes of men. Direct personal relations, in which the god commands, inspires, or blinds a man, moving on the same plane as it were, are clearly not in point. Some mode of conceiving divine causation in general is required. Μοῖρα and Αἶσα are usually not spoken of in direct relationship with the gods, and where they are they do not appear to throw any light on the present question. In one passage,[1] indeed, Zeus is described as mixing the lives of men from jars on or in the ground, but that does not help. There remains only one other expression, with several kindred phrases that will be considered later. It is ἐπεκλώσαντο θεοί, 'the gods spun', which with slight modifications occurs eight times in Homer: Il. xxiv, 525; Od. i, 17, iii, 208, iv, 208, viii, 579, xi, 139, xvi, 64, xx, 196. Thus in Od. i, 16 the poet describes how Calypso detained Odysseus:

> ἀλλ' ὅτε δὴ ἔτος ἦλθε περιπλομένων ἐνιαυτῶν
> τῷ οἱ ἐπεκλώσαντο θεοὶ οἶκόνδε νέεσθαι
> εἰς Ἰθάκην, οὐδ' ἔνθα πεφυγμένος ἦεν ἀέθλων.

It is the same image that is used of Μοῖρα and Αἶσα, an image which seems to dominate ancient thought concerning the making of fate by the gods. Here on *a priori* grounds the seeker might expect to find the explanation of a phrase, the only certain meaning of which is that the determination of the future rests with the gods. Thus 'Would that it might be mine' says Telemachos 'to avenge the insolence of the suitors', and proceeds:

> ἀλλ' οὔ μοι τοιοῦτον ἐπέκλωσαν θεοὶ ὄλβον,[2]

or, when he is less certain of his fate,

> ἀλλ' ἤτοι μὲν ταῦτα θεῶν ἐν γούνασι κεῖται.[3]

What is the process of spinning? The details of method in any particular age of Greece are by no means clear, and for the Homeric and earlier ages there is virtually no direct evidence. Only thus much is clear, that it was usually done sitting, since so almost always Homer describes the spinners.[4]

---

[1] *Il.* xxiv, 527 ff.   [2] *Od.* iii, 205 ff.
[3] *Od.* xvi, 129. Cf. i, 267.
[4] See *Od.* iv, 123, vi, 52 f., 305 f., vii, 105 f., xvii, 97, xviii, 315 f.

As I have shown elsewhere[1] the instruments used were a basket and a spindle. Under such conditions there are certain essential details which may be accepted from known practices. Since there was no distaff to hold it up, the unspun wool was apparently in the basket to one's left. In any case some of it would be taken by the left hand and with the spindle attached would be spun by the right hand either over the knees or hanging down past the right knee. For this spinning of men's fate Homer uses not only ἐπικλώθειν but also νεῖν and ἐπινεῖν. From this last is formed ἐπίνητρον, an instrument used later, placed on the knee to assist in dealing with the wool. Thus Pollux[2] says ἐφ' οὗ δὲ νήθουσι ἢ νῶσι ἐπίνητρον καλεῖται· καὶ ὄνος; Hesychius ἐπίνητρον· ἐφ' ᾧ τὴν κρόκην τρίβουσιν; and the Et. Magn.[3] ἐπίνητρον· τὸ ἐπὶ τῶν γονάτων ἐφ' οὗ τὴν κρόκην ἔνηθον. We may also illustrate the use of the knee from Theocritus:[4]

> πολλαὶ Ἀχαιιάδων μαλακὸν περὶ γούνατι νῆμα
> χειρὶ κατατρίψοντι ἀκρέσπερον ἀείδοισαι
> Ἀλκμήναν ὀνομαστί.

That the knees played a part in the spinning process is thus clear. There is further confirmation in a passage hitherto neglected by Homeric scholars—Plato's picture[5] of Ἀνάγκη in the whorls of whose spindle are set the stars and planets. Of this spindle he says στρέφεσθαι δὲ αὐτὸν ἐν τοῖς τῆς Ἀνάγκης γόνασιν, and it is with it that the μοῖρα, the 'portion' or fate of each soul about to be born, is made valid by the spinning (ἐπικλώθειν) of the Μοῖραι, Κλωθώ and Ἄτροπος. Of Ἄτροπος the word used is νῆσις.[6] Such adaptation of Homer is

---

[1] 'On the Knees of the Gods', *Class. Rev.* 1924, p. 6, where (pp. 2 ff.) I have discussed this phrase and the processes of spinning at much greater length. Here I am merely abstracting some of the more important evidence.

[2] vii, 32.   [3] 362, 20.

[4] xxiv, 74 ff. Or we may compare the ivory statuette found on the site of the temple of Artemis at Ephesus. 'The right hand with fingers extended rests flat upon the thigh and between it and the thigh passes the thread with spindle hanging from it nearly to the feet', Cecil Smith in *British Museum Excavations at Ephesus*, D. G. Hogarth, 1908, p. 158, Pl. XXIV, 1 a, b.

[5] *Rep.* x, 616 ff.   [6] 620 E. See note 4, p. 418 below.

completely in the Platonic manner and it appears almost certainly deliberate when we compare such lines as *Od.* VII, 197 f.:

πείσεται ἄσσα οἱ Αἶσα κατὰ Κλῶθές τε βαρεῖαι
γεινομένῳ νήσαντο λίνῳ ὅτε μιν τέκε μήτηρ.

For νήσαντο ἐπένησε is twice used in similar contexts of the *Iliad*[1] with Αἶσα and Μοῖρα respectively, but in Homer it is with the gods rather than either of these last that the verbs ἐπικλώθειν, etc., are most frequently used. Here, then, Plato would seem to be following him, save that he has substituted the Pythagorean Ἀνάγκη for the gods or Μοῖρα, retaining the latter as helping to spin. It seems just to infer that this was his interpretation of the phrase θεῶν ἐν γούνασι κεῖται—one which, perhaps as traditional, he expected to be recognised and to add authority to his myth. This is made the more likely in that he uses the word ἠλακάτη for the shaft of the spindle, whereas its ordinary meaning was 'distaff', an article which he does not mention, and, as I have shown elsewhere,[2] for Homer also the spindle was ἠλακάτη and there was no distaff. A few lines after saying that the spindle turns ἐν τοῖς τῆς Ἀνάγκης γόνασιν Plato refers again to knees. From the knees of Lachesis are taken 'lots' and βίων παραδείγματα. The lots merely determine the order in which the souls choose and they have no connection with knees in Homer[3] or indeed elsewhere. The βίων παραδείγματα, on the other hand, are actually the μοῖραι, the portions which are spun,[4] the destinies which men must experience. This is further evidence that for Plato the fate that 'lay on the knees of the gods' was what was spun.

At this point we may return to the apparently foolish scholion mentioned above. It is the Schol. P. *ad Od.* I, 267 and 400, and it runs thus: θεῶν ἐν γούνασι. ταῖς τῶν ἀστέρων κινήσεσιν ἀπὸ μεταφορᾶς τῶν γονάτων. ἀπὸ γὰρ τῆς τῶν ἀστέρων κινήσεως γίνονται τοῖς ἀνθρώποις τὰ εἱμαρμένα. For

[1] xx, 127 f., xxiv, 210.
[2] *Class. Rev. loc. cit.* pp. 4 and 6. See also p. 39 above.
[3] They are shaken in a helmet.
[4] See below, pp. 403 f.

this there is, of course, no foundation in Homer. For him the stars have nothing whatever to do with Fate, and are not brought into relation with the gods. The scholiast himself, indeed, was probably acquainted with the underlying assumption of astrology, but such a fanciful comparison of knees and stars, with no middle term, is unthinkable. Hence the suggestion has been ignored as unworthy of consideration. Let us turn to Plato, however. Commentators, while stressing the irreconcilability of the two conceptions, the spindle of Necessity and the shaft of light, which is the axis of the revolving heavens, yet fail to observe his reason for the union and its fitness despite discrepancies of detail. Thus in a single image he fuses the astrological notions of the East and the early Hellenic idea of fate as spun.[1] Here indeed we have a convenient middle term for the scholiast, one which, coming fresh from the glowing mind of Plato in such a myth, is indeed easily understood, but which, if omitted in a rather matter-of-fact and discontinuous commentary on Homer, leaves the two extremes incongruous and foreign to each other. It appears not unlikely that the Alexandrian critics had seen the connection between the Homeric phrase and Plato's spindle of the starry heaven moving on the knees of Necessity, but that in the process of tradition the middle term or image combining them was forgotten, so that the scholiast, true to the tradition as far as he knows it, is driven to invent one for himself, very curiously indeed, in the common motion of knees and stars. Proclus in his commentary on the *Republic*[2] definitely associates the two phrases ταῦτα θεῶν ἐν γούνασι κεῖται and στρέφεσθαι δὲ αὐτὸν ἐν τοῖς τῆς Ἀνάγκης γόνασιν.

There is no need for evidence in Homer that spinning was ever done by men. Spinning and weaving can be traced back to the neolithic age and even earlier. In the dim past, from which such a concept as this almost certainly comes, it may

---

[1] Compare the less successful combination of Ovid, *O duram Lachesim, quae tam grave sidus habenti/fila dedit vitae non breviora meae* (*Trist.* v, 10, 45 f.), which is faithful to the orthodox astrology.

[2] Ed. Kroll, vol. II, p. 227. For a fuller examination of his view see *Class. Rev. loc. cit.* p. 5.

well be that the male ancestors of the Achaeans, with the Egyptians[1] of old and some comparatively primitive peoples to-day, partook in or even wholly performed the spinning. The internal evidence of Homer is sufficient to show that his gods were habitually conceived as spinning what is to be.

[1] See Herodotus, II, 35; Soph. *Oed. Col.* 339 f.

CHAPTER II

Πείρατα

Ζεὺς μὲν ἄρα Τρώεσσι καὶ "Εκτορι βούλετο νίκην,...
'Αργείους δὲ Ποσειδάων ὀρόθυνε μετελθών,...
τοὶ δ' ἔριδος κρατερῆς καὶ ὁμοιΐου πτολέμοιο
πεῖραρ ἐπαλλάξαντες ἐπ' ἀμφοτέροισι τάνυσσαν,
ἄρρηκτόν τ' ἄλυτόν τε, τὸ πολλῶν γούνατ' ἔλυσεν.[1]

'This highly-wrought metaphor', explains Monro, 'is suggested by the Homeric use of τανύω and kindred words to express the "tension" or "strain" of an equal combat. The contest in which the two armies are joined (ὁμὸν νεῖκος, line 333) is spoken of as a piece of rope (πεῖραρ) passed over both by the two gods (ἐπαλλάξαντες) and drawn tight (τάνυσσαν), by which accordingly they are knit together inseparably. For the notion of a god *stretching* or *drawing tight* a battle, cf. XI, 336, ἔνθα σφιν κατὰ ἶσα μάχην ἐτάνυσσε Κρονίων; XIV, 389 f., δή ῥα τότ' αἰνοτάτην ἔριδα πτολέμοιο τάνυσσαν/κυανοχαῖτα Ποσειδάων καὶ φαίδιμος "Εκτωρ.' But it is somewhat difficult to conceive how a rope stretched over two armies can 'knit them inseparably together' or indeed—a different image—how two armies pressing in upon each other can be compared to a taut rope the tendency of whose two ends is to part. Further, the rope is itself variously qualified by genitives, πτολέμοιο, ἔριδος, νίκης, ὀλέθρου, etc., qualifications which show that the tension of war as root conception is inadequate. Indeed the governing notion of τανύειν, here as more often in Homer even in the passages cited by Monro, would seem to be not that of 'tension' or 'strain', but rather that of 'extending, spreading out'.[2] It is the area covered (ἐπ' ἀμφοτέροισι, XIII, 359; κατὰ ἶσα, XI, 336; ἐπὶ ἶσα, XII, 436 and XIV, 413; ἶσον, XX, 101) which is emphasised rather than the tightness of the strain. In addition

[1] *Il.* XIII, 347–60.
[2] See e.g. *Il.* XVI, 567, XVII, 547 f.

to this last, we are told, 'a further touch is given by πεῖραρ ἐπαλλάξαντες, a play between the literal sense "end of a rope" and the abstract sense which we have in ὀλέθρου πείρατα, "the ends of destruction" (= *utter* destruction), πεῖραρ ὀϊζύος, "crisis of woe" (*Od.* v, 289); cf. τέλος θανάτοιο, τέλος πολέμου, τέλος μύθου, etc. The same double use of πεῖραρ is seen in vii, 102, νίκης πείρατ᾽ ἔχονται, "the ends of victory are held" = "victory is controlled" and xii, 79, ὀλέθρου πείρατ᾽ ἐφῆπται = "destruction is made fast, secured" (cf. ii, 15, κήδε᾽ ἐφῆπται)'. Were the above an isolated instance or were it Homer's wont to use such verbal tricks, talk of a play between different senses might be admissible; but the many instances, of which these are some, point rather to a habitual mode of conceiving the fortunes of men.

Of ἐπαλλάξαντες the exact force is somewhat difficult to fix. 'The sense', says Monro, 'of passing the rope over the two sides (so as to join them) which is adopted by La Roche is satisfactory in every way.' In itself ἐπαλλάσσειν might conceivably have that meaning, but it would then remain to ask what the participle adds that would not be given by ἐπ᾽ ἀμφοτέροισι τάνυσσαν alone, a difficulty which perhaps inspires the rival interpretation 'swaying to and fro', supported among other venerable authorities by Tertullian,[1] Apostolius,[2] Liddell and Scott. This at least gives the word some value in its context—a value, indeed, which it would be hard to find in ἐπαλλάσσειν elsewhere—but it also, as Monro points out, requires a different tense. It therefore cannot stand. Van Leeuwen's '*utrinque finem tenentes*' is at best a paraphrase and need not be discussed. The scholiasts and Eustathius acknowledge the difficulty of the passage by the abnormal length of their explanations, but they reveal a virtual unanimity on the meaning of ἐπαλλάσσειν: that it refers to some manner of tying or fastening as in making a knot or bond (δεσμός, ἄμμα). The rival interpretations given above find no support or indeed mention with them. They have, indeed, at best but remote parallels in the rest of Greek literature. On the other hand

[1] See p. 338 below.　　　　[2] See *ibid.*

Plato (*Sophist*, 240 c) appears to have equated ἐπάλλαξις with συμπλοκή. Xenophon (*Eq. Mag.* 3, 3) refers to holding or placing δόρατα...ὡς ἥκιστα ἂν ἀλλήλοις ἐπαλλάττοιτο, i.e. 'cross each other', and Plutarch's ἐπηλλαγμέναις δι' ἀλλήλων ταῖς χερσί (*Lucull.* 21), 'with arms crossed', is closely parallel to Euripides' (*Hec.* 836) πούς ἐπαλλαχθεὶς ποδί, 'foot crossing foot', of serried ranks interlocked in battle. The scholiasts' 'tying' fits the notion of 'crossing' which appears to predominate in these various instances. The interpretation of Aristarchus is given thus: ὁ Ποσειδῶν καὶ ὁ Ζεὺς τὸν πόλεμον τῇ ἔριδι συνέδησαν, τὸ πέρας τῆς ἔριδος καὶ πάλιν τὸ τοῦ πολέμου λαβόντες καὶ ἐπαλλάξαντες ἐπ' ἀμφοτέροις, ὥσπερ οἱ τὰ ἄμματα ποιοῦντες τόδε ἐπὶ τόδε. They put the two ends, rope-ends, or ropes—whatever πείρατα may mean here—one over the other as in making a knot. The scholiasts or their sources also use ἐπιπλέκειν, συμπλέκειν, συνάπτειν to express the same idea. Dr Leaf has followed them: 'The words seem to mean literally *crossing over* a rope upon itself.' A single rope whose ends or halves, dubbed severally ἔρις and πόλεμος, are crossed to form a knot or loop, τόδε ἐπὶ τόδε, is perhaps the simplest interpretation of Aristarchus' words. For him and his fellows the double genitive appears to have complicated the problem, but it is the obscure meaning of πεῖραρ which is at the root of the trouble.

Briefly put, the position is that there are passages—according to the editors mentioned above, the vast majority—in which the context seems satisfied by the abstract 'end, limit' (the usual sense of the later form πέρας), e.g. πείρατα γαίης, *Il.* VIII, 478, and there are others which no less certainly demand something concrete like *rope, rope-end* or *knot*, i.e. *Od.* XII, 51, 162, 179, ἐκ δ' αὐτοῦ [sc. ἱστοῦ] πείρατ' ἀνήφθω, in the binding of Odysseus before passing the Sirens. To this phrase it is usual to add from the Hymn to Apollo (129): οὐδ' ἔτι δεσμά σ' ἔρυκε, λύοντο δὲ πείρατα πάντα. Between these two groups lie several passages, of which that before us is chief, in more or fewer of which different editors feel the need of allusion to something concrete. Doederlein, Schulze, and others hold that there are two distinct words meaning 'rope or knot' and 'end or limit' respectively. 'The alternative theory', says Dr Leaf, 'is that πεῖραρ from the abstract sense of *end* has acquired the technical meaning rope's end.' This view is elaborated by Merry and Riddell:[1] 'The simple interpretation of the *Etym. Mag.*: πεῖραρ, πέρας—τέλος—τὸ πέρας τοῦ σχοινίου, will be found quite satisfactory'. Of the explicit instances of the second group cited above—*Od.* xii, 51, etc.—'the solution is that πείρατα signifies the "rope-ends", not the whole length of the rope except by implication'; and of the present passage, despite the singular πεῖραρ, they say: 'Thus we have in *Il.* xiii, 358 the gods dragging at the *ends* of a rope'. 'The conclusion', says Dr Leaf in his note on vii, 101 f. (αὐτὰρ ὕπερθε/νίκης πείρατ' ἔχονται ἐν ἀθανάτοισι θεοῖσιν), after reviewing the three groups given above, 'seems to be that the use of πεῖραρ in xiii, 359 does convey, by an extension of the metaphor in τανύσσαι, a distinct allusion to the meaning *rope-end* or *knot*,[2] but that in every other case including the present the purely abstract sense "issue, consummation" or the like is possible and on the whole preferable; though even then the existence of the concrete sense will lend a certain colour.' For some peculiar reason the notion 'end, limit' is supposed to become attached to ropes in particular and develop a special meaning 'rope-end', of which however no instance can be found. If it could, the further development to the meaning 'rope' or 'knot' would not naturally follow. Also in the traceable early history of language the concrete usually precedes the abstract[3] —'first the natural and then the spiritual'. These attempts have ignored what scanty evidence surviving literature affords us of the sequence in time of the various usages of the word, as they do also the help which comparative philology might give. That there was a time when πεῖραρ meant 'limit, end' and had not yet acquired secondary more concrete associa-

---

[1] On *Od.* xii, 51. Cf. the view of Ameis-Hentze-Cauer quoted below (note 5, p. 323).

[2] Schulze (*Quaest. Epic.* p. 110) would reject line 360 and take πεῖραρ even in this passage as equivalent to 'limit'.

[3] Merry and Riddell instance the later use of ἀρχή for 'rope-end'.

tions, no text has endured to show; but that there was a time when that concrete meaning was forgotten and the colourless abstract was a commonplace of commonplaces almost all literature after Homer and—an infinitesimal but significant fraction of it—the varying puzzled attempts to interpret him are our witness. If we examine the cognate πειραίνω in Homer, we find it used twice (*Od.* xxII, 175, 192) in an undeniably concrete sense of knotting or fastening a cord and once in a context fitted perfectly well by the sense of 'accomplish', later universally associated with περαίνω, the form which like πέρας prevailed. Are we to suppose that a derivative sense of 'rope-end' had also infected the verb? Unfortunately the latter does not mean to 'end' a rope but to tie or fasten and seems not unconnected with the still unexplained sense of 'knot' which Schulze and others find in the πείρατα of the Hymn to Apollo cited above. There is yet another Homeric word which, *if* it be Indo-European,[1] would seem akin—πείρινς (*Il.* xxiv, 267), the wickerwork body of a wagon, πλέγμα τὸ ἐπὶ τῆς ἁμάξης (Hesychius), ἐκ ῥιπῶν δέ φασιν αὐτὸ πλέκεσθαι (schol. and Eustath.). In principle and origin weaving and wickerwork are one[2]—their essence may be described as a tying or binding. The Sanscrit stem, to which πεῖραρ and πειραίνω appear to be related, is *parvan-*,[3] meaning 'knot, link, joint'. We may also compare the Zend *parvand*, meaning 'belt, girdle, band'.[4] The sense of 'rope, knot, or bond' is clearly primitive as might have been expected. Endeavours to derive noun or verb from an abstract notion of ending or limiting are futile. That the two groups, each comprising noun and verb, are quite distinct though identical in form has an *a priori* improbability and lacks adequate support in kindred languages for any πεῖραρ

[1] It has been usual to regard -νθ- as a sign of non-Hellenic origin; but here the root and the meaning harmonise with πειραίνω, etc.

[2] See H. Ling Roth, 'Studies in Primitive Looms', *Journ. R. Anthrop. Inst.* XLVI, 1916, *init.* and Hoops, *Reallexicon der germanischen Altertumskunde,* s.v. *Webstuhl.*

[3] The primary sense appears to have been 'knot', see Collitz, *Beiträge z. Kunde der indogerm. Sprachen,* herausgeg. A. Bezzenberger u. W. Prellwitz, x, p. 60, n. 1. Boisacq compares also Sanscrit *par-u-s* in the same sense (*Dict. ét. de la langue gr.* s.v.).   [4] See p. 455 below.

with an original sense of 'end'. The third possibility is that the abstract was derived from the concrete. It only remains to show a possible mode of transition.

A bond around anything is a limit marking its outline and *circumscribing* its activity,[1] and a belt of cord is not only an obvious modern method of staking out a piece of ground but was also habitual with the ancients[2] in defining a *precinct* or τέμενος. Liddell and Scott support the meaning 'end' for πέρας by the preposition πέρα, the appropriateness of which is by no means obvious. If we would seek such kin we might suggest rather περί with its Sanscrit equivalent *pari*. Previous attempts to deal with the word have perhaps in part been baffled by the notions usually associated, in English for instance, with the word 'end'—a limit in one dimension and one direction only—no true limit in a world of three-dimensional space. In that world gravity and other factors confine man for the most part to motion in two dimensions over the plane of the earth's surface, and a ring or band[3] is the natural bound or limit. A ring or bond suffices to confine anything.

The earth itself for Homer, as we have seen,[4] was surrounded by Ὠκεανός, the river with an in-dwelling god apparently of serpent form. Epimenides of Crete taught[5] that Styx, female offspring of Okeanos, was mated with Πεῖρας and their offspring was the snake Ἔχιδνα. So, for the Sumerians long before, Hubur, the world-encircling stream of salt water, gave

---

[1] See e.g. the Black Dog's confession in Dekker's *The Witch of Edmonton*:
'Though we have power, know it is circumscribed
and tied in limits' (II, 1),
with which we may compare Theognis, 139 f. (Bgk.):
οὐδέ τῳ ἀνθρώπων παραγίνεται, ὅσσ' ἐθέλησιν·
ἴσχει γὰρ χαλεπῆς πείρατ' ἀμηχανίης.

[2] See instances in Pauly-Wissowa-Kroll, *Realencykl.*[2] XI, pp. 2139 ff. (Pfister) with the legend of the origin of Byrsa (Livy, XXXIV, 62; *Aen.* I, 368, etc.).

[3] The fundamental unity in idea of a band or bond and a knot is clear. What is a bond when something is enclosed within its loop becomes a knot if allowed to run in upon itself and drawn tight. ἅμμα can mean a knot (Herodotus, IV, 98), a noose (Eurip. *Hippol.* 781), a girdle (*Anth. Pal.* 7, 182), and a measure of length.

[4] Pp. 247 ff.   [5] B 6, Diels.

birth to Viper, Raging Serpent,[1] etc. With 'Ωκεανός is his consort Tethys, and Homer twice speaks of them as the πείρατα γαίης. Hera says: 'I am going to see the πείρατα of the pasture-abounding earth, Okeanos, generation of the gods, and mother Tethys who reared me, etc.'

εἶμι γὰρ ὀψομένη πολυφόρβου πείρατα γαίης
'Ωκεανόν τε, θεῶν γένεσιν, καὶ μητέρα Τηθύν,[2]

which in the past has been translated 'the limits of the earth, etc.', but may now be reinterpreted 'the bonds (or binders) of the pasture-abounding earth', a more natural description of what are clearly conceived of not as parts of the earth but as distinct beings encircling it. For Homer the earth appears to be conceived as a fairly shallow cylinder. Hesiod[3] tells us that Okeanos is 'wound' (εἰλιγμένος) nine times round it, as Euripides says of the serpent round the tree of the Hesperides ἀμφελικτὸς ἕλικ' ἐφρούρει,[4] where Hesiod's expression is πείρασιν ἐν μεγάλοις παγχρύσεα μῆλα φυλάσσει.[5] When at the beginning of *Iliad* xx all the gods assemble on Olympos, there is only one who does not or cannot come, Okeanos, and Porphyry[6] explains that Okeanos had to hold things together: 'For the poet says "Okeanos in which the whole earth is bound" ('Ωκεανός, τῷ πᾶσα περίρρυτος ἐνδέδεται χθών)'. In an Orphic hymn the circle of Okeanos is a belt around the cosmic deity,

ζωστὴρ δ' ἄρ' ὑπὸ στέρνων ἀμετρήτων
φαίνεται 'Ωκεανοῦ κύκλος, μέγα θαῦμα ἰδέσθαι.[7]

Further evidence in this direction has been discussed above.[8] Though men gradually realised that not a river but an ocean lay around the world, this conception of Okeanos as a bond continued long. E.g. ὁ 'Ωκεανὸς...σφίγγει τὴν οἰκουμένην (*de Mundo*, 393 b). The elder Seneca in his first *Suasoria* speaks

[1] See S. Langdon, *The Epic of Creation*, 1923, p. 85. The myth of a serpent girdling the earth is widespread later. Such legends as that among the sea-going people of the North, of the *Miðgarðsormr* 'lying in the sea around all lands and biting its tail' (*Gylfaginning*, 34), may lie behind the expectation of seeing a 'sea-serpent'.   [2] *Il.* XIV, 200 f.

[3] *Theog.* 790 f. Cf. περιελιχθέντα περὶ τὴν γῆν ὥσπερ οἱ ὄφεις, Plato, *Phaedo*, 112 D, E.   [4] *Herc. Fur.* 399.   [5] *Theog.* 335.

[6] See schol. *ad Il.* XVIII, 490. The poet appears to be Euphorion (Fr. 122 Powell).   [7] *Orphic. Fr.* (Kern), 239, 14 f.   [8] Pp. 248 ff.

of it as *totius orbis vinculum terrarumque custodia*[1] and the younger Seneca (*ad Marciam*, xviii, 6) speaks of *vinculum terrarum Oceanus* and in his *Medea* says:

> *venient annis saecula seris*
> *quibus Oceanus vincula rerum*
> *laxet et ingens pateat tellus.*[2]

The survival in Greek philosophy of the conception of a 'bond' or 'bonds' about the universe is traced below.[3]

From this sense of circumscribing 'band' or 'bond' to 'boundary', 'limit', the transition is easy. To be surrounded by was to be bound by. So Catullus *silvis redimita loca*, and *urbis vincula*[4] = Τροίης κρήδεμνα. The outline of anything is naturally conceived as a line or thread around it. For the Romans it was quite explicitly *filum*, 'thread', e.g. *mulieris filum* (Plautus), *solis filum* (Lucretius). Already in the *Odyssey* we find πείρατα used in a sense like 'bounds', 'limits'. 'Poseidon smashed my ship, hurling it on the rocks on the πείρατα of your land'[5] (ὑμῆς ἐπὶ πείρασι γαίης). We can thus also understand two Latin words which have not hitherto been satisfactorily related: *ora*, 'cord', and *ora*, the 'edge', 'boundary' of anything, e.g. *orae extremae partes terrarum, id est maritimae, dicuntur*[6] (cf. *vestis/candida purpurea talos incinxerat ora* (Catull. LXIV, 307 f.) and *formarum oras* (Lucr. IV, 135) with *filum*), also the use[7] of *ora* like that of *cingulus*, 3ώνη, as 'belt', 'zone' round the earth.[8] For *finis* see pp. 510 f.

To return to our original problem: if πεῖραρ be such a cord or bond, ἐπαλλάξαντες will mean the crossing over of it upon itself, making actual that function of tying or binding from which, like ἄμμα, it derives its name. Dr Leaf translates: '*the two gods knotted the rope of strife and war and drew it tight*[9] *for both sides*....For the metaphor see the note on VII, 102; the gods

---

[1] *Init.* Cf. a little later *terras velut vinculum circumfluat*, and Tacitus, *Germ*. 45.

[2] 375 ff. See also *cingere nexu* of *Oceanus* in note 1 on p. 250.

[3] P. 332. See also pp. 248, 443 and 453, n. 1.

[4] LXIII, 3, LXIV, 367.   [5] *Od.* IX, 283 f.

[6] Festus, s.v. (196, 31 ff. Linds.).

[7] Cf. Cic. *Rep.* VI, xx, 21 with *Tusc.* I, 28, 68. Another use of *ora* appears on pp. 388 f. Cf. *umbrosis Heliconis oris* (Hor. *Od.* I, 12, 5) with *silvis redimita loca*.

[8] Cf. pp. 250 ff., 332.   [9] Cf. the rev. Liddell and Scott, s.v. τανύω.

tie the two armies to the rope of strife and try to pull them
backwards and forwards. A somewhat similar[1] explanation
was given by Aristarchus, only he distinguished two ropes....
The general sense of the passage would be better given if we
could translate ἐπαλλάξαντες *alternately*.[2] The use of ἀλλάσ-
σειν makes this possible but we should require the present
participle in place of the aorist'. Yes—and we may add that
with ἐπαλλάξαντες thus accounted for we should be left with
a straight rope over the two armies as in Monro's rendering,
the only difference being that it would be pulled backwards
and forwards above their heads. As the scholia indicated and
his translation recognises, ἐπαλλάξαντες must here express
the crossing over upon itself or tying of the rope to form a loop
or open knot, so that there remains only ἐπ᾽ ἀμφοτέροισι
τάνυσσαν, which he renders 'drew it tight for both sides'.
There is, therefore, according to his own rendering no hint
in the Greek that the gods 'tried to pull them backwards and
forwards'. His note on VII, 102 runs: 'Apart from the use of
πεῖραρ it seems necessary to admit the concrete metaphor by
which the tide of battle is pulled backwards and forwards not
by the combatants themselves as in the game of "Tug of War",
which is commonly compared, but by the gods who thus
become the "wire-pullers" of the battle'. This merely repeats
the idea without adducing any evidence in its favour. Moreover, if the gods are 'wire-pullers' of the battle and there was
a single rope knotted around both armies, the repertoire of
their puppet-show must have been somewhat limited; and
there is no evidence that a puppet-show of any kind was part
of the familiar experience of Homer's audience to justify its
habitual use, often by the merest allusion, to illustrate the

[1] We may note that the 'similarity' of Aristarchus' explanation (that
already quoted) does not extend beyond the translation of ἐπαλλάξαντες
and has no reference to the suggestion that the gods 'pull the armies
backward and forward'.

[2] This is the rendering of Ameis-Hentze who interpret πεῖραρ as 'das
Leitseil des Kampfes', whereby the gods rein or guide the battle to the
destruction now of this side, now of that. In their note to *Il.* VII, 102 they
also imply something like a tug of war. To them also apply the objections to Dr Leaf's view.

fortunes of war. Further, against this and still more against the idea of a 'tug of war' is the use of τανύειν, in what is accepted as the same image, in several other passages where only a single god is concerned, e.g. *Il.* xi, 336 : ἔνθα σφιν κατὰ ἶσα μάχην ἐτάνυσσε Κρονίων; cf. xvi, 662, xvii, 441, xx, 101. Let us look again at ἐπ' ἀμφοτέροισι τάνυσσαν. If we are to conceive of the rope as forming an open knot or loop, the natural meaning of this is 'extended it over both armies': ἐπέτειναν ἀμφοτέροις, ἐξαπτόμενα κατ' ἀμφοτέρων τῶν στρατευμάτων, τείναντες κατ' ἀμφοτέρων τῶν στρατῶν, ἥπλωσαν αὐτὸ ἐπ' ἀμφοτέρων τῶν στρατιωτῶν. Κράτης δὲ ἐπ' ἀμφοτέρων τῶν στρατευμάτων, ἐτάνυσαν ἐπ' ἀλλήλους.[1] So the scholia, and τανυσθῆναι καὶ οἷον ἐπιρριφθῆναι τοῖς μαχομένοις μέρεσι, κατὰ τῶν πολεμούντων ταθῆναι, Eustathius.[2] If such be the force of ἐπί it is unnecessary, not to say difficult, to interpret τάνυσσαν 'drew it tight'. If we are to think of the knot being *drawn tight* above the heads of the combatants, ὑπέρ would be more natural; if around them, περί. It is of *extending* the loop or bond over both the hosts, laying it on them both, that ἐπί is most naturally used, as in Ζεὺς δ' ἐπὶ νύκτ' ὀλοὴν τάνυσε κρατερῇ ὑσμίνῃ.[3] Thus we are left with 'They looped the rope (or "bond") of strife and war and extended it over both armies'. By 'looped' is meant, as is explained above, the making of a loop by tying or crossing the two ends. It is this loop or noose, band or bond, which is thus extended. Such a bond enclosing its victims might well be called ἄρρηκτόν τ' ἄλυτόν τε τὸ πολλῶν γούνατ' ἔλυσεν, which description the supporters of the 'tug of war' or 'wire-pulling' theories

[1] This last is from Porphyry, who obviously accepts the variant τοὶ... ἐπ' ἀλλήλοισι which need not be discussed. Evidence below will show that the image refers to the activity of the gods.

[2] Van Leeuwen appears to have realised this to be the force of ἐπί... τάνυσσαν, for he translates *rixae bellique restim pugnantibus intendunt*, yet explains the image of a tug of war and gives references for διελκυστίνδα.

[3] *Il.* xvi, 567. Cf. *Od.* xi, 19. The other instances of τείνω or τανύω with ἐπί in Homer appear to be *Od.* i, 441 f., iv, 134, xv, 282, xviii, 92. We may compare ταινία, a 'band', apparently something 'extended' (see s.v. in Gk. Index) and the use of *tendo* for the extending, spreading of a net or snare, *tendicula*, 'a little noose or snare'. Cf. Virg. *Aen.* ii, 236 f., iv, 506 and Stat. *Silv.* v, 1, 155 cited on p. 374, n. 3.

have never ventured to explain. We are reminded of the trap of cords spread for Ares by Hephaistos, *Od.* VIII, 280: κόπτε δὲ δεσμοὺς / ἀρρήκτους ἀλύτους. Out of the confusion of the scholia may be selected this sentence: ἔδησαν ἰσχυρῷ δεσμῷ ὅς δεσμὸς πολλοῖς αἴτιος ἀπωλείας ἐγένετο. As in a magic circle, of which indeed the outline is sometimes defined by just such a cord, the properties of the bond or band are valid not merely at its circumference but also for all contents of the area enclosed.

In the nine other passages with τανύειν or τείνειν which Monro, Leaf, and others recognise as bound up with that before us, ἔρις, πτόλεμος, etc. occur as direct objects of the verb, apparently implying that conception of them as πείρατα which is here explicit. The nine passages are *Il.* XI, 336, XII, 436, XIV, 389, XV, 413, XVI, 662, XVII, 401, 543, 736, XX, 101. In four[1] of them the verb is in the passive and no agent is explicitly given, but it remains clear that the gods are understood, e.g.

ὣς μὲν τῶν ἐπὶ ἶσα μάχη τέτατο πτόλεμός τε,
πρίν γ' ὅτε δὴ Ζεὺς κῦδος ὑπέρτερον Ἕκτορι δῶκεν.[2]

The ἔρις, etc. is spoken of as something concrete spread out by Zeus or the other gods over the battlefield.

There are eight further obviously relevant instances of πεῖραρ to be considered, all of which Dr Leaf thinks satisfied by the 'purely abstract sense *issue, consummation* or the like'. ὀλέθρου πείρατ' ἐφῆπται or ἐφῆπτο occurs four times, *Il.* VII, 402, XII, 79; *Od.* XXII, 33, 41. Though it came when the siege seemed most hopeless, Diomedes bids the Achaeans reject the Trojan offer of terms ὡς ἤδη Τρώεσσιν ὀλέθρου πείρατ' ἐφῆπται.[3] When Odysseus shot Antinoos, the other suitors thought it was an accident: τὸ δὲ νήπιοι οὐκ ἐνόησαν / ὡς δή σφιν καὶ πᾶσιν ὀλέθρου πείρατ' ἐφῆπτο.[4] It is used of men for whom destruction is certain, but not yet actual. 'πείρατα', say Merry and Riddell,[5] 'retains its real meaning there like τέλος θανάτοιο, as may be inferred from the variant of the same expression in Τρώεσσι δὲ κήδε' ἐφῆπται, *Il.* II, 15.' τέλος θανάτοιο and κήδε' ἐφῆπται will be discussed below.[6] The real

---

[1] XII, 436, XV, 413, XVII, 543, 736.   [2] *Il.* XII, 436 f.   [3] *Il.* VII, 402.
[4] *Od.* XXII, 32 f.   [5] In a note to *Od.* XII, 51.   [6] Pp. 334, 379, 426 ff.

meaning of πεῖραρ, if by 'real' is intended 'original', we have perhaps shown to be not 'limit' as they imagine but 'cord, band, or bond'.[1] That sense fits ἐφῆπται here perfectly—which e.g. 'issues' (Leaf) does not—and is thereby itself confirmed. ἀν-ῆπτο is used of the unequivocally concrete πείρατα which bind Odysseus to the mast (*Od.* XII, 51, 162, 179). In *Il.* XII, 79 we learn from the scholia that, instead of πείρατα, Zenodotus and Aristophanes read the singular, πεῖραρ. The text runs:

Ἕκτορι πάντες ἐπώμεθ' ἀολλέες· αὐτὰρ Ἀχαιοὶ
οὐ μενέουσ', εἰ δή σφιν ὀλέθρου πείρατ' ἐφῆπται.

The change would assimilate the ὀλέθρου πεῖραρ to the ἔριδος κρατερῆς καὶ ὁμοιΐου πτολέμοιο πεῖραρ in *Il.* XIII, 358 above. Whether the singular or plural is used, the basic identity of conception is obvious—that of a bond or bonds. The plural is unchallenged in the other instances and has all other authority on its side here. In these four passages, the conception is of people not surrounded by a single bond but enmeshed in many as in a net. There are two further passages in which ὀλέθρου πείρατα feature, *Il.* VI, 143, XX, 429, which issue the courteous invitation ἆσσον ἴθ' ὥς κεν θᾶσσον ὀλέθρου πείραθ' ἵκηαι. Editors who waver over the concrete associations of ἐφῆπται have no qualms with ἵκηαι—the abstract fits—to reach the 'uttermost bounds of destruction', or the 'ending of death'! What little these add to ὀλέθρου is not very happy. How much more graphic and Homeric in spirit is 'to reach the bands (or bonds) of death'! These are bonds prepared for the individual. It is scarcely Homer's wont to change his meaning for a phrase like ὀλέθρου πείρατα from point to point, and its meaning in the other four passages, as also the original meaning of πεῖραρ, has been shown. A man may walk into a net or snare of cords as Ares did (cf. *Od.* XXII, 468 ff.) or they may be cast over him and fastened upon him.[2] In the Book of Job it is said of the wicked: 'He is cast into a net by his own feet and he walketh

---

[1] Autenrieth (*Hom. Lex.*) renders *laquei exitii* and Ameis-Hentze (*ad loc.*) 'die Schlingen des Verderbens', which does not harmonise with their rendering of ἔριδος κρατερῆς καὶ ὁμοιΐου πτολέμοιο πεῖραρ (see p. 318, note 2). [2] Cf. p. 363 below.

upon a snare' (xviii, 8), and in the next chapter (*v.* 6) Job says of himself: 'God hath overthrown me and hath compassed me with his net'.[1] In Homer man is for the most part regarded as passive to his fate but sometimes as in a sense active. We may compare *Il.* xxii, 303, νῦν αὖτέ με μοῖρα κιχάνει, with the recurring πότμον ἐπισπεῖν, or *Il.* iv, 321, νῦν αὖτέ με γῆρας ἱκάνει, with *Od.* xv, 246, οὐδ' ἵκετο γήραος οὐδόν, and so too ὀλέθρου πείρατ' ἐφῆπται and ὀλέθρου πείραθ' ἵκηαι.[2] The two instances of the latter confirm what we observed in the four instances of the former, namely that we are here dealing with a slight variation of the conception seen in xiii, 358. It is not a single noose or bond encircling a whole host but a multiplicity of bonds either awaiting or already fastened over the individual or the host. In this also we are inevitably drawn to compare the multiple δεσμοὶ ἄρρηκτοι ἄλυτοι which Hephaistos made ready for Ares and Aphrodite, a network of cords likened to a spider's web, ἠΰτ' ἀράχνια λεπτά (*Od.* viii, 280). In some such way[3] we must conceive the ὀλέθρου πείρατα.

[1] See also p. 364, note 2.

[2] Here too perhaps belongs οὐ γάρ πω πάντων ἐπὶ πείρατ' ἀέθλων/ ἤλθομεν (*Od.* xxiii, 248 f.) though the secondary meaning 'limits' might fit. See also πείρατ' ἀέθλων on p. 341.

[3] When he first appears (*Il.* v, 471 ff.), Sarpedon reproaches Hector for leaving the brunt of the battle to the allies and not urging on his country-men in whose cause they are fighting:

μή πως, ὡς ἀψῖσι λίνου ἁλόντε πανάγρου,
ἀνδράσι δυσμενέεσσιν ἕλωρ καὶ κύρμα γένησθε.

The quantity and dual form of ἁλόντε may point to some corruption in the text, as has been suggested; but as it stands these lines (487 f.) mean something like 'Beware lest being caught as in the meshes of an all-capturing λίνον you become a prey and a spoil unto the enemy'. ἀψῖσι seems to demand for λίνου a sense of something net-like with loops or meshes. The image resembles that under discussion but is softened by ὡς—'caught as in the meshes'—unless indeed that be part of the corrup-tion (? τῆς). Tryphiodorus (674) with obvious allusion to this passage writes

ἀλλ' οἱ μὲν δέδμηντο λίνῳ θανάτοιο πανάγρῳ,

which is as direct as ὀλέθρου πείρατ' ἐφῆπται (cf. *Od.* xxii, 383 ff. with 32 f., 41), and Quintus Smyrnaeus (xiii, 494 f.) of the Trojans slain:

περὶ γὰρ λίνα πάντοθε Μοῖραι
μακρὰ περιστήσαντο, τά περ βροτὸς οὔποτ' ἄλυξε.

λίνον will be discussed below (p. 336).

We may now better understand some passages of Aeschylus. The Chorus speak of Cassandra as 'caught in the snare of fate' (ἐντὸς δ' ἀλοῦσα μορσίμων ἀγρευμάτων);[1] and she in her vision of Agamemnon's murder under the robe asks whether it is 'a net of Hades' (τί τόδε φαίνεται; /ἦ δίκτυόν τι "Αιδου;);[2] and Aigisthos speaks of him as 'lying in the woven robes of the Erinyes' (ὑφαντοῖς ἐν πέπλοις Ἐρινύων/τὸν ἄνδρα τόνδε κείμενον);[3] and Hermes warns the Chorus in the *Prometheus Vinctus*: 'You will be entangled in the impassable net of ἄτη' (εἰς ἀπέραντον δίκτυον ἄτης/ἐμπλεχθήσεσθε).[4]

In *Od.* v, 288 f., when Poseidon sights Odysseus at last approaching Phaeacia and the end of his wanderings, he reflects bitterly:

καὶ δὴ Φαιήκων γαίης σχεδὸν ἔνθα οἱ αἶσα
ἐκφυγέειν μέγα πεῖραρ ὀϊζύος, ἥ μιν ἱκάνει.

Here too it has been customary[5] to interpret πεῖραρ as the abstract 'end' or 'limit', but what then is the point of μέγα we may ask. Monro endeavours to save himself by translating 'crisis', but that, while it may give sense to μέγα, is neither equivalent to 'end' or 'limit' nor suitable to the context. Poseidon has not yet thought of the wreck which is his final blow directly at Odysseus though apparently the idea strikes him in the next line. At the moment of his reflection, Odysseus is peacefully approaching safety after wanderings that had as much danger at the outset as at the close. 'End' and 'crisis' clearly will not do; πεῖραρ ὀϊζύος has a *prima facie* likeness to πεῖραρ ἔριδος and a similar translation gives us 'where it is his lot to escape from the great bond of misfortune which is upon

---

[1] *Ag.* 1048.

[2] 1114 f. Hades is referred to as a hunter, ἀγραῖος, by Aeschylus according to *Et. Gud.* p. 227, 41; *Anecd. Oxon.* II, p. 443, 12. If the robe is not part of the original history, it may as conceivably have grown out of earlier statements that he was thus snared by fate as out of the 'Αραχναῖον αἶπος suggested by Verrall.

[3] 1580f. For the Erinyes binding cf. pp. 368, 442 with 394, 400.

[4] 1078 f. For ἄτη as binder or bond in Homer see p. 327.

[5] Ameis-Hentze-Cauer, however, (*ad loc.*) has πεῖραρ 'ist "Ende" oder "Seil"; auch in unserer Seemannssprache heisst ein Tau ein "Ende". Hier wie χ 33, Z 143 die aus dem Ende geknüpfte Schlinge'.

him'.[1] He is at last to emerge, to obtain release, to become free. For the use of ἱκάνει of such a bond, the instances and illustrations dealt with just above should suffice; it is tantamount to ἐφῆπται. Just as γῆρας can either approach (ἱκάνει) or be approached (ἵκετο), so πεῖραρ ὀϊзύος and ὀλέθρου πείρατα can be either subject to ἱκάνει or object to ἵκηαι. Just as we saw that the individual or a host could fall a victim to the plural ὀλέθρου πείρατα, we now see that the individual no less than the host (XIII, 358 ff.) can be encompassed by a single bond.[2]

There remains *Il.* VII, 101 f.:

> τῷδε δ' ἐγὼν αὐτὸς θωρήξομαι· αὐτὰρ ὕπερθε
> νίκης πείρατ' ἔχονται ἐν ἀθανάτοισι θεοῖσιν.

Leaf, Schulze, Doederlein, and others are here also content with the 'issues' of victory, but ὕπερθε, obviously spatial, has given some editors pause. Merry and Riddell think that the abstract would fit well enough but that 'possibly the idea of a rope is contained...suggested by the graphic ὕπερθε'. There should be now no doubt. We have seen the πεῖραρ πολέμοιο extended over the hosts and the ὀλέθρου πείρατα fastened upon or awaiting them. πείρατα νίκης represents the other kind of fortune in war. How success no less than failure can be conceived as a cord or a bond must be considered presently.[3]

All these passages are descriptions of fate and are satisfied by the same image, that of *binding*; πεῖραρ is the *bond*. The solution is uniform and consistent, needing neither to compromise in 'rope-ends' nor to retreat upon a colourless abstraction—'limit', 'issue', 'crisis', 'sum'. Instead of vague periphrastic and unnecessary abstractions, it presents the concrete, a graphic image. To realise its nature is vitally

---

[1] For the present ἱκάνει of something continually present or which has already come we may compare the frequent use of ἵκει, e.g. *Od.* xx, 228: γιγνώσκω δὲ καὶ αὐτὸς ὅ τοι πινυτὴ φρένας ἵκει, or *Od.* ii, 28: τίνα χρειὼ τόσον ἵκει; cf. *Il.* x, 142. Even were it necessary to regard the πεῖραρ as a reference to something yet to come, i.e. the approaching wreck, the fitness of the sense 'bond' would be undiminished.

[2] For this particular 'bond' see further pp. 363 f. below.

[3] See pp. 333 ff., 365 ff.

important. 'This somewhat grossly corporeal conception must be regarded solely as a figure of speech', says Dr Leaf of the 'wire-pulling' which he thinks involved; 'the Homeric gods employ in fact more subtle powers'. To Monro it is a 'highly-wrought metaphor' or 'figure of speech'. It is an ἀλληγορία; μετενήνεκται μὲν οὖν ἀπὸ τῶν δεσμῶν say the scholiasts, μεταφορά, παραβολὴ ἀλληγορική says Eustathius. But what is Homer's practice in the matter? In contrast to his use of simile his metaphors are almost negligible—a very few, simple and brief, not going beyond single words,[1] the commonplaces of ordinary speech, offering nothing of such length or elaboration as the passages under discussion. These are abnormal and are recognised as such by the scholiast: μικτὴ ἡ ἀλληγορία. ἔχει δέ τι ἴδιον ἡ παραβολή· οὐ γὰρ ἰδίᾳ περὶ ἑκατέρου εἶπε τῆς τε εἰκόνος καὶ τοῦ εἰκονιζομένου πράγματος, ὅτι ὥσπερ οἱ ἐξασφαλιζόμενοι τοὺς δεσμούς...οὕτω καὶ οἱ θεοὶ κ.τ.λ. (schol. to XIII, 358; cf. Eustath. 937–8 ff.). What then is the solution? We should, I suggest, take the words at their face value and not try to explain them away as ῥητορικὴ ἀλληγορία or any other 'figure of speech', take them as no passing figments of the poet's brain but allusions to one of the images under which a whole people interpreted life and saw the working of fate, the action of the gods in things human, an image created and appreciated indeed by that same faculty which 'gives to airy nothings a local habitation and a name', an image which might lose credence as truth and pass into a metaphor, but which began as no such mere aid to literary description but rather as a popular belief of what actually happens on that plane where divine and human meet—the mystical and, to the unprivileged eye, invisible. It is in short a part of the national religion, of the philosophy of the race. To such a belief allusive reference would naturally be made and instantly comprehended. The obscurity which marks even the most explicit references we possess and has led to such curious and varied interpretations is thus easily explained, since it exists only when the reader or hearer has not already

[1] E.g. κύων applied in reproach to human beings.

the image in question as part of his mental furniture, as one of those *représentations collectives* which the individual receives from the community. If we would seek a parallel, we might compare the Διὸς τάλαντα, the reality of which happily the poet has left in no doubt,[1] but of which we may surmise the probable interpretation had no more explicit mention survived than *Il.* xvi, 656 ff. Zeus has decided upon temporary defeat for the Trojans,

> Ἕκτορι δὲ πρωτίστῳ ἀνάλκιδα θυμὸν ἐνῆκεν·
> ἐς δίφρον δ' ἀναβὰς φύγαδ' ἔτραπε, κέκλετο δ' ἄλλους
> Τρῶας φευγέμεναι· γνῶ γὰρ Διὸς ἱρὰ τάλαντα.

Even despite the evidence of the other passages, Monro says: ' No visible sign is meant here; the phrase is a concrete way of representing the decisive influence of Zeus', and Dr Leaf: 'Τάλαντα. Here the word practically means little more than *will*. The backward and forward movements of the battle, which Hector perceives,[2] answer to the fluctuations of Zeus' will, which themselves are typified by the figure of a balance swinging up and down'. It is not a question of Hector seeing a pair of scales but of what he believed Zeus to use in deciding. In the interpretation of early literature, a readiness to see mere figures of speech in phrases which depart from our conceptions of reality is not a virtue, though in later times when the hypotheses of primitive fancy have, relatively speaking, yielded before a closer scrutiny of fact, and when, also, the relation of language to thought has become less severe, it may be commendable caution.

We have not, however, yet exhausted the evidence of the image under consideration, that of binding. Their fate

---

[1] See *Il.* viii, 69 ff., xix, 223 f., xxii, 209 ff. discussed on pp. 397 ff. below.

[2] But Hector is the first (πρώτιστος) to flee, the first to be demoralised; the defeat did not begin till he fled, ἔνθ' οὐδ' ἴφθιμοι Λύκιοι μένον κ.τ.λ. There was therefore no movement to observe. If not of actual vision— and with γνῶ it is safer to assume not—it must be understood of perceiving the movement of something else, perhaps the sinking of his own heart from what we should regard as natural, physical, or psychological causes, but which to Homer's contemporaries seemed the interference of the gods. See p. 303.

(πόλεμος, ὀϊʒύς, ὄλεθρος, etc.) is a bond (πεῖραρ) fastened upon men. There are in Homer a number of passages in which the verbs πεδάω or ἐπιδέω, ἐνδέω, καταδέω, etc. are used to express exactly this idea. In a man's fortunes, death is the supreme event; it is fate *par excellence*, and in many tongues the word 'fate'—e.g. μοῖρα, μόρος, *fatum, šimu* [1] (Babylon.)—may be used alone to express it. It is therefore also the 'bond' *par excellence*, the 'bond' without qualification, e.g. *Il.* IV, 517–26:

> ἔνθ' 'Αμαρυγκείδην Διώρεα μοῖρ' ἐπέδησεν.
> χερμαδίῳ γὰρ βλῆτο...
> ...τὸν δὲ σκότος ὄσσε κάλυψεν. [2]

But the poet may be more explicit, just as for μοῖρα he may use μοῖρα θανάτου.[3] Thus Amphinomos is warned to flee and has foreboding of what awaits the suitors:

> ἀλλ' οὐδ' ὣς φύγε κῆρα· πέδησε δὲ καὶ τὸν 'Αθήνη,
> Τηλεμάχου ὑπὸ χερσὶ καὶ ἔγχεϊ ἶφι δαμῆναι.[4]

While the ἀοιδός is with her, Clytemnestra lives chastely:

> ἀλλ' ὅτε δή μιν μοῖρα θεῶν ἐπέδησε δαμῆναι,[5]

he was marooned to die and she joined Aigisthos. But the bond may be of a different character. Twice before the assembled hosts, Agamemnon complains:

> Ζεύς με μέγα Κρονίδης ἄτη ἐνέδησε βαρείη,[6]

and the δαίμων ῎Ατη may be the power that binds. Agamemnon blames her for his treatment of Achilles:

> κατ' ἀνδρῶν κράατα βαίνει,
> βλάπτουσ' ἀνθρώπους· κατὰ δ' οὖν ἕτερόν γε πέδησεν.[7]

On the field of battle the presence of the bond may be felt as a kind of physical paralysis. When the day is going against

---

[1] For details see Fichtner-Jeremias, 'Der Schicksalsglaube bei den Babyloniern', *Mitteil. der Vorderas.-Aegypt. Gesellschaft*, II, 1922, pp. 61 ff.

[2] *Il.* IV, 517–26. For the difficulty of distinguishing μοῖρα, a bond laid upon a man by a god or gods, from μοῖρα a personal power, see pp. 379, 392 ff., 399 f. [3] *Od.* II, 100, III, 238, XVII, 326, etc.

[4] *Od.* XVIII, 155 f.

[5] *Od.* III, 269. The reference of μιν and, with it, the sense of δαμῆναι cannot be determined with certainty. [6] *Il.* II, 111, IX, 18.

[7] *Il.* XIX, 93 f.

him, Agamemnon knows the cause. It was well for kings when they had such a refuge. Again it is Zeus:

ᾔδεα μὲν γὰρ ὅτε πρόφρων Δαναοῖσιν ἄμυνεν,
οἶδα δὲ νῦν ὅτε τοὺς μὲν ὁμῶς μακάρεσσι θεοῖσιν
κυδάνει, ἡμέτερον δὲ μένος καὶ χεῖρας ἔδησεν.[1]

We may compare:

Ἕκτορι πάντες ἐπώμεθ' ἀολλέες· αὐτὰρ Ἀχαιοὶ
οὐ μενέουσ', εἰ δή σφιν ὀλέθρου πείρατ' ἐφῆπται.[2]

This physical sense and the virtual equation of the mystical to a physical bond are strikingly revealed by one passage.[3] Melampous undertakes to 'lift' the cattle of Iphikles but is caught:

...χαλεπὴ δὲ θεοῦ κατὰ μοῖρα πέδησε
δεσμοί τ' ἀργαλέοι[4] καὶ βουκόλοι ἀγροιῶται.
ἀλλ' ὅτε δὴ μῆνές τε καὶ ἡμέραι ἐξετελεῦντο
ἂψ περιτελλομένου ἔτεος, καὶ ἐπήλυθον ὧραι,
καὶ τότε δή μιν ἔλυσε βίη Ἰφικληείη
θέσφατα πάντ' εἰπόντα· Διὸς δ' ἐτελείετο βουλή.

A similar physical effect is given where the restriction is local,[5] spatial. The Trojans flee before Achilles into the city:

Ἕκτορα δ' αὐτοῦ μεῖναι ὀλοιὴ μοῖρ' ἐπέδησεν,
Ἰλίου προπάροιθε πυλάων τε Σκαιάων.[6]

To this may be cited an exact counterpart on the purely physical plane, one which also confirms us in connecting these passages with the image of πείρατα. As they approach the isle of the Sirens, Odysseus instructs his comrades:

ἀλλά με δεσμῷ
δήσατ' ἐν ἀργαλέῳ, ὄφρ' ἔμπεδον αὐτόθι μίμνω,
ὀρθὸν ἐν ἱστοπέδῃ, ἐκ δ' αὐτοῦ πείρατ' ἀνήφθω.[7]

The binding of Hector must not, however, be regarded as a bodily incapacitation, a paralysis of the kind that may be implied by χεῖρας ἔδησεν (Il. xiv, 73) cited above. The effect of the bond of fate was that Hector willingly remained without. Physical paralysis may, however, be stated quite explicitly as

---

[1] Il. xiv, 71 ff.   [2] Il. xii, 78 f.   [3] Od. xi, 292–7.

[4] Should we, with a like transition, reinterpret Simon. 132 (Bergk) ἔργμασιν ἐν πολέμου ('in coils—enclosing bonds; cf. εἰργμός, ἕρκος—of war'; cf. pp. 310 ff., 432 ff.) δεσμῷ ἐν σιδηρέῳ, an inscription with actual fetters? Cf. δαμάω, p. 438, n. 1.

[5] Here and later I use the word 'local' not in the sense of 'partial, limited in extent', but of being tied to one place.

[6] Il. xxii, 5 f.   [7] Od. xii, 160 ff.

the means whereby the bond holds a man motionless.[1] Thus
of Alkathoos we read:

τὸν τόθ' ὑπ' 'Ιδομενῆϊ Ποσειδάων ἐδάμασσεν
θέλξας ὄσσε φαεινά, πέδησε δὲ φαίδιμα γυῖα·
οὔτε γὰρ ἐξοπίσω φυγέειν δύνατ' οὔτ' ἀλέασθαι,
ἀλλ' ὥς τε στήλην ἢ δένδρεον ὑψιπέτηλον,
ἀτρέμας ἑσταότα στῆθος μέσον οὔτασε δουρί.[2]

Spatial fixation may also be secured by physical means outside
of the victim's personality and against the will of the victim.
The weather-*bound* Menelaos asks Proteus:

ἀλλὰ σύ πέρ μοι εἰπέ (θεοὶ δέ τε πάντα ἴσασιν),
ὅς τίς μ' ἀθανάτων πεδάᾳ καὶ ἔδησε κελεύθου,[3]

To Penelope Odysseus sums up the past:

ἐμὲ Ζεὺς ἄλγεσι καὶ θεοὶ ἄλλοι
ἱέμενον πεδάασκον ἐμῆς ἀπὸ πατρίδος αἴης.[4]

We may revert in thought to the μέγα πεῖραρ ὀϊζύος[5] from
which in Phaeacia he was delivered and enabled to return
home. Frequently after a word with a final vowel, a verb
occurs which may be either (ἐ)- πέδησε or (ἐπ)- έδησε, the
aorist of either[6] πεδάω or ἐπιδέω. This might complicate the
discussion but for the fact that in sense πεδάω is virtually
identical with δέω. The image is unaffected, since a shackle
or hobble which the former verb implies is merely a specialised

[1] With this we may contrast *Il.* xii, 78, where, so far from rooting them
to the spot, the effect to be expected from the ὀλέθρου πείρατα is retreat
or flight. For a Norse parallel to the conception of paralysis as a binding
see below, pp. 353 ff.

[2] *Il.* xiii, 434 ff.   [3] *Od.* iv, 468 f.

[4] *Od.* xxiii, 352 f. Cf. xiv, 61, vii, 272.   [5] See above, pp. 323 f.

[6] There appears to be no clear instance in Homer of ἐπιδέω in a form
which cannot also equally well belong to πεδάω; the latter, on the other
hand, appears, as we see, several times in forms that admit no doubt. This
is perhaps not absolutely conclusive, but when united to the fact that
ἐπιδέω elsewhere is comparatively rare and has the sense, which we might
expect, of binding something upon something else (τι ἐπί τι), e.g. ἐπὶ τὰ
κρανέα λόφους ἐπιδέεσθαι, Herodotus, i, 171 (cf. Aristoph. *Frogs*, 1038), or
of bandaging, e.g. Hipp. *V.C.* 13, it suggests very strongly that it is to
πεδάω that Homer's doubtful ἐπέδησε must be referred. It is usually
considered an open question. Merry and Riddell assume that in *Od.* xxi,
390, ὅπλον...βύβλινον ᾧ ῥ' ἐπέδησε θύρας, it must perforce belong to
ἐπιδέω, but πεδάω may just as well describe the fixing, making fast of
a door as the stopping of a ship (*Od.* xiii, 168) or the hindering of a chariot
(*Il.* xxiii, 585). Since this note was in proof the revisers of Liddell and
Scott have come down on this side.

form of bond aiming at local restriction and applied more particularly to the feet. Poseidon stalls his horses:

ἀμφὶ δὲ ποσσὶ πέδας ἔβαλε χρυσείας
ἀρρήκτους ἀλύτους, ὄφρ' ἔμπεδον αὖθι μένοιεν.[1]

In accordance with usage the equipment and appurtenances of the gods are of gold,[2] but the epithets ἀρρήκτους ἀλύτους are precisely those which in the much discussed passage above are applied to πεῖραρ and also, as there observed, to the δεσμοί which Hephaistos *forged* (κόπτε) for Ares. To πεῖραρ we have compared the Sanscrit *parvan-*, *par-u-s* and *pari*; to these we may now add *para*, meaning precisely a hobble or shackle used e.g. for elephants. πεδάω occurs sometimes unequivocally as in *Od.* iv, 469 and xxiii, 353 just cited. Where, as in the former of these, there would seem to be a distinction from δέω, it is precisely in the direction of more markedly local restriction.[3]

[1] *Il.* xiii, 36 f.

[2] See e.g. Artemis χρυσηλάκατος, *Il.* xvi, 183, also Leaf's note on *Il.* v, 387 and 723 and Rogers on Aristoph. *Thesm.* 300 and above, pp. 106, 156, n. 2, 165 f., 183, n. 1.

[3] In vengeance for its convoy of Odysseus, Poseidon λᾶαν θῆκε καὶ ἐρρίζωσεν ἔνερθε the Phaeacian ship; upon which an observer from the land exclaims: 'ὤ μοι, τίς δὴ νῆα θοὴν ἐπέδησ' ἐνὶ πόντῳ
οἴκαδ' ἐλαυνομένην; καὶ δὴ προυφαίνετο πᾶσα.'
Od. xiii, 168 f.

The image appears here to be passing into a mere metaphor but we shall find a curious parallel (p. 355) to the present passage bearing witness the other way and evidence warning against the assumption of mere metaphor (p. 370, note 1). πεδάω can, however, be used unequivocally of human acts producing physical hindrance without the use of πέδαι. Tricked into defeat in the chariot race by something approaching a 'foul', Menelaos challenges Antilochos:

'ὄμνυθι μὴ μὲν ἑκὼν τὸ ἐμὸν δόλῳ ἅρμα πεδῆσαι'.
Il. xiii, 585.

This use would grow out of the fact that in the ordinary world of men and things binding or hobbling is the mode *par excellence* of hindering action or motion or confining locally, just as bonds form the obvious and historically primitive method of imprisonment, witnessed not only by the numerous particular instances, e.g. *Od.* xv, 444, xiv, 345, but by the idiom persisting into later ages of calling a prison δεσμοί, δεσμωτήριον, *vincula*, etc. and a prisoner δεσμώτης, though this is in part due to that caution which makes assurance doubly sure by using fetters even within imprisoning walls, e.g. *Il.* v, 385 ff. For fixation as binding see also p. 371.

The 'binding' of the gods is no mere trick of language but a literal description of an actual process, their mode of imposing fate upon mortals, a religious belief and not a metaphor. The longer expressions involving πεῖραρ τανύειν, etc. are merely more explicit references to the same. Sometimes they concern not a single individual, whose experience might adequately be described by a simple verb ἔδησε, ἐπέδησε, etc. with or without a dative or infinitive to define the bond, but rather a multitude, more or fewer of whom may be affected. It may then be necessary or desirable to say how many are involved, e.g. whether both armies and whether equally. To express this the simple verb 'to bind' is resolved and becomes 'to spread a bond over'. Of the other phrases we are perhaps justified in regarding πείρατ' ἐφῆπται as from a different angle an equivalent of ἔδησεν, and the whole phrase (τινι) ὀλέθρου πείρατ' ἐφῆπται as an equivalent of (τινα) μοῖρα θεῶν ἐπέδησε δαμῆναι. In Il. xxii, 5 ὀλέθρου is represented in the epithet of μοῖρα: ὀλοιὴ μοῖρ' ἐπέδησεν, and instead of the infinitive the dative of a noun, e.g. ἄτη, may with the verb of binding form the counterpart to the genitive defining πεῖραρ. Thus all these varieties of expression may be referred to the same image and belief: fortune in its different forms is a cord or bond fastened upon a man by the powers above.

The popular idiom expressing necessity reveals this very image. It is the so-called impersonal δεῖ.[1] Homer uses it once, τί δὲ δεῖ πολεμιζέμεναι Τρώεσσιν/'Αργείους; (Il. ix, 337–8). The usual translation, 'Why need the Argives fight?' misses the true meaning, i.e. 'what binds them to fight?' If we give to δεῖ the force which is habitual in δέω we find ourselves at once on common ground with Homer's ἐπέδησε δαμῆναι, μεῖναι, etc. and similar uses of ἔδησε, κατέδησε, ἐνέδησε, etc. dealt with at length above.[2] This original force of δεῖ is perhaps still clearer in the variant form of the idiom δεῖ σε ὅπως τοῦτο

[1] This connection with δέω, 'I bind' (see e.g. Plato, Phaedo, 99 c), is however by no means universally accepted, though given by Liddell and Scott. Boisacq and others connect it with δέομαι, δεύομαι, 'to lack, request'.

[2] δεῖ is clearly used of fate in Herodot. ii, 161; ix, 109; Soph. O.T. 825, etc.

ποιήσεις. The subject is probably the god as in ὕει and νίφει.[1] Both forms persist throughout classical Greek literature.

The etymology of ἀνάγκη, commonly translated 'necessity', is uncertain but a connection with ἄγχειν, 'to strangle', has been suggested, in which case the binding cord (or serpent) would not be far to seek. The Orphics, Pythagoreans and others conceived of a personal power Ἀνάγκη supreme over all. Parmenides speaks of his reality as remaining fast, 'for mighty Ἀνάγκη holds it in bonds of the πεῖραρ which encloses it around' (κρατερὴ γὰρ Ἀνάγκη / πείρατος ἐν δεσμοῖσιν ἔχει, τό μιν ἀμφὶς ἐέργει).[2] Alternatively he says it is 'immovable in πείρατα of huge bonds' (ἀκίνητον μεγάλων ἐν πείρασι δεσμῶν)[3] and gives what we have seen to be Homer's equivalent for extending a πεῖραρ or πείρατα, saying that there is nothing outside it 'since Μοῖρα has bound it to be whole and immovable' (τό γε Μοῖρ᾽ ἐπέδησεν / οὖλον ἀκίνητόν τ᾽ ἔμεναι).[4] This conception, of a πεῖραρ or πείρατα around the world binding it, is, we may believe, related to Homer's conception of Ὠκεανός and Τηθύς as 'bonds' binding the earth (πείρατα γαίης) traced above.[5] To the latter we have already[6] related the Orphic conception of the serpent Χρόνος wound around and its mate Ἀνάγκη, and the probably cognate Pythagorean doctrine that Ἀνάγκη 'lies around the universe' (περικεῖσθαι τῷ κόσμῳ),[7] and may now relate Plato's conception of the universe with the spindle of Ἀνάγκη as its axis and girt around by a 'bond' (ξύνδεσμος, δεσμοί)[8] of light, perhaps to be identified with the Milky Way (γαλαξίας κύκλος).

The Latin term for that which must be, *necesse*, would most naturally be related[9] to *necto*, *nexus*, with an original reference

---

[1] Liddell and Scott thus explain χρή, 'the god delivers an oracle', or as we should perhaps say, 'destines'. Compare Homer's θέσφατον.

[2] B 8, ll. 30f. (Diels).   [3] L. 26.

[4] Ll. 37f.   [5] See pp. 315ff.   [6] Pp. 249ff.

[7] *Aet.* I, 25, 2. The idea had a long history. Cf. *Orphic. Fr.* 166 (Kern), etc. According to the *Theologoumena Arithmeticae*, 60 (pp. 81, 19ff., ed. V. de Falco), attributed to Iamblichus: τὴν Ἀνάγκην οἱ θεολόγοι τῇ τοῦ παντὸς οὐρανοῦ ἐξωτάτη ἄντυγι ἐπηχοῦσι.   [8] *Rep.* 616bf.

[9] See *Anzeiger f. indogerm. Spr. u. Altertumsk.* hg. v. W. Streitberg (*Beiblatt* of *Indogerm. Forsch.* hg. v. K. Brugmann u. W. Streitberg), XXIII,

to binding or being bound. *Necessitas*, elevated into a goddess of fate like the Greek 'Ανάγκη, appears in Horace associated with the *mortis laquei*.[1] Our 'destiny, predestination', etc. are also of Latin origin in the verb *destino* which was used of 'binding', e.g. *antemnas ad malos* (Caesar, *B.G.* III, 14, 6; cf. the use of πείρατα in *Od.* XII, 51, etc.), and had as primary meaning 'fix'. Its application to human 'destiny' appears in phrases like *ad horam mortis destinatam* (Cic. *Tusc.* v, 22, 63) and *destinata deo* (Tac. *Hist.* IV, 84). We may glance aside for a moment at an idiom of our own tongue which we use daily without guessing its significance[2] in the dim past of the race. Of that which we regard as destined, necessary, certain, we say 'it is *bound* to happen', 'he is *bound* to lose, to be killed, etc.' (and in dialect 'tied to lose', etc.), just as Homer said ἐπέδησε δαμῆναι, Τρώεσσιν ὀλέθρου πείρατ' ἐφῆπται, etc. What one must do is what one is 'bound to do'.

In *Il.* VII, 94 ff. Menelaos, notwithstanding that Hector πολὺ φέρτερος ἦεν, rises to meet him with the words:

τῷδε δ' ἐγὼν αὐτὸς θωρήξομαι· αὐτὰρ ὕπερθεν
νίκης πείρατ' ἔχονται ἐν ἀθανάτοισι θεοῖσιν.

---

pp. 34, 115. Walde, *op. cit.* s.v., prefers *ne-ced-tis*, 'unausweichlichkeit', but the bulk of evidence here collected of the primitive tendency to think of fate or constraint as a binding and such expressions as *maiestatis crimen subdebatur, vinclum et necessitas silendi* (Tacitus, *Ann.* III, 67) should make what he admits as a possibility, a certainty. He thinks *necessitas, necessitudo, necessarius* used of kinship inconclusive, since ἀναγκαῖος has similar force. For ἀνάγκη itself see above. We may reply that there is no obvious relation between compulsion or necessity and kinship, but that both have a natural point of contact in binding which implies not only constraint but also union and proximity. Of the universal application of terms of binding to kinship, 'the bonds of affinity which are the links and ties of nature' (Bacon, *Political Fables*, II Expl.), we need not go far in search of examples: Sanscr. *bándhu-ḥ*, 'kinsman', etc. Walde himself translates *necessarius* 'eng verwandt, verbunden' with which we may compare the 'connection' of Lewis and Short, and Liddell and Scott's translation of ἀναγκαῖος: 'connected by necessary or natural ties'. See also below, pp. 374f., 438f.

[1] Hor. *Od.* III, 24, 5 ff. cited on p. 374 below.

[2] Skeat and Murray are apparently not concerned to explain the idiom, but in the light of the early Norse and Anglo-Saxon beliefs (see pp. 353 ff., 381, 440) the above solution appears certain.

334 ΠΕΙΡΑΤΑ

The significance and tone of this are almost exactly those of Hector's speech, when he too dares to meet a mightier than himself: οἶδα δ' ὅτι σὺ μὲν ἐσθλός, ἐγὼ δὲ σέθεν πολὺ χείρων.
ἀλλ' ἤτοι μὲν ταῦτα θεῶν ἐν γούνασι κεῖται,
αἵ κέ σε χειρότερός περ ἐὼν ἀπὸ θυμὸν ἔλωμαι.[1]

ταῦτα as defined in the following line is precisely νίκη. In similar fashion for slightly different situations three other passages[2] suggest that victory or the fortunes of war 'lie on the knees of the gods'. Perhaps even closer in form to this expression is the fragment of Archilochus:

καὶ νέους θάρσυνε· νίκης δ' ἐν θεοῖσι πείρατα.[3]

What lies 'upon the knees of the gods' is the fate that the gods spin (θεοὶ ἐπέκλωσαν).[4] πείρατα should, we might now suspect, be related to the spinning. πεῖραρ is always qualified by some genitive: ὀλέθρου, Od. XXII, 33, 41; Il. VI, 143, VII, 402, XII, 79, XX, 429; ὀϊζύος, Od. V, 289; νίκης, Il. VII, 102; ἔριδος καὶ πτολέμοιο, Il. XIII, 358. If, however, we look at the eight passages in which θεοὶ ἐπέκλωσαν or a slight variation is used, we find that (except when instead there is a dependent infinitive, e.g. ʒώειν, Il. XXIV, 515, cf. Od. I, 17, or an equivalent pronoun τὰ μέν or τά γε, Od. XI, 139, XVI, 64) ἐπέκλωσαν is followed by a defining accusative ὄλεθρον, Od. VIII, 579; ὀϊʒύν, Od. XX, 196; ὄλβον, Od. III, 208, IV, 208. There is thus striking similarity, in two cases actual identity, between the objects[5] of ἐπέκλωσαν and the determinate πείρατα. With the infinitives after ἐπέκλωσαν we may compare those after ἔδησε or ἐπέδησε, e.g. μεῖναι, δαμῆναι, etc. What, however, are the products of spinning? Thread and—the same on a large scale

---

[1] Il. xx, 434 ff.   [2] Il. xvii, 514; Od. i, 267, xvi, 129.
[3] 55 (Bgk.).   [4] See pp. 305 ff., 418.
[5] Above (p. 320) Merry and Riddell cite Τρώεσσι δὲ κήδε' ἐφῆπται, Il. II, 15, to show that πείρατα in Τρώεσσιν ὀλέθρου πείρατ' ἐφῆπται has the abstract sense which they think original. (τινι) κήδε' ἐφῆπται occurs also Il. II, 32, 69, VI, 241 and we may add XXI, 513, ἔρις καὶ νεῖκος ἐφῆπται, where the image is applied to the gods themselves (see p. 392). With an image familiar as a racial belief, there was no need to be explicit every time. πεῖραρ could perfectly well be implied in a verb like ἐφῆπται, as it unquestionably is in ἐπέκλωσαν with the apparently abstract ὄλβον, etc.

—rope or cord, a recognised meaning of πεῖραρ. Thread or wool also, though as yet unsuspected, might be, and indeed is, covered by the same term.[1] The important point for the moment is that the same fortunes which the gods spin for men, they also fasten upon them in the form of a cord or bond.

Of the passages with ἐπικλώθειν cited above, except for those whose significance is general and as it were timeless (i.e. *Il.* xxiv, 525; *Od.* iv, 208, xx, 196), all have the verb in the past tense, implying that the spinning by the gods was anterior in time to the actualisation in life. One of these exceptions is more explicit:

> ῥεῖα δ᾽ ἀρίγνωτος γόνος ἀνέρος ᾧ τε Κρονίων
> ὄλβον ἐπικλώσῃ γαμέοντί τε γιγνομένῳ τε.[2]

This is supported by *Il.* xx, 127, xxiv, 210; *Od.* vii, 197, in which the fortunes of men are spun not by the gods but by Αἶσα, Μοῖρα, or the Κλῶθες, and which unite in referring the spinning to the time of birth. The addition of marriage (γαμέοντι) in the first is natural enough, since it opens a new chapter of life to the married and initiates the birth of another generation.[3] The essential fact is that the spinning was thought of not as simultaneous with but as anterior to the fortunes spun. Something more was required for actualisation. We might expect that something to be one of the processes which naturally follow spinning among men, since there too spinning is but a preliminary. What is spun has still to be used. What are the normal uses of thread or cord? To bind and to weave. Binding is the fundamental purpose, the ἔργον, which gives a cord its significance, and to binding weaving itself and still more obviously the kindred process of net-making may be reduced or analysed. It is exactly this process, binding, which for the gods in Homer does, as we have seen, follow[4] spinning.

---

[1] See pp. 338 ff.　　[2] *Od.* iv, 208 f.　　[3] Cf. Catull. lxiv, 305–383.

[4] Apparently, the binding might take place at any point in the interval between birth or the spinning and actualisation. It could be said in the hour of their success and apparent safety:

> ὡς ἤδη Τρώεσσιν ὀλέθρου πείρατ᾽ ἐφῆπται,　　*Il.* vii, 402,

to which may be added *Od.* xxii, 33 and 41, where Homer balances it with the *mot* νῦν τοι σῶς αἰπὺς ὄλεθρος, line 28. Clearly the bond could

We can perhaps understand thus Euripides[1] speaking of
Atreus, 'for whom the goddess carded and spun bands (or
"wreaths"), strife, warfare against Thyestes, his own brother':

ᾧ στέμματα ξήνασ' ἐπέκλωσεν θεὰ
ἔριν, Θυέστῃ πόλεμον ὄντι συγγόνῳ
θέσθαι.

These varied passages of Homer are thus found to harmonise,
the difficulties of interpretation in particular instances disappear, and instead of a jumble of metaphors, figures of speech,
which no one has thought of coordinating, there emerges a
complex yet self-consistent and not ungraceful image, the
form under which the race for which Homer wrote had
conceived the making and fulfilment of human destinies.
At birth the gods or fates spin the strands of weal or woe which
a man must endure in the course of his life, strands conceived
quite literally as λίνον,[2] as threads:

τὰ πείσεται ἅσσα οἱ Αἶσα
γιγνομένῳ ἐπένησε λίνῳ, ὅτε μιν τέκε μήτηρ.

Later they bind them upon him no less literally as bonds,
πείρατα—for Quintus Smyrnaeus the ὀλέθρου πείρατα, the

be fastened long before taking effect. In other passages we should perhaps
infer that the binding was immediately antecedent to or coincident with
the fate which it ensured, e.g.

ἔνθ' Ἀμαρυγκείδην Διώρεα μοῖρ' ἐπέδησεν.
χερμαδίῳ γὰρ βλῆτο παρὰ σφυρὸν ὀκριόεντι, κ.τ.λ.

Il. IV, 517 f.

See below, p. 356.
[1] Orestes, 12 ff. στέμματα cannot mean merely unspun wool on a distaff.
Cf. pp. 376 f. and 402 ff. below.
[2] Il. XX, 127. Cf. XXIV, 210; Od. VII, 197; Theoc. I, 139, etc. It is believed that the cry λίνον or αἴλινον was not in origin a lament for a person
Linos but had a more general significance, since it was used where clearly
someone else was concerned (e.g. Aesch. Ag. 121; Soph. Aj. 627; Eurip.
Hel. 171). The current solution is just that it is the Semitic ai lanu, 'woe to
us', based on Eurip. Or. 1395 ff.: αἴλινον, αἴλινον ἀρχὰν θανάτου βάρβαροι
λέγουσιν Ἀσιάδι φωνᾷ. But the Greek cry appears to have been λίνον as
early as Homer (Il. XVIII, 570 without αἴ), not lanu ('to us'). αἴ is Greek
also: 'alas!' Whether with such Semitic background or not, Greek λίνον
or αἴλινον was, I suggest, at first used with a sense 'The thread!' 'Alas,
the thread!' (or 'net', see p. 322, note 3) crying out upon fate exactly
as later men lamented the μίτος of the Μοῖραι (see e.g. p. 349 and note 7
on p. 352). This is supported by the fact that weavers used to sing it
(Epicharm. 14 Kaibel). Cf. αἰνόλινος, δεινόλινος.

bonds encompassing doomed warriors, are the λίνα[1] of the Μοῖραι—bonds not less real because they are not visible. 'Second sight'[2] or privileged eyes may behold them as they may the gods, but to ordinary mortals these things are hid or the future would have no secrets. Their presence is witnessed by their effects. We may cite the snare which was prepared for Ares by Hephaistos and which, since it was to entrap a god, was made invisible even to the eyes of gods:

> κόπτε δὲ δεσμοὺς
> ἀρρήκτους ἀλύτους, ὄφρ' ἔμπεδον αὖθι μένοιεν...
> ἠΰτ' ἀράχνια λεπτά, τά γ' οὐ κέ τις οὐδὲ ἴδοιτο,
> οὐδὲ θεῶν μακάρων, περὶ γὰρ δολόεντα τέτυκτο.[3]

ἆσσον ἴθ', ὥς κεν θᾶσσον ὀλέθρου πείραθ' ἵκηαι runs the invitation elsewhere (*Il.* VI, 143, etc.). The victims cannot see the bonds spread for them, but when the latter take effect, they are paralysed, reft of power to move as is the warrior on the battlefield:[4]

> οὐδέ τι κινῆσαι μελέων ἦν οὐδ' ἀναεῖραι.[5]

Even so invisible[6] to men are the mystic bonds of fate, the threads divinely spun.

Looking back we may now compare with Homer's 'The πείρατα of victory are held above among the immortal gods'[7] the inscription 'Such is the wretched life of mortals, so unfulfilled their hopes, over which the threads of the Μοῖραι hang'[8] (αἴ[ς] Μοιρῶν νήματ' ἐπικρέμαται), and with the ὀλέθρου πείρατα Simonides' 'Inescapable death is hung over us; for of it good and bad have equal portion allotted'[9] (ὁ δ' ἄφυκτος ὁμῶς ἐπικρέμαται θάνατος, / κείνου γὰρ ἴσον λάχον μέρος οἵ τ'

---

[1] See note 3 on p. 322 and compare Statius, *Silv.* v, 1, 155 ff., cited on p. 374 below.

[2] Cf. p. 354 below and the anticipatory vision of Theoklymenos (p. 181).

[3] *Od.* VIII, 274 ff.   [4] See e.g. *Il.* XIII, 434 cited on p. 329.

[5] *Od.* VIII, 298.

[6] It would, however, be a mistake to assume that the invisibility was a matter of fineness, smallness. In the μέγα πεῖραρ ὀϊζύος to which Odysseus was subject (*Od.* v, 289, pp. 323 f. above), the epithet may be conceived in a physical sense, 'huge', 'great', to suit the greatness of misfortune involved.

[7] See p. 324.   [8] *Epig. Gr.* (Kaibel), 151.

[9] Fr. 39 (Bgk.). For his fate hanging over a man see pp. 402 f. below. It might be conceived as a band or a web (see pp. 426 ff.).

ἀγαθοί / ὅστις τε κακός). In a παροιμία, which survives, πεῖραρ appears to have been replaced by μίτος. The παροιμία is: μίτος ἔριδος τότ᾽ ἦν, of which the reference is given by Apostolius[1] as ἐπὶ τῶν ἐριζόντων καὶ διατεινομένων. The best parallels Leutsch could find are from Tertullian, variations of *funem contentiosum alterno ductu in diversa distendere*.[2] This, as also the διατεινομένων of Apostolius, perhaps points back to the ἔριδος πεῖραρ of the Homeric crux (*Il.* XIII, 358 ff.) discussed above and to a misinterpretation of it, still current, with which we have dealt, that of the 'Tug of War'. That misinterpretation, however, is absent from the παροιμία itself. Indeed μίτος so far from being the equivalent of *funis*, a rope, that would be necessary for a 'Tug of War', appears never to mean anything stouter than a thread or string. The ἔριδος πεῖραρ was a bond laid upon the hosts involving them in strife. Instances of μίτος as the thread of fate after κλώθειν are given below.[3]

It can also be shown that πεῖραρ could mean a woof-thread and at the same time a difficulty of interpretation is removed from a passage of Pindar. In the first Pythian occurs the statement:

καιρὸν εἰ φθέγξαιο, πολλῶν πείρατα συντανύσαις
ἐν βραχεῖ, μείων ἕπεται μῶμος ἀνθρώπων,[4]

on which Gildersleeve[5] remarks: 'A homely figure seems to underlie πείρατα συντανύσαις. Of this commentators have made nothing satisfactory though the general drift is clear enough: "summing up the chief points of many things in brief compass". The metaphor of a rope-walk would explain συντανύσαις, πείρατα being the ropes or strands'. In his note to the passage he translates 'twisting the strands of many things into a short compass', but unfortunately there is no hint of twisting or of the scholiast's συμπλέξας in συντανύσαις and the image thus presented is not very happy. For Farnell the πείρατα are 'ends', yet his rendering rests upon the idea of Gildersleeve by which the πείρατα are 'ropes or strands':

[1] 11, 62 in Schneidewin and Leutsch, *Paroemiographi Gr.*
[2] *De Pudic.* 2. Cf. *adv. Marcion.* IV, 4 and *ad Jud.* I.
[3] P. 349 and p. 352, n. 7. [4] Ll. 81 f.
[5] *Pindar, Olympian and Pythian Odes*, p. xviii, note I.

'gathering together the loose ends of many matters in a single plait'. But συντανύσαις no more expresses 'plaiting' than 'twisting', and πείρατα is not 'loose ends'. Also, apparently without being aware of a fundamental inconsistency, Farnell in his translation of the whole ode interprets 'in brief utterance straightening out a tangled skein'; but the Greek says nothing of straightening, tangling, or skein; and such a process does not very happily fit the 'brief utterance'. On the other hand perfect sense is given if πείρατα means woof-threads; and weaving is just such a 'homely figure' as is recognised to be necessary. The point of πολλῶν πείρατα... ἐν βραχεῖ now appears. In antiquity owing to the lack of mechanical devices, the insertion of woof-threads was a tedious business, so that cheaper cloths tended to have very few of the former in proportion to the threads of the warp. The better the cloth, the greater the relative number of woof-threads in a short length. This is admirably shown by the varieties of cloth which have survived in the tombs of Egypt.[1] We need not, however, go so far afield for an exact parallel to Pindar's advice, showing the literal basis of the metaphor. Speaking of winter, Hesiod[2] says: 'Wear a warm cloak'— στήμονι δ' ἐν παύρῳ πολλὴν κρόκα μηρύσασθαι, where στήμων and κρόξ (hypothetical) or κρόκη are the usual words for warp and woof respectively. τείνειν or τανύειν, used by Homer for the analogous processes of stringing a lyre or bow, naturally describes the stretching or drawing of the woof-thread across the warp, and Pollux[3] to describe what appears to be this process gives τείνειν and μηρύεσθαι, Hesiod's word,

[1] See Sir G. Wilkinson's *The Ancient Egyptians*, ed. Birch, II, pp. 161 f.: 'The number of threads in the warp invariably exceeded those in the woof, occasionally even by four times that quantity.... This structure so different from that of modern cloth, which has the proportions nearly equal, originated probably in the difficulty and tediousness of getting in the woof, when the shuttle was thrown by hand'.

[2] *Works and Days*, 538.

[3] *Onomasticon*, VII, 32. It is just possible that both words may here refer to part of the spinning process, since he is giving terms for the whole process including spinning and weaving. Were it so, it would not affect the use of both, indisputably evidenced in the case of μηρύεσθαι, for weaving.

together. Pindar and Hesiod are thus in slightly different terms giving the same advice, 'weave closely; make good cloth,[1] with many woof-threads in a short length of warp', though Pindar means it metaphorically: 'If you speak to the point and pithily—with much matter in a little space, with the texture of your speech close, well knit—less cavil follows'. If this interpretation be accepted, it would appear that πεῖραρ, like Latin *licium*, is used as well of the woof-thread which binds the warp as of a bond about the body. The 'weaving' of speech or song is a familiar image, old as Homer (*Il*. III, 212) and employed explicitly by Pindar himself several times elsewhere, e.g. ὑφαίνω δ' Ἀμυθαονίδαις ποικίλον ἄν-δημα.[2] He repeatedly[3] refers to his song as ποικίλος and thinks of it as embroidery (ποικίλλειν).[4] πολλῶν πείρατα 'threads of many things' may have implied for him here a complex small-scale design closely woven. See also pp. 343 ff.

[1] If τανύειν be used for the stretching of the woof-thread across the warp it may explain the adjective τανaüφής. This the lexicons interpret as λεπτοüφής and from them it has with general approval been restored by Wunder in Soph. *Trach*. 602 for what is probably a gloss, εὐüφῆ. Deianeira applies it to the πέπλος she is sending to win back the love of Herakles. Blümner (*Term. und Techn.* p. 160), however, identifying λεπτοüφῆ with *levidensia*, interprets both τανaüφῆ and λεπτοüφῆ as 'thinly woven cloths' in contrast to συγκρουστά, *pavitensia*, those in which the woof-threads are close together, being beaten into place by the σπάθη. But as Sir G. Wilkinson (*loc. cit.*) remarks of Egyptian weaving, 'little attention was bestowed on the disposition of the threads in cloths of ordinary manufacture'; συγκρουστά therefore represents the better and more expensive kind and its correlative the cheaper and inferior. τανaüφῆ, however, as we have seen, appears to be an epithet of praise and λεπτοüφῆ should naturally mean, not 'thinly, i.e. loosely woven' but 'finely, i.e. closely woven', of fine threads close together as in συγκρουστά—a desirable quality and to the point in Soph. *Trach*. (cf. the πολύμιτοι πέπλοι of the Danaids, Aesch. *Suppl*. 432, with Pliny's account, *plurimis liciis texere quae polymita appellant, N.H.* VIII, 48 (74), 196). Blümner does not discuss the force of the prefix τανα- in τανaüφής; but excellent sense is given if, in connection with the use of τανύειν above, it signifies cloths in which the woof-threads are carefully stretched across the warp producing a tight and close as against a loose or open texture.

[2] Fr. 179. Cf. *Nem*. IV, 44 (cf. *Pyth*. IV, 275 and the scholiast's comment on *Nem*. VII, 79, ἐπεὶ τὸ ποίημα ὑφάσματι παρέοικεν; Lat. *texere*, etc.).

[3] E.g. *Ol*. III, 8; VI, 86f.; *Nem*. IV, 14; V, 42; Fr. 194 (206), 2 f.

[4] *Nem*. VIII, 15. Cf. *Pyth*. IX, 77, also pp. 368 f. below.

πεῖραρ is used by Homer in three more contexts, which
scarcely allow precise interpretation: (1) On the Shield two
men quarrel about blood-money, ἄμφω δ' ἱέσθην ἐπὶ ἵστορι
πεῖραρ ἑλέσθαι,[1] with which I would relate Pindar's reference
to Aiakos: ὃ καὶ δαιμόνεσσι δίκας ἐπείραινε.[2] The idea may
be of a bond, a binding decision, a fastening or closing of the
dispute. (2) Nestor advised his son when about to attempt an
ἄεθλον (chariot-race): ᾧ παιδὶ ἑκάστου πείρατ' ἔειπε,[3] with
which we may relate Pindar's account of Medea helping
Jason: πείρατ' ἀέθλων δείκνυεν πατρωΐων.[4] Here something
like 'strands' or 'fastenings' might suffice, means by which
each feat had been fastened, constructed, or might be tra-
versed, accomplished (see pp. 383 f.). Cf. our 'show him
the ropes', γρῖφος,[5] δόλον ὑφαίνειν (Il. VI, 187, etc.), also
μύθους ὑφαίνειν (Il. III, 212) above. Empedocles, after a brief
statement of doctrine, says ἔειπα πιφαύσκων πείρατα μύθων
(B. 17, 15. Cf. Parmenides' use of πεῖραρ on p. 332 above).
?'Threads'; but possibly 'outlines' (cf. p. 317) will serve.
(3) Nestor wished to sacrifice an ox with gilded horns:

> ἦλθε δὲ χαλκεὺς
> ὅπλ' ἐν χερσὶν ἔχων χαλκήϊα, πείρατα τέχνης,
> ἄκμονά τε σφῦράν τ' εὐποίητόν τε πυράγρην,
> οἷσίν τε χρυσὸν ἐργάζετο.[6]

If, as is generally assumed, ὅπλα means 'tools', πείρατα τέχνης
may mean 'fasteners', 'accomplishers of art'. In all the
other twelve instances, however, in the Odyssey, ὅπλον means
'cord' or 'piece of ship's tackle'. Thus Odysseus professed
to have been bound ὅπλῳ ἐϋστρεφέϊ[7] and Philoitios tied
(ἐπέδησε) the doors of the palace with ὅπλον νεὸς ἀμφιελίσσης/
βύβλινον.[8] If ὅπλον had that sense here and the reference
were to strips of metal or wires, 'bonds', 'fasteners of his
craft' would harmonise with the then current mode of making
joins or fastenings in metal work by bonds, δεσμοί (Il. XVIII,
375. Cf. Od. VIII, 274, also p. 371 below). Later (about
400 B.C.) Zeuxis said εἰ δέ τις ἀνδρῶν/ἡμετέρης τέχνης πείρατά

[1] Il. XVIII, 501. [2] Isthm. VIII, 24f. [3] Il. XXIII, 350.
[4] Pyth. IV, 220. Cf. p. 322, n. 2. [5] P. 369 below.
[6] Od. III, 432ff. [7] Od. X, 346. [8] Od. XXI, 390f.

φησιν ἔχειν,/δείξας νικάτω,[1] possibly 'has the threads of my craft' or more vaguely 'means of execution'. Some of these instances of πεῖραρ may have grown out of the fact that πεῖραρ, a cord or bond, was the commonest means of construction (whence conversely ὅπλον signified 'cord'; see p. 371; it was by πείρατα that the gods effected the fates of men), or out of the primitive sense 'go through' or 'round' (whence 'accomplish') suggested below[2] for the verb πειραίνειν.

[1] See *Poet. Lyr. Gr.*⁴ II, p. 318 (Bergk).   [2] Pp. 383 f.

CHAPTER III

Καιρός

Pindar's πολλῶν πείρατα συντανύσαις, κ.τ.λ. began καιρὸν εἰ φθέγξαιο.[1] καιρός is supposed to mean 'due measure', 'fitness', 'opportunity', etc. But, if we look to the early evidence we shall find reason to believe that it is not a mere abstraction. It never occurs in Homer, only once in Hesiod: καιρὸς δ' ἐπὶ πᾶσιν ἄριστος,[2] from which little can be inferred. But Pindar and the tragedians have many instances, some vague like Hesiod's and some more instructive. Thus Pindar says 'I have lighted upon many themes, hitting the καιρός with no false word (καιρὸν οὐ ψεύδει βαλών)',[3] and in the *Agamemnon*, after the fall of Troy, Aeschylus says that Ζεὺς ξένιος (against whom Alexander = Paris had offended) has taken vengeance

> ἐπ' Ἀλεξάνδρῳ
> τείνοντα πάλαι τόξον, ὅπως ἂν
> μήτε πρὸ καιροῦ μήθ' ὑπὲρ ἄστρων
> βέλος ἠλίθιον σκήψειεν,[4]

and Euripides speaks of men 'aiming the bow beyond the καιρός (τόξον ἐντείνοντες...καιροῦ πέρα)'.[5] It is clear that καιρός meant something like 'mark, target'. This could not arise out of a sense 'due measure' or 'opportunity'. On the other hand 'mark', while it may explain the use approximating in significance to 'due measure' as in our 'wide of the mark', 'overshoot the mark', etc., will explain neither 'opportunity' nor the use by which Euripides refers to a part of the body where a weapon can penetrate to the life within (above all, within the head) as a καιρός, speaking of a man as εἰς καιρὸν τυπείς,[6] 'struck in(to) a καιρός'. This description of the places

---

[1] See p. 338. [2] *Works and Days*, 694.
[3] *Nem.* 1, 18. The point is not affected if καιρόν is construed also with ἐπέβαν.
[4] 363 ff. Cf. 785 ff. referred to below, p. 347, n. 2.
[5] *Suppl.* 745 f. [6] *Androm.* 1120.

where penetration was most easy the Romans appear to have translated literally, if not very intelligently, by their word for what was the common meaning of καιρός in their day, *tempus*,[1] whence our 'temple'.[2] This use of καιρός instanced in Euripides appears to be older than the use commonly translated by 'opportunity' or 'due measure'. For in the vicissitudes of Homer's epics there are countless possibilities for the sense 'due measure', 'opportune', etc.; but neither καιρός nor any derivative is used thus. Homer's references to καιρός are confined to his use of καίριος in four different contexts[3] to describe a place in the body where a weapon could easily penetrate to the life within. This use must be related to the early use of the noun traced above, to describe that at which a weapon was aimed in practice; but it does not refer to the 'target', 'point aimed at', or to the part in question as aimed at. It shows that the essential meaning of καιρός was not 'target', 'objective' (σκοπός). καιρός described where a weapon might fatally penetrate and described that at which archers aimed in practice. But what was the latter if we omit birds and beasts? At what were the archers to aim in the great shooting contest for the hand of Penelope?[4] At what was Odysseus in the habit of aiming on other occasions?[5] At a

[1] This may not be as absurd as it appears if there lingered any sense that *tempus* expressed something 'cut' (cf. *templum*, τέμενος, τέμνω). The origin here suggested for καιρός and καῖρος fits a connection with κείρω, 'cut', or κρίνω, *cerno*, 'separate, part'. Cf. διαχωριστικά in Hesychius' explanation of καίρωμα (p. 346 below) and our name for the opening in the warp: 'shed' (cf. *scheiden*, 'to part, separate'). Ernout and Meillet, not realising the use of καιρός and καίριος, think *tempus*, 'temple', and *tempus*, 'time', must be quite distinct words despite their identity in form. Of *tempus*, 'temple', they say: 'Le rapprochement avec lit. *tempiu* «je tends» est possible mais ne se laisse guère préciser pour le sens (cf. le groupe de *teneo, tendo*). Comparant le gr. κρόταφος qui appartient à une racine signifiant «battre», M. Benveniste, *Mél. Vendryes*, p. 56, a proposé de rattacher *tempus* à la racine *(s)*temb*(h)- «heurter, écraser en frappant», cf. entre autres skr. aor. *astambhit*, gr. στέμφω, στόβος, v. sl. *tepǫ*, etc. Le rapprochement est séduisant'. (*Dict. ét. de la langue latine*, s.v.)

[2] The temples appear to be the weakest point in the skull. Thus it was by driving a tent-pin through his temples that the woman Jael slew Sisera (Judg. iv, 21).

[3] *Il.* iv, 185, viii, 84 f., 325 f., xi, 439. For καιροσέων, *Od.* vii, 107, see p. 345. [4] *Od.* xix, 576 ff., 587; xxi, 76, 420 ff., etc. [5] *Od.* xix, 573 ff.

penetrable opening, an aperture, passage through the iron of an axe or rather of twelve axes set at intervals in a straight line. It would appear that the early Greek archer practised and tested his skill by aiming at an opening or a series of openings. Thus he must aim not only true but with power or his shaft, though entering, would not penetrate through. καιρός, as appears from Pindar, Aeschylus, etc., described that at which he aimed. Such a sense of καιρός will help to a better understanding of Pindar's καιροῦ μὴ πλαναθέντα,[1] 'not deviating from the καιρός'. It will explain καιρός and καίριος of parts of the body through which weapons could penetrate to the life within. It will explain καιρός apparently with a sense like 'parting, division'.[2] It will also explain the use of καιρός to express 'opportunity', εἰς καιρόν, κατὰ καιρόν, etc. We, ourselves, speak of 'an opening' in just this sense (cf. also 'loophole'). It will also explain the uses in which καιρός has been translated by 'due measure', etc. Such an opening is limited. ὁ γὰρ καιρὸς πρὸς ἀνθρώπων βραχὺ μέτρον ἔχει,[3] says Pindar. The shaft that misses the opening (i.e. that goes παρὰ καιρόν) either hits the iron around it or, in the case of the body, hits something against which it is ineffective, or it misses altogether. The καιρός thus is what is right, the right aim, the right way. καίριος was used of that which reaches, enters a καιρός: blows, etc. It, too, was used metaphorically. Aeschylus speaks of γλῶσσα τοξεύσασα μὴ τὰ καίρια[4] as Sophocles of φώνημ' ἰὸν πρὸς καιρόν,[5] etc.

There is another word, καῖρος, quite distinct, as everybody believes, from καιρός. Definitions attempted in late antiquity have survived, but they are rather vague. What is certain is that it was something important in weaving, which is the art of sending the woof-thread through the warp. For Callimachus καιρωστρίς was a weaver. Homer speaks of καιροσέων ὀθονέων,[6] apparently an expression of praise, 'καιρος-woven linen cloths'. Hesychius says καῖρον τὸν μίτον φασίν· οἱ δὲ τὰς παρυφὰς τῶν ἀμπεχόνων. οἱ δὲ εὖ κεκαιρωμένων τοῦτ'

---

[1] *Nem.* VIII, 4.   [2] See Eurip. *Hipp.* 386 f.   [3] *Pyth.* IV, 286.
[4] *Suppl.* 446.   [5] *Oed. Rex*, 324 f.   [6] *Od.* VII, 107.

ἐστι εὖ ὑφασμένων (an explanation of καιροσέων). καιρώματα γὰρ τὰ διαχωριστικὰ τῶν στημόνων πλέγματα. καῖρος was evidently in some sense the warp or something in the warp (μίτος), something to do with the 'parting' of its threads. It is generally taken to mean the row of thrums which draw the odd warp-threads away from the even, making in the warp a triangular opening, a series of triangles, together forming a passage for the woof. But these thrums according to Hesychius were καιρώματα, and the singular καῖρος would more naturally describe the opening itself, the hole in the warp. If it originally did, people who looked for some *thing* corresponding to the name might attach it to the more permanent row of thrums responsible for the opening and running along its widest part. From meaning 'spindle' ἠλακάτη was later attached to the distaff;[1] and φρένες originally meaning the 'lungs' was attached to the diaphragm bounding them.[2] Through the opening, the passage through the warp, should be the path of the shuttle with the woof, as the proper path for the arrow was through the series of apertures in the axes. The analogy is even closer. Arrow-shaped and arrow-named (ἄτρακτοι) spindles were used as spools (πηνίον ἄτρακτος εἰς ὂν εἰλεῖται ἡ κρόκη, Hesych., cf. Suidas s.v.), and the casting of the spool or shuttle thus through the opening between the warp-threads is still known as a 'shot', a single woof-thread thus cast as a 'shoot'[3] (cf. German *Schussfaden*), and 'shuttle' itself derives from the same verb. We may now suspect that καῖρος and καιρός, which we have seen reason to believe meant the opening, the passage through which archers sought to shoot, were originally the same. The differentiation by those who gave the accents proves no more for their origin than in the case of δημός and δῆμος above,[4] μυρίοι and μύριοι, etc. The use in weaving will better explain the sense 'critical time', 'opportunity' (cf. καιροφυλακέω, etc.); for there the opening in the warp lasts only a limited time, and the 'shot' must be made while it is open. The belief in the weaving of

---

[1] See p. 307.   [2] See pp. 24, 39 f.

[3] See Mary M. Atwater, *The Shuttle-Craft Book of American Hand Weaving*, p. 57. There was also in antiquity as now a 'pick'.   [4] Pp. 211 f.

fate with the length of the warp-threads representing length of time[1] may have helped this use of καιρος. In the *Agamemnon* Aeschylus makes his chorus, foreboding, say of itself (the heart) οὐδὲν ἐπελπομένα ποτὲ καίριον ἐκτολυπεύσειν,[2] where ἐκτολυπεύσειν means something like 'unwind off the spool', as was done with the woof-thread in weaving. In the passage of Pindar, with which we began, καιρος, used with the same force as in φώνημ' ἰὸν πρὸς καιρον (cf. γλῶσσα τοξεύσασα μὴ τὰ καίρια) above, is combined with words which we have seen refer to the weaving of speech:

καιρον εἰ φθέγξαιο, πολλῶν πείρατα συντανύσαις
ἐν βραχεῖ, μείων ἕπεται μῶμος ἀνθρώπων.

Our use of 'opening' apart, 'opportunity' appears to have been expressed in English by something like the Greek use of καιρος. A 'nick' means a slot or hollow in anything. It was used thus: 'There is a nick in Christianity to the which whosoever cometh, they see and feel more than others do'.[3] 'There are some nicks in time which whosoever finds may promise to himself success.'[4] 'Most fit opportunity—her grace comes just in the nick'[5] (cf. in the *Ajax* καιρὸν δ' ἐφήκεις,[6] ἐς αὐτὸν καιρόν... πάρεισιν,[7] καιρὸν ἴσθ' ἐληλυθώς,[8] etc.). 'He came in the nick of opportunity to beg for grace.'[9] The 'nick' also is spoken of as if it were aimed at: '*Schol.* "Does the sea stagger ye?" *Mast.* "Now ye have hit the nick."'[10] 'The wisdom of God...hits the very nick of time for his application.'[11] I would compare also the German *einschlagen*, 'to strike in', *Einschlag*, 'woof', with the metaphorical *einschlagen*, 'to hit the mark', and the adjective *einschlägig*, 'appropriate'.

Reference to an opening, passage through, appears to explain also the Latin *opportunus*, *opportunitas*. The root meaning

[1] See pp. 349 ff.
[2] 1031 f. In *Ag.* 786 f. also μήθ' ὑπεράρας μήθ' ὑποκάμψας καιρὸν χάριτος perhaps fits weaving better than archery.
[3] *Rutherford Letters* (1862), I, LXX, 183 cited by the *Oxf. Eng. Dict.* for the year 1636. I have borrowed the following examples from the same source.
[4] *Feltham Resolves*, II, VIII, 19 (A.D. 1628).
[5] Ford, *Love's Sacrifice*, II, 2.   [6] 34.   [7] 1168 f.
[8] 1316.   [9] Carpenter, *Soules Sent.* 40 (A.D. 1612).
[10] Fletcher, *Pilgrim*, III, 6.
[11] Flavel, *Meth. Grace*, XI, 231 (A.D. 1681).

of *porta*, *portus* (*angiportus*) is 'entrance', 'passage through'. *Opportunus*[1] would thus describe what offers an opening, or what is in front of an opening ready to go through. The antithesis is *importunus*, describing that which is 'in (i.e. blocking) the opening' or 'without (i.e. not affording) an opening'.

Here too, perhaps, is the origin of the association of the goddess of fortune in Rome's earliest days with a building called *porta fenestella*, apparently a *porta* or opening above ground level (as a window is), a symbol or the embodiment of a religious idea rather than for use, a divine or universal 'opening'.[2] Roman tradition explained it as the opening through which Fortune passed, more particularly for Servius Tullius.[3] In speech *fenestra* was used symbolically in the sense of 'opening', 'opportunity', e.g. *quantam fenestram ad nequitiam patefeceris*.[4] πόρος, cognate with *porta*, *portus*, etc., meant 'passage, way, means'. Contrast ἄπορος, ἀπορία. Akin[5] is also the use of *locus*, 'room, space', in the sense of 'opportunity', e.g. *dare locum* with a genitive 'to give room for', so 'opportunity for', something.

[1] Ernout and Meillet, *op. cit.* s.v. *portus*, suggest that *opportunus* meant originally 'which pushes towards the haven', but that does not fit very well the uses known and makes the explanation of *importunus* on the same lines difficult. The latter, if a negative, should be the negative not as they suggest of *opportunus*, but of *portunus*. Portunus was associated with doors.

[2] Cf. the divine or universal *ianua* or *Ianus*, e.g. the *geminae portae* that were opened for war. Was it to open ways for, remove obstacles from the path of, the army of Rome in the world outside?

[3] See Plut. *de fort. Rom.* x (322 E); *Quaest. Rom.* xxxvi (273 B–C); Ovid, *Fasti*, vi, 577 ff.

[4] Terence, *Heaut. Tim.* 481. Cf. Sueton. *Tib.* 28, and the use of *ianua*. E.g. the younger Pliny (*Ep.* i, 18, 4) of one of his first pleadings: *illa actio mihi aures hominum, illa ianuam famae patefecit*, 'opened a way of fame for me'.

[5] Thought of an opening, division, may explain also the Greek use of ἁρμός, 'joint' or 'chink', in ἁρμοῖ meaning 'just at the time'. Cf. Latin *articulus* used of time. For the carver the joint is the way in or through. *In ipso articulo* meant 'in the nick of time'. Thus, probably in imitation, 'Something must be done and now was the nicke and joynt of time' (*Lancash. Tracts of Civil War*, Chetham Soc. 177, A.D. 1644). There may have been the further idea that the joint is the critical point between two lengths, periods, of time, the hinge of fate as it were. Cf. uses of *cardo* (e.g. *Aen.* i, 672 *haud tanto cessabit cardine rerum*; Servius explains *in tanta rerum opportunitate* and *a ianua tractam quae motu cardinis hac atque illac impelli potest*).

CHAPTER IV

The Weaving of Fate

From later Greece there survives evidence for this variation of the binding process on the part of the powers determining man's fate. The Μοῖραι are thus addressed: περιώσι' ἄφυκτά τε μήδεα/παντοδαπᾶν βουλᾶν ἀδαμαντίναισιν ὑφαίνετε κερκίσιν.[1] To this weaving of the Μοῖραι epitaphs allude. It is not always clear, however, whether binding or weaving is in point, e.g. οὐδὲ πικρὸν μοιρῶν μίτον ἔκφυγον,[2] or again οὐκ ἔφυγον δ' ἀτρεκέως μοιρῶν μίτον ὅς μοι ἐπεκλώσθη,[3] or μοιρῶν οὐκ ἔφυγον τρισσῶν μίτον.[4] In Phaeacia, we may remember, it was Odysseus' lot ἐκφυγέειν μέγα πεῖραρ ὀϊζύος, i.e. the πικρὸς μίτος, that was upon him. But often it is the length of a man's life which is represented by the thread,[5] e.g. ἑπτὰ δέ μοι μοῖραι...ἐνιαυτοὺς ἐκλώσαντο.[6] On the loom this would seem to mean the vertical, i.e. the warp-threads. In the web of the Norse fate-goddesses we shall see that from each of these was suspended, as loom-weight, a head.[7] We are reminded

[1] Fr. Mel. Adesp. 5 (Diehl). Who weaves is sometimes not defined, e.g. τὶν δὲ τούτων ἐξυφαίνονται χάριτες, Pind. Pyth. IV, 275.
[2] Epig. Gr. (Kaibel), 324, 5.   [3] Id. 339, 5.   [4] Id. 642, 6.
[5] A curious parallel to this exists among the Koryaks (N.E. Asia), who believe that the Supreme Being sends down from the sky the souls of departed ancestors to be reborn. He keeps a supply suspended from the cross-beams of the house; and as is the length of a soul's strap so will be the length of his life when he is reborn into the world. See The Jesup N. Pacific Expedition, vol. VI, part 1, and Jochelson, The Koryak, p. 100.
[6] Epig. Gr. 153. Cf. 287, 6 and (qu)od si longa magis duxissent fila sorores, C.I.L. III, 9259, 4, also 2628.
[7] See p. 355. This appears to mean that each warp-thread represented an individual life. How length of life could be related to the spinal cord we have seen (p. 213). Or the conception might be made easier by the association or identification found elsewhere of a man's hair with the threads of his fate, the thought successfully exploited by Meredith in The Shaving of Shagpat and 'the Identical', the one hair on which Shagpat's fate depends (cf. pp. 107, 134). Hinduism speaks of a 'thread-soul', sûtrâtmâ (see Vedantasara, Manual of Hindu Pantheism, trans. G. A. Jacobs,

of the proverb ἀπὸ λεπτοῦ μίτου τὸ ʒῆν ἤρτηται[1] and its Latin equivalent   *omnia sunt hominum tenui pendentia filo.*[2]

Warp-thread and the thread from which the spindle hangs are the same, but the Latin epitaphs appear to refer to the loom, e.g.   *stamina ruperunt subito tua candida Parcae.*[3]

Juvenal[4] speaks thus of Nestor, who finds his span too long:

> *attendes quantum de legibus ipse queratur*
> *Fatorum et nimio de stamine.*

A different feeling but the same image is involved by *Parcarum putria fila querens.*[5] If the length of life be represented by one or more warp-threads, what of the woof, those threads which are intertwined with and in some kinds of weaving bound round, knotted round, the individual warp-threads?[6] In these it would be natural to see the various phases of fortune which are his lot while he lives and of which the last is death, fortunes which are bound about his life-thread just as we have

pp. 61 ff.), and in the Hindoo rite of adoption into the wife's kin the bridegroom's height is measured by a thin thread which the bride's mother swallows, maybe with the suggestion that she thus 'conceives' him (see H. Risley, *Bengal*, 1891, p. 150). Perhaps with similar thoughts the Bulgarians, instead of the human victim found elsewhere, bury under their foundations a thread equal in length to the shadow of some stranger (see H. G. Trumbull, *The Threshold Covenant*, p. 53).

  [1] Suidas, s.v. μίτος.   [2] Ovid, *ex Pont.* IV, 3, 35.

  [3] *C.I.L.* VI, 25063, 17.

  [4] X, 251 f., where *stamen* does not, however, decisively imply weaving.

  [5] *C.I.L.* IV, 21521.

  [6] Kimakowicz (*Mannus Bibliothek*, 1910, 'Spinn- und Webewerkzeuge, Entwicklung und Anwendung in vorgeschichtlicher Zeit Europas', p. 35) describes such under the term 'knot-weaving' (*Knupfweberei*); and Otto Jannasch (*Verhandl. der berliner Ges. f. Anthropologie u.s.w.*, 1888, p. 90), discussing the methods of the Swiss pile-dwellers which show a resemblance on other points to those of the early Greeks and Norsemen, says that 'the woof-thread could either be drawn straight through the warp in the ordinary way or wound round every third thread and knotted'. In English weaving still different patterns are spoken of as different *ties*. G. B. Leitch, *Chinese Rugs*, 1928, p. 8, says 'The yarn which forms the substance of the rug is tied around the warp-threads forming knots' and, again (p. 117), 'Technically speaking, the rug is not woven, it is tied'. Historically Lucretius is almost certainly right, *nexilis ante fuit vestis quam textile tegmen* (V, 1350).

seen them bound about the man himself. To such binding threads the grave inscription[1] appears to refer: *cunctis fila parant Parcae nec par⟨c⟩itur ullis.* The Latin for woof-thread as opposed to *stamen* or warp-thread is *subtemen.* Horace[2] represents Chiron forecasting to Achilles the death that lies before him:

> *te manet Assaraci tellus,...*
> *unde tibi reditum certo subtemine Parcae*
> *rupere nec mater domum caerula te revehet.*

His hope of return is cut short, precluded by death, the *certum subtemen* which the Fates have already woven, the last woof-thread bound about the warp that is his life, as in the variant form given by Horace elsewhere[3] the *laquei mortis* are bound about the man himself. On him ἤδη ὀλέθρου πείρατ᾽ ἐφῆπται. 'The woof of war' of the Norse represents only one phase of life, though that perhaps the most significant, as fraught with the supreme fate. It confirms our interpretation since in it the hosts—a man to a thread, as we have seen—form the warp, and blood, or wounds and death, the woof. 'Upon it (the loom) has been stretched a warp of human-beings, a warp grey with spears, which the valkyries are filling with weft of crimson',[4] valkyries who are elsewhere[5] said to 'bind' the warriors that are doomed.

[1] *C.I.L.* III, 9623, 7.
[2] *Epod.* XIII, 13 ff. Cf. Catullus, LXIV, 327 f.:
> *sed vos, quae fata sequuntur,*
> *currite ducentes subtemina, currite fusi.*
[3] See p. 374. [4] See p. 355. [5] See pp. 353 ff.

CHAPTER V

Other Peoples—Fate and Magic

Of the two parts of the image traced in Homer, the earlier, the spinning of fate, is so widespread and well known that it scarcely needs illustration. The old Norse goddesses, the Norns, spun [1] the fates of men at birth. The wealth of legend that grew up around this belief would make mockery of any attempt to regard it as a mere figure of speech. The Slavs also had goddesses [2] who performed the like office, e.g. Siwa; so too apparently the ancient Hindoos [3] and the Gypsies. [4] In Roman poetry, where however Greek influences were at work, the spinning of the Parcae [5] at birth is a commonplace. How very real and fundamental this conception was among the Indo-European peoples is clear. In modern Greece [6] fate is still spun by goddesses at birth and in classical times the Μοῖραι divided that office with Εἰλείθυια, [7] the goddess of childbirth. By-forms

[1] See H. Ploss, *Das Kind*[3], I, p. 42; Du Chaillu, *The Viking Age*, II, pp. 30, 32; R. M. Meyer, *Altgermanische Religionsgeschichte*, pp. 154 ff.

[2] H. Ploss u. M. Bartels, *Das Weib in der Natur u. Völkerkunde*[4], II, p. 26.

[3] See e.g. *Grihya Sutras, Gobhila*, II, 1, 18; *Hiranyakesin*, I, 1, 4, 2, trans. H. Oldenberg, *Sacred Books of the East*, vol. xxx.

[4] See the *Kesalyi* discussed by Guntert, *Kalypso*, p. 253.

[5] *Parca=par-i-ca*, goddess of childbirth (*pario*); see Stolz, *Archiv f. lateinische Lexicographie*, x, p. 162 A and Walde, s.v. As evidence of the prevalence of the conception see e.g. the Latin dictionary of Lewis and Short, s.v. *filum*; but it is difficult to define what is original and how much is borrowed from the Μοῖραι. For references to the spinning of fate in Latin poetry see E. Steinbach, *Der Faden der Schicksalsgottheiten*.

[6] See J. C. Lawson, *Modern Greek Folklore*, etc., p. 124, and B. Schmidt, *Volksleben der Neugr.* p. 212.

[7] For the close relations and virtual identity of Eileithuia and the Moirai see Weizsäcker in Roscher's *Lexicon d. gr. u. röm. Myth.* s.v. Moira, 3091. In art the Moirai often appear with spindle and distaff. From Hesiod onward Κλωθώ is the habitual name for one of their number. The Platonic conception elaborated in the *Republic* is but little removed from the Homeric (see *Class. Rev.* Feb. 1924). In the *Laws* (960 C) τὰ κλωσθέντα is used of a man's destiny. οὐκ ἔστιν ἀλύξαι/ἀνθρώποις, ὅτι Μοῖρα κατὰ κλωστῆρος ἐπείγει, says Theocritus, xxiv, 68 f. Popular

of these need not trouble us. In Homer, as we have seen, the goddess or goddesses of fate vaguely termed Αἶσα, Μοῖρα, Κλῶθες spun, and there also the time favoured was birth. The last name and the form later more common, Κλωθώ, witness how essential was the image to the representation of fate. More frequently however, but in an exactly similar fashion, Zeus or an indeterminate δαίμων or the vague plural θεοί are introduced as the spinners. These instances of the image have been regarded as a mere figure of speech—'nur ein bildlicher Ausdruck'[1]—unjustifiably, as we have seen.

The second and final process, binding (or weaving), is less familiar, but if we turn our eyes once more to the North we find remarkable parallels. It was in her girdle that lay the great strength of the heroine Brunhild as did that of Thor in the *megin-giarðar*. Saxo Grammaticus preserves the story that king Hother having met three Nymphs (i.e. Norns) and complained of his lack of success in battle, obtained from them 'a girdle of victory'[2] and immediately overcame his enemy. From another power, Miming, he obtained a bracelet the mysterious virtue of which was that its owner became wealthy.[3] This or that fortune was thus believed to be put about a man as a concrete bond. The Norse *Disir* (Old High German *Idisi*) are Norns of the battle, valkyries. Sitting above the armies, they decide their fate, preparing fetters for the side they do not favour. 'Just as the Norns "spin", so they "bind", bind the (individual) foeman or the host and unbind the fetters of the captured friend, thus deciding the battle.'[4] One of them is named *Hlokk*,[5] i.e. 'Chain', and another *Herfjotr*, i.e. 'Host-bond'. Their fetters paralyse and prevent flight. The victim

epitaphs make constant reference to the belief, e.g. μοῖρα ζωῆς κλῶσε μίτοισι χρόνον, *Epigr. Gr.* 287, 6 (Kaibel); τίς μοιρῶν μίτον ὕμμιν ἐκλώσατο; *ib.* 478; cf. 470, 2; 153, etc.; [Aristot.] *Mund.* 401 b, 16 ff.; Babr. p. 11, 69; *Anth. Pal.* VII, 14, etc.

[1] Weizsäcker, *loc. cit.* 3086. He opposes it to the spinning of the Moirai which he accepts. For male spinners see *Class. Rev.* Feb. 1924, p. 5.

[2] III, 77, also a 'belt of splendour'; cf. Olaus Magnus, *de Gent. Sept.* III, 9.

[3] Saxo Grammaticus, III, 70 f.

[4] R. M. Meyer, *op. cit.* p. 159.

[5] See e.g. *Grimnismal*, verse 36.

is doomed[1] and perishes. We could scarcely ask for a better description of Homer's gods in the passages examined; the single πεῖραρ enveloping whole hosts and the multiple πείρατα fastened upon individuals alike are here. As in Homer, the gods also bind. Indeed, one of the old Norse names for them was '*Bönd*',[2] i.e. the binders or bonds. Roman knowledge of this conception might explain the words of the German Arminius as reported by Tacitus (*Ann.* I, 65, 4): *en Varus eodemque iterum fato vinctae legiones.* The alternative is that the image was also Roman[3] and the quotation invented. The German death-goddesses drag off the dead by a rope and are provided with cord and net.[4] How vividly real these bonds were to the old Norsemen is strikingly shown in the region of magic. 'Witchcraft-knowing women were accustomed to rub with their hands the whole body of the man who was to go to war or fight; by this means they found the most vulnerable part of the body; for they believed that on this place they could find a knot, which was supposed to be the spot that was to be wounded, and if they found such a knot, they had a special protection made for it.'[5] These beliefs die hard. Maurer[6] remarks that the valkyrie *Herfjotr* (i.e. 'Host-bond') lived on to the beginning of the thirteenth century, at least in so far that her name was given to paralysis by a demonic power by

[1] *Sturlunga Saga*, I, 387, II, 47; *Hordar Saga*, II, 103 ff. See also Maurer's discussion in the *Zeitschr. f. deutsch. Myth.* II, pp. 341 ff.

[2] See e.g. E. H. Meyer, *Mythologie der Germanen*, p. 285.

[3] The expression is abnormal in native Latin literature. But see also Lucr. v, 873f. and pp. 373f. below. It is impossible to say how much influence there had been from the Greek thought traced above.

[4] J. Grimm, *Deutsche Mythologie*[4], II, p. 705, III, p. 254 (English trans. Stallybrass, p. 845). For the cord of Hel see *Njals Saga*, cap. 177. The conception persisted on through the Middle Ages: Death carried a rope. See Rochholz, *Deutsche Glaube u. Brauche*, I, p. 142 and below, pp. 357, 431.

[5] Du Chaillu, *op. cit.* I, p. 441. The *Merseburger Sprüche* (collected probably in the tenth century) give a spell to be uttered by one, already a prisoner, who wishes to free himself. Here, as in the case of Melampous, there seems a tendency to confuse the invisible fetters of the *Disir* with those of human captors. See E. H. Meyer, *op. cit.* p. 270. For the later German use of *ligaturae* in magic see Grimm, *op. cit.* (pp. 1172 and 1663 in English trans.).

[6] *Die Bekehrung des norwegischen Stammes zur Christentum*, II, p. 401.

which those ripe for death are attacked while fighting or fleeing; and, in support, he cites *Sverris-saga* (c. 68, 176): 'they could not tell the reason why the ship did not move onward; some thought that *Herfjoturr* had come above them and that they would all be unmanned, but in actual fact the explanation was that the anchor was hanging over the side'. We are reminded of Poseidon's vengeance upon the Phaeacian ship: ὤ μοι, τίς δὴ νῆα θοὴν ἐπέδησ' ἐνὶ πόντῳ, κ.τ.λ.[1]

and at the same time of the demoralisation or paralysis wherewith the binding of the gods affected the warriors of the *Iliad*.

Not only do the Norns[2] 'spin' and 'bind', they also weave. Their web hangs over every man.[3] As 'weird sisters' or *Disir*, they weave the 'woof of war' and spread it over the field. Let us look at their song in *Njals Saga*. On Good Friday Brian's Battle was fought at Dublin. On the same Good Friday a man Daurrud at Caithness saw them weaving on such a loom as they describe:

A loom has been set up, stretching afar and portending slaughter...and a rain of blood is pouring. Upon it has been stretched a warp of human beings—a warp grey with spears which the valkyries are filling with weft of crimson. The warp is formed of human entrails and is heavily weighted with human heads. Bloodstained javelins serve as heddles, the spool is shod with iron, the *hræll* is formed of arrows and it is with swords that we must sley this web of battle. Hildr is going to weave and Hjörþrimul, Sanngridr and Svipul with drawn swords....We are weaving, weaving the web of the spear. Young is the king who owned it in the past. Forth must we step and make our way into the battle where the arms of our friends are clashing....We are weaving, weaving the web of the spear while the standard of the valiant warrior is advancing....I declare that death is ordained for a mighty prince. Even now the earl has been laid low by the spears. The Irish too will suffer a sorrow which will never be forgotten by men. Now the web is woven and the field dyed crimson. The

---

[1] *Od.* XIII, 168; see p. 330 above.

[2] I am accepting R. M. Meyer's (*op. cit.* pp. 157 f.) interpretation of the *Disir* as Norns of the battle; see above, p. 353.

[3] See R. M. Meyer, *op. cit.* p. 156; W. Golther, *Handbuch der germ. Mythologie*, p. 105.

news of disaster will travel through the world. It is ghastly now to look around when blood-red clouds are gathering in the sky. The air is being dyed with the blood of men while the maidens of battle are singing. Many spells of victory have we chanted well for the young king. May we have luck in our singing.[1]

The phase of fortune here portrayed is battle, 'the woof of war'. We have therefore no colourless weaving but, successfully transferred, all the horrors of the field. At times, e.g. at the end, it would seem that the weaving preceded the battle, at others as if it were coincident and identical with it, e.g. 'Death *is ordained* for a mighty prince. Even now the earl *has been laid low* by the spears. The Irish too *will*, etc.' In Homer there was similar vagueness[2] about the time of binding. The modern thinker finds it so difficult to separate cause and effect in time that we may well excuse his predecessors a little uncertainty. Antecedence in time is sometimes definitely expressed, but the connection between the mystical action of the powers above and the experience of its effect by men appears to be felt as a logical necessity rather than a temporal sequence. What relation subsists between this weaving and the binding? The two images are parallel and interchangeable, to some extent identical;[3] both are expressions of the last step towards the actualisation of fate. When the web is spread over the battle, the position is much the same as when the multiple πείρατα are thus extended, as when the bonds of the 'army-fetterers' are fastened upon the victims. The loom represents the field of battle and the weaving the actual fighting, which is thus controlled by the valkyries. The host is the warp; they bind the crimson woof where they will and thus they 'choose the slain'—μοῖρα πέδησε δαμῆναι.

The same conceptions appear among our Anglo-Saxon forefathers. Fate was woven—*gewif*. In *Beowulf*, granting success in battle, God is said to give to the warriors 'webs of war-speed' (*wigspeda gewiofu*),[4] while pain, age, and affliction

---

[1] The *Darradarljod*, trans. by Miss N. Kershaw, *Anglo-Saxon and Norse Poems*, pp. 123 f. For the context see chap. 156 in Dasent's translation, *The Story of Burnt Njal*.

[2] See above, p. 335.   [3] See pp. 349 ff.   [4] Line 697.

are spoken of as bonds.[1] The belief in the 'bond' of death long survived. Thus in the thirteenth century 'Moyses...hente ðe cherl wið hise wond, And he fel dun in dedes bond'.[2] The belief that this or that good fortune could thus be bound about one (see p. 353) appears to be the explanation of our old proverb 'Ungirt, unblest'.[3] In the song of *The Maypole* lasses and lads who had danced and kissed 'bound themselves with love-knots/To meet the next holiday'.

There are evidences of similar beliefs among the Celts. Deserted and wounded by Maelduin, Congal says: 'It is the cutting of the thread of life and a change of time to me, that the person from whom I least expected it should thus attack and mutilate me...'.[4] There is also supernatural control by binding. Thus in one of the legends of Fionn a large woman in a coracle says: 'Fionn, I put you under bands and spells that you will go three times of your own accord to the kingdom of the Big Men and three times against your own wishes'.[5]

---

[1] See ll. 975, 1742, 2111 (cf. *Deor*, 24, etc.), and *leger-bedde fæst* (1007), *deað-bedde fæst* (2901), etc. In the thoughts traced above lies perhaps the explanation of an obscure passage (*Beowulf*, 1936 ff.) according to which if any man (except her husband) dared look at Thryth, 'he might reckon death-bonds prepared for him, hand-twisted (*him wæl-bende/ weotode tealde/hand-gewriþene*); speedily then after his arrest (*mund-gripe*) was sword appointed that the engraved sword might make it clear, make known the death-bale', i.e. not that one man's death was effected both by cords (strangling) and by the sword but he might realise, when he had looked upon her, that on him ὀλέθρου πείρατ' ἐφῆπται (cf. pp. 320 ff. above), his fate was sealed, and it was soon made manifest by his actual murder with the sword. Some survivals of this way of thinking are dealt with on p. 333 above and on pp. 381, 401, n. 1, 440 f.

[2] *Gen. and Ex.* 2716. In the anonymous

'Of a rose, a lovely rose
Of a rose is al myn song'

(*circa* 1350) Mary is prayed to 'shyld us fro the fyndes bond' (*Early English Lyrics*, Chambers and Sidgw. p. 104). Cf. *Guthlac* (*A*), 540 on p. 381 below.

[3] E.g. '"Ungirt, unblest"', says the proverb'; Cuddy Banks in *The Witch of Edmonton*, II, I. Cf. the Hindoo rite on pp. 359 f. below. Men changed themselves into wolves by putting on themselves ointment (p. 290, n. 3) and a girdle. See R. Verstegen, *Rest. of Decayed Intelligence* (1603), p. 207.

[4] *The Banquet of Dun Na N-Gedh and the Battle of Magh Rath*, (text and) trans. by John O'Donnovan, Irish Arch. Soc. 1842, p. 303.

[5] *The Fians or Stories, Poems and Traditions of Fionn and his Warrior Band*, collected by J. G. Campbell, Argyllshire Series, No. IV, p. 227.

Similarly in *A Tale of Manus* the maiden in the green kirtle, after wrestling with him, says: 'I will put you under spells, I lay on you as spells and crosses and as nine fetters of a fairy travelling wandering woman that a little fellow more timid and more feeble than yourself deprive you of your head, your ears, and your power of life...'.[1] He is fettered with his fate. To this thought probably belongs the practice of putting a taboo upon anything, prohibiting its use, by tying a withe around it. This was done in distraint for debt: e.g. 'if an anvil, a little withe was tied on it to prohibit its use...if distress was on a religious order, a withe tie was put on their bell-house or at the foot of the altar'.[2] One could be invested with strength in the form of a garment. Thus fairy women give three men three shirts, 'and when they have on the shirts the combat of a hundred men is upon the hand of every one of them. But they must put off the shirts every night and put them on the backs of chairs; and if the shirts were taken from them, they would be next day as weak as other people'.[3] As we might expect, the shirts *are* taken from them.

Among the Aryan invaders of India similar conceptions prevailed. In the *Satapatha Brahmana*[4] the symbolical victims of the Purushamedha sacrifice are given thus: 'To the priesthood he consecrates a Brahman, to the nobility a Kshatriya (i.e. member of the caste in question)...to darkness a thief, to hell a manslayer,...*to Fate a rope-maker, to Death a huntsman*'. The death-god Yama has a loop or noose wherein he takes men. He is the huntsman and binds them and leads them away in bonds;[5] the rope is made or spun by Fate. Many gods, e.g. Varuna, and demons, e.g. Grahi, are similarly provided and

---

[1] *The Fians, etc.*, Argyllshire Series, No. II, p. 347. Cf. No. III, pp. 2 and 35.
[2] *A Soc. Hist. of Ireland*, by P. W. Joyce, p. 203. Cf. below, pp. 364, n. 2, 439.
[3] *The Fians, etc.*, Argyllshire Series, IV, p. 182. See also p. 360, n. 7 *inf.*
[4] XIII, 6, 2, 20. For commentary and further references see Weber, *Indische Streifen*, I, p. 76 (to which we may add 'Fate binds a man with adamantine cords and drags him upwards to the highest rank or downwards, etc.' *Ramayana*, VII, 37, 9. Monier Williams). Of the *Sat. B.* I cite J. Eggeling's translation in the *Sacred Books of the East*, hereinafter referred to as *S.B.E.*
[5] E.g. Satyavant in the Savitri episode of the *Mahabharata*. See p. 385.

show their power by binding men with disease, ill-fortune, or death. It is one of the aims of prayer and sacrifice[1] as of magic to remove these bonds.[2] Nirriti is the goddess of destruction. To release a man from her fetters you must take a rope of grass in your hand and say: 'The indissoluble fetter which the goddess Nirriti has bound about your neck, this do I unbind for life and strength, etc.'[3] A golden[4] bond is the sacrificial present after the offering which frees a warrior from the bond laid upon him by the gods before birth. The gods bind a warrior thus lest he should slay all his foes. We could scarcely have stronger evidence of the reality and concreteness attached to the mystical bonds thus removed. As we have seen, ἄτη, 'sin, infatuation', is in Homer[5] a bond in which Zeus binds men; such also is it in the *Rig Veda*: 'Unloose sin from me as a cord, unloose evil from me like the cord which holds captive a calf' (II, 28, 5). 'Unloose, unbind the error committed which is attached to my body' (I, 24, 9). Such prayers are exceedingly frequent. Bergaigne[6] points out that it is no mere metaphor but a 'myth' which they incorporate. There is an interesting passage in the *Kausika-sutra* (46, 26–9), where the sin of overslaughing (i.e. a younger brother has married before the elder) is ceremonially removed—the priest ties two fetters of munjagrass upon the limbs of the offending parties as they sit upon the edge of a body of water, and, washing them by means of bunches of grass, rinses them off. 'Placing the fetters upon the foam, he lets them float away.' In the *Satapatha Brahmana* (XIII, 9, 2) the sacrificer, bathing, lets his garment float away thus: 'so he plucks him from out all evil'.[7] Black magic also

---

[1] See e.g. *Apastamba-crauta-sutra*, VIII, 5, 41.

[2] For this among the Greeks see p. 385.

[3] *Kausika-sutra*, 46, 19; cf. *Atharva Veda*, VI, 63, 1 f. (trans. Whitney, Harvard Oriental Series) and the action of the god (Marduk, etc.) in the Babylonian evidence on p. 364 below.

[4] *Black Yajus Veda*, II, 4, 13 (trans. Keith, Harvard Oriental Series).

[5] See above, p. 327.

[6] *La religion védique d'après les hymnes du R.V.* III, p. 163. I have myself avoided the word 'myth' as having more limited associations—it is rather an 'image', a concrete form under which their minds conceived qualities, states, affections, etc., indeed more than a metaphor; it is the physical form in which they believed these to exist and operate.

[7] This will help us to a better understanding of Juv. VI, 519–21.

uses the same conception: 'Childlessness...guilt, barrenness
—that do thou attach to our enemy as having made a garland
from a tree'.[1] 'What evil-dreaming is in us, what in our kine
and what in our horse, that let him who is not of us, the god-
reviler, the mocker, put on like a necklace.'[2] 'Let him not be
released from the fetter of perdition...ill-success...extermina-
tion...calamity, let him not be released from the fetter, the
shackle of death.'[3] One girdle might be used for binding an
enemy[4] for Yama, but another might also bind with blessings:
'Do thou, O girdle, assign to us thought, wisdom. Thou whom
the ancient being-making seers bound about, do thou embrace
me in order to length of life, O girdle';[5] which reminds of the
old English proverb above.[6] The different kinds of fortune are
conceived as something bound or wrapped[7] about a man.

[1] *Atharva Veda*, VIII, 6, 26.   [2] *Ibid.* XIX, 57, 3.   [3] *Ibid.* XVI, 8.
[4] *Ibid.* VI, 133.   [5] *Ibid.*   [6] P. 357.
[7] Cf. e.g. among Latin authors the use of *induere seditionem, societatem*;
exuere fidem, amicitiam, etc., in Tacitus alone (cf. pp. 373 ff., 439 f. below),
and among the Hebrews: 'He put on righteousness as a breast-plate and a
helmet of salvation upon his head; and he put on garments of vengeance
for clothing and was clad with zeal as a cloke', Is. lix, 17; cf. Job xxix,
14, etc., and the mantle of Elijah (I Ki. xix, 19, II Ki. ii, 13), also p. 367.
This conception of attributes as *clothing* a man appears in the name of
the ancient Irish hymn still used for general purposes and sometimes
in *investing* with ecclesiastical dignity: 'St Patrick's Breastplate' or
'Corselet'. There is added the thought of defence. 'Bind' is not a literal
translation but expresses the use to which the hymn was put.

> 'I bind upon myself to-day
> The strong name of the Trinity...
> I bind upon myself to-day
> The virtues of the starlit heaven,
> The glorious sun's life-giving ray,
> The whiteness of the moon at even', etc.

Here, despite the Christianity, we are standing on pagan ground. It ends in
the manner of a spell: 'Christ be with me, Christ within me, Christ behind
me, Christ before me', etc. The following is an account of a *zagovor* from
Russia: 'The utterer goes forth in the early morn to "the open field"...
he washes himself in the morning dew, dries himself in the sunlight and
becomes "clothed with the clouds" and girdled with the countless stars....
Then he addresses himself to the elements asking the earth—Mother
Earth bright with flowers and full of vigorous life—to make his life bright
and vigorous; asking the strong blue sea to strengthen him and the wild
winds to brace his courage and the stars—the eyes of heaven—to make
his eye-sight keen', W. R. Ralston, *Songs of the Russian People*[2], p. 360.

Instead of a cord, a garment might be the instrument. In the *Satapatha Brahmana* above it was the embodiment of evil. In the *Atharva Veda*,[1] whence I have drawn these later instances, 'They (goddesses) who spun, wove and stretched the web, let them wrap thee in order to old age; as one long lived, put about thee this garment'.

To return for a moment to Homer, we there saw that μοῖρα πέδησε with or without a following infinitive was used as equivalent to 'doomed to death', the image being of fetters about the feet—πέδαι.[2] The same conception is Vedic also. 'We rescue thee from the toils of Nirriti by means of our divine utterance. Rise up hence, O death! Casting off the foot-shackles of death, do not sink down' (*Atharva Veda*, VIII, 1, 3, trans. Bloomfield, *S.B.E.*). On the field of battle there is the same thought. The following spell is used to 'tie up enemies' in a battle-rite for victory. The commentators explain that fetters are thrown down in places where the hostile army will pass: 'I tie together the highest, together the lowest, also together the middle ones. Indra hath encompassed them with a tie; do thou, Agni, tie them together. They yonder who come to fight, having made their ensigns in troops, Indra hath encompassed them with a tie. Do thou, O Agni, tie them together'.[3] Here we have one army praying and working magically that the god or gods may encompass the other in a bond, i.e. πεῖραρ, and actual fetters are thrown down presumably to effect the mystical binding of individuals. Indra is here the equivalent of Zeus. Again 'Great forsooth is the

---

[1] XIV, 1, 45. Cf. *Grihya-sutra of Hiranyakesin*, I, 1, 4, 2.

[2] See pp. 329 f. This will explain the tragic fragment ἐμπεδὴς γαμόρος μάρψεν 'Αἴδης (Adesp. 208, Nauck), whether with Schmidt we read ἐν πέδῃς or compare ἔμπεδος, 'fettered'. Death may have been represented like the dead as in mediaeval Europe and among the Finns (see p. 428).

[3] *A.V.* VI, 103 trans. Whitney. Cf. *Paipp.* XIX and *Kaus.* 16, 6. It is followed by a similar charm. 'With tying-up, with tying-together, we tie up the enemies; the expirations and breaths of them, lives with life, have I cut off. This tying-up have I made, sharpened up with fervour by Indra; our enemies that are here—them, O Agni, do thou tie up. Let Indra-and-Agni tie them up, and king Soma allied; let Indra and the Maruts make tying-up for our enemies' (*A.V.* VI, 104).

net of great Sakra, who is rich in steeds: with it enfold thou
all the enemies, so that not one of them shall be released....
With this net of Indra I enfold all those (enemies) yonder in
darkness. With great dejection, failure, and irrefragable misfortune; with fatigue, lassitude, and confusion do I surround
all those (enemies) yonder. To death do I hand them over;
with the fetters of death they have been bound. To the evil
messengers of death do I lead them captive...scattered here
are the fetters of death; when thou steppest upon them thou
shalt not escape. Into the (snare of) death they shall fall, into
hunger, exhaustion, slaughter and fear. O Indra and Sarva,
do ye with trap and net slay yonder army'.[1] The *Kausika-
sutra* (16, 15 ff.) describes the acts which these words accompany, i.e. the strewing of fetters, traps, and nets upon the path
of the advancing enemy. Here in addition or equivalence to
the fetters we have a huge encompassing net reminding of the
Homeric ὀλέθρου πεῖρατ' ἐφῆπται, etc. We are left in no doubt
of the concreteness of the fetters believed to be imposed by
the gods. The net is as it were a weapon, an instrument of
chase and capture.[2] Death is a huntsman, Yama rides with
a noose or lasso[3] seeking his victims. This is how the laying-on
of the cord, which is itself death, may be conceived.

Like conceptions appear in Slav magic in the use of knots.
'I attach five knots to each infidel sharp-shooter. Do ye, O
knots, bar the shooter from every road and way, lock fast every
arquebus, entangle every bow, involve all warlike weapons so
that the shooters may not reach me with their weapons, etc.'[4]

---

[1] *A.V.* VIII, 8, 4 ff., trans. Bloomfield. Cf. also XI, 9, 3, etc. We see here,
as in several instances above, that the same two possibilities as in ὀλέθρου
πεῖρατ' ἐφῆπται and ὀλέθρου πεῖραθ' ἵκηαι occur side by side.

[2] In pursuit of this aspect, Scheftelowitz ('Das Schlingen- und Netzmotiv
im Glauben und Brauch der Völker', *Religionsgesch. Versuch. u. Vorarb.* XII)
has collected a wealth of parallels from other races; but the image of fate
in general and the questions we are discussing are not his object and are
missed.

[3] Men used them. The Cossacks continued to use the noose or lasso
as a weapon of war long after fire-arms had been introduced. See e.g.
Gogol's *Taras Bulba*, trans. B. C. Baskerville, pp. 170, 174, 231.

[4] Cited by Ralston, *op. cit.* p. 388. See also above, p. 360, n. 7.

Among the ancient Iranians, also, similar beliefs prevailed. 'The old Persian war-god Verethragna fetters the hands of the foeman behind his back. The death-demon Astōvīdōtūs binds the dying. According to the Iranian Epic Ahriman has a Net. While Tus and Feribur seize the castle of the Deva Bahman, the mighty Ahriman spreads out his air-like net. Likewise the god of fate is equipped with noose and net. "Even the world-destroying lion and the dragon cannot free themselves from the net of Fate." "This is the manner of lofty fate: in his hands is the diadem and also the noose; the moment a man sits gaily with the crown, Fate snatches him from the throne with his noose." [1]

The Norse and the Vedic deities alike are conceived as setting free from bonds no less than as imposing them. Theirs is 'power to bind and power to loose'. This power delegated to the Apostles [2] resembles that which we have found assumed by the workers of magic. The conception lived on through the Middle Ages, but the mercy of God could unbind what his human agents imposed: *quem excommunicationis catena constringit, miseratio tuae pietatis absolvit.*[3] Homer's gods also deliver from evil—the verb used is λύω. Hermes cheers Odysseus in his distress:

ἀλλ' ἄγε δή σε κακῶν ἐκλύσομαι ἠδὲ σαώσω.[4]

His enemy knew, as we saw, that it was his fate ἐκφυγέειν μέγα πεῖραρ ὀϊζύος in Phaeacia. Later the hero complains to Athene that after the sack of Troy she had left him to bear his troubles alone:

ἀλλ' αἰεὶ φρεσὶν ᾗσιν ἔχων δεδαϊγμένον ἦτορ
ἠλώμην, ἧός με θεοὶ κακότητος ἔλυσαν·
πρίν γ' ὅτε Φαιήκων....[5]

---

[1] Scheftelowitz, *op. cit.* p. 8, quoting from *Yast*, 14, 63; *Vendidad*, v, 8 f.; *Shahnameh*, ed. Vullers, II, 758, v, 136, I, 97, v, 665, I, 512, v, 1324 f. To his citations from the *Avesta* I would add *Vendidad*, XIX, 29 with the scholium, from which it appears that it is the wicked, the deva-worshippers, who have most to fear from the bond at death.

[2] Matt. xvi, 19; xviii, 18; cf. Luke xiii, 16 (p. 365), Prov. v, 22 (p. 439, n. 5).

[3] Cited by C. Wordsworth, *Salisbury Processions and Ceremonies*, p. 258. Cf. Berengarius Turonensis, *Ep.* XXII (Sudendorf). See also pp. 440 f. below.

[4] *Od.* x, 286.   [5] *Od.* XIII, 320 ff.

The same expression is used by Antinoos when the plot to waylay Telemachos had failed:

ὦ πόποι, ὡς τόνδ' ἄνδρα θεοὶ κακότητος ἔλυσαν.[1]

We may perhaps compare the general prayer of the *Atharva Veda* (VI, 121)—'for release from evil': 'An untier, do thou untie off us the fetters that are highest, lowest, that are Varuna's; remove from us evil-dreaming and difficulty'. As in ancient India, so in Babylonia, disease was often conceived as a bond attached by a demon. 'They spread out their net; where the anger of the gods weighs, there rush they in with a loud cry. If a man be abandoned by his god, they fall upon him, envelop him as with a garment, rush at him, spout poison over him, bind his hands, fetter his feet.' Under such a calamity prayer goes up to the gods: 'Open his bonds, loosen his fetters, etc.'[2] Not very far removed perhaps is the Homeric situation:

ὡς δ' ὅτ' ἂν ἀσπάσιος βίοτος παίδεσσι φανήῃ
πατρός, ὃς ἐν νούσῳ κῆται κρατέρ' ἄλγεα πάσχων,
δηρὸν τηκόμενος, στυγερὸς δέ οἱ ἔχραε δαίμων,
ἀσπάσιον δ' ἄρα τόν γε θεοὶ κακότητος ἔλυσαν,
ὡς 'Οδυσῆ' ἀσπαστὸν ἐείσατο γαῖα καὶ ὕλη, κ.τ.λ.[3]

We shall see[4] that δαίμων = κήρ was regularly conceived as binding with disease or other evil. There is a passage of the 'Shield of Herakles' which gives a significant alternative under the general head κακότης:

ὡς δ' ὅτ' ἀνὴρ ἀσπαστὸν ὑπεκπροφύγῃ κακότητα
νούσου ὕπ' ἀργαλέης ἢ καὶ κρατεροῦ ὑπὸ δεσμοῦ,
ὡς ῥα τότ' 'Αμφιτρύων χαλεπὸν πόνον ἐκτολυπεύσας
ἀσπασίως τε φίλως τε ἑὸν δόμον εἰσαφίκανε.[5]

---

[1] *Od.* XVI, 364.

[2] O. Weber, *Die Dämonenbeschwörung bei den Babyloniern und Assyriern*, p. 15. So too 'Headache like a garment will envelop him, the pain and shivering like a net' (R. C. Thompson, *Devils and Evil Spirits of Babylonia*, p. 55); 'The evil spirit hath set a net...so that the wanderer hath fallen sick of a headache' (*ibid.* p. 59). Cf. Hebr. *ḥebhel* 'pain', lit. 'bond'; Job xxx, 18, etc. For binding in Babylonian (Assyrian) magic see p. 372. With the Hindoo rite on p. 359 compare the mode of freeing a man from a taboo: 'His limbs are bound with a double cord of black and white threads twisted on a spindle. The cord then appears to be cut by the hands of Marduk who releases the man from the taboo' (R. C. Thompson, *Semitic Magic*, p. 165).

[3] *Od.* v, 394 ff. Cf. *Il.* xv, 262 ff.   [4] Pp. 400 ff.   [5] 42 ff.

He has unwound the πόνος off him.[1] In all these instances of λύω the basis of thought and imagery is unquestionably the same as in the ritual formulae elsewhere, and fits our interpretation of the other Homeric passages. Evil is a fetter upon a man and its removal an unloosing and unbinding. 'The Cyclops thought to catch us coming out of the cave', says Odysseus:

αὐτὰρ ἐγὼ βούλευον ὅπως ὄχ' ἄριστα γένοιτο,
εἴ τιν' ἑταίροισιν θανάτου λύσιν ἠδ' ἐμοὶ αὐτῷ
εὑροίμην.[2]

The naturalness of the image and the vividness with which the fetters might be conceived may be illustrated by two dreams, manifestations of the same faculty which created the image. When Xenophon with the Ten Thousand was in great danger and difficulty, unable to advance or retire, he dreamed that 'he was bound in foot-shackles but these fell off him of their own accord so that he was loosed and could walk freely'[3] (ἐν πέδαις δεδέσθαι, αὗται δὲ αὐτῷ αὐτόμαται περιρρυῆναι, ὥστε λυθῆναι...). In the morning this was interpreted as a good omen for their present plight and, when presently news of a way out arrived, he offered libation to the gods who had shown the dream. Nearly a thousand years later Gregory of Tours in his account of St Julian tells of a woman who could not walk for her infirmity. In a vision of the tomb of Julian it appeared to her that 'a multitude of chains fell off her limbs to the ground and she, awakened by the noise this made, became aware that she had recovered complete soundness in all her limbs'[4] (*multitudo catenarum ab eius membris solo decidere; a quo etiam sonitu expergefacta sensit omnium artuum recepisse plenissimam sanitatem*).

In the vast majority of the Homeric passages dealt with, it is evil fortune which the gods bind upon men. The πείρατα νίκης are an exception. Among the fortunes spun also—the objects of ἐπέκλωσαν, etc.—the ill predominates. Of this there are in chief two causes. The poems are prevailingly tragic in tone dealing with the perils and hardships of flood and field,

---

[1] See pp. 387 f.   [2] *Od.* IX, 420 ff. See also pp. 384 f. below.
[3] *Anab.* IV, 3, 8 ff.   [4] *De virt. s. Iul.* IX, p. 568, 21. So Luke xiii, 16.

sad alike in their course and in their issue. If we review their incidents, the pessimism of Pindar becomes an optimism: ἓν παρ' ἐσλὸν πήματα σύνδυο δαίονται βροτοῖς ἀθάνατοι.[1] The other cause lies deeper—in human nature itself which is ever ready to take the good for granted, to assume it as a right or to ignore it, but, when evil comes, to mark it all too well and to excuse it as the infliction of some power without. Centuries later, when Greek thought had reached its full stature, it was still necessary for Aristotle[2] in discussing the freedom of the will to urge that if evil acts were to be imputed to an external cause, so also must the good: γελοῖόν τε τὸ αἰτιᾶσθαι τὰ ἐκτὸς ἀλλὰ μὴ αὑτὸν εὐθήρατον ὄντα ὑπὸ τῶν τοιούτων, καὶ τῶν μὲν καλῶν ἑαυτόν, τῶν δὲ αἰσχρῶν τὰ ἡδέα. Evil fortune is felt as friction is felt, as a limitation, a restriction, a fetter, something hemming in the self and preventing its expression or free play.[3]

It might be objected that while natural enough when what it imposes is some restriction or evil, a bond has no apparent fitness when a blessing is conferred. To this the answer is simple. It is not then a bond in the sense of a fetter but merely something bound about a man as a girdle, necklace, crown, or bracelet is bound about him, as a garment is wrapped around him. If in the region of magic we would seek the beneficial counterpart to the fetter, it is the cord-amulet, taking one of the forms we have suggested—girdle, etc. W. Wundt noted it as characteristic of amulets that they have restricted powers, one protecting from ill health, another from wounds and so forth.[4] Elsewhere[5] he says: 'The fact that a simple cord was used among primitive people and still prevails in present-day superstitions makes it probable that the original amulet was the cord itself fastened about the neck or less frequently about the loins or arm'; but he made the mistake of thinking of the amulet negatively, merely as a *Schutzmittel*. Such a cord has and confers positive virtue or power (e.g. health or strength) and so exempts or protects

---

[1] *Pyth.* III, 81 f.   [2] *Eth. Nicomach.* 1110 b, 13 ff.
[3] See also pp. 437 f.   [4] *Völkerpsychologie*[2], IV, 1, p. 292.
[5] *Elements of Folk Psychology*, English trans. p. 228.

from the opposite. It endows its owner magically with the good qualities or luck it represents, exactly as do the mystical bonds of fate. God and medicine man use the same means and no less in blessing than in cursing. A girdle[1] might be used magically to bind an enemy for Death or to bind oneself with wisdom and long life. In the other form of the image there is the same twofold potentiality. A headache or sickness could be conceived as a garment, and a garment could be worn as a vehicle of long life.[2] In the Old Testament the image is frequent:[3] 'It is God that girdeth me with strength and maketh my way straight' (Ps. xviii, 32); 'Thou hast loosed my sackcloth and girded me with gladness' (Ps. xxx, 11); 'And righteousness shall be the girdle of his loins and faithfulness the girdle of his reins' (Is. xi, 5, cf. lxi, 10, etc.). In the Apocalypse the Bride is 'clad in fine linen', 'and the fine linen is the righteous acts of the saints',[4] and he that is faithful unto death receives a crown of life,[5] i.e. a crown that is the vehicle of life, confers life; which may indeed be the purpose behind the ancient and widespread custom of giving a crown or wreath of living leaves or evergreens to the dead.[6] In the Hebrew *Book of Enoch*[7] it is asked concerning a certain angel 'Why is he called "Azbuga"? Because in the future he will gird (clothe) the righteous and pious of the world with the garments of life and wrap them in the cloak of life that they may live in them an eternal life'.

In later Greece[8] cord-amulets survive, and in Homer also

---

[1] See above, p. 360.   [2] See above, p. 361.

[3] II Sam. xxii, 40; Ps. lxv, 6, xciii, 1, etc. So investing with a material girdle in the middle ages: *continentiae cingulum per hoc lineum meum a Deo accipe continentiaeque strophio ab hac deinceps die per Wiboradam tuam te praecinctum memento* (*Ekkehardi IV casus S. Galli*, 3 in Pertz, *Monum. Germ. Hist.* ii, 107). Cf. Malory, *Morte d'Arthur*, xvi, 1 and 3.

[4] xix, 8.   [5] ii, 10. Cf. James i, 12.

[6] Cf. pp. 451 ff. below.   [7] Edited and trans. H. Odeberg, xviii, 22.

[8] For literary evidence, see esp. Heckenbach, '*De nuditate sacra sacrisque vinclis*', *Religionsgesch. Versuch. u. Vorarb.* and on the archaeological side P. Walters, 'Faden u. Knoten als Amulett', *Archiv f. Relig.-Wiss.* Bd. viii, 1905. The 'Sacral Knots' worn in Minoan times are probably evidence for this thought. It explains the knot (*nodus*) on a thong (*lorum*) round the neck, which protected the poorer Roman child, a badge of freedom (Juv. v, 165, etc.).

evidence is not lacking. When Odysseus is buffeted in the deep by Poseidon, the nymph Leukothea brings a saving charm, her 'immortal head-band':

τῆ δέ, τόδε κρήδεμνον ὑπὸ στέρνοιο τάνυσσαι
ἄμβροτον· οὐδέ τί τοι παθέειν δέος οὐδ᾽ ἀπολέσθαι.[1]

When he reaches land, he is to 'unloose' it and cast it back. By its virtue he endures the sea for three days. How such a bond or amulet is equated or identified with the qualities or powers it confers (just as we saw ἔρις, ὀϊзύς, etc., obviously identified with an explicit or implicit πεῖραρ) is, however, better exemplified by Hera's request to Aphrodite:

δὸς νῦν μοι φιλότητα καὶ ἵμερον, ᾧ τε σὺ πάντας
δαμνᾷ ἀθανάτους ἠδὲ θνητοὺς ἀνθρώπους.[2]

'I cannot refuse', says Aphrodite:

ἦ, καὶ ἀπὸ στήθεσφιν ἐλύσατο κεστὸν ἱμάντα
ποικίλον, ἔνθα τέ οἱ θελκτήρια πάντα τέτυκτο·
ἔνθ᾽ ἔνι μὲν φιλότης, ἐν δ᾽ ἵμερος, ἐν δ᾽ ὀαριστὺς
πάρφασις, ἥ τ᾽ ἔκλεψε νόον πύκα περ φρονεόντων.[3]

Hera need only carry it in her bosom and its powers are hers. Similar[4] was the girdle of Ištar—when she removed it in the underworld, reproduction ceased above.

There are other traces in Homer of the association of magic with binding. The name of the Sirens appears to mean that they are the 'binders, enchainers'[5] (σειρά); their song, like that of the Erinyes,[6] is a ὕμνος δέσμιος. Even an incantation is conceived as a bond or binding.[7] This is perhaps made easier since weaving, as we have seen, is itself a form of binding and ὕμνος is said to be 'woven'[8] (ὑφαίνω). The idiom μύθους ὑφαίνειν (Il. III, 212) recalls δόλον ὑφαίνειν and the δόλος, bonds,[9] woven or spread for Ares. Just as he met Kirkē's φάρμακα with the moly, so Odysseus defeats the song of the

---

[1] Od. v, 346 f. For further discussion see below, p. 454.
[2] Il. xiv, 198 f.   [3] Ibid. 214 ff. For love as a band see pp. 373, 403.
[4] The girdle of Hippolyta, queen of the Amazons, had like powers.
[5] So Gruppe, Griechische Mythologie u. Religionsgesch.⁴ I, p. 344 and Guntert, op. cit. p. 175. Homer's account is Od. XII, 38–54, 158–200.
[6] Aesch. Eum. 306 and 331.   [7] See also p. 372, n. 2 below.
[8] See e.g. Bacchyl. v, 9 f., XVIII (XIX), 8 and p. 340 above.
[9] See Od. VIII, 274–82.

'binders' by other bonds, concrete and material (*Od.* XII,
160 ff.). The arch representative of magic in the poems is
Kirkē. It can scarcely be accidental—though apparently no
significance has hitherto been attached to it—that the only
lore beyond directions for his voyage that Kirkē is reported
to have imparted to Odysseus is a piece of this same craft—
a knot—which he used to safeguard Arete's gifts:

αὐτίκ' ἐπήρτυε πῶμα, θοῶς δ' ἐπὶ δεσμὸν ἴηλεν
ποικίλον ὅν ποτέ μιν δέδαε φρεσὶ πότνια Κίρκη.[1]

The 'Sphinx' of Theban legend can also now perhaps be
better understood. She is usually[2] explained as the 'Throttler',
'Choker', but was rather, I suggest, the 'Tight-binder', the
meaning naturally indicated by σφίγγω and fitting, as we
see,[3] her character of death-demon,[4] ἁρπάξανδρα κήρ.[5] It
fits also the possibly later version of her as singing deadly
riddles, ποικιλῳδός,[6] ῥαψῳδός.[7] We may compare στραγγαλίς, 'tight band', 'knot' with Photius' citation from
Pherecrates long before: στραγγαλίδες: τὰ δύσλυτα ἅμματα·
Φερεκράτης Αὐτομόλοις: Ὑμεῖς γὰρ ἀεὶ στραγγαλίδας ἐσφίγ-
γετε (21 Kock). For his ability to dispose of the difficulties
propounded by the Academics Chrysippus was called a 'knife
to cut Academic στραγγαλίδες': τῶν Ἀκαδημιακῶν στραγ-
γαλίδων κοπίδα.[8] With somewhat similar thought the Greeks
conceived of a riddle or trap of words difficult to deal with
as a woven rush-basket, γρῖφος (cf. Latin *scirpus, nodus, solvere*).

[1] *Od.* VIII, 447 f.
[2] See e.g. Liddell and Scott, s.v.; Gruppe, *op. cit.* pp. 522 f.; J. E. Harrison,
Prolegomena, etc., p. 211. Throttling, choking, would rather demand πνίγω.
Also it was not the appropriate act of woman, lion or bird. The singing,
the wings, the woman's head, and the self-destruction of some versions are
features shared by the Sirens. The history of the varying art form and
the etymology of Φίξ do not concern us here but rather the significance
of Σφίγξ and the background of ideas into which that name fitted.
[3] For death as a bond see pp. 327, 372 f., 405, 427 ff.; for the κῆρες
pp. 399 ff.   [4] E.g. Eurip. *Phoen.* 810 f.
[5] Aesch. *Septem*, 776 f. For the κῆρες binding, see pp. 401 f.
[6] Soph. *Oed. Rex*, 130.
[7] *Ibid.* 391. Cf. κακόπτερε μοῦσα θανόντων in the lines quoted in the
Hypoth. to Eurip. *Phoen.*
[8] See the quotation in Plut. *de Stoic. Rep.* II (1033 E).

In the various spells from the *Atharva Veda*, etc., cited above, magic is much more a living reality than for Homer. They are written for and by men who practise it in full belief. Yet the Homeric evidence, often indirect and more or less vestigial as it is, witnesses to the earlier existence of exactly the same mystical mode of thought. How real and concrete were the mystic bonds which these other peoples imagined as the vehicles of fate is revealed by the real bonds[1] which they used by way of

[1] In Homer there is nothing quite so pronounced but we have seen approximations. He seems to assimilate or confound the bonds of fate and those material fetters actually imposed on Melampous by the βουκόλοι ἀγροιῶται. We must be wary of interpreting the verb of 'binding' as a mere metaphor or extended use signifying really no more than a vague 'hold, restrict, hinder'. Exactly parallel to ἥ γὰρ τοῦ γε θεοὶ κατὰ νόστον ἔδησαν (*Od.* xiv, 61) is the language used of Athene when helping Odysseus in his distress off the coast of Phaeacia:

ἥτοι τῶν ἄλλων ἀνέμων κατέδησε κελεύθους,
παύσασθαι δ᾽ ἐκέλευσε καὶ εὐνηθῆναι ἅπαντας·
ὦρσε δ᾽ ἐπὶ κραιπνὸν Βορέην, πρὸ δὲ κύματ᾽ ἔαξεν.
                                                    Od. v, 383 ff.

How literal and concrete could be the meaning of ἀνέμων κατέδησε κελεύθους may be seen by the kindness of Aiolos, the ταμίας ἀνέμων:

τεῦχε δὲ πομπήν.
δῶκέ μοι ἐκδείρας ἀσκὸν βοὸς ἐννεώροιο,
ἔνθα δὲ βυκτάων ἀνέμων κατέδησε κέλευθα·
κεῖνον γὰρ ταμίην ἀνέμων ποίησε Κρονίων,
ἠμὲν παυέμεναι ἠδ᾽ ὀρνύμεν ὅν κ᾽ ἐθέλησιν.
νηῒ δ᾽ ἐνὶ γλαφυρῇ κατέδει μέρμιθι φαεινῇ
ἀργυρέῃ, ἵνα μή τι παραπνεύσῃ ὀλίγον περ·
αὐτὰρ ἐμοὶ πνοιὴν Ζεφύρου προέηκεν ἀῆναι.   *Od.* x, 18–25.

They could also be unbound. While Odysseus slept, his comrades

ἀσκὸν μὲν λῦσαν, ἄνεμοι δ᾽ ἐκ πάντες ὄρουσαν.   *Ibid.* 47.

There can here be no question of metaphor. The bond is as grossly material as those of Hindoo or Babylonian sympathetic magic. We are in the region of weather-medicine, the province of the rain-maker. Indeed this very magic was actually practised by the Lapps down to the nineteenth century. See J. Grimm, *Deutsche Mythologie*⁴, iii, p. 182; cf. i, p. 532 and for various parallels Frazer, *The Magic Art and the Evolution of Kings*, i, pp. 321 ff.; E. Samter, *Volkskunde in altsprachlichen Unterricht*, i Teil, *Homer*, 1923, pp. 11–14; also Heckenbach, *op. cit.* p. 101. Without a bag simple knots, the very form of magic we have been discussing, sufficed. See Olaus Magnus, *de Gent. Sept.* iii, 15, and cf. the knotted cloth in a legend cited by Samter from Müllenhoff, *Sagen, Märchen u. Lieder der Herzogtümer Schleswig-Holstein u. Lauenburg*, p. 222; and, still more close, the knots of the Vinlanders cited by Grimm and Heckenbach.

sympathetic magic to change fate or attain like ends. Centuries after Homer Greeks used such real bonds for the same purpose.

A piece of string was one of the most useful and precious possessions of uncivilised man no less than of the modern boy. With it he did countless things for which the advancing arts of woodwork and metalwork, etc., have found better methods. It is ὅπλον, the 'instrument' *par excellence*. In the *Odyssey*[1] and occasionally later, ὅπλον is used without further qualification in the sense of 'rope, cord'. If two things had to be joined together or fixed relatively to each other, binding was the obvious means. Of how true this still was there are abundant examples, e.g. locking a door (*Od.* XXI, 241), locking a chest (*Od.* VIII, 443), fastening its body (πείρινς) on a wagon, also the yoke to the yoke pole (*Il.* XXIV, 266–74). In such a world binding was almost coextensive with fixation or fastening,[2] and, when better methods were devised, the term would naturally be extended to cover them, e.g. δεσμός of a rivet or union in metal work (*Il.* XVIII, 379) and the similar use of the verb for nailing, pinning, e.g. δῆσεν ἅλοις (Pind. *Pyth.* IV, 71). This nailing was also used in magic and is apparently the origin of the Latin term *defixio*. Many effigies thus pierced have survived alike the victims they represented and those whose will they served. It is nevertheless almost certainly wrong to say with Jevons[3] that 'the verb καταδέω and the substantives κατάδεσις, κατάδεσμος must be used in the sense of hammering a nail in or fastening with a nail and are not used in this connection to mean simply "tying up"'. In support he cites the use of δῆσεν by Pindar above; but we have seen that the verb is used by Homer to describe the mystical binding by the gods, and if we examine later Greek and Latin

---

[1] See above, pp. 341 f.

[2] It seems to be almost the only way the gods possess of dealing with each other when relations become unfriendly (see *Il.* I, 399 ff., v, 385 ff., VIII, 24 ff., xv, 16 ff.). Among men binding was the usual mode of confinement or imprisonment, e.g. *Od.* XIV, 345, XV, 444, XXII, 189 ff., etc.

[3] In his chapter on 'Greek and Italian Magic' in *Anthropology and the Classics*, p. 109.

literature we find no dearth of allusion to magical binding
with threads. The general formula of the curse was καταδῶ
τὸν δεῖνα. Many actual effigies with their limbs bound have
survived.[1] In many languages[2] the general notion 'magic'
is expressed by the term for 'binding'. It has been noted[3]
that it is the commonest process of bewitchment. It would
therefore be foolish to say that καταδέω in these curses meant
just nailing. In Homer death or destruction is fate *par ex-*

[1] See Daremberg et Saglio, figs. 4786–9; also Heckenbach, *op. cit.*
pp. 87 f. For inscribed curses see e.g. R. Wünsch, *Defixionum Tabellae
Atticae*, and *Verfluchungstafeln aus Rom*; Audollent, *Defixionum Tabellae*.

[2] Scheftelowitz (*op. cit.* pp. 17 f.) cites instances. For further evidence
of the importance of tying in magic see the long chapter on 'Knots and
Rings tabooed' in *The Golden Bough. Taboo*, pp. 293 ff. We may note that
in English a spell itself may be described as 'binding' (cf. 'spell-bound'),
as is the song of the Sirens and the ὕμνος δέσμιος of the Erinyes. In *Rig
Veda*, I, 61, 4, *tataina* 'signifie que l'hymne est un lien qui retient Indra'
(Bergaigne, *op. cit.* II, p. 200). The Romans sometimes actually bound
a god. Apollodorus, according to Macrob. I, 8, 5, said, *Saturnum alligari per
annum laneo vinculo et solvi ad diem sibi festum atque inde proverbium ductum deos
laneos pedes habere.* The binding might oblige positively to this or that. In
the proverb and perhaps in the case of Saturn the binding might be
thought to check activity. Petronius seems to have related it with *religio*,
the binding felt by some, who thus are *religiosi* (pp. 439 ff.), but not felt by
others: *itaque dii pedes lanatos habent, quia nos religiosi non sumus* (44), i.e. the
gods are fettered, slow to act, because we do not feel our obligations
towards them. Greeks also bound images of their gods (e.g. Paus. III, 15,
7 and 11) perhaps to control them, as in magic they bound the effigy of
a man. We may instance this to be whispered over a meal effigy (*Die
assyrische Beschwörungsserie Maqlû*, ed. K. L. Tallquist):

> 'They have used all kinds of magic,
> To tie me as with ropes,
> To catch me as in a snare,
> To bind me as with cords,
> To overpower me as in a net,
> To strangle me as with a noose,
> To tear me as a fabric.
> But I by the command of Marduk, lord of charms,
> By Marduk, the master of enchantment,
> Both the wizard and the witch
> As with ropes I will tie,
> As in a snare I will catch,
> As in a net I will overpower,
> As in a noose I will strangle,
> As a fabric I will tear'.

[3] By W. Wundt in *Völkerpsychologie*[2], I, pp. 278 f.

cellence, the bond *par excellence;* for the action of μοῖρα, πέδησε is explicit enough; so too in these binding spells, classical and otherwise, the verb καταδῶ, etc., may stand alone without further definition of the evil that is to befall the victim.

It is interesting to find once again that the human worker of magic employs the instrument favoured also by the gods, the divine destiny.[1] Love above all minor πάθη is felt as a bond. The goddess herself bound Tibullus:

> *ipsa Venus magico religatum bracchia nodo*
> *perdocuit* (i, 8, 5 f.; cf. ii, 2, 17 ff.; ii, 4, 3 f.).

And the lovelorn man or maid may seek to bind the loveless, using an effigy as in Virgil:

> *coniugis ut magicis sanos avertere sacris*
> *experiar sensus....*
> *terna tibi haec primum triplici diversa colore*
> *licia circumdo, terque haec altaria circum*
> *effigiem duco....*
> *necte, Amarylli, modo et 'Veneris' dic 'vincula necto'*
> (*Ecl.* viii, 67 ff.).

Tibullus can also blame the girl, probably for no more than her native 'charms':

> *me retinent vinctum formosae vincla puellae*
> (i, 1, 55; cf. Horace, *Odes,* iv, 11, 23 f., etc.).

In Plautus the alternative image appears; love is a nail driven into the *animus: fixus animus clavo cupidinis (Asin.* 156). The Latin *defixio* as opposed to the Greek κατάδεσμος (cf. *devinctio*) would seem to point to a preference in Italy for the nailing method, and it is there that we find Necessity or Fate most

---

[1] It was perhaps in relation to the belief in the weaving of fate that in classical Greece and Italy threads from the loom, μίτοι, στήμονες, κλώσματα, *licia,* were particularly favoured as cord-amulets (περιάμματα); see Pley, *De lanae...usu,* pp. 92 ff., 97, and Heckenbach, *op. cit.* pp. 108 f. This is perhaps further exemplified by the κροκοῦν or binding with κρόκη in the mysteries, for which see Photius, *Lex. s.v.;* Lobeck, *Aglaoph.* p. 703; Bekker, *Anecd.* i, p. 273 and below, p. 454.

often represented with a nail in her hand, though the image is not strange to Greece.[1] Thus Horace:[2]

> te semper anteit saeva Necessitas
> clavos trabales et cuneos manu
> gestans aena, etc.;

and once again, where we may note that he combines and virtually equates her nail with the cords of death, the other instrument of κατάδεσμος:

> si figit adamantinos
> summis verticibus dira Necessitas
> clavos, non animum metu,
> non mortis laqueis expedies caput.[3]

The life-soul, the head, is pierced, is noosed. Binding and nailing are often applied to the same effigy.[4] We may compare *quod semel destinavi clavo tabulari fixum est* (Petronius, 75). With this the evidence of art is at one. On an Etruscan mirror,[5] Athrpa (= Atropos) is seen driving the *clavus trabalis* into the head of Meleager, dooming him as the binding of the gods dooms the Homeric hero. This is perhaps[6] the original explanation of the hammer in the hand of the Etruscan death-god, Charun. We have seen that victory is one of the phases of fortune which is signalised by Fate, e.g. the πείρατα νίκης of Homer and Archilochus, and the 'war-winning woof' of *Njals Saga*. Victory, with whom the *Disir* have much in

---

[1] See e.g. Aesch. *Suppl.* 944 f.; cf. 439 f. and Aristoph. *Knights*, 461.

[2] *Odes*, I, 35, 17 ff. Cf. the references given by Saglio, as mentioned in note 2 on p. 375 below; also in the Norse: *merkja â nagli Nauð* (Necessity), *Sigdrifumal*, verse 7, and *á Nornar nagli, ibid.* 17.

[3] *Odes*, III, 24, 5 ff. For the head cf. pp. 133 f. The thoughts traced help to a better understanding also of Statius' picture of Priscilla dying (*Silv.* v, 1, 155 ff.):

> furvae miseram circum undique leti
> vallavere plagae, tenduntur dura sororum
> licia et exacti superest pars ultima fili.

For further Latin evidence of the conception see pp. 403, 437 ff., 447 f.

[4] See e.g. R. Wünsch, 'Eine antike Rachepuppe', *Philologus*, 1902, pp. 126 ff.   [5] Gerhard, *Etrusk. Spiegel*, Plate CLXXVI.

[6] But it was perhaps merely an apt explanation of ordinary death, an instrument rendering lifeless without drawing blood. Cf. Milton's 'Death with his mace petrific' (*Paradise Lost*, x, 294).

common,[1] appears on coins[2] affixing a nail into the head of a trophy as Atropos into that of Meleager. Trophies can now be better understood. Each was an effigy of the vanquished;[3] it here undergoes the fate of a victim in effigy. The nailing is perhaps an expression of *devotio* and meant irreversible rout (τροπή) or destruction. So *pestilentiam quondam clavo ab dictatore fixo sedatam* (Liv. VII, 3, 3) and each year the *praetor maximus* must drive a nail (*clavum pangat*) on the Capitol (*ibid.* 5) as was done at Volsinii (*ibid.* 7) in the temple of Nortia, goddess of fate.

We can now better understand another Latin imaging of fate as a post or pillar fixed fast.

> *veter fatorum terminus sic iusserat*[4]

says Accius. And Virgil makes Dido say:

> *si tangere portus*
> *infandum caput ac terris adnare necesse est*
> *et sic fata Iovis poscunt, hic terminus haeret,*
> *at...,*[5]

while in the *Carmen Saeculare* Horace prays to the Parcae:

> *quod semel dictum est stabilisque rerum*
> *terminus servet, bona iam peractis*
> *iungite fata.*[6]

As in πεῖραρ (πέρας), boundary and fate have the same mechanism. Thus Lucretius tells how his master explored the universe,

> *unde refert nobis victor quid possit oriri,*
> *quid nequeat, finita potestas denique cuique*
> *quanam sit ratione atque alte terminus haerens.*[7]

---

[1] See R. M. Meyer, *op. cit.* p. 159.

[2] For this and allied Roman superstitions and practices concerning nails see Saglio in Daremberg et Saglio, s.v. *clavus*, col. 1240 f. The coin (of Agathocles) is given (fig. 1614) and a fuller representation (fig. 1615) from a Pompeian fresco. Nails were fixed in the heads of actual trophies, see Daremberg et Saglio, s.v. *tropaeum*, col. 4502. How good fortune might be represented thus appears in modern Italy. A lemon is taken and if it is desired to produce good luck, 'thou shouldst stick in it many pins of varied colours. But if thou wilt that evil befall anyone, put in it black pins' (recorded by C. Leland in *Aradia or the Gospel of the Witches*, p. 31). Cf. the coloured threads in note 2, p. 396 below.

[3] See e.g. Virgil, *Aen.* XI, 5–16, 83 f.   [4] 481 (Ribbeck).

[5] *Aen.* IV, 612 ff.   [6] 26 ff.

[7] I, 75 ff. Cf. ὅρος, 'determination', on pp. 464 f. The debtor assumed an

Attention was paid to the head because it contained the ψυχή.[1] Euripides conceived of the particular fate, phase of fortune, as spun and given by the deity to a man as a wreath of wool, a στέμμα.[2] By the thought traced that a phase of fortune was such a band and might be put about one in that form we can now explain the human custom of binding, wreathing the head with a ταινία or fillet, wreath, or crown. Thus, of a victor in the games Simonides says: 'Who of the present generation hath in contest of the neighbouring folk bound upon himself so many victories with leaves of myrtle or wreaths of roses?'[3] (τοσάσδε ἢ πετάλοισι μύρτων ἢ στεφάνοισι ῥόδων ἀνεδήσατο νίκας;); and of another Pindar says: 'One swift day set three glorious deeds about his hair'[4] (τρία ἔργα ποδαρκὴς ἀμέρα θῆκε κάλλιστ' ἀμφὶ κόμαις) and, in life itself, he who receives good fortune receives a μοῖρα, a crown:

> τὸ δὲ παθεῖν εὖ πρῶτον ἀέθλων·
> εὖ δ' ἀκούειν δευτέρα μοῖρ'· ἀμφοτέροισι δ' ἀνὴρ
> ὃς ἂν ἐγκύρσῃ καὶ ἕλῃ,
> στέφανον ὕψιστον δέδεκται.[5]

We can thus also better understand a number of other passages. In epitaphs Simonides says: 'This is the grave of that Adeimantos through whose counsel Greece put around her (head) the crown of freedom'[6] (ἐλευθερίας ἀμφέθετο στέφανον), and 'striving to put around Greece freedom (i.e. the band or crown that is freedom) we lie'[7] ('Ελλάδι γὰρ σπεύδοντες ἐλευθερίην

---

obligation, was 'bound' (pp. 438 ff.) and gave *pignus*. This seems characteristically to have been a ring (cf. Hor. *Od.* I, 9, 23; Juv. VI, 27; pp. 438, n. I fin.; 457, n. 3). *Pig-nus* (cf. *fe-nus*, p. 124) looks as if it were related to *pango, pepigi, pactum*, i.e. 'drive in fast', 'fix' e.g. *clavum, terminum*. If so, *pignus*='ring' is the same equation of nailing and binding. Among ourselves, 'She was nailed down to write the thing' (Meredith, *The Tragic Comedians*) or 'George comes on Wednesdays...but I cannot nail down to that day' (Longfellow, *Life*, II, 386). A custom of marking a date, or promising a time for fulfilment, by driving in a nail would explain our 'to pay on the nail'.

[1] See pp. 95 ff.   [2] See p. 336.   [3] 10, I.
[4] *Ol.* XIII, 38 f. Cf. Plat. *Rep.* 614 C on p. 427, *Od.* VIII, 244 f. on p. 380.
[5] *Pyth.* I, 98 ff. Victory (Νίκη), herself crowned (cf. Aphrodite wearing κεστὸς ἱμάς and Eros on p. 403), was represented (e.g. by Phidias, Paus. V, 11, 7) holding out or bringing a ταινία or wreath. Cf. pp. 333 f., 402.
[6] 98 (Bgk.).   [7] 100.

περιθεῖναι/κείμεθα), and of others that they 'died in order that their Greece might not take from her dying head freedom'[1] (i.e. that band—ἵνα σφίσι μὴ καθέληται/Ἑλλὰς ἀποφθιμένου κρατὸς ἐλευθερίαν), and others again 'after putting inextinguishable fame about their dear fatherland'[2] (i.e. that band—ἄσβεστον κλέος οἵδε φίλῃ περὶ πατρίδι θέντες). So too Euripides' Andromache,[3] taken from her home by the Greeks, speaks of herself as 'putting about her head hateful slavery' (δουλοσύναν στυγερὰν ἀμφιβαλοῦσα κάρᾳ), while other characters speak of putting about (περιβάλλειν) a person this or that fate, kingship (τυραννίδα),[4] safety (σωτηρίαν),[5] etc. The thought survives in the prose writers also. Thus, according to Herodotus, to the Samians, whom he is making free, Maiandrios says: τὴν ἐλευθερίην ὑμῖν περιτίθημι[6] and Astyages abuses Harpagos for his folly and injustice: εἰ παρεὸν αὐτῷ βασιλέα γενέσθαι... ἄλλῳ περιέθηκε τὸ κράτος...εἰ γὰρ δὴ δεῖν πάντως περιθεῖναι ἄλλῳ τέῳ τὴν βασιληίην καὶ μὴ αὐτὸν ἔχειν, δικαιότερον εἶναι Μήδων τέῳ περιβαλεῖν τοῦτο τὸ ἀγαθὸν ἢ Περσέων.[7] The kingship is a band put about a person, who thus becomes king. In fact βασιλεία 'kingship' was used of this physical band; it designated the diadem.[8] So we have the origin of the royal crown and of the importance of 'coronation'. Further evidence appears below.[9] The putting of a ταινία or crown elsewhere, e.g. upon a ship or a housedoor, can also now be understood as intended to confer or embody a happy fate.

[1] 103, 3 f. This is the manuscript reading which has been variously emended, e.g. Planudes ἀποφθιμένοις κάρτος ἐλευθερίας, Jacobs ἀπ' ἰφθίμου, Bergk ἀποφθιμένη. But our evidence that the head was regarded as the seat of the life vindicates the MS.   [2] 99, 1.

[3] *Androm.* 110 (cf. *Phoen.* 189). To this on pp. 146 f. I have related the Roman custom of putting a band about the head of a person when making him a slave and again another band when he was made free.

[4] *Ion*, 829.   [5] *Herc. Fur.* 304. Cf. *Or.* 1031, *I.T.* 788.
[6] III, 142.   [7] I, 129. Cf. also *Od.* III, 205–8 on p. 380.
[8] E.g. Diod. Sic. I, 47.   [9] Pp. 402 ff., 431 ff.

CHAPTER VI

Μοῖραν ἐπιτιθέναι, πεπρωμένος, etc.

There remain to be considered Homer's other expressions for fate. εἵμαρται, 'it has been apportioned', and θέσφατόν ἐστι, 'it is ordained', need not be discussed. What however of μοῖρα and αἶσα? Their obvious meaning, and that which in other contexts they possess, is just 'portion'. Of the personified powers thus named, as also of simple expressions such as ὡς γὰρ οἱ μοῖρ' ἐστὶ φίλους ἰδέειν (*Od.* v, 41), we need say little, since they, like εἵμαρται, reveal nothing as to the form under which the μοῖρα is conceived. If we exclude these, there are left several expressions hitherto unexplained. Helen says to Hector: 'Sit; for you are wearied on account of my shameless self and of the ἄτη of Paris, on our account,

> οἷσιν ἐπὶ Ζεὺς θῆκε κακὸν μόρον ὡς καὶ ὀπίσσω
> ἀνθρώποισι πελώμεθ' ἀοίδιμοι ἐσσομένοισι';[1]

similarly Odysseus seeks to comfort Aias for his wrongs:

> οὐδέ τις ἄλλος
> αἴτιος, ἀλλὰ Ζεὺς Δαναῶν στρατὸν αἰχμητάων
> ἐκπάγλως ἔχθαιρε, τεῒν δ' ἐπὶ μοῖραν ἔθηκεν.[2]

The expression is clearly spatial 'placed upon', yet commentators are content with a vague paraphrase 'assigned to' and make no attempt to explain the image. What however are Homer's other uses of ἐπι-τιθέναι with a personal object?

> αὐτὰρ ἐπὶ στεφάνην κεφαλῆφιν ἀείρας
> θήκατο χαλκείην.[3]

And under what form have we seen a man's portion, his fortunes, to be conceived? As a thread or bond placed upon him by the gods, a πεῖραρ signifying νίκη, ὄλεθρος or ὀϊζύς, etc., as the case might be. Indeed with reference to such, quite

---

[1] *Il.* VI, 357 f.   [2] *Od.* XI, 558 ff.
[3] *Il.* X, 30 f. Cf. *Od.* XXII, 123; Hymn to Aphrodite (VI), 7.

explicit, the πεῖραρ ἔριδος, we have had an almost identical expression; for this the gods ἐπ᾽ ἀμφοτέροισι τάνυσσαν. That the μοῖρα was conceived thus as a bond, or πεῖραρ, is, however, clearly shown, though unrecognised, in passages already discussed, e.g. in the fate of Melampous:

χαλεπὴ δὲ θεοῦ κατὰ μοῖρα πέδησε
δεσμοί τ᾽ ἀργαλέοι καὶ βουκόλοι ἀγροιῶται,[1]

where χαλεπὴ μοῖρα is parallel to the adjacent δεσμοί ἀργαλέοι and the personified power is precluded by θεοῦ. So too in the story of Clytemnestra:

ἀλλ᾽ ὅτε δή μιν μοῖρα θεῶν ἐπέδησε δαμῆναι.[2]

Other passages also in which μοῖρα is usually translated Fate, as if a person or agent, may well be parallel, e.g.

ἔνθ᾽ Ἀμαρυγκείδην Διώρεα μοῖρ᾽ ἐπέδησε.[3]

'Then his fate (in the form of a πεῖραρ or δεσμός) bound Diores, son of Amarynkeus.' Plato, as I have shown elsewhere,[4] follows the Homeric conception very closely and he is quite explicit: the μοῖρα is the thread spun.[5]

To this same image allusive reference was natural. Just as the πεῖραρ can be implied so that κήδε᾽ ἐφῆπται can stand no less than ὀλέθρου πείρατ᾽ ἐφῆπται, μοῖρα can be replaced by a specific fortune or fate. Peleus was blest above other men:

ἀλλ᾽ ἐπὶ καὶ τῷ θῆκε θεὸς κακόν, ὅττι οἱ οὔ τι
παίδων ἐν μεγάροισι γονὴ γένετο κρειόντων.[6]

This background of thought will help us also to understand why Pindar[7] speaks of a man's αἰών 'fastening upon him a fate of childlessness' (πότμον ἐφάψαις ὀρφανὸν γενεᾶς), and why Semonides of Amorgos[8] says of man's evil fate in marriage:

Ζεὺς γὰρ μέγιστον τοῦτ᾽ ἐποίησεν κακόν
καὶ δεσμὸν ἀμφέθηκεν ἄρρηκτον πέδης.

---

[1] *Od.* xi, 292 f.   [2] *Od.* iii, 269.
[3] *Il.* iv, 517.
[4] Pp. 306 f., 403 f., and 'On the Knees of the Gods', *Class. Rev.* Feb. 1924, pp. 3 ff.
[5] See pp. 307, 403 f.   [6] *Il.* xxiv, 538 f.
[7] *Ol.* ix, 60 f. See p. 405 below.
[8] vii, 115 f. (Bgk.). See p. 434 below.

Alkinoos tells Odysseus wherein the advantages, good points, of the Phaeacians lie, that he may tell another,

> ἡμετέρης ἀρετῆς μεμνημένος, οἷα καὶ ἡμῖν
> Ζεὺς ἐπὶ ἔργα τίθησι.[1]

We may compare from the Old Testament 'It is God that girdeth me with strength', 'And righteousness shall be the girdle of his loins',[2] etc., and for the use of ἐπί Archbishop Leighton's description of the righteousness attributed to a man by God: 'A Righteousness that is not in him but upon him. He is clothed with it'.[3] The bond can be spoken of as already upon a man ere fulfilment comes. It could be said of a man enjoying the sweets of life that upon him ἤδη ὀλέθρου πείρατ' ἐφῆπται. When Lykaon begs for mercy, Achilles refuses: 'Patroklos, a better man, has died, and I, the goddess-born:

> οὐχ ὁράᾳς οἷος καὶ ἐγὼ καλός τε μέγας τε; ...
> ἀλλ' ἔπι τοι καὶ ἐμοὶ θάνατος καὶ μοῖρα κραταιή'.[4]

'Upon me also death has been placed' (or fastened). Age and death indeed are placed or fastened upon all mankind:

> χαῖρέ μοι, ὦ βασίλεια, διαμπερὲς εἰς ὅ κε γῆρας
> ἔλθῃ καὶ θάνατος, τά τ' ἐπ' ἀνθρώποισι πέλονται.[5]

They are part of the usual lot of misery. That it is a bond that is 'put upon' men by the gods is confirmed by the fact that just before saying of Peleus that ἐπὶ καὶ τῷ θῆκε θεὸς κακόν Achilles refers to the *spinning* of evil by the gods for men:

> ὡς γὰρ ἐπεκλώσαντο θεοὶ δειλοῖσι βροτοῖσι
> ζώειν ἀχνυμένοις.[6]

Similarly Telemachos says:

> αἳ γὰρ ἐμοὶ τοσσήνδε θεοὶ δύναμιν περιθεῖεν
> τίσασθαι μνηστῆρας. ...
> ἀλλ' οὔ μοι τοιοῦτον ἐπέκλωσαν θεοὶ ὄλβον.[7]

---

[1] *Od.* VIII, 244 f. Cf. *Il.* I, 509, II, 39 f., etc.
[2] See p. 367 above.
[3] See Coleridge's *Aids to Reflection*, Aphorism LXXIII, p. 96.
[4] *Il.* XXI, 108 ff. With pp. 376 f., 457 ff., cf. *Hom. Hymn to Dem.* 150, etc.
[5] *Od.* XIII, 59 f.   [6] *Il.* XXIV, 525 f.   [7] *Od.* III, 205–8. Cf. pp. 376 f.

The thread spun is laid upon or around (περιθεῖεν) individuals or hosts, and of some kinds a portion upon every man.

Horace was familiar with fate as a bond.[1] The image traced behind Homer's Ζεὺς ἐπί...τίθησι, etc. perhaps underlies his words:

> sed satis est orare Iovem quae ponit et aufert:
> det vitam, det opes; aequum mi animum ipse parabo,[2]

which have been interpreted[3] of a banquet at which Jupiter 'sets before us and snatches from us', though the nearest parallel adduced is his picture of the winged goddess of Fortune removing a crown from one and placing it upon another (cf. pp. 402 ff., 431 ff.):

> hinc apicem rapax
> Fortuna cum stridore acuto
> sustulit, hic posuisse gaudet.[4]

In the Norse where, as we have seen, the gods are called 'the Binders' and the Norns spin, weave, and bind, and battle fraught with death is their web, there may be a parallel to this expression also; for one of the terms for the fate apportioned by them is *örlög*, 'that which is laid from the first' upon men,[5] i.e. 'fate' or 'battle'. Cf. Anglo-Saxon *orlæg*, and *orlege*.[6] In the poem (A) about Guthlac, the saint first is 'under the close fetters of hateful spirits' (540) but presently in his turn 'he bound the ministers of darkness with afflictions, laid distress upon them' (*nyd onsette*, 696 f., cf. *nyd[e]...gebunden*,[7] etc.). *Örlög* etc. are currently[8] interpreted as metaphorical, referring to commands or behests. But how the physical sense passes into

---

[1] See p. 374.   [2] *Epist.* I, 18, 111 f. The MSS. show also *qui* and *donat*.
[3] See Reid in Wilkins' note, also Wickham.
[4] *Odes*, I, 34, 14 ff. The conception of her gifts as bands or wrappings (see below pp. 420 ff.) may explain his alternative: *si celeres quatit/ pennas, resigno quae dedit et mea/virtute me involvo* (III, 29, 53 ff.).
[5] See e.g. *Helgakv. Hundingsb. i.f.*, verses 3 f. Cf. 'ez gêt keinem anders dan im wirt *ûfgeleit*', Mich. Beham's *Vom Unglauben*, 4.
[6] Also Dutch *oorlog* to which Professor Rose has drawn my attention.
[7] Gnomic Verses 38 in the Exeter book. See also Riddle, III, 13 ff. (101 b), xx, 29 f. (105 b) in the *Exeter Book* (ed. W. S. Mackie).
[8] See e.g. R. M. Meyer, *op. cit.* p. 156; Golther, *op. cit.* p. 105, and Grimm, *Deutsche Mythologie*[4] (pp. 410 and 857 in trans.). The Lithuanians and Letts also call fate *likkimas*, *liktens*, from *lik-t*, 'to lay down'.

the other may be illustrated by *iniungere*, German *einem etwas auf die Seele binden*, i.e. to *enjoin* upon one (to do something). ἐπιτιθέναι, whose parallelism does not appear to have been perceived, cannot mean merely 'command', since only in the 'middle' and that rarely—never in Homer—does ἐπιτιθέναι mean 'to lay commands upon', and that meaning is clearly impossible in the contexts cited.[1] It derives from this.

πεπρωμένος occurs twice in similar contexts. When Sarpedon and Patroklos meet, Zeus hesitates whether to rescue the former, but Hera protests:

> αἰνότατε Κρονίδη, ποῖον τὸν μῦθον ἔειπες.
> ἄνδρα θνητὸν ἐόντα πάλαι πεπρωμένον αἴσῃ
> ἄψ ἐθέλεις θανάτοιο δυσηχέος ἐξαναλῦσαι;
> ἔρδ᾽· ἀτὰρ οὔ τοι πάντες ἐπαινέομεν θεοὶ ἄλλοι.[2]

In *Il.* xxii, 178–81, with the last three lines the same and the rest of the scene scarcely changed, Athene protests when Zeus contemplates saving Hector in his turn. Current explanations and translations of the crucial phrase are not very satisfactory, e.g. 'a mortal man long doomed to fate dost thou desire to deliver again from death of evil name?' (Lang). πέπρωμαι is treated as derived from πόρω, a 'present' non-existent but postulated for ἔπορον and so bearing the meaning 'I give'. But if we render 'a man long given to fate', we are unable in Homer to find any parallel[3] to such a thought, and such a rendering is precluded by *Il.* iii, 309, xviii, 329 below, and the use of ἡ πεπρωμένη and τὸ πεπρωμένον. Instead, fate is given to, laid upon, men. Myers, apparently finding Lang's version unsatisfactory, in *Il.* xxii, 179 f. rendered 'a man that is mortal, doomed long ago by fate, wouldst thou redeem back from ill-boding death?' 'A man

---

[1] For the use of τίθημι of 'placing' fate, i.e. determining what happens, see also pp. 434 f. Perhaps Θέμις, Θέτις, and even θεός itself derive from this root and the conception of the gods as 'placers'. Thus Homer constantly expresses causation by τίθημι (e.g. *Il.* i, 2, iii, 321, xii, 450). Cf. Hdt. ii, 52: θεούς...ὅτι κόσμῳ θέντες τὰ πάντα πρήγματα καὶ πάσας νομὰς εἶχον.

[2] *Il.* xvi, 440 ff.

[3] The nearest approach is perhaps μ᾽ οὗτος ἀνὴρ κατὰ δῶμα κιόντα/ οὔ τι κακὸν ῥέξαντα βαλὼν ὀδύνῃσιν ἔδωκεν, *Od.* xvii, 566 f. Cf. xix, 167; *Il.* v, 397. Pindar speaks of one man giving another to death, *Nem.* i, 66; *Ol.* ii, 82. They are not given by Fate.

given *by* fate (αἶσα)?' To whom? To death? Whatever answer we imagine, there is no parallel to the thought and the sense of 'given' (πάλαι) is strained, since it is applied to the living. ψυχὴν Ἄϊδι δοῦναι, twice used (*Il.* v, 654 and xi, 445) of him who dies, means the act of dying. It might also be asked how would Myers render ὁμῇ πεπρωμένον αἴσῃ in its context (*Il.* xv, 209, pp. 385f. below). 'Given by the same fate' makes nonsense. If then we try to make the verb mean 'endow' and the phrase 'long ago endowed with fate', we can find in the uses of ἔπορον no shadow of a parallel for either the meaning or the construction. πέπρωται and πεπρωμένος are, moreover, never used of anything except fate, which, were they passive parts of ἔπορον, would scarcely be so, while ἔπορον itself is rarely used of human fortunes but habitually of ordinary material objects. It has the sense 'give' with the accusative of the thing given and the dative of the recipient. Lastly, while modern philologists explain thus, apparently without realising the difficulties, ancient testimony knows little or nothing of such explanation, but is equally unanimous in quite a different direction, e.g. πεπρωμένον. εἱμαρμένον· ὡρισμένον, πεπερασμένον ὑπὸ μοίρας εἰς πέρας (Photius, Suidas, etc.); πεπρωμένον· σημαίνει τὸ εἱμαρμένον καὶ ὡρισμένον καὶ οἱονεὶ πεπερατωμένον· ἀφ' οὗ γίνεται κατὰ συγκοπὴν πεπρωμένον (*Et. Magn.*); πεπρωμένην δὲ διὰ τὸ πεπερατῶσθαι πάντα καὶ μηδὲν ἐν τοῖς οὖσιν ἄπειρον εἶναι (*de Mundo*, 401 b, 10 f.), with which we may compare the opinion preserved by Eustathius (1200, 10) πεπρωμένην ὅτι πάντα εἰς πέρας φέρει. Ancient etymologies are often wild and false, but it may well mean something that the Greeks naturally looked towards the stem of πέρας and πεῖραρ for a solution, though, as might be expected, thinking only of its later meaning. πεπερασμένον or πεπερατωμένον would scarcely become πεπρωμένον. It may not be possible to determine the exact form of the present stem. πεπρωμένον might be a perfect participle passive of a verb περόω (cf. κεράω = κεράννυμι, κέκραμαι, etc.). πειραίνω, as we have seen, with an original sense of 'bind' or 'fasten', also comes to mean 'accomplish', perhaps with a basic notion 'to cross, traverse' or 'to go round'.[1] In this form the verb is rare but it is exceedingly common as περαίνω with meanings 'accomplish', 'cross' or 'traverse', and 'penetrate'. These are also the meanings of the form περάω with an 'Epic' form περόω. Exactly so ὑφαίνω has a variant ὑφάω with 'Epic' form ὑφόω.[2] If περόω was really used in or before Homer's day, we might expect that like πειραίνω it could also mean 'bind'. Whatever the form of the present, there is reason to think that πεπρωμένον originally meant 'bound'.

Let us return to the crucial instances given above:

> ἄνδρα θνητὸν ἐόντα πάλαι πεπρωμένον αἴσῃ
> ἂψ ἐθέλεις θανάτοιο δυσηχέος ἐξαναλῦσαι;

In current interpretations the vague 'doomed', explained by the almost impossible 'given', is balanced by the equally vague 'redeem' or 'deliver' for its reversal in ἐξαναλῦσαι. This last should naturally mean 'to unloose from (a bond one who is bound)'. We have already[3] seen the relation to our image of θεοὶ κακότητος ἔλυσαν, etc. On the interpretation offered, unless we take αἴσῃ as personal: 'bound by Fate'—which the parallel we are about to consider (Il. xv, 208 ff.) makes improbable—it will be an instrumental dative: 'a man who has long been bound with his fate', i.e. on whom his μοῖρα (death) has been placed, on whom ἤδη ὀλέθρου πείρατ' ἐφῆπται. This use of the dative is exactly parallel to what we saw above:

> Ζεύς με μέγα Κρονίδης ἄτῃ ἐνέδησε βαρείῃ.[4]

Zeus wants to unbind, set free, Hector and Patroklos from the doom with which they have been bound. There appears to be confirmation in the scholia (L. ad xvi, 442): ἐξαναλῦσαι· ἀναλῦσαι τοῦτο ἀπὸ τῶν μίτων τῶν Μοιρῶν, with which we may compare Eustathius: ἀφορμή ἐστιν ἀπὸ τοῦ τῶν Μοιρῶν μίτου, as also on the parallel passage: ῥηθὲν μεταφορικῶς ἀπὸ τῶν ἀναλυομένων ὑφασμάτων. ἀναλύειν is the word used by

---

[1] I.e. to traverse in three dimensions the surface of anything finite (such as a cylinder or sphere). Cf. πέρα, περί, Sanscr. pari, para. πεῖραρ is a girdling bond or the 'cross-thread' of the loom (see pp. 338 ff.), the latter, however, perhaps only incidently. The sense of 'limit' both in this and in the verb appears to result from the confining circumference. See also pp. 314 ff. and 342 above.

[2] Od. vii, 105.   [3] Pp. 363 ff.   [4] Il. ii, 111, ix, 18.

Homer of Penelope undoing her web.[1] ἐξαναλῦσαι itself is used thus in an epitaph:

ούδεὶς γὰρ δύναται μοιρῶν μίτον ἐξαναλῦσαι.[2]

Tibullus writes of the

Parcae fatalia nentes
stamina non ulli dissolüenda deo.[3]

Later magic sought, we are told,[4] λύειν τὰ τῆς εἱμαρμένης, and to his deliverer, Isis, Lucius says *fatorum etiam inextricabiliter contorta retractas licia*.[5] The explanation of the Homeric scholiast and Eustathius—which has, apparently, been hitherto dismissed as worthless—seems to involve a conception of the man as entangled in the woof. They know little or nothing of the simple binding by the gods to which we have found so frequent allusion and which satisfies the present passage, and therefore they have recourse to that form of the image more familiar in their time, the weaving of the Fates. They do, however, perceive the clear implication of some form of binding from which the victim is to be 'unloosed', if Zeus dares. After describing how Apollo, 'binding the son of Thetis with bold death' (παῖδα... Θέτιος... θρασεῖ φόνῳ πεδάσαις), staved off the fall of Troy, Pindar[6] says: 'Zeus, the warder of the gods, does not dare to unloose fates' (μόρσιμ᾽ ἀναλύεν Ζεὺς ὁ θεῶν σκοπὸς οὐ τολμᾷ). In the *Mahabharata* the Hindoo death-god, Yama, won over by the devotion of Savitri, releases her husband Satyavant from the bonds with which he has bound him, i.e. allows him to live.[7]

There remain two other Homeric passages, one in which Poseidon considers his lot and that of Zeus:

ἀλλὰ τόδ᾽ αἰνὸν ἄχος κραδίην καὶ θυμὸν ἱκάνει
ὁππότ᾽ ἂν ἰσόμορον καὶ ὁμῇ πεπρωμένον αἴσῃ
νεικείειν ἐθέλῃσι.[8]

---

[1] *Od.* II, 105, XXIV, 145.   [2] *Epigr. Gr.* 588, 8.   [3] I, 7, 1 f.
[4] Porphyr. cited by Eusebius, *Praep. Ev.* VI, 4, p. 241 a. See also Iamblichus, *de Fato*, p. 179. Cf. pp. 437 ff. below.
[5] Apul. *Met.* XI, 25. Cf. Dionysos on pp. 405, 441, 452.
[6] *Paean* VI, 83 ff. For other examples of the binding of fate in Pindar see pp. 376, 405 ff., and for the weaving pp. 349 ff.
[7] See pp. 358 ff. Compare the spell to recall the dead to life: 'Loosing the bands of death ...I lengthen out thy existence' (*Atharva Veda*, VIII, 2, 2).   [8] *Il.* XV, 208 ff.

'Bound with the same fate' (a fate shared by both) is perfectly satisfactory. The πεῖραρ ἔριδος, as we saw, was laid over two parties, ἐπ' ἀμφοτέροισι.[1] Upon Odysseus there had been μέγα πεῖραρ ὀϊзύος. 'I can', says he, 'tell Penelope about her husband; for ὁμὴν ἀνεδέγμεθα ὀϊзύν.'[2] ξυνὰ δὲ καὶ μοίρης λαχέτην λίνα, says Agathias[3] much later. In weaving it would be natural to think of two or more warp-threads as bound by the same woof. αἶσα is clearly not personified here. By whom they are 'bound' is left vague. Another application of the image to divine fortunes has already[4] been cited: ἀθανάτοισιν ἔρις καὶ νεῖκος ἐφῆπται.[5] The problem it raises will be discussed below.[6]

The remaining instances differ slightly. Priam says he cannot endure to watch the combat of his son with Menelaos.

> Ζεὺς μέν που τό γε οἶδε καὶ ἀθάνατοι θεοὶ ἄλλοι,
> ὁπποτέρῳ θανάτοιο τέλος πεπρωμένον ἐστίν.[7]

The tone is much that of Menelaos and of Hector in the passages whose exemplification of the image has already[8] been discussed:

> τῷδε δ' ἐγὼν αὐτὸς θωρήξομαι· αὐτὰρ ὕπερθε
> νίκης πείρατ' ἔχονται ἐν ἀθανάτοισι θεοῖσιν,[9]

> ἀλλ' ἤτοι μὲν ταῦτα θεῶν ἐν γούνασι κεῖται
> αἵ κέ σε χειρότερός περ ἐὼν ἀπὸ θυμὸν ἕλωμαι,[10]

and the meaning of the last line, 'for which of the two the τέλος of death is bound', is virtually ὁπποτέρῳ ὀλέθρου πείρατ' ἐφῆπται. τέλος is discussed below.[11] A man's fate may be expressed through a verb as something he is to do or suffer. We saw that ἐπικλώθειν could be followed by the infinitive οἴκόνδε νέεσθαι (Od. I, 17), зώειν (Il. xxvi, 525 f.), and that similarly the dative of the noun defining the particular fate could with ἐπέδησε be replaced by the infinitive μεῖναι, δαμῆναι, etc. So too with πέπρωται the noun subject can be replaced by an infinitive, explaining what fate has been bound,

---

[1] Il. xiii, 359.
[2] Od. xvii, 563.
[3] Anth. Pal. vii, 551, 3.
[4] P. 334.
[5] Il. xxi, 513.
[6] Pp. 392 f.
[7] Il. iii, 308 f.
[8] Pp. 333 f.
[9] Il. vii, 101 f.
[10] Il. xx, 435 f.
[11] Pp. 426 ff.

what bond has been fastened, e.g. 'that both should redden the same earth':

ἄμφω γὰρ πέπρωται ὁμοίην γαῖαν ἐρεῦσαι.[1]

In post-Homeric literature πέπρωται and πεπρωμένος gradually became colourless; they survived as the English 'bound' (e.g. 'he is bound to conquer') has done,[2] but the image was forgotten.[3]

To the same conception of fate as thread or cord (πτολέμοιο πεῖραρ, πεῖραρ ὀϊзύος, etc.) appears to belong the use of τολυπεύειν, 'to wind into a ball (τολύπη)'. Thus Agamemnon, having felicitated Achilles on his honourable end, says: 'But what joy is this to me that I wound up the (thread of) war (ἐπεὶ πόλεμον τολύπευσα)? For at my returning Zeus devised evil doom for me'.[4] It is not just our 'wind up'='make an end'. Odysseus says of the Achaeans besieging Troy: 'Zeus hath given to us that from youth even to old age we should wind grievous wars'[5] (τολυπεύειν ἀργαλέους πολέμους). The

---

[1] Il. xviii, 329.   [2] See p. 333.

[3] Nevertheless if we examine the passages in which they occur (see e.g. those cited by Liddell and Scott), we find that an original sense 'bound' satisfies all of them, while an original sense 'given' is in some cases exceedingly difficult, e.g. πεπρωμένον βασιλέα (Pind. Pyth. iv, 61 f.); 'destined king', 'bound (as) king', like 'crowned (as) king', meaning 'bound with the fortune of kingship' (see pp. 376 f., 447 f., 457 f.), gives perfect sense. If the attempt be made to apply 'endowed' universally—a sense which ἔπορον never bears—it fails in almost every instance. We can say that a fetter or bond is fastened (cf. σειρὴν πειραίνειν, Od. xxii, 175, etc.) no less than that a person is fastened. This already has been instanced in θανάτοιο τέλος πεπρωμένον ἐστίν, and it occurs frequently, πεπρωμένος being applied to the fortune in question, βίος, ἀρετά, etc., e.g. τὴν πεπρωμένην δὲ χρὴ αἶσαν φέρειν (Aesch. P.V. 103 f.). From this come the use of ἡ πεπρωμένη (sc. μοῖρα or αἶσα) alone and its personification like that of Αἶσα and Μοῖρα themselves and of Εἱμαρμένη. In the personification, as in that of μοῖρα, the association of the thread was perhaps still felt. Pausanias remarks that Olen made a hymn ἐς Εἰλείθυιαν, εὔλινόν τε αὐτὴν ἀνακαλεῖ, δῆλον ὡς τῇ Πεπρωμένῃ τὴν αὐτήν (viii, 21, 3).

[4] Od. xxiv, 95; cf. i, 238, iv, 490, xiv, 368.

[5] Il. xiv, 86; cf. xxiv, 7. 'Just as a woman rolls thread into a ball, so their days rolled on till it came to their turn to be rolled' ('Little Fool Ivan', one of the Skazki of Polevoi). Cf. p. 352 (Slav goddesses spinning fate). The sense is slightly different when Penelope (Od. xix, 137) says of her weaving 'I wind snares' (ἐγὼ δὲ δόλους τολυπεύω; cf. δόλους ὑφαίνειν, ῥάπτειν, πλέκειν and pp. 341, 368).

context of ἐκτολυπεύειν in the 'Shield of Herakles' suggests
that the evil fortune is fastened about a man and he winds it
off himself (see pp. 364 f.):

> ὡς δ' ὅτ' ἀνὴρ ἀσπαστὸν ὑπεκπροφύγῃ κακότητα
> νούσου ὑπ' ἀργαλέης ἢ καὶ κρατεροῦ ὑπὸ δεσμοῦ,
> ὣς ῥα τότ' Ἀμφιτρύων χαλεπὸν πόνον ἐκτολυπεύσας
> ἀσπασίως τε φίλως τε ἑὸν δόμον εἰσαφίκανεν.[1]

In Latin we find not only the fates spinning or winding,
e.g. *sic volvere Parcas*,[2] but also human beings might ask to
suffer their old fate again, wind it again. Thus Jupiter is asked
on behalf of the Trojans:

> *Xanthum et Simoenta*
> *redde, oro, miseris iterumque revolvere casus*
> *da, pater, Iliacos Teucris.*[3]

To go through fate again in speech was also 'to wind it again',
as one unwinds and rewinds a ball of wool:

> *sed quid ego haec autem nequiquam ingrata revolvo?*[4]

It is now perhaps possible to solve the problem of a line of
Ennius: *quis potis ingentis oras evolvere belli?*[5] and of Virgil's
imitation:

> *vos, o Calliope, precor adspirate canenti*
> *quas ibi tum ferro strages...*
> *et mecum ingentis oras evolvite belli.*[6]

It has been assumed that *oras* meant 'edges, extremities', and
an attempt has been made to explain the metaphor as unrolling the edge of a picture or a manuscript; but the war is
not a manuscript or a picture, if it was natural to speak of
unrolling a picture; and why speak of the 'mighty edges' of
either? If for Ennius and Virgil, as it did for Livy, etc., *ora* could
mean 'cord', equivalent to Homer's πεῖραρ (see pp. 315 ff.), the
image is natural—it is the coil of war, a slightly transmuted
reminiscence of the ἔριδος κρατερῆς καὶ ὁμοιίου πτολέμοιο
πεῖραρ (see pp. 310 ff. and the μέγα πεῖραρ, pp. 323 f.), war
which as a cord or thread Homer himself, in the passages just

---

[1] 42 ff.
[2] *Aen.* I, 22; cf. III, 375.
[3] *Aen.* X, 60 ff.; cf. IX, 391.
[4] *Aen.* II, 101.
[5] *Ann.* VI, *init.* (174 Vahlen).
[6] *Aen.* IX, 525–8.

discussed, speaks of 'winding' (τολυπεύειν). This the Latin poets contemplate unwinding (cf. *fusos evolvere*, etc.). We may compare the opening of the Finnish epic:

> Shall I now the end unfasten
> Of this ball of ancient wisdom,
> These ancestral lays unravel...?[1]

For Virgil's appeal to the Muses *mecum ingentis oras evolvite belli* we may recall that in the Sixth Eclogue (3 ff.), when he wanted to sing of kings and war, Apollo told him rather *deductum dicere carmen* i.e. to 'sing song of slender thread', pastoral. For the 'weaving' of song see above.[2]

---

[1] *Kalevala*, trans. Crawford, p. 4. Cf. the end, *ibid.* p. 735.
[2] Pp. 340, 368 f.

CHAPTER VII

Ὑπὲρ μόρον and the Relation of the Gods to Fate

This reinterpretation of πέπρωται, particularly in *Il.* xvi, 440-3 and xxii, 178-81, will help to a better understanding of the much disputed relationship of the gods to fate, the problems whether the gods are subordinate to fate or fate to the gods, and of the supposed violation of fate. We see that the gods, above all Zeus, spin and bind fate. Physically Zeus is irresistible and what he has bound he can unbind. But it is essential to the conception that the allotment once made be respected. There is a moral sanction intrinsic in it. αἶσα is the expression of an ordered world, 'measure' that should be observed. ὑπὲρ αἶσαν means not only 'beyond the measure allotted', 'beyond what is fated', but also 'beyond measure' (Ἕκτορ, ἐπεί με κατ' αἶσαν ἐνείκεσας οὐδ' ὑπὲρ αἶσαν,[1] etc.), and αἴσιμος 'proper, right' as well as 'fated'. Allotting is like promising; once done, one must stand by it. We may compare Zeus' statement:

οὐ γὰρ ἐμὸν παλινάγρετον οὐδ' ἀπατηλὸν
οὐδ' ἀτελεύτητον, ὅ τί κεν κεφαλῇ κατανεύσω.[2]

Otherwise the validity of allotment and the order it implies disappear. Thus it is that Zeus is restrained. He cannot 'play fast and loose'.[3] It is not that there is a stronger external deity. The society of the gods morally supports the established order and they actively intervene in human affairs to see that the measure which Zeus has allotted is fulfilled. There is the possibility that human spontaneity, if not checked, may overstep it. E.g.

ἔνθα κεν αὖτε Τρῶες ἀρηιφίλων ὑπ' Ἀχαιῶν
Ἴλιον εἰσανέβησαν ἀναλκείῃσι δαμέντες,

---

[1] *Il.* iii, 59, vi, 333.

[2] *Il.* i, 526f. Cf. the sanctity of the *terminus* (p. 375), and the Stoic view of Zeus, almost the last word of classical thought on fate: the power that determines our destinies *eadem necessitate et deos alligat...ille ipse omnium conditor ac rector; scripsit quidem fata sed sequitur* (Sen. *de Prov.* 5).

[3] Cf. *Od.* iii, 236-8, where the μοῖρα of death which the gods cannot avert is apparently nevertheless μοῖρα θεῶν (269; cf. 205-9, etc.).

'Αργεῖοι δέ κε κῦδος ἕλον καὶ ὑπὲρ Διὸς αἶσαν
κάρτεϊ καὶ σθένεϊ σφετέρῳ· ἀλλ' αὐτὸς 'Απόλλων....¹

ἔνθα κε δὴ δύστηνος ὑπὲρ μόρον ὤλετ' 'Οδυσσεύς,
εἰ μὴ ἐπιφροσύνην δῶκε γλαυκῶπις 'Αθήνη.²

This conception of the imposing of fate as a binding with it
allows us to conceive of the binding as not all-inclusive so as
to exclude freedom. Not all things need be bound or bound
in every respect; some may be loose.³ So much evil may be
in a man's fate, but he may make additional trouble for himself ὑπὲρ μόρον, 'beyond what is fated', not, as it is sometimes
interpreted, 'contrary to what is fated'. Thus Zeus can say to
the other gods: 'What blame mortals lay upon the gods! For
they say that evils come from us. But they themselves by their
own follies have woes beyond what is fated (ὑπὲρ μόρον ἄλγε'
ἔχουσιν), as even now Aigisthos beyond what was fated (ὑπὲρ
μόρον) married the wedded wife of Atreus' son and killed the
latter on his return, knowing that it was sheer destruction for
himself, since we had warned him, sending Hermes...'.⁴
Hector tries to cheer Andromache: 'No man shall launch me
to Hades beyond my fate (ὑπὲρ μόρον). His fate I say no man,
brave or coward, hath escaped, once he hath been born'.⁵
The case of Aigisthos is like that of a man sentenced to die on
a certain date and allowed a comfortable existence until then.
He can before that hurt himself by his own action or even kill
himself. The measure of evil fixed may be exceeded by a man's
own choosing. Apollo warns Aeneas to retreat before Achilles
μὴ καὶ ὑπὲρ μοῖραν δόμον ᾿Αϊδος εἰσαφίκηαι.⁶ The gods inter-

---

¹ *Il.* xvii, 319 ff.   ² *Od.* v, 436 f.
³ Cf. *Aen.* xii, 819 ff. A man may feel that two fates are with him till
he chooses between them, e.g. either to stay at home or to go to the
war and die (see *Il.* ix, 410 ff. and xiii, 665 ff., and for the κῆρες pp. 398 ff.
Cf. p. 265).
⁴ *Od.* i, 32 ff. We may prefer Hardy's account. Dick Dewey says:
'If we be doomed to marry, we marry; if we be doomed to remain single,
we do.' To which Geoffrey Day: 'That's not the case with some folk....
There's that wife o' mine. It was her doom not to be nobody's wife at
all in the wide universe. But she made up her mind that she would and
did it twice over. Doom?...Doom is nothing beside a elderly woman—
quite a chiel in her hands!' *Under the Greenwood Tree* (Pocket edition),
pp. 131 f.
⁵ *Il.* vi, 487 ff.   ⁶ *Il.* xx, 335 f.

vene to prevent accidental overstepping of fate[1] and warn men so that the responsibility is theirs. In this, as in all attempts to combine some predestination with some human freedom, there are weaknesses.[2]

Thus, speaking generally, human fate is the work of the gods. This is seen in such passages as Lykaon's speech to Achilles:

νῦν αὖ με τεῆς ἐν χερσὶν ἔθηκε
μοῖρ' ὀλοή· μέλλω που ἀπέχθεσθαι Διὶ πατρί
ὅς με σοὶ αὖτις δῶκε,[3]

and in Διὸς αἶσα, μοῖρα θεῶν, etc. ὑπὲρ θεόν is used much like ὑπὲρ μοῖραν: πῶς ἂν καὶ ὑπὲρ θεὸν εἰρύσσεσθε / Ἴλιον αἰπεινήν; [4] says Apollo to Aeneas. We must distinguish this primary belief from the answer which has to be found when the gods, clearly defined in their respective powers and provinces, have been so vividly conceived as doing and suffering like men that they in their turn have their fates and the same language is naturally employed. See p. 334, n. 5 (cf. men's binding of gods, p. 372, n. 2) and the words of Ares going to avenge his son:

εἴ πέρ μοι καὶ μοῖρα Διὸς πληγέντι κεραυνῷ
κεῖσθαι ὁμοῦ νεκύεσσι....[5]

In *Il.* xv, 208 ff. Poseidon complains that Zeus threatens him, though ἰσόμορον καὶ ὁμῇ πεπρωμένον αἴσῃ, but the allotting powers are not defined. Just before (189 ff.), however, he has described how he and his brothers, Zeus and Hades, divided the world between them by the shaking of lots:

ἤτοι ἐγὼν ἔλαχον πολιὴν ἅλα ναιέμεν αἰεὶ
παλλομένων· Ἀΐδης δ' ἔλαχε....

---

[1] In all other passages the possibility beyond what was fated is mentioned by Homer only to be prevented by the intervention of a god or gods. In *Il.* xvi, 777 ff. the Achaeans and the Trojans fought, both sides with equal success in the earlier part of the day, but as the sun moved to its setting τότε δή ῥ' ὑπὲρ αἶσαν Ἀχαιοὶ φέρτεροι ἦσαν. ἐκ μὲν Κεβριόνην βελέων ἥρωα ἔρυσσαν, which may be satisfied by 'then the Achaeans prevailed beyond their share' (which had been equality) or 'beyond measure' (cf. *Il.* iii, 59, vi, 333 quoted on p. 390). If it means 'beyond the share allotted to them', it illustrates, with *Od.* i, 32 ff., the elasticity admitted with the margin of human freedom.

[2] E.g. on what in *Od.* i, 32 ff. is spoken of as the spontaneous folly of Aigisthos appears to depend the *fate* of someone else in *Od.* iii, 269 ff. This may be an oversight. [3] *Il.* xxi, 82 ff. [4] *Il.* xvii, 327 f. [5] *Il.* xv, 117 f.

The shaking of lots might then, as the spinning of a coin more commonly now, be merely the acceptance of a decision by impartial chance. But that is most unlikely.[1] More probably the lots[2] (and possibly the vessel from which they were shaken) were either credited with a virtue of their own, possibly even a consciousness, ensuring the right decision as the balance might,[3] or thought to be controlled by higher powers who thus revealed their will. The former belief perhaps preceded the latter and may suffice for the shaking of lots to decide between Zeus, Poseidon, and Hades. Homer does not raise the question. When, however, lots are shaken amongst men to decide which of the Achaean champions shall do battle with Hector, Zeus is expected to control the lots:

Ζεῦ πάτερ, ἢ Αἴαντα λαχεῖν ἢ Τυδέος υἱόν...[4]

another indication that it is Zeus who controls fate. Sometimes the quasi-human situations, in which the poet represents the gods, require that they should appeal to other powers, as men to them. Thus, protesting to Zeus her innocence of Poseidon's action, Hera calls to witness Earth and Ouranos and the down-pouring water of Styx and the sacred head of Zeus and their bridal bed.[5] More important for the problem of fate are Μοῖρα, Αἶσα, Κλῶθες.[6] Not superior to Zeus but rather subordinate,[7] they are personifications (like Ἄτη,[8] the Ὧραι,[9] etc.), dynamic agencies of the 'thread' or 'portion'; and sometimes instead of Zeus, or vaguely Zeus and the gods, they are spoken of as allotting fate to a man. Their functions are discussed further below.[10] Their sex would follow from the gender of μοῖρα and αἶσα and fits in with the activity of women[11] as spinners and the natural association of the allotting of destiny

[1] See e.g. *Il.* VII, 169 ff. and the oracular use of lots later.
[2] The use of beans, κύαμοι, perhaps originated in the belief that they contain ψυχαί (see pp. 112 f.), for the prophetic power of which see e.g. pp. 101 ff.
[3] See pp. 397 ff., esp. note 4 on p. 398.   [4] *Il.* VII, 179.
[5] *Il.* XV, 35 ff. See too the Erinyes in XV, 204. Cf. XIX, 258 f.
[6] For instances see pp. 335, 399, etc.
[7] See e.g. Hesiod, *Theog.* 904.
[8] See pp. 327, 404.   [9] See pp. 412 ff., 460.   [10] See pp. 403 f., 410, 416 ff.
[11] For the gods and other male spinners see pp. 308 f. above and *Class. Rev.* 1924, p. 6.

with birth.[1] Later they were identified with goddesses attending at childbirth.[2] They may thus represent subsidiary folk-belief[3] which Homer has combined, but not precisely related, with his prevailing idea of the allotting of fate by Zeus, etc. By their side should be mentioned the Erinyes, the dark powers who guard the established order and punish him who oversteps it.[4]

[1] E.g. *Od.* vii, 197 f.

[2] See e.g. Eileithyia on pp. 352, 387, n. 3 and cf. *Parcae* on p. 352. In Egypt, long before Homer's time, it was believed that goddesses attending at childbirth announced gifts, parts of its fate, to the child. See e.g. the stories on pp. 44, 156, 161 f. of *The Literature of the Ancient Egyptians*, by Adolf Erman, trans. into English by A. M. Blackman.

[3] See pp. 352 f., 416 ff.

[4] See e.g. *Il.* xix, 87 f., 418, xv, 204; *Od.* xvii, 475, etc. and later Heraclitus, B 94 (Diels). See also below p. 424, n. 7.

CHAPTER VIII

The Jars of Zeus, the Scales of Zeus, and the Κῆρες

If the single image thus explains these many expressions, there yet remains a passage, describing the assignment of fate, which is universally treated as standing alone and explained without reference to any part of the conception detailed. It is the account of the πίθοι of Zeus whence he gives 'gifts', fortunes good and evil, to mortals. The context has passed unnoticed.

ὡς γὰρ ἐπεκλώσαντο θεοὶ δειλοῖσι βροτοῖσι
ζώειν ἀχνυμένοις· αὐτοὶ δέ τ᾽ ἀκηδέες εἰσί.
δοιοὶ γάρ τε πίθοι κατακείαται ἐν Διὸς οὔδει
δώρων οἷα δίδωσι, κακῶν, ἕτερος δὲ ἑάων.
ᾧ μέν κ᾽ ἀμμίξας δώῃ Ζεὺς τερπικέραυνος
ἄλλοτε μέν τε κακῷ ὅ γε κύρεται, ἄλλοτε δ᾽ ἐσθλῷ...
ὡς μὲν καὶ Πηλῆϊ θεοὶ δόσαν ἀγλαὰ δῶρα
ἐκ γενετῆς· πάντας γὰρ ἐπ᾽ ἀνθρώπους ἐκέκαστο...
ἀλλ᾽ ἐπὶ καὶ τῷ θῆκε θεὸς κακόν, ὅττι οἱ οὔ τι
παίδων ἐν μεγάροισι γονὴ γένετο κρειόντων.[1]

The reflection begins explicitly with the conception of human fortunes as threads spun by the gods, and the manner of the giving is defined by an expression (ἐπὶ τῷ θῆκε) which, as we have already seen, refers to the placing of the thread spun (μοῖρα or πεῖραρ) upon the individual. Elsewhere the gods are sometimes replaced by the personified Fates whose mode of creating human fortunes was, unquestionably, spinning, usually at birth, e.g.

πείσεται ἅσσα οἱ Αἶσα κατὰ Κλῶθές τε βαρεῖαι
γεινομένῳ νήσαντο λίνῳ ὅτε μιν τέκε μήτηρ.[2]

These threads are their 'gifts' which they 'give'. Twice Hesiod names them:

Κλωθώ τε Λάχεσίν τε καὶ Ἄτροπον αἵτε βροτοῖσι
γεινομένοισι διδοῦσιν ἔχειν ἀγαθόν τε κακόν τε.[3]

---

[1] Il. xxiv, 525–39.
[2] Od. vii, 197 f. Cf. Il. xx, 127, xxiv, 210, etc.
[3] Theog. 218 f., 905 f.

In Homer, with Peleus' fate, whose later days in marriage Zeus marred thus with evil, we may compare his 'gift' to Nestor:

ῥεῖα δ' ἀρίγνωτος γόνος ἀνέρος ᾧ τε Κρονίων
ὄλβον ἐπικλώσῃ γαμέοντί τε γεινομένῳ τε,
ὡς νῦν Νέστορι δῶκε διαμπερὲς ἤματα πάντα
αὐτὸν μὲν λιπαρῶς γηρασκέμεν ἐν μεγάροισιν,
υἱέας αὖ πινυτούς τε καὶ ἔγχεσιν εἶναι ἀρίστους.[1]

The πίθοι need create no difficulty. Wine, with which πίθοι are perhaps most frequently associated, would in any case be excluded by the fact that fusion and a homogeneous whole would result from combination. Similar difficulties[2] would arise with oil or any other liquids. Excavations in Crete and at Mykenai, etc. have shown that πίθοι were used for storing various kinds of wealth, and pots and jars of various shapes have been used by various peoples[3] for containing what is spun. The Homeric housewife spinning had what she wanted for the time being in a basket of silver or other material.[4] To the πίθοι we shall return.[5]

[1] *Od.* IV, 207 ff.

[2] They appear in George Herbert's imitation:

> 'When God at first made Man
> Having a glass of blessings standing by
> Let us (said He) pour on him all we can...
> So strength first made a way,
> Then beauty flowed, then wisdom, honour, pleasure,' etc.

It was 'a pretty pickle'. In the combination of threads, 'mixing' (ἀμμίξας), e.g. of different colours, is a natural expression most obviously of weaving but even of the spinning of fate; we find with *stamina de nigro vellere facta mihi* (Ovid, *Trist.* IV, 1, 64; cf. V, 13, 24, etc.), *postquam Parcae meliora benigna/ pensa manu ducunt hilares et staminis albi / lanificae* (Juv. XII, 64 ff.). Shakespeare's 'The web of our life is of a mingled yarn, good and ill together' (*All's Well*, etc. IV, 3), Prior's 'a life parti-coloured, half pleasure, half care' (*For my own Monument*), and Landor's 'Years, many parti-coloured years, some have crept on,' etc. (*Years*), illustrate the survival of the thought. Cf. p. 375, n. 2. It is difficult to conceive an appropriate unity, except a mere aggregate of wealth (or a meal?), in which other heterogeneous articles stored could be combined. It is unnecessary to labour the point since the things in question appear to be 'spun' and 'placed upon' Peleus.

[3] See e.g. Kimakowicz, *Spinn- u. Webewerkzeuge, Entwicklung u. Anwendung in vorgesch. Zeit Europas*, 62 f.

[4] See *Class. Rev.* 1924, p. 6.   [5] Pp. 404 and 410.

There remains one further instrument of fate, which the unity found elsewhere suggests may also originally have belonged to this same conception. It is the Διὸς τάλαντα:

ἐς δίφρον δ' ἀναβὰς φύγαδ' ἔτραπε, κέκλετο δ' ἄλλους
Τρῶας φευγέμεναι· γνῶ γὰρ Διὸς ἱρὰ τάλαντα.[1]

ἄμητος δ' ὀλίγιστος, ἐπὴν κλίνῃσι τάλαντα
Ζεύς, ὅς τ' ἀνθρώπων ταμίης πολέμοιο τέτυκται.[2]

The most explicit are two closely parallel passages:

καὶ τότε δὴ χρύσεια πατὴρ ἐτίταινε τάλαντα·
ἐν δ' ἐτίθει δύο κῆρε τανηλεγέος θανάτοιο,
Τρώων θ' ἱπποδάμων καὶ Ἀχαιῶν χαλκοχιτώνων,
ἕλκε δὲ μέσσα λαβών· ῥέπε δ' αἴσιμον ἦμαρ Ἀχαιῶν.
[αἱ μὲν Ἀχαιῶν κῆρες ἐπὶ χθονὶ πουλυβοτείρῃ
ἑζέσθην, Τρώων δὲ πρὸς οὐρανὸν εὐρὺν ἄερθεν·]
αὐτὸς δ' ἐξ Ἴδης μεγάλ' ἔκτυπε, κ.τ.λ.[3]

καὶ τότε δὴ χρύσεια πατὴρ ἐτίταινε τάλαντα,
ἐν δ' ἐτίθει δύο κῆρε τανηλεγέος θανάτοιο,
τὴν μὲν Ἀχιλλῆος, τὴν δ' Ἕκτορος ἱπποδάμοιο,
ἕλκε δὲ μέσσα λαβών· ῥέπε δ' Ἕκτορος αἴσιμον ἦμαρ,
ᾤχετο δ' εἰς Ἀΐδαο, λίπεν δέ ἑ Φοῖβος Ἀπόλλων.
Πηλείωνα δ' ἵκανε θεὰ γλαυκῶπις Ἀθήνη.[4]

On both occasions there has been an *impasse*, equality or balance between two contending parties. The τάλαντα are used and a decision follows, produced (or, at least, accompanied) by the accession or withdrawal of divine support. Current commentaries are content to compare the ψυχοστασία of Aeschylus and the Egyptian belief, or to dismiss it as a mere device of the poet to present the decision more vividly to the imagination of his audience.[5] For the second course there is no justification. In any illustration of this length Homer uses a simile; and there is here no suggestion of a mere figure of speech. Zeus' action is described circumstantially, as when he nods, lightens, etc., and the allusive references above presuppose a belief instantly recognisable. The ψυχοστασία of Aeschylus also sheds no light, being obviously derivative. In that work not Hector but Memnon is opposed to Achilles,

---

[1] *Il.* xvi, 657 f.   [2] *Il.* xix, 223 f.; cf. also xi, 509, xiv, 99.
[3] *Il.* viii, 69–75.   [4] *Il.* xxii, 209 ff.
[5] See e.g. p. 326 above and Van Leeuwen, *ad loc.* Cf. schol. A.D. to *Il.* viii, 69: τάλαντα· τὴν τοῦ Διὸς διάνοιαν.

and not the κήρ (something external and hateful[1]) or ἦμαρ but the ψυχή or soul itself is set in the balance.[2] Leaf and others have suggested that Aeschylus was influenced by the Egyptian belief[3] since Memnon was king of the Aethiopians. Among the Egyptians, however, the weighing is a very different matter, as those who have used the parallel seem scarcely to have realised. There, more reasonably, it is not till after death that the soul is weighed and then not against another soul for victory but against the feather of Maat, a standard weight as it were, and the trial is one of moral qualification, a judgment.[4] No supreme god or Zeus but the scribe Thoth does the weighing. Here, clearly, though we may[5] find the source of Aeschylus' substitution of ψυχή, it would be folly to look for any connection with the Homeric belief.

[1] See e.g. *Il.* I, 228, III, 454; *Od.* XVII, 500.

[2] We may add that in Homer a heavier κήρ or ἦμαρ is prejudicial to its owner, whereas a greater or heavier ψυχή might be expected to be advantageous and confer victory—unless indeed Aeschylus reverses the relation of the scales to the battle; but of such change no hint reaches us.

[3] A Greek would, perhaps, be encouraged to assimilate or fuse the Homeric with the Egyptian conception by the fact that, while in the former it is the κήρ which is placed in the balance, in the latter it is the heart (i.e. κῆρ). For apparent assimilation of κήρ and κῆρ in Greek thought later see Quint. Smyrn. *Posthom.* II, 570, XI, 105 f.; for the heart-soul p. 280, n. 3; for it and various forms of the external soul in folk-tales, Frazer, *Golden Bough, Balder,* II, pp. 97 ff. Such a soul is necessary to life. It is its *destruction* which means death to the owner.

[4] To it we may compare the writing upon the wall (Dan. V, 27) or, better, the early Hindoo belief of a moral weighing in the next world. See e.g. *Sat. Brahm.* XI, 2, 7, 33 ff. There is in the same quarter admirable illustration of the powers attributed to the balance. In a trial by ordeal the accused is put into one scale and earth or a similar substance into the other, till apparent equivalence is effected, when the man is taken out. He is then placed in the balance again and the balance is thus adjured: 'Thou art called *dhata* (a balance) which appellation is synonymous with *dharma* (justice)....Thou knowest the bad and good actions of all beings....Thou art superior to gods, demons, and mortals in point of veracity...therefore mayest thou deliver him lawfully from his perplexity', *The Institutes of Vishnu,* x; cf. *Narada,* I, 260–84. We may thus better understand the Pythagorean command 'not to violate the beam of the balance' (see Diog. Laert. VIII, 17) and 'the scale of Justice is watching' (ῥοπὴ δ' ἐπισκοπεῖ Δίκας, Aesch. *Choeph.* 61).

[5] See, however, note 8 on p. 405.

In the latter the κήρ is in each case presumably analogous to that of which the dead Patroklos says that it was appointed at birth:

ἐμὲ μὲν κὴρ
ἀμφέχανε στυγερή, ἥ περ λάχε γιγνόμενόν περ·
καὶ δὲ σοὶ αὐτῷ μοῖρα, θεοῖς ἐπιείκελ᾽ ᾽Αχιλλεῦ,
τείχει ὕπο Τρώων εὐηφενέων ἀπολέσθαι[1]

or of which Achilles says:

κῆρα δ᾽ ἐγὼ τότε δέξομαι, ὁππότε κεν δὴ
Ζεὺς ἐθέλῃ τελέσαι ἠδ᾽ ἀθάνατοι θεοὶ ἄλλοι.
οὐδὲ γὰρ οὐδὲ βίη Ἡρακλῆος φύγε κῆρα...
ἀλλά ἑ μοῖρ᾽ ἐδάμασσε καὶ ἀργαλέος χόλος Ἥρης.
ὣς καὶ ἐγών, εἰ δή μοι ὁμοίη μοῖρα τέτυκται,
κείσομ᾽ ἐπεί κε θάνω.[2]

It is obviously very closely related[3] to the μοῖρα, the thread which also is spun at a man's birth and later bound upon him, e.g.

ἀλλ᾽ οὐδ᾽ ὣς φύγε κῆρα· πέδησε δὲ καὶ τὸν ᾽Αθήνη
Τηλεμάχου ὑπὸ χερσὶ καὶ ἔγχεϊ Ἶφι δαμῆναι.[4]

The μοῖρα is also spoken of as if it were an agent (cf. perhaps the πεῖραρ which ἱκάνει, Od. v, 288) and further defined (cf. πεῖραρ ὀλέθρου, etc.), e.g.

μοῖρ᾽ ὀλοὴ καθέλῃσι τανηλεγέος θανάτοιο,[5]

and

Ἄργον δ᾽ αὖ κατὰ μοῖρ᾽ ἔλαβεν μέλανος θανάτοιο.[6]

So too the κήρ is τανηλεγέος θανάτοιο in the passages under discussion and μέλανος θανάτοιο elsewhere.[7] Again we may compare

νῦν δ᾽ ἔμπης γὰρ κῆρες ἐφεστᾶσιν θανάτοιο
μυρίαι, ἃς οὐκ ἔστι φυγεῖν βροτὸν οὐδ᾽ ὑπαλύξαι[8]

with

ἤ τ᾽ ἄρα καὶ σοὶ πρῶϊ παραστήσεσθαι ἔμελλε
μοῖρ᾽ ὀλοή, τὴν οὔ τις ἀλεύεται ὅς κε γένηται,[9]

and

μήτηρ γάρ τέ μέ φησι θεὰ Θέτις ἀργυρόπεζα
διχθαδίας κῆρας φερέμεν θανάτοιο τέλοσδε[10]

---

[1] Il. XXIII, 78 ff.   [2] Il. XVIII, 115–21.
[3] Of the κήρ here Stephanus, ed. Valpy, s.v., says idem μοῖραν vocat in versu sequenti.
[4] Od. XVIII, 155 f.   [5] Od. II, 100, III, 238.
[6] Od. XVIII, 336.   [7] See e.g. Il. II, 834, XI, 332, XVI, 687.
[8] Il. XII, 326 f.   [9] Od. XXIV, 28 f. Cf. Il. XXIV, 131 f.
[10] Il. IX, 410 f. Cf. II, 302; Od. XIV, 207 f., etc.

with

τὸν δ' ἄγε μοῖρα κακὴ θανάτοιο τέλοσδε,[1]

the verb of which (ἄγειν) is used also of κῆρες.[2] That κήρ and μοῖρα can be virtually interchanged we find something like proof in Hesiod:

καὶ Μοίρας καὶ Κῆρας ἐγείνατο νηλεοποίνους
Κλωθώ τε Λάχεσίν τε καὶ Ἄτροπον αἵτε βροτοῖσι
γεινομένοισι διδοῦσιν ἔχειν ἀγαθόν τε κακόν τε,[3]

and earlier:

Νὺξ δ' ἔτεκε στυγερόν τε Μόρον καὶ Κῆρα μέλαιναν,[4]

which are supported by the 'Shield of Herakles',[5] in which Clotho, Lachesis and Atropos are grouped with the κῆρες on the battle-field. For Quintus Smyrnaeus at a much later date the assimilation was complete. The κῆρες spin destiny[6] and ὑπὲρ κῆρας is used[7] as equivalent to the Homeric ὑπὲρ αἶσαν, ὑπὲρ μόρον. Both μοῖρα and κήρ alike, as we have seen, were conceived as dragging or leading a man to his fate, above all to death. In some passages[8] μοῖρα, where it is commonly interpreted as the personified power, is said to bind (πεδάαν) a man. ἄγειν suggests that carrying or dragging off by a cord which was characteristic of the German death-goddesses analogous to the κῆρες, of the Iranian death-demon, and of the Hindoo death-god Yama. In the Hindoo conception fate binds a man and drags him with the cord to this fortune or that; and there, as also in the Babylonian and other beliefs, the manner in which spirits of disease, etc. attack a man is by binding the disease or other evil upon him as a bond which they bring. Examination of the other extant Greek evidence[9] shows that

[1] Il. XIII, 602. Cf. V, 613 f.
[2] E.g. Il. II, 834, XI, 332.
[3] Theog. 217–19. Unaware of this interchangeability, many editors have thought that Hesiod could not have written the passage—they do not suggest why anyone else should—and want to cut out the whole or lines 218–19, which also occur as 904 f. Wieseler emended to καὶ μογερὰς δὴ κῆρας. For equivalence of Μοῖραι, Κῆρες, and Ἐρινύες cf. Aesch. P. V. 516 ff.; Septem, 975 ff., 1055 f., etc.
[4] Theog. 211.
[5] 258 ff.
[6] See e.g. XIII, 234.
[7] E.g. VII, 289, XI, 296.
[8] E.g. Il. IV, 517, XXII, 5. Cf., however, pp. 327, 379.
[9] It may be found s.v. 'Ker' in Roscher's Lexicon (Crusius) or in Pauly-Wissowa-Kroll, Realencykl. Supplementb. IV, 883 ff., 1924. Malten there

κῆρες were such spirits or demons, severally representing and inflicting different fortunes, old age, sickness, etc., of which death is only one. They too bind their victims with the evil in question as a bond,[1] e.g. in a poem attributed to Linus:[2]

κῆρας ἀπωσάμενος πολυπήμονας αἵ τε βεβήλων
ὄχλον ἀϊστῶσαι ἄταις περὶ πάντα πεδῶσι.

This carrying, bringing of bonds, will explain the thought of Mimnermus: 'For a little while man enjoys his youth',

κῆρες δὲ παρεστήκασι μέλαιναι,
ἡ μὲν ἔχουσα τέλος γήραος ἀργαλέου
ἡ δ' ἑτέρη θανάτοιο.[3]

Lycophron speaks of a κηρουλκὸς πάγη, noose or springe, in describing the action of Aphrodite:

ἥ μιν παλεύσει δυσλύτοις οἴστρου βρόχοις,
ἔρωτας οὐκ ἔρωτας, ἀλλ' Ἐρινύων
πικρὰν ἀποψήλασα κηρουλκὸν πάγην.[4]

The passage of Mimnermus suggests and the mass of other evidence[5] confirms that the κῆρες severally represented different

points out that the Attic θύραζε κῆρες at the Anthesteria is satisfied on this interpretation, as a more or less abusive address to departed spirits whom one was thus driving away, as elsewhere with blows. But see p. 406 below.
[1] The fullest description of a κήρ in Homer is in the battle on Achilles' shield:

ἐν δ' Ἔρις ἐν δὲ Κυδοιμὸς ὁμίλεον, ἐν δ' ὀλοὴ κήρ,
ἄλλον ζωὸν ἔχουσα νεούτατον, ἄλλον ἄουτον,
ἄλλον τεθνηῶτα κατὰ μόθον ἕλκε ποδοῖιν·
εἷμα δ' ἔχ' ἀμφ' ὤμοισι δαφοινεὸν αἵματι φωτῶν.
Il. XVIII, 535 ff.

The κήρ appears to have been conceived as possessing only one pair of hands and, if anything, considerably less than human stature, so that we are almost driven to think of it here as 'holding' its many victims as one 'holds' (ἔχει) horses or dogs by halters or leashes or as dragging by the πέδαι around the feet. The doomed but as yet unscathed (ἄουτος) was already in her power. On such, as we saw, it was said ἤδη ὀλέθρου πείρατ' ἐφῆπται. In the Teutonic belief 'the dead march like captives in Death's bonds' (Grimm, *op. cit.* cap. XXVII, p. 705). At death the κήρ ἀμφέχανε the victim (*Il.* XXIII, 78 f.). The writer of the 'Shield of Herakles' (248 ff.), seeking horrid effect, makes them blood-sucking demons fastening on a body and tossing it behind them when drained dry.
[2] Stob. *Flor.* v, 22 M. Quintus Smyrnaeus, whose assimilation of κήρ to μοῖρα we have seen, tells how Laokoon remains to face the serpents: πέδησε γὰρ οὐλομένη κὴρ/καὶ θεός, XII, 473 f.
[3] Fr. 2, 5 ff. For τέλος see below, pp. 426 ff.   [4] *Alex.* 405 ff.
[5] See e.g. for κῆρες as different forms of death *Od.* XI, 171 ff., 398 ff.

kinds of fortune, just as did the bonds which they appear to have carried and as did the bonds which the gods imposed.

This will help us to understand a great variety of vase-paintings[1] in which a figure, usually winged, is seen bringing a band closed as a wreath or open, a ταινία extended, to some-one or hovering with it above him or her. We can now inter-pret that it is a κήρ or δαίμων come to bestow this or that fortune, this or that bond.[2] Homer conceived beauty, χάρις, as a wreath or crown about things even when the things

Fig. 1. Ariadne being deserted by Theseus

were words.[3] The dynamic agencies of χάρις were themselves Χάριτες. Art represented them as goddesses each holding out a wreath or crown.[4] Meleager thus conceived three χάριτες, gifts of the three Χάριτες:

> αἱ τρισσαὶ Χάριτες τρισσὸν στεφάνωμα συνεῖραν
> Ζηνοφίλᾳ, τρισσᾶς σύμβολα καλλοσύνας·
> ἁ μὲν ἐπὶ χρωτὸς θεμένα πόθον, ἁ δ' ἐπὶ μορφᾶς
> ἵμερον, ἁ δὲ λόγοις τὸ γλυκύμυθον ἔπος.[5]

Tibullus represents Cornutus praying that his wife may have love for him (*amores*) and the prayer is answered: 'Do you see

---

[1] See e.g. Pfuhl, *Malerei u. Zeichnung d. Griechen*, figs. 194, 557, 562, 617, 620, 628, 744, also 143, 169, 569, or Miss Harrison, *op. cit.* figs. 40, 71, 78, 86, 168, 172. For such bands put upon men by men see pp. 372 ff. For further discussion see pp. 431 ff., 446 ff.   [2] Cf. pp. 375, 431.

[3] See *Od.* VIII, 175. Cf. 170 and pp. 461, n. 8; 464, n. 3.

[4] See e.g. the relief in Roscher's *Lex.* s.v. 880.

[5] *Anth. Pal.* v, 194. So, perhaps, Hesiod, *W.D.* 73f. and *cuiusvis leporis Liber diademam dedit* (Pompon. 163 Ribb.).

how Love comes on rustling wings bringing *flava* bonds to your wife?'

> *viden ut strepitantibus advolet alis*
> *flavaque coniugio vincula portet Amor?*[1]

Love bestows love upon her by binding her with it.[2] Thus too we can better understand the first of the *Anacreontea*, a dream of Anacreon, the lover (φίλευνος), led by Love ("Ερως) and wearing a wreath which the dreamer receives from him and binds about his brow and with it himself receives love (ἔρως), becomes a lover:

> τρέμοντα δ' αὐτὸν ἤδη
> "Ερως ἐχειραγώγει.
> ὁ δ' ἐξελὼν καρήνου
> ἐμοὶ στέφος δίδωσι·
> τὸ δ' ὦз' 'Ανακρέοντος,
> ἐγὼ δ' ὁ μωρὸς ἄρας
> ἐδησάμην μετώπῳ.
> καὶ δῆθεν ἄχρι καὶ νῦν
> ἔρωτος οὐ πέπαυμαι.

In Plato's myth of Er the virtual equivalence of the thread and its dynamic counterpart, the δαίμων or κήρ, is clearly shown; for after taking the βίων παραδείγματα from the *knees* of Lachesis for the souls to choose, the προφήτης speaks as if in choosing the βίοι they were choosing δαίμονες: δαίμονα αἱρήσεσθε. πρῶτος δ' ὁ λαχὼν πρῶτος αἱρείσθω βίον, ᾧ συνέσται ἐξ ἀνάγκης (617 D f.). He places the βίων παραδείγματα on the ground, whence each soul according to his turn picks up that which he chooses. In so doing, however, he is choosing a δαίμων (620 D): ἐπειδὴ δ' οὖν πάσας τὰς ψυχὰς τοὺς βίους ἡρῆσθαι, ὥσπερ ἔλαχον ἐν τάξει προσιέναι πρὸς τὴν Λάχεσιν, ἐκείνην δ' ἑκάστῳ ὃν εἵλετο δαίμονα, τοῦτον φύλακα συμπέμπειν τοῦ βίου καὶ ἀποπληρωτὴν τῶν αἱρεθέντων. The δαίμων is thus a dynamic counterpart or equivalent of the βίος. But under what form were conceived the βίοι themselves, strewn on the ground and also coming from Lachesis, from her *knees*?

---

[1] II, 2, 17 f. *flavus* was the colour of the *flammeum*, the colour of love (see pp. 151 ff., cf. 146 f.). *flavus* was used of a blush (Sen. *Hipp.* 652) as for Ovid the *rubor* of the bride's *multo splendida palla croco* is that of a blush (*Her.* xx (xxi), 162, 168). Bridal attire was dyed with *crocum rubentem* (*Georg.* iv, 182). 'The three divisions of the style, which are the only part in use, are of the colour of fire' (Martyn *ad loc.*).

[2] For love as a bond see pp. 368, 373. Cf. sleep on p. 422.

Plato's next words show that it was as unspun wool, the μοῖρα to be spun by Clotho: ὅν πρῶτον μὲν ἄγειν αὐτὴν πρὸς τὴν Κλωθὼ ὑπὸ τὴν ἐκείνης χεῖρά τε καὶ ἐπιστροφὴν τῆς τοῦ ἀτράκτου δίνης κυροῦντα ἣν λαχὼν εἵλετο μοῖραν.

The equation of the δαίμων (=κήρ)[1] to the μοῖρα, the allotted thread, will also explain the alternative text for Homer's account of the jars of Zeus.[2] Plato in the second book of the *Republic*[3] quotes them not as jars, δώρων οἷα δίδωσι κακῶν, ἕτερος δὲ ἐάων but as κηρῶν ἔμπλειοι, ὁ μὲν ἐσθλῶν αὐτὰρ ὁ δειλῶν. Instead of 'gifts' (δῶρα), which the context shows[4] were conceived as 'spun' and 'laid upon' a man, we have κῆρες. It will also throw light upon Hesiod's[5] story of Prometheus and Πανδώρα with her garlands and necklaces and the jar containing what, including Ἐλπίς, appear to be κῆρες; and with it, I suggest, will throw light upon a passage of Pindar concerning the alternations of fortune: 'καὶ θνατὸν οὕτως ἔθνος ἄγει μοῖρα. From Zeus clear sign cometh not for men; yet we set our feet upon paths of prowess, bent upon many deeds; δέδεται γὰρ ἀναιδεῖ ἐλπίδι γυῖα· προμαθείας δ' ἀπόκεινται ῥοαί'.[6] In Hesiod's story Ἐλπίς is singled out as blind aspiration contrasted with the clear foresight represented by Prometheus. So ἄτη was binder or bond.[7] We can now under-

[1] In Homer δαίμων, though of much wider range, sometimes appears to mean κήρ, e.g. πάρος τοι δαίμονα δώσω (*Il.* VIII, 166; cf. XVIII, 115), and we can scarcely doubt the existence of some relationship between the κήρ which in Homer is assigned to a man at birth (apparently as the spirit which is leading him to death and will at death seize him) and the δαίμων which in later popular belief was the personification of its destiny allotted to each soul at birth (see e.g. Plato, *Rep.* 617 D ff.; *Phaedo*, 107 D f.). In a famous passage (Fr. 550 Kock) Menander urges that this is beneficent:

ἅπαντι δαίμων ἀνδρὶ συμπαρίσταται
εὐθὺς γενομένῳ, μυσταγωγὸς τοῦ βίου
ἀγαθός· κακὸν γὰρ δαίμον' οὐ νομιστέον
εἶναι βίον βλάπτοντα χρηστόν,

a protest against the popular blaming of a κακὸς δαίμων (e.g. αἰαῖ τῷ σκληρῷ μάλα δαίμονος ὅς με λελόγχει, Theocr. IV, 40). Cf. the compounds εὐδαίμων, κακοδαίμων, etc. and above pp. 185, 265.

[2] See pp. 395 f.　　　[3] 379 D.　　　[4] See p. 395.

[5] *Works and Days*, 47–105. The scholiast (94) identifies her jar with that whence portions of fate are allotted to men and compares Homer's jars.

[6] *Nem.* XI, 42 ff. ῥοαί might come to his mind as something better from a πίθος, perhaps with a trace of the ideas above (e.g. pp. 48, n. 2, 61 ff., 68, n. 7).　　　[7] See p. 327.

stand also Pindar's thought in ἀμφὶ δ' ἀνθρώπων φρασὶν ἀμπλακίαι ἀναρίθμητοι κρέμανται¹ and φθονεραὶ θνατῶν φρένας
ἀμφικρέμανται ἐλπίδες² (for the verb cf. p. 337) and why he
speaks of the 'Loosing God' (Dionysos) 'loosing the cord of the
μέριμναι hard to bear' (τὸ τῶν δυσφόρων σχοινίον μεριμνῶν).³

The belief traced in Homer that this or that fate, above all
death, is a bond fastened upon men, lies behind Pindar's
statements that Apollo delayed the capture of Troy by
'binding with bold death the son of Thetis' (παῖδα...Θέτιος
...θρασεῖ φόνῳ πεδάσαις),⁴ and that Oenomaos 'slew thirteen
men but was himself bound (i.e. subjected to the bond of
death) by the fourteenth' (πέφνε δὲ τρεῖς καὶ δέκ' ἄνδρας·
τετράτῳ δ' αὐτὸς πεδάθη).⁵ The variant just discussed in
which the δαίμων binds with fate appears in a (? tragic)
fragment: 'Ο δαίμων to whose lot I fell (ὅς μ' εἴληχας), how
evil you are, how you vex me ever, binding me with poverty
(τῇ πενίᾳ συνδέων)!'⁶ Pindar tells us that Zeus begot a child
for Lokros 'lest his αἰών should pull him down having fastened
upon him a fate of childlessness (μὴ καθέλοι μιν αἰὼν πότμον
ἐφάψαις ὀρφανὸν γενεᾶς)',⁷ where and elsewhere⁸ αἰών appears

¹ Ol. VII, 24 f. While vaguely the whole person or the body could be
referred to, the mind was identified particularly with the φρένες (see
pp. 23 ff.). We may compare these expressions with Homer's ὕπνος...λύων
μελεδήματα θυμοῦ (Il. XXIII, 62, etc.) and φρεσὶν εἱμένος ἀλκήν, etc., on p. 420.
² Isth. II, 43. See also Fr. 214 (Schr.) with pp. 407 f. below.
³ Fr. 248 (Schroeder). Cf. λῦσον ἐκ μεριμνᾶν, Sappho, I, 25 f., λυσιμέρι-
μνος, the 'Loosing God' on pp. 441, 452, solutis curis, Catull. XXXI, 7, Hor.
Epod. IX, 37 f., Od. I, 22, 11, etc. with curas laqueata circum tecta volantis (II, 16,
11 f.; cf. 21 ff.) where laqueata might carry an unrecognised suggestion or
reminder of laquei (cf. III, 24, 8). For φροντίδες, μελεδῶναι, etc., as little
winged creatures like κῆρες, see pp. 67, 85 ff.
⁴ Paean VI, 81 ff.   ⁵ Fr. 135 Schr. (Schol. ad Ol. I, 127).
    Quoted by Alciphr. 3, 49, 1 (Adesp. 17, Nauck).   ⁷ Ol. IX, 60 f.
    Cf. Soph. Trach. 34 f.; Phil. 1348 f., etc. In Isth. VIII, 14 f. Pindar says
'over men there hangs wileful αἰών making the path of life to wind (δόλιος
γὰρ αἰὼν ἐπ' ἀνδράσι κρέμαται/ἑλίσσων βίου πόρον)', which Bury interprets: 'The figure is a wind hanging about the course of mariners but
ἐπικρέμαται is chosen with reference to the preceding metaphor of the
Tantalean stone'. But such a mixture is not happy and I would compare
rather the winged δαίμων hovering with a ταινία above a man in vase-
paintings (see pp. 402 f., 431 f.) and the αἰών which guides a man straight
along the path of his fathers (πατρίαν...καθ' ὁδόν...εὐθυπομπὸς αἰών,
Nem. II, 6 ff.). In ἐλᾷ δὲ καὶ τέσσαρας ἀρετὰς ὁ θνατὸς αἰών (Nem. III, 74 f.)
and αἰὼν δ' ἔφεπε μόρσιμος (Ol. II, 10) the image appears to be that of

to mean something like δαίμων. If in this passage πότμος is the bond or thing fastened on, the interchange with a corresponding living agency, a dynamic counterpart, may again be seen in passages[1] where πότμος expresses the latter. Man is linked with it, must go with it. Pindar, speaking of the

a charioteer (cf. *Il.* XVI, 724, 732 and the description of αἰών preserved in Nonnus, probably from earlier sources, as ἡνίοχος βιότοιο, *Dionys.* XXIV, 267) which fits the frequent variation of our image about to be discussed (pp. 407 f.), the conception of fate as a yokestrap or yoke, or that to which one is yoked. From this conception of αἰών possibly derives Plato's conception of the highest part of the ψυχή controlling the spirited and appetitive elements as a winged charioteer driving horses (*Phaedr.* 246 ff.; cf. Parmenides, B 1, Diels, with Sext. VII, 112 f., also Anacr. 4). In the *Timaeus* that highest part of the ψυχή (as we have seen, pp. 95 ff., originally the ψυχή itself), which 'dwells' in the head, is said to be given to each as his δαίμων (αὐτὸ δαίμονα θεὸς ἑκάστῳ δέδωκεν, τοῦτο ὃ δή φαμεν οἰκεῖν μὲν ἡμῶν ἐπ' ἄκρῳ τῷ σώματι, 90 A; cf. ψυχὴ οἰκητήριον δαίμονος, Democr. B 171, Diels, and pp. 118 f., 185, n. 1). How did αἰών come to bear the meaning above? From the sense of life-substance, life, it might come to mean lifetime (see pp. 200 ff.) and so time or portion, fate (cf. pp. 411 ff.). But for Pindar αἰῶνος εἴδωλον, distinct from waking consciousness, was the divine element in man and foreshadowed to him the future (pp. 102 ff.). This would naturally be conceived as δαίμων, a controlling spirit like the *genius* (pp. 150, n. 1; 159 ff., 185). Pindar by that description is referring apparently to the old conception of ψυχή, which, like the *genius*, was associated with the cerebro-spinal marrow or αἰών. There is a good deal of evidence which suggests that among the earliest Greeks the ψυχή was conceived as δαίμων (e.g. pp. 184 f.). This would make easier the claims of Orphics and others that the ψυχή was divine, also the identification of ψυχή and δαίμων in the *Timaeus*. Against the original conception of the ψυχή as δαίμων are the likeness of the later δαίμων to the Homeric κήρ allotted to each at birth and the difference between ψυχή and κήρ in Homer (pp. 398, 408). If that difference was not original, or if a man's ψυχή was a κήρ but there were other κῆρες affecting him (cf. *cerritus*, *larvatus*, note 5 on p. 148), we could thus explain ἀκήριος (*Il.* XI, 392) having the sense of 'lifeless' (= ἄψυχος), Aeschylus' substitution of ψυχαί for κῆρες (see pp. 397 f.), and the Attic reference to ancestral ψυχαί after the Anthesteria as κῆρες (see Photius and Suidas, s.v. θύραзε). Then, as φήρ to *fërus*, κήρ might be related to *cerus*= *genius* (see pp. 125 ff.), *cerebrum*, etc., having been originally used as a general term for generative or causative spirits (cf. pp. 97, 138 ff., 188 ff.), and so agencies of fate, and having already acquired among the Homeric Greeks evil associations as had μοῖρα, μόρος, etc. See also Hesiod (*W. and D.* 823) on p. 413. For the relation to ψυχή (= σκιά, p. 95) cf. ἡ σκιὴ παρέστηκεν (Herodas, I, 16, said by one who is old) with pp. 95, 399 (*fin.*), 415.

[1] E.g. Pind. *Nem.* IV, 42, V, 40, VI, 6 f.; *Isth.* I, 39 f. The conception of the winged dynamic spirit of fate (cf. πέτομαι, πότμος) compelling man like

differences among men, says: 'Different things shut off different men, each yoked with (? by) his fate' (εἴργει δὲ πότμῳ ʒυγένθ' [Schmid: ʒυγόν θ' MSS.] ἕτερον ἕτερα).[1] Euripides makes Helen say: 'With what πότμος was I yoked?' (τίνι πότμῳ συνεʒύγην;),[2] and Andromache: 'my hard δαίμων with which I was yoked' (στερρόν τε τὸν ἐμὸν δαίμον' ᾧ συνεʒύγην),[3] while Dionysius of Halicarnassus[4] even speaks of κῆρες fastened to a man by the δαίμων (ἑτέρας οὐκ εὐτυχεῖς κῆράς τε καὶ ἄτας προσῆψε). We saw (p. 364) that, like the Greeks, the ancient Babylonians conceived of sickness, among

a charioteer and turning the scale (cf. the κήρ in the scale of Zeus) appears in the *Nemesis* of Mesomedes:

Νέμεσι, πτερόεσσα βίου ῥοπά...
ἃ κοῦφα φρυάγματα θνατῶν
ἐπέχεις ἀδάμαντι χαλινῷ....

[1] *Nem.* VII, 6. The unity of thought behind the human custom of binding the head, and the belief that fate was imposed upon man in the form of a bond or στέμμα constraining to this or that (pp. 331 f., 336, 375 f., 401 ff.), will explain Pindar's statement (*Ol.* III, 6 ff.) 'the wreaths bound about my hair exact from me this god-wrought obligation that I mingle the varied utterance of the lyre, etc.' (χαίταισι μὲν ʒευχθέντες ἔπι στέφανοι πράσσοντί με τοῦτο θεόδματον χρέος/φόρμιγγα...συμμῖξαι). Some have taken the wreaths as those about the head of the victor or the horses (see scholia), but the poet elsewhere speaks of himself as singing wreathed (*Isth.* VII (VI), 39) and as taking part in a κῶμος (*Nem.* IX, 1; *Isth.* IV, 72, etc.); and ʒευχθέντες would scarcely be used except to suggest compulsion upon the wearer. In being crowned as a singer or member of the κῶμος he is bound with a particular fate, obligation as well as power (pp. 444 ff.).

[2] *Hel.* 255. In the Gnostic *Pistis Sophia* his μοῖρα leads a man to death 'by the bonds with which they have been bound by Εἱμαρμένη' (284. Cf. 286f.). We have traced the original form of the 'causal *nexus*'.

[3] *Androm.* 98. What holds the creature yoked is the noose or loop, ʒεύγλη. Thus a fragment attributed to Pindar (132, Schroeder) says that the ψυχαί of the impious flit about 'in deadly pains beneath inescapable yokenooses of evils' (πωτῶνται ἐν ἄλγεσι φονίοις/ὑπὸ ʒεύγλαις ἀφύκτοις κακῶν). Aeschylus says of Agamemnon required to sacrifice his daughter 'when he had got into the yokestrap of necessity' (or 'fate', ἐπεὶ δ' ἀνάγκας ἔδυ λέπαδνον, *Ag.* 218). His Prometheus says: 'Giving boons to men, I have, alas, been yoked in these necessities' (ἀνάγκαις ταῖσδ' ἐνέʒευγμαι, *P.V.* 107 f.), and his Io to Zeus: 'Why, O son of Kronos, didst thou yoke me in these woes?' (ταῖσδ' ἐνέʒευξας...ἐν πημοσύναις; *P.V.* 577 f.); cf. *Choeph.* 794 ff.; Moschion, 2, 2 f. (Nauck), etc.; also Euripides, *Hipp.* 237f., Virgil, *Aen.* VI, 78ff., Horace, *Odes*, IV, 1, 4–7, etc.

[4] *Antiq. Rom.* VIII, 61, 1. For μελανόʒυγ' ἄταν (Aesch. *Suppl.* 530) cf. p. 396, n. 2.

other evils, as a bond attached by a demon, i.e. κήρ. We may now compare the prayer to Tammuz for release from sickness: 'The evil spy, the adversary who with me is bound and stands against me for evil, yea the evil spy, the adversary who with me is bound...from me may he be detached. Grant me the breath of life and from my body remove him...'.[1]

The natural interchange[2] of the bond of fate and the dynamic agency by which or with which a man is bound, the κήρ or δαίμων, is thus clear. It is also clear that the κῆρες put into the scales of Zeus were such dynamic agencies of fate and not the ψυχαί of the combatants as has been maintained.[3] That the thread of fate or its dynamic agency should be weighed is what we might expect from other expressions. Alike

[1] See S. Langdon, *Tammuz and Ishtar*, p. 35.

[2] The thread was itself personified and spoken of as spinning: Μοίρης μοι φθονερὸς τοῦτ' ἐπέκλωσε μίτος (*Epigr. Gr.* 144, Kaibel; cf. 127, etc., and the Κλῶθες).

[3] Lest any should imagine that in these passages of the *Iliad* there is any support for this view we should note that VIII, 73–4 have been rejected by Aristarchus and modern commentators on account of the fact that, while they add nothing to line 72, the plural κῆρες is also inconsistent with line 70 and that the dual ἐξέσθην implies two κῆρες for the Achaeans; for which no reason can be conceived unless it be a misunderstanding of line 70. In any case this last line, indisputably genuine, makes it clear that there was not a κήρ for each warrior (cf. *Il.* IX, 411) and that therefore the κήρ could not be identical with the ψυχή. In XXII, 213, ᾤχετο δ' εἰς ᾿Αΐδαο has been interpreted of the αἴσιμον ἦμαρ in the sense of *vergebat deorsum* (Van Leeuwen), but this is already given in 212. Rather, I would suggest that the κήρ, to which Homer thus refers, was thought actually to go to the house of Hades (cf. τὸν κῆρες ἔβαν θανάτοιο φέρουσαι/ εἰς ᾿Αΐδαο δόμους, *Od.* XIV, 207 f.), possibly with the ψυχή, the expression being proleptic (cf. *Il.* IX, 413, XIII, 772, etc., and for the time relation more generally pp. 335, 356 above). Most commentators (e.g. Leaf and Monro) think that it refers to Hector proleptically. But the αἴσιμον ἦμαρ in the scale is clearly not Hector's ψυχή nor Hector. Though speculating upon other points, the scholiasts (*Il.* XXII, 209, VIII, 70) are rather emphatic that Homer κήρας τὰς μοίρας λέγει, οὐ τὰς ψυχὰς ὡς ἐξεδέξατο φαύλως Αἰσχύλος; and modern commentators, where they do not try to interpret it as a weighing of ψυχαί, speak vaguely of the weighing of 'lots' (e.g. *sortem*, Van Leeuwen; *Los*, Ameis-Hentze). In his imitation of this passage Virgil (*Aen.* XII, 725) substitutes *fatum* for κήρ as if he interpreted it as μοῖρα. αἴσιμον ἦμαρ he renders by *letum*. αἴσιμον ἦμαρ is discussed below (pp. 413ff.). If the bond was fast about the victim (πάλαι πεπρωμένον αἴση, see pp. 382ff.), it would be easier to speak of the κήρ as put in the scales.

κῆρες[1] and the personified Κλῶθες[2] are spoken of by Homer as βαρεῖαι. βαρυδαίμων, βαρυδαιμονέω and βαρυδαιμονία show that, in the time of Alcaeus and later, to be unfortunate was to have a 'heavy δαίμων'. Of the unpersonified bond of fate Agamemnon twice[3] complains that it is heavy:

Ζεύς με μέγα Κρονίδης ἄτῃ ἐνέδησε βαρείῃ,

and Odysseus laboured under μέγα πεῖραρ ὀϊзύος.[4] We perhaps to-day should not naturally think of wool as a thing to be weighed, indeed the one thing most commonly weighed. But in Homer's only other mention of τάλαντα in the sense of scales and his only instance of their use among men, that use is the weighing of wool spun or to be spun:

ἀλλ' ἔχον ὥς τε τάλαντα γυνή χερνῆτις ἀληθής,
ἥ τε σταθμὸν ἔχουσα καὶ εἴριον ἀμφὶς ἀνέλκει
ἰσάзουσ' ἵνα παισὶν ἀεικέα μισθὸν ἄρηται,[5]

and this appears to have been the commonest and characteristic use of scales in ancient Rome also, a use daily familiar in every household. *Pensum* without qualification, 'the thing weighed', meant the wool weighed out by the mistress or housekeeper (Gk. ταμίη) to be spun in a day, and doubtless when spun 'checked' by weighing again. Zeus is the ταμίης πολέμοιο, a title used with explicit[6] reference to his τάλαντα, and he himself spins[7] just as does the γυνή χερνῆτις, spins πόλεμος, ὄλεθρος, etc. His office of ταμίης is elaborated in the description of the two πίθοι, whence, as we saw,[8] he apportions fortunes good and evil,[9] periods of prosperity or adversity, to

---

[1] *Il.* XXI, 548.   [2] *Od.* VII, 197.   [3] *Il.* II, 111, IX, 18.
[4] *Od.* V, 289. See pp. 323, 337, n. 6.   [5] *Il.* XII, 433 ff.
[6] See e.g. *Il.* XIX, 223 f., quoted on p. 397.
[7] E.g. *Od.* IV, 208.   [8] See pp. 395 f. and 404.
[9] Not merely war and death but the blessings of peace also are thus apportioned. In the *Iliad* the τάλαντα appear merely for war's decisions since the poem is concerned with nothing but war. Of other issues Theognis speaks:

Ζεύς γάρ τοι τὸ τάλαντον ἐπιρρέπει ἄλλοτε ἄλλως,
    ἄλλοτε μὲν πλουτεῖν, ἄλλοτε μηδὲν ἔχειν.   157 f.

On this side the concept of 'heaviness' is confusing. In the Homeric conception the bond that was felt as heavy was evil and evil fate was felt as a burden.

a man under the form of threads, or, alternatively, as quoted by Plato, κῆρες. In the Roman conception or imitation, *pensum* is used explicitly of the thread of fate, e.g.:

> *durae peragunt pensa sorores*
> *nec sua retro fila revolvunt.*[1]

Sometimes instead of Zeus, as we have seen, Moira, Aisa or the Κλῶθες are spoken of as spinning; and in later art[2] the τάλαντα and a horn wherefrom to weigh, instead of a πίθος or πίθοι, appear as the attributes of Lachesis (cf. Τύχη[3]), as the spindle and distaff of Klotho. Of the τάλαντα the obvious origin that yet does not seem to have been suggested is in the action of the χερνῆτις, the weighing of the portion of wool to be spun, the *pensum*. In Homer it is the gods, and above all Zeus, who spin and allot fate. The evidence as to the nature of the κήρ and its replacing (or renaming) in the scale on each occasion by αἴσιμον ἦμαρ suggest that the original function of Zeus' τάλαντα was the weighing of human fortunes, portions assigned from the πίθοι under the forms shown, in which case all the various images of fate in the poems would appear to be not alternative and independent myths, still less alternative fantasies[4] of the poet, but coherent parts of a single all-embracing image. Not only the unspun wool but the spun also[5] or its dynamic agency, κήρ, could be weighed in the scales, that of one man, his fate, or of one host against that of another. Thus Zeus could demonstrate to others or remind himself to which he had assigned the heavier portion.

---

[1] Seneca, *Herc. Fur.* 181 f. Cf. Statius, *Silv.* III, 3, 172, etc.

[2] See e.g. the sarcophagus illustrated in Roscher, *op. cit.* II, col. 3099, where the horn seems to contain wool; but this may be due to faulty reproduction.

[3] Pindar seems to have identified her with Lachesis (Fr. 41, Schroeder = Paus. VII, 26, 8). An anonymous lyric fragment addressing Τύχα speaks of τὸ τεᾷ πλάστιγγι δοθέν (Adesp. 139, 6, Bgk.), just as Homer speaks of what Zeus 'gives' to men from his πίθοι (see pp. 395 f.). Dio Chrysostom says that the horn of Τύχη (from which she distributed) was 'full of times' (πλήρης καὶ βρύον ταῖς ὥραις, *Or.* 63, p. 205, Dind.). It is time that is fate, Ἕκτορος αἴσιμον ἦμαρ, etc., that Zeus weighs (see pp. 413 ff. below).

[4] For this view see e.g. Van Leeuwen on *Il.* VIII, 69.

[5] Cf. the checking, by weighing, of the wool spun and ready for use when it was returned by the slave or hired spinner.

CHAPTER IX

Time—Ἦμαρ

In modern European thought there has prevailed the conception of time as a homogeneous medium analogous to empty space. Bergson and Einstein have from different angles helped to dethrone that concept. For the Homeric Greeks time was not homogeneous; it had quality; it differed at large for the whole world within the horizon. There are all the changes of the day from dawn to the end of night, all the changes of the year from the beginning of spring on through summer, autumn, and winter. For the Romans time was weather, weather time, *tempus, tempestas*; and the thought survives in the modern French idiom: *il fait mauvais temps*, etc. Whatever came man could neither bring nor avert. Neither chaotic nor mechanically regular, it appeared to be the work of other minds, and above all of the power in the sky, Zeus. The day changes in intelligible order but with ceaseless variation of detail, so too the year. And it is not merely the sky above—blue aether, sun, moon, and stars—which changes, but the wind blowing from this quarter or that, soft or strong or not at all, maybe clouds, thunder and lightning, rain, hail or snow, the earth becoming light or dark, moist or dry, hot or cold, the waters changing, too, and all things that live—plants springing from the seed and growing to flower and seed again, animals mating and giving birth and growing up and growing old, all in due season, becoming active with the spring or hibernating, opening or wakening with the dawn, falling asleep or closing with the night. The early Greeks felt that different portions of time had different quality and brought this change or that, favoured this activity or that, ὧραι. With a good deal of incidental moralising the *Works and Days* of Hesiod is a study in this conception of time, first of the year, the changes of the sun and

the stars and therewith of man's environment on the earth and
his *works* accordingly, e.g.:

> ἦμος δὴ λήγει μένος ὀξέος ἠελίοιο
> καύματος ἰδαλίμου, μετοπωρινὸν ὀμβρήσαντος
> Ζηνὸς ἐρισθενέος, μετὰ δὲ τρέπεται βρότεος χρὼς
> πολλὸν ἐλαφρότερος· δὴ γὰρ τότε Σείριος ἀστὴρ
> βαιὸν ὑπὲρ κεφαλῆς κηριτρεφέων ἀνθρώπων
> ἔρχεται ἠμάτιος, πλεῖον δέ τε νυκτὸς ἐπαυρεῖ·
> τῆμος ἀδηκτοτάτη πέλεται τμηθεῖσα σιδήρῳ
> ὕλη, φύλλα δ' ἔραζε χέει, πτόρθοιό τε λήγει·
> τῆμος ἄρ' ὑλοτομεῖν μεμνημένος· ὥρια ἔργα,[1]

and then of the month, the changes of the moon, the *days*:

> ἤματα δ' ἐκ Διόθεν πεφυλαγμένος εὖ κατὰ μοῖραν
> πεφραδέμεν δμώεσσι· τριηκάδα μηνὸς ἀρίστην
> ἔργα τ' ἐποπτεύειν ἠδ' ἁρμαλίην δατέασθαι,
> εὖτ' ἂν ἀληθείην λαοὶ κρίνοντες ἄγωσιν.[2]

Here too the assumption that the different portions of time
have different quality is so strong that the various days of the
month, first, second, third, etc., are boldly characterised as
good or bad for this or that, although we can see no indication
in external nature of that quality. Occasionally some divine
event or the activity of some animal on that day is given as a
sign of the quality of the day, of the work that belongs to it.
Thus the poem continues:

> αἵδε γὰρ ἡμέραι εἰσὶ Διὸς πάρα μητιόεντος·
> πρῶτον ἔνη τετράς τε καὶ ἑβδόμη ἱερὸν ἦμαρ·
> τῇ γὰρ Ἀπόλλωνα χρυσάορα γείνατο Λητώ·
> ὀγδοάτη τ' ἐνάτη τε· δύω γε μὲν ἤματα μηνὸς
> ἔξοχ' ἀεξομένοιο βροτήσια ἔργα πένεσθαι·
> ἑνδεκάτη τε δυωδεκάτη τ'· ἄμφω γε μὲν ἐσθλαί,
> ἠμὲν ὄϊς πείκειν, ἠδ' εὔφρονα καρπὸν ἀμᾶσθαι·
> ἡ δὲ δυωδεκάτη τῆς ἑνδεκάτης μέγ' ἀμείνων.
> τῇ γάρ τοι νεῖ νήματ' ἀερσιπότητος ἀράχνης
> ἤματος ἐκ πλείου, ὅτε τ' ἴδρις σωρὸν ἀμᾶται.
> τῇ δ' ἱστὸν στήσαιτο γυνή, προβάλοιτό τε ἔργον.[3]

The day has a certain quality, gives something, and he who
is wise cooperates by acting so as to receive the good and avoid
the evil. Different days bring different gifts available for

[1] 414 ff.   [2] 765 ff.   [3] 769 ff.

different kinds of people, animals, or plants. So two lines later:

ἕκτη δ' ἡ μέσση μάλ' ἀσύμφορός ἐστι φυτοῖσιν,
ἀνδρογόνος δ' ἀγαθή· κούρῃ δ' οὐ σύμφορός ἐστιν
οὔτε γενέσθαι πρῶτ' οὔτ' ἄρ γάμου ἀντιβολῆσαι.
οὐδὲ μὲν ἡ πρώτη ἕκτη κούρῃσι γενέσθαι
ἄρμενος ἀλλ' ἐρίφους τάμνειν καὶ πώεα μήλων
σηκόν τ' ἀμφιβαλεῖν ποιμνήϊον ἤπιον ἦμαρ·
ἐσθλὴ δ' ἀνδρογόνος· φιλέει δέ τε κέρτομα βάζειν
ψεύδεά θ' αἱμυλίους τε λόγους κρυφίους τ' ὀαρισμούς.[1]

Thus the fortunes or activities of human beings on a day were attributed to that day. It was spoken of as if it were alive, a personal spirit, δαίμων (cf. ⁵Ὧραι, etc.). After specifying certain good days of the month the *Works and Days* at its close says:

αἵδε μὲν ἡμέραι εἰσὶν ἐπιχθονίοις μέγ' ὄνειαρ,
αἱ δ' ἄλλαι μετάδουποι, ἀκήριοι, οὔ τι φέρουσαι.
ἄλλος δ' ἀλλοίην αἰνεῖ, παῦροι δέ τ' ἴσασιν.
ἄλλοτε μητρυιὴ πέλει ἡμέρη, ἄλλοτε μήτηρ.[2]

That the other days are spoken of as ἀκήριοι, 'without κήρ', is important. It throws light upon and receives light from Homer's equation[3] of κήρ and ἦμαρ in *Il.* xxii, 209 ff. and viii, 69 ff. It implies that to the particular portion of time there corresponded a κήρ and suggests that, though a κήρ in Homer usually represented an evil fate, it could also represent this or that good fortune.

In *Il.* xxii, 209 ff. the ἦμαρ is not the day of the month nor is it shared by others, it is the time, the destiny experienced by an individual, Hector; and it is time of a specified kind, 'fatal', 'of fate': Ἕκτορος αἴσιμον ἦμαρ equated to κῆρ τανη-λεγέος θανάτοιο...Ἕκτορος; while in *Il.* viii, 69 ff. a κήρ affects the Trojans in common and another κήρ the Achaeans in common; the two κῆρες are weighed against each other, ῥέπε δ' αἴσιμον ἦμαρ Ἀχαιῶν. Hesiod defines the qualities of recurring seasons and days for whole classes of beings. Homer is concerned with individual men and individual times, recognising that time differs for different persons or collections of persons, even though they may be near together in space, e.g. victor and vanquished; for each it is coloured with this or

[1] 782 ff.   [2] 822 ff.   [3] See pp. 397 ff.

that, is experienced as this or that fate.[1] The particular phase
of fortune had duration, was time experienced. The most
natural unit is the day. Homer identifies the 'day' with the
fate experienced, speaks of the fate as the ἦμαρ. αἴσιμον ἦμαρ
(cf. μόρσιμον ἦμαρ, ὀλέθριον ἦμαρ) means not the date, but
the fate of death, visualised, conceived as concrete, put in a
balance and weighed. In such phrases ἦμαρ is the fate
experienced by the individual, not the daylight universally
shared, and it does not last just a day but is a phase of fortune
of greater or less duration. To the Phaeacians entertaining him
Odysseus says: 'Now first I will tell you my name that you
also may know it and I, when I have escaped from beneath
the νηλεὲς ἦμαρ, may be your guest-friend, though dwelling
in a far country'.[2] The νηλεὲς ἦμαρ is the evil fate that long
has been and still is upon him, fate conceived as a bond[3] with
a dynamic agency, κήρ.[4] Hector says to Patroklos: 'You said
you would destroy our city and from the women of Troy take
the day of freedom (i.e. "their freedom", the fate which has
hitherto been theirs, ἐλεύθερον ἦμαρ ἀπούρας) and bring them
in ships to your dear fatherland—Fool! In front of them were
the swift horses of Hector straining to battle; and with my
spear, I, Hector, am conspicuous among the war-loving
Trojans, I who ward off from them the day of compulsion'[5]
(i.e. of slavery, ἦμαρ ἀναγκαῖον). Elsewhere a husband is said
explicitly to 'ward off the day of slavery' (ἀμύνειν δούλιον
ἦμαρ),[6] i.e. slavery itself, that fate. Similarly with other phases
of fortune. ἦμαρ defined by an adjective is the particular
fate of the individual during a particular time. It is virtually
equivalent to αἶσα, the particular 'portion', lot, fate. Just as
the verbs of 'spinning' or 'binding' fate (ἐπεκλώσαντο,
ἐπέδησε, etc.) are followed by the infinitive expressing the fate
in question,[7] or as αἶσα or μοῖρα is defined by an infinitive
(μοι αἶσα τεθνάμεναι, οὐ γάρ πώ τοι μοῖρα θανεῖν, etc.), we find

---

[1] How passive the individual felt himself to time and his particular fate
may be seen e.g. in Penelope's words to the disguised Odysseus, *Od.* xix,
510–17, 589–93.   [2] *Od.* ix, 16 ff.
[3] See *Od.* v, 288f. on pp. 323f. So perhaps also the day coming suddenly
upon one as a snare (Luke xxi, 34). Cf. pp. 321f. (Job), 362, etc.
[4] See pp. 397 ff.   [5] *Il.* xvi, 830 ff.   [6] *Il.* vi, 463.   [7] See p. 334.

νῦν δὴ εἴδεται ἦμαρ ὑπὸ Τρώεσσι δαμῆναι[1] and νῦν ἡμῖν πάντων Ζεὺς ἄξιον ἦμαρ ἔδωκε/νῆας ἐλεῖν.[2] Zeus is the dispenser of time, of fate to each and all.[3] Odysseus reflects how the temper of a man changes with his fortune: 'The mind of men upon earth is such as the day (ἦμαρ) which the father of gods and men bringeth upon them'—not weather, but fate—

τοῖος γὰρ νόος ἐστὶν ἐπιχθονίων ἀνθρώπων
οἷον ἐπ' ἦμαρ ἄγῃσι πατὴρ ἀνδρῶν τε θεῶν τε,[4]

with which we may relate Eumaios' perception of the depraving effect of slavery: 'Far-sounding Zeus takes away half a man's virtue when the day of slavery seizes him':

ἥμισυ γάρ τ' ἀρετῆς ἀποαίνυται εὐρύοπα Ζεὺς
ἀνέρος, εὖτ' ἄν μιν κατὰ δούλιον ἦμαρ ἕλῃσιν.[5]

Here the ἦμαρ is spoken of as active, an agent (cf. μοῖρ' ὀλοὴ καθέλῃσι τανηλεγέος θανάτοιο, etc.[6]). Elsewhere the μόρσιμον ἦμαρ is said to 'come upon' (ἐπελθεῖν)[7] a man, and of Hector, who was to die on the morrow, it is said that 'already Pallas Athene was rousing against him a day of fate (οἱ ἐπώρνυε μόρσιμον ἦμαρ[8]) beneath the might of Peleus' son'. Odysseus declares that the suitors will not heed good advice: 'For indeed their day of fate stands beside them' (δὴ γὰρ παρίσταται αἴσιμον ἦμαρ),[9] as elsewhere[10] the κήρ or μοῖρα is said to 'stand beside' a man. So too, as the κήρ or μοῖρα is said to 'carry' or 'take' a man,[11] φέρεσκέ μιν αἴσιμον ἦμαρ.[12] The use of these verbs implies the conception of the ἦμαρ as a living agent, which will also explain the equation of κήρ and ἦμαρ in the scales. Time will be discussed further below.[13]

[1] Il. XIII, 98.   [2] Il. XV, 719 f.   [3] E.g. Od. XII, 399 ff., XV, 477 ff.
[4] Od. XVIII, 136 f. Cf. Tac. Ann. VI, 20 (26) qualem diem, etc.
[5] Od. XVII, 322 f.   [6] See p. 399.   [7] Od. X, 175.   [8] Il. XV, 613.
[9] Od. XVI, 280 f.   [10] See p. 399.   [11] See pp. 399 f.   [12] Hymn to Apollo, 356.
[13] See esp. pp. 443 ff. There is, of course, much and varied evidence later for this attitude to time. E.g. with more science than Hesiod, Virgil in the Georgics (esp. 1) describes the times and seasons for the farmer and the sailor. The interest of the individual or group in the quality of a particular time ahead, month or day or hour, for him or them is reflected constantly in divination, astrology, etc., e.g. Juv. VI, 517 f.; 566–81 qui mensis damnis, quae dentur tempora lucro etc. For the early Romans morning was the 'good' time, mane, and the first portion of the night was characterised as concubia, apparently 'time for embracing, lying with'. Cf. the wide recognition of the Evening star as the power of sexual love, Ištar, Aphrodite, etc. It was followed by nox intempesta, time for no action.

CHAPTER X

Lachesis, Klotho, and Atropos

The original functions of the differentiated Moirai, Λάχεσις, Κλωθώ, Ἄτροπος, can now be explained. They have been referred by later Greeks and modern scholars to the past, present, and future[1] (a reference which has some justification in the names of the Norns, Urðr, Verðandi, Skuld[2]) or in the reverse order.[3] The names lend no support to either. Their activities were originally, we may suggest, first the assigning of the portion, the λάχος or μοῖρα, by Λάχεσις with scales[4] as by Zeus with his,[5] then the spinning of it by Κλωθώ,[6] and lastly the binding or weaving of it by Ἄτροπος. Apart from the evidence already adduced, Aeschylus provides confirmation that the λάχος was the wool to be spun:

τοῦτο γὰρ λάχος διανταία
Μοῖρ' ἐπέκλωσεν ἐμπέδως ἔχειν....

γιγνομέναισι λάχη τάδ' ἐφ' ἁμὶν ἐκράνθη.[7]

Klotho's part in the process is clear in her name. The fate has thus been allotted and made up, spun. Its bringing, fastening to the victim, i.e. the binding (or weaving) process, and Ἄτροπος, 'she who cannot be turned'[8] aside or backward, remain. Antipho speaks of τῆς τύχης...ἣν οὔτ' ἂν ἐγὼ οὔτ' ἄλλος οὐδεὶς οἷός τ' ἂν εἴη ἀποτρέψαι μὴ οὐ γενέσθαι ἥντινα

---

[1] See note 1 on p. 418.

[2] Verðandi and Skuld appear, however, to be later additions. See R. Jente, *Die mythol. Ausdr. im altengl. Wortsch.* p. 199.

[3] E.g. *de Mundo*, 401 b, 16 ff.

[4] See p. 410. Possibly also by the lot (see pp. 392 f.).   [5] See pp. 397 ff.

[6] The assigning might alternatively but less probably be thought to follow the spinning.   [7] *Eum.* 334 f. and 349.

[8] Homer's gods are the binding agents, the powers that act directly upon men. Phoenix thought that men might 'turn aside' (παρατρωπῶσι) the gods by sacrifice (*Il.* IX, 500). ὅ τι δεῖ γενέσθαι ἐκ τοῦ θεοῦ, ἀμήχανον ἀποτρέψαι ἀνθρώπῳ·...ἑπόμεθα ἀναγκαίῃ ἐνδεδεμένοι says Herodotus (IX, 16). 'There is no turning aside of death (οὐκ ἔστιν θανάτου παρατροπά) for my unhappy self' say the chorus in Euripides' *Ion* (1229 f.).

δεῖ ἑκάστῳ,[1] and an inscription[2] of the ἀμε(τά)τροπα δῶρα of Τύχη. We have seen[3] that the 'gifts' of Zeus or the Μοῖραι are threads. She who comes to bind unswervingly, inflexibly, or who plies thus the woof about the warp-threads, weaving the pattern in the tapestry of fate, would be well named Ἄτροπος.[4] It is this merciless course of the shuttle which is stressed in the fragment already cited for the weaving of the Μοῖραι:

ἑζόμεναι περιῶσι' ἄφυκτά τε μήδεα
παντοδαπᾶν βουλᾶν ἀδαμαντίναισιν ὑφαίνετε κερκίσιν.[5]

For this process of tapestry-weaving or pattern-embroidery the verb γράφειν was used,[6] and this verb is used of fate in combination with ἄτροπα and in association with ἐκλώσαντο:

ἑπτὰ δέ μοι μοῖραι περιτελλομένους ἐνιαυτοὺς
ἐκλώσαντο μίτοις ἄτροπα γραψάμεναι,[7]

but here actual writing may have been intended since to that, when the image in its full complexity was growing dim, the transition was natural. In the representation cited[8] of Λάχεσις with the τάλαντα and Klotho with spindle and distaff, Atropos appears with a scroll.[9]

> The moving finger writes; and, having writ,
> Moves on: nor all thy piety nor wit
>   Shall lure it back to cancel half a line,
>   Nor all thy tears wash out a word of it.[10]

If we now look to the vision of Er, the thought behind becomes clearer and we shall see how its details naturally arise from reminiscences of such an image. The souls pass to their

[1] VI, 15.   [2] *Inscr. Gr.* XII, 5, 302.   [3] Pp. 395 f.
[4] In the earliest literature, as we have seen, the fating of death was conceived as a binding, the chief binding. For the later idea that death was the *cutting* of the thread there appears to be no evidence there. It would arise and Atropos be identified with the ending power thus conceived when the spinning was thought to be the complete process of fate or to go on throughout the life spun and its ending to signify the end of the latter. Cf. pp. 349 ff. For the *certum subtemen* Etruscans substituted her nail (p. 374).   [5] Fr. Mel. Adesp. 5 (Diehl).
[6] See e.g. Aesch. *Choeph.* 231 f.   [7] *Epigr. Gr.* 153, 3 f. (Kai.).   [8] P. 410.
[9] Cf. πότμος...ἔγραψε, Pind. *Nem.* VI, 6 f., etc., the 'Fata Scribunda' referred to by Tertullian, *de Anima,* cap. 39, 'swa hem Wyrd ne gescraf', *Beowulf,* 2574, and the Babylonian 'Tablets of Fate'.
[10] From E. Fitzgerald's translation of the *Rubaiyat* of Omar Khayyam.

life in the other world with 'symbols' (σημεῖα) of their sentence (i.e. their destiny) or of their actions 'tied around them' (περιάψαντας) by their judges (Plato, *Rep.* 614 C; cf. 616 A). How, when all is fulfilled there, they pass with new fates to life in this world is described at greater length. Lachesis, Klotho, and Atropos are all concerned with the thread and share in the spinning but their offices differ.[1] To Lachesis the souls go first and from her knees are taken not only κλῆροι—flung merely to determine the turn in which the soul chooses and having no parallel in Homer[2]—but also βίων παραδείγματα, lives complete with their various vicissitudes of fortune (see e.g. 618 A ff., 619 B f., etc.). What Lachesis thus gives we have seen[3] to be the unspun wool with its dynamic counterpart; and Klotho spins it exactly as we have suggested. It is only in the last stage that Plato seems to deviate[4] from the natural sequence pursued in the ancient Greek image as in that of other Indo-European peoples. What he substitutes is palpably inadequate. Atropos becomes almost superfluous; she merely spins again what Klotho had spun[5]—and the natural meaning of her name is perverted: ταύτης δ' ἐφαψάμενον αὖθις ἐπὶ τὴν τῆς 'Ατρόπου ἄγειν νῆσιν, ἀμετάστροφα τὰ ἐπικλωσθέντα ποιοῦντα. To express his meaning he is forced to use a quite different verb

[1] Here already Lachesis is said to sing of the past, Klotho of the present and Atropos of the future; but in the working out of the myth no indication of why this should be is given except the order of their offices which follow in this sequence. That this order was the basis for Plato's thought we may suspect from a passage in the *Laws* (960 C) in which he refers to an old tradition: τὸ Λάχεσιν μὲν τὴν πρώτην εἶναι, Κλωθὼ δὲ τὴν δευτέραν, τὴν "Ατροπον δὴ τρίτην, in which also they are concerned with τὰ κλωσθέντα, but there is no reference to past, present and future.

[2] λαγχάνειν does not necessarily imply the lot but long before Plato's day Lachesis may have been thought to assign fates with it.

[3] See pp. 403 f.

[4] Perhaps he did so because to picture Atropos advancing inexorably to bind the unborn soul with its fate would suggest too strongly that the soul was a victim and not itself responsible as he urged. A loom could not conveniently have been introduced, when the spindle had assumed such a great and central position in the Universe.

[5] 620 E. I suggest that Plato intends Atropos' function to be that for which the ἐπίνητρον was used (see above, p. 306, and *Class. Rev.* Feb. 1924, p. 3). Her action is νῆσις.

of turning, στρέφω, properly applied to such turning on an axis, rotating or spinning,[1] and cannot use τρέπω, which means 'turning' in the sense of turning (aside or backward) from a path of movement, e.g. that of one advancing to bind or guiding a shuttle.

Such distribution of offices may be illustrated by a slightly more complex form[2] of the myth from Lithuania: 'The *deiwes walditojes* were seven goddesses, the first one spun the lives of men out of a distaff given her by the highest god, the second set up the warp, the third wove in the woof, the fourth told tales to tempt the workers to leave off, the fifth exhorted them to industry and added length to the life, the sixth cut the threads, the seventh washed the garment and gave it to the most high god, and it became the man's winding-sheet'.

[1] See *Od.* VI, 53, 306, VII, 105, XVIII, 315, etc.

[2] Elements not appearing in the Greek but easily paralleled elsewhere may be ignored. The myth is cited by Grimm, *op. cit.* chap. XVI, p. 345 from *Ausland*, 1839, No. 278. For the winding-sheet of fate see pp. 425 ff. below and Gray's

> 'Weave the warp and weave the woof,
> The winding-sheet of Edward's race.
> Give ample room and verge enough
> The characters of hell to trace', etc.

The idea is still imaginatively effective. In Masefield's *The Widow in Bye Street*, when Jimmy met the woman who was to provoke him to murder there was

> 'Death beside him knitting at his shroud',

and, when he fell in love with her,

> 'Death stopped knitting at the muffling band.
> "The shroud is done," he muttered, " toe to chin."
> He snapped the ends and tucked his needles in.'

Belief that delay in the completion of the web prolonged the life might contribute to the story of Penelope and Laertes' winding-sheet (*Od.* II, 94 ff.). Cf. our 'a nail in his coffin'.

CHAPTER XI

Phases of Body and Mind, Sorrow, Sleep, Death, etc.

Σπεῖρον, a 'winding-sheet' or strip of cloth to wrap around one, is closely related to σπεῖρα, 'a cord, coil', etc. The principle is the same[1] whether it is a narrow strip or a wide one that is wrapped around a man, one band (πεῖραρ ὀϊзύος, etc.) or a number of bands (ὀλέθρου πείρατα, etc.). Beside changes of external fortune (victory, poverty, freedom, power, etc.), man is subject to changes in his own person, different states of body and mind. The narrow band is more fitted to inescapable outward fortune or to hampering of body or mind, the wide band or cloak, wrapping, to more pervasive states of body or mind. When a man's hands are stricken with weakness, or his limbs are paralysed, they are 'bound'[2] by a god; he who is deluded in mind is 'bound' with ἄτη[3] or ἐλπίς.[4] On the other hand he puts on, clothes himself or is clothed with, steadfastness, energy, shamelessness, etc. (δύσεο δ' ἀλκήν,[5] κρατερὸν μένος ἀμφιβαλόντες,[6] ἀναιδείην ἐπιειμένος,[7] etc.). In such cases it is consciousness and thus the organs of consciousness that are primarily affected; and so Homer speaks of Achilles as φρεσὶν εἱμένος ἀλκήν[8] as Pindar speaks of ἐλπίδες[9] or ἀμπλακίαι[10] 'hung about' the φρένες. So for Homer love is a covering about the φρένες:

ὡς δ' ἴδεν, ὡς μιν ἔρως πυκινὰς φρένας ἀμφεκάλυψεν,[11]

---

[1] See e.g. pp. 360 f., 364, 366 ff. [2] See pp. 327 ff.
[3] See p. 327. [4] See pp. 404 f.
[5] Il. xix, 36; cf. ix, 231. [6] Il. xvii, 742.
[7] Il. i, 149. Cf. ix, 372; Homeric Hymn to Hermes, 156; also ἐπιειμένοι ἀλκήν, Il. vii, 164, viii, 262, xviii, 157; Od. ix, 214, 514, and αἰδοῖ πεπυκασμένος, Epigr. Gr. 875, 2. So συνεκδύεται καὶ τὴν αἰδῶ (Herodot. i, 8), ἀρετὴν ἀντὶ ἱματίων ἀμφιέσονται (Plat. Rep. 457 A), etc.
[8] Il. xx, 381. This notion of clothing the φρένες might be helped by the pleura, the χιτών in which each lung is clothed (see p. 25, n. 2).
[9] See p. 405. [10] See ibid. [11] Il. xiv, 294; cf. iii, 442.

and grief:

Ἕκτορα δ' αἰνὸν ἄχος πύκασε φρένας ἀμφὶ μελαίνας.[1]

This covering or wrapping was perhaps conceived as vaporous, as indeed was the stuff of consciousness.[2] It is important to recognise this way of thinking of vapour or cloud as a garment or wrapping. In such stuff on occasion the gods clothe themselves. With expressions like ἀμφ' ὤμοισιν ἑέσσατο δέρμα λέοντος[3] we may compare ἀμφὶ δ' ἄρ' ἄρρηκτον νεφέλην ὤμοισιν ἕσαντο,[4] εἰμένος ὤμοιιν νεφέλην,[5] νεφέλῃ εἰλυμένος ὤμους,[6] πορφυρέῃ νεφέλῃ κεκαλυμμένος εὐρέας ὤμους,[7] etc. The αἰγίς or 'goatskin', the defensive covering of the sky-god Zeus, is most naturally understood as in origin an interpretation of the storm-cloud[8] even as his offensive weapon was the lightning. The substance of the 'dogskin' helmet of Hades his brother, Ἄϊδος κυνέη, also appears to have been vaporous.[9] The Latin word for 'cloud', nubes, appears to mean 'veil' (cf. nubere). Conversely for the Greeks a fine net was a 'cloud', νεφέλη. To return, it was by such a wrapping of cloud that a man was covered when he was suddenly subject to grief. When Laertes was reminded of Odysseus 'a black cloud of grief covered him' (τὸν δ' ἄχεος νεφέλη ἐκάλυψε μέλαινα).[10] It veils

---

[1] Il. xvII, 83.

[2] See pp. 44 ff. This conceiving of changes of state of the body or the φρένες as various wrappings does not affect the recognition of physiological or psychological changes within. He upon whom 'the bands of destruction are fastened' is pierced by a spear, etc.

[3] Il. x, 177; cf. I, 17, etc.   [4] Il. xx, 150.   [5] Il. xv, 308.

[6] Il. v, 185.   [7] Homeric Hymn to Hermes, 217.

[8] See e.g. Aesch. Choeph. 591 f.; Il. II, 148; Od. xv, 293; the uses of καταιγίς, καταιγίζω, etc. and below p. 424. Cf. Aristoph. Clouds, 343 and the connection of Νεφέλη with the Golden Fleece. At one time the αἰγίς is bright (μαρμαρέη, Il. xvII, 593 f.; χρυσείη, xxIV, 21); at another 'dark' (ἐρεμνή, Il. IV, 167) as a cloud is. It is shaggy (Il. xv, 309) and serves the god as a λαισήϊον. For its θύσανοι (Il. II, 448, cf. θυσανόεσσα, xv, 229, etc.) cf. 'the locks of the approaching storm' (Shelley, To the West Wind). In Aen. vII, 142 f. Virgil was perhaps thinking of the αἰγίς (Il. xvII, 593–6, etc.).   [9] See pp. 424 f.

[10] Od. xxIV, 315. Cf. κὰρ ῥά οἱ ὀφθαλμῶν κέχυτ' ἀχλύς, Il. xx, 421. This explains Ἀχλύς (Shield of Herakles, 264 ff.), usually termed a personification of grief but it is rather a personification of the mist enveloping him who faints in distress through famine (see Plaut. Curc. 309 in n. 4 on p. 182), grief, etc. Cf. Stesichorus, Fr. 93 quoted on p. 430, n. 2.

the eyes. When Koon's brother falls, κρατερόν ῥά ἑ πένθος/ ὀφθαλμοὺς ἐκάλυψε.[1] Grief is itself the veil, the covering of mist.[2] Another such fate affecting the person is sleep. It too is a covering, a soft covering:

ἥ με μάλ' αἰνοπαθῆ μαλακὸν περὶ κῶμ' ἐκάλυψεν.[3]

It is wrapped about one by the spirit of Sleep: αὐτῷ ἐγὼ μαλακὸν περὶ κῶμ' ἐκάλυψα.[4] It veils the eyes and also binds fast,[5] motionless, him who is thus enwrapped. 'Why do you waken me?' asks Penelope:[6]

ἐξ ὕπνου μ' ἀνεγείρεις
ἡδέος ὅς μ' ἐπέδησε φίλα βλέφαρ' ἀμφικαλύψας;

Even such is death, and one might pray that it too might be such a soft covering:

ἥ με μάλ' αἰνοπαθῆ μαλακὸν περὶ κῶμ' ἐκάλυψεν.
αἴθε μοι ὡς μαλακὸν θάνατον πόροι Ἄρτεμις ἀγνή.[7]

How natural it was to conceive these phases of fate, sleep and death, in this way may be seen in later writers. E.g.

et cum te fusco Somnus velavit amictu.[8]

'Now blessings light', says Cervantes,[9] 'on him that first invented this same sleep: it covers a man all over, thoughts and all, like a cloak...there is only one thing that I dislike in sleep; it is that it resembles death.'

Darkness was believed to be substantial, mist.[10] The darkness which veils the eyes in swoon or death seems to be outside, to envelope the victim. In Eugene O'Neill's *Bound East for Cardiff* Yank, who is dying in the ship's forecastle from a fall, says to his friend Driscoll 'How'd all the fog git in

---

[1] *Il.* xi, 249 f. Cf. *Il.* xx, 282.
[2] Cf. Ovid, *Trist.* i, 3, 11 ff., 91 f.; v, 5, 22.
[3] *Od.* xviii, 201.   [4] *Il.* xiv, 359.
[5] Τὸ Ὕπνε...σώματα δεσμεύων ἐν ἀχαλκεύτοισι πέδῃσι appeals an Orphic hymn (xxxv, 85). Cf. Soph. *Aj.* 675 f., ἐν δ' ὁ παγκρατὴς ὕπνος λύει πεδήσας, and in Platonic prose καθ' ὕπνον...πεδηθεὶς δύναμιν (*Tim.* 71 e), Ennius, *Annal.* 5 (Vahl.): *somno levi placidoque revinctus*; and, a metaphor in our own tongue, Moore's
'Oft in the stilly night
Ere slumber's chain hath bound me', etc.
[6] *Od.* xxiii, 16 f.   [7] *Od.* xviii, 201 f. See also below, pp. 426 ff.
[8] Tibullus [Lygdamus], iii, 4, 55.
[9] *Don Quixote*, chap. lxviii. Cf. *habes somnum imaginem mortis eamque cotidie induis* (Cic. *Tusc.* i, 38, 92).   [10] See p. 95.

here?' It was thought of as a veil of mist enwrapping the head. When a man died, 'black darkness veiled his eyes' (τὸν δὲ κατ' ὀφθαλμῶν ἐρεβεννὴ νὺξ ἐκάλυψεν).[1] To kill a man was 'to veil him with black darkness' (τινα ἐρεβεννῇ νυκτὶ καλύψαι).[2] This veil is spoken of as itself 'death': 'death veiled him about' (θάνατος δέ μιν ἀμφεκάλυψε).[3] The subject of ἀμφι-καλύπτειν with just the accusative is the wrapping, covering. Men who chose to die κυάνεον θανάτου ἀμφεβάλοντο νέφος.[4] There can be no doubt of the substantive reality, the exter-nality, of this covering: ἀμφὶ δέ μιν θάνατος χύτο θυμοραϊστής.[5] We may compare ἀμφὶ δὲ δεσμοὶ τεχνήεντες ἔχυντο[6] (the net covering Ares and Aphrodite), ἀμφὶ δ' Ἀθήνη / πολλὴν ἠέρα χεῦε φίλα φρονέουσ' Ὀδυσῆι / μή τις... ἀντιβολήσας / κερτομέοι,[7] etc. The doomed man usually becomes aware of it imme-diately before he becomes unconscious but the observer with 'second sight' might 'fore-see' it. This appears to be the explanation when Theoklymenos sees the heads (and knees[8]) of the doomed suitors 'wrapped about with darkness' (νυκτὶ... εἰλύαται).[9] Our Anglo-Saxon forefathers[10] seem to have had a similar belief. It will explain wælmist, the 'death-mist'. Thus in the short poem, 'The Fates of Men', he who dies on the gallows is described dead, torn by ravens, hanging without feeling, 'surrounded by a death-mist (bewegen wælmiste)'. In Exodus over the Egyptians who perish pursuing the Israelites there is a 'death-mist'. There are striking parallels among the Celts also. Thus in Oided mac n Uisnig (The Death of the Sons of

---

[1] Il. v, 659, xiii, 580; cf. xiv, 438 f., etc.

[2] Il. xiii, 425. Virgil's Aeneas slays a foe, ingentique umbra tegit (x, 541), and Eurydice, doomed, cries feror ingenti circumdata nocte (Georg. iv, 497).

[3] Il. v, 68.   [4] Simonides, 99, 2 (Bgk.⁴).

[5] Il. xiii, 544, xvi, 414, 580.   [6] See Od. viii, 296 ff., 278 f., 282.

[7] Od. vii, 14 ff.   [8] See pp. 181 f.

[9] Od. xx, 351 f. So too the doomed Marcellus: nox atra caput tristi circum-volat umbra (Aen. vi, 866). Before battle the doomed inque vicem voltus tenebris mirantur opertos/et pallere diem galeisque incumbere noctem (Lucan, vii, 177f.). His witch mingles with the dead, herself maestum tecta caput squalenti nube (vi, 625). This death-mist is also the explanation, e.g., of the stricken Persians' cry: Στυγία γάρ τις ἐπ' ἀχλὺς πεπόταται· νεολαία γὰρ ἤδη κατὰ πᾶσ' ὄλωλεν (Aesch. Pers. 667 ff.; so Choeph. 52 f.), and of the traditional oath at Priene: ὁ παρὰ δρυὶ σκότος, since a multitude died in battle by the oak (Plut. Q.G. 20).

[10] Cf. Wordsworth's Happy Warrior, 'while the mortal mist is gathering'.

Usnech) before the fatal encounter Deirdre says: 'Sad I deem what I now perceive, thy cloud, O Naisi, in the air, and it is a cloud of blood'.[1] Elsewhere Congall threatens Dubhdiadh that but for a certain obligation 'it would be from the rapid motion of my hand that thy heavy clouds of final dissolution would be brought'.[2] In battle Conan was visited by an 'omen of death', 'a whirling cloud grew and closed around the inlets of his sight and observation', and the writer explains 'that it was the bowels and entrails of Conan that were riddled and pierced by Cellach's first shot in the combat and that in consequence mists and death-clouds came upon him which closed a dark and gloomy veil over the open inlet windows of that prince's sight'.[3] The conceiving of the darkness or cloud about one's head at death as a substantial covering or wrapping will explain the enveloping head-covering, the peculiar attribute of the Greek death-god, Ἄϊδος κυνέη, the 'dogskin' bonnet, which characteristically in myth he lends to other people's heads and which according to the Hesiodean 'Shield of Herakles' was νυκτὸς ζόφον αἰνὸν ἔχουσα[4] (περιέκειτο δὲ ἐπὶ τὴν κεφαλὴν νέφος ἤγουν ἀορασία Schol.) and according to the Homeric scholia[5] was νέφος. Tibullus conceived the death-god thus with a wrapping = darkness about his head: tenebris Mors adoperta caput.[6] We said that the αἰγίς or 'goat-skin' covering of Hades' brother, the storm-god Zeus, was most naturally understood as the stormcloud. It is goats that the Norse storm-god Thor drives across the sky; and in Njals Saga, when Swan is pursued by Oswif, 'Swan took a goatskin and wrapped it about his own head and said "Become mist and fog, become fright and wonder mickle to all those who seek thee." Now it must be told how Oswif, his friends, and his men are riding along the ridge; then came a great mist against them...a mighty darkness came before their eyes, so that they could see nothing.'[7] The wrapping about the head

[1] See op. cit. in Irische Texte, II, 2, p. 162 (ll. 269 ff.).
[2] The Banquet of Dun Na N-Gedh and the Battle of Magh Rath, (text and) trans. by John O'Donnovan, Irish Archaeol. Soc. 1842, p. 191.
[3] Id. p. 269.   [4] Line 227.   [5] Ad Il. v, 845.   [6] I, 1, 70.
[7] Trans. Dasent (Chap. 12). Cf. the Tarnkappe, Nebelkappe, Helkappe of legend (Grimm, Deutsche Myth.[4] p. 383). In the Edda (Alvissmal,

of the death-god with which he wraps, or which he lends to, others is related to that which enwraps a man at death much as the band (κεστὸς ἱμάς) of the love-goddess, which she also lends,¹ is related to the band² with which she binds with love the ordinary mortal. Homer seems to identify the wrapping of darkness about the head of the doomed with a μοῖρα, band of fate,³ here that of death: 'him the μοῖρα of evil name veiled about under the spear of Idomeneus' (μιν μοῖρα δυσώνυμος ἀμφεκάλυψεν / ἔγχεϊ Ἰδομενῆος),⁴ as elsewhere⁵ the μοῖρα is spoken of as a band upon the doomed, said to 'bind' (ἐπέδησε) him. More precisely it covers the eyes: τὸν δὲ κατ' ὄσσε/ἔλλαβε πορφύρεος θάνατος καὶ μοῖρα κραταιή.⁶ Describing the coming of sleep to an eagle, Pindar says... 'poured a dark cloud over his curved head, a pleasant bar across his eyes' (κελαινῶπιν δ' ἐπί οἱ νεφέλαν/ἀγκύλῳ κρατί, γλεφάρων ἁδὺ κλάϊστρον, κατέχευας).⁷ Baltic Slavs still conceive of diseases, particular forms of death, 'in the shape of grey smoke flying about in a thick cloud, spread out like a broad belt of linen, and he upon whom the cloud falls must die at once'.⁸

31) one name for Night is 'Hood' or 'Cowl' (*grima*). Cf. Anglo-Saxon *niht-helm*. The skin-bonnet of Hades (cf. αἰγείη κυνέη, *Od.* xxiv, 231) rendered him upon whom it was placed invisible (cf. the explanation of Ἀΐδης as 'Unseen One'). This we can now understand in conjunction with Homer's frequent representation of a hero as rendered invisible by some god, while moving amongst his fellows, by being wrapped in cloud, which apparently was itself not seen (e.g. *Od.* vii, 15 f., 39 ff., 139–45). Compare Ἀθήνη/δῦν' Ἀΐδος κυνέην μή μιν ἴδοι ὄβριμος Ἄρης (*Il.* v, 844 f.) with a god's usual means of moving invisible among the combatants, clothing himself in cloud that is itself not seen (*Il.* v, 186, xv, 308, xvii, 551). Not seeing and not being seen are often confused by the unsophisticated and it is the property of the cloud that covers one at death that it too cannot be seen by the ordinary person outside.

We can also now better understand ἠεροφοῖτις Ἐρινύς, i.e. they were not 'blood-haunting' (J. E. Harrison, *Prolegomena, etc.* p. 215) nor 'Storm-clouds' (Roscher, *Lex.* s.v.) but thus invisible, δαίμονες who avenge sin against the established order and also bless with fertility and wealth (e.g. Aesch. *Eumen.* 895 ff.). They are much as the dead of the χρύσεον γένος who become δαίμονες...οἵ ῥα φυλάσσουσί τε δίκας καὶ σχέτλια ἔργα/ἠέρα ἐσσάμενοι πάντη φοιτῶντες ἐπ' αἶαν/πλουτοδόται (Hesiod, *Works and Days*, 122 ff. Cf. 223, *Il.* xiv, 282, etc.).   ¹ See p. 368.
    ² See pp. 373, 401, 403.   ³ See pp. 378 f.   ⁴ *Il.* xii, 116 f.
    ⁵ See p. 327.   ⁶ *Il.* v, 82 f.; xvi, 333 f.; xx, 476 f.   ⁷ *Pyth.* i, 7 f.
    ⁸ Loring, Fucher, and Lehr-Splawinski, *The Cassubian Civilisation* (1935), p. 284.

CHAPTER XII

Τέλος

There has been one almost invariable feature in discussions of πεῖραρ, an endeavour to support the abstract meaning by citing parallel phrases with τέλος, the abstractness of τέλος itself never being questioned. It is, however, a word which puzzles philologists. Indeed to them it is not one word but several. Unable to harmonise and correlate the widely varied meanings, they are driven to assume more than one original. Boisacq, for instance, distinguishes three originally distinct words (related to three different words or groups of words in various Indo-European languages) meaning (1) 'end', (2) 'troop', and (3) 'payment'; and these are but the central points of three series of meanings. It was the first of these which was called in to throw light on πεῖραρ. Πολέμου τέλος and τέλος θανάτοιο have been quoted to show that ἔριδος... καί...πτολέμοιο πεῖραρ and ὀλέθρου πείρατα mean respectively 'the issue of war' and 'utter destruction', which we have seen they do not. Indeed such abstract and periphrastic expressions are far to seek in Homer.

We have already[1] seen that Priam's remark about the impending duel between Paris and Menelaos: 'Zeus knows this and the other gods, for which of the two the τέλος of death is πεπρωμένον', probably involves the image of fate, death, as a band or bond. Another formula deserves attention. It occurs four times:[2]

ὣς ἄρα μιν εἰπόντα τέλος θανάτοιο κάλυψε.

τέλος is here habitually translated 'end', 'consummation', etc.; yet to talk of the 'end' or 'consummation' of death 'covering' anybody is very strange even now when the abstract rules and words are used as intellectual symbols

[1] P. 386.
[2] Il. xvi, 502, 855, xxii, 361 and, slightly varied, v, 553, where if it is the same τέλος that covers two, compare the parallels on pp. 385 f. above.

without much imagining of the images they may involve, much more strange in the age revealed by Homer with its clinging to the concrete and its vivid realisation of what is said. In one passage[1] the literal spatial force of κάλυψεν is proved, though even there it has passed unnoticed:

ὡς ἄρα μιν εἰπόντα τέλος θανάτοιο κάλυψεν
ὀφθαλμοὺς ῥῖνάς τε.

'The τέλος of death covered his eyes and nostrils as he was speaking.' It is impossible to think of any abstraction doing just that. We have seen that in fact death was conceived as a band[2] or a wrapping of vapour, cloud.[3] Aeschylus represents the girls of Thebes hoping death may come: νύκτερον τέλος μολεῖν.[4] The other instances about to be considered preclude any meaning like 'cloud' for τέλος in Homer and indicate that it should mean something like 'band' or 'wrapping'. A band or wrapping would produce darkness. Cf. the Baltic Slavs' conception: 'cloud spread out like a broad belt of linen, and he upon whom the cloud falls must die at once' (p. 425). How natural such an image of death is may be seen e.g. in a poem of T. E. Brown, *Ex Ore Infantis*:

> To-day beneath the piteous gaze of morn
> Her child is dying. On his little brow
> Descends the veil, and all is over now;

or in George Eliot's, 'as she was bending to kiss him, the thick veil of death fell between them' (*Scenes of Clerical Life*, XXIV *fin.*). In sympathetic magic men used bands or wrappings to produce the effects produced also by the mystic bands or wrappings of fate.[5] To the 'τέλος θανάτοιο covering eyes and nostrils' should perhaps be related the later Greek custom of veiling the head of the dead[6] and, earlier, 'the gold[7] bands with eyes

---

[1] *Il.* xvi, 502 f.   [2] P. 327.   [3] Pp. 421 ff.
[4] *Sept.* 367.   [5] See pp. 353 ff., 441 f., etc.
[6] See p. 133. Euripides associates the drawing down of the lids over the eyes of the dying with the darkness. To his mother Polyneikes says: 'Draw together my eyelids with your hand, mother'—he places it himself upon his eyes—'and goodbye. For already darkness envelopes me' (ἤδη γάρ με περιβάλλει σκότος), *Phoen.* 1451 ff. Cf. Virgil, *Georgic* IV, 496 f.
[7] Was the gold intended to be a band of life instead? Cf. pp. 106; 156, n. 2; 164 ff.; 183, n. 1; 330; and the crown or wreath, pp. 367, 449 ff.

marked on suggesting a special religious usage' found at Knossos. 'The incised eyes clearly indicate that they were intended to serve as a bandage over the eyes of the dead person.'[1] Pindar speaks of sleep as external, 'a bar across the eyes' (p. 425), and, of Zeus releasing from death, says ἀνὰ δ' ἔλυσεν μὲν ὀφθαλμόν, ἔπειτα δὲ φωνὰν χαλκομίτρα Κάστορος.[2] A doubtful passage[3] of Aeschylus seems to ask that the dead Agamemnon may 'see clearly from the dark veil' (δνοφερὰ καλύπτρα). The myth attributing an enveloping head-covering to the death-god, the Ἄϊδος κυνέη, lent to cover the heads of others, may thus be related to the funeral custom of covering the head of the dead. There is a striking parallel in the North. Among the Finns the death-god was Tuoni, represented as remarkable for his hat, which he wore drawn down to his shoulders,[4] and in the *Kalevala* the dead man is said to enter Tuoni's realm 'with Tuoni's hat upon him'.[5] The custom of enveloping the head of the dead is referred to in northern sagas[6] and exemplified in graves that have been opened.[7] The equation of the wrapping of fate given by the gods with that with which men wrapped the dead was exemplified in the Lithuanian belief that the goddesses who spun and wove a man's fate 'gave it to the most high god and it became the man's winding-sheet'.[8] Like the Greeks, the Italians also veiled the dead or doomed,[9] and on Roman and Etruscan monuments there can be seen to come to the dying or dead

[1] Sir A. Evans, *The Palace of Minos at Knossos*, I, pp. 96 f.

[2] *Nem.* x, 90. Cf. Soph. *Aj.* 706 with p. 421 above.

[3] *Choeph.* 809 ff. Antigone speaks of her father τὸν ἀεὶ κατὰ γᾶς σκότον εἱμένος (Soph. *Oed. Col.* 1701). Phaedra in her distress says to her nurse πάλιν μου κρύψον κεφαλάν and the nurse replies κρύπτω· τὸ δ' ἐμὸν πότε δὴ θάνατος/σῶμα καλύψει; (Eurip. *Hippol.* 243–251).

[4] See J. M. Crawford, *Kalevala*, Introd. p. xxvi.

[5] *Ibid.* I, p. 230.　　　　　　　　　　[6] See p. 154.

[7] See Du Chaillu, *op. cit.* pp. 90, 92; also Addendum IX, pp. 509 f.

[8] See p. 419. Cf. σπεῖρον p. 420 and the etymology of τέλος given below. In mediaeval representations, e.g. English monumental brasses, the soul is often represented naked and held in a sheet by the Almighty Father (see *A Manual for the Study of Monumental Brasses...'rubbings' in the possession of the Oxf. Architectural Soc.*, Oxf. 1848, p. xlix).

[9] See pp. 132 f.

daemons, sometimes winged, carrying a cloth as if to 'cover' or wrap him.[1] All this supports the natural interpretation that the 'τέλος θανάτοιο covering eyes and nostrils' was a band or wrapping of some kind.[2]

If so, and if it was related to or identical with the bands or bonds, different phases of fate, misfortune, age, death, etc., brought and put upon men by the gods or κῆρες,[3] the picture presented by Mimnermus[4] can be better appreciated: 'The

[1] See F. Poulsen, *Etruscan Tomb Paintings* (trans. I. Anderson), pp. 55 ff. Cf. Tib. on pp. 422, 424 with p. 423, nn. 2, 9. The ideas traced probably explain the cloth often shown extended behind a bust of the dead. In one case (see *Rev. Archéol.* 1844, Pl. 17) Charun with his hammer is leading the horse on which the soul is riding with head incompletely muffled. *Persona* (mask covering the whole head. Cf. pp. 135 and 146) has been explained to be the same as Etruscan *Phersu* (see Pauly-Wiss. *Realencykl.* VI, 775). In the Tomba degli Auguri (Poulsen, pp. 12 f.) Phersu is portrayed. His association with death suggests that he is an Etruscan version of Hades and that, as Hades was characterised by his helmet, he is a death-god who takes the heads, i.e. souls (see pp. 100 and 135 ff.), of his victims. Cf. also *larva* = 'mask' and 'ghost' (p. 135; cf. p. 154, n. 4) and Praxidike = Persephone conceived as a head (p. 114, n. 5). In the tomb he is represented with a dog which is fighting with a man who is entangled in a cord, apparently the leash of the dog, held by Phersu. We can now perhaps better understand why the man's head is completely covered by a cloth or bag. Since he is wielding a club we may suggest that he is Hercules and the dog Cerberus. The man's head is covered as a man's head was covered when he entered the world of death (see p. 133, n. 1. Was Hercules' image *operto capite*—see Serv. *ad Aen.* III, 407, VIII, 288, Macrob. III, 6, 17—like this? The rest of the painting shows that Phersu runs away as Hades did (e.g. Roscher, *Lex.* s.v. Kerb. 1121), i.e. that the man with the club prevails (as Hercules did, *Od.* XI, 623 ff., *Aen.* VI, 395 f., etc.). In art Hercules often holds the dog by a leash (e.g. Rosch. *ibid.* fig. 2).

[2] Not only the Greeks and Romans but also the Jews put a cloth over the head of the dead (see S. John, xi, 44; xx, 7). The Greeks and Romans also put a cloth thus over the head of the doomed (see note 1, p. 133 above). So was it done to Haman (Esther, vii, 8). By the conception of death as such a covering (cf. Job xvi, 16; Ps. xliv, 19) we can perhaps explain Isaiah's prophecy (xxv, 7 f.) that God will save mankind. 'And he will destroy in this mountain the veil that veils all peoples and the covering that is over all the nations. He will destroy death for ever.' For Jewish thought of fate as a band or wrapping see pp. 360, n. 7, 367, 437, n. 3, and 439, n. 5. Cf. perhaps also the cloth to envelope the dead, or his head, on tombs at Palmyra (Clermont Ganneau, *Ét. d'arch. or.* I, p. 113; Seyrig in *Berytus*, III, pp. 139 f., Pll. XXXII f.).

[3] See pp. 401 ff.   [4] Fr. 2, 5 ff. (Bgk.[4]).

black κῆρες stand near, the one holding the τέλος of grievous old age (γῆρας), the other the τέλος of death', where τέλος cannot mean 'end' but is something concrete, the form under which the particular phase of fortune was visualised, something carried by the κῆρες:

κῆρες δὲ παρεστήκασι μέλαιναι,
ἡ μὲν ἔχουσα τέλος γήραος ἀργαλέου,
ἡ δ' ἑτέρη θανάτοιο.

Another fragment[1] of the same also tells of γῆρας:[2]

τὸ δ' ἀργαλέον καὶ ἄμορφον
γῆρας ὑπὲρ κεφαλῆς αὐτίχ' ὑπερκρέμαται
ἐχθρὸν ὁμῶς καὶ ἄτιμον, ὅ τ' ἄγνωστον τιθεῖ ἄνδρα,
βλάπτει δ' ὀφθαλμοὺς καὶ νόον ἀμφιχυθέν.

Here the picture is clearly of something first hanging or hung over a man and then enveloping him, the last line recalling Homer's 'τέλος θανάτοιο covering his eyes and nostrils'.[3] We have already[4] explained thus Simonides' 'Inescapable death is hung over us, for of it good and bad have equal portion allotted':

ὁ δ' ἄφυκτος ὁμῶς ἐπικρέμαται θάνατος,
κείνου γὰρ ἴσον λάχον μέρος οἵ τ' ἀγαθοί
ὅστις τε κακός.

We have seen[5] that our forefathers likewise conceived of disease, death etc. as bonds put about men. There appears to

[1] 5, 5 ff.
[2] That γῆρας was conceived as a veil, or skin over the body, is confirmed by Homeric Hymn to Aphrodite, 224, according to which Eos forgot to ask for youth for Tithonos and to 'scrape away baleful γῆρας'. See too Il. IX, 446. Cf. Aristoph. Peace, 336 and above p. 290, n. 1. Later the slough or skin cast by a snake was called γῆρας. For old age binding see Laberius, 122 f. (Ribbeck) with Catullus, LXI, 33 ff.
[3] Cf. in the Homeric Hymn to Aphrodite (244 f.):

νῦν δέ σε μὲν τάχα γῆρας ὁμοίιον ἀμφικαλύψει
νηλειές, τό τ' ἔπειτα παρίσταται ἀνθρώποισιν,

where there appears to be transition insensibly from the band or wrapping to the κήρ or dynamic agency, for which compare pp. 399 ff., 415 and such Homeric passages as Il. XIV, 233 f. If it is related to any Greek word, the name of the τελχῖνες, evil δαίμονες or workers of magic in Crete, perhaps goes back to these associations of τέλος. For magic as binding see pp. 367 ff., also note 4 on p. 446. Stesichorus, we are told, τὰς κῆρας καὶ τὰς σκοτώσεις τελχῖνας προσηγόρευσε (Fr. 93, Bgk. = Eust. ad Il. IX, 525). Cf. τελχίν· καὶ ἡ εἰς θάνατον καταφορά, Et. Magn. s.v. (751, 34).
[4] P. 337.   [5] Pp. 356 f., 381.

be a remarkable parallel to Mimnermus' picture of the κήρ bringing his wrapping to the victim in the Anglo-Saxon charm[1] against the coming of a dwarf, the embodiment of a disease:

> Here comes a spider-wight walking in:
> He had his covering (*hama*) in his hand.
> He said that you were his horse.
> He puts his bands on your neck....
>
> (Cf. pp. 405 ff. above.)

Fig. 2. Europa on the Bull

In Homer, instead of covering a man, the τέλος of death is sometimes said just to 'reach' him. To the dying Sokos Odysseus says: 'The τέλος of death was too quick in reaching you nor did you escape from beneath it':[2]

φθῆ σε τέλος θανάτοιο κιχήμενον οὐδ' ὑπάλυξας.

So a man who tries to save himself is said to 'avoid the τέλος of death'[3] as forty lines before he was said to 'escape from the great bond (πεῖραρ) of misfortune which reached him'.[4] We have seen that the early Greeks believed that the threads or

---

[1] It is in the *Lacnunga* ('Healings') of MS. Harl. 585 published by O. Cockayne, *Leechdoms, Wortcunning and Starcraft of Early England*, Vol. III, p. 42. *hama* was used of a garment, covering or skin, e.g. that cast by a snake.

[2] *Il.* XI, 451.   [3] *Od.* V, 326.   [4] 289 (see p. 323).

bands of fate were held or hung thus over men[1] and that the gods, κῆρες, etc. put bands of this or that fortune upon men,[2] and that the belief that the various phases of fortune came to men in this way at the hands of god, δαίμων, κήρ, μοῖρα, explains the many vase paintings in which a figure (usually winged) brings a circle, crown, or ταινία to someone or holds it over him or her.[3] Thus to Europa on the bull that is bearing her off to be married there is seen coming, hastening to reach her, such a figure carrying a crown or circle or an open band. Marriage was a τέλος. In the *Odyssey* Aphrodite asks for the τέλος θαλεροῖο γάμοιο for the daughters of Pandareus, going to Zeus. 'For he knows well what fate is given or denied (μοῖράν τ' ἀμμορίην τε) to mortals' (xx, 73 ff.). Struck by Antinoos, Odysseus says: 'May the τέλος of death reach Antinoos before marriage'.[4] Pindar says: 'We differ each in nature, one receiving as his lot this, others that. But for one man to win all happiness is impossible. I cannot say to whom Fate hath held out this fast (i.e. "secure") τέλος (τίνι τοῦτο Μοῖρα τέλος ἔμπεδον ὤρεξε)',[5] which recalls p. 376 (cf. pp. 444 f.) and the figure

---

[1] P. 337.   [2] Pp. 319 ff., 400 ff.

[3] P. 402. This perhaps lies behind τὸ φέρον (Soph. *O.C.* 1693, etc.), τοῦτο ἔφερεν αὐτῷ...τοῦτο τούτῳ ἐφέρετο (Marc. Ant. v, 8), and the names *Fors, Fortuna* (Virg. *Aen.* II, 34, 94, Ov. *Trist.* I, 3, 101), Horace's *volucrisque fati tardavit alas* (*Od.* II, 17, 24 f.), etc. Cf. pp. 381, 403.

[4] *Od.* XVII, 476. In Homer just as it could be said not only that the πεῖραρ or πείρατα, 'bonds', of 'misfortune' or 'destruction' 'reached' a man or were fastened upon him (see pp. 320 ff.) but also that the man 'reached the πείρατα' as if they were extended waiting for him (see pp. 321 f.), so not only could it be said that the τέλος of death 'reached' or 'covered' a man but also that an 'evil μοῖρα led him to the τέλος of death' (τὸν δ' ἄγε μοῖρα κακὴ θανάτοιο τέλοσδε, *Il.* XIII, 602). Within a few lines Achilles speaks of himself as 'being carried to the τέλος of death' and of the τέλος as 'reaching' him. 'My mother Thetis says that two κῆρες are carrying me to the τέλος of death. If I stay here and fight round the city of the Trojans, my return is lost but my glory will be imperishable; but if I go home to my dear fatherland, my glory is lost but I shall live long nor will the τέλος of death quickly reach me' (*Il.* IX, 411 ff.).

[5] *Nem.* VII, 54 ff. For τέλος of a desirable item of fate we may compare Homer's 'For I say that there is no more beautiful (χαριέστερον) τέλος than when there is mirth among all the folk and the feasters listen...' (*Od.* IX, 5 f.).

holding out the crown or band on vase-paintings. Another relic of this sense may perhaps be seen in Herodotus' statement that, when their mother had prayed that the god might bestow upon Kleobis and Biton the happiest fate, they fell asleep and οὐκέτι ἀνέστησαν ἀλλ' ἐν τέλει τούτῳ ἔσχοντο (1, 31. Cf. τῇ πάγῃ ἐνέχεσθαι, 11, 121 and Hdt. on pp. 376f., 416, n. 8).

To show that Homer's ἔριδος καὶ πτολέμοιο πεῖραρ meant 'the issue of war' Monro and others cite his parallel use of πολέμου τέλος. Urged to meet Achilles, Aeneas says that Achilles cannot be faced because he receives divine help;

εἰ δὲ θεός περ
ἶσον τείνειεν πολέμου τέλος, οὔ κε μάλα ῥέα
νικήσει· οὐδ' εἰ παγχάλκεος εὔχεται εἶναι,[1]

where Monro interprets '"stretched even the decision of the war", i.e. pulled evenly at each end of the line. The metaphor of a rope is a favourite one; see on 13.358'. There, as we have seen, while πεῖραρ is interpreted 'end', Monro's idea is of a rope stretched across two armies fastening them together. Here however he supposes that the gods are not 'pulling evenly', quite a different idea. We have seen that in XIII, 358 it is not a matter of 'pulling' thus at all but of a bond extended. The language in the two passages is so closely parallel that Monro cannot avoid finding an allusion to the same 'metaphor', and Leaf too, while translating τέλος by 'issue'. Instead of ἔριδος...καὶ...πτολέμοιο πεῖραρ we have πολέμου τέλος; instead of ἐπ' ἀμφοτέροισι we have ἶσον, and there is the same verb τανύειν, τείνειν. In the one passage the meaning of πεῖραρ has been shown to be concrete. No less is demanded in the other passage for τέλος; yet all have been content with something like a 'decision' or 'issue' to be 'stretched', which is un-Homeric, not to say nonsense. There is, indeed, actual proof that τέλος cannot here mean 'end' or 'issue' or 'decision'. According to Hesiod[2] the gods and Titans 'fought continuously for ten years':

οὐδέ τις ἦν ἔριδος χαλεπῆς λύσις οὐδὲ τελευτὴ
οὐδετέροις, ἶσον δὲ τέλος τέτατο πτολέμοιο.

---

[1] *Il.* xx, 100 ff. [2] *Theog.* 637–8.

'Nor was there any loosing of the dire ἔρις nor end for either side, but the τέλος of war was extended evenly.' λύσις, 'loosing', implies that what is loosed is a bond and is used of the bonds of fate.[1] Any sense of 'end', 'issue', 'decision', for τέλος is precluded by οὐδὲ τελευτή. Eustathius remarks of the Homeric passage: πολέμου δὲ τέλος οὐκ ἔστι νοῆσαι τὴν νίκην ἐνταῦθα, τὸν πόλεμον δὲ αὐτὸν περιφραστικῶς. In what sense πεῖραρ could be identified with πόλεμος in the 'defining genitive' we have seen.[2]

'Above, the bands of victory are held among the immortal gods (ὕπερθε/νίκης πείρατ' ἔχονται ἐν ἀθανάτοισι θεοῖσιν)',[3] says Homer. 'The bands of victory are among the gods (νίκης δ' ἐν θεοῖσι πείρατα)',[4] says Archilochus. Sailing is safe between midsummer and autumn, says Hesiod, 'unless Poseidon, the earth-shaker, or Zeus, king of the immortals, wishes to destroy you; for among them (or "in their hands") is the τέλος alike of good fortune and of bad (ἐν τοῖς γὰρ τέλος ἐστὶν ὁμῶς ἀγαθῶν τε κακῶν τε)'.[5] And Semonides of Amorgos not only says of men's misfortune in marriage:

Ζεὺς γὰρ μέγιστον τοῦτ' ἐποίησεν κακόν
καὶ δεσμὸν ἀμφέθηκεν ἄρρηκτον πέδης,[6]

but also elsewhere: 'Loud-thundering Zeus holds the τέλος of all things that are and places it where he will (τίθησ' ὅπη θέλει',[7] cf. pp. 378 ff. above), which we may set beside 'Zeus, he

[1] See pp. 363 ff., 384 f., 441 f.
[2] Pp. 320 ff.
[3] Il. VII, 101 f. See pp. 333 f.
[4] Fr. LV, Bgk.[4]
[5] Works and Days, 667 ff.
[6] Fr. VII, 115 f., Bgk.[4] See pp. 379 f. above.
[7] Fr. I, I f. Cf. Eurip. Orestes, 1545 f. If τέλος need not mean the act of fulfilment (for which sense see below, pp. 460 ff.) but can refer to the band of fate causing fulfilment, we can explain the reply which on three occasions in Homer (Il. XIV, 195 f., XVIII, 426 f.; Od. V, 89 f.) one deity gives to another when asked to do something as yet unspecified. 'Tell me what is your wish. My spirit bids me τελέσαι, that is if I am able τελέσαι and εἰ τετελεσμένον ἐστίν', which last is currently (see e.g. Ameis-Hentze-Cauer ad Od. V, 90) interpreted 'if it can be accomplished' as if the perfect participle passive were the verbal adjective in -τός. But there is no evidence for such a use of the perfect participle passive anywhere in Homer and this meaning for τετελεσμένος makes nonsense of e.g. μῦθος ὁ δὴ τετελεσμένος ἐστί, describing a promise already fulfilled (Il. I, 388). The perfect participle naturally implies that the τέλος already exists or

who plies (or "distributes") the bands both of life and of death':

Ζεὺς ὁ καὶ ʒωῆς καὶ θανάτου πείρατα νωμῶν.[1]

The besieged Theban maidens of Aeschylͺs, crying out to each of their gods in turn at this or that sign of the onset, shout 'The air is raging with the shaking of spears. What is happening to our city? What will befall? Whither and what τέλος is a god bringing? (ποῖ δὲ τί. τέλος ἐπάγει θεός; Tucker or "whither now is...ποῖ δ᾽ ἔτι κ.τ.λ.") E-e-e-eh! Stones are hurled at the battlements. Oh, Apollo! At the gates there is clashing of bronze-bound shields and from Zeus in battle the holy τέλος fulfilled by war (πολεμόκραντον ἁγνὸν τέλος ἐν μάχᾳ)';[2] then they call more generally upon the gods to hear and defend them, to the δαίμονες who 'loose' (λυτήριοι), etc. To the suppliant Danaids, who ask him to protect them from the pursuing sons of Aigyptos, the king of Argos says: 'If against your kin, the sons of Aigyptos, I stand before the

has been given. This τέλος must therefore be something slightly different from that which is to be the work in the future of the speaker (εἰ δύναμαι τελέσαι). We have seen that fate was spun in advance and a band was already fastened upon one before one experienced the event or phase of fortune it represented, and that the gods subordinate to the arch-binder Zeus were concerned to fulfil the fate that was already bound and not to contravene it (pp. 390 ff.). The reply would thus mean 'if I can give τέλος (in the sense of "perform the act that is the τέλος", for which sense see below, pp. 460 ff.) and if the τέλος (i.e. band of fate) is already given, exists'. The slight shift of meaning would immediately be understood by the hearer who shared these beliefs just as, to take a more familiar image, were the causation in both cases a matter of 'ordaining', we should understand 'my spirit bids me ordain it, that is if I can ordain it, and if it has been ordained' (sc. by the powers of fate). Cf. Soph. O.C. 1693 f. In Aen. v, 796 ff. Venus asks Neptune to allow the Trojans safe passage to their city in Italy si concessa peto, si dant ea moenia Parcae. 'His μοῖρα subdued even Herakles' says Achilles, ὡς καὶ ἐγών, εἰ δή μοι ὁμοίη μοῖρα τέτυκται, / κείσομ᾽ ἐπεί κε θάνω (Il. xviii, 119 ff.), and Menelaos, about to fight Paris, ἡμέων δ᾽ ὁπποτέρῳ θάνατος καὶ μοῖρα τέτυκται, τεθναίη (Il. iii, 101 f.). τετελεσμένον ἦμαρ (Hesiod, Works and Days, 799) is perhaps the reverse of ἡμέραι ἀκήριοι (823). See pp. 399, 413 ff. (κήρ interchangeable with μοῖρα=bond).

[1] Fragm. Mel. Adesp. 86 in Anthol. Gr., Hiller-Crusius[4]. πείρατα has in the past been translated 'ends', etc. here, but the concrete meaning has much more point and the passage evidently belongs to the present group.

[2] Septem, 155 ff.

walls and go through the τέλος of battle (διὰ μάχης ἥξω τέλους),
is it not a bitter price to pay...?'¹ Of the Corinthian warriors
who fought, some on one side, some on the other, at Troy,
Pindar says that they 'were reputed to cut the τέλος of battle
in both directions (ἐδόκησαν/ἐπ' ἀμφότερα μαχᾶν τάμνειν
τέλος)'.² The meaning of τέλος was gradually developing, as
we shall see, but these expressions recall the πολέμου τέλος
'extended' by the gods in Homer and 'extended' and opposed
to λύσις in Hesiod.

Τέλη λύει (cf. λυσιτελεῖ) can perhaps now be explained. Its
force is shown, by the contexts in which it appears, to have
been something like 'it profits, is advantageous'. In the past³
it has been explained as 'it indemnifies for expenses incurred'
or 'it pays what is due' and so 'it pays', i.e. profits, avails. But
unfortunately against this explanation, which Plato⁴ quotes,
we appear to have no evidence⁵ that λύειν meant 'to pay'.
Plato himself⁶ preferred to interpret of that which 'looses the
τέλος (i.e. "end") and keeps movement free', i.e. frees from restriction. Earlier Sophocles not only says⁷ φεῦ, φεῦ, φρονεῖν ὡς
δεινὸν ἔνθα μὴ τέλη/λύῃ φρονοῦντι, but also says of Oidipous,
when he suddenly passed from his unhappy existence, that he
'blessedly loosed the τέλος of life⁸ (ὀλβίως γ' ἔλυσε τὸ τέλος...
βίου)', where 'paying' is quite inappropriate and the closest

¹ Suppl. 474 ff. If τέλος could mean something like the 'circle', 'band',
or 'wrapping' of fate, we might perhaps reinstate the manuscript reading
of a fragment of Aeschylus (151, Nauck): 'Death (?) will peel off the
τέλος of the immortals', τέλος ἀθανάτων ἀπολέψει, i.e. as Hesychius
explains, τὸ ἐκ τῶν θεῶν τέλος, the τέλος given by the gods. For ἀπολέψει,
'peel off', the current reading is the conjecture of Musurus, ἀπολείψει,
from the context (Hesychius' interpretation according to the sole MS.).
A Babylonian prayer (5th tablet, Maqlû series, ed. Zimmern, pp. 25 ff.)
reads 'May the bewitchment through the charm of Ea be peeled off like
an onion.... May it be removed like a husk'.
² Ol. XIII, 56 f.
³ See e.g. the revised Liddell and Scott, s.vv. λυσιτελέω, λύω V₂.
⁴ See Crat. 417 B f.
⁵ See p. 440 below, and for the use of τέλος of payment, fulfilment of
a promise, pp. 460 ff. These secondary senses of the two words are not found
combined to express discharge of an actual obligation, payment, and do
not give good point in the idiom under consideration.
⁶ Crat. 417 B f.   ⁷ Oed. Rex, 316 f.
⁸ Oed. Col. 1720.

parallels appear to be αἰῶν' ἔλυσεν[1] and λύειν βίον,[2] which seem to imply that this life itself is a bond loosed at death 'when we have shuffled off this mortal coil'.[3] Pindar's θνατὸν διέρχονται βιότου τέλος is discussed below.[4] The τέλος is life, not the end. A portion of fate is a portion of time.[5] Τὸ γὰρ τέλος τὸ περιέχον τὸν τῆς ἑκάστου ζωῆς χρόνον οὗ μηδὲν ἔξω κατὰ φύσιν αἰὼν ἑκάστου κέκληται, says the Aristotelian *De Caelo*[6] later. We have seen that the fundamental meaning of τέλος is not 'end', and that Hesiod relates τέλος to λύσις where there is no possibility of 'end' or 'paying' but τέλος seems to mean something like 'band', 'bond'. Can we explain τέλη λύει thus as originally meaning 'it looses bands', i.e. 'it delivers' and so 'it is advantageous'? Yes. Death and other forms of ill[7] fortune were conceived as bands, τέλη, and λύειν is used in Homer and later of deliverance from such.[8] Thus we can understand how λύει alone could be used with the same force as τέλη λύει but more frequently, e.g. λύει γὰρ ἡμᾶς οὐδὲν οὐδ' ἐπωφελεῖ...θανεῖν (Soph. *Electra*, 1005 f.), φημὶ τοιούτους γάμους/λύειν βροτοῖσι (Eurip. *Alcestis*, 627 f.), etc. What is the Latin for 'it profits, is advantageous'? *Expedit*, meaning originally just this, 'it unfetters, frees from fetters'. So, as we have seen,[9] Horace says: *non mortis laqueis expedies caput*. Attempts are currently[10] made to explain the Latin noun meaning 'advantage, profit', *lucrum* (*lucrum facere*, etc.) by way of ληΐζομαι, λεία, or ἀπολαύω, etc.; but it has the same relation to *luo*, 'I loose' as *inuolucrum* to *inuoluo*,[11] *simulacrum*

---

[1] Bacchyl. 1, 43.

[2] Eur. *Iph. Taur.* 692. See also the 'crown of life' (pp. 367, 453).

[3] *Hamlet*, III, 1, 64. Cf. ἐκτολυπεύω (pp. 364 f., 387 f.) and 'Mine age (*dor*) is removed and is carried away from me as a shepherd's tent: I have rolled up like a weaver my life' (Isai. xxxviii, 12). *dor* 'lifetime' originally = 'circle' (cf. pp. 367, 429, n. 1, 442 ff., 451 f.).

[4] P. 459.   [5] See pp. 347 ff., 411 ff., 443 ff.   [6] 279 a, 25.

[7] For man's sense of being bound, his feeling of evil around him rather than good, see pp. 365 f. In these idioms advantage is release from evil rather than something positive.

[8] See pp. 363 ff., 384 f., 441.   [9] P. 374.

[10] See e.g. Ernout and Meillet, *op. cit.*; Walde, *op. cit.* s.v. and F. Muller, *Altital. Wörterbuch*, s.v. *lutlom*.

[11] Or, to follow the convention I have used elsewhere for the benefit of non-classical readers, *involucrum*, *involvo*. Cf. *dissolüenda* on p. 385.

to *simulo*, etc., and we may now realise that it goes back to just this idea of 'loosing', and originally meant 'that which looses'. This thought will explain why in Plautus one who has previously been normally prosperous and has just made a profitable transaction, bringing him money, refers to it by saying 'I have disentangled (or "loosed") my *res* (*explicavi meam rem*) *lucro*',[1] and will throw light upon some of the most fundamental terms in Roman law. The man under obligation for debt was described as 'bound' (*nexus*), e.g. *liber qui suas*

---

[1] *Poen.* 750. It occurs to me that the opposite of *lucrum*: *damnum* (e.g. Plaut. *Capt.* 327) may be related to δέω, κρήδεμνον, 'head-band'; Sanscr. *dāman* 'bond', and, perhaps, Latin *redimio* 'bind'; and in origin meant 'binding' and, according to the thought traced, restriction, ill-fortune. He who inflicts it 'gives *damnum*' to the other, and undoes it by 'loosing', 'unloosing' it. Thus time and again in old Latin. E.g. *si quid redemptoris opera domino damni datum erit, resolvito* (Cato, *Agr.* 144, 3; cf. 145, 3; 149, 2). Cf. Tacitus, *Ann.* II, 26 and, perhaps, with point hitherto obscured Lucan I, 106. For the verb *damno* compare ἐπιτιθέναι of imposing a penalty with pp. 378 ff. above and 'lay on' etc. in the Gaelic instances on pp. 357 f. Its reverse also is 'I loose', i.e. *absolvo* ('acquit', cf. p. 440). *damno* sometimes appears to have a sense like *obligo*. See e.g. Virgil, *Ecl.* v, 80: *damnabis tu quoque votis* with *obligatos* and *alligabis* in Servius, and Hor. *Od.* II, 7, 17; 8, 5 f.; IV, 2, 54; *Sat.* II, 3, 85 f. (*damnati*= *obligati*; cf. Ov. *Tr.* I, 2, 83) with p. 457, n. 3, and *votum solvere* (p. 439). Cf. later *arta legis catena damnati* (Fulg. *Aet. Mund.* p. 134) and Hebrew *eşar* 'decree', 'vow', lit. 'bond' (cf. Acts xx, 22), also *lex*, if from √*lig* (cf. *Aen.* VII, 203; XII, 30). Current theories have been reviewed thus: 'Quoi qu'on en dise parfois, aucun rapport n'est senti en latin entre *damnum* et *dare*. L'expression *damnum dare* n'est pas une figure étymologique: le sens est «causer un dommage»...il est donc impossible d'appuyer sur les sens et emplois attestés à date historique un rapport entre *do* et *damnum*. On a rapproché gr. δάπτω «je partage», δαπάνη «dépense», δαψιλής «généreux». Le rapprochement avec *daps*, souvent proposé, est indémontrable' (Ernout and Meillet, *op. cit.* s.v.).

δάμνημι, δαμάω; *domo*; Sanscr. *dam* etc.; applied to 'subduing', also, I suggest, originally had the meaning 'bind'. Old Irish used *damnaim* 'I bind' also (*a*) as 'I subdue' and (*b*) as 'I condemn', while in German 'to subdue' is *bändigen*. *Vinco*, I suggest, is similarly related to *vincio*. Cf. *condo* and *condio* etc., *vinciturum* (Petron. 45) = *victurum* (cf. p. 450, n. 1) and, for *vici* etc., the compound of *vincio*: *cervicis* etc. Attempts are currently made (see Walde, also Ernout and Meillet s.v.) to explain *vinco* as identical with Anglo-Saxon *wig*- 'to fight', old Irish *fichim* 'I fight' etc.; and, for the idea of 'mastering', compounds (*ubarwehan* etc.) are adduced, but there, unfortunately, it is the *prefix* which makes the difference (cf. *debellare*). Subjugation was naturally conceived as 'binding' (pp. 353 ff., 371).

operas inservitu te pro pecunia quadam debebat, dum solveret, nexus vocabatur (Varro, *Ling. L.* VII, 105), and property held subject to obligation was *nexum*.[1] There was restriction upon him or it, a 'bond', *nexus* (cf. *obligatio est iuris vinculum quo necessitate adstringimur*, etc., Justinian, *Instit. Pr. de Oblig.* III, 13), in which he or his *res* was entangled. When he paid he was said to 'loose' (*luo, solvo*) himself or his *res*. Hence the common uses of *solvo* in respect of payments. We still use 'lien' and 'bond'[2] (cf. p. 457, n. 3, and Hesych. ὑποδέσματα, ὑποδέσμιος, ὑποδῆσαι). The doomed man was *fatis debitus* or, as we have seen, 'bound'.

Among the ancient Hindoos to be released from evils was to be loosed from bonds.[3] For them too a debt was a bond. Thus in the *Atharva Veda* a formula 'to set free from debt' runs: 'What I eat that is borrowed, that is not given back; with what tribute of Yama I go about—now, O Agni, I become guiltless as to that; thou knowest how to unfasten all fetters',[4] and a formula 'for relief from guilt or obligation' (VI, 119): 'I make it known to Vaiçvanara, if there is on my part promise of debt to the deities; he knows how to unfasten all bonds'. Quite clearly also in evidence already quoted[5] they conceived sin as a bond with which the sinner was bound. This thought will explain the Romans' use of *luo*, 'I loose' (*noxam, stuprum*, etc.), of atoning for an offence. The offence was a bond 'loosed' by undoing the harm done or by the offender suffering like harm, as the 'bond' of debt was 'loosed' by payment (cf. *luella, poena* = ποινή). We can thus also better understand *religio*, their sense of a mystic 'binding'[6] from this or that. E.g. after

---

[1] Cf. the concrete bonds used by Celts (p. 358) and *religio*, etc. below.

[2] So the defaulter: *adde Cicutae/nodosi tabulas centum, mille adde catenas:/effugiet tamen haec sceleratus vincula Proteus* (Hor. *Sat.* II, 3, 69 ff.).

[3] See pp. 358 ff. above.   [4] VI, 117 (trans. Whitney).

[5] Pp. 359 f. See also Bergaigne, *op. cit.* III, pp. 157 ff. and cf. the Biblical 'His own iniquities shall take the wicked and he shall be holden with the cords (*hebhel*) of his sin' (Prov. v, 22; cf. Is. v, 18; lviii, 6; Acts viii, 23).

[6] That this was the root idea is suggested by *religare*. Cf. p. 372, n. 2. More important, this will best explain the uses, e.g. with *obstringo* and *solvo* as cited, or Cicero's *religione impediri* (*Verr. II*, IV, 122; *ad Fam.* IV, 12), *religione se implicare* (*de Domo S. ad Pont.*, XL, 105), *religione obligare* (XLI, 106), *religione religare* (XLVII, 124). With his *qui autem omnia quae ad cultum*

the capture of Veii, according to Livy, Camillus said that he
had vowed a tenth of the booty to Apollo. The booty was,
however, all held by the people. Thus there was a *religio* upon
them. The pontiffs 'were of opinion that the people must be
loosed from the *religio*' (*pontifices solvendum religione populum
censerent*), so it was decided that everyone 'who wanted to loose
(*exsolvere*) himself and his house from the *religio*' should hand
over one tenth of his share (Livy, V, 23. Cf. XL, 29, etc.; *nulla
mendacii religione obstrictus*, Caes. *B.C.* I, 11, etc. and ὅρκος p. 457,
n. 3). Here *religio* seems to refer to the objective bond. The
latter was felt subjectively and with advancing rationalism this
aspect prevailed.[1] Lucretius claims *artis religionum animum nodis
exsolvere*, I, 931 f., IV, 6 f., and fears that Memmius may be
religione refrenatus (V, 114). This sense of a binding is also a
sense of powers that bind and so became 'religion'. In our
own land for Britons and Angles and Saxons in Christian
times sin and debt were bonds. Thus Gildas: *immanium
peccatorum funibus compediti* (*De Exc. Brit.* 109). Cynewulf
wrote[2] that he had been *synnum asaeled* 'fettered by sins' but
God *bancofan onband* 'unbound my body.' Thus too in the York
Bidding Prayer in the Layfolks Mass Book we read 'We sal
pray...for all þaes þat er bun in dette or in dedely syn', and
later 'A synnar bund with the band of syn...is oblissit to thole
pain for his syn'.[3] So Dante, *Purg.* XVI, 24, XXIII, 15. Still in the
Book of Common Prayer: 'O Lord, we beseech Thee, absolve

---

*deorum pertinerent diligenter retractarent et tanquam relegerent, sunt dicti religio-
si ex relegendo* (*de Nat. D.* II, 28, 72) cf. *superstitiosi* from *superstites* (*ibid.*).

[1] *superstitio* I would explain, by similar development, as in origin describing the action of an external power standing over, dominating one.
Cf. Lucr. I, 65 with Serv. *ad Aen.* XII, 817. ἐφίσταμαι was used of κῆρες
(p. 399; cf. pp. 402, 405, n. 8, 430 f.) or of supernatural messengers above
one's head (see e.g. pp. 102 f.). Cf. 'obsession' from *obsessio* (mediaev.) by
such a power (demon, etc.). Subjection to such a power will explain the
early use; *superstitiosus* meant a prophet, one liable to be possessed, with
knowledge beyond that of ordinary mortals (e.g. Plaut. *Amph.* 323, *Curc.*
397, *Ru.* 1139). Ennius' Cassandra says *missa sum superstitiosis ariolationibus,/
namque Apollo fatis fandis dementem...ciet* (42 f. Ribb.; cf. *Trag. Inc.* 19 Ribb.).
Pacuvius seems to balance *superstitio* with frenzy (*vecors*, 216, Ribb.). Cf.
Aen. VI, 78 ff., 100 f.

[2] *El.* 1244 ff. See p. 439, n. 5, but the idea would be natural to these
peoples. See pp. 353 ff., 381, 457, n. 3.   [3] Archb. Hamilton, *Catech.* 263.

thy people from their offences; that through thy bountiful goodness we may all be delivered from the bonds of those sins which by our frailty we have committed'.[1] He who has not loosed himself or been loosed still carries his bond till death. The thought appears vividly in *The Divine Providence* of Swedenborg: 'He who has introduced himself more intimately and deeply into the communities of hell [sc. by willing and doing evil] becomes as it were bound with cords; but so long as he lives in the world he does not feel these bonds; they are like soft wool or smooth threads of silk which are pleasant to the touch; but after death these bonds instead of being soft and pleasant become hard and galling'.[2] Finally among the Greeks themselves just as other evils were bonds from which one might be loosed, so debt and sin. Hesiod[3] speaks of the 'loosing of debts' (χρειῶν λύσις), and later we find λύω μισθόν implying not mere paying over but the 'loosing', removal, of an obligation (cf. *solvo, luo*); and thus we can understand, as with *luo* above, why a sin or hurt done is said to be 'loosed' by the sinner undoing it or suffering the like or paying a price, e.g. λύσων ὅσ' ἐξήμαρτον ἐν τῷ πρὶν χρόνῳ (Soph. *Phil.* 1224), φόνῳ φόνον πάλιν λύοντας (*Oed. Rex*, 100f.; cf. Eurip. *Orestes*, 510f.). The λύτρον[4] is often a sacrifice. In Plato's day 'prophets' professed not only for slight cost to inflict calamity upon others by incantations and 'bindings' (καταδέσμοις), persuading the gods to do their will (i.e., apparently, by sympathetic magic making the gods bind the victim with evil fortune; cf. pp. 345 ff., 387 ff.), but also to 'loose and cleanse men from their sins' (λύσεις τε καὶ καθαρμοὶ ἀδικημάτων) during life and also after death by sacrifices and rites 'which loose us from the evils yonder'[5] (i.e.

---

[1] Coll. for the 24th Sun. after Trin.   [2] § 296.   [3] *W. and D.* 404.
[4] Aesch. *Choeph.* 48. See also *lustrum* and *delubrum* in Addendum x, p. 510.
[5] *Republic*, 364 cff. Cf. *Phaedr.* 244 D; also pp. 363 ff. above and the Orphic fragment preserved by Olympiodorus (*in Plat. Phaed.* II, 11, p. 87, 13 ff., Norv.= Fr. 232, Kern), ὅτι ὁ Διόνυσος λύσεώς ἐστιν αἴτιος· διὸ καὶ Λυσεὺς ὁ θεός, καὶ ὁ Ὀρφεύς φησιν...

ὄργιά τ' ἐκτελέσουσι λύσιν προγόνων ἀθεμίστων
μαιόμενοι· σὺ δὲ τοῖσιν ἔχων κράτος, οὕς κ' ἐθέλῃσθα
λύσεις ἔκ τε πόνων χαλεπῶν καὶ ἀπείρονος οἴστρου.

He 'looses the cord of the μέριμναι hard to bear' (see p. 405).

in the world of the dead, αἳ τῶν ἐκεῖ κακῶν ἀπολύουσιν ἡμᾶς).
Thus Christian priests claimed the power *supra mundum alligandi cum in mundo reos alligaverint et solvendi cum paenitentes solverint.*[1] Later in the *Republic* Plato represents the dead as judged on entrance to the other world and the righteous passing on 'with symbols of the fate adjudged them fastened about them in front, the wicked with symbols of their deeds [fastened] behind' (σημεῖα περιάψαντας τῶν δεδικασμένων ἐν τῷ ἔμπροσθεν, τοὺς δὲ ἀδίκους...ἔχοντας καὶ τούτους ἐν τῷ ὄπισθεν σημεῖα πάντων ὧν ἔπραξαν).[2] Pythagoreans of apparently the same date taught that the fate of unpurified souls was 'to be bound in unbreakable bonds by the Erinyes' (δεῖσθαι ἐν ἀρρήκτοις δεσμοῖς ὑπὸ 'Ερινύων).[3]

The usages already quoted suggest that τέλος originally meant something like 'band'. τελαμών, 'band' or 'bandage', is usually related to τλάω, 'I endure' or 'dare', which however scarcely fits 'bandage'. Apart from this, however, and its own derivatives, the Greek words nearest in form to τέλος, to which one might therefore naturally look for a clue as to its origin, are τέλλω (and its cousin πέλομαι), of which the basic idea appears to be that of 'turning', 'circling', and τέλσον, the edge or boundary of a ploughland, apparently as the place where one *turns round* in ploughing (cf. δινεύοντες...στρέψαντες...στρέψασκον of the τέλσον, *Il.* xviii, 544 ff., Latin *versura* and Hesych. τέλσας· στροφάς, τέλη, πέρατα). Philologists, we saw, finding no connection between the meanings, have concluded that there are three originally distinct words of the form τέλος. An attempt has been made to explain the τέλος which means 'end' as the 'place where one makes a half-turn in the race or in ploughing' (see Boisacq, *loc. cit.*) and so the 'end, limit'. But neither the uses already discussed nor that of the Homeric passages about to be discussed in which τέλος

---

[1] Gildas, *op. cit.* p. 32. Cf. p. 405, Matt. xvi, 19, John xx, 23, Rev. i, 5, p. 363 above.

[2] 614 c. Cf. *Ol.* xiii, 38 f. (p. 376) and *Od.* viii, 244 f. (p. 380). Perhaps to be related is the fable in Phaedr. iv, 10; Horace, *Sat.* ii, 3, 299, etc.

[3] Quoted by Diogenes Laertius (viii, 31) from Alexander Polyhistor.

means something like 'fulfilment' (e.g. ἐπ' ἀρῇσι τέλος ἡμετέρῃσι γένοιτο, *Od.* XVII, 496) naturally arise out of 'the place
at which one turns'. Instead I would suggest that with
this root notion of 'turning round' τέλος meant 'circling' or
'circle' (cf. στροφή, στροφάς, etc., and σπεῖρον), which sense
is to be seen in the cognate πόλος and περιπλομένου δ'
ἐνιαυτοῦ, περιτελλομένων ἐνιαυτῶν, which imply the 'circle of
the year' (ἐνιαυτοῦ κύκλον, Eurip. *Orestes*, 1645; *Phoen.* 477;
τὸν ἐνιαύσιον κύκλον, *Phoen.* 544; ἑπτά...καρπίμους ἐτῶν
κύκλους, *Hel.* 112; τὸν στέφανον τοῦ ἐνιαυτοῦ,[1] etc. Cf. Latin
annus with *anulus*, etc.), perhaps also in Homer's τελεσφόρον
εἰς ἐνιαυτόν, i.e. 'circle-bearing year'[2] (cf. τοξοφόρος, πυρο-
φόρος, also κυκλοφόρος, etc.), so complete year. Thus, too,
when Hesiod[3] speaks of 'Ὠκεανός as τελήεις ποταμός it will
mean not the 'perfect river' or the 'river in which all others
end' but the 'circling river' which Liddell and Scott recognise to be the meaning, though they can arrive[4] only by
way of 'ending in itself', which τελήεις could scarcely express.
'Circling' is the meaning of the Semitic word which the Greeks
made into 'Ὠκεανός.[5] Compare also 'Ὠκεανοῦ κύκλος above.[6]

If τέλος thus meant 'circle', 'band', we can also explain its
use to designate a body of men; which τέλος has been treated
as a distinct word related to Sanscrit *kula-m*, 'herd' (see
Boisacq, *loc. cit.*). We may instead compare our use of 'band',
'circle', 'ring', 'knot', etc., German *Bund*, Hebrew *ḥebhel*
('cord', 'band',[7] and so 'band', 'company' of men, I Sam.

[1] See Brightman, *Liturgies Eastern and Western*, p. 127. With περιπλομένου
δ' ἐνιαυτοῦ compare περιπλομένοιο κύκλοιο, Emped. B 26, 1, Diels, with
pp. 451 ff. below. See also Hermipp. (Fr. 4 Kock, Stob. *Phys.* 1, 8, 36).

[2] 'Fulfilment-bringing' has little point when e.g. Thetis says: 'even if
he [the dead Patroklos] lies for a τελεσφόρος ἐνιαυτός, his flesh will ever
be firm or even better' (*Il.* XIX, 32 f.; cf. *Od.* IV, 86, X, 467, XIV, 292,
XV, 230). The sense demanded by the various contexts is rather that of
a complete year—'full circle'. See also below, p. 447.   [3] *Theog.* 242, 959.

[4] They are no more happy about τελεσφόρος: '*bringing to an end*; used
by Homer always in phrase τελεσφόρον εἰς ἐνιαυτόν for the space of a
year's *accomplishing its round*, for a *complete* year'.   [5] See pp. 249f.

[6] Pp. 249f., 316. Here too Homer might instead use πεῖραρ.

[7] Cf. pp. 367, 437, n. 3, 439, n. 5; *ṣephirah*, 'circle', 'diadem', 'fate'
(Ezek. vii, 7, 10).

444

TΕΛΟΣ

x, 5, 10; Ps. cxix, 61, cf. ᵃ*guddah*). That an assembly of men
was conceived in some such way is shown by Homer's expression for its breaking up; it is 'loosed' (λῦσαν δ' ἀγορήν,
λῦτο δ' ἀγών, etc.). Homer uses τέλος thus: ἐλθεῖν ἐς φυλάκων
ἱερὸν τέλος, *Il.* x, 56; δόρπον ἔπειθ' ἑλόμεσθα κατὰ στρατὸν ἐν
τελέεσσι, *Il.* xi, 730. It is unnecessary, if τέλος signified 'circle'
or 'band' thus, that it should always refer to a geometrical
'circle', any more than the English word (cf. *circulus*). But the
early Greeks, when they assembled, did form into a 'circle'.
When Menelaos was wounded, περὶ δ' αὐτὸν ἀγηγέραθ'
ὅσσοι ἄριστοι/κυκλόσε (*Il.* IV, 211 f.). And a circle appears
to have been the ritually desirable form for a gathering.
When they assembled in peace οἱ δὲ γέροντες/ἥατ' ἐπὶ ξεσ-
τοῖσι λίθοις ἱερῷ ἐνὶ κύκλῳ, *Il.* xviii, 503 f. Cf. κυκλόεντ'
ἀγορᾶς θρόνον, Soph. *Oed. Rex*, 161; ἀγορᾶς...κύκλον, Eurip.
Orestes, 919, etc., also the circular form of the πρυτανεῖον or
θόλος.[1]

If it thus meant 'circle', τέλος when used of a phase of
fortune, while conceived thus visually as a circle or band about
a man, yet represented a portion of time and was experienced
as a process or an event by the person upon whom it was placed.
It was apparently, like πεῖραρ, the fate spun; the different
'bands' or 'circles' were different portions of life and so of
time.[2] The band, circle, itself naturally symbolic of completeness and continuity,[3] would represent the complete phase of
fortune. We have seen[4] that just as 'victory', 'liberty', and the
various other phases of fortune were bands fastened upon men

[1] πόλις itself, one might suggest, originally connoted 'ring-wall'. Cf.
πόλος and τὸν Ἀθηνέων κύκλον (Herodot. I, 98, Thuc. II, 13, VI, 99, etc.),
στέφανος (Pind. *Ol.* VIII, 32, Anacr. 72), etc. for 'city'. *urbs* too perhaps
in origin expressed 'circle' as *orbis*. For the vowels cf. *orca, urceus*. 'Town'
originally connoted a surrounding fence (cf. Germ. *Zaun*).
[2] See pp. 347ff., 411ff., 436.
[3] διὰ τέλους, διατελέω, etc., imply for τέλος the complete process, not
merely the 'end'.
[4] Pp. 375ff. The putting of a band about one as a symbol of his
fortune is perhaps the origin also of our northern custom (cf. pp. 353ff.)
whereby the champion, the victor, receives a belt, 'holds the belt'. See
also pp. 448, n. 5, 455, n. 6.

by god or μοῖρα, etc., so the band, the 'crown' or 'circle'[1] that was put upon the head of the victor in the games, etc., was conceived by Pindar and Simonides as itself the 'deed' or 'victory'. But Pindar seems to speak of this crown as τέλος. In the first Isthmian he says that Kastor and Iolaos were often victorious in the games, the races with and those without armour and the hurling of the spear and of the discus: 'For there was no pentathlum then but for each several feat there was its τέλος; with the twigs whereof often binding their hair, etc. (ἐφ' ἑκάστῳ ἔργματι κεῖτο τέλος· τῶν ἀθρόοις ἀνδησάμενοι θαμάκις ἔρνεσιν χαίτας κ.τ.λ.)'.[2] Here Farnell translates: 'But each several feat had its own issue of victory determined for itself', and comments: 'Again we may note the signs of hurry in the prosaic form of the statement'; but Fennell and Bury see that τέλος must in some way mean the prize and the scholia say τέλος δὲ λέγει τὸ νικοφορῆσαι ἢ τὸν ἐφ' ἑκάστῳ τιθέμενον στέφανον...ἐφ' ἑκάστῳ ἀγωνίσματι καὶ ὁ στέφανος ἦν...τὸ δὲ κεῖτο τέλος ἀντὶ τοῦ ἦν ἰδιάζων καὶ ὁ στέφανος. Again, in the tenth Olympian, Pindar asks 'Who was it then who received the fresh crown (ποταίνιον ἔλαχε στέφανον) with hands and feet and chariot?...Oionos, son of Likymnios, was best in running a straight course with his feet and Echemos it was who gave glory to Tegea by wrestling and Doryklos carried off the τέλος of boxing (Δόρυκλος δ' ἔφερε πυγμᾶς τέλος)',[3] where Farnell renders 'was triumphant in the issue of boxing'. In both these passages it is natural to take τέλος of the crown, which, exactly as the invisible band or circle given by the gods, represented the particular deed or fortune and expressed its fulfilment.

For Pindar the ceremony at the games was τελετή,[4] the action described by the verb τελέειν, the putting on of the τέλος.[5]

---

[1] In *Orph. Arg.* 325 wreaths are referred to as κύκλοι, cf. *circulus* and *terque focum circa laneus orbis eat*, Prop. IV, 6, 6, etc. We have seen (p. 336) that Euripides preserves the conception of fate as embodied in στέμματα. This thought may perhaps also explain a little later in the same play:
κύκλῳ γὰρ εἰλιχθεῖσαν ἀθλίοις κακοῖς
οὐπώποτ' ἄλλην μᾶλλον εἶδον ἑστίαν. (*Orestes*, 358 f.)

[2] *Isth.* I, 26 ff. [3] *Ol.* x, 60 ff.
[4] *Ol.* x, 51; *Pyth.* IX, 97; *Nem.* x, 34. [5] See p. 461.

The thought traced will perhaps also throw light on the use of τέλος, τελέειν, τελετή in connection with the mysteries. The τέλος was not given to the god nor was it, as usually explained, a 'making perfect' of the initiate which would be τελείωσις. It was analogous to the τέλος of marriage (pp. 431 f.)— alike the person married[1] and the person initiated[2] were said τελεῖσθαι—but that, as we have seen,[3] in Homer was analogous to the τέλος of war, the τέλος of old age, etc., received by human beings. It was, we might thus infer, a new state, a new fate received, embodied in a band or wrapping fastened around or covering the recipient. In fact in the classical period the person married and the person initiated alike received such a band or wrapping,[4] and it should according to our earlier

---

[1] E.g. in an inscription of Cos (Paton, 386).

[2] E.g. Demosth. De Cor. § 265.   [3] Pp. 431 ff.

[4] To wrap the head was to invest the ψυχή (pp. 133 f., 144 f.) with a new fate. That which went round a person might merely bind or might cover him (cf. μίτρα, κρήδεμνον, etc., and p. 420). If the band or covering (see p. 274, μύστης, etc.) were thus originally the τέλος, it will explain such later uses of τελέειν as, in the prescription of a magical papyrus: 'Be in clean linen, covered with an olive-crown and make the πέτασος thus: take clean linen and write on its side the 365 gods and make it as a covering (or "canopy"); go beneath it for τέλος' (ποίησον ὡς καλύβην ὑφ' ἣν ἴθι τελούμενος, Pap. Gr. Mag. Vol. II, XIII, pp. 96 ff., Preis. Thus perhaps the 'witch's hat', Paus. v, 27, 6 etc.); or the account of Perseus slaying Medusa in Joannes Malalas (Chron. II, 35, Mig.): Perseus'cut off her head and taking it he immediately ἐτέλεσε τὴν κάραν αὐτὴν μυστικῶς'. The traditional story, which is apparently thus interpreted, was merely that he immediately covered the head, wrapped it up (e.g. in the 'Shield of Herakles', 224 f., ἀμφὶ δέ μιν κίβισις θέε θαῦμα ἰδέσθαι. Cf. the story of the Korybantes or Kabeiroi on p. 101 above, perhaps the αἰτία for procedure in their mysteries). In late Greek also τέλεσμα was something 'loosed' (see Ducange, and Manetho, 5, 128, Andreas Cret. in S. Palaioph. 206 B). If τέλος were originally the band or covering, it might explain references to the initiation as τελεσφορία and to the initiate as τελεσφόρος (cf. στεφανηφόρος, etc., and Homer's use of τελεσφόρος, p. 443 above) and perhaps also the name of the healing god, worshipped in Asia Minor, Τελεσφόρος (cf. Μιτρηφόρος, a name of Dionysos, Diod. IV, 4, 4), whose appearance was unique. He was represented almost completely enveloped in a garment with a cowl or hood over his head, a covering, possibly, similar to that originally put on by worshippers as the τέλος, the new state which they wished to be theirs. This form of covering may have been Thracian—it is suited to cold weather. It is perhaps that Thracian covering elsewhere called ζειρά, which Herodotus (VII, 75) and Xenophon (Anab. VII, 4, 3 f.)

argument[1] represent and confer the new state, a new fate. In Homer the maiden is distinguished by a particular form of band, the παρθενίη ζώνη, which is 'loosed' at marriage,[2] and on her wedding day Andromache received another band, a 'head-band', κρήδεμνον, from the goddess of love herself,[3] Aphrodite, who carried her peculiar properties about in the form of a band, the κεστὸς ἱμάς, and passed them on to others in that form.[4] Among the Romans a maiden was distinguished by one form of 'fillet' (*vitta*), the bride or married woman by another.[5] To such bands there is no lack of parallels. Thus 'the Semangs and Senoi of the Malaccan forests are invested with the head-fillet by the medicine-man who exchanges it for another at particularly important turning-points of life, such, for example, as the entrance of the youth into manhood or of the woman upon marriage. If the woman be widowed, her

---

imply enveloped the body to the feet and perhaps also the head. *Gloss. Herod.* explains it as μίτρα, ταινία, διάδημα, ἱμάτιον, ζώνη, πορφυροῦν ἔνδυμα. In the light of pp. 426 ff. above we may perhaps understand why Hades is called ζειροφόρος by Antimachos (Fr. 88, Kinkel). Cf. Yama on pp. 358 ff., also pp. 323, 361, n. 2.

[1] E.g. pp. 331, 375 ff.

[2] *Od.* XI, 245. Cf. Suidas, s.v. λυσίζωνος. It was apparently not put on till the marriageable state was reached (see Callim. *Hymn to Artem.* 14). Cf. the thought in *Ekkeh.* and Malory on p. 367, n. 3.

[3] *Il.* XXII, 470 ff. In Homer women who wear the κρήδεμνον are married with the possible exception of the δμῶαι who accompany Nausikaa. If they count as maidens, possibly as in Rome a different form of 'head-band' was put on at marriage. Mystical correspondence between the head-band and the fortune or state of the wearer we may illustrate by a legend in Uhland's *Balladen und Romanzen*, 'Der Kranz': 'Es pflückte Blümlein manigfalt', in which a wreath, bound by a fairy or Fate about a maiden's head, buds in her virginity, blossoms at wedlock, bears fruit when she becomes a mother, and fades when she is a widow.

[4] See p. 368.

[5] *virgineae vittae*, Virg. *Aen.* II, 168; Val. Flac. VIII, 6; and for the *vitta* of marriage, Prop. IV (v), 11, 34 *altera vitta* and 3, 15; Plaut. *Mil. Glor.* 791 f.; Tib. I, 6, 67; Ovid, *ex Pont.* III, 3, 51, *Ars Am.* I, 31, *Trist.* II, 247 and 252, *Rem. Am.* 386. The same thought might appear when the wrapping was wide, a garment (see pp. 360 f.). The Romans had their *toga virilis* as opposed to the *praetexta*, etc., whence e.g. *condicio* (i.e. social rank) *quae vestis modo nobis circumdata est* (Sen. *Ep. Mor.* XLVII, 16). Cf. *munia* (functions, office) *ducis induere* (Tac. *Ann.* I, 69, 2), *seditionem induere* (II, 15), *exuere fidem, amicitiam*, etc.; also Juv. VI, 519 ff. cited on p. 359.

former fillet is placed upon her head [i.e. instead of the marriage fillet]. This signifies the annulment of the magical union that existed throughout the period of marriage'[1] (rather, I suggest, annulment of the marriage condition and potency, then a reinvesting with the other). 'The Krens maiden wears a band round her knees and on marriage exchanges it for a head-band',[2] i.e. a kind of παρθενίη ζώνη for a κρήδεμνον. In Java divorce is effected by the priest's cutting of the 'marriage cord'.[3] 'The Snood was a ribband with which a Scotch lass braided her hair, and which was the emblem of her maiden character. When she married, she changed the snood for the curch or coif; but if she lost the name of virgin before she obtained that of wife she "lost her silken snood" and was not privileged to assume the curch.'[4] Among primitive peoples such outward trappings are no mere symbols but rather vehicles of magic power endowing the wearer with the attributes proper to his class.[5] Indeed the belief and the mode of thought behind the putting on of these various 'bands' are exactly those seen above[6] in magic. They are here pressed into

[1] Wundt, *op. cit.* p. 89.

[2] See Ploss, *Das Kind*, ii, p. 70. Is this the meaning on the Mycenaean ring (*J.H.S.* (1901), fig. 51)?

[3] See Crawley, *Mystic Rose*[1], p. 323.

[4] Brewer, *Dictionary of Phrase and Fable*, s.v. Snood. Cf. Scott, *The Lady of the Lake*, iii, 5; *The Heart of Midlothian*, xxii, *init.* etc.

[5] Sometimes it was also physically useful, e.g. the 'belt' of the earl or knight (see p. 455, n. 6). Clothes probably have a similar history. If or where man began to wrap such about him first in a warm climate, he probably attributed to the wrapping some magical effect, not merely decoration or the protection of his body from the weather or blows. Skins (see p. 235, n. 4) would precede woven cloth. Aprons of fig-leaves (Gen. iii, 7, cf. p. 109, n. 4) and the like would first be worn not from motives of decency but in respect for the power in the sexual organs (cf. pp. 109, n. 2; 153, nn. 1, 2; 234, n. 9), which explains also their exposure in magic, e.g. by ancient Irish (cf. pp. 156 f.) and Arab women in the face of an enemy army (*Táin Bó Cú.* trans. Dunn, pp. 77 f., Well-hausen, *R. arab. Heid.*[2], pp. 159 f., 195 f.) and their representation as amulets (*fascinum*, etc.) and in apotropaic gestures.

[6] Pp. 353 ff. A ring is merely one form of such bands. Thus a ring was given by Morgue la Faye to Ogier the Dane endowing him with youth just as in the same romance Papillon was to have 'la couronne de joye de laquelle ils usoient en faerie' (cf. Ogier's own crown, the putting on

the service of the social organisation. With advancing civilisation the charm passes into the mere symbol or badge.

To return to the mystic τέλος, in the *Clouds*[1] of Aristophanes there is a well-known parody of initiation. Strepsiades has come to Socrates to be initiated into the mystery of the φροντιστήριον, to become an adept in tricky speech.

Socrates. Now take this crown.

Strepsiades. A crown—what for? Goodness! Socrates, don't sacrifice me like Athamas.

---

of which changed his state and made him completely forget his past). And thus we can understand the wedding ring itself, put on to 'change the state' of a person. In *The Doctrine of the Masse Booke*, from Wittonburge, by Nicholas Dorcastor, 1554, the ring is spoken of thus: 'Halow thou, Lord, this ring, which we bless in thy holye Name, that what woman soever shall weare it, may stand fast in thy peace and continue in thy wyl, and live and grow and waxe old in thy love and be multiplied into that length of daies, thorow our Lord, etc. Then let holy water be sprinkled upon the ryng' (see Brand's *Popular Antiq.*, rev. Ellis, ed. Bohn, Vol. II, p. 106). It is still the instrument of the change of state. Thus at the climax of the English rite the man puts the ring upon the woman's finger and, holding it there, says: 'With this Ring I thee wed, with my body I thee worship, and with all my worldly goods I thee endow: In the Name of the Father, and of the Son, and of the Holy Ghost. Amen'. This band was put upon the finger originally perhaps not merely because it was most convenient there, but also because, as we see (pp. 97, n. 10, 177, 198, n. 1, 226, n. 1, 477, n. 2, 478, n. 2), the *hand* had peculiar sanctity. For binding of the hand see also pp. 135, 226, n. 1, 453 f. According to Aulus Gellius (x, 10) the Greeks and Romans wore a ring on the fourth finger of the left hand, and Apion explained that from that one finger a thin *nervus* extended to the heart. The Hereford, York, and Salisbury Missals explain that in that finger is a vein going to the heart. Apparently in these the ring was thought to bind the central consciousness (see pp. 23 ff., 79 ff.) as a girdle might or as what was put upon the head was thought to affect the life-soul, the ψυχή or *genius* (see pp. 98 ff., 132 ff.). The 'true-love knot' also was a physical expression of binding in love (see pp. 357, 373, 403). The ring bound the recipient with the new state, the new fate, but the giver, who had it first, might also be bound. We shall see (p. 457, n. 3) that at Rome a promise or oath, an obligation assumed, was embodied in a ring and given. It was *pignus* (p. 375, n. 7). A Roman promising marriage gave a plain iron ring; the woman took it to herself, wore it, an 'engagement ring'. See Juv. VI, 27; Plin. *N.H.* XXXV, 12. A gold ring was the symbol of equestrian rank at Rome. Cicero (*Verr.* II, iii, 176) says *anulum invenit* for *eques factus est.*

[1] 254 ff. Cf. Photius, s.v. νεβρίζειν: ὡς τοῦ τελοῦντος τοὺς τελουμένους τούτῳ καταζωννύντος.

Socrates. No, No. We do all these things to people receiving
τέλος (οὐκ ἀλλὰ ταῦτα πάντα τοὺς τελουμένους ἡμεῖς ποιοῦμεν).
Strepsiades. Then what do I gain by it?
Socrates. You will become a polished speaker, chatterbox.

Thus a στέφανος or στέμμα was put upon the victim to be
sacrificed and rendered it holy;[1] a στέφανος was put upon
the initiate and invested him with his new state, new fate.
A good deal later we are told[2] that initiation consisted of
(1) purification, (2) the passing on of the rite, (3) the
ἐποπτεία, (4) τετάρτη δέ, ὃ δὴ καὶ τέλος τῆς ἐποπτείας, ἀνά-
δεσις καὶ στεμμάτων ἐπίθεσις, and (5) the resultant εὐδαιμονία.
The conscious sense of the word has changed but it is to the
putting on of crowns that τέλος is applied. That the initiation,
like the receiving of the τέλος of marriage, was felt as a
change of fate is clear. Alike in the Athenian marriage
ceremony[3] and in the initiation described by Demosthenes[4]
was used the formula 'Evil have I fled, better have I found
(ἔφυγον κακόν, εὗρον ἄμεινον)'. Sophocles' Oidipous 'blessedly
loosed the τέλος of life'.[5] The dead man in his grave might
claim that he had 'loosed the cords of τύχη from himself'
ὠ[κ]υμόρου τύχης πείσματα λυσάμενος.[6] The initiate is sure of
a happy fate after death. Thus of the initiation at Eleusis the
Homeric Hymn to Demeter says: 'Blessed is he among men
who hath seen these things. But he who is without τέλος of the
rites, who is without a portion, hath not ever share of like fate
though dead beneath the dank gloom':

> ὃς δ' ἀτελὴς ἱερῶν, ὅς τ' ἄμμορος, οὔ ποθ' ὁμοίων
> αἶσαν ἔχει φθίμενός περ ὑπὸ ζόφῳ εὐρώεντι.[7]

In Homer we saw[8] reason to believe that the τέλος, the 'band'

---

[1] So perhaps the oracle ἔστεπται μὲν ὁ ταῦρος, ἔχει τέλος, ἔστιν ὁ θύσων
(Paus. VIII, 7, 6). Cf. pp. 228, n. 1, 236, 456, n. 2. The Romans did the
like and some explained *victima*, perhaps rightly (see p. 438, n. 1), as *quae
vincta adducatur ad altare* (Fest. 508 L.).
[2] Theo Smyrn. *Mathem.* I, p. 18.
[3] See e.g. Suidas, s.v. ἔφυγον referring to an evil wreath.
[4] *De Corona*, § 313.   [5] See p. 436.
[6] See *Bulletin de Corr. Hell.* xxv, p. 327.
[7] 480 ff. Cf. Soph. Fr. 837 on pp. 273 f.
[8] Pp. 320 ff., 426 ff.

or 'circle', might bind either an individual or a multitude as a bond or magic circle affecting all within its periphery. These thoughts will help us to understand the claim of the Orphic (?) initiate on the tablet found in a grave in South Italy: 'I flew forth from the circle¹ of grief and pain. I stepped with swift feet upon the crown desired':²

κύκλο⟨υ⟩ δ' ἐξέπταν βαρυπενθέος ἀργαλέοιο,
ἱμερτο⟨ῦ⟩ δ' ἐπέβαν στεφάνο⟨υ⟩ ποσὶ καρπαλίμοισι.

It is a change of fate thus visualised.

¹ The τέλος was not only conceived visually as a circle around a man but also experienced as a period (cf. περίοδος) of time in which the fate was fulfilled (pp. 429 ff., 444 f.). The latter sense may be seen e.g. in τὸ τέλος τὸ περιέχον τὸν τῆς ἑκάστου ζωῆς χρόνον οὗ μηδὲν ἔξω κατὰ φύσιν αἰὼν ἑκάστου κέκληται (de Caelo, 279 a, 25). Propertius speaks of the life of Marcellus as a 'circle': tot bona tam parvo clausit in orbe dies, III (IV), 18, 16. So Seneca: tota aetas partibus constat et orbes habet circumductos maiores minoribus: est aliquis qui omnis complectatur et cingat; hic pertinet a natali ad diem extremum. est alter qui annos adulescentiae [ex]cludit. est qui totam pueritiam ambitu suo adstringit. est deinde per se annus in se omnia continens tempora quorum multiplicatione vita componitur. mensis artiore praecingitur circulo. angustissimum habet dies gyrum (Ep. Mor. XII, 6). Cf. Hor. Sat. II, 6, 26; Hebrew dor (p. 437, n. 3).

οὕνεκ' ἀμειβομένη ψυχὴ κατὰ κύκλα χρόνοιο
ἀνθρώπων ζώιοισι μετέρχεται ἄλλοθεν ἄλλοις·
ἄλλοτε μέν θ' ἵππος...τότε δ' ὄρνεον αἰνὸν ἰδέσθαι,

says an Orphic fragment (224 b, Kern) concerning the various incarnations, lives of the ψυχή. The belief that portions of time, of fate, were 'circles' would be encouraged by the view that the fate of the world in general was a matter of 'circles', the 'circle of the year', etc. (see p. 443). Thus Aristotle: φασὶ γὰρ κύκλον εἶναι τὰ ἀνθρώπινα πράγματα, καὶ τῶν ἄλλων τῶν κίνησιν ἐχόντων φυσικὴν καὶ γένεσιν καὶ φθοράν. τοῦτο δὲ ὅτι ταῦτα πάντα τῷ χρόνῳ κρίνεται καὶ λαμβάνει τελευτὴν καὶ ἀρχὴν ὡσπερανεὶ κατά τινα περίοδον· καὶ γὰρ ὁ χρόνος αὐτὸς εἶναι δοκεῖ κύκλος τις. τοῦτο δὲ πάλιν δοκεῖ διότι τοιαύτης φορᾶς ἐστὶ μέτρον καὶ μετρεῖται αὐτὸς ὑπὸ τοιαύτης (Phys. 223 b, 24 ff.). Fate, time (cf. tempestas, temps, etc.) changed as the circle in the heavens changed. χρόνος was perhaps originally expressive of that which touched one's surface (cf. χραίνω, χράω, χροΐζω, χρώς, etc.), what one experienced (cf. contingo), and perhaps extended to that which touched the surface of the world. Cf. p. 250 and χρόνου περιιόντος, Hdt. II, 121, 2, etc. So Κρόνος from κραίνω.

² Orph. Fr. 32 (c), 6 f. (Kern). The difference of terms perhaps represents the difference between the invisible 'circle' of fate from which the initiate escaped and the visible wreath within which he had placed himself. The tablet continues: 'I passed beneath the bosom of the Lady, the Earth-queen. With swift feet I stepped from (ἀπέβαν) the crown desired. Fortunate and blessed one, thou shalt be a god instead of a

The idea of a man's fate as a circle within which he is bound will help to explain the 'wheel' of Ixion and the sympathetic magic[1] by which a bird ἴυγξ[2] was bound in a 'circle' (wheel) and the 'circle' then turned in the belief that as a result the person intended would be bound and moved with love.

ποικίλαν ἴυγγα τετράκναμον Οὐλυμπόθεν
ἐν ἀλύτῳ ζεύξαισα κύκλῳ
μαινάδ' ὄρνιν Κυπρογένεια φέρεν
πρῶτον ἀνθρώποισι,

says Pindar (*Pyth.* IV, 214 ff.; cf. *Nem.* IV, 35) and describes Ixion's fate—the wheel—for his love of Hera thus:

τὸν δὲ τετράκναμον ἔπραξε δεσμόν
ἑὸν ὄλεθρον ὅγ'· ἐν δ' ἀφύκτοισι γυιοπέδαις πεσὼν τὰν πολύκοινον
ἀνδέξατ' ἀγγελίαν

(*Pyth.* II, 40 f.; cf. the fate of Tityos in relation to his passion pp. 85 f. above). The 'wheel' is a form of bond which moves perforce. We have seen (p. 441, n. 5) that for the Orphics Dionysos was 'the Looser' (Λυσεύς), from whom by rites (ὄργια ἐκτελέσουσι) men sought that he would 'loose their unrighteous forefathers' (λύσιν προγόνων ἀθεμίστων):

σὺ δὲ τοῖσιν ἔχων κράτος, οὕς κ' ἐθέληισθα
λύσεις ἔκ τε πόνων χαλεπῶν καὶ ἀπείρονος οἴστρου.

In these ideas we have also probably the origin of the Orphic conception of the κύκλος (cf. p. 451), the 'circle' or 'wheel', in which a man is bound and suffers undesirable fate. Proclus (*in Plat. Tim.* 42 C, D = Orph. Fr. 229, Kern) tells us that

οἱ παρ' Ὀρφεῖ τῷ Διονύσῳ καὶ τῇ Κόρῃ τελούμενοι τυχεῖν εὔχονται
κύκλου τ' ἂν λῆξαι καὶ ἀναπνεῦσαι κακότητος, (*sic*)

---

mortal'. If ἀπέβαν be correct and it is to the initiation that the claim refers, we must understand that while alive he had in the 'mystery' staked a claim to a happy fate after death by being temporarily, ritually, received into it. Cf. Lucius' claim after initiation into the mysteries of Isis: 'I went to the confines of death and trod the threshold of Proserpine and was borne through all the elements and I came back. I saw the sun shining brightly in the middle of the night. I came to the nether gods and to the supernal gods face to face and I worshipped them at close quarters' (Apul. *Met.* XI, 23). [1] See Theocr. II, Hor. *Epod.* XVII, 7, etc.

[2] The choice may be explained by the fact that the Greeks saw it as σεισοπυγίς and interpreted it sexually (cf. κιναίδιον) as potent to excite another. Cf. old Norse *Friggjar-elda*, a bird identified as the wagtail, lit. 'fire (?) (cf. p. 156) of Frigg', the goddess of love (pp. 475 f.). Cf. English 'to frig' = to wriggle and 'wag-tail' = a wanton woman.

and Simplicius:[1]

ἐνδεθῆναι δὲ ὑπὸ τοῦ τὸ κατ' ἀξίαν πᾶσιν ἀφορίζοντος δημιουργοῦ θεοῦ ἐν τῷ τῆς εἱμαρμένης τε καὶ γενέσεως τροχῷ οὗπερ ἀδύνατον ἀπαλλαγῆναι κατὰ τὸν Ὀρφέα μὴ τοὺς θεοὺς ἐκείνους ἱλεωσάμενον οἷς ἐπέταξεν ὁ Ζεὺς κύκλου τ' ἀλλῆξαι καὶ ἀναψῦξαι κακότητος.

The initiate exchanged the 'circle' for a 'crown'. We have seen[2] that Plato conceived of the souls of the righteous after death as having 'symbols of the fate adjudged them fastened around them'. It may be a survival of this thought that the souls of the blest are elsewhere represented with fillets or garlands,[3] which, as we saw,[4] were on earth the embodiment of a happy fate. Thus Pindar describes them on the flowery Islands of the Blest: 'with strings thereof they entwine their hands and with crowns by the righteous decisions of Rhadamanthys who on the judgment seat...':

ὅρμοισι τῶν χέρας ἀναπλέκοντι καὶ στεφάνοις
βουλαῖς ἐν ὀρθαῖσι 'Ραδαμάνθυος[5]....

---

[1] In [Aristot.] de Caelo, II, 1, 284 a, 14 (= Orph. Fr. 230, Kern). The 'circle' of the individual fate was perhaps not clearly distinguished from the cosmic 'circle'. We have seen (pp. 250 f. and 332) that Ἀνάγκη was conceived of as encircling and binding the world and as the 'mate of Χρόνος', itself conceived as a serpent wound round (ἑλικτός). See Orph. Fr. 54, 58 (Kern) and p. 332 above. The world of γένεσις and of mortal change appeared to be bounded and dominated by the 'circle' of the heavens, identified with the κύκλος ζωδιακός, the solar ecliptic, the κύκλος γαλαξίας or αἰθὴρ σφίγγων περὶ κύκλον ἅπαντα (Emped. B 38, 4, Diels). The ideal and eternal world to which the soul aspires is, as Plato indicates, outside the 'circle'. See Plato, Phaedr. 246 ff. with Procl. in Plat. Tim. 33 B. Cf. Hermetica (ed. W. Scott), I, 8 and 13 f.   [2] Pp. 441 f.

[3] E.g. Virgil, Aen. VI, 665. Not, as Norden explains, 'because they are feasting'. That is incidental to their fate. Cf. Plato, Rep. II, 363 c f. and Aristoph. Frogs, 329 f.

[4] Pp. 375 ff. The mysteries apart, we have seen (p. 367) that this was probably the original meaning of the crown, wreath, or band, put upon the head of the dead. 'Friends used to send ταινίαι for the dead' says the schol. to Aristoph. Lys. 602 ff. Cf. Copa, 35 f., Prop. III, 16, 23, etc. Burial was thought vitally important to the fate of the soul. No less apparently was crowning. Kreon, in his vindictiveness against Polyneikes, proclaims:

ὃς ἂν νεκρὸν τόνδ' ἢ καταστέφων ἁλῷ
ἢ γῇ καλύπτων, θάνατον ἀνταλλάξεται.

Eurip. Phoen. 1632 f.

[5] Ol. II, 74 f. There are variants: στεφάνους and (possibly a gloss) κεφαλάς. Perhaps Pindar wrote not χέρας but γέρας. Cf. lines 48 f. Ὀλυμπίᾳ μὲν γὰρ αὐτὸς /γέρας ἔδεκτο; Pyth. V, 30 f. ἀρισθάρματον... γέρας

They bound, we are told, the right hand and the left foot of initiates with thread. This binding was κροκοῦν.[1] That some such binding was a principal part of the Eleusinian mysteries is shown by the fact that the priestly families administering the rites comprised not only Κήρυκες and Εὐμολπίδαι, descendants of Εὔμολπος, but also Κροκωνίδαι, descendants of Κρόκων. In the Samothracian mysteries[2] a ταινία was used and was usually put round the waist of the initiate (περὶ γὰρ τὴν κοιλίαν οἱ μεμυημένοι ταινίας ἅπτουσι πορφυρᾶς), but Odysseus, we are told, used a 'head-band' (κρήδεμνον) instead. The sea-goddess Ino Leukothea was worshipped in Samothrace. According to Homer[3] she had been a mortal, 'but now in the salt sea she had received a portion (ἔμμορε) of honour from the gods'. She told Odysseus to strip off all the clothes he was wearing and lent him her 'immortal head-band' and bade him fasten it beneath his chest and said he would thus be safe. By its virtue he was able to endure the sea for three days (till he reached land). With this we may relate the fact that in the island of Cythnos still 'it is the μπόλια or scarf worn about the head which alone is believed to invest Nereids with their distinctive qualities'.[4]

That, amid the other observances, the binding of the initiate was a vital part of the τελετή is confirmed by its importance in the initiation rites of kindred Indo-European races. Among the ancient Hindoos a boy was initiated as a Brahmin, became a *dvipa* or 'Twice-born', by having a sacred thread put upon or about him and this is still[5] the practice. This thread was

ἀμφέβαλε τεαῖσιν κόμαις and VIII, 78, etc. The accusative after πλέκω and its compounds is normally the thing woven or plaited.

[1] See *Anecdota Graeca* (Bekker), I, p. 273.
[2] See Schol. *ad* Apoll. Rh. I, 917; Orph. Fr. 296 (18) (Kern).
[3] *Od.* v, 333 ff.
[4] Lawson, *op. cit.* p. 138, quoting Βαλληνδὰς, Κυθνιακά, p. 123. We may compare the Mandaean myth of the demon Ur who lost all his power when he lost his crown; for all his strength was in the latter (W. Brandt, *Mandaische Schriften*, pp. 174f., 178). Cf. p. 455, n. 3.
[5] See S. Chunder Bose, *The Hindoos as they are*, pp. 181 ff. He must always wear it. 'If the thread should break, the wearer is supposed to remain immovable, without breathing or speaking, till a fresh thread is brought to him' (*The Rites of the Twice-born*, Mrs S. Stevenson, p. 33). There is, as there was in the Greek 'mysteries', a great deal else in the ceremony.

'endowed with a mystic virtue of the first importance'.[1] So among the ancient Persians as among the Parsees to this day. 'At the age of fifteen the boy or girl was solemnly admitted to the community of Zoroastrians by being girt with the sacred thread',[2] itself as it were the embodiment of the new state received, the religion itself, and related to the band *parvand* (= πεῖραρ)[3] around the heavens.[4] In the ancient *Avesta* Haoma is thus addressed: 'Forth hath Mazda borne to thee the star-spangled girdle, the spirit-made, the ancient one, the Mazda-yasnian faith',[5] and in the Pahlavi *Ẓad-Sparam*, it is said of the archangel Spendarman: 'tied to her waist she wore a golden girdle which was the religion of the Mazda-worshippers itself'.[6]

[1] Oldenberg, *op. cit.* p. 399.   [2] Geiger, *Ostiranische Kultur*, p. 238.

[3] See pp. 314, 332. The white headband of the Mandaeans (cf. p. 454, n. 4) represented the light of the great first Life. It is Wisdom (*Mand. Lit.* ed. Lidzbarski, pp. 5 ff.).

[4] *Dadistan-i Dink*, chap. XXXIX, discusses the reasons for tying on the sacred thread-girdle (*kustîk*) and refers to an old tradition that when the demons rushed up towards the heavens 'they saw multitudes of luminaries and also the barricade and rampart of the glory of the religion and the girdle (*parvand*) of the wishes and good works of all, where it is arrayed like a brilliant thread-girdle (*kustîk*) and all its luminaries are girded (*parvasta*) by the girdle as the girdle of the omniscient wisdom has girded the all-intelligent angels' (trans. E. W. West, *Pahlavi Texts*, II, *Sacred Books of the East*).   [5] III, *Yasna*, IX, 25 (trans. L. H. Mills).

[6] XII, 4. (*Pahlavi Texts*, V.) We may explain the twisted thread put upon the baptised in Armenia and indeed the girdle *characteristic* of Christians in Asia (*J. Asiat.* XIII, pp. 404 f.) as going back to these practices. The Indo-Persian god Mithras was identified with the heavenly light and with righteousness. His name suggests the Greek μίτρα signifying a 'belt' or 'head-band' and, when his cult spread into the Graeco-Roman world, at the initiation of a 'soldier' a crown was presented to the candidate, but he let it go on to his shoulder saying 'Mithras is my crown'. See Tert. *de Cor.* 15; *de Praesc. Haer.* 40. In the west the Cathari (καθαροί) or Albigenses taught that the aim of the soul is to regain the garment of its heavenly state. At the initiation rite (*consolamentum*), by which one became *perfectus* (τέλειος), the initiate was girt about the body with a thread, which was called his 'garment' (see C. Schmidt, *Histoire et Doctrines de la Secte des Cathares ou Albigeois*, II, p. 127). The initiation of a Templar consisted of girding him with a white cord which had been in contact with, placed around, the divine head (see p. 144). This cord the Templar wore ever after day and night (see Michelet, *op. cit.* I, p. 92). It was regarded as *salutifera* (see Loiseleur, *La Doctrine Secrète des Templiers*, p. 178). In the cult of the witches (cf. p. 208, n. 2, p. 240, n. 7) he who achieved divinity was invested with string or garter (see M. A. Murray, *The God of the Witches*,

That the 'mystery', μυστήριον, was embodied or involved in the band or στέμμα is indicated by a passage of Euripides. It was usual for a suppliant to make himself holy by taking a στέμμα, and, when Adrastos is a suppliant before Theseus, the Theban herald brings the command 'to loose the holy μυστήρια of the wreaths and drive him forth from the land':

λύσαντα σεμνά στεμμάτων μυστήρια
τῆσδ' ἐξελαύνειν.[1]

He who bore the wreath became *ipso facto* holy. In the *Plutus* of Aristophanes a slave says to his master: 'I'll give you trouble; for you won't hit me while I have got a crown' (στέφανον ἔχοντά γε), and the master replies: 'No indeed I won't; but if you annoy me at all, I'll take away your crown and then hit you'.[2]

pp. 75 ff. For the leg see pp. 174 ff., 246 above). The belt or *cordon*, etc., of any Order of Knighthood appears to derive from the ideas and practices we have traced (cf. the ring of the Roman knight in n. 6, p. 448). So too the 'apron', the symbol of Freemasonry.

[1] *Suppl.* 470 f. Cf. the reference of μύστης to the wrapping of the head (p. 274, n. 2; p. 446, n. 4 above), also *Suppl.* 32–40, *Ion*, 1310 f., etc. στέφανον μὴ τίλλειν (Porph. *Vit. Pythag.* 42) can now be better understood.

[2] 20 ff. In *Il.* I, 11 ff. Chryses comes as suppliant, 'carrying στέμματα of far-shooting Apollo on a golden sceptre' (wood studded with gold. Cf. 234–46. For the gold see pp. 106; 156, n. 2; 165 ff.; 330 etc.), but Agamemnon spurns his request: 'Let me not catch you by the ships...lest the sceptre and the wreath of the god avail you not'. Possibly the plant in its life and vigour might be thought an embodiment of the god himself. Cf. the *capita deorum* consisting of *verbena*, the *verbena* put upon the head of the *pater patratus* and carried by the *fetialis*, pp. 141 f., and the herald's sceptre (*Il.* VII, 277); our practice, 'touching wood', when fearing some harm, appears to be a survival from the belief that one thus makes contact with and is protected by the life-power. The sceptre was 'imperishable' (*Il.* II, 46, 186). By it one swears (*Il.* I, 234 ff., VII, 412, X, 321, 328) and from it one receives power and inspiration. The prophet has it (Aesch. *Ag.* 1265). (So the poet's ῥάβδος, Hes. *Theog.* 30 ff., P. *Isthm.* IV, 38.) Inspired as a poet (*Theog.* 80 ff.), the king (or judge) holds it, and he who addresses the assembly (*Il.* I, 234 ff., II, 101 ff., XVIII, 504–8, XXIII, 568; *Od.* II, 37). It was the life-power in *striking transmissive* form. So the thyrsus (p. 221) inspiring (cf. Ov. *Am.* III, 1, 23, *Tr.* IV, 1, 43 f., Juv. VII, 60, etc.) and the magic 'wand', e.g. of Kirke (*Od.* X, 238 f., etc.), the golden twig of Hermes (*Od.* V, 47 f., XXIV, 2 ff., Hom. *H. to Herm.* 529 ff.) or of Athene (*Od.* XVI, 172 ff.). The 'olive branch' (e.g. Aesch. *Eum.* 43) is originally the power in which the suppliant trusts and which he hopes the other will respect. The

With the change of fate and state received by him who was 'initiated' we may relate that of the priest. His holiness, his new role, new fate, appears likewise to have been embodied in the band or crown about his head. That is the one thing usual. Indeed priests are often called just 'crown-wearers', στεφανηφόροι.[1] How the office was embodied in the band around the head may be seen in Tacitus' account of a young German who had been made priest of a Roman cult but then revolted, renouncing his office by breaking the fillets: *sacerdos apud aram Vbiorum creatus ruperat vittas, profugus ad rebelles.*[2] Among the Greeks not only did priests wear crowns or headbands but also when, as very frequently was the case, an ordinary layman wished to sacrifice, it appears to have been the rule for him to assume holiness, religious power, for the time being, by putting on a crown.[3] 'So essential was the crown

golden branch of *Aen.* vi, 136ff., can now be better understood. Initiates (cf. *Aen.* vi, 258) visited the underworld (p. 451, n. 2) as did Hermes. The branch carried by an initiate is called βάκχος (Xenophan. B 17), the name of the god (so *te quatiam*, Hor. *Od.* i, 18, 11f.), and wreaths are βάκχοι (e.g. βάκχοισιν κεφαλὰς περιάνθεσιν ἐστέψαντο, Nic. Fr. 130) and the initiate thinks himself thus βάκχος. So Orph. Fr. 5 in *Phaedo*, 69c. The wreath is the vehicle of a particular kind of divinity and he who bore it was invested with that divinity. The initiate is said τελεῖσθαι Διονύσῳ, etc., and he who is σώφρων is said metaphorically τελεῖσθαι σωφροσύνῃ, Xen. *Oec.* xxi, 12. Orestes' branch (Aesch. *Eum.* 43ff.) is itself wreathed with wool. Cf. the wreathing of a bowl full of holy liquid (Soph. *O.C.* 473ff., Theoc. ii, 2). For the use of wool cf. pp. 107f., 130f., 231ff., esp. note 4, p. 235.

[1] See e.g. Stengel, *Gr.Kult.*[3] pp.46f.   [2] *Ann.* i, 57. Cf. Plut. *Vit.Iul.* 47 f.

[3] See the references in Stengel, *op. cit.* p. 108. Cf. the Roman practice of covering the head to sacrifice, pp. 133f. above. Among the Norsemen, who had a like conception of fate as a bond imposed and who took to themselves this or that fate in the shape of a material bond, girdle, bracelet, etc. (see pp. 353 ff.), there was kept in the temples a huge ring or bracelet, which was worn by the priest at all meetings. It was also touched by him who swore an oath. To this I would relate Early Irish *mind* 'diadem, oath' (cf. Welsh *minn* 'wreath') and ὅρκος, that which is sworn by or the oath itself felt as 'binding' (e.g. ὁρκίοισι μεγάλοισι ἐνδεδέσθαι, Herodot. iii, 19, μεγάλοις ὅρκοις ἐνδησαμένα τὸν κατάρατον πόσιν, Eurip. *Med.* 161 ff. Cf. ὅρκοισι περιβαλοῦσά με, *I.T.* 788 with p. 376), with cognate ἕρκος 'enclosure, necklace', mediaev. *ligamen*, 'oath of allegiance', also the *orbes* dedicated to Semo Sancus (Liv. viii, 20) and the *urfeta* (= *orbita*), the ring given as a binding promise (Ter. *Eun.* 541 with pp. 375, n. 7, 448, n. 6 *fin.*), and perhaps Avestan *mithra* = 'oath' with p. 455, n. 6. Cf. *religio* on pp. 439f., Numbers xxx, 2ff., and *The Maypole* on p. 357.

in cult that λαβεῖν (ἀναδέξασθαι, etc.) τὸν τοῦ θεοῦ στέφανον is equivalent to assuming the priesthood (Dittenberger, *Orientis Graec. Insc. Sel.* vol. II, Leipzig, 1905, no. 767, note 14), and στεφανηφόροι include all professional priests and all magistrates who in virtue of their office take part in public rites (*ibid.* no. 322, note 24).'[1] This is not all the truth. While there were priests, ministers of a particular temple or cult, who were nothing more, yet from the time of Homer onwards the holders of political power were also normally the chief religious officials of the state. The king or magistrate sacrificed on its behalf. His power was religious as well as secular— indeed in the remote past there would be virtually no distinction, since magic or daemonic agencies were to be met with in all things—and he was apparently invested with it, as was the priest or sacrificer, with a crown or band about the head. To make a man ruler was περιτιθέναι (or περιβάλλειν) αὐτῷ τὴν βασιληΐην or τὸ κράτος, etc.[2] The crown is still the symbol of kingship.[3] We can now understand why. It was originally its embodiment, a band, the concrete form under which men believed that different kinds of fate were bound about them by the higher powers[4] or might magically be bound about them by men themselves.[5] The mayoral 'chain' is the survival of a variant form of such a band. Evidence that Pindar regarded the crown about one's head as binding, constraining to a function or office, has been cited above.[6] The distinctive feature common to holders of office in Greece—the various magistrates, archons, etc.—was the wearing of a band or crown,[7] and this was expressive of

[1] G. F. Hill, s.v. Crown (Greek and Roman), in Hastings' *Encycl. of Rel. and Ethics.* He refers the practice to 'the mere instinct of decoration', 'a natural expression of a joyful state of mind'. We can now better understand the Christian tonsure in this form: *corona*, that word being used to mean also *dignitas clericalis, sacerdotalis, pontificialis, quia corona est insigne praecipuum clericatus et sacerdotii* (Maigne D'Arnis, *Lex. Man.* s.v.).

[2] See pp. 376 f.

[3] For the 'throne' see pp. 280 f. and for the sceptre p. 456, n. 2. They are combined in *Il.* XVIII, 504–8. For 'anointing' see pp. 188 ff.

[4] See pp. 327 ff.   [5] See e.g. pp. 353 ff.   [6] P. 407, n. 1.

[7] See Aeschines, *In Tim.* 19 with schol.; Plut. *Lyc.* 26; *Quaest. Rom.* XL=274; Aristoph. *Clouds,* 625; Aristot. *Ath. Pol.* LVII, 4, etc.

political office[1] and not merely of religious duties. But in the idiom of the fifth century the holders of office were οἱ τὰ τέλη ἔχοντες or οἱ ἐν τέλει, where τέλος cannot mean 'end' and so 'supreme power' as has been suggested.[2] It is like the τέλος received by the initiates, a phase of fortune or fate received when a man was invested with it, his office. Thus Demosthenes can say 'each man was eager τελεσθῆναι στρατηγός'.[3] Not only does Pindar say that 'with the help of a god the sons of Kleonymos pass through the mortal τέλος of life (θνατὸν διέρχονται βιότου τέλος) flourishing with virtues always'[4]— where the τέλος is like 'the τέλος of old age',[5] etc., and 'the τέλος of life' which according to Sophocles[6] Oidipous 'loosed' at death—but also, when Aristagoras becomes πρύτανις at Tenedos, Pindar prays that he (Arist.) may 'with heart unscathed pass through the twelve-month τέλος with glory'[7] (σὺν δόξᾳ τέλος δωδεκάμηνον περᾶσαι); and, as we have seen,[8] he speaks of the victor's crown as τέλος. For Aeschylus a person having office or authority is τελεσφόρος[9] and an office is referred to as τέλος.[10] The lexicon of Photius explains τέλος· ἀρχή, πρᾶξις. τέλος· καὶ τὸ διδόμενον τοῖς βασιλεῦσι (cf. Suidas). If we are right, originally the τέλος was at once the circle, crown, or band, put upon a man by the powers above or his fellows, and the fate or office, event or activity in time[11] of which that band was the embodiment. Mimnermus, two lines

[1] Exactly as the private citizen might, by putting on a crown, change his state for the time being, invest himself with power such as the official priest possessed, in order to sacrifice, so, in order to intervene for the time being in state affairs by addressing the assembly, he put on a crown (see Aristoph. *Eccl.* 130 ff., 163). Cf. the holding of the sceptre on similar occasions (note 2 on p. 456) and the counsellors' 'thrones' (p. 281).

[2] Liddell and Scott, s.v. The officials themselves are sometimes referred to as τὰ τέλη.   [3] XIII (περὶ συνταξ.), 19.

[4] *Isth.* IV, 4 f. For life as a circle see note 1 on p. 451.

[5] See pp. 429 f.   [6] See pp. 436, 450.   [7] *Nem.* XI, 9 f.

[8] Pp. 445 f.   [9] *Choeph.* 663.

[10] *Ag.* 908 f., δμωαί...αἷς ἐπέσταλται τέλος/πέδον κελεύθου στρωννύναι πετάσμασιν; cf. 1202, μάντις μ' ᾿Απόλλων τῷδ' ἐπέστησεν τέλει; *Choeph.* 760, κναφεὺς τροφεύς τε ταὐτὸν εἰχέτην τέλος, etc. Did ἐν-, ἐπι-τέλλω originally mean 'wind upon', so 'bind upon', 'enjoin'? Cf. pp. 376 ff., 438, n. 1, 442 f.

[11] See pp. 427 ff., 444 ff.

after speaking of 'the black κῆρες standing near, one holding the τέλος of grievous old age, the other the τέλος of death',[1] says of youth (ἤβη) 'when this τέλος of the prime shall pass (ἐπὴν δὴ τοῦτο τέλος παραμείψεται ὥρης), 'twill be better to die straightway than to live'. Here the one aspect, there the other, predominates, and, as the original belief fades, τέλος comes to mean little more than 'phase of fortune' (a unitary item of fate) or 'office', 'activity'.

In Homer and later τελέειν means something like 'to produce the τέλος of' and is equated to τέλος ἐπιτιθέναι, 'to add the τέλος to'.[2] That the fundamental meaning of τέλος is not 'end' has been shown by the evidence already cited and may be seen in the use of τελέειν. Thus in contexts which show that only *two* days and nights have passed there recurs the phrase: 'But when at last fair-tressed Dawn τέλεσε the third day',[3] by the side of which we may set Poseidon's reminder to Apollo that they had once undertaken to serve Laomedon for a year at a specified remuneration (μισθῷ ἐπὶ ῥητῷ), 'but, when the joyful Horai were bringing out the τέλος of the remuneration (μισθοῖο τέλος... ἐξέφερον), then he by force robbed us of all the remuneration'.[4] The Horai, as the deities specially concerned with the passage of time, of day and night, the seasons, etc., through the sky and to the earth, were the doorkeepers of heaven[5] and so would 'bring out the τέλος'. There was the promise but nothing more till there came the τέλος, the circle that was the event, fulfilment. Of the long and indecisive struggle with Troy Agamemnon says: 'It is shameful for those who come after to hear that such and so great a host of Achaeans wages ineffective war, battling against foes that are fewer, and not yet has any τέλος been revealed (τέλος δ' οὔ πώ τι πέφανται)'.[6] Men become aware of this or that τέλος in the decisive event. Agamemnon, who could have 'ended' the war at once, says that he will fight at Troy 'till I reach a (or

[1] See p. 429.
[2] See e.g. *Il.* XIX, 107, XX, 369 f., cited on p. 461 below.
[3] *Od.* V, 390, IX, 76, X, 144. Cf. τελευτάω below (note 4, p. 461).
[4] *Il.* XXI, 443 ff.
[5] See *Il.* V, 749 ff., VIII, 393 ff.　　　　　[6] *Il.* II, 119 ff.

"the") τέλος of war' (or 'of the war', τέλος πολέμοιο κιχείω).[1] These passages[2] indicate how τέλος could come to be interpreted and mean 'fulfilment', 'completion', and so 'end'. The circle, itself naturally expressive of completeness, represented a process. Thetis finds Hephaistos with twenty tripods he had designed. They had wheels beneath. 'Thus far they had τέλος, but the curiously wrought handles were not yet attached.'[3] As with the μισθοῖο τέλος, so with any promised or purposed event. Twenty lines after Odysseus has said 'May the τέλος of death reach Antinoos before marriage',[4] Eurynome says of all the suitors 'Oh that to our prayers there might be a τέλος (εἰ γὰρ ἐπ' ἀρῆσιν τέλος ἡμετέρῃσι γένοιτο). Then would none of these men reach the fair-throned Dawn'. Hera says to Zeus who has promised something: 'You will be false and will not put τέλος to your word (ψευστήσεις οὐδ' αὖτε τέλος μύθῳ ἐπιθήσεις)'.[5] So a human being who brings something to pass is said τέλος ἐπιτιθέναι or τελέειν. When Achilles threatens the Trojans, Hector tells them that Achilles is not like the gods, strong in action, 'he will not put τέλος to all his words (οὐδ' Ἀχιλεὺς πάντεσσι τέλος μύθοις ἐπιθήσει) but to this he does (τὸ μὲν τελέει) and that he cuts short half way',[6] i.e. before its fulfilment (μεσσηγὺ κολούει). Men themselves, as we saw,[7] bestowed τέλος, an actual crown.[8] In English

---

[1] *Il.* III, 290 f.

[2] So Nestor tells Diomedes that he is a good speaker for a young man: 'None of the Achaeans will find fault with your speech or gainsay it; but you have not reached the τέλος of speech (μύθων)' (*Il.* IX, 55 f.). 'Obey me as I put the τέλος of (my?) speech (μύθου) in your φρένες' (*Il.* XVI, 83), says Achilles to Patroklos who, in turn, reproaches Meriones who is talking on the battlefield, 'for in hands (sc. action) is the τέλος of war, in council the τέλος of speech' (ἐν γὰρ χερσὶ τέλος πολέμου, ἐπέων δ' ἐνὶ βουλῇ, XVI, 630).   [3] *Il.* XVIII, 378 f.

[4] *Od.* XVII, 476, cited on p. 432 above. Τελευτάω is used by Homer, much like τελέω, of the whole of a process and not confined to its ending; thus ἀλλὰ τά γε Ζεὺς οἶδεν... εἴ κέ σφι πρὸ γάμοιο τελευτήσει κακὸν ἦμαρ (*Od.* XV, 523 f.). For κακὸν ἦμαρ=death, see pp. 414 f.

[5] *Il.* XIX, 107.   [6] *Il.* XX, 369f.   [7] Pp. 444 ff.

[8] This was felt by later Greeks to be τέλος as a completion. On the fact that men wore a crown when sacrificing, Athenaeus (XV, 674) quotes Aristotle (Fr. 98, Rose): οὐδὲν κολοβὸν (cf. Homer's κολούει above) προσφέρομεν πρὸς τοὺς θεοὺς ἀλλὰ τέλεια καὶ ὅλα. τὸ δὲ πλῆρες τέλειόν

itself 'crown' has developed the meaning 'fulfilment, completion, perfection, end' and 'The end crowns all', *finis coronat opus*. If we turn to Chapman's translation of the *Iliad* it is striking to find him time and again rendering a passage with τέλος or τελέειν by 'crown', though thinking that τέλος itself means 'end'. Thus for Agamemnon's words just quoted he says: But how vile such and so great an host
Will show to future times that, matched with lesser numbers far,
We fly, not putting on the crown of our so long-held war
Of which there yet appears no end.

So two hundred lines later he translates Calchas' interpretation of the serpent and sparrows:

Thus he interpreted this sign and all things have their crown
As he interpreted till now,

where Homer's words are κεῖνος τὼς ἀγόρευε· τὰ δὴ νῦν πάντα τελεῖται. And in Hector's contrast of the gods and Achilles already cited:

And they may make works crown their words, which holds not
in the war
Achilles makes.

Thus it is in our own day:

The lad came to the door at night,
When lovers crown their vows....[1]

Finally, τέλος 'payment' is, as we saw, currently explained as a quite different word from τέλος, 'end', and formed from a different root visible in τλάω, τάλας, etc. It is thus supposed to have meant originally 'what was endured'[2] and so 'toll',

ἐστιν. τὸ δὲ στέφειν πλήρωσίν τινα σημαίνει. Ὅμηρος (*Il.* I, 470) κοῦροι δὲ κρητῆρας ἐπεστέψαντο ποτοῖο. καὶ (*Od.* VIII, 170) ἀλλὰ θεὸς μορφὴν ἔπεσι στέφει. τοὺς γὰρ αὖ τὴν ὄψιν ἀμόρφους, φήσιν, ἀναπληροῖ ἡ τοῦ λέγειν πιθανότης· ἔοικεν οὖν ὁ στέφανος τοῦτο ποιεῖν βούλεσθαι. For μορφὴν ἔπεσι στέφει see p. 402, also 464, n. 3.

[1] A. E. Housman, *A Shropshire Lad*, LIII.
[2] Boisacq (*op. cit.* s.v.) compares for this sense φόρος. But the sense of that is quite different: that which is brought—cf. Homer's δῶρα φέρειν (*Od.* VIII, 427), χάριν φέρειν (*Il.* IX, 613), etc., Attic εἰσφορά (Aristoph. *Birds*, 191), etc.—rather than that which is borne as a burden. It was the name by which the voluntary confederates of Delos called their contributions to the common fund (Thuc. I, 96).

'tax'. But there is no hint of such a word or meaning in the earliest literature and the supposition is unnecessary. We have seen[1] that a debt was conceived as a bond, which might help this use of τέλος. But there is another possibility. For Pindar[2] the victor's crown was the τέλος of his victory, its embodiment, fulfilment. In the *Trachiniae*[3] of Sophocles after Herakles has sacked Oichalia Lichas reports that his master is in Euboia and there ὁρίζεται/βωμοὺς τέλη τ' ἔγκαρπα Κηναίῳ Διΐ; and in the *Antigone*[4] it is said that the attacking leaders slain ἔλιπον/Ζηνὶ τροπαίῳ πάγχαλκα τέλη. In both cases it is an offering to the god, its fulfilment, actual payment. From Homer[5] onwards it was customary in the hour of trial to vow something, to promise to the god, if he would help to victory, the arms or other spoils of the enemy and after victory to fulfil the promise, i.e. to pay. We have seen[6] that in Homer the τέλος of the μισθός, i.e. the event promised, the payment, is clearly related to these other Homeric uses of τέλος. And for this same payment Homer uses τελέειν, which also has been regarded[7] as of different origin from the other uses of τελέειν, but unnecessarily: 'we departed', says Poseidon, 'angry because of the μισθός which having promised he did not τελέειν (μισθοῦ χωόμενοι τὸν ὑποστὰς οὐκ ἐτέλεσσε)'.[8] Similarly the Aitolians promised gifts to Meleager if he would help them, but he refused till the enemy were burning the town, then he helped them, τῷ δ' οὐκέτι δῶρ' ἐτέλεσσαν.[9] And when gifts have been promised to Odysseus, Alkinoos asks him to wait εἰς ὅ κε πᾶσαν/δωτίνην τελέσω.[10] The actual payment was τέλος. From payment, the act, to what was paid the transition is natural and easy (cf. our 'offering', etc.).

Thus the various uses of τέλος can be explained and derived from a single root idea. The problem is complex, the evidence is fragmentary, and certainty as to the precise connotation of the word in every context quoted is impossible.

[1] Pp. 438 ff. [2] See pp. 445 f. [3] 237f.
[4] 142 f. [5] See e.g. *Il.* x, 460 ff. and 571, vii, 81 ff.
[6] Pp. 460 f. with 427 ff. [7] See e.g. Ebeling, *Lex. Hom.* s.v.
[8] *Il.* xxi, 457; cf. ix, 157. [9] *Il.* ix, 598. [10] *Od.* xi, 351 f.

Through this discussion of details there is visible the relationship of the early conception of fate to the practices of magic, a fundamental unity in the methods of mystical influence, whether exerted by gods or by men. In those methods and in the fossils of language, we appear to have tapped a lower level of thought, to have reached a mode of apprehending reality different from that familiar to civilisation. It is but a single image though complex; yet such is its importance and universality as an expression of human experience that we are perhaps justified in making this general inference. The distinguishing characteristic, if we would be more definite, appears to be a need of concreteness or materiality in the objects of thought, an incapacity for thinking the abstract.[1] A mere determination, qualification of something else, which has no visible form apart from that which it affects or qualifies, is given substantial existence and shape as a thing *per se*, as something superadded,[2] wrapped around the other thing,[3] as a πεῖραρ. Troubled by the problem of predication Antisthenes said ἵππον μὲν ὁρῶ, ἱππότητα δὲ οὐχ ὁρῶ,[4] 'I see a horse; horsiness I do not see'. It is perhaps not without significance that when later Greek thinkers—the Pythagoreans—first consciously faced the problem of 'univer-

[1] It is that tendency which constantly re-emerges in symbolism. The fundamental difference is that we do not now regard the image as the objectively real form of that which we so present. Cf. p. 359, n. 6 above.

[2] We may compare Kant's definition of a predicate, 'a conception of something which is capable of being added to the conception of a thing', and the English idiom, 'a man with great sensibility', etc.

[3] In the Homeric poems the interest is naturally concentrated upon human beings, but the same mode of thought was inevitably applied to all living things (a class including many things—see e.g. pp. 247 ff.—we should exclude from it), and we find it applied even to such entities (see p. 67) as words (pp. 402, 461), and later we know that ταινίαι, crowns, etc. were put upon sacrificial victims (p. 450), bowls (p. 456, n. 2), ships, etc. Where there was pervasive change (see pp. 420 ff.) by a physical element added (or withdrawn, see e.g. note 2, p. 430), that element was appropriately conceived. Thus Athene pours beauty over Odysseus:

ὡς δ' ὅτε τις χρυσὸν περιχεύεται ἀργύρῳ ἀνήρ...
ὡς ἄρα τῷ κατέχευε χάριν κεφαλῇ τε καὶ ὤμοις.
Od. vi, 232–5. Cf. ii, 12; Pind. *Ol.* vi, 76, etc.

[4] Simplic. *in Arist. Cat.* 8 b, 25 (p. 208, 28 ff. Kalb.).

sals', before a 'Theory of Ideas' had been evolved or the distinction of ὕλη and μορφή = εἶδος had become fashionable, its solution[1] once again was spatial and its terms were Homer's πεῖραρ and περαίνω, namely τὸ πέρας[2] or τὸ περαῖνον, and that which receives this, ἄπειρον; which terms Plato accepts[3] and from which the Aristotelian φαμὲν τὸ μὲν περιέχον τοῦ εἴδους εἶναι, τὸ δὲ περιεχόμενον τῆς ὕλης[4] is not far removed.[5] Like the Homeric πείρατα, Plato's εἴδη satisfied the mind's demand for substantive reality in the objects of thought and gave to qualities, etc. a separate substantive existence in the region of the gods above. Of one or other of them the individual partook (μετέχειν), shared (κοινωνεῖν), as long before[6] he had his share (μοῖρα) of this or that πεῖραρ in the jars of Zeus.[7] In the earlier solution of the problem there are already distinguished the formal cause, the πεῖραρ, and the effi-

[1] See Philolaus, Fr. 1 f. (Diels, *F.V.S.*). In ancient India where also we found (pp. 358 ff.) the conception of fate as bonds put about the individual, philosophers, amid much that was very different, conceived of qualities or moods as cords, strands (*guṇa*).

[2] For 'definition' = ὅρος (lit. 'boundary'), cf. Lucr. 1, 670f. and p. 375.

[3] *Philebus*, 23 c ff.   [4] *De Caelo*, 312 a, 12 f. Cf. *Phys.* 211 b, 10 ff.

[5] Cf. πεῖραρ, *filum, ora* on pp. 315 ff.

[6] See e.g. pp. 378 ff. The earliest instances of μετέχειν (Aeol. πεδ-) appear to be Sappho's taunt to a wealthy woman who has no μοῖρα of poetry (cf. p. 376): 'Of you there will be no remembrance; for you share not in the roses from Pieria' (i.e. have not received a crown, a wreath from the Muses: οὐ γὰρ πεδέχεις ῥόδων/τῶν ἐκ Πιερίας, Fr. 68 Bgk.), and Alcaeus' lament for an evil fate: ἔμε δείλαν ἔμε πασᾶν κακοτάτων πεδέχοισαν (Fr. 59 Bgk.). Pindar not only says of victors ὀκτὼ στεφάνοις ἔμιχθεν ἤδη (*Nem.* II, 22) but also νόσοι δ' οὔτε γῆρας οὐλόμενον κέκραται/ἱερᾷ γενεᾷ (*Pyth.* x, 41 f.) and—of a man—ἰδέᾳ τε καλὸν/ὥρᾳ τε κεκραμένον (*Ol.* x, 103 f. Cf. *Pyth.* IX, 71 f. etc.). So Sophocles: δειλαίᾳ δὲ συγκέκραμαι δύᾳ (*Antig.* 1311; cf. *Aj.* 895. For Aristophanes' οὕτω πολυφόρῳ συγκέκραμαι δαίμονι, *Plut.* 853, cf. e.g. p. 407 above). In the *Philebus* (23 c) Plato unites πέρας and ἄπειρον in ἐξ ἀμφοῖν τούτοιν ἕν τι συμμισγόμενον. To these conceptions, this tendency to give a separate substantive existence to qualities, etc. we may relate also σώματα εἶναι τὰ σχήματα ὥσπερ τὰ ἄλλα ποιά (Simplic. *in Cat.* 10 a, 11, p. 271, 21 Kalb.), the Stoic doctrine that each attribute or property (ἕξις, ποιότης, e.g. virtue, cruelty) of a thing is itself a substance (οὐσία), a body (σῶμα) gaseous in nature, a πνεῦμα, mingled (μῖξις, κρᾶσις) with that in which it is. For their teaching that affections of a living creature, emotions, etc., were themselves living creatures, ζῷα (see e.g. Plut. *De Comm. Not.* 45), cf. Ἔρως, etc.

[7] See pp. 395 f.

oo   30

cient cause, dynamic agent, god,[1] even as for Plato there are εἶδος and θεός. Homer is on the way to a single efficient cause, θεός, the god Zeus, but there survive the many, each to its kind. It is striking how close is the function of his eternal Ἔρως, Ὕπνος, Χάρις, etc., each respectively with an unfailing supply of ἔρως, ὕπνος, χάρις, etc. for transient individuals, to that of Plato's θεός and εἴδη also eternal and unfailing.

[1] See pp. 319 ff., 399 ff.

ADDENDA

I. 'WINGED WORDS'

(Addendum to pp. 67 f. (esp. n. 4 on p. 67) and p. 86)

While this is in proof, Professor J. A. K. Thomson (*Cl. Quarterly*, 1936, 1 ff.) has explained ἔπεα πτερόεντα as an image of words as arrows feathered and so flying true to their mark, τῇ δ' ἄπτερος ἔπλετο μῦθος as also an image of an arrow unfeathered and so swerving from the mark: 'the speech...did not lodge itself in her understanding'. But this does not fit the passages in question. The μῦθος did reach the mind intended. His interpretation that the hearer did not understand what was said does not fit in with the words missing their mark, unless, indeed, the mark was a different *portion* of the mind or a subsequent event ('their' being understood). Nor do the contexts (*Od.* xvii, 45–60, xix, 15–32, xxi, 380–7, xxii, 394–400) admit even this. In each case the speaker achieves his object and is understood. If there was an element in the general situation which the hearer did not understand, the speaker, it is clear, did not aim his words to enlighten her upon that. If, however, ἔπεα πτερόεντα προσηύδα, etc. referred to the words or thoughts flying rapidly as little winged creatures across to the hearer (see p. 67), τῇ δ' ἄπτερος ἔπλετο μῦθος will mean that the thought (so μῦθος commonly in the *Odyssey*; cf. pp. 13 f. and 67 f. above) did not fly but remained still in the hearer. This does fit the contexts. The hearer understands and does not answer but quietly acts as bidden. It is quite a different setting in which Aeschylus (*Ag.* 276) makes his Chorus ask Clytemnestra ἀλλ' ἦ σ' ἐπίανέν τις ἄπτερος φάτις; Perhaps elliptically 'rumour that moves rapidly though it is not a bird, not winged', which may also explain ἀπτερέως and ἄπτερος in contexts which seem to require a reference to swiftness (Ap. Rh. iv, 1765, etc.). Aeschylus' Erinyes move ἀπτέροις ποτήμασιν (*Eum.* 250) while Virgil more boldly visualises the swiftness of Rumour by giving it wings: *Fama...pernicibus alis...volat,* etc. (*Aen.* IV, 173–190). If ἄπτερος φάτις were (as Professor Thomson claims it must be, yet his 'aimless rumour' is not) a synonym of the Homeric ἄπτερος μῦθος, we might take φάτις like μῦθος and reference to unspoken thought might fit. His views are discussed by Mr George Thomson in *Cl. Quart.* XXX, 1936, p. 105 and by Mr E. C. Yorke, *ibid.* p. 150.

II. MARS, WOODPECKER, WOLF

(Addendum to pp. 146–167)

The thought traced in this chapter will perhaps also explain the remarkable importance of the woodpecker (*picus*) in Italy: *Picus, Piceni,* etc. It was believed to have prophetic power and to have *quiddam divinum* so that no nail would remain in a tree in which it nested.[1] With it, more particularly with one species, the *picus Martius,* the great god Mars was identified. Its cry is not remarkable and its pecking beak will not suffice to explain why it should have been singled out and honoured thus. The significance which we have seen to be attached to the head and to the appearance of fire there suggests attention to a remarkable characteristic of the different European species: that they are marked with scarlet on the head, most strikingly in the case of the Great Black Woodpecker, the *picus Martius* of Linnaeus. It is wholly black except for the head which is flaming scarlet. Whether the ancient explanation of Mars' name by *mas, maris*[2] be true or not, many difficulties concerning him, e.g. his connection both with fertility and with

---

[1] See e.g. Isidore, *Or.* XII, 7, 47. It was apparently too potent for any *defixio* (see pp. 373 ff.).

[2] E.g. Varro, *de Ling. Lat.* V, 73; cf. *Maspiter = Marspiter, ibid.* VIII, 49, IX, 75, X, 65; and *maspedis = marspedis* (Fest. 152 f. ?'male foot', cf. pp. 246, 280, n. 2). I suggest that *Mavors* was *mas = mars* or √*ma* (p. 177, n. 9) with *ver* as in *verres* (*ibid.*). The *ver sacrum* was usually his. Cf. *vorto, verto,* etc. The compound is intensive. Cf. *Mamers, Marmar,* etc., and such deities as *Aius Locutius* (*aio, loquor*) and *Vica Pota* (*vinco, potior*: Cic. *de Leg.* II, 11, 28).

war,[1] may be resolved if he was a god of virility, of generative power, which, as we have seen (pp. 147 ff., 187 ff., 238 f., 243 f.), manifests itself alike in fertility and in strength and fierceness and which was associated with an appearance of fire in the head.[2] The head of the horse, also sacred to Mars, was decked and set up apparently as a source of fertility, more particularly corn fertility.[3] The other animal with which Mars was peculiarly associated or identified was the wolf (*lupus*).[4] This too combines obvious fierceness with fertility, fitting it to be an embodiment of that power. 'As salt [i.e. lecherous] as wolves in pride', says Shakespeare,[5] which helps us to explain *lupa*, i.e. lewd woman, *lupari*, *lupanar*. By such associations may be explained the fertilising activity of the *Luperci* who at the *Lupercalia* ran through the city rendering women fruitful by their blows[6] and the custom whereby the Roman bride[7] anointed with wolf's fat the doorposts of her

---

[1] See e.g. Cyril Bailey, *Ovid, Fasti*, iii, pp. 33 ff.   [2] See pp. 147 ff.

[3] See pp. 126, 142, n. 3. It is noteworthy that the female deity of generation, fertility, corresponding in form to *cerus*, i.e. *Ceres*, was also identified with corn (p. 125). Cf. *faenum* on pp. 124, 142, n. 3.

[4] As the natural form of his mate in early beliefs we can perhaps explain the she-wolf which suckled his sons (cf. n. 6). Bulls were offered to him (see e.g. the evidence in Roscher, *Lex.*, s.v., 2431 f.). If the interpretation of *faenum* on p. 142, n. 3 is correct, the *faenum* put upon the horn (cf. pp. 243 f.) of a fierce bull (Hor. *Sat.* 1, 4, 34) perhaps originally signified Mars' possession. The throwing of corn or grass-stalks—*festucae* (Pers. v, 175, Plaut. *Mil. G.* 961, Plut. *de Sera Num. Vindicta*, 550)—at a slave to restore his *caput*, i.e. *genius* (pp. 145 f. and Addendum iii), was perhaps a bestowal of the procreative power (cf. p. 456, n. 2) identified with Mars.

[5] *Othello*, iii, 3, 404.

[6] See pp. 198, 235, n. 4. The first were reputed to have been Romulus and Remus begotten by Mars and mothered by a she-wolf (e.g. Ov. *Fasti* ii, 361–422), *Luperca dea* according to Varro (Arnobius iv, 3) in the *Lupercal*, 'the cave of Mars' (*Aen.* viii, 630 ff., cf. *deum bellicosum*, Serv. *ad Aen.* viii, 343), whence the *Luperci* set out. For their name cf. *Mamercus* etc. Whether the goat and dog victims were substitutes for wolves that could not so easily be procured (cf. p. 472, n. 2), the dog next of kin, the goat equivalent in sexuality—'as prime (i.e. "ruttish") as goats' says Shakespeare in the above context—or natural victims for a wolf-god or had quite other significance can scarcely be guessed.

[7] The above interpretation of Mars may also throw light upon the parting of the bride's hair (cf. p. 232 with 123 ff., 197 f.) with a spear, *hasta caelibaris*—Mars was represented by and in fact identified with a

husband's house, from which custom she was believed to derive her name *uxor*.[1] Fat or marrow was identified with seed.[2] Pliny[3] tells us that there was believed to be in the wolf *amatorium virus*, in the tail. Better known is the *amatorium virus* of the horse (*hippomanes*) identified with seed[4] and such interpretation explains, we have suggested,[5] the use of the liquid from the tail of the October horse.

III. *LIBER, LIBER*, 'FREE', *FREYR*, ETC.

(Addendum to pp. 146, 154 f., 202, etc.)

If, as appears, for the early Romans freedom was the affair of the procreative spirit in a man, his *genius*, and slavery in some sense denied or put out of action the latter, one may guess that *liber*, the term applied to a man or to his head when the procreative spirit in him was naturally active thus, and

spear (Plut. *Vit. Rom.* 29, etc.)—also perhaps upon the use of *mavors, mavorte*, etc. for a woman's head dress, the veil or scarf (cf. *flammeum*, etc. pp. 153 f., 403) covering a married woman's head (*Corp. Gloss.* IV, 517, 29, etc.). *vocatum autem mavortem quasi martem; signum enim maritalis dignitatis et potestatis in eo est* says Isidore (*Orig.* XIX, 25, 3 f.). The male thus perhaps secured himself (cf. p. 153, n. 2) or his wife and her love (cf. I Corinth. xi, 10).

[1] See Serv. *ad Aen.* IV, 458; Pliny, *N.H.* XXVIII, 9, 142. For the apparently later alternative use (*ibid.* 135) of fat from the pig, see pp. 154 f., 177, n. 9. It may originally have been hers to anoint also her husband himself.

The current explanation of *mulier* by *mollis* 'soft' does not satisfy. *Mulier* was, I suggest, in the primitive family simply the 'miller', 'grinder' (cf. *molire*) of the corn, the basic food. This was the main task of the women; the men hunted, herded or cultivated the land. Cf. the royal ménage in Homer, *Od.* VII, 103 ff., XX, 105 ff. with Plaut. *Merc.* 396, 416 etc. This grinding seemed to the Romans the main part of bread-making. *pistores Romae non fuere ad Persicum usque bellum annis ab urbe condita super DLXXX. ipsi panem faciebant Quirites, mulierumque id opus erat sicut etiam nunc in plurimis gentium* (Plin. *N.H.* XVIII, 11, 107). For the relation of *mulier* to *molere*, *mola* etc. cf. e.g. *colo, cultor, tollo, tuli*, etc., Umbrian *kumultu* = Latin *commolito*, μύλη = 'mill' etc. Cf. our 'spinster' = 'an unmarried woman'.

[2] See pp. 178 f., 187, 190 ff., 205 f., etc.
[3] *N.H.* VIII, 22, 83.
[4] See p. 245.   [5] Pp. 126 f., 207 f., etc.

Liber, the word used to designate the procreative or fertility god (see pp. 126 f., 145, 218, 264), were one,[1] and that it originally expressed a natural state, a distinctive activity or attribute of the procreative spirit or deity. Altheim's contention (*Terra Mater*, pp. 17 ff.) that *Liber*, the distinctive personal name of the Italians for their fertility god, was merely a translation of an unimportant and scarcely recorded epithet of the Greek god Dionysos, Ἐλευθέριος, does not satisfy; and what we mean by the word 'free' is not natural as the distinctive attribute of the procreative spirit. What would be? The stem of *libare*, 'to pour liquid', Gk. λείβειν, by which the ancients and some moderns have explained *Liber*, instantly suggests itself (cf. *macere, macer; scabere, scaber; gignere, gen-, gener*, etc.), and is supported by the forms *Leiber* (Cista Praenest.) for *Liber* and *loebertatem, loebesum* for *libertatem, liberum* (Varro, *Ling. Lat.* vi, 2; Paul. Fest. 108, 5 Linds.), *Loebasius* for *Liber* (Serv. *ad Georg.* i, 7), recalling λοιβή, etc. But how 'pouring liquid'? This, we saw (ἔραμαι, λείβεσθαι, etc. on p. 202; cf. p. 177, n. 9), was the aspect of sexual desire, which in Greek gave desire its name, and we may now suggest that it will also explain λίπτεσθαι, which has that sense: 'to desire', and that λίψ, which means 'desire', is the same word as λίψ, which means 'a pouring of liquid, a stream'. This will perhaps explain also the apparently cognate *libet* or *lubet*, *libido*, etc.,[2] and German *lieben*, our own 'lief', 'love', and

---

[1] Thus we can also explain why for the young the attainment of membership of the community as a free citizen was identified with the attainment of procreative power and the outward emblem was the *toga virilis* or *libera* and it was assumed at the festival of *Liber* (p. 264). A relationship of *līber* and *Līber*, whether for slaves or free men, is suggested also by a fragment of Naevius: *libera lingua loquimur ludis Liberalibus (Com. Fr.* 113 Ribb.).

[2] So too, I suggest, *deliciae, delicia*, etc. (whence Fr. *délices*, our 'delicious' etc.), meaning something like 'pleasure', 'delight', and used often specifically of sexual pleasure (e.g. Plaut. *Rud.* 426; Cic. *pro Cael.* xix, 44; Catull. xlv, 24; lxxiv, 2). It was sometimes transferred, like *amores* or *voluptas*, to the cause, the beloved. The word is currently explained by *allicio*, etc., 'draw, attract'; but that sense does not fit its uses (contrast *illecebra*); and *deliciae* in fact was in use, meaning 'a water-course', orig. 'down-flowings', from *liqui* (cf. *colliciae*). We may compare, for example,

their obvious kin. In any case, if *liber*, the distinctive attribute of the procreative spirit when fulfilling itself, not denied,[1] meant originally, with such a physical basis, 'desiring' or 'procreative', there is a remarkable parallel among our own forbears of northern Europe, for whom, as we have seen (pp. 100, 154 f.) and shall see, the head had much the same significance as for the Romans. We can thus understand our own word 'free', German *frei*, etc. Anglo-Saxon *freó* not only means 'free, noble' (of rank) but also occurs in the sense and must mean in the first place 'having desire, joy';[2] for it is

homines deliciis diffluentes (Cic. *de Amic.* xv, 52), *deliciis permaduimus* (Sen. *Epist. Mor.* xx, 13) with such expressions as *per laetitiam liquitur animus* (Atil. 2 Ribb.), *voluptate cum liquescimus fluimusque mollitia* (Cic. *Tusc.* ii, 22, 52), *laetitiae exsultantes languidis liquefaciunt voluptatibus* (*ibid.* v, 6, 16). The 'melting' is not limited to the pleasures of love. So too, I suggest, *delicatus* (whence our 'delicate', etc.) naturally belongs to *delicare*=*deliquare* 'to make liquid, melt'. Cf., for example, *libidinosae et delicatae iuventutis* (Cic. *ad Att.* i, 19, 8), *delicatis et obscenis voluptatibus* (Cic. *de Nat. Deorum* i, 40, 111) with, for example, *qui* (*animus*) *luxuria et lascivia diffluit* (Ter. *Heaut.* 945 f.), and, for both *deliciae* and *delicatus*, *ebrios ocellos* (Catull. xlv, 11; see pp. 202 f. above) and the examples on p. 35, n. 6, also the uses of *fluens* and *udus*, and of *voluptas* for the liquid, the male seed. For the freer physical working of emotion, secretion, that lies behind and for the frank naturalism of expression see, for example, pp. 3 f., 18, 108, 123 f., 201 ff. All this may explain *laetus*, orig. 'moist', so 'fat', 'fruitful' (Cato, *Agr.* 61, etc.), 'glad'. For the suggested relation of *libet* to *lībare*, cf., e.g., that of *placet* to *plācare*; and for *libet* and *līber* cf. the *loufir* of *Tab. Bant.* 8 (apparently part of the Oscan form of *libet* or *lubet* and meaning *vel*, which originally = 'wish') with Paelignian *loufir* = *līber*. Justinian, *Inst.* i, 3, defined *libertas* as *facultas eius quod cuique libet*, cf. Cic. *Par.* v, 1, 34 etc.

[1] Slaves in fact lost their sexual rights or initiative and power to refuse in the early Greek and Roman and other societies. See, for example, the elder Seneca, *Contr.* iv, 10: *impudicitia in ingenuo crimen est, in servo necessitas* with Hor. *Sat.* i, 2, 116 ff., Petron. 45, 8; 75, 11, etc. and pp. 4, 225, n. 2 above and the customs of making women concubines and men eunuchs. But it was not only thus that the life-soul was denied in slavery. Cf. p. 145 (the *genius*' loss of control of a man) and nn. 1 and 2 on p. 475.

[2] For the linking of joy with desire see p. 21 (*lust*, etc.). Our 'frolic' = 'sportive, joyful' meant also 'free', Anglo-Saxon *freólíc*. Cf. German *froh*, etc. That freedom meant desire, joy in him that had it was felt by John Barbour in the fourteenth century (*Bruce*, 225 ff.):

A! Fredome is a noble thing!
Fredome mays (='makes') man to haiff liking...
A noble hart may haiff nane ese (=no ease)
Na ellys nocht (=nor naught else) that may him plese

clearly related to *fréon*, 'to love' (our 'friend', German *Freund*, *Freier*, etc.). We may relate no less the variant *fri*, 'free, noble', and *fria*, 'lord, master', with *fria*, 'to love'; and *frig*, 'free, noble',[1] with *frig*, 'love, affection', and *Frig*, the goddess of sexual desire or love and of fertility. The connection is not less clear in old Norse or Icelandic. There the word applied to those who are not slaves is *frjáls* (=*fri-hals*, where *hals* = 'neck', for which see below) or *frí*, but *frí* also means 'lover' and *frjá* 'sweetheart', and the physical aspect appears in *frjó*, *freó*, 'seed' (Eng. 'fry'), *frjór*, 'fertile',[2] etc. *Freyr* and *Freyja*

> Gyff (=if) fredome fail; for fre liking
> Is yarnyt our (=yearned for over) all othir thing.
> Na he that ay has levyt fre
> May nocht knaw weill the propyrte,
> The anger, na the wrechyt dome,
> That is couplyt to foul thyrldome.

[1] For the sense that the freeman, master, or noble, was one who followed his own desires we may compare the ancient Hebrew *nadhibh*, 'noble' (in rank thus) from an earlier sense 'willing'.

[2] If Welsh *rhydd*, 'free', be, as appears, cognate with *fri*, etc. we may perhaps compare *rhyal*, 'procreation', *rhyderig*, 'apt to copulate', used more particularly of a female animal desiring the male. In *Indogerm. Forsch.* IX, 1898, Anz. 172 f., Schrader, glancing at the possibility that *liber* might be related, explained ἐλεύθερος as 'belonging to the people' by relating it to Old Slav. *ljudŭ* = *populus*, O.H. German *liut*, Anglo-Saxon *léod* = 'folk', etc. He compared Gothic *freis* (= 'free') and explained that as 'dear, loved, desired' on the basis of Sanscr. *priyá* and so 'belonging to friends, i.e. to the community or race', as opposed to slaves regarded as of different stock. But *priyá*, which may well be related, means 'loving' or 'loved', *pri* = 'to love' or 'to delight', and he ignores the obvious interpretation of ἐλεύθερος by direct relation to ἐλεύθω, as θαλερός to θάλλω, τολμηρός to τολμάω, etc. with a probable sense 'mobile, able to go, at large' in contrast to the slave as restricted or 'bound' (see δμώς and p. 439), or possibly 'generative' (cf. the relation of *cresco* to *creo*, φύω), if Fick's explanation of ἐλεύθω as originally meaning 'grow' or 'mount' (*Wörterbuch*, I⁴, 122, 298, 534; *Zeitschr. f. vergl. Sprachforsch.* ed. Kuhn, XIX, 249 ff.) be correct. In any case Schrader's conjecture about the meaning of *freis* runs against the actual uses in Anglo-Saxon and Old Norse. It is now the fashion to equate *liber* etymologically to ἐλεύθερος (see e.g. the revised Liddell and Scott s.v.). In *Rev. des ét. lat.* XIV, 1936, pp. 51 ff., E. Benveniste, more confidently than Schrader, explains *liber* by Sanscr. *rodh-*, Gothic *liudan* = 'grow' and O.H. German *liuti* = 'people', etc. From these he extracts the idea of 'birth' and so 'birth in a group, membership of a society', and explains *Liber* as 'he who ensures birth or growth' but *liber* and *liberi* (for which see p. 225 above) as 'born in the group' and

(cf. *Frig*), the names of the god and goddess of love, procreation and fertility (cf. pp. 154 f.), are currently explained as merely expressions of rank: 'lord, master' and 'lady'; but we have seen that in these formations above (Anglo-Saxon *freó*, *fria*, etc., so Germ. *Frau*, etc.), those meanings are secondary to the sense 'desiring, loving' and it is natural to believe (as in the case of *Liber* and *Frig*) that these deities originally were singled out, from others no less exalted, to receive these names because the latter described just them, the powers of love and fertility. If,as in the explanation of *Liber* and Ἔρως, etc. (p. 202), the physical aspect seen in *frjó*, *freó*, Engl. 'fry' came first, a relation to *freyða*, 'to foam' (cf. *froða*, 'foam, slaver' and *frodig*, 'sappy' on p. 68, n. 7) is possible. Cf. p. 233, n. 5 (slaver = seed) and p. 121 (seed = foam).

It was urged above (pp. 100, 153 ff.) that Angles, Saxons, Norsemen, etc. believed that the procreative life-soul was in the head (with its neck, cf. p. 124, n. 4 and below). We can thus understand[1] why Norsemen referred to sexual intercourse in terms of the head (e.g. *hélt höfði við hringbrota, Oddrúnargrátr*, 23; cf. *caput limare cum aliqua*, etc., pp. 123 f.) and, perhaps, why Angles and Saxons spoke of a consort as a 'neckbedfellow' (*heals-gebedda*, cf. *heafod-gemæca*, p. 154). If, as we

---

so 'legitimate'. He compares γνήσιος, which is not, however, strikingly parallel. Besides being remote and difficult in the matter of form and inconsistent in the meanings, this explanation ignores other uses of *liber*. E.g. when it is applied to a place by Plautus, it is a place for sexual indulgence (*Bacch.* 82, *Cas.* 533, 535, 537, *Mil. Gl.* 678, *Per.* 805, *Poen.* 177, 602, 657, *St.* 662). If *Liber* were related to *liudan*, etc., the sense 'generative' might, as we have seen, fit the free man no less than the god.

[1] It will perhaps also explain the idiom *heita í höfuð á einum* of naming after one. Cf. pp. 145, 183, n. 4, 264. We have seen there that for the Romans the name was intimately related to or identified with the procreative life-soul and was received or restored when the latter was received or restored. If the relation of name to head in the North be so interpreted, it fits the belief that the luck (cf. p. 477, n. 2) of the person whose name was given was thus attached to its new bearer (see e.g. Du Chaillu, II, p. 31, and cf. *heill*, 'luck', *heili*, 'brain' on p. 477, n. 2 below) and we can perhaps explain the ceremony with which the name was given, the pouring or sprinkling of water (O.N. *ausa vatni*) upon the child, as originally a bestowal of the life-element (cf. pp. 200 ff., 271 ff., 283, n. 1, 290, n. 3, 477 ff.).

have just argued, freedom was for these peoples too a condition of that procreative element, we can explain, in much
the same way as we can the Roman evidence about *caput,* etc.
(pp. 144 f.), e.g. why Angles and Saxons used the expression
heafod niman, 'to take (his) head', with the significance 'to
accept as slave', while one who surrendered himself thus into
the power of another was said by the Norsemen *foera einum
höfud sitt,* 'to bring his head to one'. The hair of thralls was
cut short (cf. pp. 129 f., 145, 229 ff., 478, n. 2). Thus, too, we can
understand why a band or bond (cf. pp. 353 ff., 381, 457, n. 3)
was put about the neck of the thrall as by the Romans about
his head (p. 145, cf. 439); and emancipation, liberation, was
'neck-loosing', *háls-lausn*; and terms for 'freedom' (Gothic
freihals, Anglo-Saxon *freóls,* etc.), for 'free-man' (O.H. German
frihals, etc.), and for 'free' (Old Norse *frjáls*), all originally
meant just 'free-neck', the adjectival element of which has
been explained above. Thus, too, we can understand the
importance of the head in ceremonies of emancipation. The
old Norse Frostathing Law (IX, 12) lays it down that the
thrall must kill a wether and get a freeborn man to cut off
the wether's head and his master shall take the 'neck-loosing'[1]
(*háls-lausn,* i.e. the price of freedom, ransom money) from
the neck of the wether. For the substitution cf. p. 218, n. 1
above. And in the laws of the Gulathing (61) the thrall or
bondwoman is to pay the value in money and to be taken to
church and a book (gospel) shall be placed on his or her head
and he or she shall be given his or her freedom.

This reference of freedom to the procreative life-element
suggests that to it should also be related the other distinctive
feature of the process of liberation among the Norsemen: the
thrall drank 'freedom-ale' (*frelsisöl*) with free men. We have
seen that Angles and Saxons drank such liquid as in some
sense the stuff of life, of health and fertility (p. 277, *wæs hal*[2]),

---

[1] The significance attributed to the neck will explain also the Anglo-
Saxon fine: *heals-fang,* lit. 'neck-taking', and the old Norse expression for
'fine fellows': *góðir hálsar,* lit. 'good necks'.

[2] If we interpret Old Norse *heill,* Anglo-Saxon *hál,* etc., signifying 'hale,

and other Germanic peoples certainly regarded ale as the stuff of fertility.¹ In any case it is clear that water (pp. 118, 203, 218 ff., 229 ff., 247 ff., 252, etc.) and wine (pp. 215 ff., etc.) were among the Greeks ceremonially identified with, and believed to replenish, the procreative life-element in man. But there too, apparently, it was this element in the head which was believed to be primarily concerned in slavery or freedom.²

healthy', as originally connoting not just 'wholeness' or 'completeness' nor merely 'health' but the positive and desirable potency of life (cf. the strength, vitality, intrinsic in the concept of the ψυχή or *genius*, pp. 97 f., 138 ff., 179 f., 187 ff., *valeo*, and the Swedish identification of the soul with 'the strength', p. 196) we can understand in relation to it as originally expressive of such power: (1) the Old Norse noun *heill* usually translated 'good luck' (cf. p. 476, n. 1) or 'omen' and sometimes carrying the sense of a personal power; (2) the Old Norse adjective *heilagr*, Anglo-Saxon *hálig*, our 'holy', German *heilig*, etc. and the nouns: Old Norse *helgi*, etc. = 'holiness, sanctity' (cf. ἱερός, 'holy', originally 'strong, powerful' and pp. 284, n. 5; 109 with n. 2); and lastly, in the light of the significance of the head and its fluid contents for the Norsemen, (3) their term for the brain: *heili*. It was, or contained, the potency of life. Cf. pp. 157, 193 f., ἰφθίμους κεφαλάς, etc. Identification of this potency with the procreative element would explain the Anglo-Saxon use of the middle finger (i.e. *digitus impudicus*, cf. pp. 139, n. 4, 198, n. 1, 226, n. 1, 233, n. 5) to salute another with. Cf. p. 132 (*Salve!*, *Viva!* etc.) and p. 185 (greeting with knee or head) and pp. 492 ff. It was termed *hálettend* (*hálettan*, 'to salute, hail').

¹ See, for example, *Handwörterb. d. deut. Abergl.* s.v. *Bier* 1269, 1273–7.
² Like thoughts may explain why the ancient Babylonians, who used the same Semitic root for 'head' as the Jews and with them regarded it as 'source' (p. 234) and spoke of slaves as 'heads' (*rešu*), marked the slave on his forehead, cutting his hair (see Holma, *Die Namen d. Körpert. im Ass. Bab.* p. 55). Alternatively they might mark the ears (*ibid.* p. 28, cf. Exod. xxi, 6, also the binding of the head, I Kings xx, 31 f., with *sub corona*, p. 145). To emancipate was to 'clean the forehead' (Holma, *op. cit.* pp. 14, 55). Among the Arabs (cf. pp. 103, 234, n. 9 above) what distinguishes a freeman is the lock on his forehead; the slave's forehead is shaved (Welhausen, *op. cit.* p. 198). The Babylonians viewed the hand as seat of strength (Holma, *op. cit.* p. 112) and stuck out the finger with magic potency and in insult (*ibid.* p. 123, cf. Isa. lviii, 9 and above pp. 198; 226, n. 1; 233, n. 5; 448, n. 6; 477, n. 2). This suggests that they, like the Greeks, Romans, and Jews (pp. 97; 198, n. 1; 494 ff.), associated the hand also with the life-soul (cf. p. 197 above). They marked slaves upon it (Holma, p. 120) as an alternative to the head. These practices explain in the Apocalypse the seal (σφραγίς), mark, or name of God, or of 'the beast', put upon the forehead or hand (vii, 3; ix, 4; xiv, 1, 9; xiii, 16; xx, 4; xxii, 4, cf. Ezek. ix, 4; Exod. xxxviii, 36 ff.). The recipients were 'slaves', δοῦλοι (Rev. vii, 3), 'purchased', ἠγορασμένοι (xiv, 3). The other place for a name was

For so we explained 'putting hateful slavery about one's head' (p. 145) and the 'crown of freedom', etc. (pp. 375 f.) and can explain the δουλείη κεφαλή of Theognis (535) and the custom of cutting slaves' hair short (e.g. Aristophanes, *Birds*, 911 with schol.). If, then, this procreative element identified with water or wine was believed to be restored when a man was freed, we can understand as a taking or replenishing of that (cf. pp. 290 f.) the Greek rite of achieving freedom—for such it seems—by drinking water or wine. Instead of 'May I become free!' one might say 'May I drink the water of freedom!' (ὕδωρ πίοιμι ἐλευθέριον, Antiphanes, Fr. 25 Kock). We are told explicitly of Argos that slaves, when being set free, drank of a certain fountain (see Paus. II, 17, 1; Hesych. s.v. ἐλεύθερον ὕδωρ). And it is natural to explain by such a rite with wine not only another fragment of Attic Comedy, a prayer to 'drink the wine of freedom and die' (ἐλεύθερον πιοῦσαν οἶνον ἀποθανεῖν, Xenarch. Fr. 5 Kock), but also in Homer the prayer for liberation from the Achaeans and slavery (cf. e.g. p. 414), 'to set up the wine-bowl of freedom in the halls after driving the well-greaved Achaeans out of Troy':

κρητῆρα στήσασθαι ἐλεύθερον ἐν μεγάροισι
ἐκ Τροίης ἐλάσαντας ἐϋκνήμιδας Ἀχαιούς,
(*Il.* VI, 528 f.),

also perhaps the titles Ἐλεύθερος, Ἐλευθέριος, Ἐλευθερεύς occasionally given to the wine-god, Dionysos.[1] Plato was familiar with the thought; for so we may explain a famous passage: ὅταν οἶμαι δημοκρατουμένη πόλις ἐλευθερίας διψήσασα κακῶν οἰνοχόων προστατούντων τύχῃ, καὶ πορρωτέρω τοῦ δέοντος ἀκράτου αὐτῆς μεθυσθῇ, τοὺς ἄρχοντας δή, ἂν μὴ πάνυ πρᾶοι ὦσι καὶ πολλὴν παρέχωσι τὴν ἐλευθερίαν, κολάζει... (*Rep.* 562 c f.). Cf. τὸ λεγόμενον ἐλευθέριον ἑλκύσας, Athenaeus 687 b, with Livy xxxix, 26, 7 f., etc.

upon the thigh (Rev. xix, 16), for which cf. pp. 183 f. The same relations of head and hand to the life-soul may explain their wrapping in Ezek. xiii, 18. Cf. the veiling of the head on pp. 103, 153 f. and of the hand on p. 133.

[1] His names implying 'loosing' may refer to wine's wider power to let a man loose (cf. pp. 385, 405, 441, 452) and not merely to the change in one who has been a slave.

The Greek associations of wine may have contributed to Horace's *libera vina*:

> *Musa dedit fidibus divos puerosque deorum*
> *et pugilem victorem et equum certamine primum*
> *et iuvenum curas et libera vina referre.*
>
> (*Ars Poet.* 83 ff.)

But we are not far from where we began. *Liber* was identified peculiarly with wine: *fruges Cererem appellamus. vinum autem Liberum, ex quo illud Terentii* (*Eun.* 732): '*sine Cerere et Libero friget Venus*' (Cic. *de Nat. Deorum* II, 23, 60).

A relation of freedom to generative liquid in plants and men, identified with water, will explain also why slaves were taken to the temple of Feronia, goddess of water[1] and fertility,[2] to have their heads shaved and covered with the *pilleus* (cf. p. 145) and become free (see Servius *ad Aen.* VIII, 564). Promising to free his slaves, Trimalchio says *cito aquam liberam gustabunt* (Petron. 71), and Seneca's last act glances at these ideas: *stagnum calidae aquae introiit, respergens proximos servorum addita voce libare se liquorem illum Iovi liberatori*[3] (Tac. *Ann.* xv, 64).

IV. ANCIENT JEWISH CONCEPTIONS OF THE MIND OR 'SOUL', THE 'SPIRIT', THE 'HOLY SPIRIT', THE BODY, AND THE DIVINITY OF CHRIST

(Addendum to pp. 103, 144, 188 ff., etc.)

The importance to the world of the Jewish conceptions of 'soul' and 'spirit' embodied in the Christian tradition makes it desirable, if we can, to understand these conceptions more fully. The development and fusion of ideas make it extremely

---

[1] E.g. *ora manusque tua lavimus, Feronia, lympha*, Hor. *Sat.* I, 5, 24. Cf. *collegium aquatorum = Feronienses*, *C.I.L.* v, 8307 f.

[2] See e.g. Livy XXVI, 11, 8 f.; for her name cf. the use of *fero* = 'I bear offspring' and *ferax, fertilis*.

[3] A Stoic's views of Jupiter, and of death as release in such circumstances, and a recollection of the last act of Theramenes (p. 276) and the last wishes of Socrates (Plato, *Phaedo* 117Bf., 118), both of whom like Seneca had drunk hemlock, explain the other elements. Thrasaea poured similar libation with his blood (Tac. *Ann.* xvi, 35).

difficult, as with θυμός and ψυχή, *animus* and *anima*, to discover the original thought. We must beware of preconceptions created by translation. It has been impossible to convey more than a part of the meaning; in many contexts it has been necessary to use a word which implies much that is alien to the original.

Nephesh is, in hundreds of passages of the Old Testament, translated 'life' or 'soul'. It is clearly something in man (or any other animal) which is necessary to life and with which life is closely bound up. So Michal, David's wife, told him: 'If thou save not thy *nephesh* to-night, to-morrow thou shalt be slain' (I Sam. xix, 11); and David said to Jonathan: 'What is my sin before thy father that he seeketh my *nephesh*?' And he said unto him: 'God forbid; thou shalt not die' (xx, 1 f.). But it is not only necessary to life; it is the chief designation of the conscious self, feeling and thinking. So, for example, Jonathan continues: 'Whatsoever thy *nephesh* desireth, I will even do it for thee.' Occasionally the English versions use 'mind' (Gen. xxiii, 8; II Sam. xvii, 8, etc.).

What is its physical nature? It is several times explicitly identified with or closely related to the blood (Gen. ix, 4 f.; Lev. xvii, 11, 14, etc.). But it is clear from its root that it was something of the nature of 'breath' or 'exhalation'. Cf. Isa. iii, 20; Jer. xv, 9; Job xi, 20; xli, 21, etc. The *nephesh* was associated with the heart (e.g. Joshua xxii, 5; xxiii, 14). At Ras Shamra, in a fourteenth-century Phoenician text, the *nephesh* is in the chest (see Dussaud, 'La notion d'âme chez les Israélites et les Phéniciens', *Syria*, xvi, p. 276). In the kindred Assyrian the corresponding *napištu* was applied to the throat through which one breathes. Thus far, we can see, *nephesh* comes very close to or is identical with the conception of θυμός and *animus* traced above (pp. 44 ff., 54, 61 ff., 80 f., 168 ff.), identifying the ordinary consciousness with the breath in direct relation to the blood. Because the connection of the *nephesh* with blood was still felt after death, it was forbidden to eat blood (Gen. ix, 4; Deut. xii, 23, etc.). Blood shed was said to cry out from the ground (Gen. iv, 10; cf. Heb. xi, 4, etc.). Though the *nephesh* is in several passages spoken of as dying (Judges xvi, 30, etc.), it is, according to others, still present with the body after death, at any rate when the latter has not lost its blood. So apparently Job xiv, 22; Lev. xxi, 11, etc. It seems to have been believed to be in the grave or *Sheol* (Pss. xvi, 10; xxx, 3; Job xxxiii, 18, 22, 30, etc.). It has been pointed out (e.g. by Dussaud, *op. cit.* p. 270) that a Syrian inscription from Zendjirli, perhaps of the eighth century B.C., implies a prayer that the dead man's *nephesh* may eat and drink with the god Hadad. In this survival it is unlike θυμός and *animus*. It is not, I think, as θυμός and *animus* were, said to leave the body during life. Elijah restored it to the son of the widow of Zarephath after he had died (I Kings xvii, 17-22).

With a root sense of 'blowing', the noun *ruaḥ*, like *anima*, connoted sometimes a 'wind' or 'blast' (e.g. Gen. iii, 8; Exod. x, 13, etc.) and sometimes 'breath' (Exod. xv, 8; Isa. xi, 4, etc.). There are other passages where it is difficult to exclude such a merely physical sense but in which it might be, and sometimes has been, translated 'spirit' (II Kings xix, 7; Job iv, 15, etc.); and there are others where the merely physical 'breath' or 'wind' will not satisfy, but something like 'spirit' or 'soul', implying life or consciousness or both, is needed, and our English versions usually translate 'spirit'. But it is extremely difficult to define the conception. Some scholars have maintained that *ruaḥ* was basically identical with *nephesh*. It certainly appears in later ages to have been assimilated in some respects or fused with the latter, much as we saw ψυχή was with θυμός and *anima* = *genius* was with *animus*. Specialist scholars do not seem yet to have established the original conception or the precise stages of its development, and it would be rash without such scholarship to attempt it; but, in the light of our experience in the classical field and what we seem to have found already of ancient Jewish beliefs, we may perhaps venture something, leaving to others the task of tracing the stages more precisely. There are a number of points which differentiate *ruaḥ* from *nephesh*. It is, for example, never like the latter identified with the blood or even brought into any relation with it. Also at quite an early stage it is used to signify the 'spirit' of Yahweh entering a man to possess him to prophesy (e.g. I Sam. x, 6, 10 ff.) or, what may be much the same thing, to fill him with wisdom (for example, Judges iii, 10; II Sam. xxiii, 2) or to fill him with strength.[1] *Ruah* might also be used of another spirit subordinate to Yahweh and sent into a man to trouble him or lead him astray, sometimes in prophecy. See, for example, I Sam. xvi, 14–23; xviii, 10; I Kings xxii, 20–24.

For both the Greeks and the Romans strength belonged to the procreative life-soul, ψυχή, *genius* (pp. 187 ff.). We have already seen reason in the Biblical, Rabbinic and other evidence to believe that for the ancient Jews the 'spirit' = life-soul was associated with the head, believed to be in the head (pp. 103, 144, 153, 183, n. 4), which saw visions, was prophetic (p. 103, where 'the visions of the head' were visions of the *ruah*, Dan. ii, 1, 28); also that it was on the one hand—in a sneeze[2] (pp. 104 f.)—conceived of as of the nature of vapour, fitting the name *ruah* and its Greek version πνεῦμα, and on the other hand conceived of as liquid identical with the seed or life-fluid in the head and spine (pp. 144, 189 ff., 234 f., 287). By this identification we explained the linking of death with sexual shame in the Fall (Gen. ii, 17–iii, 19 on

---

[1] E.g. Judges xiv, 6, 19; xv, 14. There is other evidence that vitality and strength were identified with the *ruah*. When the faint and strengthless are revived, their *ruah* returns to them. For example, when Samson, dying of thirst, had drunk, 'his spirit (*ruah*) came again and he revived' (Judges xv, 19; cf. I Sam. xxx, 12 with xxviii, 20, 22, etc.). Encouraging Jerusalem, Isaiah implies that 'spirit' means strength: 'the Egyptians are men, and not God; and their horses are flesh, and not spirit...and they all shall fail together' (xxxi, 3).

[2] It is interesting to find in the Rabbinic tradition possession conceived of as the entry of a spirit in the form of a small fly through the nostrils into the brain (see L. Blau, *Das altjud. Zauberwesen*, p. 160), with which we may compare the Arab story of the punishment of Nimrod by the sending of a fly through his nostrils into his brain so that 'he wandered to and fro as a madman' (see J. Meyouhas, *Bible Tales in Arab Folklore*, p. 43). Josephus tells how Eleazer draws out the spirit from one possessed by putting to his nostrils a ring having beneath its seal a root indicated by Solomon (*Antiq. Jud.* VIII, 2).

p. 109, n. 4) and the belief that it is the tail-end of the spine which grows into a new body in the Resurrection (pp. 126, n. 3; 208; 287 f.). We also saw that strength and vitality were identified with the procreative life-soul (= 'spirit') in the head and hair[1] (pp. 234f.). Thus far the conception is almost identical with what we have traced as underlying the ψυχή and the Roman *genius*.

We saw also that this liquid of life and strength, the seed, was conceived of as 'oil' and that a new 'spirit', even the 'spirit' of Yahweh, was believed to be transmitted to the head by anointing it with holy oil (pp. 189ff.), and that this 'oil' = seed was naturally derived also from the thighs (marrow or fat, pp. 108, 184, 189f.), also from the fat, more particularly that around the kidneys (p. 188). Scarcely less naturally was it to be derived from the *omentum*, the fat which covers the belly like an apron (cf. pp. 188, n. 2; 208, n. 2; 280; 282), and from the other fat parts there. Among the ancient Hindoos the *omentum* was the essential part of the sacrificial victim, the life-principle—with it the *ātman* was identified (*Taittirīya Saṃhitā*, VI, 3, 9, 5. Cf. the self = the seed on p. 196 above)— and it with the rest of the fat of the body was gathered up to be burned for the gods (p. 280, n. 1). Among the Greeks it was the marrow and this fat identified with the ψυχή and the seed, the life-stuff, that were offered to the gods (pp. 279 ff.); and it is these that among the ancient Jews must not be eaten but must be offered to Yahweh. See p. 287 with, for example, I Sam. ii, 15 ff. and 'thou shalt take of the ram, the fat and the fat tail and the fat that covereth the inwards and the caul of the liver and the two kidneys and the fat that is upon them and the right thigh, for it is a ram of consecration'. It is placed on Aaron's hands, then burned upon the altar (Exod. xxix, 22 ff.; cf. xxiii, 18; with Lev. iii, 3–5, 9–11, 14–17; iv, 8–10; vii, 3–5, etc.). If we look, we find that the seed is spoken of as coming not only from the loins and thighs

---

[1] Samson's strength depended on the presence of the spirit of Yahweh in him, upon the presence of his hair that was Yahweh's (Judges xiii, 5; xiv, 6, 19; xv, 14; xvi, 15–20, 22 ff.).

(pp. 108, 184, 189) but also as coming from the belly and its parts or organs, from the *me'im*.[1] For example, Yahweh says to David: 'I will set up thy seed after thee, which shall proceed out of thy *me'im*' (II Sam. vii, 12; cf. xvi, 11); and to Abraham: 'He that shall come forth out of thine own *me'im* shall be thine heir' (Gen. xv, 4). In a woman, also, *me'im* describes that part from which the child is born (Gen. xxv, 23; Ruth i, 11; Isa. xlix, 1; Ps. lxxi, 6). Another word for 'belly, abdomen' is *beten*, which in many contexts (for example Gen. xxv, 23 f.; xxx, 2; Judges xiii, 5; xvi, 17; Job i, 21) is used of that part of the mother in which the child is, and whence it is born; in other contexts it is the source in the father, for example: 'The Lord hath sworn unto David in truth; he will not turn from it: Of the fruit of thy *beten* will I set upon thy throne' (Ps. cxxxii, 11). 'Shall I give my first-born for my transgression, the fruit of my *beten* for the sin of my soul?' (Mic. vi, 7). 'Thy *beten* is like a heap of wheat', says the Song of Songs (vii, 2) of the beloved. We can now understand the ancient Rabbinic curse, 'May thy seed be as that of a man whose navel is sunken [drawn in] and as that of a mule which is sterile!' (See Blau, *op. cit.* p. 74.)

With *ruah* as the procreative life-soul,[2] that has a wisdom of its own, we can explain its location in this part of the body (cf. Prov. xx, 27 and below, p. 500). So, in Job, Elihu must speak, 'For I am full of words. The spirit [*ruah*] of my belly [*beten*] constraineth me. Behold my belly [*beten*] is as wine which hath no vent. Like new wine-skins it is ready to burst. I will speak that I may be refreshed' [lit. 'breathe'] (xxxii, 18 ff.). With a similar reference to the wind-like *ruah*, Eliphaz said, 'Should a wise man make answer with know-

---

[1] This has been inadequately rendered 'bowels' (cf. p. 486, n. 1 below), which has had a curious consequence: the use of 'bowels' (cf. Fr. *entrailles* etc.) for 'children', for example: 'thine own bowels which do call thee sire' (Shakespeare, *Meas. for Meas.* iii, 1, 29).

[2] This side of *ruah* may throw light upon Mal. ii, 15 f., speaking of 'the residue of the spirit': 'He sought a goodly seed. Therefore take heed to your spirit and let none deal treacherously against the wife of his youth. For I hate putting away, saith the Lord.'

ledge of wind [i.e. that is but wind] and fill his belly [*beṭen*] with the east wind [*ruaḥ*]?...They [the wicked] conceive mischief and bring forth iniquity, and their belly [*beṭen*] prepareth deceit' (xv, 2, 35). The image of generation was appropriate there. Job himself says: 'my *ruaḥ* is strange unto my wife and my supplication to the children of my belly [*beṭen*]' (xix, 17). It is apparently of the belly as the place whence the prophetic wisdom is to be uttered that when a roll is handed to Ezekiel, the voice says of it: 'Cause thy belly [*beṭen*] to eat and fill thy *me'im* with this roll...go get thee unto the house of Israel and speak with my words unto them'[1] (iii, 3–4). The image, 'eating', for the intaking of the prophetic

---

[1] In Proverbs not only wisdom but titbits of scandal may go down to that part, that is, to the *ruaḥ*: 'The words of a whisperer are as dainty morsels and they go down into the chambers of the belly' (xviii, 8; cf. xxii, 17 f.). If the above interpretation of *ruaḥ* is correct there was in time a blurring of the difference from the *nephesh* and the ordinary consciousness. But the deeper emotions and the thoughts from the depths, that seemed alien to the consciousness that received them, were perhaps by the Israelites, as by the Babylonians, always referred to these parts (for example the 'reins' or kidneys) more commonly than by the Greeks and Romans (see pp. 84 ff.). As we might expect, the *me'im* are affected by love. In the Song of Songs: 'My beloved put in his hand by the hole [of the door] and my *me'im* were moved for him' (v, 4). This part of the body is the place of tender feelings, pity (for example Jer. iv, 19; xxxi, 20). It is striking how, as for the Babylonians, the belly is the seat of compassion. In Assyrian the same word *rêmu* meant both 'compassion' and 'womb'. Obviously cognate, in Hebrew the singular *reḥem* means 'womb', and its plural is in most contexts translated 'mercies' or 'tender mercies', of God or man. This is an inadequate paraphrase for the parts or organs to which the feelings were attributed, for instance in 'the tender mercies of the wicked are cruel' (Prov. xii, 10). Sometimes, where reference to a physical organ is inescapable, the rendering has been 'bowels'. Thus, when Joseph saw Benjamin, 'his bowels did yearn upon his brother' (Gen. xliii, 30); and 'her bowels yearned upon her son' (I Kings iii, 26). A reference to the intestines will not suffice, as the invariable reference of the singular to the womb, the generative part of the woman that bears a child, shows. The association of tenderness with love, with the organ and supposed source of sexual love, and with maternal and paternal feelings ('like as a father pitieth his children', Ps. ciii, 13), with the seat of maternity or paternity, is natural. For the Greeks and Romans the knees, sources of generation (pp. 174 ff.), addressed in appeals for pity (pp. 174, 180 f.) and by later interpreters referred to *misericordia* (p. 149, n. 3), were, as I have shown, seats not of emotion but of the procreative life-soul.

wisdom, is determined by the destination of the latter, the belly, its proper place and source.

It is now more easy to understand the strange words attributed to Jesus: 'If any man thirst, let him come unto me and drink. He that believeth on me, as the scripture hath said, out of his belly shall flow rivers of living water. But this spake he of the Spirit, which they that believed on him were to receive.' (John vii, 37–9; cf. iv, 10–14 and pp. 287 f. above. For the 'drinking' of the Spirit cf. I Cor. xii, 13, etc. on p. 493 below.)

The word *ruaḥ* itself and its other uses imply something of the nature of wind or breath as does ψυχή. In this last we saw that the original reference was probably to sneezing (pp.103 ff., 120) and flatulence (p. 112, n. 2) and perhaps chiefly to the supposed 'breath' of procreation (pp. 120f.). There appears to be evidence for a similar conception among the Semites. The Arabs identified the surviving life-spirit, conceived of as a *gânn* (pl. *ginn*), with the head (this is implicit in evidence which appears in Welhausen, *Reste arabischen Heidentums*[1], pp. 178, 185), and regarded the *ginn* as responsible for love and madness and prophecy (*ibid.* p. 156). They veiled the head in prophecy (*ibid.* p. 135). But they also associated the *ginn* with the abdomen; 'Stinks are their element and they eat excrement' (*ibid.* p. 150). They were particularly to be guarded against by one easing himself (*ibid.* pp. 158, 173). To 'possess' a man, render him mad, a witch blew into his genital organ and the man went off, crazed, into the wilderness (*ibid.* p. 159). After death the surviving life-soul or spirit was believed to be capable of procreation. Syrians believed that a widow might conceive by her husband for nine months after his death (see S. T. Curtiss, *Primitive Semitic Religion To-day* (1902), p. 115). A *weli*, a departed local saint or sheikh, might be resorted to. At the so-called Baths of Solomon near Karyaten, places where hot air comes out of the ground, 'one of these, called Abu Rabah, is a famous shrine for women who are barren and desire children. They really regard the *weli* of the shrine as the father of the children born after such a visit.' They 'allow the hot air to stream up their bodies, saying "Oh, Abu Rabah...with thee is the generation, with us the conception"' (*ibid.* p. 117).

We can now better understand the Rabbinic evidence for the practice of consulting the spirit of one dead by means of a skull (cf. p. 103 above) or alternatively the male organ. Buxtorf (*Lex. Chald. Talm. Rabb.* p. 348) cited some of the evidence, for example *Sanhedrim* 65 b, thus: *Python qui ascendere facit (mortuum) per virilitatem et qui ascendere facit per cranium*, and again *educit ex sepulchro et collocat mortem super membrum virile suum. Hoc modo magicam exercebant et per mortuum divinabant.* This interpretation—that of Rashi—was disputed by some. We may compare *Midrash Rabbah Gen.* xi, 5: 'Let him who brings up (the dead) by his male organ prove it, for every day he (the dead) comes up but not on the Sabbath.'

The thought traced may also throw light upon the word '*obh*, in some passages naturally translated by our versions 'familiar spirit', in others 'one that hath a familiar spirit'. This appears to be a secondary and later use. In both cases the spirit of one of the dead seems to be involved, for example, at Endor (I Sam. xxviii, 7–20) or 'When they shall say unto you "Seek unto them that have familiar spirits and unto the wizards that chirp and that mutter", should not a people seek unto their God? On behalf of the living should they seek unto the dead?' (Isa. viii, 19). Compare xix, 3; xxix, 4; Lev. xix, 31; xx, 6, etc. It is natural to interpret '*obh* in the light of Job xxxii, 19, cited above, where the word is used with the meaning 'skin-bottle' or 'bag'. That passage may, indeed, furnish the clue; that it is the conception of the spirit in the bag of the belly—our word 'belly' originally meant such a bag—which lies behind, or perhaps rather the conception of a bag, a receptacle, in the belly,[1] into which the spirit entered and thence spoke.

[1] It can scarcely be the sort of bag in which Odysseus kept the winds, a part of the wizard's apparatus outside himself. Explicitly in Lev. xx, 27 the '*obh* is in the person; and, as we have seen, the word comes to be used of the person who contains the spirit (for example, I Sam. xxviii, 3). The current suggestion that '*obh* expressed the conception of the spirit (after it

This would explain why the Seventy, to express the Jewish conception of a prophesying spirit within (i.e. to translate *'obh* in its primary sense), used ἐγγαστρίμυθος, 'one speaking in the belly'[1] (I Sam. xxviii, 8), and used the same word also

has left the body at death) as a skin, full of wind, is possible but scarcely compatible with the inevitable basis, what is experienced of the 'spirit' in oneself during life and what is witnessed when the life departs from another. Such a 'skin' suggests something both visible and tangible, palpable. Contrast pp. 93 f., 262 and, probably closely parallel to the Jewish *ruah*, the Babylonian idea of the departed spirit as a wind. See for example p. 196. *'obh* is not used of a departed spirit in any other connection.

[1] The Greeks had this same conception of a prophet with a prophetic spirit in the belly, ἐγγαστρίμαντις or ἐγγαστρίμυθος (see Aristoph. *Wasps*, 1019 f. with Schol.; Plat. *Soph.* 252c with Schol. etc. Cf. στερνόμαντις on p. 66). This may explain Zeus with Μῆτις in his belly (or 'womb', νηδύς) to counsel him (*Theogony* 899 f.) and should perhaps be related to the evidence cited in the latter half of n. 2 on p. 112, especially the flatulent beans not to be eaten as containing ψυχή, and *Works and Days*, 757–9: the taboo [μηδέ ποτ' ἐν προχοῆς ποταμῶν μηδ' ἐπὶ κρηνάων οὐρεῖν, μάλα δ' ἐξαλέασθαι·] μηδ' ἐναποψύχειν, and in *Hom. Hymn to Hermes*, 295–303, from the belly wind breaking, the equivalent to a sneeze, which last we saw was best understood as an outgoing of or utterance from the prophetic ψυχή (see pp. 103 ff.; 131 f.; 138 f.; 184, etc.). This and a sneeze both confirm Apollo's words. Young Hermes in Apollo's arms

> οἰωνὸν προέηκεν ἀειρόμενος μετὰ χερσί
> τλήμονα γαστρὸς ἔριθον ἀτάσθαλον ἀγγελιώτην.
> ἐσσυμένως δὲ μετ' αὐτὸν ἐπέπταρε.

Apollo hurriedly put the lad down and said εὑρήσω καὶ ἔπειτα βοῶν ἴφθιμα κάρηνα τούτοις οἰωνοῖσι. Hesiod implies direct connection between Zeus's belly and his head; for Metis's offspring emerged there (*Theog.* 888 f., 924). This belief in the ἐγγαστρίμαντις might be explained by his or her procreative ψυχή, which had prophetic knowledge beyond the ordinary consciousness = θυμός and was identified with the seed (see pp. 102 ff.; 185; 108 ff.; 197 f.; 188, n. 2); or the ψυχή might be supposed to be displaced by an alien spirit. Later at any rate such a spirit in vaporous form was believed to enter the womb of the Pythia and be responsible for her prophecies. She is 'pregnant' with it. Thus the author of 'On the Sublime' (XIII, 2) describes it as ἀτμὸν ἔνθεον breathed from a cleft in the earth, and the Pythia αὐτόθεν ἐγκύμονα τῆς δαιμονίου καθισταμένην δυνάμεως παραυτίκα χρησμῳδεῖν κατ' ἐπίπνοιαν. A source quoted by Suidas refers to the possessing spirit as Python thus (s.v.): Πύθωνος δαιμονίου μαντικοῦ. 'τάς τε πνεύματι Πύθωνος ἐνθουσιώσας καὶ φαντασίαν κυήσεως παρεχομένας τῇ τοῦ δαιμονίου περιφορᾷ ἠξίου τὸ ἐσόμενον προσαγορεῦσαι....' If the serpent, Python, was believed to be the 'possessing' spirit before Apollo's victorious coming, it may originally have been no more than the form under which the ψυχή of one of the great dead, such as Melampous or Teiresias, was conceived (see pp. 206 f.,

of the human being possessing such (i.e. *'obh* in the secondary sense—e.g. *ibid.* 3) and described them as 'which speak from the belly': οἳ ἐκ τῆς κοιλίας φωνοῦσιν[1] (Isa. viii, 19).

By the thought that this wind-like spirit inside would act as a 'float', changing the specific gravity of the body, we can explain why the way to discover the possession of such a spirit was to put the suspect in water. Its possession was proved if the person floated. Thus for example, among the Arabs, at Kufa the Caliph Valid I threw those who were thought to be witches into the water and put to death those that floated but fetched

233), possibly a divine 'spirit' of fertility, conceived as e.g. Zeus Meilichios (pp. 233f.), in serpent form even as the human generative spirit. The persistent belief in a natural vapour exhaled from the earth in the shrine at Delphi (cf. p. 66, n. 5) is unsupported by any trace to-day. It arose, I suggest, out of an original belief that a 'spirit' or ψυχή, conceived of in vaporous form (pp. 93 ff., 104, 262), rose out of the earth and entered into and 'possessed' the Pythia. In Acts xvi, 16, at Philippi Paul encountered a young woman who had a 'Python spirit' (ἔχουσαν πνεῦμα Πυθῶνα), wherewith she prophesied. The pretence to possess such a spirit explains 'ventriloquism', i.e. 'speech in the belly (*venter*)'. The latter consists of mere tricks of the voice, which were referred to the belly only because of this background of belief.

[1] Among the Karens of Burma similar considerations seem to have led to the same basic scheme, though the context of life and thought is remote from those of the Greeks, Romans, Jews, Babylonians and their kin. The conscious self responsible for ordinary actions is the *thah* in the heart in the breast. The life-soul or 'spirit', the presence of which means life and strength, and to which procreation and fertility belong, is the *la* or *kalah* associated with the head. It passes through the fontanelle and is associated with the skull. Every animal, every plant has its *la*. In a man it is active during sleep. Then it may wander from the body and be sexually united with another. It is responsible for dreams, visions; for insanity, reckless folly or courage (cf. pp. 147 ff.); for shamelessness and lust. It is that which survives death, that with which the person is then identified. It is associated also with the belly, seat of passions. That of the wicked chooses its next form of life after death by picking up entrails from a heap— the *kephoo* is 'the stomach of a wizard which at night in the repulsive form of a human head and entrails sallies forth in quest of food'. They 'formerly supposed that every human being found having a "paunch" or "stomach" was a witch or wizard'. See *A Dictionary of the Sgau Karen Language*, p. 69 and E. B. Cross in *Journ. of Amer. Or. Soc.* IV, 1854, pp. 309–12; F. Mason in *Journ. of Asiat. Soc.* XXXIV, 1865, pp. 196–202, 208; C. J. F. S. Forbes, *British Burma and its People*, 1878, pp. 252, 276; H. I. Marshall, *The Karen People of Burma*, 1922, pp. 156, 169, 204, 219–22, 229, 232, 245, 276 f.

out and saved those that sank (Welhausen, *op. cit.* p. 160). In England the same method was employed. It is described, with examples, by Sir Walter Scott in his *Letters on Demonology and Witchcraft* (chap. VIII): 'The suspected person was wrapped in a sheet, having the great toes and thumbs tied together, and so dragged through a pond or river. If she sank, it was received in favour of the accused; but if the body floated (which must have occurred ten times for once, if it was placed with care on the surface of the water), the accused was condemned.'

The Jews, for whom, we have seen reason to believe (pp. 109, 183 f., 189), the thighs contained the seed and spirit or soul, seem to have given similar value to the knees. A mother gives birth to a child on to the knees of one, who by receiving it thus assumes its parentage (Gen. xxx, 3–6; cf. l, 23; Job iii, 12). The Hebrew word for 'knee', *berekh*, pl. *birkayim*, is clearly one with Bab. *birku*, 'knee' or 'generative organ'[1] (pp. 124, n. 6, 176), and appears to be related to Hebr. *bᵉrekha*, 'pool', perhaps as containing liquid that meant fertility (pp. 177f.). Why were the knees or kneeling vitally important to the act of blessing? The verb *barakh, bērēkh* (Pi'el), 'knee'[2] or 'kneel', is used mainly in the sense 'bless'. It does not mean 'pray' or 'worship'. It is used either of actually making fruitful and prosperous or of the bestowal of such 'blessing' with words: 'I will bless her, and moreover I will give thee a son of her: yea, I will bless her, and she shall be a mother of nations...as for Ishmael, I have heard thee: behold, I have blessed him, and will make him fruitful, and

[1] Some passages in which this translation has been deemed necessary can perhaps be referred just to the knees with the significance we have traced.
[2] We can now perhaps understand this with not only the ancient Irish custom of raising the knee or thigh, source of generation, to greet or hail (p. 186 with p. 175), but also the Egyptian custom of blessing or hailing in greeting (προσκυνέουσι) by lowering the hand to the knee (Herodotus II, 80). Cf., among the Finns, the putting of hands to knee to create (p. 177). For the Egyptians the thighs were seats of the seed and life (pp. 183, 280) and the hieroglyph for the *ka* (= *genius*) was just a pair of hands and arms out-stretched (see p. 495 below with p. 284 above) and they transmitted life by the hands and arms (see p. 208, n. 3). We may compare also the Anglo-Saxon use of the middle finger (= *digitus impudicus*) to greet or bless with life and health (pp. 477 n. 2 and 494 ff. below).

will multiply him exceedingly; twelve princes shall be beget'
(Gen. xvii, 16, 20); 'He smelled the smell of his raiment, and
blessed him, and said, See, the smell of my son is as the smell
of a field which the Lord has blessed: and God give thee of
the dew of heaven, and of the fatness of the earth, and plenty
of corn and wine' (Gen. xxvii, 27 f.; cf. 38 f.); 'Eli blessed
Elkanah and his wife, and said, The Lord give thee seed of
this woman for the loan which was lent to the Lord. . . .And
the Lord visited Hannah, and she conceived, and bare three
sons and two daughters' (I Sam. ii, 20, etc.). Blessing seems
indeed to have been thought of as an outpouring of liquid, of
fruitfulness: 'The Almighty, who shall bless thee, with blessings
of heaven above, blessings of the deep that coucheth beneath,
blessings of the breasts, and of the womb' (Gen. xlix, 25);
'Passing through the valley of weeping they make it a place
of springs; yea, the early rain covereth it with blessings'
(Ps. lxxxiv, 6); 'Like the dew of Hermon, that cometh down
upon the mountains of Zion: for there the Lord commanded
the blessing, even life for evermore' (Ps. cxxxiii, 3); 'For
I will pour water upon him that is thirsty, and streams upon
the dry ground: I will pour my spirit upon thy seed, and my
blessing upon thine offspring: and they shall spring up among
the grass, as willows by the watercourses' (Isa. xliv, 3);
'And I will make them and the places round about my hill
a blessing; and I will cause the shower to come down in its
season; there shall be showers of blessing. And the tree of the
field shall yield its fruit' (Ezek. xxxiv, 26); 'Prove me now
herewith, saith the Lord of hosts, if I will not open you the
windows of heaven, and pour you out a blessing' (Mal. iii,
10); 'The soul of blessing shall be made fat: and he that
watereth shall be watered also himself' (Prov. xi, 25); 'Let
thy fountain be blessed, and rejoice in the wife of thy youth'
(*ibid.* v, 18).

These passages strongly suggest that to give a blessing was
to give liquid that is life, seed. Isa. xliv, 3 equates 'blessing'
with 'spirit', both 'poured'. We saw elsewhere how the life-
soul (= 'spirit') was identified with the seed (pp. 108 ff.,

123 ff., 174 ff., 189 ff., 234, etc.). That identification will explain Isa. xxxii, 15: 'Until the spirit be poured upon us from on high and the wilderness become a fruitful field' (cf. xliv, 3 f. and pp. 189 ff.). This is naturally understood of Yahweh as the husband of the land (cf. Isa. lxii, 4 f.) even as the Canaanite Baal was believed to be and as we have seen on occasion the Greek Zeus (p. 230, n. 8). See also p. 288. Very near is Ps. civ, 30: 'Thou sendest forth thy spirit, they are created, and thou renewest the face of the ground.' Cf. Gen. i, 1 ff. (a conflation of this with creation by the spoken word).

To come back to the other aspect of the spirit—but it is still liquid—'It shall come to pass afterwards that I will pour out my spirit upon all flesh; and your sons and your daughters shall prophesy' (Joel ii, 28). In the New Testament the 'spirit' of God, 'the Holy Spirit', is 'poured' (Acts ii, 33; x, 45, etc.), 'making anew' with 'the bath of regeneration' (Titus iii, 5f.), and it is absorbed as liquid, 'drunk' in (I Cor. xii, 13; cf. Acts i, 5; xi, 15f.; II Cor. iii, 3, etc.).

A father about to die 'blessed' his sons (Gen. xxvii, 4 ff., xlviii, 9 ff. etc.). He might then be thought to transmit not merely fruitfulness but soul or 'spirit'. In anointing a king, the spirit was given by pouring actual liquid representing seed into one who thus becomes a 'son' (pp. 189 ff.). It is not the legal fiction of adoption but a magically effective bestowal of seed=spirit (cf. pp. 109, n. 4; 111, n. 6). Elijah is told: 'Elisha, son of Shaphat...shalt thou anoint to be prophet in thy room' (I Kings xix, 16). In fact, as Elijah departed, Elisha asks for and obtains a double portion of Elijah's 'spirit' (II Kings ii, 9-15). We can thus understand his cry 'My father, my father'; also perhaps 'the sons of the prophets' (*ibid.* 3, 15; I Kings xx, 35 ff., etc.; cf. I Sam. x, 11 f.) and the 'begetting' of 'sons' or 'children' by this or that Apostle (e.g. I Cor. iv, 14-17, Philemon 10), who transmits the 'spirit' of God, the Holy Spirit (II Tim. i, 2, 6f., 14, etc.), and is himself thus a 'godfather', 'his fader spirituel' as Chaucer's Persone (835 [908]) calls him. This appears to be the ultimate source of 'godfathers'.

The spirit might be transmitted into the head (seat, apparently, of prophetic soul and seed, pp. 102 ff., 234, etc.) either by anointing or by laying the hand upon it. Joshua 'was full of the spirit of wisdom; for Moses had laid his hands upon him' (Deut. xxxiv, 9). It was through his hands that he, who 'blessed' his son or grandson before he died, transmitted his gift (Gen. xlviii, 13 ff.; cf. xlix, 26, etc.). The hand was for the Jews, with the knees, the seat of strength (e.g. Job iv, 3 f., Isa. xxxv, 3) or of 'life' (Isa. lvii, 10), both of which were naturally associated with the seed (pp. 108f., 189, 235; cf. 478, n. 2). It had sanctity, being given as a pledge (II Kings x, 15; Ezek. xvii, 18, etc.) as among the Greeks, Romans and others. For these, we have found reason to believe, it represented, was in some way identified with, the procreative life-soul (pp. 97; 177; 198, n. 1; 226, n. 1; 233, n. 5; 477, n. 2; cf. 478, n. 2). And we may now guess that it represented this also among the Jews and their neighbours. That will explain how it could be that we are told in the *Talmud* (*Soṭa* 36 b) that, when Potiphar's wife invited Joseph to lie with her and he suppressed his desire, 'the seed came out of his finger nails'. Cf. *Midr. Rabb. Gen.* 87: 'his seed was scattered and issued through his finger nails.'[1] Its survival will explain the doubtless ancient belief, universal comparatively recently amongst the Nusairiyeh in Syria,

---

[1] It also perhaps explains how the phylactery on the hand (see below, p. 497, n. 1) could be interpreted as representing 'restraint of lust' (see I. Abrahams in Hastings' *Encycl. of Religion and Ethics* xii, 144, citing Shūlḥān 'Ārûkh I, ch. 25). Similar thoughts to the above perhaps lay behind the Slav story that Satan created his following of demons by washing his hands and letting the water drip from his fingers behind him. From these drops the demons arose. (See Hastings, *op. cit.* iv, 622 b.) This evidence may be added to that on p. 246 that, like horns, the finger-nail and toe-nail, Latin *unguis*, and the talon, or hoof, Latin *ungula*, were believed to be outcrops of the life-fluid ('oil' as we have seen). One is tempted to suggest that the early Latins felt a relation with *unguo* = 'I anoint'. If they originally conceived of 'anointing', as did perhaps the Greeks, as 'piercing, penetrating' (cf. χρίω, pp. 211 f.), that sense would fit the nails and talons, which may suffice to link *unguo* with *unguis* and *ungula*. In English and other Germanic languages the word for 'nail' in this sense also describes a piercing spike as if piercing were a prime characteristic of finger-nails.

that their Sheikhs have no ordinary sexual union, but 'their children are begotten through passes which they make with their hands over the bodies of their wives'[1] (Curtiss, *op. cit.* p. 107, citing E. E. Salisbury, *Journ. of the Amer. Orient. Soc.* VIII, 1866, p. 297). This, too, will throw light upon the story of Epaphos, told by Aeschylus and others, that Zeus begot him upon Io with a touch of his hand: ἐφάπτωρ χειρὶ φιτύει γόνον (Aesch. *Supp.* 313), πατὴρ φυτουργὸς αὐτόχειρ ἄναξ (*ibid.* 592), ἐπαφῶν ἀταρβεῖ χειρὶ καὶ θιγὼν μόνον (*P.V.* 849). The two lands with which the Greeks particularly associated Epaphos were Egypt and Syria (see, for example, Apollod. *Bibl.* II, 9 Wagn.). In Egypt the texts and pictorial representations show that life was transmitted by the hand (p. 208, n. 3), and from the earliest times the hieroglyph for the *ka* (= *genius*; for example, 'he is thy son whom thy *ka* hath begotten for thee', *Instruction of Ptahhotep*[2] 12) was two hands and arms outstretched thus: ⎩⎭. The evidence we have just set out shows the beliefs the Greeks would find in Syria. These might well make them think of Epaphos there or have been part of any basis they found for the story there.

There are two other pieces of early evidence which may be relevant. In Isa. lviii, 9, current evil practices are attacked: 'the putting forth of the finger and speaking wickedly'. Among the Babylonians the finger was stuck out to annoy or insult (as the *digitus impudicus* at Rome, see p. 198, n. 1) and

---

[1] This begetting by moving the hand over may perhaps be linked with the begetting by anointing, since the verb 'anoint' *mashah* in other contexts means 'smear' or 'stroke'. In anointing a king the oil originally was probably stroked, smeared, on the head with the hand.

[2] See A. Erman, *The Lit. of the Anc. Egyptians*, trans. Blackman, p. 59. Circumcision was performed by a priest of the *ka* (see Budge, *Osiris etc.* II, p. 220). The *ka* was apparently identified also with the head. Cf. pp. 105, 203, 278, 284 above. The king's *ka* was represented sometimes in human form carrying a cane, at the top of which is a head surmounted by the hieroglyphic sign meaning 'royal *ka*'. Sometimes the *ka* was represented (for example over the head of the king in battle) just by a fan (see for example Naville in Hastings, *Encycl. Rel. and Eth.* III, 431). We can perhaps explain this as a symbol for the wind-like 'spirit', the source of wind. Cf. ψυχή (ψύχειν, pp. 120 f.), *anima, ruah*, with *flabellum* (*flabrum*), *éventail*, etc.

originally it was credited with magic potency.[1] The other evidence consists of a very curious practice at burial unearthed in Palestine. 'In a number of tombs, all about 1200 B.C., there were found with the vessels containing food exactly identical vessels containing one or more human bones. In one, for instance, was a small earthenware jug containing the finger-bones of an infant.'[2] There was part of a skull fitted into a bowl but for the most part they were finger-bones of children or adults. This reminds us of the Roman custom of *os resectum*, the custom of cutting off a finger before burning: the presence of this one 'bone' rendered the house *funesta* until it was burned (p. 267). Festus reports it thus: *membrum abscidi mortuo dicebatur cum digitus eius decidebatur ad quod servatum iusta fierent reliquo corpore combusto* (Festus s.v. p. 135 Linds.). It is perhaps natural to relate this preservation of finger-bones with the identification of the hand or a finger with the 'spirit' or procreative life-soul. With both I would link the ancient Jewish practice of giving the name 'hand' to a stone set up for the dead. Thus: 'Absalom in his life-time had taken and reared up for himself a pillar...for he said: "I have no son to keep my name in remembrance" and he called the pillar after his own name and it is called "Absalom's hand" unto this day' (II Sam. xviii, 18; cf. I Sam. xv, 12) and in Isa. lvi, 4 f.: 'For thus saith Yahweh of the eunuchs that keep my Sabbaths...: Unto them will I give in mine house and within my walls a hand and a name better than sons and daughters.' These suggest that the pillar was intended as a permanent embodiment or representative of the procreative life-soul or spirit, and with this the 'name' was identified (cf. pp. 145, 264). Some of the extant pillars at graves are clearly themselves phallic.[3] This use of 'hand' in the above passages has been interpreted as implying that the representation of a hand

---

[1] See H. Holma, *Die Namen der Körperteile im Assyr-Bab.* p. 123.
[2] *Palestine Exploration Fund Quarterly Statement*, 1905, pp. 32 f.
[3] See the examples cited by S. A. Cook in his notes to the third edition of W. Robertson Smith, *The Religion of the Semites*, 1927, p. 688, also Curtiss, *op. cit.* p. 188, etc.

was put upon the tombstone as we know it was upon the
stelae dedicated to the Phoenician Baal and Tanith. These last
were fertility powers, and I suggest that the hand in their case
was not merely apotropaic or a pointer but expressive of the
procreative life-power in the god as in a man. And with this
I would link the remarkable practice of representing the
fertility god Sabazios by a hand or in the form of a man
carrying a hand on a sceptre (see Roscher's *Lexicon* s.v., also
p. 198, n. 1 above). The inclination of the Jews to worship him
and to identify his name with *Sabaoth* may have been helped by
their ideas about the hand. It is interesting for what we shall
say about blessing with the hand upraised that the Sabazios
hand has the curious gesture (the two first fingers up and apart
and the thumb outstretched but the two smaller fingers bent
towards the palm) which has down the centuries been used
for 'blessing' in the Christian Church of the West.

This relation of the hand to the procreative life-soul =
'spirit'[1] will help us to understand its use amongst men
(cf. p. 208, n. 3) no less than anointing, in transmitting the
spirit or vital power, also how instead of the frequent 'the
spirit of Yahweh came upon him' (Judges iii, 10; vi, 34; I Sam.
x, 6; xvi, 13, etc.) we find 'the hand of Yahweh came upon
him, and he said' etc. (II Kings iii, 15 f.; Ezek. i, 3; iii, 22;
viii, 1 f.; xxxvii, 1, etc.), and why, reporting the defence
of Jesus, when attacked for casting out evil spirits, Luke can
make him say 'But if I by the finger of God cast out devils'
(xi, 20) where Matthew has 'But if I by the spirit of God cast
out devils' (xii, 28). We can also understand how Jesus and
the Apostles by 'laying on of hands' transmitted the spirit

[1] With the above evidence for the association of the procreative life-
soul = 'spirit' with the head, thighs and hand we have already (p. 478,
n. 2) related the practice of putting a seal or mark or name upon the head,
thigh or hand of the slave. With it should naturally also be related the use
of phylacteries, the fastening of protective amulets upon the head and the
hand or arm (see p. 494, n. 1; Blau, *op. cit.* pp. 92, 151; cf. Exod. xiii, 9, 16;
Deut. vi, 8; xi, 18) and the curious passage of Ezek. xiii, 17 ff. against women
who prophesy out of their own heart and 'sew bands (? amulets, charms)
upon all hands and make wrappings for the heads of every stature to
hunt souls...'.

(Acts viii, 17; ix, 17; xix, 6, etc.) even as it was transmitted by anointing. They also by laying on of hands transmitted— another aspect of the same thing (pp. 196 ff., 477, n. 2)—life, health (Mark v, 23; vi, 5; xvi, 18, etc.). Here also their 'laying on of hands' has the same value as their anointing (see p. 287, n. 2). With, doubtless, the same original significance hands were uplifted to 'bless' or 'hail', i.e. to bestow life and health, at a distance.[1] In early Christian art God the Father, or perhaps rather his 'Spirit', is often represented by just a hand.

The Holy Spirit became visible as fire—at Pentecost. *ruaḥ* meant 'wind'; and the 'spirit' (*ruaḥ*) of a man or of Yahweh was, as we saw, of this nature. So, 'suddenly there came from heaven a sound as of the rushing of a mighty wind and it filled all the house where they were sitting and they saw tongues parting asunder (i.e. distributing themselves) like as of fire and it sat upon each of them and they were all filled with the Holy Spirit' (Acts ii, 2–4). It was the 'baptism with the Holy Spirit' (i, 5). According to Matthew (iii, 11) and Luke (iii, 16), John the Baptist had the same conception: 'I indeed baptise you with water unto repentance; but he that cometh after me...shall baptise you with the Holy Spirit and fire (ἐν πνεύματι ἁγίῳ καὶ πυρί)'. This can now be related to the belief we have already traced in the Talmud (*Niddah* 30 b: see p. 153, n. 1 with pp. 147 ff.): that when a child is in the womb, a light burns on its head, in which the life-soul (= 'spirit') is; that is, in a human being his own spirit is manifest as fire. With this we related not only similar beliefs among other peoples but also the belief about Moses that when he came down from Mount Sinai, 'the skin of his face

---

[1] Lev. ix, 22 f., II Kings iv, 29 etc. Cf. pp. 181, n. 1; 186; 477, n. 2; 491, n. 2. This beneficent act, bestowal of life, may have been the original meaning of the Roman greeting by holding up the hand, perhaps the finger (*digitus salutaris*), towards another, i.e. *salutare*, 'to give *salus* to', our 'salute'. *Salus* and *salve!* = 'Hail!' (pp. 277, 477, n. 1), Homeric οὖλε, expressed originally 'wholeness', the fulness of life. Cf. p. 477, n. 2 and the greeting 'Live!' taken over by the Romans as *ave* from the Carthaginians (see Plautus, *Poen.* 998, 1141 and, for example, Walde-Hofmann s.v.).

shone and they were afraid to come nigh him'[1] (Exod. xxxiv, 30). It was, apparently, his spirit manifest in power; but the spirit of Yahweh possessing one would naturally be conceived in the same form, as of fire. We can now better understand the 'glory', or halo.[2]

An oil-lamp was put on their tombs by the Jews in the first centuries of our era to represent the spirit.[3] The equation had been made long before in a way which grimly convinces of its reality. We saw that in the sacrifice it was the fat, which was identified with the 'spirit', that was offered (pp. 287, 484 f.). 'In the period contemporaneous with Egyptian rule in Canaan, deposits of lamps placed between two bowls begin to occur under the corners of thresholds of houses, in positions where formerly sacrificed infants were buried. It is clear that these are intended as substitutes for child-sacrifice. The lamp, the symbol of life, takes the place of the life of the child....Lamp and bowl deposits become increasingly frequent in the upper Canaanite

[1] It is in harmony with the above interpretation of head and hands that early Christians believed that in holy men praying at night the head and uplifted hands flamed (see examples in Reitzenstein, *Hist. Monach. u. Hist. Laus.* pp. 56 f.).

[2] See p. 167. In the New Testament, δόξα 'glory' is used of shining radiance as *kabhodh* 'glory' is in the Old. See e.g. Acts xxii, 11; Luke ix, 29-32; I Corinth. xv, 41. Paul speaks of himself and his fellows as ministers not, as Moses was, of death, the letter of the Law that killeth, but of the spirit of the living God that giveth life. Therefore they shine with glory not less than Moses: 'If the ministration of death in letters, engraven on stones, came with glory so that the children of Israel could not look steadfastly upon the face of Moses for the glory of his face, how should not rather the ministration of the spirit be with glory?...We all with unveiled faces reflecting as a mirror the glory of the Lord are transformed into the same image from glory to glory even as from the spirit of the Lord (or "from the spirit which is the Lord" ἀπὸ Κυρίου πνεύματος)....God, who said "Light shall shine out of darkness", hath shined in our hearts to give the light of the knowledge of the glory of God in the face of Jesus Christ' (II Corinth. iii, 7, 18; iv, 6). The 'glory', *kabhodh*, δόξα (LXX), of Yahweh was visible fire (Exod. xxiv, 16f.; Ezek. i, 27f., x, 4 etc.). Cf. Isaiah x, 16 with passages in which *kabhodh* is used apparently of the soul or spirit in a man, e.g. Gen. xlix, 6; Ps. vii, 5 and xvi, 9, in which last it is rendered by the LXX as 'tongue', γλῶσσα.

[3] See for example Hastings, *op. cit.* xII, 144 *b*.

and Israelite levels, and jar-burials [i.e. of infants] decrease in the same ratio, until, about the time of the Exile, jar-burials cease altogether and only lamp and bowl deposits remain.'[1] The lamp is not just a 'symbol of life' but equivalent 'spirit', life-stuff, to serve instead. This equation, which links the oil or life-fluid in a man with the spirit, with which, as we saw on very different evidence, it was identified in belief (pp. 189 ff.), and which links it with the flame, as which both oil and spirit could be manifest, also perhaps lies behind 'The spirit (*n^eshama*) of a man is a lamp of Yahweh searching all the innermost parts of the belly (*beṭen*)', Prov. xx, 27.

There remains the dove. When Jesus was baptised by John, Mark tells us that 'Coming up out of the water, he saw the heavens rent asunder and the Spirit as a dove descending upon [or "into"] him. And a voice came out of the heavens: "Thou art my beloved son; in thee I am well pleased". And straightway the Spirit driveth him forth into the wilderness' (i, 10–12). It is perhaps now unnecessary to urge that here, too, the explanation is to be found in the conceptions of the spirit in man, i.e. that at this time the spirit of an ordinary human being was conceived of as taking the form of a dove so that the spirit of God to possess a man was thought of in the same form. There is clear evidence that in Palestine and Syria the spirit outside the body, the departed spirit, was thought of as a dove. There were *columbaria* with niches for the urns or ashes of the dead; and actual dovecots were joined to graves.[2] This thought was continued among the early Christians. In the Catacombs we find the spirit drinking the water of life represented by a dove drinking from a basin.[3] There are two

---

[1] . L. B. Paton in Hastings, *op. cit.* III, 187, citing *Palestine Exploration Fund Quarterly Statement*, 1903, pp. 10 f., 228, 299, 306 ff.

[2] See Gressmann, *Taufe u. Taubengöttin, Archiv für Religionswiss.* xx, pp. 328–30. The departed spirit appeared in the form of a dove in old Germanic and Slav (Polish) beliefs (see Grimm, *Deutsche Myth.*[4] pp. 690 f. with *Nachtr.* p. 246). If, as appears likely, the Erinyes were originally departed ψυχαί of human beings (cf. p. 424, n. 7), the association of dark-coloured doves with them and the fate goddesses (Aelian, *Nat. Anim.* x, 33) points to a similar Greek belief.

[3] See, for example, Hastings, *op. cit.* XII, 134*b*.

obvious reasons for this belief. The dove is remarkable for its mating ways, its loving habits. In the Song of Songs (i, 15; ii, 14; iv, 1; v, 2; vi, 9) it is the type of the beloved, of the tenderness of love. It was, therefore, as natural to see in it an embodiment of the departed procreative 'spirit' as it was to see in that form the spirit of love and fertility in all things, the goddess Aštarte, Atargatis, etc. (cf. the relation of the procreative life-soul, *juno*, and the great goddess of procreation, *Juno*, pp. 142 f.). The other reason is its low mournful note. This is its other most frequently mentioned attribute in the Old Testament. It 'mourns' (Isa. xxxviii, 14; lix, 11; Ezek. vii, 16; Nahum ii, 7). One of the words (*hagha*) used to describe this sound of doves (for example, Isa. xxxviii, 14) is one of two— it is translated 'mutter'—used of the sound of soothsayers who prophesied with the aid of a departed spirit (Isa. viii, 19). The other verb used of the sounds of the latter, *çaphaph* (Isa. viii, 19; xxix, 4), which has been translated 'whisper', 'peep' or 'chirp', is from its other instances (*ibid.* x, 14; xxxviii, 14) clearly a term for birds' utterance. The characteristic utterance of the Arab soothsayer is known as *saj'*, of which the normal meaning is the 'cooing' of a dove.

In the earliest Gospel, Mark, Jesus was the son of Joseph born again of water and the Spirit as Son of God at baptism, the *Messiah*, χριστός i.e. 'Christ' = 'anointed' [1] (see pp. 189f.). When the Gospels of Matthew and Luke were written, a new and more impressive story appears. According to Matthew, when Mary was only betrothed, she was found to be with child, and Joseph was warned by an angel: 'Fear not to take unto thee Mary thy wife; for that which is begotten in her is of the Holy Spirit', and Joseph took her 'and knew her not till she

[1] In this version the spirit, that in the original *Messiah* was apparently conceived of as oil infused (pp. 189 ff.), takes the form of a dove. If the Baptist actually anointed Jesus, the coming of the dove is a visualisation of the divine counterpart coming as when Samuel 'anointed him in the midst of his brethren and the spirit of the Lord (Yahweh) came mightily upon David...' (I Sam. xvi, 13; see p. 190). It was slightly delayed in the case of Saul (I Sam. x, 1–13). There is nothing to preclude that at baptism Jesus was deeply moved, had a profound religious experience in which he felt himself called as *Messiah* (pp. 190 f.).

had brought forth a son' (i, 18–25). In Luke i also Jesus is the Son of God from the womb. There is no hint of any message to Joseph, but Gabriel says to Mary: '"Fear not, Mary: for thou hast found favour with God, and behold thou shalt conceive in thy womb and bring forth a son and shalt call his name Jesus. He shall be great and shall be called the son of the Most High"...and Mary said unto the angel "How shall this be, seeing I know not a man?" And the angel answered and said unto her, "The Holy Spirit shall come upon thee and the power of the Most High shall overshadow thee; wherefore also that which is to be born shall be called holy, the Son of God"' (i, 26–38).[1] So for John (i, 14, 18; iii, 16, 18) and others later Jesus was 'the only begotten son of God'. God is the father; and his 'spirit'—that in a man, to which, as we have seen, procreation belongs, and part of which passes to be the 'spirit' of his son (cf. p. 109, esp. n. 3; p. 111, n. 6; pp. 492 f.)—is naturally involved in this begetting. These appear to be the original basic interrelations of the Trinity, of Father, Son, and Holy Spirit. The Spirit is the link no less in the other version of Jesus' sonship (pp. 190 f.). Luke's expression 'The Holy Spirit shall come upon you' is that which in Acts i, 8 describes the entry[2] of the Spirit into the Apostles (ii, 3 f.). Even this account of

[1] Somewhat inconsistently Matthew and Luke retain the alternative story of Jesus' divine sonship. They represent him as receiving the Spirit and acknowledged by God as his son only after his baptism by John (Matt. iii, 16 f.; Luke iii, 21 f.). Contrast John the Baptist 'filled with the Holy Spirit even from his mother's womb' (Luke i, 15).

[2] In harmony with what we saw (pp. 119 f. and with note 14) of procreation as 'breathing', Mary was apparently believed by some quite late to receive the Holy Spirit as breathed into her womb. Ambrose in the 4th century in his hymn 'Veni redemptor gentium':

> Non ex virili semine
> Sed mystico spiramine
> Verbum Dei factum est caro
> Fructusque ventris floruit,

and it recurs e.g.

> Aura sancti spiritus
> Crescit venter caelitus
> Nulli viro cognitus.

(See Analecta Hymnica Medii Aevi, ed. Blume and Dreves, v, p. 58.)

the divine fatherhood, given by Luke with great dignity and beauty, fitted into existing thought. The occasional visiting of a woman by Yahweh to bring to birth a son seems to be implicit in Paul's interpretation (Rom. ix, 7–9; cf. Gal. iv, 22–9) of the story of Yahweh's promised visit to Sarah and the consequent birth of Isaac (Gen. xviii, 10–15; xxi, 1–3), son not of the flesh (of Abraham) but 'of the promise'. Philo of Alexandria, an older contemporary of Jesus, saw in such passages actual begetting by God.[1]

The last stage in this progressive exaltation[2] of Jesus into God represents him as 'begotten before all worlds' without naming a mother or explaining how this fact was known: 'the firstborn of all creation; for in him were all things created in the heavens and upon the earth...all things have been created through him and unto him; and he is before all things and in him all things consist...in him dwelleth all the fulness of the Godhead bodily' (Coloss. i, 15–17; ii, 9; cf. Hebr. i, 2, etc.); 'who being in the form of God...emptied himself, taking the form of a servant, becoming in the likeness of men' (Philipp. i, 6 f.). 'In the beginning was the Word [λόγος, "*Logos*"] and the Word was with God and the Word was God. The same was in the beginning with God. All things were made by him [δι' αὐτοῦ] and without him was not anything made...and the Word became flesh and dwelt among us and we beheld his glory, the glory as of the only begotten from the Father' (John i, 1–3, 14). This last stage is crystallised in the equality of the three Persons of the Trinity, Father, Son, and Holy Ghost or Spirit, e.g. in the 'Athanasian Creed': 'Whosoever will be saved, before all things it is necessary that he hold the Catholick Faith; which Faith

---

[1] See, for example, A. S. Carman, 'Philo's doctrine of the divine Father and the virgin mother', *Amer. Journ. of Theol.* 1905, pp. 491 ff.

[2] There has also, somewhat later, been progressive exaltation of Mary the mother of Jesus into the Mother of God. So, in the Roman Catholic Church, her 'immaculate conception', disputed since the second-century *Protevangelium* or *Book of James*, was proclaimed by the Pope in 1854; and the taking up of her body as well as her soul into heaven is even now in 1950 at last proclaimed as a dogma by the Pope, assured of the support of a majority of bishops.

except everyone do keep whole and undefiled, without doubt he shall perish everlastingly. And the Catholick Faith is this: that we worship one God in Trinity and Trinity in Unity... and in this Trinity none is afore or after other, none is greater or less than another, but the whole three Persons are co-eternal together and co-equal.' It is a magnificent, though difficult, conception. It made it easier for men to worship Jesus and to find power in him; it linked him with the cosmic *Logos* of the Stoics or of Philo; but it was apparently no more than the confidently expressed thought of St Paul or a contemporary, which was almost inevitably welcome to his followers. It is no more certainly true than some of St Paul's other pronouncements, for example: 'neither was the man created for the woman, but the woman for the man' (I Corinth. xi, 9). More important, it was apparently undreamed of by Jesus himself, who according to the earliest and most trustworthy evidence, when addressed as 'Good Teacher', said 'Why callest thou me good? None is good save one, even God' (Mark x, 18; Luke xviii, 19; cf. Matt. xix, 17), and, when crucified, said 'My God, my God, why hast thou forsaken me?' (Mark xv, 34; Matt. xxvii, 46).

To trace the genesis of certain beliefs and to explain their form is not to discredit the truth most of them image, though imperfectly, the essential Christian vision of God and of men in relation to Him and to each other, a vision already in great part seen by the noblest Jewish prophets and Greek philosophers but most simply and movingly proclaimed and lived by Jesus. Through Him and his disciples and apostles the ancient superstition that the king is son of a god became a way for all men to know God as their Father[1] (pp. 190f.), and the ancient and rather selfish idea of sacrifice, redeeming oneself by the life of a fellow-creature, became through the self-offered 'Lamb of God' self-sacrifice: 'that a man lay down his life for his friends', and all men are these. This vision is in the present writer's opinion

[1] This image too, of course, is imperfect. Its maleness, its anthropomorphism, its suggestion of a being of the same order as man, these are not intrinsic to ordinary experience of the universe or to the mystic's awareness of God.

moreuniversal and profound than any of the arrogant ideologies or timid scepticisms of the modern world, and it needs to be proclaimed anew, freed from the inessential details that have been outgrown. They prevent its acceptance by critical minds and, scarcely less, by the mass of men. These now depend upon their own devices and the inertia of a tradition whose credentials have become dubious. To 'cut away the dead wood' and reveal the still solid core of truth would be worth much. 'I am the true vine and my Father is the husbandman. Every branch in me that beareth not fruit, he taketh it away; and every branch that beareth fruit he purgeth it that it may bear more fruit' (John xv, 1 f.). A man is not helped to know God or to love his neighbour as himself if he is required to believe, for instance, that an insane person is 'possessed of an unclean spirit' or 'devil', or by eight, or by a legion of them, and that once these last were obligingly transferred by Jesus from one man into two thousand swine, that were innocently feeding near, and in the swine rushed to drown them all (Mark v, 2–14), or that Jesus blasted a fig-tree because it had not borne fruit out of season when he wanted some (*ibid.* xi, 12–23). If the superstitions of Palestine nineteen centuries ago are understood, seen for what they were, they need not discredit the unageing truths, which had already then been perceived and with which they were then inevitably joined. Jesus himself applied a fearless common sense and humanity to venerable but unhelpful superstitions, 'the tradition of men' (see for example Mark ii, 23–iii, 6; vii, 1–23). Fearlessly to follow common sense and humanity, never allowing either to be sacrificed to a doctrine or to personal or sectional or national ends, seems to be the chief need of this age.

V. *PRAECORDIA* AND THE LIVER

(Addendum to pp. 42 and 89)

We saw that for the Romans the organs of consciousness were the heart and the liver and the *praecordia*; and we interpreted *praecordia* as originally meaning not the diaphragm but the lungs. This explains and is itself confirmed by five

tabellae defixionis or curse-tablets which were published by
M. W. Sherwood Fox in the *American Journal of Philology*
(Suppl., vol. xxxiii, 1912) and have been kindly brought to
my notice by Mr F. H. Sandbach in time for insertion here.
They appear to have been inscribed in or near Rome perhaps
70 years B.C. In more or less identical terms each of them for
a different occasion consigns to Proserpine the various parts
of a victim's body, indicating their functions: for example,
'the mouth, lips, tongue so that the victim may not be able
to say what is causing her to suffer' (*ni dicere possit quit sibi
doleat*), her feet so that she may not be able to stand, and so
on. Thus 'her chest, liver, heart and lungs so that she may
not be able to understand (or "perceive") at all what is
causing her to suffer' (*pectus, iocinera, cor, pulmones ni possit quit
sentire quit sibi doleat*). These organs were consulted for knowledge of the future (p. 60, n. 2).

VI. ΒΡΟΤΟΣ, 'GORE', AND THE 'ICHOR' OF THE GODS

(Addendum to pp. 46 ff., 61, 298 f.)

We have seen that in man while the life-soul, the ψυχή, is
the divine, the immortal, factor, the θυμός is mortal, 'destroyed' and 'shattered' by death. Death itself is characterised
as 'θυμός-shattering' (p. 95). But θυμός is in direct relation
to, is an emanation of, blood (pp. 46 ff., 61). This relation of
θυμός, the mortal factor, to blood may help us to explain
βρότος, 'gore' (blood that has run from a wound and is dry
apparently), i.e. that it is in origin one with βροτός, related
to *mors* and meaning 'mortal' or 'dead'. Its θυμός has been
destroyed, and it is parted from the ψυχή. For the accents
cf. pp. 211, n. 9; 343 ff. If βρότος expressed originally only
what is 'mortal' or 'dead', the *Iliad*'s invariable definition of
it by αἱματόεις is natural. Homer seems to have understood
βρότος in some such way. His gods have no 'blood' that is
mortal, only a counterpart that is ἄμβροτον, 'immortal', i.e.
ichor, which is why they are known as 'immortal'. This

liquid, ichor, issues when, in *Il.* v, 339ff., Aphrodite is wounded:

ῥέε δ' ἄμβροτον αἷμα θεοῖο
ἰχώρ, οἷός πέρ τε ῥέει μακάρεσσι θεοῖσιν·
οὐ γὰρ σῖτον ἔδουσ', οὐ πίνουσ' αἴθοπα οἶνον,
τοὔνεκ' ἀναίμονές εἰσι καὶ ἀθάνατοι καλέονται.

These last two lines recall Kirke's bidding: 'Eat food and drink wine till once more you get θυμός in your chests...but now you are dry and lacking θυμός' (*Od.* x, 460ff.; p. 48). The liquid in the bodies of the gods, ἰχώρ, is perhaps related to αἰών, the liquid of the immortal life-soul (pp. 200 ff.), and to the water of life (pp. 288 ff.). The cicada, τέττιξ, was believed to live on dew and to be without blood (Aristot. *Hist. An.* 532b 13; Theoc. ιν, 16; *Anth. Pal.* νι, 120, etc.) and free from suffering and age; it was like the gods:

ὀλίγην δρόσον πεπωκὼς
βασιλεὺς ὅπως ἀείδεις...
τὸ δὲ γῆρας οὔ σε τείρει,
σοφέ, γηγενής, φίλυμνε·
ἀπαθὴς δ' ἀναιμόσαρκε
σχεδὸν εἰ θεοῖς ὅμοιος.

Anacreontea, 32 Bgk.

VII. *APOCOLOCYNTOSIS*

(Addendum to pp. 123 ff.)

We have traced among the Romans the belief that the life-soul which survives death is in or is the head and is a god, so that the person can be said at death to become a god, the emperor a god not merely for his family but for the Roman people (so Vespasian, aware that he is dying: *vae, puto, deus fio*, Suetonius, *Vesp.* 23). His head, radiant, ascends to heaven, a god, *numen* (pp. 137 ff.). This belief will, I suggest, explain *Apocolocyntosis*, 'Pumpkinification', the title of Seneca's mocking account of Claudius' degradation at death instead of *apotheosis*, 'deification'; i.e. his head, instead of passing thus radiant to heaven, a god, *qua caput Augustum, quem temperat orbe relicto, | accedat caelo faveatque precantibus absens* (Ov.

Met. xv, 869f.; cf. pp. 135, 163f.), is dishonoured, 'becomes a pumpkin'. Jeering at Claudius' official deification, Juvenal says, of the mushroom that poisoned him: *tremulum caput descendere iussit in caelum* (p. 136). Seneca himself thinks of death as the departure of the head: *cur caput tenebris grave | non mitto ad umbras Ditis aeternas?* (p. 134), and wishing to flatter Nero sees his head radiant, i.e. divine: *flagrat nitidus fulgore remisso | vultus et adfuso cervix formosa capillo* (*Apocol.* 4; cf. p. 166). In the *Apocolocyntosis* he is, I suggest, referring to the emperor's head that should be divine. The resemblance of head to pumpkin (κολοκύνθη, *cucurbita*) and the identification of a worthless head with a pumpkin were familiar. Thus in his *Metamorphoses* Apuleius (cf. p. 130) has *cucurbita calviorem* 'more bald than a pumpkin' (v, 9) and *nos cucurbitae caput non habemus ut pro te moriamur* (i, 15), referring to the empty head of madness (cf. p. 148, n. 4) or meaning 'mine is not a worthless life, as good as no life-soul, to sacrifice for you' (cf. *caput pro aliquo offerre*).

VIII. *MORTARIUM*, 'MORTAR'

(Addendum to pp. 249, n. 9; 281, n. 1)

The belief traced on pp. 249 (esp. n. 9) and 281 (esp. n. 1) that not only roots, seeds, etc. but stone, minerals, possess life may enable us to find the true explanation of Lat. *mortarium* (our 'mortar') meaning (*a*) the vessel in which things are crushed, disintegrated; (*b*) that which has been crushed or mixed—drugs or cement. I suggest that like other Latin words beginning with *mort-* it originally referred to death and meant that in or with which a thing was 'deaded' or 'dead' (cf. *frigidarium, sacrarium, vivarium,* etc.), also the resultant 'dead' substance (cf. *bellaria, pulmentarium,* etc.). This would obviously fit the vessel for crushing roots or fruit or grain (e.g. Cato, *Agric.* 74) or the substance resulting in these cases (e.g. Juv. VII, 170). Nonius remarks (449, 19) that 'The ancients laid it down on strong authority that even *inanimalia* [i.e. objects later deemed so] can be "killed" and "slain" (*interfici* and *occidi*)', citing, for example, *durum molle voras, fragmenta interficis panis* (Lucilius 1157 Marx). Thus it is, apparently, that Homer speaks of 'mill-slain' barley (μυλη-φάτου ἀλφίτου ἀκτῆς, *Od.* II, 355). The early Romans did this to their grain with a *mortarium*. A baker was *pistor*. The same explanation fits no less (*a*) that with which stones, etc. were crushed and mortar made, and (*b*) the resultant mortar. We have seen that stone was conceived as alive. *Viva*, 'quick', was applied explicitly to *calx*, lime, with which mortar was made, when the *calx* was *exstincta* (e.g. Vitr. II, 5). The alchemists, who based their researches upon a persisting belief in the 'life' of stones (see p. 281), termed the residuum of their processes *caput mortuum*. 'Deads' is the English mining term for the stone, earth, etc. containing no ore and thrown up in working. The vein with ore in it was 'quick'. Ovid speaks of *saxo quod adhuc vivum radice tenetur* (*Met.* XIV, 713). On Virgil's *vivoque sedilia saxo* (*Aen.* I, 17) Henry notes that 'in Italy at the present day any stone no matter whether *in situ* or not is denominated *vivo*, provided only it possesses the qualities popularly attributed to pure and perfect stone, in other words provided it is hard, durable, fine-grained, and free from admixture of earth, sand or other extraneous substance...while on the other hand any stone not possessing these properties is denominated *morta*'.

IX. THE 'BILLIE BLIND' OR 'BELLY BLIND', 'THE AULD BELLY-BLIND MAN'

(Addendum to p. 428 with p. 429, n. 1)

The Billie Blind or Belly Blind (see *Engl. and Scot. Pop. Ballads*, ed. F. J. Child, vols. I, pp. 63, 67, 466; II, p. 472; IV, p. 494; V, p. 239, etc.), a household spirit who appears at the bed or elsewhere to approve a marriage and attests or denies the bride's virginity or good birth, was, I suggest, in origin an ancestral spirit or *Lar* (p. 158, n. 5. Cf. the interest of the *Lar*, Plaut. *Aul. prol.*, 385 ff., *Rud.* 1206 f., etc.) with a wrapping over his eyes, since the dead had such. It is an old name for Blind Man's

Buff = Hoodman Blind. Billy or Belly is, I suggest, just our
'Belly', originally = 'bag', here that with which the head of
the dead was believed to be covered and with which the head
of the corpse was customarily covered and with which upon
his head the dead was visualised returning (see pp. 427 ff.).

X. *DELUBRUM* AND *LUSTRUM*

(Addendum to pp. 437 ff.)

Clytemnestra sent a sacrifice as λύτρον πεσόντος αἵματος
(Aesch. *Ch.* 48). In *religio* and the basic Roman thought of
evil, sin, and debt, as bonds to be 'loosed' (pp. 439 ff.), lies,
I suggest, the explanation of the word for a shrine, place of
sacrifice, *delubrum*, i.e. a 'place of loosing' (cf. p. 125), as also of
the rite *lustrum* (*lustrare*, etc.), a 'loosing', as Varro thought (*de
L.L.* vi, 11), not a 'purification'. There is no trace of 'washing'.
Ennius translated ["Εκτορος] λύτρα apparently by *lustra*.[1] For
luere: *lustrum* cf. *fluere*: *flustrum*. The taking of the *suovetaurilia*
around, for example, an *ager* in *lustratio* might be conceived as
unbinding it or as bringing all of it into contact with them
and into benefit; the sacrifice itself would be conceived as
λύτρον, paying, 'loosing'. Cf., for example, *habes cuius rei causa
fecerim hecatomben: in quo ego puto, quoniam est luere solvere, lutavi*
(Varro, *Menipp.* 100) and *lustramurque Jovi votisque incendimus
aras* (*Aen.* iii, 279), *piaculum solvunt, hoc est enim diis lustrari,
offensa eorum liberari* (Serv. *ad loc.*).

XI. *FINIS, FIMUS*

(Addendum to pp. 313 ff.)

This evidence (pp. 313 ff.) suggested to me in 1925 that
finis = 'limit' was originally identical with *funis* = 'cord'. So
fimus = 'dung' with *fumus* = 'smoke' (see alternatives in

---

[1] The *lytra* of some MSS. is currently read after Bergk (*Op. Philol.*
I, 295 f.), who unjustifiably assumes that *lustrum* from √*lu-* 'loose' did not
and could not exist. It undeniably existed from √*lu-* in the much rarer
sense 'wash'.

Walde-Hofmann, s.v.). Dung smokes and reeks, is that which in a quite distinctive way gives off, 'breathes out' (pp. 74 f.) a smell, as does more pleasantly for the Greeks that to which they gave such name (cf. p. 44), θύμος, 'thyme' (for the difference of accent cf. pp. 211, n. 9; 343 ff., 506). The French have found it natural to express 'dung' as *fumier*, 'to dung' as *fumer*. The same thought is, perhaps, also the true explanation of the German *Mist* = 'dung'. Akin to *fumus* are *suffire*, *suffimentum*, etc.; and there is in Latin clear evidence of the tendency of original *u* to become *i*. In many words the transition is clear, both forms surviving: for example, *infumus*, *infimus*; *decumus*, *decimus*; *recuperare*, *reciperare*; *lubet*, *libet*; *clupeus*, *clipeus*; *lacruma*, *lacrima*; in harmony with which *fumus* would become *fimus* and *funis* *finis*. In 1931 Niedermann explained *finis* by *funis* (*Glotta* XIX, 7) but for want of this background of thought it has found no favour. Instead a derivation from *figo* is current (see Walde-Hofmann, also Ernout and Meillet, s.v.).

XII. ANCIENT HINDOO CONCEPTIONS OF THE SOUL

(Addendum to pp. 280, 484)

As we have seen (pp. 280 n. 1, 484), among the ancient Hindoos the *omentum* was the essential part of the sacrificial victim, the life-principle—with it the *ātman* was identified (*Taittirīya Saṃhitā*, VI, 3, 9, 5. Cf. the self=the seed on p. 196 above)—and it with the rest of the fat of the body was gathered up to be burned for the gods. We may compare not only the similar practice of the Greeks[1] and the Jews (pp. 279 f., 484 f.) but particularly those of the more

---

[1] The *omentum* was offered by the Romans also to their gods (p. 282). The name, perhaps a shorter form of *ovimentum* as *momentum* of *movimentum*, may be explained if the Latins saw, as the Jews apparently did, in this fat the source of seed or offspring. If the ultimate root is that of *aug-* (*ōg-*, cf. *Claudius*, *Clodius*; *caudex*, *codex*, etc.) that might have the sense of 'seed, sperm' which is seen in the Icelandic *auki*, etc. Cf. *incrementum* and our 'increase' = 'offspring'.

closely kindred Persians who, according to Strabo (xv, 3, 13 = 732 Casaub.), divided the sacrificial animal amongst themselves, leaving only its ψυχή to the deity: 'Nevertheless, as some say, they put a bit of the *omentum* on the fire.' Cf. *Vendidad*, xviii, 70. When a man died, the Hindoos sacrificed a cow and put its heart on the man's heart and its *omentum* round his head and face (see *Grihya Sutra* of Āśvalāyana, iv, 3, 17). Scholars have found it difficult to define the original Vedic notions of the soul. Already in the *Rig Veda* it appears that the *manas*, the conscious mind that perceives and thinks and feels emotions, resides in the chest, in the heart. Cf. the 'breaths' of speech, of seeing, of hearing, etc., in the Upanishads on pp. 75 f. above. The *asu*, which is mentioned as other than the *manas* and which appears not to be concerned in consciousness, is the life, the vitality and strength (see *Rig Veda*, i, 113, 16; 140, 8) and is that which Agni, the funeral fire and fire-god, is characterised as leading to the world of the dead in the heavens. It is clearly something wind-like and so has been thought (see, e.g., Oldenberg, *Relig. des Veda*[4], p. 526) to have referred originally to the ordinary breath of respiration, which is *prāṇa*. We may now guess that it—and perhaps *ātman*, which in the *Rig Veda* is something of the nature of wind and later is the most important word for 'soul'—was originally much the same as we have traced to be the ψυχή, *anima = genius*, etc. of other 'Indo-European' peoples, i.e. the procreative life-soul conceived of as vaporous and as 'breathing' in procreation (pp. 119 f.) and associated particularly with the head. This would explain above the putting of the *omentum* about the head of the dead. We have seen (p. 100) that the closely related Persians associated the immortal part with the head and (p. 105) that when a man sneezed, Hindoos cried 'Live!' much as did Greeks and Romans, for whom a sneeze was an emission through the nostrils of the life-soul in the brain. While among the early Hindoos cremation was usual, the bodies of young children and ascetics were buried; but first the skull was split (see Caland, *Die altind. Todten- u. Bestattungsgebr.* § 50), apparently to release the soul. If the latter were originally identified with ordinary breath, this opening of the skull would be unnatural. In the *Mahabharata*, xiii, 168, 1 ff., when Bhisma dies, his *ātman* makes a way out for itself through his head, and in the great sacrifice of the Horse (*aśvamedha*), when the latter is slain by Bhima, its head rises and disappears into the heaven, while its body is cast into the sacrificial fire. We may compare in the *Rig Veda* (i, 116, 12; 117, 22; 119, 9) the horse's head which is given to Dadhyañc and prophesies, reveals the truth. We have indeed already seen, in the parting of a woman's hair to secure an easy birth (p. 232, n. 4), that for the ancient Hindoos the head was involved in procreation. In the *Grihya Sutra* of Sānkhāyana (i, 19, 1), to secure a child, a powdered root is put into the wife's nostril with the words 'Into thy breath I put the sperm.' Cf. Pāraskara, i, 13, 1; and Āśvalāyana, i, 13, 2, where the sap of a plant is used thus. In the *Atharva Veda*, iii, 23, an arrow is broken over the wife's head with the words 'Into thy womb let a foetus come, a male one, as an arrow to a quiver.' Finally, it may now perhaps be guessed that the Vedic words for 'head' *çira-h*, etc., Avestan *sarah-*, which have been recognised as cognate with κάρα, κέρας, *cerebrum, cornu*, our 'horn', etc., were, as we have seen the latter were, originally expressive of generation. Cf. Sanscrit *çrṅgam* = 'horn', and Avestan *gaokerena* = 'ox-horn', source of fertility (p. 241 n. 1).

GENERAL INDEX

Acheloos, the prime river-god, 240, 249

adoption by taking child on the knees, 175–6

age: conceived as a drying process, 214–15, 219–21, as a slough to be cast off, 291, 430 n. 2, as a bond, 401, 429, 459–60

aiōn (αἰών): identified with the life-fluid, 200–6, 212–15, 251, 254, 507; meaning approximates to 'fate', 204–5, but definitely becomes 'spinal marrow', 205–6, 208; associated with snake form, 206–7, 251; development of meaning to 'life', 208–9; cognate words, 209; related to anointing, 209–12; diminishes with age, 213–16; relation to river-worship, 230 and n. 8, to Ὠκεανός, 247–53; departs with death, 254; equated with δαίμων, 405–6

alchemy, origin of, 281 n. 1, 508–9

Alcmaeon of Croton, 71, 76 and n. 9, 80 n. 6, 115 and n. 7

Ambrose, Saint (quoted), 502 n. 2

ambrosia, 74, 292–9

amulets: horns and phalli as, 240 n. 1; bands or wrappings, 357–61, 366–77; and the significance of clothing, 448 n. 5; as protective phylacteries, 497 n. 1

Anaxagoras, 83, 84, 238, 253

Anaximander, 248 n. 3, 251–2

Anaximenes, 32, 115 n. 7, 248 n. 3, 252

Ancren Riwle (quoted), 202 n. 2

anger: breathed, 50, 52; as fire in the eye, 77; associated with bile, 88; as fire in the brain, 147–50

Anglo-Saxons. See s.v. English in General Index, and in Index of Words, p. 530

anima: name for departed soul, 132; hospes comesque corporis, 161 n. 2; true significance and relation with animus, 168–73, 209 n. 3

animus: affected by emotion, 34–5; associated with lungs, 42–3, 168–71; related to blood?, 63, to vision, 79, to speech, 139 n. 2; dualism of animus and genius, 148 n. 2, 168; true significance and relation with anima, 168–73, 209 n. 3; and Jewish nephesh, 481–2

Anna Perenna, festival of, 216, 227

Anthesteria, festival of, 218 n. 3, 400 n. 9, 405 n. 8 fin.

Arab beliefs, 103 nn. 2, 3, 188 n. 2, 448 n. 5, 483 n. 2, 487, 490

Aristotle: theory of hearing, 72–3; explanation of sneeze, 104; doctrine of the ψυχή, 111 n. 6; on Thales' view of water as primary substance, 247–8; freedom of the will and an external cause, 366. See also Index of Passages, p. 541

Armenian beliefs, 180 n. 1, 189 n. 2 fin., 290 n. 3

Athene: birth from the head of Zeus, 111, from the chin of Zeus, 233

athletes, reasons for anointing, 210–11

Australian native belief, 188 n. 2

Babylonians: divination by entrails, 60 n. 2; notion of the liver, 89, of head and knee, 124 n. 6, 176, of strength, 196, of the vine, 217 n. 2; treaty-curses, 218 n. 1; earth encircled by a serpent, 249 n. 5; funeral practices, 284–7; disease conceived as a bond, 364, 400; prayer quoted, 436 n. 1; slaves marked on the forehead, 478 n. 2; seat of compassion in the belly, 486 n. 1; departed spirit conceived as wind, 487 n. 1. See also Index of Words, p. 530

Baganda beliefs, 236

baldness: related to drought, 231 n. 1, to loss of seed, 232

baptism, 189 n. 2 ad med., 228 n. 1, 299, 498–501

Barbour, John (quoted), 474 n. 2
barley-groats: 'the marrow of men',
222, 228 n. 1, 229, 274 n. 2, 279
n. 5; identified with the life-
substance, 228 n. 1
battle: lust for, 21–2; imaged as living
creature, 187 n. 8; controlled by
πείρατα of the gods, 310–11, 317–
20, 324–8, 337, 356; 'woof of war',
351, 355–6, 374; use of magic in
battle-rites, 361 and n. 3, 362–3;
significance of trophies, 375; 'coil
of war', 388–9; πολέμου τέλος, 433–6,
460–1
beans (κύαμοι), 112 and n. 2, 113 n. 1,
393 n. 2, 489 n. 2
beauty: as a wreath or crown, 402,
461 n. 8; poured about a person,
464 n. 3
belly: treated as independent being,
88; seat of spirit and seed, 485–90;
originally = 'bag', 510
Beowulf (quoted), 38, 68–9, 100, 154
and n. 10, 155 n. 4, 196 n. 4, 209
n. 3, 356–7, 417 n. 9
blood: its relation to breath and consciousness, 47–9, 61–3, 481–2, to
sense of touch, 81, to character,
121–2; represented by wine and
food, 218 n. 1, 272 n. 1, 278 n. 2;
part of 'moisture' lost at death,
255; related to ichor, 506–7
blush: manifestation of genius, 146;
and flammeum, 153 and n. 2, 403 n. 1
boar, associated with fertility, 154–5
bond: round the earth as serpent or
'Ὠκεανός, 248–50, 251 n. 11, 315–17,
332; of strife, victory, 310–11, 317–
20, 324–8, 433–6; as a mesh or net,
321–3; of fate round men, 322–4,
331–8, 349–51, 378–82, 390–4; expressed by images of binding, 324–
33, 386–7; invisible to victims of
the gods, 337 and n. 6; related to
woof-threads of fate, 338; in beliefs
of the Norse, 353–6, 363, Anglo-
Saxons, 356–7, Celts, 357–8, Hindoos, 358–62, 363–4, Slavs, 362,
Persians, 363; gods' 'power to
loose', 363–5, 384–5; girdle, amulet,
of good fortune, 366–8, 371 n. 3;

and Homeric associations with
magic, 368–73; binding co-extensive
with nailing, 371–5; love as, 373;
as wreath or crown, 376–7; of the
κῆρες, 400–8; as winding-sheet,
420; sleep as, 422 and n. 5; τέλος
θανάτοιο, 426–31, 432 n. 4; of old
age, 430, 459–60; loosed when one
is benefited, 436–7; of debt, obligation, 437–9, 441, 463; of sin,
440–2, 510; of initiation, 446–56,
459. See also s.vv. crown, ring
bones: importance after death, 80 n. 1,
260–3, os sacrum, 126 n. 3; fire and
'chill trembling' in, 150–2; identified with manes, 267–70; hope of
new life from, 271–4; anointed with
wine after burning, 277–9; offered
with fat to the gods, 279–80, 283;
seat of youth and strength, 287–8;
preservation of finger-bones, 496
Book of Common Prayer (quoted),
189 n. 2 fin., 440–1, 448 n. 6
brain: cause of nodding in sleep,
104 n. 5; a fluid mass, holy, 108;
origin of the seed, 115 and n. 7;
conceptions of fire in, 146–9, and
cf. 158–60; identified with boldness
and impudence, 156–7; seat of the
genius, 162–3; origin of English
name, 193 n. 3; believed to be
source of hair, 234–5, of horns,
237–9
breath: as the stuff of consciousness,
24, 31, 33, 44–6, 482; related to
blood, 46–8, 209 n. 3; affected by
emotion and thought, 49–56; as
vehicle of sense perceptions, 67–79;
effect on the liver, 87–8; of procreation, 119–20, 132, 169, 487 and n. 1,
502 n. 2; of the dying, 128, 171–2;
and distinction between anima and
animus, 168–72; surrounds the
earth, 252. See also s.v. thymos
Brown, T. E. (quoted), 427
Browne, Sir T. (quoted), 213 n. 1,
242 n. 3
Browning, E. B. (quoted), 153 n. 3
burial customs: hair plucked and
heaped on corpse, 98–9; preservation of the head, 99–102; wrapping

of the head, 133 n. 1; setting up of
oscilla, 135–6; protection of head in
the grave, 135 *and* n. 9; cremation,
256–70; treatment of the burnt
bones, 271–2, 277–83; rites of the
Egyptians, 283–4, Babylonians,
284–7, Jews, 287–8, Bulgarians,
349 n. 7 *fin.*
Burns, Robert (quoted), 222 n. 3
Burton, R. (*Anatomy of Melancholy*),
85 n. 2

Caesar-worship, 136–8, 166
Camenae and *Carmentis*, water and
inspiration, 35, 67
candle, offering of, 265 n. 2 *fin.*, 287
and n. 3
capping ceremonies, 145 n. 10,
376–7
Carpenter, John (quoted), 347
castration, 109 n. 2, 177 n. 9, 187 n. 8,
233 n. 5, 238–9
Celts: beliefs about the head, 100–1
and n. 4, 104 n. 1, 156–7, 236 n. 2;
conception of lightning, 143 n. 3;
'flame of valour', 158; beliefs
about the knees, 185–6, the marrow,
193 n. 6, 289 n. 5; 'Auld Hornie',
240 n. 7; use of skulls for drinking
vessels, 241 n. 2; view of fate as a
bond, 357–8; belief in 'death-
clouds', 423–4. *See also s.vv.* Irish,
Scotland
Ceres, 125–6, 153 n. 4, 471 n. 3
Chaucer (quoted), 69, 493
chest (thorax): seat of consciousness,
26–7, 73, 117, 168–71; moist with
sleep, emotion, 30–3; concerned in
anger, 147–9; significance for Germanic peoples, 209 n. 3
children: funerals of, 136, 263–4; of
slave women by Roman citizens,
225 n. 2, 475 n. 2; assumption of
toga virilis, 264, 473 n. 1. *See also s.v.*
youth
Chinese: doctrine of knowledge, 76
n. 9; notion of shadow-soul, 95 n. 4;
belief in aphrodisiac qualities of
rhinoceros horn, 245 *and* n. 7
Chronos (Χρόνος): Pherekydes' teaching about, 248 *and* n. 6, 251; and

Orphic cosmogony, 250, 332–3,
453 n. 1; related to αἰών, 251;
original meaning, 451 n. 1 *fin. See
also s.v.* time
Cid, Chronicle of the, 51 n. 2, 234
circle: of 'Ὠκεανός, 247–8, 251 n. 11,
443; time and fate as, 251, 443,
451–3, 460; meaning of τέλος,
442–4; wreath or crown of victory,
444–5; 'wheel' of Ixion, 452. *See
also s.vv.* crown, ring
cold: connected with detestation and
fear, 46 n. 6, with the term ψυχή,
94–5, 120 n. 4, with the dead, 95,
with the brain, 120 n. 4, with
chastity, 150 n. 2
Conrad, Joseph (quoted), 51 n. 2
corn: assimilation of men to, 113–14;
offered to Ceres, 125–6; October
Horse ceremony, 126; associated
with Mars, 142 n. 3, 471; stalks
thrown to restore freedom to slaves,
471 n. 4
Cowper, William (quoted), 105 n. 5
cremation: reasons for, 256–62; Italian
and Roman practices, 262–70
cross-bones, skull and, 186
crown: consecrates head, 133 n. 1 *fin.*;
significance of radiate, 165–6;
στεφάναι of Parmenides, 251 n. 11;
of life, 367; 'head-band' of Leukothea, 368; of victory, freedom,
kingship, 376–7, 458; of Fortune,
381, 432–3; beauty conceived as,
402; of singer in a κῶμος, 407 n. 1;
τέλος, 444–51, 453–4, 461–2; used
in Mithras cult, 455 n. 6; worn by
priest, magistrate, king, 457–60
cuckold's horns, 243–4
cups: inscribed with '*vivas*', etc., 216–
17; on Spartan grave reliefs, 272
n. 7, 285; of eternal life, 299

daimōn (δαίμων): contained in the
head, 119, 144; relation to the
genius, 162–5; κακοδαίμων, 185 n. 1,
404–7; two attend each person,
266–7; identified with a κήρ, 402–
10; in Plato's myth of Er, 403–4;
carries cloth to cover the dead,
428–9

death: causes disappearance of φρένες and θυμός, 59–61, 117, of ψυχή and θυμός, 93–5; coldness of, 95 *and* n. 5; linked with sexual shame, 109 n. 4, 483; Roman beliefs about, 133–8, 507–8; covering of head at, 132–3, 154; last breath caught by relative, 171–2; portended by mist or darkness, 181–2, by shudder down the spine, 207–8; Heraclitus' view of, 252 n. 11; causes body to dry up, 254–6, 269–70; cremation after, 256–64; calling of name of the dead, 264; and the use of '*manes*', 264–9 (esp. 265 n. 2); as a bond round men, 327, 354–63, 372–3, 380, 405, 417 n. 4; its bonds equated with the nail of Fate, 374–5; dead recalled to life, 385 *and* n. 7; κήρ of appointed at birth, 399, and drags victim to his fate, 400–1; as an enwrapping cloud or vapour, 422–5, 427; τέλος θανάτοιο, 426–31, 460–1; spirit of the dead consulted, 488. *See also s.vv.* burial customs, cremation, *genius, psyche*

Dekker, T. (quoted), 240 n. 7, 315 n. 1

Delphi: victim required to tremble, 227 n. 12; oracular *omphalos* stone, 281

Democritus, 88, 118, 121, 237, 250 n. 2, 253

desire: connected with delight, 21 *and* n. 3, 474 n. 2, with movement, 21 n. 5, 22; manifestation of the *animus*, 224–5; explanation of words connected with, 473–6

devotio, rite of, 132–3, 375

dew: θυμός likened to, 46–7; dead restored by, 288; food of the cicada and the gods, 507

door posts: symbolism of, 348; anointed by Roman brides, 472

dreams: phantoms related to, 102–3, 262; images of myths appear in, 183 n. 1, 187 n. 7, 365; issue through gates of horn and ivory, 242

Dyak head-hunters, 100 n. 3, 127 n. 2

ear: passes sound to the lungs, 69–72; tingles when about to hear, 197

effigies: piercing and burning of a candle, 287 n. 3; binding of, 372–5

Egyptians: beliefs about the lungs, 28 n. 1, the head, 105 n. 10, the thighs, 183, 280 *and* n. 3, 491 n. 2; birth from tears, 203 n. 5, 278 n. 1; process of embalming, 205 n. 4, 258 n. 5, 283–4; notion of spine and vital fluid, 208 n. 3, of the earth as a body, 211 n. 9 *fin.*; quality of weaving, 339 *and* n. 1, 340 n. 1; goddesses of childbirth, 394 n. 2; belief in weighing of the soul, 397–8; life transmitted by the hand, 495

Eleusinian mysteries, 113 *and* n. 1, 274 n. 2, 450, 454

Eliot, George (quoted), 427

emanations, Empedocles' doctrine of, 77

embalming, 205 n. 4, 256–8, 283–4

emotion: expressed freely in Homeric age, 3; not differentiated from cognition or conation, 14–18, 20–2; affects the lungs, 32–5, the breathing, 49–58, the limbs, 81; conceived as living creatures, 465 n. 6

English: belief in liquid going to lungs, 36 n. 12; use of 'soul' for 'lungs', 38 *and* n. 8, 39; mind in the breast, 68–9; beliefs about the head, 100, 114, 150 n. 3, 154–6; belief that marrow is the seed, 213 *and* n. 4; custom of drinking the health, 277, 477–8; 'Prophetic Stones', 281 n. 4; idiomatic use of 'to be bound', 333; belief in fate as woven, 356, in death as a bond, 357, 430–1, in 'death-mist', 423; representations of the soul, 428 n. 8; view of sin and debt as a bond, 440–1; victor 'holds the belt', 444 n. 4; use of ring in marriage service, 448 n. 6; practice of 'touching wood', 456 n. 2; association of freedom with desire, 474–6; use of middle finger in greeting, 477 n. 2, 491 n. 2. *See also* Index of Words, pp. 530–1

Erinyes: avengers of blood, 255; appealed to by the injured, 265 n. 2 *fin.*; bind victims, 368, 372 n. 2,

442; guard established order, 394, 424 n. 7; departed ψυχαί of human beings, 500 n. 2

Eskimo beliefs, 47 n. 2

Etruscans: divination by liver, 89; attach masks to cinerary urns, 135 n. 9; grave pictures, 265 n. 2 *ad med.*; representation of Athrpa and Charun, 374, 429 n. 1; wrapping of the dead, 428–9; association of Phersu with death, 429 n. 1

eye: breathes, 73–5; emits ray, 76–8; evil, 78, 233 n. 5, 243 n. 6; a lover's, 197, 203–4; veiled by grief, 422; covered or bound in death, 422–5, 427–30. *See also s.vv.* sight, tears

'Fall', unites death with sexual shame, 109 n. 4

fat: believed to be without feeling, 81; source of seed, 115, 188 n. 2, 210–12; identified with good land, 211 n. 9; put with bones of the dead, 271–2; offered to the gods, 279–81, 283, 484; Roman bride anoints with, 471–2. *See also s.vv.* marrow, oil

fate: controlled by the *genius*, 160–5, by the ψυχή, 184–5; connected with αἰών, 204 n. 4, 251–3; as Χρόνος mated to 'Ανάγκη, 251, 332–3; controlled by δαίμονες, 265, 353; fatalism in Homer, 303–4, 322, 326 n. 2, 365–6, 413; spun by the gods, Μοῖρα, Αἶσα, 304–9, 334–7, 349–51, 352–3, 387–9, 390–4; as a bond round men, 321–4, 331–8, 378–82, 425, 431–3; and the image of binding, 324–33, 386–7; its bonds invisible, 337 *and* n. 6; weaving of, 338, 349–51, 373 n. 1, 416–19; in beliefs of the Norse, 352–6, 381, Anglo-Saxons, 356–7, Celts, 357–8, Hindoos, 358–62, Persians, 363; gods' power to unbind, 363–5, 384–5; girdle of good fortune, 366–8; Fate represented with nail in hand, 373–5, as a pillar fixed fast, 375, as a wreath of wool, 376, as a crown, 377; conception of ὑπὲρ μόρον, beyond what is fated, 390–4; bestowed by Zeus from jars,

395–6, 404; the scales of, 397–8, 408–10; relation of the κήρ or δαίμων to the μοῖρα, 399–405; conceived as a yoke, 405 n. 8, 406–8; its relation to time, 413–15; winding-sheet of, 419 *and* n. 2; τέλος, 426–66

finger: as a sign, 139 n. 4; used to propitiate, 149; interlocked to hinder childbirth, 180; equated with the phallus, 198 n. 1; liquids produced by, 221; sneeze stopped by moving ring to longest finger, 226 n. 1; applies saliva to the brow, 233 n. 1; *mano cornuto,* 240 n. 1, 243 n. 6; relation to wedding ring, 448 n. 6; used in greeting, 477 n. 2, 491 n. 2; Jewish preservation of finger-bones, 496–7. *See also s.v.* hand

Finnish beliefs. *See s.v. Kalevala*

fire: in the eyes, 76–7; in anger, 147–50; soul conceived as, 155–6; 'flame of valour', 157–8; procreation by, 158–9; manifestation of *genius,* 163–7; on head of horned fertility god, 240 n. 7; cremation of the dead, 256–64; of hell, 288; Holy Spirit as, 498–9

Fitzgerald, Edward (Rubaiyat quoted), 417

Flavel, John (quoted), 347

Fletcher, John (quoted), 347

food: related to consciousness, 48; and the sense of taste, 62–3; converted by liver into blood, 85 n. 2; and the belly, 88; received by *genius,* 141 *and* n. 6, 224–5; represents blood, 218 n. 1; superstitions about, 225–6 *and* n. 1; fused with drink in idea of divine nourishment, 297–9

Ford, John (quoted), 347

forehead: touched in honouring the *genius,* 129–30, 180 n. 6, 227; rubbed when blushing, 146; charms of a low, 149 n. 5; struck in distress, 184–5; and the cuckold's horns, 243–4; marked in slavery, 478 n. 2

Freemasonry, 'apron' of, 455 n. 6 *fin.*

frogs a symbol of resurrection, 291

funeral rites. *See s.vv.* burial customs, children, cremation generation: cognate with 'knee' in Indo-European languages, 175–6; the knees as 'generative members', 175–80, 233; of bees from an ox, 207 n. 2; Homer's sense of γένεσις, 247–8. *See also s.v.* seed

genital organs: inspire reverence, 109 n. 2, 448 n. 5; in images of Hermes, 122; connected with the knees, 175–80

genius: existing interpretations, 127–9; equivalent to ψυχή, 129, 405 n. 8; survives death, 131–8; manifested in sneeze, 132, 138–40; connected with Caesar-worship, 136–8; receives food and drink, 141 *and* n. 6, 224–8; associated with blushing and burning of the brain or head, 146–9, 158–60, 163–7; foresees danger, 150 n. 1, 160–1; associated with serpent form, 159 n. 2; equivalent to 'unconscious mind', 161–2; sometimes unpropitious, 162–3; as star or comet, 163–5; and the *nimbus*, 165–7; associated with the knees, 181 *and* n. 6; responsible for quivering, throbbing, itching, 197–9; symbolised by horn of plenty, 240

Germanic peoples: old student song, 86 n. 6; beliefs about the head, 100, 106, 154–6; horns the source of seed, 240–1; death-goddesses, 354. *See also* Index of Words, p. 532

ghost: methods of laying, 100, 186, 262; modern Greek view of, 234

glove as gage of honour, 97 n. 10

Gnostics, 109 n. 4, 407 n. 2

God (of Christians): Jesus' claim to be his son, 189 n. 2, 501–3; inheriting the kingdom of, 189 n. 2; his mercy, 363, 440–1; the *Logos*, 503–4; the Father, 504–5. *See also s.v.* Jesus

godfather, origin of, 493

gods: identified with the sacrificial victim, 60 n. 2, 228 n. 1, 236–7; the *genius* a deity, 131–8; expressed by *numen*, 140–3; in the Kabbalah, 144, 234; represented with *nimbus*, 165–7; of witches, 208 n. 2, 240

n. 7, 455 n. 6 *fin.*; of the underworld, *manes*, 264–9; offerings to, 279–91; use of ambrosia and nectar, 292–9; men's fates determined by, 303–9, 322–4, 331–8, 349–51, 378–82, 390–4; power to loose from bonds, 363–5, 384–5; relation of Μοῖρα, Αἶσα, etc., to Zeus, 393–4; clothed in cloud, 421, 424–5; sceptre of, 456 n. 2. *See also s.vv. kēr*, Mars, Zeus

gold: gilding of horn and head, 106, 236; =seed, 156 n. 2; used for crowns, 165 n. 6, 166; in Mycenaean graves, 183 n. 1; the dead as χρύσεον γένος, 424 n. 7; on eyes of the dead at Knossos, 427–8; on the suppliant's sceptre, 456 n. 2

Grail legend, 109 n. 4, 157 n. 1, 187 n. 7, 220, 231 n. 1

Gray, Thomas (quoted), 419 n. 2

Greeks, ancient. *See s.v. appropriate entries in* General Index *and in* Index of Words, pp. 532–6

Greeks, modern: belief in shadow-soul, 95 n. 4; 'Last Request' of a robber, 99 n. 1; Zakynthos folktale, 178–9; conception of the returning dead, 234; vessels of water broken at the tombs of friends, 272–3; 'immortal water', 289 n. 3; fate spun by goddesses, 354

grief: expression of, in Homer, 20–1, 201–2, 421; affects the lungs, 33–5, 37; as a veil over the eyes, 421–2

hair: offered to the dead, 98–9, 107–8; of tail, associated with fertility, 126 n. 3; related to the *genius*, 130, 235 n. 4; *stella crinita*, 163; offered to river at puberty, 229, 231–2; its growth associated with sexual vigour, 232–3; parted with *hasta caelibaris*, 232 n. 4, 471 n. 7; Nazirite's offering of, 234–5; of slaves cut short, 477–9

hand: sanctity, 97 n. 10, 448 n. 6; importance of touching with, 129; used in supplication and *adoratio*, 180–1; embodiment of procreative power, 198 n. 1, 478 n. 2, 494–7; seat of strength, 494; laying on of hands, 497–8. *See also s.v.* finger

Hardy, Thomas (quoted), 391 n. 4
head: associated with the ψυχή, 95–122, 185 n. 1; seat of life, 96; holy, 97, 100–2, 108, 116; identified with the person, 98; its power to prophesy, 103–5; sacrificial, 105–6; contains the soul, 107–8, 134–6, 376, 494; source of seed, 109–16, 121–7, 144–6, 234 *and* n. 6, 237, 238 n. 1, 476–7; Zeus gives birth from, 111, 178, 183; of corn, 113–16; =flower, 114–15; as seat of consciousness, 116–17, of the *genius*, 130–1, 136–8, 226–8; covered at death or sacrifice, 132–3, 145, 427–9, 446–9, 509–10; *numen, capita deorum*, 138–44, 166, 456 n. 2, 507–8; *capitis deminutio*, 145–6, 239 n. 6; conceptions of fire in, 146–9, 158–60, 163–5; veiled at marriage ceremony, 152–3, 165, 472 n. 1; liquid in it called φλέγμα, 160 n. 4; and the *nimbus*, 165–7; seat of strength, 193–5; its itching related to sexual experience, 198–9; crowned and garlanded, 376–7, 407 n. 1, 453–9; in ceremonies of emancipation, 477. *See also s.vv.* brain, eye, forehead, horns
hearing, 43, 69–72, 87–8
heart: position of, 26–8, 54; as 'bushy', 'hairy', 28, 29 *and* n. 2; as seat of mind, 40, 56, 80, 82, 171, 225; thought to contain breath, 49 *and* n. 1, 50; χόλος in, 52; seat of *animus*, 225; heart-soul of the Egyptians, 280 n. 3, 398 n. 3; associated with Jewish *nephesh*, 481
Heraclitus, 33, 76 n. 9, 251–2
Hermes, significance of, 122
'heroes' (ἥρωες): significance for Homer and Hesiod, 8 n. 2; believed to appear in snake form, 207; not free agents in Homer, 303–4, 327–8; rendered invisible, 424 n. 7
Hindoos: beliefs about speech, sight, hearing, 75–6; and sneezing, 105; gold=seed, 156 n. 2; legend of birth from the knees, 183; strength identified with seed, 196; life-principle identified with *omentum*, 280 n. 1, 484, 511–12; conceptions

of the soul, 349 n. 7, 511–13; view of fate as a bond, 358–62, 400, 465 n. 1, of debt as a bond, 439; Savitri episode in *Mahabharata*, 385; moral weighing in next world, 398 n. 4; initiation rites, 454–5. *See also s.vv.* Indian beliefs, Upanishads *in* General Index *and* Index of Words *s.v.* Sanscrit, p. 540
Hippo of Samos, 118, 214, 248
Hippocrates; Hippocratic schools, 23, 26, 36, 39, 80 n. 6, 115 n. 7, 121
Homer: evidence for early thought, 2; some characteristics of Homeric heroes, 3–7, 20–2; nobility of spirit and barbarism of action, 7–9; and changes in word meanings, 8 n. 2, 39–40, 69–71, 116, 296, 305–6; and origins of words and thoughts, 66, 69–70; fatalism in, 303–4, 322, 326 n. 2, 365–6, 413; obscurity, 323–7; use of magic, 368–73; comes near to a single cause, 466
horns: gilded in sacrifice, 106, 236; 'of consecration', 236–7; outcrop of life-substance in the head, 237–9; cognate words, 238; sexual significance of, 239, 241–6; horn of plenty, 239 *and* n. 4, 243 n. 4; used for drinking, 241 *and* n. 2; of Lachesis, 410; of Τύχη, 410 n. 3
Housman, A. E. (quoted), 462
Hunt, Leigh (quoted), 243

immortality: water of, 289–91; in doctrine of Mithraism, 299; and the chrism in Christian baptism, 299. *See also references to* immortal soul, pp. 93–299 *passim*
incense, 282, 284, 286
Indian beliefs, 186, 245 n. 7. *See also s.v.* Hindoos
inspiration: connected with breath, 51–2, 56; manifestation of *genius*, 161–3
Irish: use brain as a missile, 157, 193 n. 6; belief that the head flames in fury, 157–8; view of the knees, 185–6; strength identified with the marrow, 193 n. 6; jawbone removed from skulls, 236 n. 2; 'marrow-vat'

Irish: *continued*
    restores life and strength, 289 n. 5;
    belief in the thread of life, 355–6;
    taboo imposed by binding, 358;
    expose sexual organs in magic, 448
    n. 5. *See also s.v.* Celts
Italians: funeral customs, 135, 262–3;
    belief in procreation by fire, 158;
    rite to produce good fortune, 375
    n. 2
Ixion's wheel, 452

jars of Zeus, 305, 395–6, 404, 409–10
jaw: cognate with words expressing
    generation, 175–6, 233; 'dropped',
    234 n. 1; Samson's jawbone of ass,
    235–6; preserved by Baganda and
    Egyptians, 236 *and* n. 2; often
    missing from skulls in Ireland, 236
    n. 2
Jesus: the son of God, 189 n. 2, 501–3;
    baptism, 500, 501 n. 1; as Second
    Person in the Trinity, 503–4; the
    self-offered 'Lamb of God', 504–5
Jews: spirit=breath, 51 n. 2, 481;
    beliefs about the head, 103–5, 144
    and n. 8, 153 n. 1, 167, 483; cir-
    cumcision, 107 n. 4; beliefs about
    the thighs, 109 n. 1, 183 *and* nn.
    4, 7; conception of seed as oil,
    188–9, 484; Jesus the son of God,
    189 n. 2, 501–3; 'Wine to your
    life!', 217 n. 2; Nazirite's offering
    of hair, 234–6; sanctity of horns,
    236 *and* n. 8, 239 n. 6; beliefs about
    fat, 281, 287–8, 484; view of fate
    as a garment, 367, 380; belief in
    'death-mist', 423; covering of the
    dead, 429 n. 2; the hand associated
    with the life-soul, 478 n. 2; con-
    ceptions of the procreative life-soul,
    481–8; nature of the *nephesh*, 481–2,
    of the *ruaḥ*, 482–3; consult spirits of
    the dead, 488–90; importance of
    knees in the act of blessing, 491–2;
    beliefs about the hand, 494–8; and
    the Holy Spirit, 498; lamp on tomb
    as a symbol of life, 499–500; the
    dove a symbol of the departed
    spirit, 500–1; three Persons of the
    Trinity, 503–4

Jonson, Ben (quoted), 193 n. 3, 231
    n. 1
Justesen, P. T., on φρένες and θυμός,
    24 *and* n. 4, 44 n. 8, 58 n. 6, 81 n. 11,
    99 n. 7

Kalevala (quoted), 177, 389, 428
Karen beliefs, 490 n. 1
kēr (κήρ): Sphinx described as ἁρπάξ-
    ανδρα κήρ, 369; weighed in scales of
    Zeus, 397–8, 415; was the ψυχή
    originally a κήρ? 398; assimilation
    of κήρ and κῆρ, 398 n. 3, 400–1;
    appointed to each person at birth,
    399; related to μοῖρα, 399–400;
    binds victims to their fates, 400–10,
    429–32, 460; Plato's myth of Er,
    403–4; =δαίμων, 404–8; connected
    with time, 413–15
kiss, 87, 123, 208 n. 2; 'last kiss',
    172–3
Klotho, significance of, 306–7, 352–3,
    410, 416–18
knees: source of seed, 111, 124 n. 6,
    175–8, 233, 246; sanctity, 149 n. 3,
    174, 181; birth from man's, 178–9,
    183; rubbed or clasped in supplica-
    tion, 180, 185; marrow-bones, 182
    and n. 5; seat of ψυχή, 184–5; raised
    in salutation, 186, 477 n. 2 *fin.*, 491
    n. 2; seat of strength, 187; thought
    behind phrase 'on the knees of the
    gods', 303–9, 334; of Lachesis in
    Platonic myth, 403; and the act of
    blessing, 491. *See also s.v.* thigh
knight, belt or *cordon* of, 448 n. 5, 455
    n. 6 *fin.*
knowledge: not differentiated from
    sentiment, 15–22; transmitted in
    last breath of the dying, 172
Koran (quoted), 288

Lachesis, 307, 410, 416–18
Landor, W. S. (quoted), 396 n. 2
Lares, ancestral *genii*: 158 n. 5, 227,
    264 n. 9, 282; origin of Billie Blind,
    509–10
leg: birth from a king's, 179; of
    eunuch believed to swell, 246; and
    cult of witches, 455 n. 6. *See also*
    s.vv. knees, thigh

Lévy-Bruhl (quoted), 19
libations: essential part of a treaty,
218 n. 1; use of skulls for, 241 n. 2;
as offerings to the dead, 271–9, to
the gods, 279, 282–6; of ambrosia,
296–7
life-principle, stuff of life: believed to
be in the head, 96–100, 123–32,
226–8, 236; as liquid in a divine
head, 144, 234; supreme embodiment in the sun, 156 n. 2; anima, not
animus, 168–71; in the knees, 174–8,
491; identified with αἰών, 200–6,
212–15; equated to wine, 216–19,
287 n. 2, to liquid, 219–23, 289–91,
492–3; manifested in horns, 237,
246; dried up at death, 254–6; hope
of renewal, 271–4, 291 n. 1; in the
omentum, 280 and n. 1, 484, 511–12;
in the bones, 287–8, 496; ambrosia
its divine counterpart, 292–3; associated with freedom, 472–80; Jewish
conceptions of, 480–5, 496; symbolised by a lamp on Jewish tombs,
499–500. See also s.vv. aiōn, genius,
psychē
light: thought to be breathed, 74–9,
250 n. 1; rays of about the head,
165–6; girdle of about the universe,
249–50, 332; Mithras identified
with, 455 n. 6
lightning, 143 n. 3, 156 n. 2
Lithuanians: word for fate, 381 n. 8;
myth of goddesses who spin and
weave, 419, 428
liver: position, 26; its significance,
84–9, 505–6; affected by love, 152
Longfellow, H. W. (quoted), 375 n. 7
lot, used in allotting fate, 392–3, 408
n. 3, 416 and n. 4, 418 n. 2
love: affects the lungs, 37, 54–5, the
belly, 88; as fire in the marrow and
head, 151–2; described as 'liquefying, melting', 202–4, 473 n. 2;
aphrodisiac power of hippomanes,
245–6, 472; cestus of Aphrodite, 368,
425, 447; bond of, 373, 402–3;
'true-love knot', 448 n. 6 fin.;
associated with tenderness, 486
n. 1
lungs. See phrenes

Luz, the bone in Rabbinic tradition,
288 and n. 3
Lykaian Zeus, 95 n. 4

madness: tossing of the head in, 104
n. 5; how conceived, 147–9, 159–60;
rage a spasm of, 148, 245 n. 2; in
relation to horns, 243–5
magic: use of skull and thigh-bone in,
186, of nail parings in, 246; sympathetic, 275, 359–61, 363, 366, 385,
427, 441, 452; detection of spot
where man will be wounded, 354;
binding by spells, 357–8, 359–63,
369–70, 427; in Homer, 368–73;
used in nailing effigies, 371–2. See
also s.vv. amulets, witches
marriage: importance of veil and
torch, 153 and nn. 2, 3, 232 n. 4,
472 n. 1; custom of drinking wine
at, 217, of sprinkling river water,
230, 272, 273 n. 2; bride's hair
combed with hasta caelibaris, 232
n. 4, 471 n. 7; the vitta and crines,
232 n. 4, 447 and n. 5; libations
poured at, 276; fate spun at, 335;
relation to fate, 391 and n. 4, 432,
448 n. 6; the head-band of, 446–8;
the wedding-ring, 448 n. 6; as
initiation, 450; origin of name uxor,
472
marrow: source of seed, 109–10, 115,
118; of same nature as the brain,
118, 149; source of strength, 149–50,
289 n. 5; burns in anger and frenzy,
150–2; in thigh-bone, 182 and n. 5;
identified with αἰών, 205–6, with
fat, 212; 'barley-groats, the marrow
of men', 222, 228 n. 1, 229, 274
n. 2, 279 n. 5
Mars: and the October Horse, 126,
472; associated with corn, 142 n. 3,
471, with woodpecker and wolf,
470–2; identified with hasta caelibaris? 471 n. 7
Masefield, John (quoted), 419 n. 2
Meredith, George (quoted), 375
n. 7
Messiah. See s.v. Jesus
meteorology, interest of early philosophers in, 248 and n. 3

Mickiewicz, Adam (*Pan Tadeusz*), 79
n. 2, 143 n. 3
milk: produced by Dionysos, 221;
offered in libations, 272 n. 4;
poured on bones, 282–3; claimed to
be ambrosia, 292 n. 3
Milton (quoted), 67 n. 8, 374 n. 6
Minoans: evidence for early beliefs, 2;
writing, 6 n. 11; and the head, 102,
105–6, 143–4; horn of Amaltheia,
239–40; use of horns as amulets,
240 n. 1; burial practices, 273, 285;
fresco from Knossos, 281 n. 4;
'Sacral Knots', 367 n. 8; gold on
eyes of dead at Knossos, 427–8. *See
also s.v.* Mycenae, Mycenaeans
Mithraism, 299, 455 n. 6
Mohammedan beliefs, 126 n. 3, 208,
288–9
Moirai (Μοῖραι): spin fates of men,
305, 307, 337, 352–3, 410; in Plato's
myth of Er, 306–8, 403–4; sometimes confused with μοῖρα spun by
a god, 327, 379, 393–4, 399; Parmenides on, 332; weaving of the,
349–50; related to goddess of childbirth, 352 n. 7, to Zeus, 393–4;
interchanged with κῆρες, 400; differentiated as Lachesis, Klotho,
Atropos, 416–19. *See also s.v.* fate
moisture: its relation to consciousness,
31–5, 46–8, 64 n. 3; τὸ ὑγρόν the
ἀρχή for Hippo of Samos, 118. *See
also s.vv.* water, wine
money-boxes, 124 n. 6
month, significance of the days of the,
411–13
Moore, Tom (quoted), 422 n. 5
Mycenae, Mycenaeans: gild the faces
of the dead, 106, the thighs of the
dead, 183 n. 1; rhytons in the shape
of animals, 241 n. 2; funeral customs, 258–61, 272. *See also s.v.*
Minoans

'nail, pay on the', explanation of,
375 n. 7
Necessity ('Ἀνάγκη): mated with
Χρόνος in Orphic cosmogony, 251,
332–3, 453 n. 1; Pythagorean conception of, 251, 332, 453 n. 1;

Plato's spindle of fate on the knees
of, 306–8, 332; Parmenides on, 332;
represented with nail in hand,
373–4; yoke of, 407 n. 3
nectar, 67, 296–9
neolithic burial customs, 136, 262–3
Nereids, scarf of, 454
Nestor's throne anointed, 280–1
New Guinea, 14, 68
nodding the head: by Zeus, 29, 97–8;
sanctity attached to, 104 *and* n. 5;
connected with use of *numen*, 138–40
Norse: beliefs about the head, 100,
476–7, the thighs, 186, the earth as
a body, 211 n. 9 *fin.*; 'whale-seed',
238 n. 1; fat the life-substance, 283
n. 1; fate-goddesses, 349; 'woof of
war', 351, 355–6; spinning and
weaving of fate, 352–6, 381; conception of fate as a bond, 457 n. 3;
conception of freedom, 475–7. *See
also* Index of Words, p. 536
nous, 38, 56, 58 n. 6, 82–3
Nubians, 191, 210

oath: sworn by the head, 96, 108, by
the source of life, 109, 247, by a
herald's sceptre, 456 n. 2, by a ring
in the temple, 457 n. 3
October Horse, 126 *and* n. 3, 127, 226
n. 5, 472
oil: seed conceived as, 188–91, 484;
used in anointing, 188–9 *and* n. 2,
210–11; connected with horns, 239
n. 6, 494 n. 1; oil or fat offered to
the gods and the dead, 271–91;
related to ambrosia, 292–5. *See also
s.v.* fat
Okeanos ('Ὠκεανός): river surrounding
the earth, 247–8, 443; of serpent
form, 248–50, 315–16; as bond encircling the earth, 251 n. 11, 316–17,
332; described as τελήεις, 443
omentum, its significance, 188 n. 2, 280
and n. 1, 282, 484, 511–12
opportunity, how conceived and expressed, 343–8
Orphism: legend of Orpheus' head,
101 *and* n. 8, 112; and the ψυχή, 112,
115, 256, 274, 405 n. 8; world-egg,
120, 250; souls pass as fire to the

heavens, 164 n. 7; cosmogony, 248
n. 6, 250–1 *and* n. 11, 316; conception of fate as Χρόνος mated to
Ἀνάγκη, 251, 332–3, 453 n. 1;
grief and pain as a circle, 451 *and*
nn. 1, 2, 452
oscilla. See Word Index *s.v. oscillum*
Osiris, 101 n. 8, 283–4
Ouranos: dome above the earth, 249
and n. 9; part of Orphic world-egg,
250; Pythagoreans on, 252; moisture
of, 258 n. 5

pain: liquid, 33–5; as an attack by
winged creatures, 85–6
palaeolithic burial customs, 136, 262–3
paying connected with λύειν and
τέλος, 436–9, 462–3
Persephone, 114 n. 5, 218 n. 3, 429
n. 1
Persians: beliefs about the head, 100,
159; spirit of water, Anāhita, 219
n. 7; the 'tree of life', 241 n. 1, 299;
bond imposed by a god, 363;
initiation practices, 455; sacrificial
practices, 511–12. *See also s.v.*
Mithraism
perspiration = exhalation of ψυχή,
196–7. *See also s.v.* sweat
Pherekydes, doctrines of, 229 n. 8,
251–3
Phersu, 114 n. 5, 429 n. 1
phrenes (φρένες): seat of thought, 13;
additional activity involving emotion, 14–15; appearance and position, 23–8; described by Homer as
πυκιναί, 28; structure, 28–30; tradition of vegetation in, 30; dryness
of, 31; and sleep, 31; and wine or
moisture, 32, 34–7, 66–7; and love,
37; described as porous, 38; identified with the diaphragm, 39–40;
subsumed in the ψυχή, 116–17;
clothed with ἀλκή, ἐλπίδες, etc.,
420 *and* n. 8
Phrygian mysteries, 113
plants: kinship with men, 113–15, 217,
267, 271–2; γόνατα of, 178 n. 1;
depend upon liquid for life, 219–22
Plato: doctrine of soul's 'vision', 18;
use of φρένες in *Timaeus*, 23, 39;

image of mind as a cage of birds,
64 n. 4, 86; theory of hearing, 71,
of vision, 77–8; doctrines about the
liver and belly, 87–8; and the importance of the head, 118–19, 144;
his river Ameles, 229 n. 8; explanation of pierced πίθος (*Rep.* 363 D),
274 n. 2; his picture of Ἀνάγκη
and the Μοῖραι, 306–8, 403–4, 417–
18, of Ἀνάγκη and the girdle of
light, 332; interpretation of τέλη
λύει (*Crat.* 417 B), 436; on prophets
who 'bind' or 'loose', 441; on
judgement of the dead, 442, 453;
'Theory of Ideas', 465–6. *See also*
Index of Passages, p. 543
poetry: inspired by drinking from
springs of Helicon, 66–7; Ennius on
the *furor* of the poet, 159; Ovid on,
173; generated in the mind, 219
n. 3; the poet's wreath, 407 n. 1, his
sceptre, 456 n. 2
praecordia: organ of consciousness for
the Romans, 40–2, 505–6; affected
by moisture, 42–3
Prior, Matthew (quoted), 396 n. 2
procreation: Homeric view of, 4; in
relation to the head, 109–16; conceived as breathing, 120, 132, 169;
in relation to the *genius*, 127–9;
Germanic god of, 155–6; surviving
life-soul capable of, 488. *See also*
s.vv. genius, seed
prophecy, 60, 66–7, 483, 485–90
psychē (ψυχή): conceived as a shadow,
59–60, 95, 224 n. 1; 'life-soul' not
'breath-soul', 93–5; associated with
the head, 95–122; no part in waking
life, 102–3; gives prophetic sign in
sneeze, 103, 138–9, 197, 489 n. 2;
contained in the head, 107–9, 236;
identified with the life-stuff, 109–16,
119, 200, 206–9, with the conscious
life, 116–17; origin of the word,
119–20; Hermes associated with,
122, 296 n. 7; analogous to the
genius, 129; associated with the
knees, 184–5; seat of strength,
195–7; responsible for quivering,
throbbing, itching, 197–9; assumes
snake form, 122 n. 3, 206–8, 233–4,

psychē: continued
249, 291 n. 1; exhaled from liquid,
252 *and* n. 11; released by cremation, 261–2; libations received by,
272; weighed, 398; conceived as
δαίμων, 405 n. 8
Pythagoreans: theories of sight, 76; on
the ψυχή, 112, 115 *and* n. 7, 118;
and 'Ανάγκη, 251, 332, 453 n. 1,
πνεῦμα, 252; source of myth of the
pierced πίθος, 274 n. 2; on justice,
398 n. 4; on the binding of unpurified souls, 442; doctrine of
πέρας and ἄπειρον, 464–5

rain: regarded as seed, 230 n. 8,
288–9; believed to come from the
horn of Amaltheia, 240
ring: power to stop sneeze, 226 n. 1;
symbol of obligation, 375 n. 7, 448
n. 6 *fin.*, 457 n. 3; wedding ring,
448 n. 6
river: receives hair as offering, 101
n. 8, 229, 231–2; source called
'head', 125, 231; ἴφθιμος used of,
194; life-begetting, 230 *and* n. 8,
240. *See also s.vv.* Okeanos, water
Romans. *See s.v. appropriate entries in*
General Index *and in* Index of
Words (Latin), pp. 537–9
Romulus, 138 n. 2, 471 n. 6
rope. *See* General Index *s.v.* bond, *and*
Index of Words *s.v.* πεῖραρ
rose, *flos genialis*, 130
Ross, W. D. (quoted), 119 n. 14
Rüsche, F., 24 n. 4, 48 n. 1, 58 n. 6,
94 n. 5

Sabazios, fertility god, 198 n. 1, 497
sacrifice: victim identified with the
deity, 60, 228 n. 1, 236, 484; treatment of the head in, 105–8, 133
n. 1; trembling of the victim, 228
n. 1; of victims to a river, 229–32;
of clothing to the dead, 259–60;
significance of offerings, 279–91; of
the divine bull by Mithra, 299;
crown used in, 457, 459 n. 1. *See
also s.v.* libations
Samothracian mysteries, 454
Samson the Nizirite, 234–5

Scandinavian beliefs, 153 n. 2, 196,
477 n. 2
Scotland: medicine drunk from a
horn, 241 n. 2; snood of maiden-
hood, 448; Barbour's *Bruce* quoted,
474 n. 2; the Billie Blind, 509–10
Scott, Sir Walter (quoted), 491
'sea-serpent', myth of, 316 *and* n. 1
seed (animal): thought to be a portion
of the life, ψυχή or *genius*, 109–12,
115–16, 118–22, 251–2; thought to
derive from fat, 115, 188–92, 472;
related to fierceness, 150–1, 158 *and*
n. 5, 471; thought to come from the
knees or thighs, 175–83, 233, 484;
identified with strength, 187–96,
235; and sweat, 192; identified with
tears, 202–3; and river water, 229–
30; relation to the hair, 231–3, to
horns, 236–46; of the universe,
247–8; bones the seed of new bodies,
269–70, 271–2; the Koran on,
288–9; derived from the belly,
485–90, from the hands, 494–5
seed (vegetable): of fruit known as the
'head', 113–15, 126, 217; equated
to human, 217–22, 253; drying of
likened to drying of bones, 267–70;
πανσπερμία a life-substance, 296
n. 7
Semele, myth of, 156 n. 2
Shakespeare (quoted), 69, 113 n. 6,
191 n. 1, 202 n. 2, 213 n. 4, 245 n. 2,
325, 396 n. 2, 437, 471, 485 n. 1
Shelley, P. B. (quoted), 421 n. 8
sight, 16–17, 73–9. *See also s.vv.* eye,
tears
Sirens, 368–9, 372 n. 2
skin: admits *immeans spiritus*, 76 n. 9;
significance of, 235 n. 4; old age
conceived as a skin to be shed, 291,
430 n. 2; of animal as clothing, 448
n. 5
slavery: affects the head, 145–6, 377,
472–3; offspring by slave women,
225 n. 2; δούλιον ἦμαρ, 414;
emancipation from, 472–80
Slavs: association of soul and head,
155 n. 2, of soul and fire, 158 n. 5,
161 n. 3; view of fate, 352, 387 n. 5;
binding by magic, 362; view of

death and disease as a cloud, 425, 427; myth of creation of demons, 494 n. 1

sleep: conceived as a liquid, 31–3; causes loss of contact with the λόγος, 76 n. 9; and the ψυχή, 102; as a veil or bond, 422 *and* n. 5, 428

smoke: anger as, 52, 87; the visible form of the life-substance in cremation, 262; life-substance transmitted as, 279–86. *See also s.v.* incense

snake: *genius* and ψυχή assume form of, 159 n. 2, 206–8, 233–4, 249, 291 n. 1; and head of Kleomenes, 207; teeth whence men are born, 233–4; 'Ωκεανός of serpent form, 248–50, 315

sneeze: prophetic, 103–5, 197; manifestation of ψυχή, 120, 483, 487, of *genius*, 132, 138–40, 225–6, 264; originates in the life-principle, 205 n. 4, 512; recalls a dish to table, 225–6; stopped by moving one's ring, 226 n. 1

snood of Scottish maidens, 448

Society Islanders, 14, 170

Socrates: doctrine of virtue as knowledge, 18; notion of the soul, 117 n. 10; 'with his Greek Daimonion', 162; view of lust, 198 n. 1; as 'midwife' of ideas, 219 n. 3

soul. *See s.vv.* anima, animus, genius, psyche, thymos

Spartan grave-reliefs, 272 n. 7, 285

spear, *hasta caelibaris*, 232 n. 4, 472 n. 1

speech. *See s.v.* words

Spenser, Edmund (quoted), 213 n. 4

Sphinx, significance of, 369

spinning: method of Homeric times described, 305–6; of fate by Αἶσα, Μοῖρα, the gods, 306–8, 334–7, 352–3, 358–9, 380–1, 387–9, 393–4, 409–10, 416; done by men, 308–9; of destiny by the κῆρες, 399–400

Spirit, the Holy. *See s.vv.* Jesus, Jews

stars: identified with the *genius*, 163–5; washed by 'Ωκεανός, 249; Anaximander's view of, 251 n. 11; and scholiast's comment on θεῶν ἐν γούνασι κεῖται, 307–8

'steatopygous' images, 183 n. 1

Stoics: notion of the soul, 47 n. 6, 77–8, of the seed, 120; and astrology, 164–5; view of fate, 390 n. 2; doctrine that each attribute of a thing is itself a substance, 465 n. 6; view of death as a release, 480 n. 3

stones: conceived as bone, 249 n. 9; polished and anointed, 280–1, 286–7; possess life, 508–9

strength: connected with breath, 51; attribute of the ψυχή and *genius*, 97, 140, 195–7; derived from marrow, 149–50; contained in the knees, 187, in the seed, 187–9, 235, in the fluid of the joints and sweat, 190–3, in the head, 193–5 identified with Jewish *ruah*, 483 *and* n. 1; in the hand, 494

Styx, river: significance of the name, 95 n. 5, 202 n. 5; of Hesiod, 229 n. 8; 'the greatest...oath for the blessed gods', 247–8; Achilles dipped in, 290 n. 3; mated with Πεῖρας, 315

Sumerian beliefs, 315–16

sun: supreme embodiment of the life-principle, 156 n. 2; in Orphic cosmogony, 251 n. 11; Aethiopian table of, 295; κύκλος ζωδιακός, 453 n. 1

sweat: origin in cerebro-spinal fluid, 160 n. 4, 193; identified with the stuff of strength, 191–3, 210; from same source as tears, 202. *See also s.v.* perspiration

Swedenborg, E. (quoted), 109 n. 3, 441

Tammuz, 286, 408

Tantalus, 294

tears: =αἰών, the life-fluid, 201–5; offered to the dead, 278 *and* n. 1. *See also s.v.* sweat

teeth, men born from, 233 *and* n. 5

Templars: charged with worshipping heads, 144, 157 n. 1; kiss of initiation, 208 n. 2, cord of initiation, 455 n. 6

testes, 109 n. 4, 176, 188

Thales of Miletus, 1–2, 248, 252

thigh: sworn by, 109 n. 1; contains seed, 182–3, 484; birth from, 183, 198 n. 1; struck in anguish, 183–4; seat of ψυχή, 184–5; skull and thigh-bones, 186; place for marking slaves, 478 n. 2, 497 n. 1. *See also s.v.* knees

thinking: conceived as speaking, 13–14, as breathing, 67–8; thoughts conceived as winged creatures, 67 n. 4, 86 *and* n. 6; modes of revealed by early evidence, 464–6

Thomson (*City of Dreadful Night*), 78 n. 2

throne, significance of, 280–1

thumbs up!, 139 n. 4

thymos (θυμός): converses in thought, 13; the stuff of consciousness in the φρένες, 23–4, 30–1, 40; identified with breath, 44–6, 49, 66–9, with blood, 47–9; as seat of the emotions, 49–56; said to 'fly', 67 n. 4; in the limbs, 79–80; superseded by brain, 116–19; and Jewish *nephesh*, 481–2

time: connected with αἰών, 208–9, 213–15; Orphic view of Χρόνος, 250–1; *tempus* (time) and *tempus* (temple), 344 n. 1; represented by warp-threads in weaving of fate, 346–7; 'nick of', 347, 348 n. 5; ἦμαρ and the scales of Zeus, 398 *and* n. 1, 408 n. 3; modern concepts of, 411; in the *Works and Days*, 411–13, 434 n. 7 *fin.*; relation to fate, 413–15, 437; in the *Georgics*, 415 n. 13; and functions of the Μοῖραι, 418 n. 1, of the Horai, 460. *See also s.vv. aiōn, Chronos*

touch, sense of: explained, 79–81; Roman practice of touching in ritual, 129, 133–4, 471

Tourneur, C. (quoted), 213 n. 4

Trinity, Holy, interrelationship of, 502–4

Tychē (Τύχη): identified with Lachesis, 410; 'gifts' not to be refused, 417; the cords of, 450

unconscious, ancient approximation to conception of, 103 n. 4, 161–2

unicorn, virtue of horn, 245–6

universals, how conceived, 464–6

Upanishads (quoted), 75–6

Valkyries, 351, 353–5

veil: on the head at death or sacrifice, 132–3, 145, 427–9, 446–9, 509–10; its use in marriage, 153 *and* nn. 2, 3, 232 n. 4, 471 n. 7; connection with *nubes* and νεφέλη, 421; of grief, 421–2; of death, 422–5, 427–9

victory. *See s.v.* battle

virginity: valued, 109 n. 4; tested by measuring head, 124 n. 4; offered to a river, 230; attested by the Billie Blind, 509. *See also s.v.* marriage

vitality. *See s.vv.* life-principle, strength

war. *See s.vv.* battle, Mars

warmth: connected with joy, 46 n. 6, with lechery, 156 n. 2. *See also s.v.* fire

water: inspires poetry, 66–7; 'generative water', 118, 229–33, 473–4; head sprinkled with, 133 n. 1, 476 n. 1; and Grail legend, 220–1; 'the best thing' (Pindar), 229; viewed by Thales as a primary substance, 247–8; as symbol of life-fluid, 272–4, 288–91, 476 n. 1; poured in libations, 274–5, 285–6; Jewish view of, 288; of freedom, 479–80. *See also s.vv.* baptism, libations, river

weaving: in essence a binding, 314, 335, 349–51, 368, 385; ancient processes of, 338–40, 345–7; connected with fate in beliefs of the Norse, 352–6, 381, Anglo-Saxons, 356–7; threads from the loom as cord-amulets, 373 n. 1; of fate by the Μοῖραι, 416–19

Welsh: belief that the soul appears as a flame, 156; version of the Grail legend, 157 n. 1. *See also s.v.* Celts

wine: damages the φρένες, 32, 35–7, 42–3; in Propertius III (IV), 152; *vita vinum est*, 216–17, 227, 275; assimilated to the seed, 218–19; represents blood, 218 n. 1, 272 n. 1, 278 n. 2; stimulates sexual appetite, 219; invalids bathed in, 222; appeases the *genius*, 227–8; poured as libations, 271–9, 282–3, 286; 'Here's your health', 277; Jewish view of, 287 n. 2; associated with nectar, 296–9; of freedom, 479–80

witches: and baptism, 189 n. 2 *fin.*; rite of kissing deity's posterior, 208 n. 2; worshipped horned fertility god, 240 n. 7; detect spot where man will be wounded, 354; blow spirits into men, 487–8; trial by water, 490–1. *See also s.v.* magic

wolf: its victim smitten with silence, 79 n. 2; men transformed into, 357 n. 3; Mars associated with, 470–2

woman: has no soul, 111 n. 6; correlation with water, 219, 230 *and* n. 4; explanation of *mulier*, 472 n. 1, of *uxor*, 472; loss of sexual rights in slavery, 474 n. 1

woodpecker, significance of, 470

words: as products of thought, breath, 13–14, 67–9, 170, 172; the *Logos*, 33, 76 n. 9; winged, 67 n. 4, 469–70; speech or song conceived as woven, 340; τέλος of speech, 461 n. 2

Wordsworth (quoted), 49 n. 5, 423 n. 10

wreath. *See s.vv.* bond, crown

Wren, Christopher, the elder (quoted), 105

writing: not used in Homer, 6 n. 11, 68; of fate, 390 n. 2, 417

Xenocrates on εὐδαίμων, 119 n. 1

Xenophon's dream, 365

Yama, Hindoo death-god, 358, 360, 362, 439

York Bidding Prayer, 440

youth: the time of liquid, of marrow, 213–15, 287–8; renewed by infusion of liquid, 289–90, by sloughing of skin, 291. *See also s.vv.* age, life-principle

Yule: boar's head at, 155 *and* n. 1; burning of log, 156 n. 2

Zakynthos, folktale from, 178–9

Zeno the Stoic, 67 n. 8, 252 n. 11

Zeus: and birth of Athena, 111, 233, of Dionysos, 183; Meilichios, 234 n. 1; Heraclitus on, 252; and the trick of Prometheus, 279; represented by a stone at Delphi, 281; Ktesios, 296 n. 7; dispenses human fate, 303, 305, 395–8, 404, 465; the scales of, 326, 397–8, 408–10; controls time, 411, 415; his aegis, 421, 424; holds the τέλος of all things, 434–5; a single efficient cause, 466; father of Epaphos, 495

Zulus, 188

INDEX OF WORDS

ARABIC

gânn, ginn, 487

ASSYRIAN AND BABYLONIAN

birku, 124 n. 6, 176, 491
qaqqadu, 124 n. 6
rêmu, 486 n. 1
rêš nâre, 234 n. 6
rêšu, 124 n. 6
ša rêši, 226 n. 3
šimu, 327
utukku, 196

ENGLISH

ANGLO-SAXON

brægen, 193 n. 3
breosthord, 68–9
cneów, 186
deað-bedde fæst, 357 n. 1
freó, 474, 476
freólic, 474 n. 2
freyða, 476
gæst, 150 n. 3
grima, 154 n. 4
hálig, 477 n. 2
hama, 431 *and* n. 1
heafod, 154 n. 5, 476–7
heals-fang, 477 n. 1
heals-gebedda, 476
hreðer, 38–9, 69 n. 1
leger-bedde faest, 357 n. 1
lith-ule, 191
lust, 21 n. 3
mearh, 182 n. 5
niht-helm, 424 n. 7
orlæg, 381
sawol, 38 n. 8, 63, 209 *and* n. 3
wælmist, 423
wæs hal, 277 *and* n. 3
wer, 177 n. 9

MIDDLE ENGLISH

braine, 245 n. 2
loke, 155 n. 1

MODERN ENGLISH

acquit, 438 n. 1
adore, 181 *and* n. 1
aeon, 200–2
aesthetic, 75
aghast, 150 n. 3
'alive and kicking', 180 *and* n. 4
altar, 282 n. 1
animate, 168–73
artery, 80–1

belly, 488, 509–10
belt, 353 *and* n. 2, 444 n. 4, 448 n. 5
bless, 491–3
blow, blower, blow-through, 120 n. 1
bonfire, 268 n. 1
bound (it is b. to happen, etc.), 333
bowels, 485–6
bust (sb.), 135 n. 9 *fin.*
brain, 245 n. 2

cap (v.), 145 n. 10, 376–7
capital, 124 n. 6
cathedral, 281 n. 3
chairman, 281 n. 3
chest, get it off one's, 69
Christ ('the anointed'), 189 n. 2
conspire, 171–3
cordon, 455 n. 6 *fin.*
cycle, 251–2, 443–4, 451–3

damn, 438 n. 1
deads, 509
democracy, 211 n. 9
destined, 333

elbow-grease, 191
engagement ring, 448 n. 6
expedient, 437

familiar spirit, 488–9
fire-drake, 155 n. 4
free, 474–80
friend, 475
frig, 452 n. 2, 475–6

genial, 129–30, 225–8
genuine, 175–6, 233 *and* nn. 2, 5
ghost, 150 n. 3
godfather, 493
green, 177 n. 9

Hail!, 277, 477–8, 498 n. 1
hale, 277, 477–8
hand (your h. upon it), 97 n. 10
health, drink one's, 216–17, 277–8, 477 n. 2
heat (sexual), 151–3, 156 n. 2, 158–9, 488
hell, 100, 273 n. 4, 286
hero, 8, 206
holy, 477 n. 2
horn, 238, 243

immolate, 228 n. 1
importune, 348 *and* n. 1
inspiration, 50–2, 171
instill, 43
invest, 360 n. 7

joint, out of, 348 n. 5

knee, 176, 186

liberty, 473–6
love, 475–6
lucre, 437–8
lust, 21, 474 *and* n. 2

maggot, 86 n. 6
male, 177 n. 9
marrow-bones, 182 n. 5
marry, 177 n. 9 *fin.*
masculine, 177 n. 9 *fin.*
mask, 135, 429 n. 1
merry-thought (wish-bone), 60 n. 2
mortar, 508–9

nail, pay on the, 375 n. 7
necessity, 332–3
nick (in the n. of time), 347, 348 n. 5
nimbus, 165–6
nuptials, 153, 232 n. 4, 472 n. 1
nymph, 34–5, 219 *and* n. 7

obligation, 438 n. 1
olive branch, 456 n. 2

personality, 146
phlegm, 160 n. 4
pluck (sb.), 69
political, 444 *and* n. 1
porridge (save your breath to cool your p.), 120 n. 4

religion, 439 n. 6, 440, 510
rival, 219 n. 7

salute, 477 n. 2, 498 n. 1
saphead, 213 n. 4
sapient, 61–3
sceptre, 456 n. 2
sinews (of war), 187 n. 8 *fin.*
solve, 369
spirit, 69, 172, 482–4
spunk, 156
superstition, 440 n. 1

temple, 344 *and* n. 1
tender mercies, 486 n. 1
throne, 281 n. 3
thumbs up!, 139 n. 4
'touch wood!', 456 n. 2
trepanning, 136 n. 3
trophy, 375 n. 2
truth at the bottom of a well, 67 n. 1

vein (of wit, etc.), 42 n. 12, 64–5
vernacular, 177 n. 9
victor, 438 n. 1 *fin.*
virgin, 177 n. 9

wagtail, 452 n. 2
wassail, 277 n. 3
wax (sb. and v.), 238 n. 1, 282 n. 9
wedding ring, 448 n. 6
Word (the *Logos*), 33, 76 n. 9, 503
words (winged), 67 n. 4, 86 *and* n. 6, 469–70

zone, 317

FINNISH

polvi, 177

FRENCH

entrailles, 485 n. 1
faire mauvais temps, 411
fouet, 141 n. 7

GERMAN

bändigen, 438 n. 1
binden auf die Seele, 382
Brunst, 156
Bund, 443
einschlagen, 211 n. 4, 347
Geist, 150 n. 3
grün, 177 n. 9
Hahnreh, 243 n. 6
Hirn, 238
Kinn, 233
lieben, 473
Lust, 21 n. 3, 474 n. 2
marag, 182 n. 5
Mist, 511
phnuht, 57 n. 1
Seele=sawol, 38 n. 8, 63, 209 and n. 3, 382
Tarnkappe, 424 n. 7
Worm, 207

GREEK
ANCIENT

ἄγαλμα (agalma), 106
ἀγγεῖον (angeion), 31
ἄγειν (agein), 400
ἄγχειν (anchein), 332
ἀδινός (hadinos), 26 n. 3
ἄητος (aëtos), 52
αἴ (ai), 336 n. 2
αἰγίς (aigis), 421 and n. 8, 424
αἰδοῖα (aidoia), 109 n. 2, 280 n. 2
αἰονάω (aionaō), 209, 230
αἶσα (aisa), 305–7, 378, 387 n. 3, 390
αἰσθάνομαι (aisthanomai), 75
αἴσθομαι (aisthomai), 75
ἀίω (aïō), 74 and n. 6, 75
αἰών (aiōn). See General Index s.v. aiōn
ἀκήριος (akērios), 405 n. 8, 413, 434 n. 7 fin.
ἄλειφα (aleipha), 279–80, 293
ἄλειφαρ (aleiphar), 281, 293–4
ἀλείφεσθαι (aleiphesthai), 210
ἀλίβαντες (alibantes), 255–6
ἀλοιφή (aloiphē), 211, 298
ἀμβροσία (ambrosia). See General Index s.v. ambrosia
ἅμμα (hamma), 315 n. 3
ἀμφιβάλλειν μένος etc. (amphiballein menos), 420–1

ἀνάγκη (anankē), 251, 307, 332–3. See also General Index s.v. Necessity
ἀνακεύειν (anakeuein), 97 n. 8
ἀνασταλύζω (anastalyzō), 33
ἀνθερεών (anthereōn), 232
ἄνθος ἥβης (anthos hēbēs), 232
ἀπαρχαί (aparchai), 107
ἁρμός (harmos), 348 n. 5
ἄτη (atē), 323, 327, 404
ἄτσα (atsa), 179
Αὐαίνου λίθος (Hauainou lithos), 256
αὗος (auos), 192 n. 1, 222, 255–6
αὔτή (aütē), 22
ἀφαυρός (aphauros), 110 and n. 2
ἀφροδίσια (aphrodisia), 121
ἀχλύς (achlys), 74 n. 6, 421 n. 10

βάκχος (bacchos), 221, 456 n. 2
βαρυδαίμων (barydaimōn), 409
βασιλεία (basileia), 377
βασσάρα (bassara), 235 n. 4
βία (bia), 196
βίος (bios), 196
βρέγμα (bregma), 193 n. 3
βρεχμός (brechmos), 193 n. 3
βροτός (brotos), 506–7
βρότος (brotos), 506–7

γαστήρ (gastēr), 88 and n. 6
γενειάς (geneias), 233
γένειον (geneion), 132, 233
γενέσια (genesia), 272 n. 8
γένεσις (genesis), 246–7, 451 n. 1
γενύς (genys), 233
γῆρας (gēras), 324, 430 and n. 2. See also General Index s.v. age
γόνατα (gonata), 175, 176 n. 4, 178 n. 1
γόνυ (gony), 175, 233
γράφειν (graphein), 417
γρῖφος (griphos), 341, 369

δαῆναι (daēnai), 18–19
δαίμων (daimōn). See General Index s.v. daimōn
δαμάω (damaō), 438 n. 1
δάμνημι (damnēmi), 438 n. 1
δαναοί (danaoi), 256
δεῖ (dei), 331
δεινόλινος (deinolinos), 336 n. 2
δέλτοι φρενῶν (deltoi phrenōn), 28 n. 6

δέω (deō), 329–30, 331 n. 1, 438 n. 1
δῆμος (dēmos), 211 n. 9, 346
διὰ τέλους (dia telous), 444 n. 3
διατελέω (diateleō), 444 n. 3
διάφραγμα (diaphragma), 39 n. 6
διερός (dieros), 254–5, 272
δόξα (doxa), 499 n. 2
δρόσοι (drosoi), 213 n. 6
δύσεο ἀλκήν (dyseo alkēn), 420–1

ἔαρ (ear), 177 n. 9
ἐγγαστρίμυθος (engastrimythos), 489
    and n. 1
ἐγκέφαλος (enkephalos), 105, 108, 115.
    See also General Index s.v. brain
ἑδανός (hedanos), 294
ἐερσήεις (eërsēeis), 254
εἶδος (eidos), 465–6
εἵμαρται (heimartai), 378, 385, 387
    n. 3, 407 n. 2
εἰσπνεῖν (eispnein), 119 n. 14
εἰσπνήλας (eispnēlas), 119 n. 14
ἐκτολυπεύειν (ektolypeuein), 347, 364,
    387
Ἐλευθέριος (Eleutherios), 473, 479
ἐλεύθερος (eleutheros), 475 n. 2, 479
ἐλεφαίρομαι (elephairomai), 242 n. 1
ἐλέφας (elephas), 242 n. 1
ἔλλοψ (ellops), 28 n. 6
ἐντέλλω (entellō), 459 n. 10
ἐξαναλῦσαι (exanalysai), 384–5
ἐπαιονάω (epaionaō), 209, 272
ἐπαλλάσσειν (epallassein), 311–12,
    317–18
ἐπί (epi), 319, 379–80
ἐπιθυμητικόν (epithymētikon), 87 n. 9, 88
ἐπικείρειν (epikeirein), 187 n. 8
ἐπικλώθειν (epiklōthein), 305–6, 334,
    386
ἐπίνητρον (epinētron), 306
ἐπίπνοια (epipnoia), 119 and n. 14
ἐπιτέλλω (epitellō), 459 n. 10
ἐπιτιθέναι (epitithenai), 378–81
ἔπος (epos), 67–8
ἐράω (eraō), 202 n. 5
ἔρις (eris), 320–1
ἕρσαι (hersai), 213 n. 6
ἔρσην (ersēn), 177 n. 9
εὐδαιμονία (eudaimonia), 295
ἐφῆπται (ephēptai), 320, 331, 379
ἐφίσταμαι (ephistamai), 440 n. 1

ζειρά (zeira), 446 n. 4
ζειροφόρος (zeirophoros), 446 n. 4 fin.
ζεύγνυμι (zeugnymi), 407
ζώνη (zonē), 317

ἡβάω (hēbaō), 218 n. 2
ἠεροφοῖτις (ēerophoitis), 424 n. 7 fin.
ἠλακάτη (ēlakatē), 39 and n. 4, 307,
    346
ἦμαρ (ēmar), 398, 411–15
ἥρως (hērōs). See General Index s.v.
    'heroes'
ἦτορ (ētor), 46 n. 6, 80–2

θάρσος (tharsos), 50, 52
θερμαίνω (thermainō), 46 n. 6
θόλος (tholos), 444
θρόνος (thronos), 281 n. 3
θυμοειδές (thymoeides), 40, 88
θυμός (thymos). See General Index
    s.v. thymos
θύμος (thymos), 511
θωρήσσεσθαι (thōrēssesthai), 36 n. 9

ἰαίνω (iainō), 46 n. 6, 48 n. 3
ἱερὰ σῦριγξ (hiera syrinx), 208
ἱερεύειν (hiereuein), 228 n. 1
ἱερὸν ὀστέον (hieron osteon), 109 n. 2,
    208
ἱκάνω (hikanō), 324
ἴυγξ (iynx), 452
ἴφθιμος (iphthimos), 194 and n. 5
ἰωή (iōē), 69–70

καιρός (kairos), 343–8
καῖρος (kairos), 344 n. 1, 345–7
καιροσέων (kairoseōn), 345
καιροφυλακέω (kairophylakeō), 346
καλύπτειν (kalyptein), 427–36
κάρα (kara), 125, 238, 242 n. 1
κάρηνον (karēnon), 238 n. 2
κατάδεσμος (katadesmos), 371–2, 442
καταδέω (katadeō), 371–2
καταιγίζω (kataigizō), 421 n. 8
καταιγίς (kataigis), 421 n. 8
καταιονάω (kataionaō), 209
κατανεύειν (kataneuein), 97 n. 8
κατείβω (kateibo), 201
κελαινόφρων (kelainophrōn), 25
κέρας (keras), 238, 242 n. 1
κεροβάτης (kerobatēs), 246

κεστὸς ἱμάς (kestos himas), 368, 376 n. 5, 425, 447
κεφάλαιον (kephalaion), 124
κήρ (kēr), 398–402. *See also* General Index *s.v. kēr*
κῆρ (kēr), 23, 26, 28–9, 86 *and* n. 6, 398 n. 3, 400–1
κηρός (kēros), 282 n. 9
κῖκυς (kikys), 255 n. 4
κλάειν μακρὰ τὴν κεφαλήν (klaein makra tēn kephalēn), 185 n. 1
κνίση (knisē), 280
κοινωνεῖν (koinōnein), 465
κολοκύνθη (kolokynthē), 215 n. 2, 508
κόρος (koros), 20–1
κραίνω (krainō), 242 n. 1
κραίνω (krainō), 194 n. 5
κράς (kras), 194 n. 5, 242 n. 1
κρᾶσις (krasis), 465 n. 6
κρήδεμνον (krēdemnon), 368, 438 n. 1
κρίνον (krinon), 215 n. 2
κροκοῦν (krokoun), 373 n. 1, 454
κρυερός (kryeros), 46 n. 6
κύαμος (kyamos), 112, 393 n. 2
κυκεών (kykeōn), 274 n. 2, 297

λανθάνεσθαι (lanthanesthai), 19
λάσιος (lasios), 28–9, 54–5
λεπτοϋφής (leptoÿphēs), 340 n. 1
λίνον (linon), 322 n. 3, 336 *and* n. 2, 337
λίψ (lips), 473
λόγος (logos), 13, 33, 76 n. 9
λουτρόν (loutron), 272
λουτροφόρος (loutrophoros), 273 n. 2
λύειν (lyein), 363–5, 436–9, 441
λύσις (lysis), 365, 434
λυσιτελέειν (lysiteleein), 436–7
λύσσα (lyssa), 25
λύτρον (lytron), 510

μελεδώνη (meledōnē), 33, 86, 405 n. 3
μέμαα (memaa), 21 *and* n. 5, 22
μένος (menos), 25, 51 *and* n. 4, 52, 194 n. 12
μέριμνα (merimna), 86, 405
μετάφρενον (metaphrenon), 27
μετέχειν (metechein), 465 n. 6
μήδεα (mēdea), 187 n. 8
μηρία (mēria), 182 n. 5

μηρός (mēros), 182 n. 5
μιμνήσκεσθαι (mimnēskesthai), 19
μῖξις (mixis), 465 n. 6
μίτος (mitos), 336 n. 2, 338, 346, 349–50, 373 n. 1, 384, 408 n. 2
μίτρα (mitra), 455 n. 6
μοῖρα (moira), 327, 378, 399–400, 425. *See also* General Index *s.v. Moirai*
μορμολυκεῖον (mormolykeion), 135 n. 4
μόρος (moros), 327, 390–1
μύειν (myein), 274 n. 2
μυληφάτος (mylēphatos), 509
μυστήριον (mystērion), 456
μύστης (mystēs), 274 n. 2, 456 n. 1
μυττός (myttos), 139 n. 2

νέκταρ (nektar), 299. *See also* General Index *s.v.* nectar
νεφέλη (nephelē), 421 *and* n. 8
-νθ- (-nth-), sign of non-Hellenic origin, 314 n. 1
νόος, νοῦς (noos, nous). *See* General Index *s.v.* nous
νοῦσος (nousos), 86
νύμφη (nymphē), 34–5, 219 n. 7
νυμφόληπτος (nympholēptos), 35 n. 5

ξηρός (xēros), 192 n. 1

οἶδα (oida), 15–18
οἶστρος (oistros), 86 n. 6
ὄνος (onos), 226 n. 5
ὅπλον (hoplon), 341–2, 371
ὅρκος (horkos), 457 n. 3
ὄσσομαι (ossomai), 16
ὀσφύς (osphys), 208, 280 n. 2
οὖθαρ ἀρούρης (outhar arourēs), 211 n. 9
οὐλοχύται (oulochytai), 228 n. 1
᾽Οφιονεύς (Ophioneus), 248 n. 6

παλμός (palmos), 197
πανσπερμία (panspermia), 253, 296 n. 7
παρθενίη ζώνη (partheniē zōnē), 447–8
παχνοῦσθαι (pachnousthai), 46 n. 6
παχύς (pachys), 81
πεδάω (pedaō), 327, 329 *and* n. 6, 330 *and* n. 3
πειραίνω (peirainō), 314, 383–4, 465

πεῖραρ (peirar), 310–42, 383, 384 n. 1, 426, 455, 464
πείρινς (peirins), 314
πεπνῦσθαι (pepnysthai), 56–9, 67, 94
πεπρωμένος (peprōmenos), 382–7
περαίνω (perainō). See s.v. πειραίνω
πέρας (peras). See s.v. πεῖραρ
περίοδος (periodos), 451 n. 1
περιτιθέναι (peritithenai), 377, 380–1
περόω (peroō), 383
πευκάλιμαι (peukalimai), 30–1
πίειραν ἄρουραν (pieiran arouran), 211 n. 9
πίθος (pithos), 273, 395–6
πίονα δῆμον (piona dēmon), 211 n. 9
πλεύμων (pleumōn), 37, 39
πνεῦμα (pneuma), 51, 54–6, 77, 95, 171, 250, 252, 465 n. 6
πνέω (pneō), 53–9, 171
ποιπνύειν (poipnyein), 56–7
πόλις (polis), 444 n. 1
πόρος (poros), 29, 348
πραπίδες (prapides), 29–30, 38
προπίνειν (propinein), 217, 275–6
προσκυνεῖν (proskynein), 181 n. 1
πτερόεις (pteroeis), 67 n. 4, 86–7, 469–70
Πύθων (Pythōn), 489 n. 1
πυκινός (pykinos), 28
πυρὸς μειλισσέμεν (pyros meilissemen), 262 n. 3
πυρόσπορος (pyrosporos), 156 n. 2

ῥάβδος (rhabdos), 456 n. 2
ῥάχις (rhachis), 234
ῥιγέω (rhigeō), 46 n. 6
ῥιζώματα (rhizōmata), 253

σιδήρεος (sidēreos), 249 n. 9
σκέλετος (skeletos), 192, 256, 261–2
σκιά (skia), 95, 195, 405 n. 8 fin.
σκληρός (sklēros), 213 n. 6
σοφός (sophos), 63 n. 6
σπαρτοί (spartoi), 113
σπεῖρον (speiron), 420
σπέρματα (spermata), 253
σπονδαί (spondai), 218 n. 1
σταλαγμός (stalagmos), 33
στέμμα (stemma), 336 and n. 1, 376, 450, 456
στεφανηφόρος (stephanēphoros), 457–8

στέφανος (stephanos), 376–7, 378, 445, 450, 456, 461 n. 8
στραγγαλίς (strangalis), 369
στρέφω (strephō), 419
στυγέω (stygeō), 202 n. 5
συντανύειν (syntanuein), 338–9
σφίγγω (sphingō), 369

ταινία (tainia), 319 n. 3, 402, 453 n. 4, 464 n. 3
τάλαντα (talanta), 326, 397, 409–10
ταμίης πολέμοιο (tamiēs polemoio), 409
ταναΰφής (tanaÿphēs), 340 n. 1
τανύειν (tanyein), 310–11, 318–20, 339, 340 n. 1, 433
ταριχεύειν (taricheuein). See ταρχύειν
τάριχος (tarichos), 258, 261
Τάρταρος (Tartaros), 249–50, 258 n. 5
ταρχύειν (tarchyein), 256–8, 261
τελαμών (telamōn), 442
τελέειν (teleein), 434 n. 7, 445–6, 459–60, 462
τελεσφορία (telesphoria), 446 n. 4
τελεσφόρος (telesphoros), 443 n. 4, 446 n. 4, 459
τελετή (teletē), 445–6
τελευτάω (teleutaō), 461 n. 4
τέλη λύειν (telē lyein), 436
τέλος (telos), 386, 426–66
τελχῖνες (telchines), 430 n. 3
τέρπεσθαι (terpesthai), 20–1
τετελεσμένος (tetelesmenos), 434 n. 7
τήκεσθαι (tēkesthai), 33–4, 48, 201–2
τίθημι (tithēmi), 382 n. 1
τόκος (tokos), 124
τολυπεύειν (tolypeuein), 387–9
τριτοπάτορες (tritopatores), 120, 158 n. 5
τριχῶσαι (trichōsai), 99 n. 2
Τύχη (Tychē). See General Index s.v. Tychē

ὑγιής (hygiēs), 215 n. 2
ὑγρός (hygros), 202–3, 213 n. 6, 251–2
ὕλη (hylē), 465
ὑπηνέμιος (hypēnemios), 120
ὑποδέσματα (hypodesmata), 439
ὑπτιάσματα χερῶν (hyptiasmata cherōn), 181 n. 1
ὑφαίνω (hyphainō), 340–1, 384

φλέγμα (phlegma), 160 n. 4

φλέψ (phleps), 80–1
φόρος (phoros), 462 n. 2
φρένες (phrenes). *See* General Index *s.v. phrenes*
φρονεῖν (phronein), 14–15, 20
φροντίς (phrontis), 86, 405 n. 3
φύσις (physis), 247, 253

χάλκεος (chalkeos), 249 n. 9
χάρις (charis), 402
χάρμη (charmē), 21–2
χέω (cheō), 423, 464 n. 3
χλούνης (chlounēs), 109 n. 4, 177 n. 9
χλοῦνις (chlounis), 177 n. 9
χλωρός (chlōros), 177 n. 9
χοαί (choai), 272, 298 n. 8
χόλος (cholos), 52, 84–5, 87
χρή (chrē), 332 n. 1
χρῖσμα (chrisma), 189 n. 2
χρίω (chriō), 211
Χρόνος (Chronos). *See* General Index *s.v. Chronos*
χρόνος (chronos), 451 n. 1
χυλός (chylos), 62
χυμός (chymos), 62

ψύχειν (psychein), 120
ψυχή (psychē). *See* General Index *s.v. psychē*; *and for etymology*, pp. 119–20
ψυχοστασία (psychostasia), 150 n. 1, 397–8
ψυχρός (psychros), 46 n. 6

Ὠκεανός (Okeanos). *See* General Index *s.v. Okeanos*
ὥρα (hōra), 393, 411–13

MODERN

ἀνάρραχο (anarrhacho), 234
μπόλια (mpolia), 454

HEBREW

ai lanu, 336 n. 2
barakh, 491
berekh, 491
beṭen, 485–6
Çaphaph, 501
dor, 437 n. 3
eṣar, 438 n. 1
hagha, 501
ḥebhel, 364 n. 2, 439 n. 5, 443

ḥelebh, 211 n. 9
kabhodh, 499 n. 2
mashaḥ, 495 n. 1
me'im, 485 *and* n. 1, 486 *and* n. 1
nadhibh, 475 n. 1
nephesh, 481–2
'obh, 488–90
panim, 144 n. 8
reḥem, 486 n. 1
rosh, 234 n. 6
ruaḥ, 482–3, 485–7, 498
yarekh, 109 n. 1, 188 n. 3

HITTITE

genu, 176 n. 3

ICELANDIC AND OLD NORSE

Bönd, 354
brundr, 156
bruni, 155–6
frelsisöl, 477
frjá, 475
frjáls, 475
froða, 63, 68 n. 7
geisa, 150 n. 3
góðir hálsar, 477 n. 1
heili, 476 n. 1, 477 n. 2
heill, 476 n. 1, 477 n. 2
heita í hofuð á einum, 476 n. 1
kné, 186
Miðgarðsormr, 316 n. 1
Oðrærir, 68 n. 7
örlög, 381
reð undir hverju rifi, 68 n. 7
safi, 63
þurr, 63
vatr, 63
ver, 177 n. 9

IRISH

allur mo cnám, 191 n. 1
damnaim, 438 n. 1
glun, 175
mind, 457 n. 3
mir, 182 n. 5
smior, 191 n. 1
smuis, 191 n. 1
tathlun, 157

ITALIAN

morta, 509

LATIN

absolvo, 438 n. 1
acerbus, 264
adnuo, 139 and n. 4
adoleo, 282 n. 1
adoratio, 181 n. 1
adorea, 142 n. 3
altare, 282 n. 1
anhelo, 171
anima. See General Index s.v.
animus. See General Index s.v.
apex, 145 n. 10
Apocolocyntosis, 507–8
aridus, 192, 225
articulus, 348 n. 5
asellus, 226 n. 5
augeo, 238 n. 1
aura, 74

bulla, 264 n. 9
bustum, 135 n. 9 fin.

capillus, 135 n. 9
capita deorum. See General Index s.v. head
capitalis, 159 n. 4
Capito, 226 and n. 3
capo, 226 n. 3
capus, 226 n. 3
caput, 123–5, 132, 135 n. 9 fin., 145, 149–50, 195 n. 2
cardo, 348 n. 5
cera, 282 n. 9
cere comminuit brum, 125
cerebrosus, 148, 244, 245 n. 2
cerebrum, 125 and n. 8, 148, 150, 238, 240 n. 7, 244
cereo, 125, 238, 240 n. 7
cereus, 282 n. 9
cerritus, 148 and n. 5
cerus, 125–6, 148, 150, 405 n. 8 fin.
clavus, 373–5
cometes, 163–4
concubia nocte, 415 n. 13
conspiro, 171
contingo, 451 n. 1
conubium, 153
cor, 40, 172, 225
cornipes, 246
cornu, 238, 244–5
corona, 458 n. 1; c. graminea, 142 n. 3; c. radiata, 166; sub c., 145, 478 n. 2

crines, 232 n. 4
cucurbita, 215 n. 2, 508

damnum, 438 n. 1
defixio, 371, 373–5
deliciae, 473 n. 2
delubrum, 510
desipere, 61
destino, 333, 374
devotio, 132–3, 375
digito caput uno scalpere, 198 n. 1
divus, 137

ebullire, 264 n. 9
evolvere, 388–9
exhalare vinum or crapulam, 43
expedire, 437
explicare, 438
exuere, 360 n. 7

faenum, 124 n. 6, 471 n. 4
fatum, 327, 408 n. 3
femen, 182
femur, 182
fenestella, 348
fenestra, 348
fenus, 124
festuca, 471 n. 4
fetialis, 142
filum, 317, 465 n. 5
fimus, 510–11
finis, 510–11
flammeum, 153 and n. 1, 165, 167 n. 4, 232 n. 4, 403 n. 1
flavus, 403 n. 1
fumus, 44, 510–11
funis, 338, 510–11

gallus, 109 n. 4
gena, 233
genialis, 129–30, 226 and n. 4
genius. See General Index s.v.
genu, 175–6, 180–1, 233
genuinus, 175–6, 233 nn. 2, 5
genus, 176
gramen, 142 n. 3

hasta caelibaris, 232 n. 4, 471 n. 7
hippomanes, 245, 472
hominium, 97 n. 10

ianua, 348 nn. 2, 4
ianus, 348 n. 2
imagines, 135, 136 n. 6, 137 n. 4, 146
immolare, 228 n. 1
importunus, 348
incrementum, 511 n. 1
induere, 360 n. 7, 447 n. 5
inflo, 171
iniungere, 382
insulsus, 62 n. 3
intempesta nocte, 415 n. 13
invidere, 79
iuba, 164 n. 6
iubar, 164 n. 6, 167 n. 4
iuno, 127–8, 129 n. 6, 143, 149, 264 n. 10

kerriios, 148

laetus, 473 n. 2
lanatos pedes habere, 372 n. 2
Lar, 158 n. 5
larva, 135, 148 n. 5, 192, 429 n. 1
larvatus, 148 n. 5
lex, 438 n. 1
libare, 285, 473 *and* n. 2
liber, 472–4, 475 n. 2, 476, 480
liber, 473 n. 2
liberi, 225 n. 2
libet, 473 n. 2
licium, 340, 373 n. 1
locus, 348
lucrum, 437–8
luela, 439
luere, 437, 439, 441
lupa, 471, 472 n. 4
lupanar, 471
lupari, 471
Luperci, 198 n. 1, 235 n. 4, 471 *and* n. 6
lustrum, 510 *and* n. 1
lympha, 34, 219 n. 7
lymphaticus, 34 *and* n. 5
lymphatus, 34–5, 67

mactare, 228 n. 1
mactus, 282
madeo, 177 n. 9
maialis, 177 n. 9
mane, 415 n. 13
manes, 132–3, 264–9

manus. *See* General Index *s.v.* hand
mare, 177 n. 9
maritus, 177 n. 9
mas, 470 *and* n. 2
masca, 135 n. 4
masculus, 177 n. 9
maspedis, 470 n. 2
mavors, 470 n. 2, 471 n. 7
Meditrinalia, 216 n. 6
medulla, 149–52, 159–60, 210, 213 n. 4, 220
membrum, 182 n. 5
mens, 172 n. 4
modius, 126 n. 2
mola salsa, 282
mortalis, 131 n. 2
mortarium, 508–9
mulier, 472 n. 1
Mutinus, 139 n. 2
muto, 139 n. 2
Mutunus, 139 n. 2

necessarius, 332 n. 9
necesse, 332–3
necessitas, 332 n. 9, 333
necessitudo, 332 n. 9
nexum, 439
nexus, 407 n. 2, 438–9
nimbus, 165–7
nodus, 367 n. 8
nubere, 153
nubes, 421
numen, 140–3

obligatio, 439
obsessio, 440 n. 1
Oceanus. *See* General Index *s.v.* Okeanos
omentum. *See* General Index *s.v.* opima (spolia), 235 n. 4
opportunus, 347–8
ora, 317, 388, 465 n. 5
oras evolvere belli, 388–9
oratio, 13
orbis, 457 n. 3
orbita, 457 n. 3
os resectum, 267, 496
os sacrum, 208
oscillum, 127, 135 *and* n. 2, 144

parens, 131 *and* n. 4, 135, 137–8

Parentalia, 132
pater patratus, 138 and n. 2, 142 and n. 1,
    218 n. 1, 456 n. 2
pectus, 40, 149
pensum, 409–10
penus, 176
perfundere, 35 n. 6
persona, 146, 429 n. 1
picus Martius, 470
pignus, 375 n. 7, 449 n. 6
pilae, 135 n. 2
pilleus, 144–5, 480
pinguis, 81, 212, 282
pitnita, 160 n. 4
plango, 185 n. 2
poena, 439
porta, 348 and n. 1
portus, 348 and n. 1
praecordia. See General Index s.v.
procapio, 124
propinare, 217, 228 n. 2, 275–6
prurire, 198–9
pudenda, 109 n. 2
pudicitia, 146 n. 5
pudor, 146 n. 5
pulmo, 41

ramites, 29
redimio, 438 n. 1
religio, 439–40, 510
rivales, 219 n. 7

Salacia, 177 n. 9 fin.
salus, 217 n. 1
salutare, 498 n. 1
sapere, 61–3, 65
sapiens, 61–3
siccus, 192, 212, 223 and n. 3
silentes, 139 n. 2
solvere, 369, 439 and n. 6, 440–1
spiritus, 76 n. 9, 171–3
spiro, 171
spolia, 235 n. 4
spondeo, 218 n. 1
stamen, 350–1
stella crinita, 163–4
stomachor, 89, 147
struppi, 141 and n. 6
subtemen, 351
sucidus, 192
sucus, 62, 85 n. 2, 192, 212, 224

superstitio, 440 n. 1
superstitiosus, 439 n. 6, 440 n. 1
supinae manus, 180
supplicatio, 137 and n. 4, 282

talem, 171 n. 5
tempus, 344 and n. 1
tendicula, 319 n. 3
tendo, 319 n. 3
testa, 135 n. 9
toga virilis, 146, 264, 473 n. 1
tropaeum, 375 n. 2
tus, 278

uber agri, 211 n. 9
umbra, 95, 132
umor, 192
unctus, 212, 278
unguis, 246, 494 n. 1
ungula, 246, 494 n. 1
unguo, 494 n. 1
urbs, 444 n. 1
uva, 218 n. 2
uxor, 472

vena, 42, 64
verbena, 141 and n. 7, 142 and n. 2, 456
    n. 2
verenda, 109 n. 2
verna, 177 n. 9, 225 n. 2
victima, 450 n. 1
vinco, 438 n. 1
vindicta, 145
vinum respersum, 278
vir, 177 n. 9
virga, 177 n. 9
virus, 177 n. 9, 187, 255 n. 4
vis, 177 n. 9, 196
viscus, 263 and n. 3
vita, 169 n. 1, 196, 224
vitalia, 277 n. 8
vitis, 218 n. 2
vitta, 232 n. 4, 447 and n. 5
volito vivos per ora virum, 173

POLISH

kolano, 176

RUSSIAN

koleno, 176

SANSCRIT

asu, 512
ātman, 484, 512–13
ayúḥ, 209
bándhu-ḥ, 332 n. 9
dam, 438 n. 1
dāman, 438 n. 1
dắti, 211 n. 9
dhūmah, 44
guṇa, 465 n. 1
kula-m, 443
māmsam, 182 n. 5
manas, 512
pari, 315, 330
prāṇa, 75, 512

Praṇayama, 76 n. 2
priyá, 475 n. 2
pupphusa-ḥ, 57 n. 1
rakta, 153 n. 3
raṇa, 22
Sīmantonnayana, 232 n. 4
vắr, 177 n. 9
vṛṣan-, 177 n. 9

WELSH

mer, 182 n. 5
rhydd, 475 n. 2

ZEND (OR AVESTAN)

Mithra, 455 n. 6, 457 n. 3

SELECT INDEX OF PASSAGES

A few of the passages on which new interpretation is offered are included in this index.

GREEK

Aelian

de Natura Animalium
  I (51), 206
  x (40), 246
Varia Historia
  XIII (22), 65 n. 1

Aeschylus (ed. Murray)

Agamemnon
  (363–6), 343; (1031–2), 347; (1048),
  (1114–15), 323; (1121–2), 84;
  (1235–6), 53 *and* n. 3; (1388–90),
  46; (1580–1), 323
Choephoroe
  (183–4), 84; (296), 258; (389–90), 54
Eumenides
  (17), 66; (380), (840–2), 74 n. 6
Fragmenta (ed. Nauck)
  (193), 87
Persae
  (667–9), 423 n. 9; (991), 82
Prometheus Vinctus
  (479–81), 213; (849), 495; (1078–9),
  323
Supplices
  (313), (592), 495

Anacreontea (ed. Bergk)

  (1), 403
  (32), 507

Anthologia Graeca Palatina

  v (194), 402
  xi (278), 243

Apollonius Rhodius

  III (683–4), 67 n. 4

Aristophanes (ed. Hall and Geldart)

Nubes
  (232–3), 48 n. 2
Plutus
  (20–2), 456

Ranae
  (194–5), 256

Aristotle

de Animalium Generatione
  746 b (21), 233
  781 a (23), 72
Fragmenta (ed. Rose)
  (98), 461 n. 8
Problemata
  867 a (23), 231
  960 b (21), 962 b (35), 72

Bion

  I (45–6), 87

Democritus (in *Frag. d. Vorsokr.* ed.
  Diels)

  A (29), 211
  B (32), 108 n. 7

Diogenes of Apollonia (in *Frag. d.
  Vorsokr.* ed. Diels)

  B (6), 80–1

Doxographi Graeci (ed. Diels)

  (589), 250 n. 2

Empedocles (in *Frag. d. Vorsokr.* ed.
  Diels)

  A (33), 203
  B (6), 203

Euripides (ed. Murray)

Andromache
  (110), 145, 377; (418), 109 n. 3;
  (1120), 343
Fragmenta (ed. Nauck)
  360, 8 (22), 113 n. 4
Hercules Furens
  (4–5), 113 n. 4; (1140), 74
  n. 6
Hippolytus
  (255), 118

Iphigenia Taurica
  (361–4), 233 n. 4
Medea
  (107–8), 74 n. 6
Orestes
  (12–14), 336; (358–9), 445 n. 1
Supplices
  (470–1), 456; (745–6), 343

Galen (ed. Kuhn)
de Placitis Hipp. et Plat.
  II (5), 67 n. 8

Heraclitus of Ephesus (in *Frag. d.
Vorsokr.* ed. Diels)
B (85), 197 n. 2

Herodas (ed. Headlam)
VIII (2–5), 222

Herodotus

I (31), 433; (129), 377
III (22–3), 290; (142), 377
IV (187), 160 n. 4

Hesiod

Fragmenta (Rzach³)
  245 (7), 73
Shield of Herakles
  (7), 73; (42–5), 364; (141), 249
    n. 7; (227), 424; (314–15), 249
    n. 7; (397), 191–2
Theogony
  (211), (217–19), 400; (535–40), 279;
    (607–9), 204; (640), (796–7), 297
Works and Days
  (122–4), 424 n. 7; (141), 131 n. 2;
    (414–22), 412; (538), 339; (608),
    193; (765–79), 412; (782–9),
    (822–5), 413

Hippolytus
Refutatio Haeresium
  V (17), 228 n. 1

Homer
Iliad
  I (3), 99; (526–7), 390
  III (39), 242; (59), 390; (299–301),
    108; (308–9), 386
  IV (517–26), 327, 335 n. 4

V (471–2), 322 n. 3
VI (333), 390; (357–8), 378;
  (528–9), 479
VII (94–5), 333–4; (101–2), 324,
  386; (402), 335
VIII (69–75), 397; (306–9), 114
XI (55), 99
XII (79), 321; (433–5), 409; (436–7),
  320
XIII (347–60), 310–11; (710–11),
  193; (769), 242
XIV (164–5), 31; (198–9), 368;
  (200–1), 316; (214–17), 368;
  (294), 420–1
XV (117–18), 392; (208–10), 385;
  (466), 186 n. 8
XVI (119), 186 n. 8; (440–3), 382,
  384; (502–3), 427; (656–8), 326,
  397
XVII (83), 421; (111–12), 46 n. 6;
  (319–22), 390–1; (327–8), 392
XVIII (535–8), 401 n. 1; (607–9),
  249 n. 7
XIX (223–4), 397
XX (100–2), 433; (435–6), 386
XXI (82–4), 392; (443–5), 460
XXII (209–14), 397; (388), 180
XXIV (197–9), 18; (514–19), 79;
  (525–6), 380, 394; (525–39),
  394
Odyssey
  I (16–19), 305
  II (237), 99
  III (74), 99; (205), 305, 380;
    (205–8), 380
  IV (208–9), 335, 396
  V (288–9), 323; (346–7), 368;
    (383–5), 370 n. 1; (394–8), 364;
    (436–7), 391
  VI (140), 79
  VII (197–8), 307
  VIII (274–8), 337; (447–8), 369
  IX (420–2), 365
  X (18–25), 370 n. 1; (493–5), 195
  XI (211–12), 20; (558–61), 378
  XIII (168–9), 330 n. 3
  XVI (129), 305
  XIX (512–13), 20; (516–17), 86;
    (562–7), 242
  XX (9–10), 184; (351–2), 181;
    (434–6), 334

Homeric Hymns

II, *To Demeter*
(275), 73–4; (480–2), 450
III, *To Apollo*
(130–2), 111
IV, *To Hermes*
(118–20), 205–6; (421–3), 70
V, *To Aphrodite*
(244–5), 430 n. 3
VIII, *To Ares*
(12–15), 117
XXVIII, *To Athena*
(4–5), 111 n. 5
Battle of Frogs and Mice
(144–5), 70

Menander
Fr. 550 (Kock), 404 n. 1

Mesomedes
Nemesis, 406 n. 1

Mimnermus (in *Poetae Lyr. Gr.* ed.
Bergk)
2 (5–6), 429–30, 459–60
5 (5–8), 430

Moschus
II (16–17), 87

Orphica (ed. Abel)
Hymns
(xv), 112

Orphicorum Fragmenta (ed. Kern.
See also General Index *s.v.* Orphism)
(21 a), 111–12
(32 c), 451
(224 b), 451 n. 1
(229), 452–3
(230), 453
(232), 441 n. 5, 452
(239), 316
(354), 203

Pindar
Fragmenta (ed. Schröder)
(111), 206
52 (*Paean* VI, 81–3), 405
Isthmians
I (26–8), 445

II (43), 405
VIII (14–15), 405 n. 8
Nemeans
I (18), 343
V (6), 232
VII (6), 407
IX (42–4), 404
Olympians
I (1), 229
II (57–8), 117; (74–5), 453
III (42), 229
VII (1–2), 217; (24–5), 405
IX (60–1), 379
X (60–2), 445
XIII (38–9), 376
Pythians
I (7–8), 425; (48), 116; (81–2), 338,
343, 347; (98–101), 376
IV (158), 232; (214–15), 452
V (51), 117
IX (31–2), 116

Plato
Laws
(960 C), 418 n. 1
Republic
(562 C), 479; (617 D), (620 D),
403
Theaetetus
(197 C), 67 n. 4

Plutarch
Lives (*Pericles*)
(VI), 237–8
Quaestiones Graecae
(XII = 294 C), 281

Pollux
Onomasticon
VII (32), 339–40

Porphyry
Vita Pythagorae
(43), 280 n. 2

Quintus Smyrnaeus
XIII (494–5), 322 n. 3

Sappho (in *Poetae Lyr. Gr.* ed.
Bergk)
(51), 276

Semonides of Amorgos (in *Poetae Lyr. Gr.* ed. Bergk)
VII (115–16), 379, 434

Simonides of Ceos (in *Poetae Lyr. Gr.* ed. Bergk)
(10), 376
(98), 376
(99), 377
(100), 376
(103), 377

Sophocles (ed. Pearson)
Ajax
  (236), 206
Fragmenta
  (837), 274

Theocritus
I (46–9), 222 n. 11
XIV (18–21), 277
XVIII (46–7), 276
XXIV (74–6), 306

Theognis (in *Poetae Lyr. Gr.* ed. Bergk)
(139–40), 315 n. 1
(729), 86
(1163–4), 70

Xenophon
Anabasis
  IV, 3 (8), 365

Zenobius
III (64), 304

LATIN

Accius (ed. Ribbeck)
(481), 375

Apuleius
Florida
  II (15), 192
de Magica
  (63), 192
Metamorphoses
  X (28), 43

Aquilius (ed. Ribbeck)
Boeot.
  (9), 223

Cato
de Agri Cultura
  66 (1), 61

Catullus
XV (16), 124
XXXV (15), 151
XLIII (16), 151
LXI (114–15), 153 n. 1
LXIV (93–4), (196–8), 160; (254–5), 34
LXVI (23–5), 150
C (7), 151

Cicero
de Finibus
  II, 8 (24), 61 n. 8
Philippic II
  (25), 42–3
de Republica
  II, 21 (37), 159
Tusculanae Disputationes
  I, 40 (96), 276

Columella
de Re Rustica
  II, 10 (11), 269

Ennius
Annales
  VI (*init.*), 388
Epigrammata
  (II), 173
Saturae
  III (1–2), 159

Horace
Ars Poetica
  (83–5), 480; (309), 65; (409–10), 64
Carmen Saec.
  (26–8), 375
Epistles
  I, 1 (43–5), 195; 15 (19–20), 42; 18 (111–12), 381
  II, 2 (188), 131 n. 2

Epodes
   III (5), 42
   XIII (13–15), 351
   XVII (25–6), 41
Odes
   I, 12 (46–8), 164; 28 (19–20), 134;
      34 (14–15), 381; 35 (17–19), 374
   II, 18 (9–10), 64
   III, 13 (3–5), 239; 24 (5–8), 374
Satires
   I, 2 (68–9), 139 n. 2; 4 (17–21), 170,
      (89), 42

Juvenal

III (36), 139 n. 4
v (49), 43 n. 16
VI (49), 124; (621–3), 136
VII (111), 170
x (62), 138 n. 1; (118–19), 65

Livy

I (39), 159
XLII (16), 42

Lucan

VII (457–9), 138 n. 1
IX (65–6), 150

Lucilius (ed. Marx)

(557), 216
(590–1), 41

Lucretius

I (37), 173; (64–5), 143; (75–7), 375;
   (412–13), 65
III (959), 134
VI (762–5), 265 n. 2

Martial

I, 39 (3–4), 64
III, 19 (6), 170 n. 2
VI, 61 (10), 162
VII, 69 (2), 64
VIII (65), 167

Ovid

Amores
   III, 9 (25–6), 65 n. 1; 10 (27–8),
      152
Fasti
   III (115–16), 142 n. 3; (523–5), 216

Metamorphoses
   XIII (929), 130
   XIV (147–9), 214 n. 1
   xv (845–9), 164; (878–9), 173
ex Ponto
   I, 2 (57), 34
   II, 5 (21–2), 64
Tristia
   III, 14 (33–6), 64

Pacuvius (ed. Ribbeck)

(83), 89

Petronius

(17), 180
(21), 211
(34), 216
(41), 227
(62), 149
(71), 480
(75), 149
(76), 161
(79), 131
(109), 130
(111), 223

Plautus (ed. Lindsay)

Amphitruo
   (462), 145
Captivi
   (80–4), 192
Mercator
   (100), 124; (590–1), 147
Miles Gloriosus
   (587), 61; (639–40), 193; (883),
      64 n. 3
Mostellaria
   (243), 151
Persa
   (801–2), 147
Poenulus
   (701), 211; (750), 438
Rudens
   (333–5), 129 n. 7; (510–11), 170

Pliny the Elder

Nat. Hist.
   II, 25 (93–4), 163
   XI, 37 (133), 120 n. 4; (212), 212;
      (213), 81
   XVIII, 2 (25), 139 n. 4

Propertius

II, 9 (26), 134; 12 [III, 3] (17), 152
III [IV], 5 (21–5), 130; 17 (9), 152;
    18 (25–6), 134, (33–4), 163
    n. 3

Prudentius
contra Symmachum
    II (1096–8), 139 n. 4

Quintilian
Inst. Orat.
    IV, 2 (123), 41

Saxo Grammaticus
XIV (564–6), 241

Seneca the Younger
Epistulae Morales
    XII (6), 451 n. 1
Hercules Furens
    (181–2), 410
Phoenissae
    (233–5), 134

Statius
Silvae
    V, 1 (155–7), 374 n. 3
Thebais
    VIII (84–5), 265 n. 2

Tacitus
Annals
    XV (64), 480

Terence
Eunuchus
    (317), 192

Theodosius I
Codices
    XVI, 10 (2), 227

Tibullus
I, 1 (55), 373; 7 (23–4), 125; 8 (5–6),
    373
II, 2 (17–18), 402–3

Varro
Fragmenta
    (57), 124

Virgil
Aeneid
    I (402), 166; (443–4), 126; (659–
    60), 152; (710), 166
    II (101), 388
    III (303–5), 265 n. 2
    IV (66–9), (101), 152; (612–15),
    375; (698–9), 134
    V (67–8), 166; (80–1), 267; (173–4),
    150
    VI (739–43), 265 n. 2
    VIII (388–90), 151; (680–1), 164
    IX (496), 134; (525–8), 388; (596), 42
    X (60–2), 388
    XII (65–6), (101–2), 147
Culex
    (214–20), 265 n. 2
Eclogues
    IV (610), 265 n. 2
    V (65–6), 265 n. 2
    VIII (67–72), 373
Georgics
    II (388–90), 127
    III (242), (258–9), (266–8), 151

ANGLO-SAXON
Beowulf
    (1327), 100; (2661–2), 100, 196
    n. 4; (2909–10), 100

THE BIBLE
Genesis
    xvii (16, 20), 492
    xxvii (27–8), 492
    xlix (25), 492
I Samuel
    ii (20), 492
    x (1–3), 189 n. 2
    xiv (12–13), 189 n. 2
    xix (11), 481
    xx (1–2), 481
II Samuel
    xviii (18), 496
I Kings
    xvii (17–22), 482
Job
    xv (2, 35), 486
    xviii (8), 321–2
    xix (6), 322; (17), 486
    xxxii (18–20), 485

Psalms
 lxxxiv (6), 492
 lxxxix (20, 26–7), 189 n. 2
 cxxxiii (3), 492
Proverbs
 v (18), 492
 xi (25), 492
 xii (10), 486 n. 1
 xviii (8), 486 n. 1
Isaiah
 xxv (7–8), 429 n. 2
 xxxii (15), 493
 xliv (3), 492
 lvi (3), 221 and n. 1; (4–5), 496
 lxi (1), 189 n. 2
Ezekiel
 xxxiv (26), 492
Daniel
 ii (1, 28), 483
Malachi
 ii (15–16), 485 n. 2
 iii (10), 492
Mark
 i (10–12), 500
 vi (13), 287 n. 2

Luke
 x (34), 287 n. 2
John
 i (1–3, 14), 503
 iii (3, 5), 189 n. 2
 vii (37–9), 487
 xix (39–40), 287 n. 2
Acts of the Apostles
 xiii (23–33), 189 n. 2
To the Romans
 i (1–4), 189 n. 2
To the Corinthians I
 xv (37–8), 270
To the Corinthians II
 iii (7, 18), 499 n. 2
 iv (6), 499 n. 2
To the Colossians
 i (15–17), 503
 ii (9), 503
To Titus
 iii (5–6), 189 n. 2
I John
 ii (20, 27), 189 n. 2
 iii (2, 9), 189 n. 2

PHILOSOPHY
OF
PLATO AND ARISTOTLE

AN ARNO PRESS COLLECTION

Aristotle. **Aristotle De Sensu and De Memoria.** Text and Translation with Introduction and Commentary by G[eorge] R[obert] T[hompson] Ross. 1906.

Aristotle. **Aristotle Nicomachean Ethics.** Book Six, with Essays, Notes, and Translation by L. H. G. Greenwood. 1909.

Aristotle. **Aristotle's Constitution of Athens.** A Revised Text with an Introduction, Critical and Explanatory Notes, Testimonia and Indices Revised and Enlarged by John Edwin Sandys. Second Edition. 1912.

Aristotle. **The Ethics of Aristotle.** Edited, with an Introduction and Notes by John Burnet. 1900.

Aristotle. **The Ethics of Aristotle.** Illustrated with Essays and Notes by Alexander Grant. Fourth Edition. 1885.

Aristotle. **The Fifth Book of the Nicomachean Ethics of Aristotle.** Edited for the Syndics of the University Press by Henry Jackson. 1879.

Aristotle. **The Politics of Aristotle.** With an Introduction, Two Prefatory Essays and Notes Critical and Explanatory by W. L. Newman. 1887.

Aristotle. **The Rhetoric of Aristotle.** With a Commentary by Edward Meredith Cope. Revised and Edited for the Syndics of the University Press by Sir John Edwin Sandys. 1877.

Bywater, Ingram. **Contributions to the Textual Criticism of Aristotle's Nicomachean Ethics.** 1892.

Grote, George. **Aristotle.** Edited by Alexander Bain and G. Croom Robertson. Second Edition, with Additions. 1880.

Linforth, Ivan M. **The Arts of Orpheus.** 1941.

Onians, Richard Broxton. **The Origins of European Thought About the Body, the Mind, the Soul, the World, Time, and Fate.** 1951.

Pearson, A. C., editor. **The Fragments of Zeno and Cleanthes.** With Introduction and Explanatory Notes. 1891.

Plato. **The Apology of Plato.** With a Revised Text and English Notes, and a Digest of Platonic Idioms by James Riddell. 1877.

Plato. **The Euthydemus of Plato.** With Revised Text, Introduction, Notes, and Indices by Edwin Hamilton Gifford. 1905.

Plato. **The Gorgias of Plato.** With English Notes, Introduction, and Appendix by W. H. Thompson. 1871.

Plato. **The Phaedo of Plato.** Edited with Introduction, Notes and Appendices by R. D. Archer-Hind. Second Edition. 1894.

Plato. **The Phaedrus of Plato.** With English Notes and Dissertations by W. H. Thompson. 1868.

Plato. **The Philebus of Plato.** Edited with Introduction, Notes and Appendices by Robert Gregg Bury. 1897.

Plato. **Plato's Republic:** The Greek Text, Edited with Notes and Essays by B. Jowett and Lewis Campbell. Volume II: Essays. 1894.

Plato. **The Sophistes and Politicus of Plato.** With a Revised Text and English Notes by Lewis Campbell. 1867.

Plato. **The Theaetetus of Plato.** With a Revised Text and English Notes by Lewis Campbell. 1861.

Plato. **The Timaeus of Plato.** Edited with Introduction and Notes by R. D. Archer-Hind. 1888.

Schleiermacher, [Friedrich Ernst Daniel]. **Introductions to the Dialogues of Plato.** Translated from the German by William Dobson. 1836.

Stenzel, Julius. **Plato's Method of Dialectic.** Translated and Edited by D. J. Allan. 1940.

Stewart, J. A. **Notes on the Nicomachean Ethics of Aristotle.** 1892.